24,77

PO 540
Music

SHOWTIME

◆

SHOWTIME

A HISTORY OF THE BROADWAY
MUSICAL THEATER

◆

LARRY STEMPEL

W. W. NORTON & COMPANY
NEW YORK   LONDON

For information about permission to reproduce selections from this book,
write to Permissions, W. W. Norton & Company, Inc.,
500 Fifth Avenue, New York, NY 10110

For information about special discounts for bulk purchases, please contact
W. W. Norton Special Sales at specialsales@wwnorton.com or 800-233-4830

Manufacturing by RR Donnelley, Harrisonburg, VA
Book design by Dana Sloan
Production manager: Anna Oler

Library of Congress Cataloging-in-Publication Data

Stempel, Larry.
Showtime : a history of the Broadway musical theater / Larry Stempel. — 1st ed.
p. cm.
Includes bibliographical references and index.
ISBN 978-0-393-06715-6 (hardcover)
1. Musicals—New York (State)—New York—History and criticism. I. Title.
ML1711.8.N3S73 2010
792.609747'1—dc22

2010019704

ISBN 978-0-393-92906-5 (paperback)

W. W. Norton & Company, Inc.
500 Fifth Avenue, New York, N.Y. 10110
www.wwnorton.com

W. W. Norton & Company Ltd.
Castle House, 75/76 Wells Street, London W1T 3QT

1 2 3 4 5 6 7 8 9 0

Meinen lieben Eltern zum Andenken gewidmet

CONTENTS

ILLUSTRATIONS

PREFACE

It's the fragment, not the day.
[. . .]
Not the building but the beam,
Not the garden but the stone,
Only cups of tea
And history [. . .]

"SOMEONE IN A TREE" (*PACIFIC OVERTURES*)
STEPHEN SONDHEIM

I began *Showtime* as the winds of cultural change gathered force on Broadway and hints of the postmodern outlook to come filled the air. Sometime in the late 1970s, I showed a very rough outline for a book on the history of Broadway musicals to Lehman Engel. He had written *The American Musical Theater: A Consideration,* the first book to analyze the working principles of a core repertoire of Broadway shows he held up as models of excellence; I considered it a revelation. He also ran the BMI Musical Theater Workshop, where, as a budding songwriter, I had been reaping the benefits of his wit and wisdom as well as the criticism of my colleagues. Because of the workshop experience, I wanted to become more familiar with the traditions in which I was working. I thought I might take a more scholarly approach than that of the few books on the subject then available. My outline represented a plan of action, but it was no more than a sketch. Little did I know then to what extent the project would take on a life of its own, and much of my life as well. Lehman (no one ever seems to have called him Mr. Engel) smiled on my ambition, but cautioned in the way of someone practiced in the vagaries of show business: Know your audience. In hindsight, I wish he might also have said: Know your subject. For only in the course of the years of work that lay ahead did I come to realize just how difficult writing such a history would be.

Simply getting a sense of what most of the musicals I would be writing about were like proved problematic. Unlike playscripts or opera scores, few comparable published sources existed for musicals before the 1940s, except for some operettas. Nor was there anything like original cast recordings of the shows (but for the special case of *The Cradle Will Rock*). Commercial movie musicals adapted from Broadway musicals abounded, some going back to the 1920s. But as movies, such "adaptations" had their own set of priorities, which involved—in whole or in part—new producers, new directors, new choreographers, new designers, new performers, new plots, new scripts, and new songs. Least among Hollywood's priorities was the preservation of any sense of the original stage shows with which these films sometimes shared little more than the title.

Above all, a Broadway musical generally achieved its fullest realization as a live entertainment—an event without the cultural authority behind it of a "work." A Broadway show simply did not have the aura of an "opus" about it. And so whatever might have been published of a given show was meant not as a record for posterity, but for immediate and practical use as a blueprint for a performance—for example, sheet music of simplified versions of selected songs from the show with the potential of becoming popular hits on their own. The documentable evidence of what held a musical together existed, if at all, largely in manuscript, typescript, and sketches.

But the musical theater was also an unstable and multidisciplinary medium in which the lines of creative authority were dispersed among the separate disciplines involved. Thus there was no single source for a show (not to mention its pre-Broadway genesis or its post-Broadway career) but rather many sources, and rarely any generally agreed upon central authority to coordinate them and hold them all together. To get any accurate, even if incomplete, sense of a show, one had to get hold of scripts or prompt books for the dialogue from one source, orchestrations for the songs from another, set designs for the staging from yet another, costume sketches for what the performers wore from still another, and so on. (Some photographs from the late nineteenth century did exist, but these were mainly posed studio shots of some of the performers rather than production shots of the shows themselves. And there were rarely any color photographs before the 1940s.)

To compound these difficulties, all such material circulated in a world motivated first and foremost by the dollar sign (or, more precisely, what it stood for). As part of the business of show business, the material seems to have been regarded as having little intrinsic value once a show had exhausted its money-making potential. At that point it became disposable stuff. Much of it was irretrievably lost; the rest was often scattered about. Additionally, even when such materials managed to survive in some recoverable form, they invariably proved unreliable: They were riddled with inconsistencies of one kind or another. Musical shows existed in a constant state of flux—cut from, added to, or simply altered in some way at almost every stage of their incarnation: in out-of-town tryouts, during Broadway runs, on subsequent tours, and in revival. Even *Show Boat*, that seeming bedrock of the modern Broadway musical, exists today in multiple versions—several by one or more of the show's original creators, in fact—no one of which can be said to be definitive.

Some shows posed few of these problems, to be sure. Most, however, posed many. And so putting together the kaleidoscope of pieces for this book involved a lot of dogged research and a bit of educated guesswork on my part. *Showtime* thus draws on a wide variety of primary materials and archival holdings of original sources (prompt books, typescripts, song sheets, orchestrations, cast recordings, photographs, films, videotapes, playbills, programs, reviews, advertisements, set designs, costume renderings, business records, personal correspondence, scrapbooks, memoirs, autobiographies, interviews in print or on recordings, and interviews that I conducted in person, by phone, and by mail). It also calls upon an extensive and ever-growing literature of secondary sources reflecting a diversity of methodologies and approaches: practical as well as theoretical, journalistic as well as scholarly, devotional as well as critical, and so on.

I had little inkling that the book before you would eventually entail all this when I first sat down to write it many years ago. The full measure of what I had undertaken eluded me early on. Only with the passing of time and my immersion in the work did I come to realize the greater implications of the enterprise I had embarked upon. And as I did, my motivation for completing the book took an important turn. I had begun by looking into the Broadway musical's past mainly for my own purposes. I now hope to provide the Broadway musical of the present with the kind of foundational history it has yet to enjoy—and which I believe it deserves.

Over the years of this undertaking, I accumulated a treasure chest of indebtedness to friends and strangers for their many contributions and kindnesses. My heartfelt thanks go out to all who helped in one way or another to bring this book to completion:

To the late Lehman Engel, whose pioneering work as a teacher and author served to reposition America's musical theater in my mind as a field for critical inquiry; and to the members of his BMI Musical Theater Workshop, whose in-class discussions and after-hours debates first piqued the curiosity that led me to probe further.

To the working professionals in the Broadway musical field who found time to grant me an interview or simply to respond to my questions with grace and frankness: Leonard Bernstein, Abba Bogin, William David Brohn, Carmen Capalbo, Agnes de Mille, Bob Fosse, Gerald Freedman, Sheldon Harnick, Jerry Herman, Peter Howard, Edward Kleban, Bruce Pomahac, Sid Ramin, Trude Rittmann, Arthur Schwartz, Stephen Sondheim, Lys Symonette, and Lee Becker Theodore.

To the libraries and collections both public and private whose staffs, by dint of their expertise and goodwill, proved indispensable to the conduct of my research: The Beinecke Rare Book and Manuscript Library of Yale University; Bertolt-Brecht-Archiv; The British Library; The Dramatists Guild; Hampden-Booth Theatre Library at The Players; Harvard Theatre Collection; The Library of Congress, Music Division; Museum of the City of New York, Theater Collection; New-York Historical Society; The New York Public Library: Manuscripts and Archives Division, Schomburg Center for Research in Black Culture, Jerome Robbins Dance Division, Rodgers and Hammerstein Archives of Recorded Sound, Billy Rose Theatre Collection, Music Division, and Theatre on Film and Tape Archive; The Pierpont Morgan Library; The Rare Book, Manuscript, and Special Collections Library of Duke University; The Rodgers and Hammerstein Organization; The Shubert Archive; Weill-Lenya Research Center; and The Wisconsin Center for Film and Theater Research.

To the organizations whose generous support ultimately made the research, writing, and publication of this book possible: The National Endowment for the Humanities for a Fellowship for Independent Studies and Research, which allowed the project to get off the ground; Fordham University for two Faculty Fellowships, which enabled the project to continue on its course and reach its goal; and Fordham University again and the American Musicological Society for the publication subventions that helped the completed project see the public light of day.

To those who by a word or a deed proved instrumental in overcoming an obstacle as it arose or in putting a piece of the puzzle in place as the book slowly came together: Randy Bigham, Maryann Chach, Carol Cornicelli, Kara Darling, Graeme Fullerton, Lawrence Greene, Kitty Carlisle Hart, Florence Leeds, Jeremy Megraw, Louis Rachow, Anne Kaufman Schneider, Susan Sommer, David Thomas, and George Zournas.

To the scholars and researchers who put their own work on hold for a while to read and comment on parts of my work-in-progress, or who put up with my incessant queries and came back with thoughtful, often thought-provoking answers: Jon Alan Conrad, Elaine Crane, Richard Crawford, George Ferencz, Joseph Kerman, Miles Kreuger, Steven Ledbetter, Glenn Litton, Robert McLaughlin, Sally Parry, Susan Ray, Deane Root, Wayne Shirley, John Shout, and Joseph Swain.

To my editor at W. W. Norton, Maribeth Payne, and the indefatigable staff whose talent, dedication, and professionalism helped to shepherd this book through seemingly endless mazes of publishing requisites and concerns: Courtney Fitch, Junenoire Mitchell, Imogen Howes, Ariella Foss, Anna Oler, Nancy Rodwan, and Charles Brock of The DesignWorks Group.

To the anonymous reviewers whose considered and invaluable suggestions helped turn my manuscript into a less imperfect book (I can name only those who at some point revealed to me who they were): Geoffrey Block, Rose Rosengard Subotnik, and, above all, Kim Kowalke, who had the unflagging generosity of spirit and the sheer perseverance to read and critique the complete manuscript in several stages of its final development.

To Claire Brook, who, with her selfless championing of this book ever since she first responded to my proposal for it from the music editor's desk at Norton in 1979, has done more than anyone to turn that proposal not just into a reality, but into a better reality than I might otherwise have hoped for. She defies categorization: When I started she was my editor, but by the time I finished she had become my muse.

And to my beloved wife Carol and daughter Rebecca. Where do I begin—or end? I thank you for all sorts of help and support, large and small, spoken and unspoken, and for your infinite patience throughout the years. I am grateful beyond measure.

Larry Stempel
Mount Vernon
October 2009

SHOWTIME

◆

BEFORE THE CURTAIN

The title of this book needs no apology—but it might warrant a little explanation. More than summing up the book's subject, it evokes its aura: houselights dimming; an orchestra starting to play; perhaps even a Bob Fosse–like character (as in the movie *All That Jazz*) psyching himself up to perform by proclaiming: "It's showtime, folks!"

Yet the title *Showtime* can also suggest something beyond the immediate relationship of a performance and a clock. It serves here to identify a particular, comprehensive history of the Broadway musical theater. Such a history has rarely been told in full; it is almost too rich to tell. It covers a range of entertainments, artful and crude, funny and sentimental, plotless and also stuffed with plot. It covers the geographic reach of the United States, even as it centers emphatically in New York City, and also goes beyond the nation's borders. And it covers a time span going back through a past of more than two centuries, and forward through an ever-changing present.

Standard histories of musical shows, which define the subject in somewhat different ways, tend to omit some vital part of this story: Kurt Gänzl's *The Musical: A Concise History*, for example, ignores the revue; Andrew Lamb's *150 Years of Popular Musical Theatre* gives short shrift to Off Broadway; and Cecil Smith's *Musical Comedy in America* gives almost no indication that there was anything even resembling musical comedy in America before the 1840s. In this book, by contrast, the history of the Broadway musical theater appears in its abundance, however it may sprawl. The word "showtime" here, then, reflects the historical trajectory that

1

holds this book together. And so the title relates not to any particular performance, but to a recurring sense of occasion specific to the theater and, by extension, to the particularity in each of the many kinds of performances that belong in these pages. Quite literally, *Showtime* tells the story of a category of show over the course of time: the kind of show we now call the Broadway musical as it changes historically in form, in style, in content, in context, in purpose, and in meaning.

"The musical" eludes easy definition. The term itself is hardly satisfactory. Apart from its grammatical awkwardness—one might reasonably ask, "The musical *what?*"—one speaks of the musical as if the term had always been in use and as if the concept was self-evident. Neither is the case. As the term of choice, "the musical" has been in circulation only for about half a century. Before the 1960s, musical comedy generally described the field; before that, light opera and comparable terms served a similar function. As a concept, moreover, the musical refers to no single form or institution but to a collection of many practices: some overlapping, some conflicting. So it is probably best to begin by defining the musical broadly as a type of performance made up of the basic creative processes that all such practices

Comedy (mask in left hand). One of a pair of allegorical figures (together with Tragedy, *opposite*) carved in wood by William Rush and installed in 1808 on the facade of Philadelphia's New Theater in Chestnut Street.

have in common. These include, above all, talking (almost always); singing (most often accompanied by unseen instruments); and dancing (generally mixed and interspersed with other kinds of movement). The Czech theorist Ivo Osolsobě put it well when he summarized the subject of his *Semiotics of the Musical Theatre* in such irreducible terms as *The Theatre Which Speaks, Sings, and Dances.*

The comparative weights assigned to song, dance, and speech in any musical and how these elements combine or keep their distance throughout reflect different norms associated with each of the musical's several genres or subgenres. These, too, resist easy definitions. For one, definitions necessarily change as genres evolve. Minstrel shows, for example, turned into substantially different diversions in late nineteenth-century America from what they had been when they first caught America's fancy before the Civil War. A proper definition would have to be flexible enough to take such change into account. Then, too, the same show may fit in more than one generic category. Opening night critics variously referred to *Oklahoma!*, for instance, as a musical comedy, a musical play, an operetta, and a folk opera. In a sense, all were correct. It's not so much that different writers define the genres differently—though at times they do—but rather that, no matter how these categories are defined, the bor-

Tragedy (mask at right foot).

ders between them tend to remain fluid rather than fixed: They borrow from each other. Nonetheless, a familiarity with genre provides a helpful tool not only to understand how different musicals work but also to enjoy such shows for what they are. A genre establishes a configuration of constraints and opportunities—the rules of the game, so to speak—by which creators create, performers perform, and audiences come to know what to expect. If one goes to a revue hoping to be moved by a story, one sets oneself up for disappointment no matter how good the show.

Whether or not a show actually has a story line can serve as a basis for distinguishing among the musical's many genres and for dividing them into two large groups for the sake of clarity. Minstrel shows, burlesque, variety, vaudeville, and revues make up some of the major types of musicals without stories, though they differ from each other in structure, style, where they are performed, and what kind of audiences they attract. Devoid of a narrative pretext, these shows present a series of discrete performances directly to an audience. And in the absence of the built-in continuity supplied by a narrative, they may either revel in the disjunction of their separate parts or strive to create a consistent look, tone, or style of presentation—a certain touch that lends a unity to their proceedings discernible only in performance. Though it may seem contradictory, many storyless musicals actually do both.

Story-telling musicals, by contrast, focus on the ways they handle the basic tension between their narrative parts (usually spoken) and their unabashedly performative parts (usually sung and/or danced). Shows of this type include (in order of increasing musicality) plays with added songs, musical comedies, musical plays, operettas, and even operas of a certain popular bent (Broadway, folk, rock, etc.). While these also differ significantly among themselves, such shows all rely on narratives for continuity; they use song and dance in specific patterns of pacing and proportion either to disrupt their story lines as they unfold or to help them along. Talking carries great weight, for instance, in plays with added songs (*Uncle Tom's Cabin*), but virtually no weight at all in pop operas that favor nonstop singing throughout

(*Les Misérables*). Here too, however, distinctions may blur. And even the litmus test of narrative itself may prove unreliable, as in the case of shows that mix elements of vaudeville and musical comedy (*Watch Your Step*), or, more recently, "concept" musicals, which borrow as much from storyless revues as they do from story-telling musical plays (*Chicago*).

All these types of shows make up the world of musical theater. The term applies both to a performance medium (the musical *theater*) and to a performance mode (a *musical* theater). On the one hand, the term privileges the stage as the arena for producing musicals and performing them in real time before an audience whose responses (in terms of laughter, applause, silence, rioting) affect the performance in turn. Musical theater signifies a live medium, one in which no two performances are ever identical however much they may be alike. Thus it refers to the stage musical rather than, say, to the film musical or the television musical. These types of musicals, by contrast, are similar but technologically based entertainments—not dead exactly, but not quite live either. They have histories of their own, though these inevitably intersect with the history of the musical theater in one way or another. A 1972 film musical, *Cabaret*, for example, so powerfully reinterpreted the 1965 stage musical *Cabaret* on the screen that it not only displaced the authority of the original in popular culture, but it also prompted changes in subsequent stage versions of the show. Moreover, a growing reliance on the use of technology outright in the theater has changed our threshold of perception for what constitutes live performance altogether. (How many who saw *The Act* on Broadway in 1978 were aware that Liza Minnelli's Tony Award–winning performance in it included, in addition to her singing, her lip-synching onstage to prerecorded songs?) Still, even as the musical theater absorbs innovations such as these, it continues to offer an experience qualitatively different from that of other media—an experience forged not only out of live performers and live audiences, but out of a special sense of intimacy shared in the coming together of the two under one roof.

On the other hand, "musical theater" also refers to a particular condition of the theater itself. Despite much historical and cross-cultural evidence to the contrary, theater in its "normal" state is now commonly thought of as an emphatically verbal form of expression. Thus to speak of a musical theater, implies a theater divided between two modes of performance: one essentially spoken; the other characteristically sung, at least from time to time, and therefore musical. This division did not become standard in American popular culture until the later nineteenth century, when several trends converged to help bring it about—the collapse of the stock company system and its diversity of stage offerings; the rise of an entertainment industry organized along highly specialized lines; a growing public taste for realism in the theater and the corollary downplaying or elimination of musical artifice. Yet such fragmentation flies in the face of earlier theater practices. Up until about the Civil War music played a prominent role in almost all stage offerings; the same companies performed both spoken and musical plays, and on the same programs. One might even make a convincing case that the normal condition of theater in America at the time was a musical one. This clearly no longer holds true. Nowadays, in fact, musical theater refers exclusively to the theater of the musical.

But not unambiguously. At times one finds the term "musical theater" used loosely to refer to other lyric stage forms as well. What might these include? For one, music theater (lifted from the German *Musiktheater*), a twentieth-century catchall usually reserved for otherwise uncategorizable stageworks of the avant-garde that are neither operas as conventionally understood nor commercial entertainments. (Igor Stravinsky's *The Soldier's Tale* provides a good example; it uses music, speech, and dance, but no singing.) For another, musical drama, a description first used widely in Italian opera of the seventeenth and eighteenth centuries (*dramma musicale*) but now applied to virtually any serious narrative work for the musical stage (Gian Carlo Menotti's *The Consul*). Or music drama, a seemingly related term but one more closely associated with the later output of Richard Wagner and that nineteenth-century ideal of a collective art form that he called the *Gesamtkunstwerk* (*Tristan and Isolde*). But lyric stage forms of these types differ from musicals in critical respects— aesthetic intentions; national and cultural traditions; performance styles and institutions—and one clouds the discussion by minimizing the differences.

Here the term "Broadway," discreetly introduced, comes in handy. It goes a long way toward dispelling ambiguities. Be it as an indicator of geography or of character, "Broadway" immediately puts any discussion of musical theater into a modern American framework that distinguishes it from all the above. Literally, it locates the street and geographic epicenter in New York City of a system of musical theater in the United States— its creation, production, and reception—that dominated the field for most of the twentieth century. Figuratively, it stands for an ethos: It identifies the utterly commercial, collaborative, and vernacular character of that musical theater wherever its practice has taken hold—whether Stateside, or as an American import in London, Sydney, Tokyo, Gelsenkirchen, or anywhere else on the planet. To be sure, Broadway's position at the hub of a now international musical theater industry no longer goes unchallenged. But Broadway's ethos nevertheless continues to represent the cultural yardstick by which almost all activity in the field is still measured. The ample story of how such a Broadway musical theater came to be—as a live entertainment, a commercial art, and a cultural practice—is the subject of this book.

Showtime considers its subject from two perspectives. The book looks at the aesthetic development of the Broadway musical theater in its own right: the changing approaches to the craft and art of creating hit shows, or at least viable productions for the medium. The book also considers the cultural conditions outside the theater that give this development broader significance: the social, religious, political, and economic forces that act on, react to, and interact with it in different ways over time. In creating *Showtime*, moreover, I have tried to balance not only *what* the book addresses but also *how* the book addresses it. Writing a history of some breadth and depth in a relatively new field of scholarship poses problems no longer deemed problematic in more established fields. My challenge throughout as author has been to bring order to a chaos of details swirling about the Broadway musical theater as a subject—to weave these separate strands into a coherent history—without forcing them to fit into a master narrative.

Major reference books cataloguing this subject from various perspectives and published in recent decades constitute a sure sign of the field's scholarly coming-of-age. Yet even the best of these are of limited use for a project such as this. They deal exhaustively with the details and, to avoid the chaos, arrange them according to a system (no matter how unrelated the system to the details). Some use the order of the letters of the alphabet to marshal their material (Kurt Gänzl's *Encyclopedia of the Musical Theatre*; Thomas Hischak's *The Oxford Companion to the American Musical: Theatre, Film, and Television*). Others look to the calendar for inspiration and do it chronologically (Gerald Bordman's *American Musical Theatre: A Chronicle*; Richard Norton's *A Chronology of American Musical Theater*). Such books prove invaluable resources to the extent that they are reliable and that their systems make the information they organize easy to access. But as they focus on ordering the information they parcel out without connecting it, they do not do the work of histories.

Histories connect the dots—or try to. Historians analyze the information and interweave it in all sorts of ways. In short, they tell stories to explain the evidence of the past and interpret its significance. Not all stories are equally plausible, however, particularly those that tend somehow to reduce the fullness of the past in order to produce grand narratives in the present. One such narrative type, for instance, sees historical change in terms of progress toward a goal. In the 1950s, Leonard Bernstein famously espoused it in a historical survey of "American Musical Comedy" on TV, suggesting that "historical necessity" underlay the aesthetic growth he saw taking place in the field. More recently, Scott Miller's *Strike Up the Band: A New History of Musical Theatre*, while political in its thrust rather than aesthetic, has continued in the Bernstein tradition, defending what it calls the "evolution of the art form." Another such story type, by contrast, sees the circumstances of history shaping the destiny of genres as they arise, develop, and inevitably run their course. Here the titles of books like Mark Grant's *The Rise and Fall of the Broadway Musical* and Denny Flinn's *Musical! A Grand Tour: The Rise, Glory, and Fall of an American Institution* speak for themselves. Yet narrative approaches of the one type or the other suggest criticism more than they do history. Indeed, it is not immediately evident why any historical change should have to amount to an improvement *or* a decline. Sometimes a change is just a change. History, after all, is a messy enterprise. And books such as these, whichever narrative scheme they adopt, ultimately approach history from their own particular coign of vantage. They may prove enormously insightful, but they tell only one part of a larger story. And to the extent that they present a limited outlook as a genuine panorma, they diminish their plausibility as histories altogether. "Don't look for *Brigadoon* or *The Sound of Music* here," cautions Miller at the start of his *New History*, for example, "they played no part in the evolution of the musical theatre."

Showtime is not a chronicle. Nor does the story it tells depend on an overarching narrative. While the book does its share of ordering information and connecting dots, I have sought in writing it to steer a course between the Scylla of outright advocacy and the Charybdis of mere description. I have tried, in fact, to construct a history of the Broadway musical theater at once coherent and critical: to shed light on the patterns of thought, behavior, and achievement that make sense of such a history without overlooking their attendant tensions, complexities, and contradictions. I have also tried to write a history at once balanced and comprehensive both in the evidence it takes into account and in its coverage of the subject. Comprehensive, however, does not mean exhaustive or encyclopedic. You won't find every show ever produced on Broadway mentioned in these pages. Instead, you'll find a careful selection of shows—virtually all the well-known ones (including *Brigadoon* and *The Sound of Music*), and a good many of the not so well known—chosen for their ability to serve as trenchant examples of each of the many styles, genres, subjects, personalities, institutions, movements, and trends that played a major role in the development of the different kinds of productions we know today as Broadway musicals.

The main sections of this book follow a broad chronological plan. Part One, "Out of the Nineteenth Century" (chapters 1–3), begins effectively before the Civil War as New York assumes preeminent status among theater-producing cities in the United States and emerges later in the nineteenth century as the hub of a new kind of show business in America. Part Two, "Into the Twentieth Century" makes up the largest portion of the book and can be divided into two subsections: The first (chapters 4–7) focuses on the creation of a self-consciously "American" musical stage in the early decades of the new century, while the second (chapters 8–11) moves into the mid-twentieth-century's so-called Golden Age of the Broadway musical. Part Three, "Toward the New Millennium" (chapters 12–16), traces the decentering of Broadway following the Second World War and the globalization of the musical later in the twentieth century and up through the start of the twenty-first. There the book doesn't end but leaves the history of the Broadway musical open to its uncertain future.

Within this overall plan, however, the individual chapters do not proceed along simple chronological lines. This is not to say that successive chapters do not appear in proper chronological sequence. They do—but not necessarily simply. The book's chapters are organized around topics rather than in decades or other fixed parcels of time. One chapter may focus on a genre ("The Script Angle" looks at approaches to the musical play); another chapter, on a stylistic period ("A Shadow of Vulgarity" relates the Jazz Age to Broadway's sense of "jazz"); another, on an institution ("Away from Broadway" surveys Off Broadway and its offshoots); and so on. Because of this, some chapters need more background than others to get started, while some require different time spans to pursue local affinities or trace long-range consequences before they play themselves out. Chronologically, then, successive chapters may overlap or backtrack somewhat. Of course, however chapters are organized, some crisscross in coverage is unavoidable. But that *Showtime*'s chapters follow a topical arrangement rather than a strictly chronological one allows for the book's development as a history of ideas as well as facts.

As the subject of a book—any book—Broadway musical theater grabs our attention. It does so not only for its intrinsic qualities as an attention-grabber but also for its remarkable hold on different segments of the public over time. In its many guises, it has remained one of the most popular ongoing forms of live entertainment in the United States—but not only the United States. Today, hit shows such as *The Phantom of the Opera* may run for twenty years or more on Broadway, delight millions of people worldwide, and generate billions of dollars. However its popularity is gauged, the Broadway musical is arguably the twentieth century's most broadly representative musical theater form on an international scale. If for no other reason, then, it warrants a history of its own, perhaps even a comprehensive one at that.

But does it warrant a scholarly history? The author of the first history of the genre, himself a critic with academic credentials, thought it did not. Such an undertaking went against the grain of "the medium itself." "If the descriptions and assessments of the pieces and people [this book] deals with are offhand rather than scholastic," wrote Cecil Smith in the author's foreword to *Musical Comedy in America*, "this is because the medium itself does not suggest *Wissenschaft* [scholarly study] and the devices of the doctor's dissertation." Writing in 1950, Smith summed up the general outlook of his age. And even at the time Smith's book was posthumously reissued and updated in 1981, both musical-lovers and practitioners of *Wissenschaft* still largely held to the view he had articulated some three decades earlier. Especially for those academics who still looked to Europe for cultural cues or who still clung to the tenets of high modernism, the very popularity of musicals—typically American, middle-class, and commodified through and through—constituted proof positive of their shallowness. Irrelevant as culture, banal as art, musicals after all were, well, musicals. They deserved no sustained scholarly attention.

How times have changed. The past few decades have seen a turnaround regarding the Broadway musical theater of unprecedented proportions. Since the 1980s, an explosion of *Wissenschaft* in the field has crystallized in the form of articles in scholarly journals, academic monographs, and, indeed, doctoral dissertations. In contrast to the writings of journalists and devotees, which dominated the relative few sustained probes of the subject earlier on, an impressive body of thoroughly professional and scholarly informed books now exists. It covers a range of approaches to the Broadway musical theater: histories of its specific genres (Jessica Sternfeld's *The Megamusical*; Elizabeth Wollman's *The Theater Will Rock: A History of the Rock Musical from "Hair" to "Hedwig"*), and of its individual shows (Tim Carter's *"Oklahoma!": The Making of an American Musical*; bruce mcclung's *"Lady in the Dark": Biography of a Musical*); studies of its specific creators (Foster Hirsch's *Harold Prince and the American Musical Theatre*; Stephen Banfield's *Sondheim's Broadway Musicals*), and of its particular constituencies (John Clum's *Something for the Boys: Musical Theater and Gay Culture*; Andrea Most's *Making Americans: Jews and the Broadway Musical*); analyses of its musico-dramatic forms (Geoffrey Block's *Enchanted Evenings*; Joseph Swain's The *Broadway Musical*), and of its social and cultural meanings (John Bush Jones's *Our Musicals, Ourselves: A Social History of the American Musical Theatre*; Raymond Knapp's two-volume *The American Musical and the Formation of National Identity* and *The American Musical and the Performance of Personal Identity*). And this amounts to just the tip of the iceberg.

What accounts for so decisive a cultural shift? More than any other single factor, perhaps, a generational change in sensibilities on both sides of the equation—in the practice of the musical itself and in the study of it. For one, nobody refers to the field as musical comedy any more—and with good reason. The sense of sheer levity, once highly prized in the field, now has to contend with forces both heavier and darker than comedy alone suggests. Indeed, a certain darkness of subject matter and in outlook, sophistication in means of expression, and high-mindedness of aesthetic ambition characterize much of the most interesting work in the field over the last generation. Such musicals virtually demand to be taken seriously. And such seriousness, in turn, has cast its shadow back over the history of the medium itself, as the movement to produce both faithful and freighted revivals of older shows on Broadway attests. At the same time, on the other side, academics across a spectrum of disciplines have subjected both the values and methods of humanistic studies to radical reassessments. Moved by the force of postmodern awareness, with its inclusionary sense of what constitutes culture and its suspicion of cultural hierarchies and historical "metanarratives," scholars no longer find only "highbrow" subjects appropriate for study, but also "lowbrow" and even "middlebrow" ones—Broadway musicals among them. In this regard, no one's work has proved more emblematic of the shift than Stephen Sondheim's. His work has imbued the field with new artistic stature as it has transformed the Broadway musical theater from within, and it has also caught the critical attention of scholars of music, theater, American culture, and other academic disciplines like no one else's previously in the history of the medium. Might the time not now be ripe, therefore, for a scholarly reassessment of the history of the medium itself?

Culturally speaking, musicals matter. How they matter and to whom may change. But the fact *that* they matter has remained fairly constant in American culture over time. While popularity may not be the sole measure of worth, their popularity attests to the degree to which they resonate with something vital in the tenor of an age. Musicals provide one way of taking the pulse of American culture. The pleasures they afford are sufficiently varied to cover a spectrum of tastes. And it is through such pleasures that audiences have traditionally taken stock of who they are at any given moment. Understanding the history of musicals can thus give some insight into the values and beliefs of those theatergoers that such entertainments once held in thrall. One may not always like what one finds a musical discloses: What one learns about the past is often more disturbing than reassuring. But it will not be untruthful. Understanding the history of musicals may have relevance for today's audiences as well. It may be crucial to a full appreciation not only of a revival of an old show, but of a new show altogether. Consider *Urinetown*, for example, which, by spoofing the conventions of past musicals, assumes a spectator's knowledge of what it spoofs. In fact, it's hard to find a show nowadays that doesn't refer to the history of the medium in some way, self-consciously, with the styles and conventions of the past used to make a point. Even theatergoers who just like to go to musicals and who might otherwise not have much interest in reading a history of them will be surprised at how their enjoyment can increase when they understand what informs the very shows they go to simply for the pleasure of it.

As a history of Broadway's musical theater, *Showtime* offers access to such an understanding. And as a comprehensive history, it does so throughout. For contemporary shows are not the only ones to derive meaning by referring directly to the spirit, styles, and structures of the musicals that preceded them. One might say that the history of the Broadway musical is littered with them. But that would be putting the conceptual cart before the horse. It is rather that such musicals constitute the very stuff that makes a history out of what would otherwise be a random collection of shows. In other words, because the Broadway musical as a category embraces such a diversity of types, the way these shows relate to each other—the way they regularly draw on one another over time regardless of their genre—creates that sense of a shared tradition that gives legitimacy to the Broadway musical as a category in the first place. *Follies*, for example, draws repeatedly and deeply on the spectacular revues of the early twentieth century; *Chicago*, on vaudeville; and *Gypsy*, on burlesque. Still earlier, *Of Thee I Sing*, the first Broadway show to win a Pulitzer Prize, drew directly on *The Mikado*, a comic opera of Gilbert and Sullivan that goes back to the late nineteenth century. And earlier still, *The Threepenny Opera*, whose success in New York virtually launched the Off Broadway musical, drew even more intimately on *The Beggar's Opera*, a ballad opera that goes back as far as the early eighteenth century—which is in fact where, chronologically, *Showtime: A History of the Broadway Musical Theater* begins.

And so what started out as "a little explanation" to introduce this book has come full circle. The show itself, as it were, can now begin. As the houselights dim and the orchestra starts to play, it's time to raise the curtain on this history of the Broadway musical theater by turning the page. It's *Showtime*, folks!

PART ONE

OUT OF THE NINETEENTH CENTURY

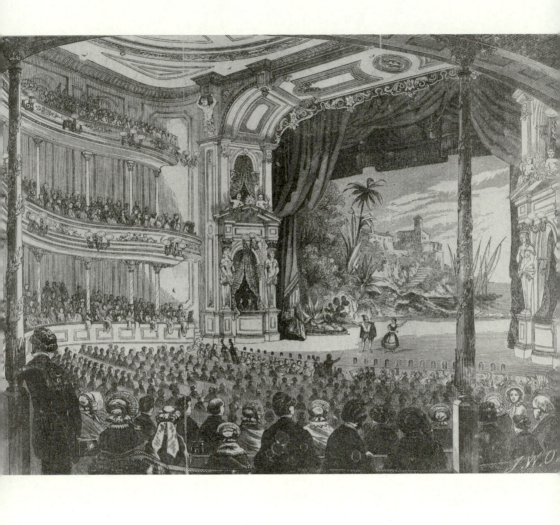

TRANSITION STAGES

MACBETH

[London, 1606?] Astor Place Opera House Production (5/7/1849–5/10/1849). **Producers:** William Niblo and James H. Hackett. **Text:** William Shakespeare. **Music:** Matthew Locke? **Director:** John Sefton. **New York Run:** 2 performances. **Cast:** Mrs. Coleman Pope, William Charles Macready. **Songs:** "Witches' Chorus"?, "Come Away, Come Away"?

UNCLE TOM'S CABIN

(7/16/1853–ca. 6/19/1854). **Producer:** Alexander H. Purdy. **Book:** George L. Aiken, adapted from the novel by Harriet Beecher Stowe. **Songs:** George C. Howard and others. **Director:** Howard. **New York Run:** 325 performances. **Cast:** Mrs. [Caroline Emily Fox] Howard, Miss Cordelia Howard, George C. Howard, Greene C. Germon, J. W. Lingard, George L. Fox. **Songs:** "Oh! I'se So Wicked," "Uncle Tom's Religion," "Old Folks at Home," by Stephen Foster.

THE BLACK CROOK

(9/12/1866–1/4/1868). **Producers:** William Wheatley, Henry C. Jarrett and Harry Palmer. **Book:** Charles M. Barras. **Music:** Thomas Baker and others. **Directors:** Wheatley and Leon Vincent. **New York Run:** 475 performances. **Cast:** Annie Kemp Bowler, Marie Bonfanti, George Boniface, Charles Morton. **Songs:** "You Naughty, Naughty Men."

1855 newspaper engraving of the interior of Niblo's Garden, the best-equipped and most fashionable theater in mid-nineteenth-century New York.

Music and theater have shared long and sometimes overlapping histories in North America. Even before Columbus first landed at the end of the fifteenth century, singing and dancing played prominent roles in all kinds of ceremonies on the continent. Later, as Europeans came to Christianize and settle the land, they also brought many of their theater-based habits with them: Original plays were being performed in New Spain by the mid-sixteenth century, and by the early seventeenth century, in New France as well. Yet it was not until later still that a recognizably musical theater developed, particularly in those English-speaking regions of North America that are now part of the United States. It took the coming together of cultural conditions in an age touched in various ways by the spirit of the Enlightenment—a worldly outlook, a time for recreation, a sense of the "public sphere" and of a marketplace not only of ideas but of entertainments—for the history of musical theater, as we now understand the term, to begin.

According to a familiar catchphrase, theater at its most basic consists of two planks and a passion. Little more was available throughout British North America; and in certain places, considerably less. Some colonies resisted theater outright. Puritan New England and Quaker Pennsylvania banned it on religious grounds: It was the "Synagogue of Satan." Other areas saw it simply as a hotbed of crime and sought to restrict the traffic in thieves, prostitutes, and like-minded entrepreneurs who used it as a base of operations. Yet even when openly permitted, theater amounted to no more than a makeshift affair. Audiences were small; performers, untrained; playhouses, nonexistent. Barns, taverns, and other public gathering spots served as the performance sites for plays. Around 1716, in Williamsburg, Virginia, the first colonial playhouse on record was built with planks that served directly as the stage. The passions played upon those boards, however, remained the work of amateurs drawn from the local community and the students of William and Mary College. Not until the 1750s or thereabouts did professional acting companies bring their expertise to the performance of stageworks in the colonies on a regular basis. In doing so, they laid the groundwork for durable institutions of English-language theater in North America.

But professional theater was an import: All theater companies came from Great Britain. They led precarious existences. With no cities in the colonies able to support them for a full season, they toured in varying orbits from Halifax, Nova Scotia, to the Leeward Islands in the Caribbean. Major stopovers included Philadelphia, New York, Williamsburg, Annapolis, Charleston, as well as Barbados and Jamaica. Their repertoires consisted entirely of British plays, which they performed in rotation. The plays ran the gamut from the tragedies of Shakespeare (*Richard III, Othello*) to the comedies of Farquhar (*The Recruiting Officer, The Beaux' Stratagem*) with a healthy dose of farces (*The Mock Doctor*) and some pantomimes (*Harlequin Collector*).

The acting companies even threw operas into the mix—at least the English version of what they called opera at the time. For in the jargon of the eighteenth-century stage, "English opera" (unlike the all-sung Italian kind) applied loosely to one of several types of plays with added songs. The ballad opera, for example, often consisted of a satirical play interspersed with simple airs, popular tunes, and broadside ballads. John Gay's landmark comedy of 1728, *The Beggar's Opera*, not only served as the prototype, it continued to influence later developments on the musical stage to such an extent that historians now tend to view it as a forerunner of the modern musical. The first opera performed in America, *Flora* (Charleston, 1735), and the first opera written by an American, *The Disappointment* (Philadelphia, 1767), were both ballad operas, in fact. Another type, the pastiche opera or *pasticcio* (literally, "hodgepodge"), favored a more sentimental play and more elaborate musical numbers (Isaac Bickerstaffe's and Thomas Arne's *Love in a Village*, 1762). Generally in both these English opera types, actors spoke the dialogue rather than sang it. Moreover, audiences recognized much of the music, as playwrights cobbled scores together by borrowing from various well-known sources rather than insisting that the music all be freshly composed. The same troupes ultimately performed both plays and operas and under the same conditions—often on the same bill—which typified American stage practice of the age. There was no functional differentiation between such theatrical genres.

The troupe that would become the foremost theater company in America first crossed the Atlantic and arrived in Williamsburg in 1752. Originally managed by Lewis Hallam (1714?–1756), the London Company of Comedians dominated the American stage for nearly half a century. It reorganized several times, however, and changed its name after Hallam's death to the American Company of Comedians, and again after the Revolutionary War to the Old American Company. Calling the company "American" stemmed in part from the desire to distance it from the taint of English decadence, which clung to theater generally in an America increasingly bent on independence from the British Crown. Yet given the basic character of the company throughout its long career—its British personnel, its British performance traditions, its British roster of plays—it could be considered American in little more than the geography of where it performed. The play on meaning here was striking—particularly at a time when, after the Treaty of Paris and the withdrawal of British troops in 1783, Americans sought to define themselves as Americans with renewed intensity as they created a new nation.

Political independence was one thing, however; cultural independence, another. To *be* American in the new republic meant laying claim

Philadelphia's New Theater, later known as the Chestnut Street Theater, opened in 1794 as the foremost home for drama in the United States.

to a distinctive sense not just of place, but of character. In the theater this would now mean, beyond simply performing for audiences in the United States of America, engaging them in plays that addressed American themes and from the perspectives and sensibilities of Americans. Plays on American subjects by playwrights born in America actually began to appear with some frequency in the Federal era. The Old American Company itself produced many of the most important—*The Contrast* (1787), by Royall Tyler (1757–1826); *André* (1798), by William Dunlap (1766–1839). But the prevailing winds of taste over the postcolonial American stage were still European. In 1794, an English visitor remarked of a performance he attended at Philadelphia's newly opened Chestnut Street Theater, by far the finest playhouse in America: "It is an elegant and convenient theatre, as large as that of [London's] Covent Garden; and, to judge from the dress and appearance of the company around me, and the actors and scenery, I should have thought I had still been in England."

Henry Wansey, the visiting Englishman, based his impression on the sights he saw about him in the Chestnut Street Theater. His impression would probably have been no different had it been based on the sounds he heard there as well. For the music director and co-manager of the company, Alexander Reinagle (1756?–1809), was himself British-born, British-bred, and thoroughly British-trained. One of the most distinguished composers then living in America, Reinagle immigrated to the United States and settled in Philadelphia. He brought a strong European sense of style and professional skill to bear in helping to shape the theater and concert life of the city, which by the 1790s had become the nation's capital and greatest center of theatrical entertainment.

Reinagle's career typified that of the best musicians active in the theaters of the United States at the start of the nineteenth century, not only in Philadelphia but in such rival centers as Charleston and New York. Theater companies everywhere employed musicians in a variety of capacities: singing actors and actresses, orchestra players, conductors, coaches, composers, arrangers. But without formal institutions on this side of the Atlantic where aspiring musicians might learn their trade, American companies looked to Europe for personnel with the professional training and experience necessary for their productions. They did not have to look long. Starting in the 1780s, qualified German, French, and above all English musicians immigrated to America in large numbers, bringing their taste and technical expertise to the burgeoning theatrical life of the United States. Foremost among them were composers who could also perform, conduct, and arrange their music—most prominently, the Frenchman Victor Pelissier (1745?–1820?), and such Englishmen, besides Reinagle, as Rayner Taylor (1747–1825), Benjamin Carr (1768–1831), and James Hewitt (1770–1827). Of their American stageworks, *The Archers* (Carr and Dunlap, 1796) is one of the earliest extant, although only the playscript and a single song survive. For both *The Voice of Nature* (Pelissier and Dunlap, 1803) and *The Aethiop* (Taylor and William Dimond, 1814), however, scripts, song texts, and music have all come down to us more or less intact. Historically, therefore, one might describe these as the first complete works of the American musical theater that we possess in some sort of written form.

But it may still be somewhat premature at this point to speak of a musical theater in the United States—at least as a distinct form of cultural practice. After all, one wouldn't use the term "musical theater" without implying its distinction from a nonmusical form of theater. Otherwise, why not simply speak of theater and have done with it? On what, then, does the distinction rest? If we begin with a spoken play—on the assumption that theater implies spoken plays above all else—we can convert that play into a potentially musical one just by adding a song to it. A song bridges the gap between words and music: Words must still be communicated, but instead of speaking them, one sings them—and by singing, changes them. Singing thus amounts to taking the first step toward opening up the theater's verbal world of discourse to musical possibilities—ultimately, even to wordless ones altogether: dancing, for example, or the sheer sound of instruments playing. Of course, spoken plays make use of singing, dancing, and incidental music, too—but with a difference. It is not that a musical theater piece must necessarily have *more* musical moments than a play (though it usually does), but rather that such moments constitute the very centers of pleasure of the work: the centers of gravity and levity. They are, said one observer, "the reason one goes to it in the first place." Such musical moments have the power to transform our whole experience of theater into something qualitatively different from what we experience when the main investment on the stage is in the words.

Such a polarized view of theater finds general acceptance today. But it probably does not reflect the experiences of English-speaking audiences in eighteenth-century America, who were drawn to popular theater forms in which musical elements freely mixed with speech (a rarity in more elite forms of English theater due to restrictions of royal licensing and pressures of aristocratic patronage). Even later, in early nineteenth-century America, there were still neither social strictures nor institutional structures to divide what was musical in stage entertainment from what was not. Apart perhaps from the opera house—at best a shaky institution in America at the time—a cultural space for musical theater as a separate entity simply did not exist. Instead, "the same facilities, the same personnel, the same techniques were used in the performance of all theatrical genres," and music in one form or another served them all, even the tragedies of Shakespeare. Today's theatrical practice may differ considerably in this respect, but, argues Deane Root, a historian of nineteenth-century music and culture, it should not blind us to the realities of our theatrical past:

> *The prevailing view [today] of nineteenth-century American theater is dominated by attention to the* words *voiced by the actors. But for most of this period theater simply did not operate from written texts alone; music was an equal and essential partner with the script. Music was so ubiquitous in the American theater throughout the nineteenth century that any understanding of the subject—or of individual works or theaters, indeed even of specific performances or performers—must take it into account.*

The rise of realism in the theater worked to change this ubiquity, as it aimed to drive any music that was not dramatically "justifiable" from the stage. So did the commercial and industrial revolutions of the same period work to change the ways of production and reception in American theater, moving them toward the lines of specialization we know today. But these developments belong to the late nineteenth century. Not until then can one speak of American musical theater in an historically informed sense—one based not only on abstract distinctions between "straight" and musical forms of theater, but based also on the development of cultural institutions to legitimize their differences in practice, each with special genres and traditions of its own.

No clear historical divide, however, separates the first signs of that specialized world of musical theater we now take for granted from the last traces of a musically ubiquitous world of theater we no longer recognize as such. There is only an ill-defined transition from the one condition to the other that, gradually and in stages, took place over the second half of the nineteenth century in America. A sampling of these stages nonetheless can help clarify the nature of this transition. Three in particular, taken from around the middle of the century, stand out from the rest with a degree of intensity and notoriety that compels us to look at them more closely: the Astor Place riot in New York; the adaptations of the novel *Uncle Tom's Cabin* for the stage; and *The Black Crook*, once widely held to be the first Broadway musical. Considered together, the three offer a vivid picture of cultural change in America as the transition was just getting under way from which musical theater in its modern sense—and with it the Broadway musical—first emerged.

THE ASTOR PLACE RIOT

"It will be a great week in New York," proclaimed the *New York Herald* on May 3, 1849. "Trade is brisk, industry is productive, the shipping interests are going ahead, and theatricals flourish along side all these elements of general prosperity." The last entry in this ledger of good fortune was not out of keeping with the rest. Theatricals figured prominently in the economic prosperity of New York even before the emergence of a commercial theater as we know it. Theatricals appealed to nearly all levels of society, and so they also had a hand in fostering the city's sense of civic well-being. In these respects, New York City resembled other great urban centers where theater activity flourished in mid-nineteenth-century America—Boston, Philadelphia, Baltimore, Charleston, New Orleans. Yet it differed from them by developing a new sense altogether of what a great urban center could be.

In 1849, New York was already well on its way to becoming a "mother city" to the nation: a *metropolis*. If it had not yet achieved the kind of cohesiveness of institutions for a truly metropolitan culture, it lacked for nothing in the sheer concentration of physical resources to qualify as a metropolis. With over half a million inhabitants, New

York City—that is, properly, Manhattan—had more, and more diverse people in it than any city in the United States. (Baltimore and Brooklyn, the next two largest cities in the nation, each had populations of less than one-third that number.) New York also had the greatest concentration of the nation's mercantile and industrial wealth: It was the country's commercial emporium, its financial center and chief port. Since the Cunard Line had relocated its western shipping terminus from Boston to New York the year before, the city had become the gateway for two-thirds of all imported goods and three-quarters of all immigrants from Europe entering the United States.

New York's population and wealth, and the entrepreneurial drive to bring the two together, formed the basis for a thriving theater culture. Rivaled only by Philadelphia earlier in the nineteenth century, New York City by mid-century boasted the foremost resident companies in the nation and a choice of theaters to accommodate them. (Theaters often took their names from the streets where they stood— the Bowery, the Park, the Chatham—or from the businessmen who ran them—Mitchell's Olympic, Niblo's Garden, Barnum's American Museum.) New York City drew first-rate visiting companies and artists from elsewhere; it also served as a major source of hit productions for the theaters of other cities—hits such as *New York As It Is* (1848), which, taking New York's own "Bowery b'hoy" tough for its hero and his working-class milieu for its subject, became the most popular play performed on an American stage up to its time. Thus, when the well-known actor-manager William Burton began shifting the base of his operations from Philadelphia to New York early in the 1848–49 season, the move symbolically confirmed New York's emergence as the undisputed capital of the nation's theatrical life.

It was all the more shocking therefore when, at the end of what was to have been that "great week in New York," theatricals actually made a shambles of the *Herald*'s forecast. Indeed, on May 10, a performance of *The Tragedy of Macbeth* at the Astor Place Opera House turned into tragedy of another kind. The trouble had already begun on May 7, at the opening of a run of Shakespeare's *Macbeth* starring William Charles Macready (1793–1873). (Macready, an Englishman, was one of the great tragic actors of the age and he behaved accordingly onstage and off, which often rubbed American audiences the wrong way.) When Macready first appeared on stage in the title role that night, several spectators created a grand disturbance in the house aimed at driving him off. Later, he indignantly noted in his diaries some of the projectiles the audience hurled at him: "four or five eggs, a great many apples, nearly—if not quite—a peck of potatoes, lemons, pieces of wood, a bottle of asafoetida which splashed my own dress, smelling, of course, most horribly." By the third act the uproar escalated: someone started flinging chairs. The first one landed in the orchestra pit where it "caused a prestissimo movement among the musicians, not set down in the original music for *Macbeth*." And as the next chairs reached the stage, Macready ordered the curtain rung down and canceled the performance.

Incensed, the actor resolved to cancel his New York engagement entirely and return at once to his native England. A committee of prominent New Yorkers intervened, assured Macready of the support of the city's respectable community, and urged him to reconsider. He did—regrettably. For when he reappeared as Macbeth in the same house three nights later, a new disturbance began to brew. This time the police took action. As Macready tells it in his diaries:

> *The police rushed in at the two sides of the parquette, closed in upon the scoundrels occupying the centre seats and furiously vociferating and gesticulating, and seemed to lift them or bundle them in a body out of the centre of the house, amid the cheers of the audience. I was in the act of making my exit with Lady Macbeth, and . . . as well as I can remember the bombardment outside now began. Stones were hurled against the windows in Eighth Street, smashing many; the work of destruction became then more systematic; the volleys of stones flew without interruption, battering and smashing all before them; the Gallery and Upper Gallery still kept up the din within, aided by the crash of glass and boarding without.*

In the street, a furious mob attacked the opera house in support of the protesters inside. In the house, Macready, defiant, strove to finish the performance:

> *In the very spirit of resistance I flung my whole soul into every word I uttered, acting my very best and exciting the audience to a sympathy even with the glowing words of fiction, whilst these dreadful deeds of*

*real crime and outrage were roaring at intervals in our ears and ris-
ing to madness all round us. . . . Going to my room [after the play's
conclusion] I began without loss of time to undress, but with no feeling
of fear or apprehension. When washed and half dressed, persons came
into my room—consternation on the faces of some; fear, anxiety, and
distress on those of others. "The mob were getting stronger; why were
not the military sent for?" "They were here." "Where? Why did they
not act?" "They were not here; they were drawn up in the Bowery."
"Of what use were they there?" Other arrivals. "The military had
come upon the ground." "Why did they not disperse the mob then?"
. . . Suddenly we heard a volley of musketry: "Hark! what's that?" I
asked. "The soldiers have fired." "My God!" I exclaimed. Another
volley, and another!*

The militia had fired point-blank on the rioters in the street. When the
smoke had cleared, more than 100 had been injured, and 22 people lay
dead or dying.

Riots were nothing new to the theater early in the nineteenth century. On the contrary, audiences were used to interacting with the stage

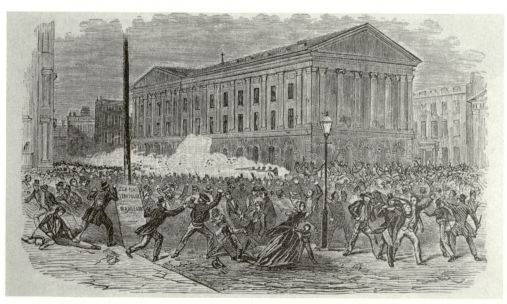

1849 newspaper engraving showing the mayhem outside the Astor Place Opera House
as militias open fire on the mob.

and making their opinions known. Spectators regularly exercised their "sovereignty" at performances through disturbances that took many different forms. Of all of these, riots were by far the most disruptive. But a theater riot was also by custom a self-regulated event, and the one in Astor Place was clearly not that. It involved crowds of angry demonstrators outside the theater as well as in it. Putting it down, moreover, involved New York's citizen militia opening fire on the people for the first time in the city's history. Thus the incident that occurred at what the *Herald* would decry as the "Massacre Opera House in Disaster Place" has also come to be regarded by historians in larger terms: not simply as another theater riot, but as a riot *about* the theater.

What was it, then, that stirred the rioters to action? Accounts vary. According to one, it was a bitter feud between two tragedians, Macready and Edwin Forrest (1806–1872), which their followers took up with a vengeance when both men starred in separate productions of *Macbeth* the same week in New York. According to another account, it was nativism run amok. Macready was British, of course, and many New Yorkers, swayed by a rising tide of nativist passion, saw him as an agent of "foreign rule" now culturally imposed by England on the United States. The native-born Forrest, by contrast, they rather identified with the heroes he portrayed in American plays who galvanized the common people to resist imposed authority in any form—the Indian chief in *Metamora* (by John Augustus Stone, 1829); Spartacus in *The Gladiator* (by Robert Montgomery Bird, 1831). A placard circulated the day after the riot revealed the nativist position with an inflammatory flair:

> AMERICANS! *Arouse! The Great Crisis Has Come!! Decide now whether English* ARISTOCRATS!! *and* FOREIGN RULE! *Shall triumph in this* AMERICA'S METROPOLIS, *or whether her own* SONS *whose fathers once compelled the base-born miscreants to succumb, shall meanly lick the hand that strikes, and allow themselves to be deprived of the liberty of opinion—so dear to every true American heart.*

According to still another account, however, the riot did not protest the sway of any foreign power so much as it did the forces of division within American society itself. The very opening of the Opera House in Astor Place in 1847 had been contentious. It represented an attempt by New York's "aristocracy" to control and divide theatergoing in the city along social and economic lines. So when leading citizens from New York's merchant and professional classes now closed ranks behind Macready's appearance there, they fanned the flames of an already combustible situation. And smoldering resentments among the city's less privileged classes erupted offstage into violence, violence that turned deadly in the streets. (Among the prime participants in the mayhem, ironically, were the "Bowery b'hoys," those working-class toughs whose bent for the rough-and-tumble had recently been so celebrated on the stage in *New York As It Is*.) What the riot really dramatized, said one source, was "an opposition of classes—the rich and the poor . . . a feeling that there is now in our country, in New York City, what every good patriot hitherto has considered it his duty to deny—a *high* class and a *low* class.

Such opposition violated an ideal of communality then prevalent in the theater. Indeed, the makeup of earlier theater audiences had been remarkably heterogeneous, even as audiences tended to gravitate toward certain playhouses along social lines. In the 1830s, for example, New York's upper sets favored the Park Theater, the "middling" classes the Bowery, and the lower classes the Chatham. Too, economic status generally determined where one sat in a given house. (This can be inferred from the scale of ticket prices, which, at the Bowery Theater in 1830, ran: 37½ cents for "groundings" in "the pit" in front of the stage, 75 cents for "gentlemen" in the tiers of boxes surrounding them, and 25 cents for everyone else up in "the gods," the uppermost gallery of the house.) Nonetheless, the different segments of the public that sought the pleasures of the stage earlier in the nineteenth century did so basically by sharing the same cultural space, however differently they may have dealt with the experience. An uneasy democracy of sorts reigned in the American theater that drew, it was said, "all ranks of the people together."

What enticed such a diversity of people to converge under a single roof was the variety of amusements that the theater offered of an evening. A typical bill at the time consisted of a *mainpiece*—often a full five-act tragedy—followed by an *afterpiece*—say, a two-act farce or comic opera. Audiences relished this unlikely coupling, one observer deeming the latter as indispensable to the former as "the wine we drink after dinner, to correct the humors and promote digestion." Additionally, a bill might begin with an instrumental overture and might be punctuated throughout by interludes and other entertainments featuring some built-in musical component. In fact, music pervaded even productions of stageworks primarily driven by spectacle or the spoken word—including Macready's *Macbeth*. Managers offered up a stew of attractions in an effort to tie their profits to the democratic ideal that one theater might serve the tastes of all—concert, song, farce, opera, variety, tragedy, dance, even "equestrian drama."

By contrast, the Astor Place Opera House was originally built and run by New York's fashionable classes as a "classic and exclusive place of amusement." The management limited the diversity of its audiences by establishing strict codes of dress and behavior; and it limited the appeal of the operas it offered by mounting them in almost any language except English. Inevitably perhaps, such snobbery provoked a reaction that in this case turned violent: the opposition of one segment of theatergoers to the restrictive practices of another—the low, as it were, against the high. Years later, Henry James would look back on the riot as representing the "instinctive hostility of barbarism to culture." Indeed, whether the riot was a catalyst or simply an indicator of cultural change, within a generation of the event each of these segments would consolidate its own distinctive venues and forms of musical theater—a "popular" one, above all, in the morally suspect concert saloon; an upright or "serious" one, in the democratically suspect Metropolitan Opera. And so the riot has come down to us as something of a cultural watershed; for it occurred precisely at a time when the effects of industrialization were starting to split apart much that had previously held together in American life. More vividly than any other event of the period, it marked the beginning of the end of theater in the United States as a conglomerate entertainment for a heterogeneous audience. "The Astor Place Riot intimated that this union was no longer possible," writes theater historian David Grimsted. "The country had grown up, and grown apart. The theater after midcentury followed this development. It expanded and divided—into legitimate drama, foreign-language drama, farce, vaudeville, circus, burlesque, minstrelsy, opera, symphony—each with its separate theater and separate audience."

The move to fragment audiences and specialize in different kinds of theater could not have succeeded without transforming the basic stock-company system that had been the institutional bedrock of the

American stage from its beginnings up until the Civil War. The stock company was a continuous, self-sufficient unit for producing plays; and it presented many plays in repertory each season. The troupe consisted of performers and artisans who were attached to a theater which the company owned or leased on a steady basis. As the personnel remained the same while the plays changed, the versatility of its members was the key to any company's success. Most versatile of all was the actor-manager who typically ran the company by taking charge of both its artistic and financial affairs: directing the plays and managing the theater. The system proved remarkably durable, though it was weakened when, with the American engagement of British actor George Frederick Cooke in 1810, independent traveling "stars" began using the resources of local stock companies for purposes of their own. Later in the nineteenth century, however, the stock system was undermined by what amounted to an alternative to it in the "combination system."

The combination system first developed in the 1860s as an efficient response to the pressures of specialization. Such pressures not only split play production and theater management into two structurally independent functions, they also forced companies to abandon repertory seasons and forced managers to dedicate their theaters to one type of entertainment in order to survive. Unlike the stock company it eventually replaced, a combination company was a discontinuous unit put together to produce one play only. Producers aimed to maximize profits by means of a "long run" during which the one play would be repeated night after night for as long as an audience would pay to see it. Then the company would take the play on tour, performing it in as many theaters as possible across the land. If the company could not keep up with the demand of theaters for a very popular play, new companies that literally duplicated the original company's production would be put together. But as the life of any combination company was limited to the working life of its play, once the play had exhausted its audience, the company would disband.

The combination system brought about a transformation of the American stage toward the end of the nineteenth century called "the industrial revolution in the theater." However simplified the comparison, there are striking parallels between the industrialization of the American economy and the restructuring of the American theater that took place at about the same time: the centralized system of play pro-

duction in New York, the standardization of product in duplicate companies, the division of labor between the production of plays and the
running of the theaters that featured them. If the making of theater
in America had been no more than a cottage industry up through the
middle of the nineteenth century, by the century's end it had become
big business: show business.

New York City emerged from this transformation with its position of leadership in the nation's theatrical affairs ever more deeply
entrenched. "Make your mark in New York," Mark Twain had advised
performers back in the 1860s. "With a New York endorsement you
may travel the country over . . . without fear—but without it you are
speculating on a dangerous issue." A generation later, nothing about
the situation had changed except the degree to which Twain's advice
had become incontrovertible. In the interim, the city had become,
besides the production capital of an entertainment industry in the
United States, its corporate headquarters. And a New York endorsement now came in the form of a three-word stamp of approval: "Direct
from Broadway." For the term "Broadway," too, had been undergoing
a transformation that amounted to a shift of emphasis in its meaning.
Broadway still referred to a street in New York, and, by extension, the
theater district through which it ran. But it now began referring to
something less tangible as well. Broadway was becoming the trademark of a certain ethos in American entertainment: a catchword for a
set of practices and beliefs aimed not only at getting the greatest value
for your money on a stage but at obliterating altogether the distinctions between commerce and art.

UNCLE TOM'S CABIN, THE MUSICAL

Uncle Tom's Cabin was the most popular American play of the nineteenth century. It is also considered the first major stage hit in America in which all extraneous entertainments were eliminated from a
program. Its very success helped establish the practice of doing away
with an afterpiece and stretching a single narrative entertainment
over the full course of an evening in the theater. The play was based
on a sentimental novel by Harriet Beecher Stowe in which Stowe combined Christian allegory and domestic melodrama to "awaken sympa-

thy and feeling for the African race" and to indict slavery in America as "a system necessarily cruel and unjust." A best-seller when first published in book form in 1852, *Uncle Tom's Cabin* had a profound and polarizing impact on America's conscience in the incendiary years before the Civil War. At the height of the conflict, in fact, President Lincoln is even said to have referred to Stowe as the little lady who actually started the big war.

Americans became acquainted with Stowe's work not only by reading the novel but also by seeing it performed in one of its many stage adaptations. Such adaptations appealed to educated audiences who may well have read the original yet still enjoyed the spectacle of the stage, and they appealed to working-class audiences who, barely literate, would have known Stowe's work only in this form. Stowe, however, withheld permission from the undertaking. She argued that if her book succeeded as a play, it would set a bad precedent because such success would desensitize the public to the moral dangers inherent in the theater itself.

> *If the barrier which now keeps young people of Christian families from theatrical entertainments is once broken down by the introduction of respectable and moral plays, they will then be open to all the temptations of those [plays] which are not such, as there will be, as the world now is, five bad plays to one good one.*

Stowe was a devout Christian as well as the daughter, sister, and wife of distinguished Calvinist ministers. Theatergoing for her was not the morally neutral act it would later become in America. She was not alone in her beliefs. Her mistrust of the stage reflected the ambiguous role theater had played not only among the religious in the United States but generally in American culture up to her time. Prohibitions against the stage had ruled everywhere in early colonial America—north, south, Puritan, Anglican—"in detestation of idleness" that diverted from the grim and necessary work of survival. By the mid-eighteenth century, opposition had relented sufficiently in colonies like Virginia and New York to permit stage presentations, though not without objections to them now as occasions for criminal and licentious acts less depicted onstage than actually performed in the audience. (Pickpockets notoriously plied their trade in the pit; prostitutes plied theirs in the third tier, traditionally reserved for "unescorted" women.) During the Revolution patriots throughout the colonies reinstated bans on theatrical activity, which now seemed a diversion of resources and energies from the war effort. Yet even after the war, opposition persisted in such pious strongholds as Quaker Pennsylvania and Calvinist New England, where it was based on the orthodox Protestant view of theater as inherently sinful. Theater was blasphemous: It mocked God by creating worlds of deception that undermined the natural order of things. And theater was idolatrous: It took pleasure in making public display of the deceit. Given so hostile a climate for the undertaking, then, professional theater had to wait until the early nineteenth century to gain a lasting institutional foothold in American culture (though in Hartford, Connecticut, it was still illegal to present a play of any kind until 1862). Stowe thus had both history and high principled ground to stand on in refusing permission. But in the absence of any copyright laws to protect her interests at the time, she had no legal ground whatever.

Thus countless *Uncle Tom's Cabin*s found their way onto America's stages in short order, with playwrights free to make whatever changes to the novel they wished. George L. Aiken (1830–1876) wrote the best remembered of these. Scripted for an acting company managed by George C. Howard (1815–1887), Aiken's play was first produced in Troy, New York, within half a year of the publication of Stowe's novel. The following summer it opened at Purdy's National Theater in New York City for a run of nearly a year, a sensation in an era when long runs were not the rule.

Aiken's *Uncle Tom's Cabin* followed the multiple narrative strands of Stowe's book. One told the story of the slave Eliza, who escapes with her son by crossing the ice on the Ohio River and makes her way to Canada. Another told the story of Uncle Tom, a slave who refuses to escape and whose resistance to slavery remains internal. Indeed, Tom maintains his dignity, morality, and religious faith despite the ordeals he endures. When Tom saves Little Eva from drowning, he is bought by the young girl's father, Augustine St. Clare. St. Clare, a kindly slave owner awakened to the ills of slavery, vows to free Tom but dies in an accident before he can do so. St. Clare's widow, however, sells Tom to the evil slave driver Simon Legree; and Legree, unable to come to terms with Tom's Christ-like goodness, eventually whips him to death. (Howard performed alongside his family in the

National Theatre!

Formerly the Chatham, in Chatham street, near Roosevelt.

Sole Lessee, Proprietor, and Manager.................... A. H. PURDY.

First and Second Dress Circles and Upper Boxes...... ...... 25 Cents
Orchestra Arm Chairs............................ ...... 50 Cents
Parquette for Colored Persons...................... ...... 25 Cents
Exclusive Private Boxes.... ....$5 :One Person to Private Box.....$1

Doors open at 7, curtain will rise at quarter before 8 o'clock, precisely.

Unprecedented! Twelfth Week of the Grand Drama.

The immense success attending the representation of the great Moral Drama of UNCLE TOM'S CABIN has induced the Manager to announce it for Every Evening during the month of October. The Youthful Wonder,

LITTLE CORDELIA HOWARD

Appearing in her original character of the Gentle Eva.

MR. J. J. PRIOR   MR. LINGARD
As George Harris.   As Uncle Tom.

MR. G. L. FOX,
As Phenias Fletcher.

MR. J. B. HOWE,
From the London Theatres, as St. Claire.

Together with

THE FULL NATIONAL COMPANY

Thursday Evening, Oct. 6th, 1853,

And Every Night (Sundays excepted,) during October,

The New and Wonderfully Successful Dramatic Version of

UNCLE TOM'S CABIN

Or, Life among the Lowly.
DRAMATIZED FROM
MRS. HARRIET BEECHER STOWE'S
world renowned work by G. L. Aiken, Esq.

IN SIX ACTS

Eight Tableaus & Thirty Scenes,

EMBRACING THE WHOLE WORK,

in which will be introduced the original songs, composed and written expressly for this piece by
G. C. Howard, entitled

TO LITTLE EVA IN HEAVEN, and
UNCLE TOM'S RELIGION.

Published by Oliver Ditson, Boston, and for sale by Perry & Co., Firth and Pond, and all the principal Music Stores in New York.

LITTLE CORDELIA HOWARD,
In her Original Character of EVA, as performed by her over TWO HUNDRED NIGHTS.

MR. J. J. PRIOR as . . . George Harris

Uncle Tom, the faithful Slave	Mr. J. Lingard	Sambo, the Slave of Legree	Mack
George Harris a Fugitive	J. J. Prior	Jumbo, the Slave driver	MacDonnell
Gumption Cute, the Yankee	h. Stone	Alf Man, the Slave purchaser	Daymon
Phenias Fletcher, the Kentuckian	G. W. L. Fox	Skegns, the Auctioneer	Lyons
St. Claire, the Southern Gentleman	J. B. Howe	Adolph, the Master's man	Mitchell
Legree, the Pirate Slave dealer	N. B. Clark	Waiter, the smart man	Cline
Mr. Wilson, the Quaker	Toulmin	Doctor, the last visitor	Smith
Deacon Perry	L. Fox	Harry, the child of the fugitive... Mast. Murray	
Marks, the Lawyer	Herbert	Slaves, Planters, Citizens, &c	
Old Shelby, the insolvent Planter	Rose		
George Shelby, the son	Mr. Blake		
Tom Loker, the Slave hunter	G. Lingard		
Haley, the Slave Trader	Mack		

EVA, the flower of the South	LITTLE CORDELIA HOWARD		
Topsy, the Girl that never was born			Mrs. Mack
Aunt Ophelia, the Vermonter			Mrs. Bradshaw
Eliza, the fugitive wife	Mrs. W. G. Jones	Marie St Claire, the victim of custom. Miss Landers	
Cassy, the distracted	Mrs. Bannister	Chloe, the wife of Uncle Tom	Mrs. Lingard
Emeline, the Quadroon Slave	Miss Barber	Female Slaves, &c.	

The Play is beautifully interspersed with Singing and Dancing.

Song, Old Folks at Home, words and Music by E. P. Christy, Esq. .... Uncle Tom
Dance and Song... Topsy
To Little Eva in Heaven, words and music by G. C. Howard .... St. Claire
Uncle Tom's Religion, words and music by G. C. Howard .... Uncle Tom

TABLEAUS IN THE DRAMA.

1st. THE ESCAPE OF ELIZA.
2nd. THE TRAPPERS ENTRAPPED.
3rd. THE FREEMAN'S DEFENCE.
4th. DEATH OF LITTLE EVA.
5th. THE LAST OF St. CLARE.
6th. TOPSY BUTTING THE YANKEE.
7th. CASSY HELPING UNCLE TOM.
8th. DEATH OF UNCLE TOM.

NOTICE.--- The Ladies and Gentlemen will please remain seated until the Curtain Descends, that every effect may be given to the Last Grand Tableaus.

N. B. The performance will conclude at Eleven o'clock Every Evening

In preparation and will be produced, when an opportunity presents itself, " The Key to Uncle Tom's Cabin," by G. L. Aiken, Esq. Little Katy, or the Hot Corn Girl, by C. W. Taylor, Esq. Paradise Lost, by C. W. Taylor, Esq., all of which have been secured by Copyright in the Southern District of New York.

original production: he played St. Clare; his four-year-old daughter played his stage daughter, Little Eva; and his wife, a cousin of Aiken's, played the slave Topsy—in blackface. The regular appearance of families together on the stage was more than an economizing measure of companies such as Howard's. It lent respectability to a profession still widely held in disrepute.)

It took Aiken no fewer than six acts, eight tableaux, and thirty scenes to adapt Stowe's novel to the stage. To fit all this into a single evening required doing away with an afterpiece. As nothing succeeds like success, this ostensibly started the practice of "one-play entertainments" for which Howard claimed the credit. According to an advertisement, moreover, the play was "moral, religious, and instructive" rather than simply entertaining. In fact, with the afterpiece eliminated, nothing else on the bill now compromised the moral thrust of the play, so "there would be no impropriety in the religious portion of the community witnessing it." The logic was apparently convincing. Along with everyone else, the pious came in droves to see it; and eventually— though, in the words of her escort, she sat "well muffled . . . in the shade of the curtains of our box"—Stowe herself.

Aiken's drama stuck to its literary source. It took up the abolitionist cause directly. (An *Uncle Tom's Cabin* by H. J. Conway that played at Barnum's American Museum rather favored the anti-abolitionist cause.) It also flouted the derisive stage Negro conventions of the period and dignified the portrayal of Tom, even though all the play's black roles were performed by the company's white actors in blackface, in accordance with the custom of the age. Yet Aiken was no man's fool in matters of the stage, and he departed from Stowe enough not to ruin his chances for success. He cut out philosophic discourses, inserted low-comedy scenes, and generally bent Stowe's vision to the moral platitudes of the melodramatic form he took as a given. If he did not reward Tom by the final curtain, he made sure at least to punish Legree by killing him off at the end. But in meting out justice to one villainous individual, Aiken deflected attention from Stowe's view of the systemic injustice in the institution of slavery itself.

1853 playbill for the Howard Company's original production of *Uncle Tom's Cabin* in New York.

The play was indeed a melodrama, a genre that captured the spirit of the nineteenth century like no other. More frequently performed than any other type of theater at the time, melodramas told unambiguous tales of right and wrong that appealed directly to the emotions. They also espoused democratic values, favored action over character development, and obeyed an absolute code of moral conduct whereby vice would not go unpunished nor virtue unrewarded. Notable American examples of the era besides *Uncle Tom* include William H. Smith's *The Drunkard* (1844, also premiered by the Howard troupe) and Dion Boucicault's *The Poor of New York* (1857) and *The Octoroon* (1859). Melodrama was also more than a pure or "straight" theatrical genre. As its name implies, a *melo*-drama was a play with music—but without singing. It called for instrumental "action music" from time to time to underscore what characters were saying as they spoke and to convey what they were thinking or feeling when they were silent. Little of this music has come down to us. Without it, however, a melodrama was just a drama—and incomplete.

As a melodrama that also included songs, however, Aiken's play used music in three significantly different ways. First, music appeared plausibly "inside" the play as part of the story. Characters in the play could thus perform such music themselves or realistically be expected to hear others performing it—today the terms *diegetic* or *source* music often describe this function. For example, as Little Eva reads to Tom from the Bible, he responds by intoning a familiar hymn. On another occasion, with no one else around, Tom sings Stephen Foster's popular "Old Folks at Home" to himself. Such musical numbers evoked a private memory or a shared cultural reference between one character and another. Neither song was unique to *Uncle Tom's Cabin* since each already had a recognizable existence apart from the play. But their insertion into the drama related directly to the mood of the scenes they were meant to enhance.

Second, music also appeared implausibly "outside" the play, as if out of nowhere—nondiegetic music, that is, meant to amplify the emotion of a scene or clarify its action. This was the *melo* part of the melodrama and, according to the conventions of the genre, such music represented the expressive focus of the play in audible terms that the audience alone could hear, *not* the characters onstage. One stage direction reads: Simon Legree "Strikes TOM with whip, three blows—Music chord each blow." Another requires continuous music from one scene to the next as the runaway slave Eliza tries to escape her pursuers. Typically, Aiken's script indicated only *where* such music was to be played, not *what* the music actually was. And so it was usually up to a house musician at each theater to compose or arrange what were known as "melos"—the "hurries," "pathetics," and other characteristic musical passages called for by the script's cues—and score them for the instrumental forces on hand.

The third use of music in Aiken's drama related to songs again—however, songs now written expressly for the drama by Howard. These songs were not diegetic, but not *unambiguously* nondiegetic either. They existed in a kind of limbo, neither quite "inside" nor "outside" the play. While sung onstage by characters in the play, they were not necessarily audible to anyone onstage, perhaps not even to the characters singing them. Consider "Uncle Tom's Religion," for example. It did not function as an independent song so much as an internal monologue that somehow took the shape of a song as Tom externalized it. It behaved more like an operatic aria, then, though written in the manner of a parlor tune of the day, and performed as part of a spoken play rather than a fundamentally musical one. In addition, the song uniquely suited not just *Uncle Tom's Cabin* but the character of Uncle Tom. Its words defined the performer who sang it as someone who spoke in dialect and who personified the submissiveness that has since come to load the very name Uncle Tom with the pejorative freight it now carries in American culture. Even the musical setting was individualized (most extraordinarily for a stage song of the period) in the pathos evoked by the tremulous piano chords that accompany Tom's final words.

> *Far away from wife and children,*
> *Still I plod my way along.*
> *Massa Clare has gone to Eva,*
> *Leaving friendless poor old Tom.*
>
> *Yet with trust and strength in heaven*
> *I remain a faithful slave.*
> *When de whip to me am giben,*
> *I'll think of him who died to save.*

"Uncle Tom's Religion" (*Uncle Tom's Cabin*)

In sum, "Uncle Tom's Religion" exemplifies what we now would call a theater song, to distinguish it from other song types. Unlike "Old Folks at Home," which Tom consciously performs as a "source" song in the play, Tom sings "Uncle Tom's Religion" almost unconsciously—as if, as a character in the play, he seems not to know that he is singing it at all.

In the mid-nineteenth century it was not unusual for an essentially dramatic play to have strong musical components. In *Uncle Tom's Cabin* these operated on many levels: diegetically, melodramatically, and approaching what we now call musical theater in a song like "Uncle Tom's Religion." Central to the play as it was originally produced, however, was not the musical theatricality of it but the drama—the "great moral drama" of the decade before the Civil War. It did not remain so. After the war, productions of the piece—"Tom shows," for short—increasingly became occasions to showcase the talent of African Americans, now emancipated, and to introduce a variety of theatrical novelties. Thus *Uncle Tom's Cabin* came to include all sorts of stage doings that had little to do with Stowe or even Aiken—from specialty numbers by black performers (banjo players, dancers, even "jubilee singers" in the slave auction scene) to animal acts (including live bloodhounds to chase after the runaway Eliza). All this tended to alter the essential spirit of the piece, to transform a moral drama into an entertainment at times resembling nothing so much as a minstrel show. Indeed, a critic remarked of the success of one such Tom show already in 1878, "The drama proper has been curtailed to such an extent that it must be difficult for anyone who has not read the novel . . . to patch together the story of it." Yet it took the better part of a generation for *Uncle Tom's Cabin* so to turn from the drama proper. *The Black Crook*, shortly to rival it in popularity, would not wait that long.

THE BLACK CROOK

From its inception *The Black Crook* celebrated the sheer theatrical thrust of theater in ways *Uncle Tom's Cabin* did not. Less focused on dramatic values from the start, *The Black Crook* made music, dance, and the sensationalization of the stage the reason for an evening in the theater. "Theatrical" and "dramatic" are not mutually exclusive terms. Yet neither are they quite the same. They go back etymologically to words that are Greek in origin: theater referring to that which "is seen," and drama to that which "is done." *Theatrical* then suggests those aspects of a play that relate to its enactment on a stage and its impact on an audience, qualities that tend to be visual or more broadly sensuous, perhaps even sensational. *Dramatic*, in turn, suggests those aspects that relate to a play's structure, plot, and action, qualities that are primarily verbal, even literary and intellectual. Both, of course, figure in the life of most plays. Some plays, however, are created with the idea not of balancing the two but rather of throwing weight more in the direction of one than the other. That was the case with *The Black Crook*.

Legend has it that *The Black Crook* began as two entertainments— a melodrama and a ballet—that came together as much by accident as by design. The melodrama, the work of playwright Charles M. Barras (1820?–1873), already seemed old-fashioned when it was new. Its supernatural tale of good and evil owed much to *Der Freischütz*, Carl Maria von Weber's German Romantic opera of 1821 and one of the most popular musical stageworks of the age. Nevertheless, William Wheatley (1816–1876), the manager of Niblo's Garden, booked *The Black Crook* for his theater. He valued Barras's play, he said in hindsight, as "just the wanted piece" to combine with something else. That something was the ballet, the work of a European dance troupe led by choreographer David Costa (1835?–1873?) and starring Marie Bonfanti (1845–1921). Booked in advance for the Academy of Music, the Europeans suddenly found themselves stranded in New York without a theater when the academy burned down. The intrigues to find a new house for the troupe and Wheatley's inspiration to house it as best he could at Niblo's by incorporating it into the frame of Barras's script thus led to the combination of costume melodrama, romantic ballet, and fairy spectacle that became the landmark production.

The Black Crook, as dance historian Barbara Cohen-Stratyner shrewdly put it, was "seminal without being particularly original." Barras's script was surely the least original element in the mix. Set in seventeenth-century Germany, Barras's play told the story of two village innocents, Rodolphe and Amina, whose love for one another is thwarted by the treacherous Count Wolfenstein. He has designs on Amina himself. He is also in league with the evil sorcerer Hertzog (aka the Black Crook), who has made a Faust-like pact with the devil to pro-

Backstage at Niblo's Garden as *The Black Crook* chorines prepare to "fly" in an aerial ballet.

vide a "fresh soul" annually, and who thus has designs of his own on Rodolphe (Hertzog: "He's mine—ha, ha—he's mine!"). In the end, however, the good Fairy Queen Stalacta and her magical subjects intervene to reunite the lovers and to defeat both the earthly forces of Wolfenstein and the supernatural ones of the Black Crook (Hertzog: "Foiled, tricked, crossed in the hour of my victory!").

From the start, no one had kind words for the play. An opening night reviewer called it "rubbish." Charles Dickens was unkinder still when he saw it later in the New York run and professed to find its goings-on beyond the reach of reason:

> [It is] the most preposterous peg to hang ballets on that was ever seen. The people who act in it have not the slightest idea of what it is about, and never had; but, after taxing my intellectual powers to the utmost, I fancy that I have discovered Black Crook to be a malignant hunchback leagued with the Powers of Darkness to separate two lovers; and that the Powers of Lightness coming (in no skirts whatever) to the rescue, he is defeated.

Surely Dickens overstated the case for humorous effect. (The show did not really feature nudity, only the suggestion of it.) Yet from Dickens's vantage as a man of letters, *The Black Crook* did have its priorities backward. It was not a piece of dramatic literature—not first and foremost a play that used musical accompaniment and scenic support, but the other way around. For Dickens that amounted to the tail wagging the dog; he called it, literally, *pre-posterous*: what belonged behind it put up front. Dramatic literature, however, was hardly what Wheatley had in mind. Less a play in its own right, *Black Crook* was really a blueprint for an occasion that emphasized other things: music, spectacle, and movement of a most alluring kind.

Music pervaded *The Black Crook*, though little of it has survived. Thomas Baker, a staff conductor at Niblo's, seems to have provided whatever the production needed: from short melos for each of the music cues in the script to full-blown instrumental sequences for the stage tableaux and ballets. Vocal numbers worked somehat differently, as singers often inserted material of their own choosing into the production. The most popular song on opening night, "You Naughty, Naughty Men," was an interpolated number for Amina's maid, in fact.

Sung by Millie Cavendish, the English actress for whom Theodore Kennick (lyrics) and George Bickwell (music) had written it, the song made light of the sexual connivances of men and the ultimate collusion of women in them. But it had virtually no bearing on the story. It was rather a saucy music hall ditty in five stanzas, each sung to different words yet always to the same music, thus following the simple strophic form beloved of popular songs of the period. For all its popularity, however, when Cavendish left the show early in the run, the song left with her. And as the show enjoyed an astonishingly long run by standards of the day, several songs came to occupy the slot that Cavendish's song originally filled. Not only did different singers bring their own songs with them regardless of the show in which they performed, but the same singers also tended to change songs during the run of a given show in order to keep their performances fresh.

Far better remembered than the melodrama or the music were *The Black Crook*'s scenic effects. Working at the cutting edge of the era's technology, the show outdid earlier theater spectacles in the daring and the impact of its stage displays. Moreover, in the spirit of the Gilded Age, the producers advertised the cost of putting on the show as if it were one of the attractions:

> the most RESPLENDENT, GRAND AND COSTLY PRODUCTION *ever presented on this continent....* THE GORGEOUS AND BRILLIANT NEW SCENERY.... THE DAZZLING TRANSFORMATION SCENE ... *at a cost of Fifteen Thousand Dollars....* THE NEW STAGE AND MACHINERY, *combining the latest improvements of Europe and America, making it equal, if not superior, to any in this world, constructed at a cost of over ten thousand dollars....* THE COMPLICATED GAS CONTRIVANCES.... THE CALCINE LIGHTS.... *The whole involving an outlay of* FIFTY THOUSAND DOLLARS.

No photographs of the production exist to give us a sense of what the scenic effects of such contrivances resembled. What we have are only verbal accounts, none perhaps more vivid than that of Mark Twain. He caught a performance of the original production in 1867 and, while he thought the scenery "gorgeous beyond anything ever witnessed in America, perhaps," he was more taken by the tableaux, especially one that climaxed the great transformation scene at the end of the show. Some thirteen minutes long, this was a wordless, musically underscored change of scene, in full view of the audience, that began in a dim "subterranean gallery" and finished up in the "Realms of Stalacta," all radiant and covered with "girls."

> *Beautiful bare-legged girls hanging in flower baskets; others stretched in groups on great sea shells; others clustered around fluted columns; others in all possible attitudes; girls—nothing but a wilderness of girls—stacked up, pile on pile, away aloft to the dome of the theatre, diminishing in size and clothing, till the last row, mere children, dangle high up from invisible ropes, arrayed only in camisa. The whole tableau resplendent with columns, scrolls, and a vast ornamental work, wrought in gold, silver and brilliant colors—all lit up with gorgeous theatrical fires, and witnessed through a great gauzy curtain that counterfeits a soft silver mist! It is the wonders of the Arabian Nights realized.*

Twain described what he saw; others, what they felt. "One grows dizzy in the blaze of splendor, and rises at the fall of the curtain with a sort of stupefied air," said one observer; another spoke of the "lavish richness and barbaric splendor" whose "luster grows as we gaze, and deepens and widens, till the effect is almost painful."

The assault on one's senses from the spectacle was rivaled by the assault on one's sensibilities by the dance. Indeed, the corps de ballet, consisting of "voluptuously-formed dancing girls, who seem to wear little else than satin slippers, with a few rose-buds in their hair," elicited a range of passionate responses—from prurience to indignation. Some of the ballerinas' costumes seemed shockingly scant. They hinted at nudity altogether in the "Demons Dance," where traditional ballet skirts were replaced by snug drawers over flesh-pink tights. As for the dance itself, some of the movements verged on the lewd. A few danseuses even lifted their legs to expose their undergarments and assumed such attitudes with danseurs as to suggest to at least one clergyman "scenes which one may read of, describing the ancient heathen orgies." The press condemned such trespasses as vehemently as the pulpit. An editorial in the *Herald* railed, "Nothing in any Christian country, or in modern times, has approached the indecent and demoralizing exhibition," and called for the police to "arrest all engaged in such a violation of public decency and morality." But the police did nothing to stop the show. And the public, drawn perhaps all the more to the theater by such notoriety, did everything in its power to keep it running.

The Black Crook enjoyed its reputation as a "naughty, naughty" entertainment. It appealed to the very middle classes whose values it transgressed. Here was a show in which not the story but "the scenery and the legs," Twain said, were "everything." And the promise of their sensationalized display brought spectators to the theater again and again to experience what was otherwise beyond the pale of middle-class forbearance—the scenery's "barbaric splendor," for example, and the

Pauline Markham poses in full regalia for her role as Stalacta in *The Black Crook* (studio photograph ca. 1869).

"demoralizing exhibition" of the legs. But it would be misleading to overlook what was *not* sensational about the piece. For what audiences actually heard and saw in the theater was mostly not so transgressive after all. Barras's play, whatever its dramatic weaknesses, gave the sensationalizing impulses at the heart of the show a narrative and highly moral frame. The fact that *Black Crook* was far more successful than shows like Laura Keene's *The Seven Sisters* (1860) or any of its predecessors that were also long on spectacle and feminine display may thus have been connected with the fact that *Black Crook* was also long on plot and moral rectitude where they were not. At the same time, however, although *Black Crook* was clearly a "one-play entertainment," the play itself was not the show's main attraction as much as the needed foil for its presentations of women, scenery, dance, and song. Perhaps the real success of *Black Crook*, then, lay in a tension between its spectacle and its melodrama—how well it spoke to bourgeois sensibilities by negotiating between competing claims of transgression and respectability in the sensationalism of its production values and the conventionality of its scripted ones.

Beyond the mix of elements that went into making it a success, *Black Crook* redefined the very meaning of success in quantifiable terms. It took in over a million dollars in box office receipts, a hitherto unimaginable return on a capital investment in the theater that dwarfed virtually all competition. What made such a profit possible was a run of 475 consecutive performances at Niblo's Garden, far exceeding that of any production before in New York (and on Broadway too in a sense, as Niblo's was located at the corner of Broadway and Prince Street). And what fed the run besides word-of-mouth was the management policy of welcoming publicity in any form that might win for the piece not just fame but notoriety. (The addition of new ballets and other attractions during the run also helped keep it going.) The original production spawned many other productions; and *Black Crook* began its first national tour in 1867, initiating some twenty consecutive seasons in which it was professionally mounted in theaters across the country. Finally came the revivals, including some ten new productions of the show over the next twenty-five years in New York alone, each one with its own set of "improvements" (1870, 1871, 1873, 1874, 1876, 1882, 1883, 1886, 1889, 1892).

A success of such unprecedented magnitude helped give rise to the cult of the long-running hit show. And the fact that that success was achieved by separating the production itself from the playhouses where it was produced gave increased momentum to the ongoing institutional restructuring of theater in the United States in the late nineteenth century. *The Black Crook* has thus assumed a mythic status in the history of the American stage, not as the earliest musical hit so much as the first blockbuster in the modern sense. Many regard it as the first Broadway musical, though the claim would be hard to sustain on purely historical grounds whatever criteria one chooses to apply. Today, however, when on the broad spectrum of American entertainment Broadway musicals are widely held to constitute a genre of their own, *The Black*

Crook takes pride of place at the start of more historical accounts of that genre than any other single work. Broadway mythmakers even accorded it that rarest of distinctions when in 1954 the story of its origins was made the subject of another musical: *The Girl in Pink Tights.* In sum, *The Black Crook* was more seminal than original; its historical importance may have less to do with what it was than what it eventually came to represent.

One might go so far as to characterize the Astor Place riot, *Uncle Tom's Cabin,* and *The Black Crook* as influential emblems of change in the transition from one kind of theater to another that took place during the second half of the nineteenth century in America. The riot at the Astor Place Opera House gave impetus to the trend toward specialization in the theater and the separation of popular culture from other cultural forms that became normative by the century's end. *Uncle Tom's Cabin* helped establish the practice of one-play entertainments through its durability and reach into theaters in virtually every corner of the nation. *The Black Crook* hastened the demise of the stock company and the rise of the combination system through the kind of profitability demonstrated by its success. None of these proved decisive in itself. Yet each contributed to alter American theater in ways that proved decisive for developing a distinct form of American musical theater around the turn of the twentieth century that has been identified with Broadway ever since.

How "musical" does musical theater have to be before it is no longer regarded simply as theater? And how "Broadway" before it is no longer simply American? Is it a question of artistic choices that creators make in shaping a production? Is it a question of cultural assumptions that audiences bring with them into a theater? There are no simple answers. Historians have consistently considered *The Black Crook* part of the musical theater because, as an extravaganza (which is how it was widely understood in its day), it was more a musicalized spectacle with narrative elements than the other way around. *Uncle Tom's Cabin* has generally not been so considered, however, because, as a melodrama, it *was* the other way around: a staged narrative with musical elements (though in the course of its production history it took on so many musical elements eventually as to warrant at least some consideration as a form of musical theater as well).

On the other hand, while *Black Crook* may have been the more musical production, it was by far the less American. Its character, subject, and setting were patently European. There was almost nothing about it of the vernacular that would soon inscribe a form of musical theater as being not only American, but specifically *of* Broadway—neither its humor, acting, singing, nor dancing. The spirit, style, and energy that were to make the Broadway musical distinctive were shaped largely in the crucible of American subcultures each with vernaculars of their own (working-class, immigrant, ethnic). These were first expressed not on the narrative stage that took a play as its point of departure but in the kaleidoscope of episodic stage forms that used music and that went by many names, of which "variety" might best serve to describe them all.

MECHANICS' HALL
472
BROADWAY, ABOVE GRAND STREET.

OPEN EVERY NIGHT
FRONT SEATS INVARIABLY RESERVED FOR LADIES

BRYANT'S

MINSTRELS

Bryant Brothers............ ....Proprietors and Managers

MONDAY EVENING, APRIL 4th, 1859
PROGRAMME—PART FIRST.

Instrumental Overture		Bryant's Minstrels
We're the boys for pleasure	Operatic	Company
Me and Eliza		Jerry Bryant
Bonny Mae		T. B. Prendergast
Yes, in a Horn		J. Unsworth
Medley Chorus, popular Ethiopian airs		Company
Only 19 Years Old		Dan Bryant
Finale--Masquerade Waltz		Full Band

PART SECOND. VARIETIES.

Pas Seul, Burlesque	H. Leslie
FADDEN MAC FADDEN......by the	MAC DILL DARROLLS
Violin Solo	P. B. Isaacs
Tambourine Duet	Jerry and Dan Bryant
Favorite Ballad	Little Arthur

WE COME FROM THE HILLS
Emmett, Prendergast, Jerry and Dan Bryant.

Flutina Solo...Neil Bryant

BURLESQUE ITALIAN OPERA

Mlle. Pickle Hominy, Prima Donna	Madame Very Angry Prendergasto
Count no-Count MacCaffery, Primo Tenor	Sig. Dani Brigudo Bryanto
Signor Houlihan Stuffhiscowl, Primo Basso	Sig. Unosro Lynckxiani
Hoer's (well) Formed, Baritone	Heer Jerro La Blatchio Bryanto
Sig. Sardinero, "Officers"	Sig. Excelocerio Emmittani
Two Distinct Orchestras, Efficent Chorus, &c.	the whole under the direction of
	Mons. Max Mush-tie-stray-cow-eelman, Signors Issaosani and Bros. Hobbes

PART THIRD—PLANTATION.

Local Banjo Song	J. Unsworth
THE SURPRISE PARTY...CARROLL, JERRY and DAN BRYANT
Wooden Shoe Dance	R. Sands

After which Mr. Dan Emmett's new and original
PLANTATION SONG AND DANCE,
DIXIE'S LAND
Introducing the whole Troupe in the Festival Dance.

The whole to conclude with
"OUR AMERICAN COUSIN" BILL
Which has been brought from "Laura Keene's Theatre," AND WILL
BE PLACED ON THIS STAGE WITHOUT ANY ALTERATIONS.

NOTICE CHANGE OF TIME!
Doors open at quarter to Seven.   Curtain will rise at quarter to Eight o'clock.

ADMSISION   25 CENTS

HERALD PRINT.

2

VARIETY STAGES

THE MULLIGAN GUARD BALL
(1/13/1879–5/24/1879). **Producers:** Edward Harrigan and Tony Hart. **Book, Lyrics and Director:** Harrigan. **Music:** David Braham. **New York Run:** 100+ performances. **Cast:** Annie Yeamans, Harrigan, Hart. **Songs:** "The Mulligan Guard," "The Babies on Our Block."

FIDDLE-DEE-DEE
(9/6/1900–4/20/1901). **Producers:** Joseph Weber and Lew Fields. **Book and Lyrics:** Edgar Smith. **Music:** John Stromberg. **Director:** Julian Mitchell. **New York Run:** 262 performances. **Cast:** Fay Templeton, Lillian Russell, De Wolf Hopper, David Warfield, Weber, Fields. **Songs:** "Come Back, My Honey Boy, to Me," "Ma Blushin' Rosie."

IN DAHOMEY
(2/18/1903–4/4/1903). **Producers:** Jules Hurtig and Harry Seamon. **Book and Director:** Jesse A. Shipp. **Lyrics:** Paul Laurence Dunbar. **Music:** Will Marion Cook. **New York Run:** 53 performances. **Cast:** Aida Overton [Walker], Bert Williams, George Walker. **Songs:** "Swing Along," "I'm a Jonah Man."

1859 playbill announces "Mr. Dan [E]mmett's new and original plantation song and dance, DIXIE'S LAND" in the program of Dan Bryant's Minstrels in New York.

When the last third of the nineteenth century began, the United States lay shattered in the wake of a civil war. By the time it ended, the United States had emerged as a world power. Historians often call the period that saw this transformation the Gilded Age, invoking the title of an 1873 satire by Mark Twain and Charles Dudley Warner. By this title, the authors meant to mock the pretensions of an age that was not at all golden.

A Golden Age glowed. The Gilded Age glittered. Its leading businessmen set about creating the "cash nexus" that shaped the era's central undertaking: mass industrialization of the American economy. They engineered the dazzling prosperity of the age. In the process, they turned themselves into the nation's first generation of corporate millionaires, and their names into household words: John D. Rockefeller (who made his fortune in oil), Andrew Carnegie (in steel), J. P. Morgan (in banking), Cornelius Vanderbilt (in shipping and railroads).

Beneath the glitter, however, lurked darker issues of a society fundamentally transformed by industrialization. For example, what did the future hold for political stability in America amid growing inequities of wealth and opportunity that polarized haves and have-nots? Or for national identity in the face of waves of immigrants who provided the needed labor force but who were ethnically diverse and unschooled in republican values? Or for social cohesion altogether as Americans abandoned the countryside and agricultural careers to migrate to overcrowded cities for more lucrative jobs in manufacturing and, once there, to compete not only for work but for its obverse, the new social construct, leisure?

The rise of leisure as a distinct cultural phenomenon resulted in part from the increased size and spending power of the urban upper and middle classes. "We may divide the whole struggle of the human race into two chapters," said America's future President James A. Garfield in 1880. "First, the fight to get leisure; and then the second fight of civilization—what shall we do with our leisure when we get it." To the latter challenge the cities of the Gilded Age responded by developing new forms of consumption, recreation, and diversion that ingeniously catered to a host of different tastes all at once. For consumption, for example: the department store. For recreation: the amusement park. And for diversion: the variety show of many types, including one that would ultimately be touted as "our most nationally representative form of theatrical entertainment," vaudeville.

FROM MINSTRELSY TO VAUDEVILLE

"Variety" has several meanings in the world of entertainment. As a structure for a performance—a variety show—it refers simply to "a succession of different things," according to journalist Bert Lowry. As an institutional structure—a variety theater—it refers to an organization for producing variety shows, whose character shifted over time: from an establishment originally offering refreshment with entertainment to one ultimately offering entertainment with refreshment. In the first sense, variety applies to many of the most beloved diversions of the nineteenth century—including circuses, minstrel shows, and burlesques. In the second sense, variety led directly from the concert saloon to vaudeville, which surely also belong on the list of beloved diversions. In truth, it is not always easy to distinguish between the different uses of "variety" as a term. Sometimes the distinction is negligible.

What distinguishes all variety shows from other performance types, however, is the focus on the act of performing itself, unencumbered by other considerations. At their peak such entertainments represented musical theater at its most carnivalesque. They did not have plots, they did not tell stories, and they did not observe the niceties of what a later generation would call political correctness. (Present-day audiences would likely find scandalous their no-holds-barred approach to matters of race, ethnicity, and gender.) Freed from these constraints, variety shows offered what more sophisticated or respectable forms of entertainment did not: indulgence in the most unbridled expressions of talent, energy, and fun ever let loose on a musical stage.

In all of the many forms variety took during the nineteenth century, from minstrelsy to vaudeville, performers always shaped their acts to the tastes and expectations of audiences. Most often, they did so in front of the very audiences they aimed to please. Dancers, gymnasts, and animal trainers, for example, did not have to worry about sticking to a script: They never used one. Actors, singers, and comedians, who might have used scripts when they rehearsed, never really felt bound by them. Variety performers of every kind relished the freedom to interact with their public while performing, feeding off audience response and feeding it in turn with all the improvisatory skill they could muster. Ultimately, theirs was an art dictated by the norms of live entertainment and the ethos of the popular stage, perhaps the only truly democratic mass medium of the period: It reached virtually all areas of the country and placed no demands of literacy on its audience.

Minstrel shows represent the earliest variety show–type to make a lasting impact on American culture and to develop into a distinctly American form of show business. In these entertainments, white northern actors portrayed southern plantation life by burlesquing Negro character types ("Zip Coon," "Jim Dandy") in song, dance, dress, and dialect. They did so, moreover—inverting the traditional whiteface makeup of circus clowns—by using burnt cork to blacken their faces, which we view today as intrinsically degrading.

Blackface acts by solo white performers had long been a theater staple. Their appeal grew particularly in the 1830s when Thomas Dartmouth Rice (1808–1860) first popularized the character of "Jim Crow" with an impersonation that surpassed the renditions of other "Ethiopian delineators." But the shift from independent solo acts to full-length ensemble shows began only in the 1842–43 season with the engagement at New York's Bowery Theater of four white Northerners who called themselves the Virginia Minstrels. Led by Dan Emmett (1815–1904), soon to win fame as the composer of "Dixie," this blackface quartet created an overnight sensation and laid the groundwork for the new diversion—the minstrel show name, its spirit of collective mayhem, and the nucleus of its performing ensemble: a fiddler, a banjoist, a tambourine player, and a player of the "bones" (castanetlike clappers).

E. P. Christy (1815–1862) later in the decade used his troupe of Christy's Minstrels to give the new entertainment a characteristic structure. He developed the three-part format that became standard in the 1850s. In part one, the company entered and formed a semicircle. At the center sat the "interlocutor," a master of ceremonies with a pompous flair and a gift for bloated rhetoric; at the ends sat the "endmen" (named Tambo and Bones for the instruments they played), who used their dialect humor to mock his pretensions. In this portion, group songs alternated with comic exchanges between the interlocutor and the endmen that doted on riddles, wisecracks, and the inexorable pun. An endman caught in a shipwreck in the Erie Canal, for instance, explained how he pulled out a bar of soap and washed himself ashore.

The second part constituted the variety section, or "olio." This consisted of a medley of specialty acts featuring a diversity of artists such as "wench" impersonators, acrobats, clog dancers, and monologists who habitually delivered sermons of non sequiturs called stump speeches. One began this way, for example:

> *Feller-fellers and oder fellers, when Joan of Ark and his broder Noah's Ark crossed de Rubicund in search of Decamoran's horn, and meeting dat solitary horseman by de way, dey anapulated in de clarion tones of de clamurous rooster.*

Finally came the third part, the afterpiece, in effect a farce with songs. Here performers often made a travesty of a popular play (*Uncle Tom's Cabin*) or took particular delight in burlesquing more prestigious stage fare, such as an Italian opera (*Lucia di Lammermoor* turned into "Lucy Did Lam a Moor") or a tragedy of Shakespeare's (*Julius Caesar* became "Julius the Snoozer"). Shakespeare's *Othello*, in fact, provided one of the most popular sources for afterpiece debunkery—and one of the most revealing. Not only was its hero black in the original play, but as its heroine Desdemona was also white, their relationship touched one of the most sensitive fault lines in American society. Where but through the minstrel's mask in nineteenth-century America could one encounter public expression of sentiments such as those found in this duet from *Desdemonum, An Ethiopian Burlesque?*

Scene I.—A street in Wennice. House of Brabantium, with practical window R.H. Night. (enter OTELLER, L., with tambourine, and musicians, who serenade and retire.)

Duet

OTELLER: Wake, Desdemonum, see de risin' moon,
    Ebrybody's snorin', nightingale's in tune;

Trow aside your lattice, show your lubly phiz;

Sing a song of welcome, while I go troo my biz!

DESDEMONUM: (at casement)

'Tel, my duck, I hear you; daddy's gone to bed.

Fotch along your ladderum, I'm de gal to wed!

Since burnt-cork am de fashion, I'll not be behind—

I'll see Oteller's wisage in his highfalutin' mind.

BOTH: De hour am propitious—come, my darlin' flame!

Dey say dat in de dark all cullers am de same.

(OTEL. throws her a rope ladder. She descends. They embrace.)

Covering a range of humor from the silly to the transgressive, the minstrel show grew in popularity before, during, and after the Civil War. En route, it spurred the creation of a fresh and memorable repertoire of songs—"Oh! Susanna" (Stephen Foster, 1826–1864), "I Wish I Was in Dixie's Land" (Dan Emmett), "Carry Me Back to Old Virginny" (James A. Bland, 1854–1911). And it enlisted the direct contributions of African Americans in developing a distinctive stage dance vernacular—the cakewalk, the soft shoe, tap. During its forty-year heyday, the minstrel show became the dominant mode of commercial entertainment in the United States until vaudeville and burlesque displaced it in national affection in the 1880s and 1890s.

Blackface minstrelsy, said William Dean Howells in the 1880s, was "our one original contribution and addition to histrionic art." By histrionic art he did not mean high art. On the contrary, minstrelsy embodied a self-consciously "popular" form of entertainment that, by means of the very unruliness of its histrionics, broke sharply with efforts to create a "legitimate" native tradition on the American stage. It represented a rude form of commerce between male working-class culture and middle-class values. And it represented an even ruder form of negotiating racial division in the United States. Frederick Douglass railed against its blackface imitators as "the filthy scum of white society, who have stolen from us a complexion denied to them by nature, in which to make money, and pander to the corrupt taste of their white fellow citizens." Yet great numbers of those fellow citizens flocked to the entertainment over the decades convinced they were getting, even if comically distorted, a dose of the real thing. Undeniably, however conflicted the messages derived from the minstrel stage, they were in no way ennobling. Indeed, the American minstrel show lent itself to "the often malicious caricaturing of an unfortunate race," as James Monroe Trotter put it, that seemed congruent with the rationale for slavery even after the Civil War, when the success of black troupes now entering the minstrel trade in large numbers ironically served to reinforce the racial stereotypes developed earlier on the stage by whites.

The minstrel show underwent many changes after the Civil War that prolonged its life as a genre even as they chipped away at its identity. It grew in size. In the 1870s, showman J. H. Haverly (1836?–1901) combined four minstrel troupes into a single company, "Haverly's United Mastodon Minstrels" ("FORTY—COUNT 'EM—40"), and won a new following for the old entertainment. It also grew in scope. Haverly especially favored lavish stage productions that emphasized visual spectacle and thus removed the minstrel show almost entirely from its rudimentary roots. Finally—the *coup de grâce*—it became refined. In the 1880s, the noted company of George Primrose (1852–1919) and Billy West (1853–1902) did away entirely with plantation and blackface material so that hardly anything of the original minstrel show remained except for the name. The minstrel show of the Gilded Age had become an entertainment in many respects indistinguishable from other variety-based entertainments of the era.

A preoccupation with refinement also played a key role in the development of vaudeville, an entertainment whose roots lay in the dubious offerings of New York's variety houses. Such establishments offered programs of diverse acts with no narrative continuity from one to the next. Starting in the 1850s, they came to provide a structure for exhibiting in one place the various talents of singers, pugilists, minstrels, dancers, gymnasts, pantomimists, comedians, and a host of other performers.

They also bore the taint of disrepute, engendered by the conditions under which the shows they staged took place. For variety shows were not necessarily the main attraction in the beer halls or "concert saloons" that typically housed them on the Bowery and lower Broadway. Venues of this sort normally catered to a rough clientele of working-class men who took at least as much pleasure in the camaraderie of where they sat together—smoking, drinking, and enjoying the services of "waiter girls"—as in the entertainment onstage. The waitresses, moreover, sometimes offered more intimate pleasures in private rooms, always illegally. (Harry Hill's Variety Theater, one of the city's foremost in the

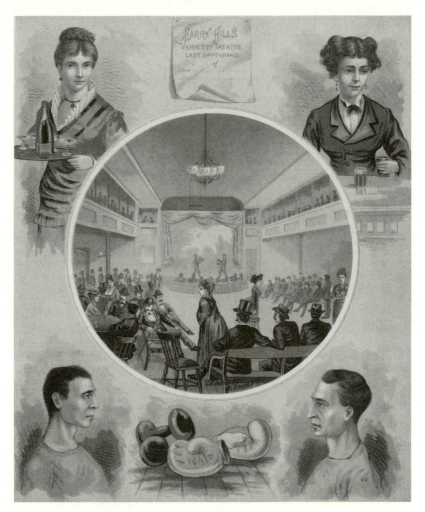

Flanked by images of barmaids and boxers, an 1878 illustration of the interior of Harry Hill's Variety Theater shows a stage, a pit, a gallery, and an overwhelmingly male audience.

1870s, held the distinction of being the only "respectable vile house" in New York: Hill made sure that any crimes arranged on his premises were committed elsewhere.) And so when the sons of the middle class also began to frequent such sites, the newspapers pulled no punches calling attention to the priorities of what they offered:

> Concert saloons . . . *under guise of singing and selling lager beer, are really the lowest and most infamous houses of prostitution, in which*

thousands of young men and boys congregate every night, and plunge into the worst excesses of ruinous and disgraceful debauchery. Some of them have licenses for theatrical performances, and resort to petty plays, gymnastic feats, dancing, &c., &c. . . . [But] the plausible cloak of music and theatrical performances [only] blinds the eyes of parents and guardians to the real character of these places, which are thus doing their work of ruin and degradation upon the rapidly increasing number of victims, with perfect impunity and even without suspicion.

By refining and thus broadening the appeal of variety, vaudeville became the most popular theater form by the end of the nineteenth century. The transformation was slow, helped along by legislation that prohibited issuing both a liquor license and a theatrical license to a single establishment, and by the work of reformers within the ranks of variety itself such as Josh Hart, Frank Kerns, and Charley White. More effectively than other reformers, Tony Pastor (1834?–1908) turned the traditional orientation of variety into one friendlier to the rising class of urban white-collar workers and their families, and so he became "the father of vaudeville." A former minstrel performer and circus clown, Pastor entered variety as a comic singer around the time of the Civil War. Then in 1865 he began managing variety houses as well. For over a decade he tried to draw a wider public to his theaters by restraining their trade in prostitution, liquor, and rowdy male behavior—thus loosening their ties to working-class culture. Yet real success in demonstrating that the "high-class" variety show he had in mind could be profitable eluded him until 1881 when he opened his last house, Tony Pastor's New Fourteenth Street Theater, just off Union Square. There he established a "clean" brand of variety, attracting an audience of middle-class patrons to see some of the finest performers anywhere in show business—among them Lillian Russell, Weber and Fields, and the Four Cohans. Russell herself was particularly taken with Pastor's new theater, and she described some of the ways it not only gave new life to variety but also made a once vulgar entertainment reputable:

Everything in Pastor's was clean and fresh and new. The seats were priced at a dollar and a half—the same as those in theatres which had drama or comic opera as their attractions. There was no smoking permitted in the theatre and the audience was usually in full dress. In an age when "variety" was considered just a little too daring for women to attend, Tony Pastor's Theatre set a standard that was unique and drew as many women as men. Every act was scrupulously clean and free from any suggestiveness; the performers were fine men and women and great artists did not hesitate to appear there.

Pastor's move to Union Square placed him and his venture directly in the heart of New York's first major theater district. By the 1880s Union Square had become the address of many of the city's important theaters—Wallack's, the Academy of Music, and now Pastor's. It had

Tony Pastor, who "fathered" vaudeville by making variety respectable, poses as the very model of a Gilded Age show businessman.

also become the prime site for transacting theater business and the hub of the theater's many support enterprises—wigmakers and costumers, print shops and photographers' studios, theatrical newspapers and booking offices—and for this it was affectionately dubbed "The Rialto" (as in the marketplace associated with the Rialto district in Venice).

Pastor himself, however, could not adjust to the new business practices already at work transforming the American theater. His undertaking was soon superseded by the efforts of a new breed of entrepreneurs led by B. F. (Benjamin Franklin) Keith (1846–1914) and E. F. (Edward Franklin) Albee (1857–1930), who together ruthlessly converted Pastor's local operation into a large-scale enterprise. Applying the principles of industrialization to the stage, they helped systematize the variety trade on a national basis—with a "circuit" of playhouses spread over a wide range of cities; performers constantly on tour to fill them; and booking agents to serve as middlemen between the two, who were thus the first theater businessmen whose job no longer involved them directly in any phase of theatrical art.

The change in institutional structure required a change in name to consolidate it in the public mind. Keith vigorously promoted "vaudeville" as a way of linguistically distancing the new entertainment from variety and its associations with working-class culture. (The word was both ancient and fashionably French, though there was no discernible connection between the American entertainment that now bore the name and the fifteenth-century vau-de-Vire songs for which it had ostensibly been coined.) As vaudeville, then, the genre reached its peak in the first decades of the twentieth century. The larger period in which vaudeville flourished, however, lasted for fifty years: roughly from 1881, when Pastor's Theater opened at Union Square, to 1932, when all-film programs replaced it at New York's Palace Theater, which was the flagship theater of the Keith Vaudeville Circuit and, by extension, the symbol of vaudeville itself.

According to the only known study of New York theatergoers in the early years of the twentieth century, the average vaudeville audience consisted of 60 percent "working" class, 36 percent "clerical" class,

---

The Palace on Broadway at Forty-seventh Street, flagship theater of the Keith-Albee circuit and the "Valhalla of Vaudeville."

and 4 percent "vagrant," "gamin," or "leisured"—though what these social categories actually meant at the time remains unclear. (By contrast, the same study indicates only 2 percent of the average legitimate theater audience was working class.) The vaudeville show that they saw consisted of a series of unrelated specialty acts—"turns," as they were called. These followed one another in quick succession and without duplication of performers or types of performance, so as to give an impression of "infinite variety." Eight to twelve acts made up a bill, with no act longer than twenty minutes. "Big-time" vaudeville (the Keith Circuit, the Orpheum Circuit) featured two bills daily, but there were several more in "small-time" vaudeville (the Pantages Circuit, the Loew Circuit) or continuous vaudeville, where bills rotated in "ferris-wheel" fashion from morning till night. The acts were interchangeable cogs in the machinery of vaudeville, but their function was fixed. The following gives a sense of their structure and what they were supposed to do in a standard nine-act show. It comes from an account by a booking agent for Keith's Palace Theater circa 1915:

1. A "dumb act" that is not dependent on being heard so it can't be spoiled by the noise of latecomers
   (e.g., animals, dancers, acrobats).
2. A "typical vaudeville" act to settle the audience down in preparation for the show to come
   (male-female singing duet or comedy team).
3. An act to wake the audience up, of a different kind entirely from the two before it
   (comic or dramatic sketch).
4. The first "big punch" of the show
   (a big-name personality act).
5. The second most important spot on the bill, something for the audience to talk about in the intermission
   (big production number, star act, novelty).

INTERMISSION

6. A start-up act to regain the previous build-up of tension, but not stronger than any of the acts still to come
   (vaudeville specialty, comedy dumb act).

7. An act to build up interest for the biggest act of the bill that follows, but by way of contrast with it
   (comedy playlet or serious dramatic playlet).
8. The chief attraction of the bill, the "big" comedy hit
   ("headliner" comedian or team).
9. A showy "sight" act to send a pleased audience home over the noise of those already leaving
   (animals, exotic costumes, trapeze artists).

Woodrow Wilson, who visited Keith's Theater in Washington weekly during most of his presidency, noted the virtue in such an arrangement. "If there is a bad act at a vaudeville show, you can rest reasonably secure that the next one may not be so bad; but from a bad play, there is no escape." As long as it was morally unimpeachable, almost any act might appear on the vaudeville stage. As theater historian Robert Allen observed, "Vaudeville was simply the aggregate of all the forms of entertainment from which it took attractions. Vaudeville existed only as a distinctive presentational, environmental, and institutional form; in terms of content, vaudeville was nothing and everything."

Vaudeville represents the culmination of the nineteenth-century variety tradition before it passed from the stage to the mass media of the twentieth century. Yet the "everything" of a vaudeville show functioned within a structure of limited possibilities given the brevity of its parts and the marked differences between them in style and content. The variety format thus challenged some of the most gifted entertainers of the Gilded Age to take up the task of making *something* out of the nothing of heterogeneous attractions. They drew upon the disparate elements of their apprenticeships in minstrel shows, dime museums, and circuses; connected these elements in a diversity of ways; and forged them into entertainments that in time replaced variety altogether: plays with song and dance, burlesques, revues, musical comedies. Three teams of comic performers perhaps best represent this project: Harrigan and Hart, Weber and Fields, and Williams and Walker. They do so not only because of the different formal paths their funmaking took, but also because they embodied the different sensibilities of those ethnic subcultures—Irish American, Jewish American, and African American—that would contribute most substantially to the development of Broadway musicals in the next century.

HARRIGAN AND HART

The shows of Edward Harrigan (1844–1911) and Tony Hart (Anthony Cannon, 1855–1891) gave comic voice to the experience of immigrant and working-class New Yorkers of the Gilded Age. They also figured prominently among the earliest sustained efforts to bring narrative continuity to the disparate elements of the variety stage. Harrigan and Hart began their fourteen-year partnership in Chicago in 1871 with an act that toured the minstrel and variety theaters of the day. They performed short skits in which Harrigan's baritone voice and dry wit served as comic foils to Hart's falsetto singing, rambunctious acting, and extraordinary gift for female impersonation in so-called wench roles. Booked into New York's Theatre Comique, a reputable variety house on lower Broadway, their act soon occupied the most important spot on the program. In time, the partners took over the management of the house, formed their own company, and expanded their skits into longer and longer pieces that ultimately displaced all the other variety acts with full-length entertainments of their own.

Harrigan led the company as an actor-manager. He produced, directed, and starred in his own productions. He wrote them, too—some forty extended plays in all. And in a permanent songwriting partnership with David Braham (1834–1905), who became his musical director and father-in-law, he provided texts for most of the songs sung in them as well—over two hundred all told. From 1873 to 1893 Harrigan productions played through every New York theater season when the company was not on national tour. In 1885, however, Hart left the company in a dispute with his partner, and he died of syphilis six years later—the very season the company achieved its greatest success with *Reilly and the Four Hundred* in a brand-new theater Harrigan had built and named after himself uptown near Herald Square.

The move of the company from its humble beginnings on lower Broadway to what was then upper Broadway was a sign not only of a growing audience for the Harrigan-Hart enterprise (even without Hart), but also of its growing acceptance in social circles. For the changing makeup of its audiences from the 1870s to the 1890s corresponded to the social and economic geography of New York that divided Manhattan theatergoing into three zones. Theaters for lower-income laborers were scat-

tered among the largely immigrant Irish and German communities down
along the Bowery from Chatham to Grand Streets; they offered variety
shows, melodramas, and assortments of ethnic plays. Theaters offering a
broader spectrum of middle-class fare lined the area of shopkeepers and
office workers along Broadway from Grand Street north up to Union
Square (Fourteenth Street). And theaters that catered to the city's more
established families of means, offering opera and serious drama among
their fare, spread out along Broadway from just below Union Square
north up to Herald Square (Thirty-fourth Street) and beyond.

By the 1890s, Harrigan's work had acquired a growing sense of cultural stature as well. He keenly felt its influence on the work of others,
especially the plays of Charles Hoyt (1859–1900). Hoyt was a newspaper reporter turned playwright who wrote eighteen works for the
stage, almost all of them hits. The most successful by far was *A Trip to
Chinatown*, which ran for 657 consecutive performances in New York
beginning in 1891. Like Harrigan's plays, Hoyt's were farces that often
featured horseplay, a variety act, and a scattering of diegetic songs. But
Hoyt's plays also painted a much broader picture of the American social
scene than Harrigan's, with more individualized characters, and, in the
later ones, a genuine sense of satire as well (*A Temperance Town*, 1893;
A Milk White Flag, 1894; *A Contented Woman*, 1897). To what extent
Harrigan's writing may have influenced Hoyt's remains unclear.

Beyond doubt, however, was the critical reception accorded Harrigan's work by such cultural luminaries of the day as novelist William
Dean Howells. He praised it on several occasions in the pages of *Harper's*
magazine, the prestigious monthly to which he contributed regularly as
an editor. "We still have no drama [we can call our own]," Howells wrote
in 1886, yet "we recognize in Mr. Harrigan's work the spring of a true
American comedy, the beginning of things which may be great things."
Howells, one of the most distinguished of America's authors and critics, championed the cause of realism in literature, and he saw the work
of Harrigan in some sense as aligned with his own. "We cannot do less
than cordially welcome reality as we find it in Mr. Harrigan's comedies.
Consciously or unconsciously, he is part of the great tendency toward the
faithful representation of life which is now animating fiction."

Realism animated much of the thought and feeling in the arts of the
late nineteenth century. As an aesthetic movement, it aimed to look at life
as it is rather than as it ought to be. Thus realism supplanted the "esthetic

of beauty" of early nineteenth-century Romanticism with an "esthetic of truth," allying itself in the process to a project of social reform and a search for truth in places previously deemed unfit for art. Its subjects embraced the sordid and unseemly, and, more startling still, the common-place. And its spirit characteristically informed the work of such eminent novelists as Émile Zola, Honoré de Balzac, and Charles Dickens, to all of whom the popular press compared Harrigan at one time or another.

Harrigan's realism, however, lacked a realist's agenda. He wrote farces about New York's working-class poor with no reformist program to improve their lot. He hoped rather to improve their disposition as they recognized themselves portrayed onstage in all their "picturesque-ness" and "local color," as he put it; and he directed his productions with an ear for accuracy in dialect and slang, and an eye for verisimilitude in costume and stage design. Above all, he peopled his plays with types of ethnic characters who lived in the tenements of Manhattan's slums: mainly immigrant Irish and Germans, whose great influx to New York had begun in the 1840s, and American Negroes, who began to migrate northward in large numbers after the Civil War. In depicting them, Harrigan kept close to the stereotypes of racial comedy from the min-strel and variety stages of his youth: the Irish, "Dutch" (German really: from *deutsch*), "Ethiopian," and other acts based on caricatures of Amer-ica's ethnic subcultures. But he eventually minimized the grotesquerie with which such types were commonly portrayed onstage, and even imbued some with a degree of humanity—especially the character of Dan Mulligan, who moved from expressions of racial prejudice in ear-lier plays to those of tolerance in later ones.

A concern for ethnicity lay at the heart of Harrigan's work. But whereas variety-based shows comically abstracted ethnic character types and ridiculed them in isolation from each other, Harrigan's shows found humor largely in the conflicts that arose by bringing them together. Indeed, the racial comedy of Harrigan and Hart proved most memorable for its inclusion of all such types within the panorama of a given time, place, and condition: the Gilded Age on New York's Lower East Side and its democracy of squalor. As one of Harrigan's song texts put it:

> *It's Ireland and Italy, Jerusalem and Germany,*
> *Oh, Chinamen and nagers, and a paradise for rats,*

All jumbled up togayther in the snow or rainy weather,
They represent the tenants in McNally's row of flats.

"McNALLY'S ROW OF FLATS,"
(*McSORLEY'S INFLATION*, 1882)

Harrigan's plays showed remarkable sympathy for the diverse racial and ethnic communities of the city—the Jews in *Mordecai Lyons* (1882), the Italians in *Waddy Googan* (1888). But it was the Irish who dominated his plays, and mostly at the expense of the other ethnic groups. (Even an admiring Howells was not blind to the fact. In Harrigan's plays, he remarked, "not all the Irish are good Irish, but all the colored people are bad colored people.") Both Harrigan and Hart were of Irish descent. So was the better part of their early audiences downtown who surely saw something of themselves in the partners' merry work. Indeed, the Irish made up the largest "foreign" ethnic group in New York at the time, but their support alone did not account for the ultimate success of the plays. What made for the Harrigan-and-Hart heyday of the 1880s, in fact, was not "popular" patronage so much as support from the "fashionable" middle classes whose sense of themselves in American society may have been confirmed by contrast with the "other half" of the social spectrum that Harrigan and Hart depicted.

That heyday began with *The Mulligan Guard Ball* (1879). It was the first of the many Harrigan and Hart plays to exceed one hundred performances at a time when an extended run in New York generally lasted a month. The show's success sparked further hits in the same mold on which the greater portion of the partners' fame would come to rest. And as the show's origin went back to "The Mulligan Guard," one of their early songs, *The Mulligan Guard Ball* encapsulates the historical development of the Harrigan-Hart enterprise itself. First came the song, a lampoon of the paramilitary social clubs popular in working-class neighborhoods, and it furnished the basis for a ten-minute skit which the duo first performed in 1873. By 1878 the skit had expanded into a forty-minute play. And when the play emerged the next year expanded as *The Mulligan Guard Ball,* that show's success led in turn to a whole spate of Mulligan-related plays that became the company's exclusive fare for three of its next five seasons:

1879–80:
The Mulligan Guard Chowder
The Mulligan Guards' Christmas
The Mulligan Guards' Surprise

1880–81:
The Mulligan Guard Picnic
The Mulligan Guard Nominee
The Mulligans' Silver Wedding

1883–84
The Mulligan Guard Ball (rev.)
The Mulligan Guard Picnic (rev.)
Cordelia's Aspirations
Dan's Tribulations

The company mounted non-Mulligan hits in seasons in between and after, too—*Squatter Sovereignty* (1882), *McSorley's Inflation* (1882), *The Leather Patch* (1886), *Reilly and the Four Hundred* (1890). But the Mulligan plays had a special draw. Because the Harrigan-Hart enterprise operated as a stock company, its actors remained constant while the roles they played tended to change from production to production. With the Mulligan series, however, the same actors kept their roles from one play to the next: Dan Mulligan (Harrigan), his wife, Cordelia (Annie Yeamens), their son, Tommy, and their Negro maid, Rebecca (Hart, often playing both roles in the same show), the German butcher, Lochmuller (Harry Fisher), etc. And so the actors and their roles often became fused in the public mind, with audiences developing a genuine fondness for them as characters whose turmoils and shenanigans they followed in installments over the years, much as viewers might follow the episodes of a TV sitcom today.

In *The Mulligan Guard Ball*, two plots intersect in the leading role of Dan Mulligan, an Irish immigrant who heads a social club named for him. (While Harrigan preferred to describe Mulligan as "honest, thrifty, home-loving, genial," the character who emerges from his plays is sufficiently bibulous, ignorant, and pugnacious to resemble most any stage Irishman of the period.) In the first plot, Dan's son Tommy elopes with the German butcher's daughter over the objections of both

HARRIGAN & HART
THE ORIGINAL
MULLIGAN GUARDS, 1879.

Costumed as Mulligan Guards, l. to r.: Tony Hart and Edward Harrigan
(with Morgan Benson in the center).

fathers, who oppose such intermarriage (Dan: "The Divil a Dutch drop of blood will ever enter this family"). In the second plot, the Skidmore Guard, a Negro social club, rents a dance hall for a ball on the same night that the Mulligan Guard rents it for a ball of its own. That night, after a tense confrontation, the Skidmores agree to move their festivities to the floor above where their dancing becomes so animated they come crashing through the ceiling onto the Mulligans below. (Harrigan staged this with dummies!) In terms of character, no one in either story undergoes a change of heart nor is any conflict resolved. In terms of action, the play doesn't end so much as it just stops (typically, Harrigan's final prompt served for a denouement: "General melee and curtain"). When a rival producer charged that a Harrigan show was less a "play" than "a prolongation of sketches," the accused countered that his work was really "a continuity of incidents." Later he admitted, "I wish a fellow could make a play without a plot. They are nightmares to me."

Over the years, Harrigan rewrote *The Mulligan Guard Ball* so that it grew in size within the repertoire of the company that first created and then repeatedly re-created it. It thus came to exist in several versions, no one of which can be considered definitive. As originally performed in one act in 1879, it shared a variety bill with such acts as Fryer's Dogs and Fred Plaisted "champion oarsman and club swinger." At that time, it also contained some three or four original Harrigan-Braham songs. For an 1883 revival it became a full-length play in two acts with about seven songs. And for an 1892 revival (now without Hart) it grew to three acts with about eight songs. The songs are fully self-contained pieces for which Harrigan first wrote the words for Braham to set to music. Typically, they follow the pattern of an explanatory verse, whose text changes with every stanza, and an exclamatory refrain or chorus, whose text remains the same. Typically, too, the songs suit the credibility of a realistic stagepiece because they are sung diegetically, that is, as "source songs" in the play. At one point, for example, Tommy asks, "I say Pop give de boys a song as a send off," and Mulligan obliges with "The Babies on Our Block." At another, Mulligan makes plans with his pal McSweeney for the upcoming Mulligan ball, then asks him, "Do you remember the old tune?" and launches into "The Mulligan Guard." Unlike "The Babies on Our Block," this song at least relates to the situation. But it has nothing to do with the scene's dramatic point: the ball. It is simply an emblem of nostalgia, as much the signature song of Harrigan and Hart themselves as of the Mulligans (Ex. 2-1).

As a rule, Harrigan and Hart show songs do not bear directly on the action. "I'll Wear the Trousers, Oh!" is an exception, however, and it comes from act 3 of *Cordelia's Aspirations* (1883), generally considered Harrigan's finest work. In the play, Cordelia entertains thoughts of moving up in society, and she gets the family to move from the tenements of Mulligan Alley up to fashionable Madison Avenue. Dan goes along with his wife's wishes though he is clearly out of place in the new

Ex. 2-1. David Braham, music, Edward Harrigan, lyrics: "The Mulligan Guard,"
The Mulligan Guard Ball

We should - er'd guns, and march'd, and march'd a - way. From
Bax - ter Street, we march'd to Ave - nue A. With
drums and fife, how sweet - ly they did play, As we
march'd, march'd, march'd in the Mull - i - gan Guard.

surroundings. Goaded by his friend McSweeney, however, Dan finally decides to take matters into his own hands and set things right.

MAC [MCSWEENEY]: Your friends would like to see you back in Mulligan Alley.
DAN [MULLIGAN]: I'd go back but for Cordelia.
MAC: Is she wearing your trousers?
DAN: (with energy) No sir. (striking table) No woman can wear my trousers.
MAC: (rising) Home rule forever.

[DAN:] SONG *I'll Wear the Trousers, Oh*

[VERSE 1] Oh, years ago, in sweet Mayo,
    I married sweet Cordelia;
    A happy wife, and a happy life,
    Our marriage was no failure.
    When we were wed, these words I said:
    Oh, take my houses, oh!
    But bear in mind, ye'll always find,
    I'll wear the trousers, oh!

[CHORUS] I'll wear the trousers, trousers, oh!
    I'll wear the trousers, oh!

So ev'ry man do all you can
To wear the trousers, oh! . . .

The song still shows the verse-and-chorus form of a self-contained musical number, but the lyrics now refer specifically to Dan Mulligan and his situation onstage ("I married sweet Cordelia"). The song also has direct consequences for the outcome of *Cordelia's Aspirations* since Dan decides to move back to Mulligan Alley after singing it. "I'll Wear the Trousers, Oh!" is thus more an expression of Dan's feeling than a source song; and as such, it works to precipitate the resolution of Dan's dilemma in the play (and the dilemma of those in the audience disturbed by the prospects of both Irish assimilation and parity between the sexes that the play raised).

"Musical comedy as we know it today began with Edward Harrigan and Tony Hart." So wrote librettist Michael Stewart a century after the fact, perhaps with a song like this in mind and the way it worked in combination with its play. (Stewart had a personal stake in the matter: He wrote the libretto for the 1980s Broadway musical *Harrigan 'n' Hart*.) But Harrigan himself did not view his undertaking as a distinctly musical one. Rather, he wrote plays whose way of using a song by its very "realism" mitigated against the special sense of unreality associated with the musical as a genre. Historians of both theater and musical theater tend to concur: Harrigan's plays are "not merely musical comedies" but closer to "straight plays" because, though "dotted with interpolated songs, and, on rare occasions, dances," they "employed none of the other appurtenances of the musical stage."

Following Harrigan's death in 1911, the *National Review* summed up his achievement in these terms: "When Harrigan came to town, minstrelsy was popular, burlesque was at its height, and variety had a large following. He conceived the idea of making up a show combining the leading elements of all three and using a connected story upon which to hang the specialties." That may not add up to musical comedy as we know it. Yet it can fairly be seen as pointing one way toward later developments by making increasingly elaborate forms of entertainment out of the storytelling devices and song-and-dance routines popular on the stages of America in the Gilded Age.

WEBER AND FIELDS

The shows of Weber and Fields combined variety and narrative elements as well. But they also played a more characteristic role in developing some of those "other appurtenances": the additional features that helped define the musical stage as a distinctive arena of amusement. They reveled, for example, in the kind of visual display we now associate with musicals, and perhaps because of which we have curiously come to call a musical "a show." For beside the sounds of speech and song to delight the ear, musicals have traditionally offered a feast for the eye through costumes, stage settings, special effects, and movement—especially the movement of chorus lines and the chorines who inhabit them. The institutionalization of such features can be traced back to the extravaganzas of the nineteenth century of which *The Black Crook* is, if not the earliest example on the American stage, surely the best remembered. Extravaganzas, however, form only a part of a larger stage tradition that has gone by the name of burlesque. And burlesques were what the Weber and Fields shows were most often called, though the word was never used with great precision.

The term "burlesque" has basically two meanings: a send-up, and a girlie show. The latter evolved out of the former. Originally, burlesque referred to anything funny whose humor derived from its relationship to an existing model. In this sense, the following taxonomy from an 1891 account suggests the range the term could cover.

> *In art caricature is burlesque, in literature parody is burlesque, in the drama comic pantomime, comic opera, travesty, and extravaganza are burlesque. All dramatic burlesque ranges under the head of farce, although all farce is not burlesque. Burlesque is the farce of portraiture on the stage; farce on the stage is the burlesque of events.*

As a theatrical form, burlesque gained its initial popularity in America in the 1840s, imported from England by such funmakers as William Mitchell (1798–1856) and John Brougham (1810–1880). (In 1840, for example, when ballerina Fanny Elssler took New York by storm dancing in *La Tarantula*, Mitchell donned a tutu to dance the lead in a mock ballet he called *La Mosquito*.) In some shows, even the songs might be burlesqued: Brougham's afterpiece *Po-ca-hon-tas* (1855) filched its music from popular tunes of the day, cannibalizing the texts but keeping the music as a point of reference. In other shows, it was not: J. Cheever Goodwin's and Edward E. Rice's *Evangeline* (1874/1877) spoofed the Longfellow poem with a set of original musical numbers. But the scripted aspects of burlesque provided much the lesser part of the entertainment. At least as important to the success of the genre as *what* appeared onstage was *how* it was presented and performed. Yet this we can know today only at second hand, if at all.

Burlesque in its original sense also related to such stage forms as travesty, pantomime, and extravaganza. Travesty thrived on cultural subversion whether or not it actually involved cross-dressing (*transvestite* comes from the same word). It might burlesque a work of highest culture, debasing it with puns and jokes of the lowest humor—the case as we saw with Shakespeare's *Othello* and *Desdemonum*, the blackface minstrel skit that called itself "An Ethiopian Burlesque." Pantomime took fairy tales and children's stories as its objects, which performers would clown their way through using an arsenal of commedia dell'arte devices—as did George L. Fox (1825?–1877) most famously in *Humpty Dumpty* (1868). Extravaganza for its part poked fun at whatever lent itself to spectacle and music, and, as even its humor was diffuse, the form seemed rather like a "burlesque without an object"—which might also apply to *The Black Crook*.

Extravaganzas produced in the wake of *The Black Crook*, however, frequently split apart the dual emphasis in that show on scenic splendor and female anatomy to focus on one or the other. On the one hand, the modern tradition of spectacular Broadway shows began effectively with the work of the Kiralfy brothers, Imre (1845–1919) and Bolossy (1847–1932), the foremost producers of opulent stageworks in the 1870s and 1880s. The Kiralfys purchased exclusive production rights to *The Black Crook* itself and mounted regular revivals of the show that outdid each other in sheer spectacle and scenic effects; and with their production of *Excelsior* (1883), they were among the first to bring electric light onto the Broadway stage, enlisting the help even of Thomas Edison in their efforts. The modern tradition of anatomical shows, on the other hand, is often said to have begun in 1868 with the arrival in New York of English dancer-pantomimist Lydia Thompson (1836?–1908) and her troupe of "British Blondes." With their productions of such shows as *Ixion*, *The Forty Thieves*, and *Bluebeard*, they created newer burlesques that traded on *The Black Crook*'s success with skirtless dancers in tights by matching such sexually transgressive displays with sexually transgressive speech and behavior. The rise of burlesque's second meaning traces its origin to these productions: the so-called leg drama, which, as the form consolidated in the 1870s and 1880s, increasingly abandoned the drama for the leg (and then other body parts).

By the turn of the century, popular demand for burlesque had split irreparably in two: between "hot" shows and "clean" ones. Hot "girlie" shows doted on blue jokes and the female form in states of disclosure that tested the limits of middle-class forbearance and so risked the periodic interventions of clergymen, politicians, and police. Such diversions shifted the emphasis from burlesque to "a burlesque show," and narrowed the focus of the entertainment offered to "striptease." Burlesque in this form reached a critical tipping point in 1931, when the foremost purveyors of ecdysiastic art, the Minsky brothers—Abe, Billy, Herbert, and Morton—leased the Republic Theater on Forty-second Street as their flagship house and famously brought striptease to Broadway itself. By 1937, no fewer than seven legitimate Broadway theaters had converted to striptease houses, which finally led to the shutdown of burlesque altogether that year by New York's Mayor Fiorello La Guardia.

Clean burlesque shows, by contrast, downplayed sexuality and so won broader audiences to the entertainment. By doing so, however, they often resembled nothing so much as a cheaper version of vaudeville. Weber and Fields turned this situation around. They presented clean burlesque (almost emblematically so when they ridiculed *Sappho*, a scandalous French drama, by inverting its morality in a lampoon they named "Sapolio," after a popular soap product). Yet their appeal grew in the face of competing kinds of entertainment as they consistently featured the most expensive star talent of the era in productions that for sheer comic energy and musical staging were unmatched by vaudeville and the early revue.

Joseph Weber (1867–1942) and Lew Fields (Moses Schoenfeld, 1867–1941) grew up as streetwise pals on New York's Lower East Side. Not yet teenagers, they already performed together in beer gardens and variety houses doing a routine that combined "knockabout" comedy with "racial" caricature. In 1884 they made their debut on the burlesque stage at Miner's Bowery Theater, where in time they perfected a "Dutch" dialect act that would catapult them to national stardom. Sporting derby hats, checkered suits, and chin whiskers, they caricatured a pair of German immigrants: the short and stocky Mike (Weber), and the tall and thin Meyer (Fields). Mike typically bore the brunt of Meyer's abuse; and the abuse was both verbal:

MIKE: I am delightfulness to meet you.
MEYER: Der disgust is all mine.

and physical:

MEYER: If I'm cruel to you, Mike, it's because I luff you. [gouges his eyes]
MIKE: If you luffed me any more, I couldn't stand it.

Their great success under various managements prompted the partners to form a Weber and Fields Own Company in 1890. By the end of the decade, they had become not only actor-managers of their own Music Hall at Broadway and Twenty-ninth Street but two of the most powerful and influential show businessmen on the New York musical stage. The partners broke up in 1904 to pursue independent careers as performers and producers. Fields was still active a generation later as the producer of several of the major new-style musical comedies (*A Connecticut Yankee*, 1927; *Hit the Deck*, 1927), for many of which his son Herbert now wrote the books.

Productions at the Weber and Fields Music Hall lasted for eight seasons (1896–1904); they proved to be the pinnacle of the partners' joint careers. The shows were brilliantly cast and staged, and presented as a full-length two-act bill. The first act gave its name to the evening. It took the form of a vaudeville-type olio—that is, a medley of different acts—yet with a tenuous plot that alternated comic sketches and musical numbers. The second act consisted of a travesty/burlesque of a recent Broadway hit—mostly a legitimate drama (*Cyrano de Bergerac* became "Cyranose de Bric-a-Brac"); less often, a musical one (*The Geisha*, "The Geezer"). Moreover, to keep up public interest in the shows, the travesty was generally replaced after several weeks with a burlesque of something more current. By 1897, Weber and Fields had put together the team responsible for creating the shows, led by composer-conductor John Stromberg, librettist-lyricist Edgar Smith, and director-choreographer Julian Mitchell. The full company numbered about fifty performers, headed by the partners themselves and half a dozen other stars, though not until 1899 did the jewel in the crown of stars join the ranks: America's "Queen of Comic Opera," Lillian Russell. The Music Hall's greatest seasons followed: *Whirl-i-Gig* (1899–1900), *Fiddle-Dee-Dee* (1900–01), *Hoity-Toity* (1901–02), and *Twirly-Whirly* (1902–03).

John Stromberg (1853–1902), the Music Hall's music director and house composer, contributed songs to the Weberfields shows that proved more serviceable than memorable. Perhaps his most interesting tunes

As German immigrants in their signature "Dutch act,"
l. to r.: Joe Weber (Mike) and Lew Fields (Meyer).

are those that capitalized on the era's craze for "coon songs"—popular songs with lyrics in a purportedly Negro dialect, and with syncopated music in a vocal adaptation of ragtime rhythms. (While apparently not considered derogatory at first when applied to people, the term "coon" came to signify blacks by the end of the nineteenth century and met with increasing resistance thereafter as being racially demeaning.) Two such songs appeared in *Fiddle-Dee-Dee*, for example: "Come Back, My Honey Boy, to Me" (sung by Lillian Russell in the first act) and "Ma Blushin' Rosie" (sung by Fay Templeton in the second). The second of these songs became one of Stromberg's biggest offstage hits, a love song whose lightly syncopated verse ("Dar's a colored bud ob beauty") charmingly contrasted with a more broadly lyrical refrain ("Rosie, you are ma posie"). Yet sung in context onstage, it must have seemed as absurd for a white woman to be singing in the narrating voice of a black man as it was for anyone to be singing a coon song at all in a travesty of *Quo Vadis* ("Quo Vas Iss?") set in ancient Rome. Such absurdities typified the comedic strategies of Weber-and-Fields burlesque.

Edgar Smith (1857–1938) authored the scripts on which the shows were based, though such scripts may have been intended more as blueprints for performers, than as definitive texts. Not only did audience reaction (or its lack) prompt the revision of scripts, in addition, actors used to the inspired anarchy of the burlesque stage rarely spoke all their lines as written. So much improvised input was expected of burlesque performers, in fact, that an accomplished actress who came to the company fresh from the legitimate theater found herself at a loss in rehearsals. "I always had a cue to work on," she complained. "I don't know where to start my lines. I'm sure I shan't know what I am doing the first night, nor any night. I never know what the others are going to do or say."

Julian Mitchell (1854–1926) actually put the shows on their feet and, doing so, may have played the biggest role in defining the special character of the Music Hall productions. Though constrained by the cramped stage of a 665-seat house, his staging brought such focus to the musical portions of the productions that they came to rival in interest the comedic thrust of the shows. Dances, sets, costumes, choruses— all were engaging as separate components, yet coordinated to common effect. Above all, Mitchell lavished his greatest care on the chorus, not only to bring out the sheer beauty of the women who made it what it was, but to make sure that what they did had the "intelligent action," as he put it, to make the chorus in effect "a part of the play."

Mitchell himself started out in the theater as a dancer, but growing deafness forced him to abandon a career as a performer for one as a stager. Prolific beyond belief, he mounted a total of approximately eighty Broadway productions in the course of a career defined largely by three long-term relationships. Charles Hoyt first engaged him in 1884 and Mitchell spent more than a decade staging the playwright's farces— including *A Trip to Chinatown*. Next came his work for the Weber and Fields burlesques (1897–1902). Last, there was a long association with producer Florenz Ziegfeld during which he staged some ten editions of the *Follies* (1907–25). Mitchell's whole career as a director can thus be seen in progressive terms: from directing farces with musical moments in them, to burlesques that called for a more eminently musical kind of staging, and finally to revues that called for what was perhaps the most tasteful and cohesively developed staging of all variety-type shows.

What distinguished the revue (originally "review") as a form from other variety-show types was its move toward a more unified style than that of vaudeville, and toward a more urbane tone than that of burlesque. While a revue consisted of songs, dances, sketches, and tableaux that were all unrelated to one another, it used and reused the same cast of performers throughout, albeit in different roles. And while a revue lacked a plot it often made use of a connecting theme to link its unrelated parts. Indeed, the very format of a "review" of the past year's social events and foibles gave the genre its name. George Lederer (1861–1938) arguably produced the first successful shows of the type, which he mounted annually at the Casino Theater starting in 1894 with *The Passing Show*. (He called it "a topical extravaganza." Others spoke of "a review, in dramatic form, of the chief events of the past year—political, historical and theatrical.") But it was not until Florenz Ziegfeld (1867–1932) set the standard with his brilliantly sustained series of *Follies* (twenty-two editions, 1907–1931) that the genre became established in American popular culture, its choruses of women raised to cult status, and its name fashionably gallicized as "revue."

The impact of the Weber and Fields Music Hall productions can thus be seen as even more significant historically than the effect Weber and Fields themselves had as comedians on several generations of comic performers. For the repeated success of the company's way of entertaining exerted the larger influence in the gradual transformation of such forms as vaudeville and burlesque into the emergent forms of revue and musical comedy—most directly perhaps in what Ziegfeld would adopt as a producer by way of Mitchell's choruses, and in what Herbert Fields would adapt as a librettist from the legacy of his father's routines.

Weber and Fields did play significant roles themselves, however, not only in the comic history of Broadway musical entertainment but also in its social history. Both were Polish Jews with German cultural backgrounds who came to the United States as children in the 1870s. Yet throughout their lives they felt compelled to deny their foreign births and to downplay their cultural heritage. Onstage and off, little about them was identifiably Judaic in a religious sense or Jewish in an ethnic one. Onstage, for example, they deliberately distanced themselves from such associations by hiring "Hebrew" comedians whose stereotypically Jewish acts were meant to contrast with their own. Indeed, "Hebrew" comedy meant one thing in variety practice and "Dutch" comedy another (though a comedian did not have to *be* Jewish, or German for that matter, to excel in either: many in fact were Irish). And as the comedy with which Weber and Fields made their reputations was decidedly Dutch—that is, stereotypically German—it differed from Hebrew comedy even in its dialect.

It was as Americans, however, that the partners aimed to pitch their appeal. They did not belong to the "new" immigration of Jews from Eastern Europe that would bring to America such future stars of the musical stage as Sophie Tucker, Al Jolson, and Irving Berlin. They belonged rather to an older generation of Central European immigrants of which they were surely the most conspicuous musical theater showmen of Jewish descent. Weber and Fields thus resisted publicly identifying themselves as Jewish immigrants altogether perhaps because they had grounds to fear that to do otherwise would have hindered their professional careers in the United States. Their experience was not unique. (Irving Berlin gave names to some of his best-remembered songs that were as psychologically revealing as was his decision to change his own name early on from Israel Baline: "God Bless America," "Easter Parade," "White Christmas.") Indeed, the experience of Weber and Fields was to be repeated time and again in one way or another by an upcoming generation of those who, like themselves, were to see in Broadway the road not only to fame and fortune but to an often more coveted form of cultural approval: assimilation.

WILLIAMS AND WALKER

For African Americans in the Gilded Age there was no general prospect of cultural assimilation. The Irish and the Jews also endured a history of violent discrimination in America—the Irish tainted by association with Roman Catholicism and an extranational allegiance; the Jews tainted by a non-English-speaking culture and a non-Christian faith. For those willing to discard such affiliations or downplay them, however, the prospect of assimilation seemed real enough. But Africans bore a burden that precluded the possibility: a past history of enslavement in the United States that they could neither discard nor downplay even after Emancipation because of the indelible taint of color. Blackness itself—being Negro—warranted multiple forms of discrimination sanctioned by both law and custom in America during an era of segregation that stretched from the end of Reconstruction in 1877 to the passage of the Civil Rights Act of 1964.

The policy of racial segregation prevailed in virtually all walks of national life. That included the theater, where to call a song-and-dance show featuring African Americans a "black musical" made sense precisely because no one in the entertainment business ever spoke of a "white musical"—one simply took it for granted. The term "black musical" thus underscores both the significance of an African American presence in musical theater and its separation from the cultural mainstream—a presence and an absence, as it were. Yet use of the term has continued on into the integration era. Shows with all-black casts have continued to be produced, albeit now for a greater variety of purposes than before. Moreover, the term itself has expanded in meaning as the perspective on it has changed. "Black musical," as the term is now generally used, signifies a show whose creation, performance, or reception pertains, in whole or in part, to any aspect of black life or culture—a show "by, about, or involving African Americans."

The history of black musicals begins effectively with the minstrel show, the earliest distinctly national form of popular entertainment in the United States. But for all its popularity, minstrelsy left a disturbing heritage in its wake. For many African Americans born in the generation after Emancipation who had professional aspirations in the performing arts, the minstrel legacy proved deeply embarrassing—

so much so that the perception of resisting it in any form became a touchstone for a new sense of cultural legitimacy. On this basis, in fact, James Weldon Johnson cited *The Creole Show* (1890) in his pioneering study, *Black Manhattan*, as the first modern black musical. (*The Creole Show* featured women singing and dancing onstage; classic minstrel shows allowed only men and female impersonators.) Many came to view any departure from minstrelsy's stereotypes as a kind of emancipation from a theatrical form of slavery itself. At times this dynamic even took on biblical overtones. Ernest Hogan (1865–1909), a leading minstrel showman who had begun as a "pickaninny" in an *Uncle Tom's Cabin* troupe, ultimately left the minstrel stage to become a star in his own right and, reputedly, the highest paid black headliner in vaudeville. Given the trajectory of Hogan's career, then, one newspaper hailed him at the end of it as a "Moses of the colored theatrical profession."

More than any exodus from minstrelsy, however, what really mattered was the entry into the promised land of Broadway. For composer Will Marion Cook (1869–1944) the moment seemed at hand the night in 1898 when a Broadway audience stood and cheered for ten minutes after the first performance of his *Clorindy*:

> *Maybe, when the pearly gates open wide and a multitude of hosts march in, shouting, laughing, singing, emoting, there will be a happiness which slightly resembles that of Clorindy's twenty-six participants. I was so delirious that I drank a glass of water, thought it wine and got gloriously drunk. Negroes were at last on Broadway, and there to stay. Gone was the uff-dah of the minstrel! Gone was the Massa Linkum stuff! We were artists and we were going a long, long way.*

Cook characteristically overstated the import of the event. With the regular season concluded for the summer (as was common in pre-air-conditioned days), *Clorindy* appeared as a late-night summer diversion at the open-air Roof Garden atop the Casino Theater—*on* Broadway, that is, but not *of* Broadway: neither in house nor in season. Nor did all agree the show had rid itself of minstrelsy's traces; Cook's collaborator, the poet Paul Laurence Dunbar (1872–1906), apparently cringed with embarrassment at the premiere on that account. *Clorindy* was, however, one of two revue-like shows produced in New York in 1898 that launched into the tributaries of Broadway's mainstream the careers of the greatest black musical showmen of the age—and through them the course of the black musical itself.

The first of these, *A Trip to Coontown*, constituted a full-length musical farce completely created, staged, and performed by blacks in an out-of-the-way theater on Third Avenue. The many talents of one of its stars, Bob Cole (1868–1911), proved central to the show's favorable reception in New York and on tour. Not long after, Cole met and joined forces with the Johnson brothers, composer J. Rosamond (1873–1954) and lyricist James Weldon (1871–1938). Working as a trio or in pairs, the three men wrote over 150 songs, many of which made it to Broadway interpolated into the shows of others. Eventually Cole partnered with Rosamond alone. As the team of Cole and Johnson, the two appeared as a high-class vaudeville song-and-dance act; and at their peak, they appeared as costars and songwriters of all-black Broadway book shows of their own (*The Shoo-Fly Regiment*, 1907; *The Red Moon*, 1909).

The second show, its full title *Clorindy; or, the Origin of the Cake-walk*, was a forty-five-minute potpourri of songs and dances starring Ernest Hogan (Reuben Crowdus). An irrepressible showman famous as the writer of the hit song "All Coons Look Alike to Me" (1896), Hogan later went on to attain Broadway stardom in all-black musical comedies to which he also contributed script material and songs (*Rufus Rastus*, 1906; *The Oyster Man*, 1907). But the script and songs for *Clorindy* were written by Paul Laurence Dunbar and Will Marion Cook, whose work Hogan actually undermined. For he ultimately took what had begun as a musical with a story, cut all of Dunbar's dialogue, and turned the remainder into a pure song-and-dance show on the order of John Isham's *Octoroons*, which had played the Casino's Roof Garden the year before. Hogan had not even been the writers' first choice for the show. Cook had tailored his material to the talents of a pair of rising stars who were unavailable at the time of *Clorindy*, but with whom his career was about to become inextricably intertwined: Bert A. Williams (1874–1922) and George W. Walker (1873–1911).

Still in their twenties by the turn of the twentieth century, Williams and Walker were the most celebrated team of black comedians in vaudeville. The pair had met in San Francisco in 1893 while performing together in a minstrel troupe and soon became a song-and-dance team. They toured vaudeville as the "Two Real Coons" to distinguish themselves from rival blackface entertainers who were not the real

thing (like Irishmen McIntyre and Heath). Working from minstrel stereotypes, the two developed the contrasting personas for which they
would become famous: Walker, the flamboyant "dandy" and glib con
artist; Williams, the dim "darky" bemused by his perpetual hard luck.
Engaged on the east coast in 1896, they swept high-class vaudeville
as cakewalk dancers in a sensational act that pitted Walker's athleticism against Williams's eccentricities. Eventually they joined the cast
of *Clorindy* after its opening and toured with it. They then formed their
own touring company to produce all-black shows that they would write
together and in which they would co-star. Although little more than
medleys of vaudeville specialties at first, these shows over time took on
some of the more cohesive trappings of musical comedy.

The duo's sixteen-year partnership ended in 1909 when sickness
forced Walker to retire from the stage. Williams continued with the company, but he seemed hamstrung without Walker's energy onstage to offset
his comic pathos, and without Walker's business sense behind the scenes
to keep the company going. By 1911, the pioneering era of all-black musicals on Broadway had come to an end as well. Hogan, Cole, and Walker
had died, their companies had disbanded, and the center for producing
black musicals in New York had moved uptown to Harlem. Williams
meanwhile had accepted an unprecedented offer from Florenz Ziegfeld
to cross the color line and enter Broadway through the front door. He
became a featured Ziegfeld comedian, the only black star in eight editions
of the *Follies* at their peak (1910–19). But the racial prejudice Williams
encountered even as a member of the company tempered his professional
triumphs. And he continued to perform in the blackface makeup audiences
had come to expect, effectively barred by his own brilliance in creating
the darky figure the public loved from appearing onstage, as he longed to
do, in a different persona. Comedian W. C. Fields, who worked with Williams in the *Follies*, called him "the funniest man I ever saw and the saddest man I ever knew." Williams spoke more wryly. "I have never been
able to discover that there was anything disgraceful in being a colored
man," he said. "But I have often found it inconvenient—in America."

The musicals of the Williams and Walker Company (1899–1909)
mixed variety acts with ongoing bits of farce. The shows featured
the same black casts, including not only Cook, Williams, and Walker,
but also their wives, Abbie Mitchell Cook, Lottie Williams, and Aida
Overton Walker (1880–1914), often considered the third most impor-

tant member of the troupe. The same nucleus of black talent also created the shows and put them on their feet: Williams wrote songs with Alex Rogers; Walker developed book ideas; Jesse Shipp actually wrote the book and staged it; Cook served as music director and "composer-in-chief"; and Aida Walker did the musical staging. The company mounted three major Broadway productions: *In Dahomey* (1903), *Abyssinia* (1906), and *Bandanna Land* (1908).

In Dahomey, by far the most successful of the shows, appears in histories of the musical stage as much as a social milestone as an artistic one. The first full-length all-black musical to play a legitimate Broadway theater in season, *In Dahomey* succeeded with audiences that were racially mixed, though separately seated. (Between 1902 and 1905 it also successfully toured the United States and England, with a seven-month engagement in London that included a command performance at Buckingham Palace.) The story centered on the attempts of some unscrupulous businessmen in Boston's black community to use less fortunate members of their race to colonize Africa. In order to help finance the scheme, they hire two detectives to locate a lost heirloom in Florida by any and by all means. It is the sleuths whose antics come to dominate the evening. They form a classic pair—one a knave, Rareback Pinkerton (Walker); the other a fool, Shylock Homestead (Williams)—and they ultimately wind up in Dahomey themselves as rulers of the African state.

The book was not fixed, however. Neither was the score, even though it appeared at the time in published form. (A theatergoer who might have seen *In Dahomey* in New York on two occasions a year apart—once before and once after its British tour—would have heard only two musical numbers in the show that remained the same; the rest were all different.) Indeed, with constant changes to both script and songs over the years it played, the show seems to have revolved about its performers more than it ever evolved as a work. As with so many variety-based entertainments of the period, *In Dahomey* represents a triumph of performance over scripted matter. But only the latter remains. And so if it is easier for us today to get a sense of Cook's music, say, than of Williams's humor, it is important to keep in mind that this is probably not how most audiences originally experienced *In Dahomey*, or were meant to. "The headliners are the whole show," wrote one critic at the time, "Williams in particular."

Nevertheless, Cook's contributions to the show give evidence of

The Boston scene from *In Dahomey*, l. to r.: George Walker (Rareback Pinkerton), Aida Overton Walker (Rosetta Lightfoot), and Bert Williams (Shylock Homestead).

one of the more distinguished musical minds writing for Broadway at the time. Cook had a rather remarkable background in European classical music. He had studied violin with Joseph Joachim in Germany and composition briefly with Antonin Dvořák in New York. But he abandoned a career in concert music and embraced Broadway, not to compete there with white artists on their terms but to develop a kind of "genuine Negro" utterance in music that might appeal to the broader audience to be found there. In this he often succeeded. Indeed, the culturally subversive sentiment of these lines from *In Dahomey*'s "On Emancipation Day" suggests Cook's ambition, albeit beneath the minstrel rhetoric that was never absent from his shows:

> *When dey hear dem ragtime tunes*
> *White fo'ks try to pass fo' coons*
> *On Emancipation day.*

Critics praised Cook's shows particularly for their spirited ensemble numbers in which choruses danced and sang at the same time. (Choruses of the period usually did one or the other.) "Swing Along!" from *In Dahomey*, a dialect song in cakewalk style, offers a fine example of such a song-and-dance number. Its refrain fits the parallel period form then prevalent in popular music. The melody, sixteen bars long, consists of two parts split evenly down the middle (AB: mm. 1–8; AC: mm. 9–16), the first halves of each part (A) being alike, and the second halves (B or C) being different. Throughout, the easy rhythmic swing of Cook's music lends itself well to the high-stepping grace of the cakewalk it was meant to support. But the second A section proves especially winning when, instead of simply repeating the conventional accompaniment of the first A (Ex. 2-2a), the bass line steps down jauntily through the notes of the scale (see accents, Ex. 2-2b) as if it were following Aida Walker's prescriptions for actually doing the cakewalk: "Joyousness should be tinged with sobriety. Horseplay should be done away with for good and all. . . . The swing, all jauntiness and graceful poise, must come from the shoulders, and the toes must turn well out."

We cannot similarly recover Williams's comedy, though we can get a sense of it through photographs, film, recordings, and from what he and others have said about it. At a time when comedians were inclined

Ex. 2-2a. Will Marion Cook, music and lyrics: "Swing Along!" mm. 1–4, *In Dahomey*

Ex. 2-2b. "Swing Along!" mm. 9–12

to overact, his humor drew an uncommon power from being measured and understated. And while he performed in blackface makeup, he avoided the racial stereotype as he transformed the sorrow of his race into the stuff of laughter. His appeal was racial without being *merely* racial. And he claimed to have discovered in the very act of putting on blackface a way of distancing himself from the character he portrayed that was the key to his sense of humor.

> *The sight of other people in trouble is nearly always funny. . . . [But] the man with the real sense of humor is the man who can put himself in the spectator's place and laugh at his own misfortunes. . . . It was not until I was able to see myself as another person that my sense of humor developed. . . . Nearly all of my successful songs have been based on the idea that I am getting the worst of it. I am the "Jonah Man," the man who, even if it rained soup, would be found with a fork in his hand and no spoon in sight.*

Into every show Williams inserted at least one such song, which he delivered patiently, half-spoken, half-sung. Most popular among them were "I'm a Jonah Man" (*In Dahomey*); "Here It Comes Again" (*Abyssinia*); and the one that became his musical signature, "Nobody" (*Bandanna Land*), with its famous refrain:

> *I ain't never done nothin' to Nobody;*
> *I ain't never got nothin' from Nobody, no time:*
> *So until I get somethin' from somebody, sometime,*
> *I'll never do nothin' for Nobody, no time.*

For historian Ann Douglas, these lines sum up the essence of Williams's art, a performance art that drew a kind of subversive strength from its implied refusal to perform.

> *[Williams would] really just as soon, as the drooping shoulders, slow shuffle, and mournfully reserved face attest, not perform at all. . . . His singing style was closer to talking than singing; his spirits were never quite high enough, it seemed, for the impudence of song; and his listeners had not, in any case, merited so supreme an effort. The last line of*

"Nobody" was Williams's comic and not so comic threat to his audience that he might resign his post as their entertainer.

Bert Williams practiced comedy in self-contained units of songs or skits that clearly made their point and ended with their final notes or punchlines. In this he was no different from other comedians of the day, great and small. But because of this his comedy tended to interrupt the narrative thrust of the musical comedies in which he starred with Walker. One critic thus questioned *In Dahomey*'s very billing as a musical comedy because, he said, "though there is plenty of music, there is no sort of coherence or development of incident which justified the name of comedy." Criticism of this kind had been levelled earlier at Harrigan's plays, and it was still pertinent though it missed the point. Musical comedy on Broadway at the turn of the century was simply not a playlike comedy with music; it often dropped any pretense of being a play at all to indulge in whatever variety-type diversions its performers brought with them to the stage. Coherence of plot may or may not have been an ingredient in the mix, but it was not the primary condition to which the entertainment aspired. And so Williams's comedy lent itself perfectly to the discrete acts in revues and on the vaudeville stage in which he appeared after Walker's death. In fact, his return to vaudeville in 1918, triumphantly now at the top of the bill at the Palace Theater, can be seen as a return to his institutional roots as a performer and, beyond, to the panoply of variety-based entertainments from which American vaudeville itself drew—variety, circuses, minstrel shows, burlesques (in both senses).

Yet American theatergoers at the time did have access to a more playlike form of comedy with music that went by the name of operetta. It, too, had a strong middle-class appeal, though its audiences often included a more cultivated and conspicuously prosperous segment as well. For it differed from the variety-type shows in everything from its aesthetic aspirations to its institutional framework and, above all, its cosmopolitan character. Rarely did its practitioners go in for the local focus and homespun verities of a Harrigan and Hart, Weber and Fields, or Williams and Walker. Ultimately, it favored the former side in America's love/hate relationship with European culture, and tellingly took its cue and half its name from opera. But it would be no less important to the development of an American musical theater for that.

THE DAILY GRAPHIC

AN ILLUSTRATED EVENING NEWSPAPER

39 & 41 PARK PLACE

| VOL. XIX. | All the News. Four Editions Daily. | NEW YORK, SATURDAY, MARCH 1. 1879, | $12 Per Year in Advance. Single Copies, Five Cents. | NO. 1852 |

THE PINAFORE CRISIS.

3

A Transatlantic Muse

LA GRANDE-DUCHESSE DE GÉROLSTEIN
[THE GRAND DUCHESS OF GEROLSTEIN]
(Paris, 1867). New York (9/24/1867–3/25/1868, performed in French). **Producer:** H. L. Bateman. **Libretto:** Henri Meilhac and Ludovic Halévy. **Music:** Jacques Offenbach. **Director:** ? **New York Run:** 156 performances. **Cast:** Lucille Tostée. **Songs:** "Voici le sabre de mon père" (The Sabre Song), "Dites-lui" (The Letter Song).

H.M.S. PINAFORE; OR, THE LASS THAT LOVED A SAILOR
[London, 1878]. New York (1/15/1879–6/14/1879). **Producer:** James C. Duff. **Libretto:** William Schwenk Gilbert. **Music:** Arthur Sullivan. **Director:** H. W. Montgomery? **New York Run:** 175 performances. **Cast:** Eva Mills, Blanche Galton, Thomas Whiffen, Henry Laurent. **Songs:** "When I Was a Lad," "I Am the Captain of the Pinafore," "He Is an Englishman."

ROBIN HOOD
(9/28/1891–ca. 11/1891). **Producer:** The Bostonians. **Book and Lyrics:** Harry B. Smith. **Music:** Reginald de Koven. **Director:** H. Dixon. **New York Run:** 40 performances. **Cast:** Caroline Hamilton, Jessie Bartlett Davis, Tom Karl, Henry Clay Barnabee. **Songs:** "Song of Brown October Ale," "Tinkers' Chorus," "Oh Promise Me."

An 1879 newspaper cartoon panel, forerunner of the comic strip, depicts "The Pinafore Crisis" in New York caused by "a ship which never would have passed quarantine unheeded had it been known what a dreadfully contagious and pernicious fever she had on board."

EL CAPITAN

(4/20/1896–ca. 7/1896). **Producer:** De Wolf Hopper Opera Co. **Book:** Charles Klein. **Lyrics:** Tom Frost. **Music:** John Philip Sousa. **Director:** Herbert A. Cripps. **New York Run:** 112 performances. **Cast:** Edna Wallace Hopper, De Wolf Hopper. **Songs:** "El Capitan's Song," "When We Hear the Call to Battle."

THE FORTUNE TELLER

(9/26/1898–ca. 11/1898). **Producer:** Alice Nielsen Opera Co. (Frank L. Perley). **Book and Lyrics:** H. B. Smith. **Music:** Victor Herbert. **Director:** Julian Mitchell. **New York Run:** 40 performances. **Cast:** Alice Nielsen, Eugene Cowles. **Songs:** "Always Do as People Say You Should," "Romany Life," "Gypsy Love Song."

MLLE. MODISTE

(12/25/1905–6/16/1906). **Producer:** Charles Dillingham. **Book and Lyrics:** Henry Blossom. **Music:** Herbert. **Director:** Fred G. Latham. **New York Run:** 202 performances. **Cast:** Fritzi Scheff, William Pruette. **Songs:** "Kiss Me Again," "I Want What I Want When I Want It."

THE RED MILL

(9/24/1906–ca. 5/1907). **Producer:** Dillingham. **Book and Lyrics:** Blossom. **Music:** Herbert. **Director:** Latham. **New York Run:** 274 performances. **Cast:** Augusta Greenleaf, David Montgomery, Fred Stone. **Songs:** "The Streets of New York," "Every Day Is Ladies' Day with Me," "The Isle of Our Dreams."

◆────────

The charm of operetta rests in the modesty of its presumption, for the very name contains both the seriousness of an ambition and the limit to that seriousness as a musical theater enterprise. It is opera with a diminutive ending—perhaps, as one observer has it, an "unassuming little opera."

Opera lay at the opposite end from variety on the spectrum of late-nineteenth-century musical theater. To American audiences of the era, opera often meant a dramatic stagework of high artistic ambition that was sung not only from beginning to end but also in a foreign language. (On both counts, presumably, Samuel Johnson had dismissed the enterprise a century earlier as "irrational" and "exotic.") This double curiosity derived in large part from traditions born of the aristocratic courts of Europe that had cultivated the genre since its inception in Italy in the seventeenth century. Surprisingly, such traditions also took root when later transplanted in the more democratic soil of the United States. Ralph Waldo Emerson's famous enjoinder to Americans of the nineteenth century that "We have listened too long to the courtly muses of Europe" could have applied to this genre quite well.

Indeed, opera thrived on this side of the Atlantic. Its very ties to European culture made it an emblem of prestige, commonly viewed as the highest form of musical theater. It also proved one of the costliest, and hence came to function as a barometer of status in the Gilded Age for an American "aristocracy" of wealth, which often substituted for the real thing. This function impinged even on the founding in New York of the Metropolitan Opera. As the story goes, a certain Mrs. Vanderbilt (of the family of railroad magnate Cornelius Vanderbilt) was denied an opera box at New York's elite Academy of Music. In high dudgeon, with her status in society thus at stake, she mobilized forces to build a rival opera house, the Metropolitan, where there would be boxes sufficient to accommodate her and those of her ilk who had been snubbed as being nouveaux riches by the city's old money. With the opening of the new house, she recovered her status as she had planned. She also had her revenge in a way she could scarcely have imagined. The Academy, after thirty-two years of operation, stopped presenting regular opera seasons in 1886. The Metropolitan, which opened in 1883, has endured to the present.

Operetta resembled opera in its narrative structure and musical sophistication, though in spirit it often moved closer to variety-type shows on the entertainment spectrum. Historians now tend to see operetta's emergence in late-nineteenth-century Europe as confirmation of the rise of a "popular" culture distinct from the aristocratic ones that had been in retreat since the French Revolution. In America, operetta occupied a more ambiguous position: It seemed too frivolous to pass as art, and too much like opera to pass for sheer amusement. Thus in 1867, at the time of the genre's first major success in the United States, The *New York Dramatic Mirror* hailed it as in some sense the highest order of *popular* musical theater. And so it would be regarded for the rest of the century and beyond as it helped to shape a distinctly American musical theater as well—first as comic opera, later as romantic operetta, and later still, arguably, as the musical play.

OPERETTA: THE GOLDEN AGE

The term "operetta" as we now use it refers to a spirited stagework in which a story unfolds in song, dance, and spoken dialogue. In its heyday, the specific kind of stagework operetta represented differed both from variety-based shows that also told stories (*The Mulligan Guard Ball, In Dahomey*), and from operas that also had spoken dialogue (*Faust* and *Carmen* in their original versions). On the one hand, variety musicals did not take their measure as entertainment from opera. Operettas did, at least in certain key respects. Operetta stories commonly dealt with courtly life and aristocratic society, as did the stories of most operas. The major roles in operettas regularly called for singers with operatic training who could sing solos and hold their own in ensemble parts. Even the music written for operettas normally required the skill of composers (not just songwriters) who could write in operatic forms— recitative; arioso; continuous movements, especially in opening numbers and finales—and also orchestrate the music they composed. In these respects operetta differed considerably from variety-based musicals.

How, then, on the other hand, did operetta differ from opera? For an influential segment of late-nineteenth-century society, opera—or, more nearly, operagoing—represented a morally uplifting occasion and musically demanding activity (even if the opera one attended was a comic one). With operettas, neither was the case. Their stories may have dealt with the nobly born, but their focus was invariably on how ignobly they behaved. Many operettas told sexually suggestive tales in which morality was compromised or, at least, teasingly made to seem so. And while operettas required singers with legitimate voices, they also demanded that such singers act, put words across (spoken and sung), and scale down the grandiloquence of operatic vocal projection. Additionally, if operettas took their musical shape in operatic forms, they also infused their music with the grace and verve of styles derived from popular dances of the period—such as galops, quadrilles, cancans, polkas, and, above all, waltzes. Even the production of operettas followed the dictates of commercial houses rather than the norms of the subsidized court and state theaters that customarily housed opera. As much a business as an art, operetta aimed not to edify but to amuse.

In its modern form, operetta flourished roughly from 1860 to 1930. It underwent several shifts in style during this period, the most significant occurring about halfway through, around the turn of the century. In the early decades, the flurry of creative activity that most clearly defined the genre came out of three great urban centers: Paris, London, and Vienna. In later decades, important operetta activity also came out of Berlin, Budapest, and New York. Yet it is only with respect to the Viennese strain of operetta that one commonly speaks in terms of the shift from a Golden Age in the nineteenth century to a Silver Age in the twentieth. (This is perhaps because Vienna—symbolically the center of German-language operetta production—so dominated the Silver Age, at least until the First World War, that Paris and London could no longer successfully compete with it internationally as they had before.) The division into Golden and Silver eras, however, may also prove useful to understanding the historical development of the genre as a whole, even if it proves less precise when applied to other centers of activity than Vienna. In this broader sense, our concern here is with operetta of the Golden Age. (We will consider Silver Age operetta in chapter 5.)

Operetta first flowered in Paris in the 1850s and 1860s. It grew out of an effort to revive the original spirit of opéra comique, a lighthearted French genre dating back to the eighteenth century that had assumed more serious ambitions in the nineteenth century. At first, the new genre consisted of only one-act sketches with a scattering of musical numbers performed by less than a handful of actors. The French fittingly referred to these staged musical miniatures as opérettes; or, since the Théâtre des Bouffes-Parisiens housed the first successes in the vein, as opéras bouffes. Jacques Offenbach (1819–1880), the theater's composer-director, extolled their virtues—brevity, wit, directness—and saw in the early popularity of his productions the promise of bigger things to come:

> *We have had some success in reviving the form of the musical sketches of the old* opéra-comique. . . . *We intend, not only to go on with this, but also to mine the inexhaustible vein of French gaiety of the past. Our only ambition is to "write short," but if you think about it for a moment, that is no mean ambition. In an opera that lasts barely three quarters of an hour, where one may only have four characters on stage, and an orchestra of thirty musicians at most [as opposed to an opera orchestra of eighty], the ideas and melodies have to be in hard cash. . . .*
>
> *Far be it from us to be reactionary or to disparage new techniques. We do not say that looking back to the past is the last word in progress; but, granted that the genre we are developing under the license of the Bouffes-Parisiens is only the first step on the ladder, there still has to be a first step if we are to climb any higher.*

In time, Offenbach did climb higher, expanding opéra bouffe both as a form of entertainment and in terms of its cultural reach. By the 1860s, it had grown into an evening's-length amusement normally in three acts, containing some twenty to thirty musical numbers, and performed by a full cast and chorus. Typically, it relied on the stage traditions of farce and literary burlesque to tell tales of sexual intrigues. Yet the practitioners of opéra bouffe also saw the lyric stage as a vehicle for satire, and they used comic impudence and musical wit to poke fun at the court of Napoleon III and the political and social foibles of France's Second Empire.

Tours of the Bouffes-Parisiens company to London and Vienna won an international following for the genre and sparked the development of operetta in those cities. By the 1870s and 1880s, each had stamped the enterprise with a distinctive genius of its own. In London, Gilbert and Sullivan emerged as the foremost creators of what they called comic operas. These, too, consisted of satirical diversions, though Gilbert was as apt to burlesque the conventions of the dramatic and operatic stage as to ridicule Victorian values and institutions. Less salacious than their French counterparts, these comic operas delighted in stories of innocent love, mistaken identity, and class conflict. But since much of their humor took the form of puns and verbal gymnastics, they tended not to travel well outside the orbit of English-speaking theaters. In Vienna, Johann Strauss II, the "waltz king," emerged as the foremost composer of what the German-speaking theaters called Operette. Redirecting his talent from the ballroom to the stage, Strauss built his theater scores around dance forms dominated by the sexually charged energy of the waltz. This fit the mood of the entertainment well since Operette, though regularly based on French farces, tended more toward the romantic than the satirical. In fact, whether placed in aristocratic, rural, or historical settings, their stories often verged on the risqué as they doted on jealousy, misunderstanding, disguise—especially women in trouser roles—and the amorous imbroglios of consenting adults.

The many genre names—opéra bouffe, comic opera, and Operette simply being the most prominent—indicated genuine differences between national schools with respect to musical and theatrical practices, conventions, and styles. Only in retrospect did theatergoers apply "operetta" generically as an umbrella term to cover all of the different strains. But while the term had first been used in the seventeenth and eighteenth centuries to describe works that were "short, or otherwise less ambitious, derivatives of opera," it no longer meant the same when applied to the substantial stagework that operetta had become by the late nineteenth century. Opera with a diminutive ending now pointed not to the brevity of a genre but to its levity: a genre quite unencumbered by the seriousness of opera's aesthetic reach. For a burgeoning middle class, then, operetta developed as an entertainment alternative—a light opera—at a time when opera otherwise conceived abandoned much of what had once made it accessible so that it might assume a certain gravitas and become, in a word, heavy.

The conflicting aims of perhaps the two most influential theater composers of the age reflected this split in the world of middle-class musical culture. Richard Wagner (1813–1883) saw musical theater as an almost sacred undertaking; Jacques Offenbach saw it in terms of an emerging "culture industry." Wagner espoused a progressive program for musical-dramatic stageworks, transforming the very nature of musical language and continuity under the rubric of an "artwork of the future." Offenbach rather looked the other way, seeking to recapture through the musical language and discontinuities of a bygone era something of the aura of eighteenth-century comic opera in a spirit of nostalgia, parody, and skepticism. Offenbach sought to develop, as he described it, a *"genre primitif et vrai"*—"primitive" in returning to the spirit of its origin in opéra comique, and "true" perhaps in both prizing simplicity and mocking pretension.

For critic Karl Kraus, writing significantly later, the "truth" of this type of operetta lay in its ability to see itself as absurd. From a rational standpoint, the combination of acting and singing made no sense at all (though, without it, there could of course be neither opera nor operetta). In Offenbachian operetta, however, this combination was undertaken knowingly and with sheer delight in the nonsense of the result. The genre was self-aware, according to Kraus. It could thus be trusted where opera could not, he argued, precisely because opera took the absurdity of singing its action seriously.

> *[Opera] is by definition nonsense. It postulates the real world and inhabits it with people who sing when seized by a fit of jealousy, when plagued by a headache, when declaring war—even in the throes of death they do not spare the coloratura. Opera reduces itself to absurdity through the incongruent pairing of a profound earnestness with the odd human habit of singing. In operetta, on the other hand, absurdity is a given. Operetta postulates a world in which the laws of causality are suspended . . . and where song is the certified means of communication.*

For English-speaking audiences, there are perhaps no more telling examples of that "world in which the laws of causality are suspended" than the tongue-twisting patter songs of Gilbert and Sullivan. In *The Pirates of Penzance*, for instance, Major-General Stanley introduces himself by singing what is surely the most famous patter song of all. In it, he satirizes the idea of the British Army officer who knows far too much of everything except what he really needs to know in his profession. He begins:

I am the very model of a modern Major-General,
I've information vegetable, animal, and mineral,
I know the kings of England, and I quote the fights historical
From Marathon to Waterloo, in order categorical . . .

Yet he concludes with an admission that undermines his credibility:

For my military knowledge, though I'm plucky and adventury,
Has only been brought down to the beginning of the century;
But still in matters vegetable, animal, and mineral,
I am the very model of a modern Major-General.

Stanley may well be a major-general, but he is certainly no modern one. Addressing audiences as a contemporary in the 1880s when *Pirates* was new, he admits the latest military exploit he knows of is the Battle of Waterloo, which took place in 1815. Nor is there a shred of shame in his confession. On the contrary, Stanley takes pride in the very artifice with which he contradicts himself, choosing his words as much for their ability to rhyme as to make sense. At the end, he even puts greater store in their ability to rhyme when he makes a point of matching "strategy" with "a better Major-General has never sat a gee," and thus undermines his claims to any competence at all as a major-general. For a "gee" is—or was—a nickname for a horse, but not a military one. Furthermore, as a performer, Stanley ultimately subverts even the sense of his words by delivering them as if they were the most natural thing in the world, but at a speed that makes them sound like gibberish. Only by imagining the

The "modern Major-General" flaunts the trappings of his useless erudition in a sketch by W. S. Gilbert himself (signed "Bab").

dizzying impact of all of this at once can one begin to appreciate that upside-down universe in which Karl Kraus says "absurdity is a given."

Patter songs like this may well be the height of light-opera lunacy, yet they have a logic of their own. So do the many other kinds of musical numbers in the Gilbert and Sullivan operettas that are not nearly so bizarre. Such numbers actually make eminent "sense" in the context of the plays in which they appear. Nor are the plays themselves at all incoherent. They tend to develop with utmost logic; however, they proceed from preposterous premises—in *The Pirates of Penzance*: a hero's sense of duty so absolute as to honor even an obvious mistake; in *The Mikado*: a Japan in which there is state-mandated execution for flirting. At their best, the plays of Gilbert and Sullivan and of others who wrote satirical operettas are literate plays. But as they originate in ridiculous assumptions and as they rely on music to get from one plot point to the next, they operate in a world turned, as Gilbert liked to say, topsy-turvy.

The play in a light opera is traditionally referred to as the libretto— the script or "little book" of all the words spoken and sung. The music is synonymous with the score. In the nineteenth century such a score consisted of a variety of numbers, from solo songs or arias to ensemble introductions and finales. The songs were often in simple strophic forms, though the technique needed to sing them was far from simple: full-throated singing was one of the delights of the genre. Numbers using more involved musical forces included choruses, ensembles of two or more characters singing independent parts (duets, trios, etc.), and concerted finales in which as many characters as possible proceeded to fill the stage at the end of an act, singing contrasting numbers one after another to reflect changes in the action. Indeed, it became most evident in the finale that the function of a light opera number might differ from that of a number in a variety-based show where singing was used less to tell a story than to divert attention from it.

Creating the text and music of light operas generally involved the work of librettists and composers who did not perform onstage but specialized in what they did behind the scenes. This marked an important division of labor. Variety-type musicals, by contrast, tended not to make such distinctions: they were more the creations of their own performers. With burlesques, revues, and even early musical comedies the two functions so often overlapped it was difficult to separate what these shows actually were as entertainments from who performed them—

and usually pointless for audiences even to try, or for such shows to be performed by anybody else. Their creators conceived them not as independent works that could endure on their own, but in the spirit of occasions that might be repeated only under certain limited conditions. Thus the scripts of even the foremost actor-authors of the age were not published as a rule, Ned Harrigan's included. And while songs to their shows did appear in print, these were commonly issued as separate pieces of sheet music, not as complete scores. It would have been impractical to do otherwise: Variety-type shows were constantly subject to change, and whatever afterlives they enjoyed beyond their initial runs were usually local in scope and of relatively short duration.

Light operas led different afterlives. With an international network of theaters and institutions through which they were marketed, they enjoyed both a broader following and a more sustained hold on audiences; and it proved profitable to publish their librettos and vocal scores. Once published, moreover, such pieces were also less apt to change (though there was still tinkering aplenty that went on from one production to the next). Like operas of the "heavy" kind, then, light operas came to be viewed as "works" apart from their original performers or any particular performance. As such, they make up the earliest important body of work for the commercial musical stage that has come down to us both textually intact (words and music) and through a more or less unbroken performance tradition. The spread in the popularity of the genre on this side of the Atlantic in the late nineteenth century can thus be said to have paved the way for the creation of the first durable repertoire of musicals made in America.

LIGHT OPERA IN AMERICA

It took the generation of the Gilded Age, roughly the last third of the nineteenth century, to develop a light opera tradition suited to an American musical theater. This involved importing European troupes and stageworks to build a regular audience for light opera in the United States, forming stable American companies to specialize in their performance, and creating a durable repertoire of American works for such companies to perform. What led to these developments can be seen in part as the consequences of three Broadway openings, each a signal moment in American acceptance of another of the European national schools that became most vital to the early growth of the genre: the French, with *The Grand Duchess of Gerolstein* in 1867; the British, with *H.M.S. Pinafore* in 1878; and the Austro-German, with *The Queen's Lace Handkerchief* in 1880.

Even before the Civil War, audiences of mostly French- and German-speaking immigrants enjoyed European light operas on a steady basis in the foreign-language theaters of New York. But the nationwide craze for the genre did not begin until 1867, when a company imported from France first presented *La Grande-Duchesse de Gérolstein* in New York, and performances in English soon followed with a sensational effect. (Even in the case of ready-made hit musicals of foreign origin, one could not hope for popular success on the commercial stage in America except by performing them in English.)

The Grand Duchess of Gerolstein told a tale suffused with eroticism, satire, and Gallic charm. Gerolstein, an imaginary state in Europe, is thrown into turmoil by its headstrong young ruler when she rejects a politically appropriate suitor and promotes a common soldier in whom she is sexually interested to become commander in chief of the army. The libretto of Ludovic Halévy (1834–1908) and Henri Meilhac (1831–97) had come under attack at home for the barbs it aimed at the political and military intrigues of the Second Empire. But the satire was all but lost on American audiences, which did not prevent them from making humorous connections nonetheless between *The Grand Duchess* and events in their own recently concluded Civil War. Ironically, some observers felt this was the main reason for the work's success in the United States.

There was no misunderstanding Offenbach's music, however. It surmounted all cultural barriers with irresistible tunes ranging from the militarily robust to the sexually suggestive—the Sword Song ("Voici le sabre") and the Letter Song ("Dites-lui"). Such songs, in the words of one commentator, were "hummed, whistled, played until the ear was worn to shreds." *The Grand Duchess's* popularity firmly established French light opera as a major theatrical attraction in the United States. It opened the way for public acceptance of more operettas by Offenbach, such as *Orpheus in the Underworld* (Paris, 1858; rev. 1874), *La Belle Hélène* (1864), *Bluebeard* (1866), *La Vie Parisienne* (1866), *La*

Périchole (1868), and by his successors, including Charles Lecocq (*La Fille de Madame Angot*, 1872) and Edmond Audran (*The Mascot*, 1880). As theatrical touring expanded after completion of the transcontinental railroad in 1869, the works of these composers provided the first experience of extended-form dramatic music for many Americans who lived beyond the east coast of the United States, and the exposure made them aware of previously unimagined levels of quality and pleasure that such entertainments might reach.

In 1870s Paris, however, Offenbach's opéras bouffes fell precipitously out of favor, casualties of the cultural backlash following France's defeat in the Franco-Prussian War. Finding himself on the verge of bankruptcy, Offenbach accepted an invitation to appear in the United States in connection with the country's centennial celebrations of 1876. In New York and Philadelphia, he conducted a series of concerts of his music and some performances of his stageworks that included *La Vie Parisienne*. (Playing in the orchestra's first violin section was the young John Philip Sousa.) The tour did much to improve Offenbach's financial situation. It also revealed what he called the "deplorable condition" of musical theater in America. As he noted in his diary, published in France the following year as *Notes d'un musicien en voyage*:

> *To have good artists, good companies, and authors, stable institutions are necessary, long training, a tradition which comes only slowly into existence. In New York, there is no permanent opera, no permanent* opéra comique, *nor even any operetta theatre which is sure of two years of life.... The theatre lives in America from day to day. The directors and their companies are nomads. Most of the artists are just visitors borrowed from the Old World, coming for one season only and then leaving.*

Offenbach was a canny observer of American mores, however. And seeing in the present situation the seeds of a more artistically vital future, he went on to predict:

> *The day when you will have established permanent theatres ... you will have done a great deal for dramatic art, for American composers and authors, but you will not harvest the fruit of your efforts immediately. Ten years, perhaps twenty years will be necessary for the estab-*

lishments that you will have founded to produce the excellent results
which you have every right to expect. But what are twenty years?
Twenty years for your students to become masters, twenty years for you
to become no longer mere tributaries of European art, twenty years for
the theatres of the Old World to come asking you for artists as today
you ask them!

What led to forming the permanent institutions Offenbach called
for was not opéra comique, however. That subgenre was soon eclipsed
by English comic opera, the second of the schools of European operetta to set off an even bigger light-opera mania in the United States.
It started with *H.M.S. Pinafore* (London, 1878), the fourth of fourteen
stageworks written by the team of William S. Gilbert (1836–1911) and
Arthur Sullivan (1842–1900) that would include *The Pirates of Penzance* (1879), *Patience* (1881), *Iolanthe* (1882), and their most durable
success both at home and abroad *The Mikado* (1885). *Pinafore*'s American premiere took place in Boston in November 1878. Within months
the craze for it had spread like a wildfire, with productions in San Francisco, Baltimore, Philadelphia, and eight different ones in New York.
Within a year it had become the single most performed operetta in the
country, with more than a hundred professional and amateur productions, and numerous competing ones in each of the larger cities.

For Americans whose national culture was still strongly influenced
by British sensibilities, *Pinafore* marked a characteristic departure from
the ways of continental light opera. The fun in Gilbert's libretto was
morally unassailable and needed no translation. The music in Sullivan's score replaced what now seemed like French froth with sturdier
English tunefulness. Its songs, choruses, and anthems found cultural
resonance even in the parlors, schools, and churches of small-town
U.S.A. *Pinafore*, wrote an American contemporary, was enjoyed by "the
most uncompromising Yankee almost as much as if he had been an
Englishman himself."

Above all, *Pinafore* acknowledged its own artifice as a satire with
a certain playfulness of spirit. It could enjoy poking fun at Victorian
society because it did so without advocating an overturn of the social
structure. It told a story of conflict between the dictates of love and
class that takes place onboard Her Majesty's Ship *Pinafore*. Defying
social norms, Ralph, a lowly sailor, falls in love with Josephine, his

high-born captain's daughter. She loves him in return, but is wooed by a suitor more suited to her station in life, First Lord of the Admiralty Sir Joseph Porter. Sir Joseph ultimately loses interest in the girl, however, when he discovers—along with everyone else—that Ralph and the captain, who were indeed born at opposite ends of the social spectrum, had also been mistakenly switched as babies by their nurse Little Buttercup. ("Love levels all ranks," Sir Joseph nervously remarks, "but it does not level them as much as that.") And so the now high-born sailor and lowly captain's daughter are free to marry.

Gilbert thought his topsy-turvy stuff "innocent but not imbecile." Boston critic John S. Dwight put it in a broader context, as if elaborating on Gilbert's words. As for innocence, Dwight said *Pinafore* "is cleverer than the French Opera Bouffe, and doubtless has done much to drive out and occupy the place of that unclean drama of Silenus." And as for its lack of imbecility, "it is a thousand times better and more entertaining than those extravaganzas of the *Evangeline* stamp, stuffed full of flat inanities and fly-blown with puns too poor to raise a laugh." In taste, artistry, and wit, *Pinafore* surpassed all the kinds of storytelling musicals that had dominated the American stage before it arrived. So, too, would those of Gilbert and Sullivan's comic operas that followed in its wake. They set a new standard altogether by which future musicals in America would be measured.

Gilbert and Sullivan had set out to do nothing less than reinvent the English-speaking comic musical. At least, so Gilbert later recalled:

When Sullivan and I began to collaborate, English comic opera had practically ceased to exist. Such musical entertainments as held the stage were adaptations of the crapulous plots of the operas of Offenbach, Audran and Lecocq. The plots had generally been bowdlerized out of intelligibility, and when they had not been subjected to this treatment they were frankly improper; whereas the ladies' dresses suggested that the management had gone on the principle of doing a little and doing it well. We set out with the determination to prove that these elements were not essential to the success of humorous opera. We resolved that our plots, however ridiculous, should be coherent, that our dialogue should be void of offence; on artistic principles, no man should play a woman's part and no woman a man's. Finally, we agreed that no lady of the company should be required to wear a dress that she

*could not wear with absolute propriety at a private fancy ball; and I
believe I may say that we proved our case.*

Pinafore may have well proved the case for Gilbert and Sullivan in
America, but the countless American productions of the work did not
earn its authors one cent. In the absence of an international copyright
law prior to 1891, *Pinafore* was protected by copyright only in the
country where it had been premiered: England. Its subsequent mountings in the United States had all been in pirated versions—legal perhaps but unauthorized. Adding artistic insult to financial injury, such
versions freely adapted the piece to suit local tastes, changing it in
one way or another, sometimes beyond recognition. (Ralph was even
played by a girl in a Boston production and, in a Baltimore one, Little
Buttercup by a man.) To forestall a similar fate to their next venture,
The Pirates of Penzance, the Englishmen sought to secure its American copyright by giving the official world premiere in New York.
Shrewdly, they preceded the premiere with a month of performances
of *Pinafore* itself. On December 1, 1879, *H.M.S. Pinafore* received its
first authorized performance in the New World—with Gilbert directing players of the D'Oyly Carte organization for which the work had
been created, and Sullivan conducting his score complete and unimproved by others.

The D'Oyly Carte productions—professional, polished, and unim-
peachably authentic—were a revelation to American audiences. Yet the
D'Oyly Carte Opera Company remained a thoroughly British enterprise throughout its long career (1879–1982; 1988–2003). While it
was to come back to perform in America at regular intervals, it would
always return home. The formation in Boston of the Boston Ideal
Opera Company (1879–1904) shortly before the first arrival of the
D'Oyly Cartes in New York would have more lasting consequences for
the growth of light opera in the United States. Put together largely by
its female impresario Effie Ober, this company was created in order to
mount a musically "ideal" production of "this *Pinafore*," as one of the
players put it, that had "been already done to death in many ways [but
had never] been really sung." The Boston Ideals' success with *Pinafore*
launched what would become one of the finest artistic ensembles for
the popular lyric stage in America. Soon it expanded its repertoire to
include English-language productions of non-English operettas (von

Suppé's *Boccaccio*, Audran's *The Mascot*) and even Italian comic operas (Mozart's *The Marriage of Figaro*, Donizetti's *Don Pasquale*). It also extended its geographic reach with tours of cities on the east coast and in the Midwest. Reorganized in 1887 as the Bostonians, the company now gave its leadership over to a triumvirate of its own players, of whom the most memorable was the comic baritone Henry Clay Barnabee (1833–1917). In time, contralto Jessie Bartlett Davis (1860–1905), basso Eugene Cowles (1860–1948), and other star-quality singers joined the company and adapted their talents to the starless ensemble style for which its productions were famous. Moreover, it now began to tour from coast to coast and to produce original works by American writers—Thomas Thorne and Clay Greene's *The Maid of Plymouth*, Victor Herbert and H. B. Smith's *The Serenade*, and the operetta that became its signature piece, Reginald de Koven and H. B. Smith's *Robin Hood*. For Barnabee, a stalwart of the troupe throughout its twenty-five-year existence, the Bostonians was "the representative light-opera company of America" in its day. It "gave the United States the most successful school for operatic study that this country has ever had," and "no other organization has done more, if as much, toward assisting American writers or opera."

While the Boston Ideals was establishing itself in the 1880s, Americans were developing a taste for the third of Europe's national light-opera schools. New York productions in 1879 and 1880 of Franz von Suppé's *Fatinitza* (Vienna, 1876) and *Boccaccio* (1879) first piqued American interest in operettas from German-speaking lands (often, if not always correctly, described as Viennese). More works of the type followed shortly with great success: *The Queen's Lace Handkerchief* (1880), *The Merry War* (1881), both by Johann Strauss II (1825–1899), *The Beggar Student* (1882) by Karl Millöcker, and many others, almost all of them originally set to librettos by the team of F. Zell (1829–1895) and Richard Genée (1823–1895). To one observer it seemed as if a "German operetta invasion" had hit New York. Yet even as German operettas lay hold of America's stages, none sparked anything like the national frenzy of *Grand Duchess* or *Pinafore*. (The United States would indeed be seized by a German operetta frenzy, but not until decades later—that is, with the arrival of *The Merry Widow* in 1907 and the "rediscovery" a few years after of Johann Strauss's masterpiece *Die Fledermaus*.)

Two New York impresarios figured prominently in the new development. One was Col. John McCaull (?–1894), a lawyer whose exemplary success in running his McCaull Opera Comique Company (1880–1890) earned him, besides a lot of money, the sobriquet of America's "father of comic opera." The other was Rudolph Aronson (1856–1919), a musician and artistic visionary who tried and failed to build a national conservatory of music, school of drama, and center for the performing arts in Washington, D.C.

McCaull brought a shrewd business sense and an eye for talent to managing the company that bore his name. He filled its ranks with promising performers, many of whom rose to fame with the troupe, then formed star companies of their own. Among them were Francis Wilson (1854–1935) and De Wolf Hopper (1858–1935), both to emerge as leading comedians of the age. Another was Lillian Russell (1861–1922), the prima donna with a stunning soprano voice and hourglass figure who became America's first great operetta diva, the "Queen of Comic Opera." The troupe was basically a stock company headquartered at Manhattan's Bijou Theater. It also toured, as Hopper recalled:

> *We played fifty-two weeks a season, twenty-two in New York City and thirty on the road. . . . Opera bouffe, light opera, operetta or comic opera, as you will, was in its hey-day. Musical comedy and the revue were yet unborn. In numbers and importance light opera ranked second only to the drama itself. Musically [however,] the United States had produced little of its own beyond Stephen Foster's negro songs, and we imported virtually all of our light operas from Austria, Germany and France.*

McCaull's even gave the local premiere of *The Queen's Lace Handkerchief,* which, though only a minor Viennese confection, proved so popular that Aronson came to see it as "the forerunner . . . of the Austro-German craze" in the United States. Aronson was not a disinterested observer. As *Handkerchief* was the inaugural production at the Casino Theater, and as Aronson had just built the house, he undoubtedly saw in the success of what the Casino offered the success of the Casino itself. Built on a grand scale in Moorish style on the corner of Thirty-ninth Street and Broadway, the Casino became New York's first legitimate theater that could accommodate musical productions year-round. Aronson built the house to be "the Home of Comic Opera," and he ran it accordingly—with mostly German and French pieces sung in English. By Aronson's reckoning, during the decade of his stewardship (1882–1892), three and a half million people saw the thirty-five operettas he mounted there in costly stagings accompanied by an orchestra of thirty musicians. The extravagance eventually bankrupted him, however, and forced him from the scene. Thereafter, the Casino was

Interior of the Casino Theater prior to 1905.

to be the home to newer forms of entertainment, such as revues (*The Passing Show*) and musical comedies (*Florodora*), though it returned to operettas in the 1920s (*The Vagabond King, The Desert Song*) before it was finally razed in 1930.

In 1883, a year after the Casino opened, the Metropolitan Opera House opened diagonally across the street from it. Any symbolism in erecting the one theater so close to the other may have been unintentional, but it could not have been more pronounced. By their proximity, the two houses flaunted the architectural differences between them in ways that reflected the cultural split in musical theater at the time. The Casino served as a comic opera house for broad middle-class patronage. It had fine sightlines from most of the orchestra and balcony that made up its auditorium. And it boasted a roof garden theater—the first of its kind in New York—that offered a welcoming outdoor ambience and refreshments along with musical entertainment on hot summer nights. By contrast, the Metropolitan served as a grand opera house and a kind of private club for fashionable society—though others, too, might be admitted (somewhat grudgingly perhaps). Its awe-inspiring interior contained more than 120 boxes piled four tiers high; and perched on top was a gallery offering more affordable seats but full views of the stage from only one-quarter of them. The cost for a partially obstructed view in the gallery of the Metropolitan was $1.50, the same price one paid for the best seat in the orchestra at the Casino.

Some of the most notable productions of the Aronson years at the Casino included *Erminie* (1886), a long-running English import in which Francis Wilson found his signature part, and a lavish revival of *The Grand Duchess* (1890), with Lillian Russell now in the title role of the French piece whose success more than twenty years before had sparked the light opera movement in America. Then in 1892 the Casino staged its first American-made operetta, *The Fencing Master*, by the team of de Koven and Smith, whose *Robin Hood* had played in London the year before. The moment seemed historically auspicious. With a well-developed audience for light opera in the United States

---

Interior of the Metropolitan Opera House in 1955. While renovated several times since it opened in 1883, the house preserved the original "golden horseshoe" layout of boxes and tiers that allowed society to see itself and to be seen.

and relatively stable institutions to perform it in place, American writers now created a body of work in the genre, some of sufficient distinction even to export eastward across the Atlantic to the lands of its origin—and just about on schedule, as Offenbach had predicted.

AMERICAN LIGHT OPERA

That American audiences preferred their operettas imported did not mean that American writers hadn't also tried their hand at the genre. Even before Offenbach and Gilbert and Sullivan came to visit in the 1870s, immigrant and native writers in the United States had created original European-style operettas; and they continued to do so after the Europeans left. A pop-

Posing in her costume for the title role in *The Grand Duchess of Gerolstein*, Lillian Russell makes the most of her hourglass figure.

ular early example was *The Doctor of Alcantara* (1862), written as an opéra bouffe in Boston by British-born librettist Benjamin Woolf and German-born composer Julius Eichberg, then revised as a comic opera sixteen years later to reflect the shift in taste resulting from the *Pinafore* craze. *Pinafore* and the Gilbert and Sullivan hits that followed, in fact, especially *The Mikado*, became models for an entire generation of American writers—Willard Spenser (*The Little Tycoon*, 1886) and J. Cheever Goodwin and Woolson Morse (*Wang*, 1891). And later still, the Austro-German influence made itself felt particularly in the output of such immigrant musicians as Gustave Kerker (*The Belle of New York*, 1897), Ludwig Englander (*The Strollers*, 1901), and Gustav Luders (*The Prince of Pilsen*, 1903). These and similar efforts, while often highly successful, were the work of practitioners of varying gifts. They were also of little more than local interest, though there were exceptions. *The Belle of New York*, a modest success at home, proved a sensation in London, Paris, and Berlin (perhaps due to the novelty in Europe of its New York setting and character types: a British observer called it "purely American—American to the backbone").

But the real blossoming of operetta composition in America began in the 1890s with the work of Reginald de Koven, H. B. Smith, John Philip Sousa, and Victor Herbert. These men constitute the earliest group of writers to create an American light opera repertoire of some durability and distinction, though they too embraced European models for the most part. They also constituted the last important group of comic opera writers to come of age honing their talents on the system of stock companies in America that specialized in the genre. McCaull's, for example, premiered some of their earliest efforts in the 1880s: Sousa's *Désirée* (1884), de Koven and Smith's *The Begum* (1887). Their more memorable creations, however, premiered by other companies, appeared in the following decade; and they include *Robin Hood* (1891), *El Capitan* (1896), and *The Fortune Teller* (1898).

Reginald de Koven (1859–1920), born into a family of wealth and cultivation, pursued a gentleman's course of study in Europe as a young man. There he came into contact with the main centers of light opera levity. He took a degree at Oxford, learned orchestration in Paris from Léo Delibes, and studied operetta composition in Vienna with Franz von Suppé and Richard Genée. In America, de Koven enjoyed a distinguished career as a music critic, conductor (Washington Symphony Orchestra), and composer of two grand operas as well as the twenty-four light ones on which his reputation mainly rests. Of his operettas fifteen had books by Harry Bache Smith (1860–1936), surely the most prolific lyricist-librettist in the history of the American stage. Smith spent some fifty years writing for the theater and claimed his total output exceeded three hundred titles—including adaptations of foreign operettas, lyrics for the Weber and Fields burlesques, scripts for Ziegfeld's *Follies*, and librettos for book shows with music by such composers in addition to de Koven as Sousa, Herbert, Kern, Romberg, and Berlin. Given the enormity of this output and the speed at which Smith had to work simply to get it out and up on the stage, it is not surprising that critics considered little of it inspired. Smith saw himself as a practical man of the theater. As such, he harbored clear-eyed views of the librettist's craft, and of his own limitations:

> *A playwright, given a story and characters, has merely to arrange his story, develop it logically and naturally, and establish certain climaxes which shall terminate his acts. A librettist must do this and much more. After constructing his play, he must take it all to pieces, find places for his songs, and then write his songs. He must also—in a real comic opera—carry on the action of his play to music and verse. He must plan the play musically and dramatically. . . . Mind you, I am speaking of really meritorious librettos. The average musical play[s] written in America nowadays [are] beneath critical consideration. . . . I have been guilty of aiding and abetting some of these conspiracies.*

The most popular of the de Koven–Smith collaborations were *Robin Hood, Rob Roy* (1894), and *The Highwayman* (1897). As operettas these works typically bucked the winds of realism that swept the theater at the end of the century. Far more genteel than gritty, they took place in an idealized British past, with lovable outlaws as heroes in the title roles. *Robin Hood* had two additional characters of note. One was the Sheriff of Nottingham, whose villainy was tempered by the comic art of the Bostonians' Henry Clay Barnabee. The other was Alan-a-Dale, a trouser role in which contralto Jessie Bartlett Davis introduced "Oh Promise Me," a hymnlike ballad that soon became an American wedding standard and was to remain so long after *Robin Hood* itself had been forgotten.

Smith claimed that, in collaborating, he and de Koven "decided to bestow . . . the sincerest flattery of imitation" on Gilbert and Sullivan. He had a way with words. Such flattery is perhaps most evident in Smith's use of patter for satirical twitting:

> *If a wretch in anguish utter steals a slice of bread—no butter—*
> *'Cause he's starving and of pie he hasn't got any,*
> *He has time for deep repentance, for the justice in the sentence*
> *Gives him twenty years in that far Bay called Botany!*
> *But it's very much more healthy for the tolerably wealthy*
> *To appropriate, embezzle and conceal;*

For Dame Justice sits and grieves, never calling people thieves
If they do not really need the things they steal.

"ON THE TRACK" (*THE HIGHWAYMAN*)

For his part, de Koven flattered many composers—Sullivan, to be sure, but also the continental light opera masters. Critics often took his music to task for being derivative and generally more lyrical than dramatic. Yet for piquancy of musical ideas and fluency in their expression, de Koven's scores are accomplished in ways earlier American stage scores are not. *Robin Hood* may not have been the first distinctly American light opera, but it initiated what de Koven's wife called "the epoch of light opera in America." The difference is telling. The musical quality and charm of the piece no less than its lasting commercial success may well have inspired the creation of a repertoire of comparable stageworks over the next four decades, the peak years of American-made operetta (1890–1930). But the work itself did not address particularly American concerns other than the ever-present one of ambivalence with respect to European culture. Nor did it speak—or sing, more importantly—in a recognizably American voice. Here de Koven did not mince words. "What we need is music in America," he proclaimed, "not American music."

For John Philip Sousa (1854–1932) the terms of de Koven's proposition were not mutually exclusive. Born, educated, and musically trained in the United States, Sousa turned down the opportunity to study abroad. His interests lay closer to home; and we tend to approach his music and his career today almost entirely from a nationalist perspective. In an age when the wind band as a cultural institution played a major role in American life, he established himself as the nation's premier military and concert bandmaster (U.S. Marine Band, 1880–1892; Sousa Band, 1892–1932). In addition, Sousa composed, especially the marches on which his fame rests, and which are still heard as distinctly American in spirit: that is, jaunty rather than stately in character ("The Washington Post," "The Stars and Stripes Forever"). Yet for much of his professional career Sousa also worked in the musical theater, though his efforts in this area remain less well known, in part because they were less successful and less clearly shaped by national influences. In the 1870s he performed and arranged works by Europe's leading light opera composers, and between 1882 and 1913 he saw produced nine full-length operettas of his own. Characteristic of the genre, all his operettas had foreign themes or exotic settings—except *The American Maid* (1913, aka *The Glass Blowers*). And characteristic of Sousa, none was an unqualified success—except *El Capitan*, which toured the country for four years.

El Capitan takes place in a mythological Peru of the sixteenth century when it was still a colony of Spain. The title is the nom de guerre of a bloodthirsty mercenary who has been hired to lead a group of insurgents against Don Medigua, the timid viceroy newly arrived from Spain. But the mercenary is secretly killed before he can join the rebels, and Medigua himself enters the enemy camp disguised as "El Capitan." His plan is to trick the insurgents under his command, deliver them to the Spanish army, reveal himself as viceroy, and have them all hanged. Should the rebels prove victorious, however, he intends to stay on as El Capitan. Inevitably, complications follow in matters of love as well as war—Medigua is married, El Capitan is eligible, and sexual propriety is the order of the day. Yet all wrongs are amicably righted in the end, and the rebels pardoned.

El Capitan was produced by the De Wolf Hopper Opera Company, a troupe formed from the remnants of McCaull's when that company disbanded, and named for the comic basso who was its star. The show succeeded in large part because Hopper himself created the double role that gave full rein to his comic versatility. Moreover, by ridiculing the rule of Spain in the New World, the story proved popular in a United States whose national mood would soon lead to the Spanish-American War. Yet as a comic opera, *El Capitan* ridiculed everything else as well—even the insurgents intent on fighting the Spanish. For example, their battle song, "When We Hear the Call to Battle," while sung in earnest in the context of the plot, was couched in such general terms as to suggest a parody—a song more *about* their patriotic fervor than a particular expression of it:

> *Onward, patriotic son!*
> *Onward, till the foe's undone!*
> *Onward, till the battle's won*
> *For your country and its glory.*

"WHEN WE HEAR THE CALL TO BATTLE"
(*EL CAPITAN*)

Sheet-music cover with a comic rendering of De Wolf Hopper
in the title role of *El Capitan*.

And when Sousa had the rebels also whistle and sing nonsense sylla-bles to imitate musical instruments at the same time, any hint of seri-ousness went up in contrapuntal tomfoolery.

Politics aside, there was no ambiguity about this number as sheer entertainment of an inspired kind. Here was a march by America's "march king" in top musical form. That, too, constituted part of the operetta's great appeal. And in an effort to match or make good on *El Capitan*'s success, Sousa wrote several more theater scores in quick suc-cession: *The Bride Elect* (1897), *The Charlatan* (1898), and *Chris and the Wonderful Lamp* (1899). While these were favorably received, a com-parable hit eluded him. Thereafter his work for the musical stage was less sustained. In the end, Sousa inclined more toward instrumental than vocal composition. He also saw himself "handicapped in my own opera-writing by the difficulty of getting first-class librettos." His tri-umph in the world of light opera, then, was robust but brief and soon eclipsed by that of another composer whom Sousa acknowledged to be "the best-equipped man of his time for this work."

He referred to Victor Herbert (1859–1924), the most gifted Amer-ican stage composer of his generation; and the most beloved. Irish-born and German-trained, Herbert was a virtuoso cellist who played in major orchestras in Stuttgart and Vienna. He immigrated to the United States in 1886 when the Metropolitan Opera company engaged his wife to sing *Aida* and offered him a job in the orchestra. He fur-ther distinguished himself in America as a bandmaster (22nd Regiment Band, New York National Guard, 1893–1900), an orchestral conduc-tor (Pittsburgh Symphony Orchestra, 1898–1904), and composer of music for the concert hall (*Second Cello Concerto*, 1894) and for the new medium of silent film (*The Fall of a Nation*, 1916).

But Herbert's most distinguished achievement of all rests in the scores to more than forty productions he composed and orchestrated for the lyric stage, among them *Babes in Toyland* (1903), *Mlle. Modiste* (1905), *The Red Mill* (1906), *Naughty Marietta* (1910), *Sweethearts* (1913), and *Eileen* (1917, aka *Hearts of Erin*). His theater output was prodigious and varied. From 1894 to 1924—except for a 1900–3 hia-tus during his Pittsburgh years—hardly a Broadway season went by without the premiere of at least one new Herbert stagework. These included extravaganzas (*Babes in Toyland*), musical comedies (*The Only Girl*, 1914), and revues (*The Century Girl*, 1916, with additional songs by Irving Berlin), as well as operas and operettas: comic (*The Serenade*, 1897), sentimental (*Naughty Marietta*), and grand (*Natoma*, 1911).

Herbert's music spoke to theater audiences across the United States with an uncommon freshness and authority. Yet it fell short of the kind of "greatness," so prized in nineteenth-century European and American culture, that went beyond competency or even excellence. It did not sufficiently transcend the practices of his day to remake the conventions that validated it. (Instant intelligibility being basic to success on the commercial stage, the music of few working in the field could have passed the test.) Herbert's music, however, bore the stamp of personality. Indeed, his was the first American musical personality to impose itself on public taste nationwide through a body of stageworks that remained in cultural currency even after their composer's death—most powerfully in sound film reconstructions (*Babes in Toyland*, 1934 and 1961; *Naughty Marietta*, 1935, with Jeanette MacDonald and Nelson Eddy), and Broadway revivals (*The Red Mill*, 1945; *Sweethearts*, 1947). In this sense, and with emphasis on the stageworks at least as much as the individual songs, Victor Herbert—unlike, say, Stephen Foster—can be considered the first great composer of the American musical theater.

Before 1900 Herbert saw ten comic operas produced, of which *The Serenade* and *The Fortune Teller* were the finest. Both featured H. B. Smith librettos with convoluted plots and foreign locales ripe for "characteristic" musical exploitation: Spain and Hungary, respectively. Like the early operettas of de Koven and Sousa, they were created for repertory companies that toured. Alice Nielsen (1870?–1943), a young, relatively inexperienced, and superb soprano, had recently joined the Bostonians and excelled in the premiere production of *The Serenade*—though not in the leading female part. A year later she left the Bostonians to form her own Alice Nielsen Opera Company and to premiere *The Fortune Teller*, in which she now starred. She played no fewer than three roles: Irma, a Budapest heiress; Musette, her gypsy look-alike; and even the brother of the man she loves, whose identity she assumes in order to thwart the plans of a count who wants to marry her for her money. Nielsen dominated vocally, too, especially in "Romany Life" ("Thro' the forest, wild and free"), which came to epitomize gypsy music on the American stage. The only number to become a hit that wasn't hers in the show, in fact, was "Gypsy Love Song," sung by Eugene Cowles. (Not coincidentally, she had taken him along with her from the Bostonians.)

Fortune Teller proved enormously successful though it played only forty performances in New York. It had premiered in Toronto, then came to New York, where it played five weeks at Wallack's Theater. Then it went off on a two-year national tour to play most of the big cities of the East and inland as far as Chicago. Traveling companies regularly booked such limited New York engagements for their productions. Culturally, New York may have given a show a cachet elsewhere unattainable; economically it represented, in effect, just another stand. "The road" was where the money was, and by the turn of the century more than three hundred traveling troupes chaotically crisscrossed the land. To impose order on this chaos, six businessmen organized a trust known as the Theatrical Syndicate in 1896. Led by producer-manager Charles Frohman (1860–1915) and booking agents Marc Klaw (1858–1936) and Abraham Lincoln Erlanger (1860–1930), the Syndicate ruthlessly proceeded to monopolize legitimate theater in the United States. By gaining booking control of most of the important legitimate houses in the country and demanding exclusive representation, the new monopoly marked the triumph of the businessman in the American theater. Indeed, the booking agent, once no more than a middleman, now exerted control over the activities of play producers and theater managers alike. In time, members of the Syndicate themselves took on the work of producers and managers, centralizing not just the booking but also the production of plays in New York, and even in the theaters that they now built, owned, or leased in the newly emerging theater district around Times Square.

The new situation spelled doom for the independent repertory company, which had provided the institutional framework for the development of light opera in America. Even the Bostonians were ultimately powerless to withstand its effects. Already weakened from within by the departure of many of the troupe's best players in pursuit of stardom, the Bostonians fought off the Syndicate's pressures to control their management from without as long as they could, only to succumb finally in 1900, and close altogether in 1904.

By the time Victor Herbert returned to the theater in 1903 after his tenure in Pittsburgh, the Syndicate governed first-class theatrical production in the United States, and he returned to a Broadway considerably different from the one he left. Economically, his stageworks now were largely created as "permanent" Broadway attractions to play in

Fritzi Scheff (Fifi) and William Pruette (Henri de Bouvray, seated) in *Mlle. Modiste*.

New York as long as possible and only then go out on the road. Artistically, they underwent several changes of style, initially in an effort to bring light opera more in line with a growing taste for still lighter musical stage forms. Herbert's two most successful shows of the decade illustrate the trend: *Mlle. Modiste* (1905) and *The Red Mill* (1906).

The two shows had much in common—including long runs at the same Syndicate-owned theater (the Knickerbocker), a two-act format where previous comic operas tended to have three, and librettos written by a bookwriter-lyricist of unusual gifts, Henry Blossom (1866–1919). The stories of both also took place in faraway Europe (France and Holland, respectively); but, unlike most earlier comic operas, the settings now were wholly modern, and the plots hinged on Americans who, while traveling abroad, helped set local wrongs to rights. In this respect they resembled musical comedies, though only *The Red Mill* was billed as such; *Mlle. Modiste* still bore the name of comic opera. These distinctions referred less to the structure of the productions than to their style, which depended above all on the performing strengths of the stars around whose talents the shows were built. *Mlle. Modiste*'s star, on the one hand, was Fritzi Scheff (1879–1954), a Viennese prima donna who had left the Metropolitan Opera Company to appear on the nonoperatic stage for the first time in Herbert's *Babette* (1903). On the other hand, *The Red Mill*'s stars were David Montgomery (1870–1917) and Fred Stone (1873–1959), a pair of vaudeville clowns who had made their debut on the legitimate stage as the Tin Woodman and the Scarecrow in *The Wizard of Oz* (1903). Thus "opera" in comic opera and "comedy" in musical comedy inscribed a difference that was demonstrably real onstage. That did not mean, of course, there was any lack of the comic element in *Mlle. Modiste* or a lack of vocal lyricism in *The Red Mill*. The difference was rather a matter of style and emphasis.

Something of that difference can be demonstrated by comparing the great waltz songs of the two shows. In *Mlle. Modiste*'s "If I Were on the Stage," a Parisian shopgirl imagines the kinds of roles she would portray as the diva she longs to be. The number ends with "Kiss Me Again," a slow, sensuous waltz whose long sustained phrases, rhythmic flexibility, and wide intervallic leaps ("ten-der-ly pressed") place heavy demands on the vocal technique of any singer. (Ex. 3-1a) In *Red Mill*'s "The Streets of New York," by contrast, two fun-loving Americans find themselves stranded in Holland and long for the "peachcrop" of women back home. Their waltz is a more spirited one (sung at about twice the speed of the other) whose short phrases, rhythmic regularity, and narrow range are all negotiable by singers with no training at all, even by comedians. (Ex. 3-1b).

Ultimately, the two songs can be heard as pointing in different stylistic directions the musical theater was taking around the turn of the century: one toward romantic operetta, the other toward musical comedy. Yet Victor Herbert reserved his finest efforts in the theater for what he continued to call comic opera, even as the genre changed and the name lost currency early in the new century. Indeed, public taste for light opera altogether was waning, and the cultural energy a generation of Americans had invested in developing the genre since the first successes of Offenbach and Gilbert and Sullivan was mostly spent. True, American creations in this vein were now exported: *Robin Hood*,

Ex. 3-1a. Victor Herbert, music, Henry Blossom, lyrics: "If I Were on the Stage: Kiss Me Again," *Mlle. Modiste*

Ex. 3-1b. Victor Herbert, music, Henry Blossom, lyrics: "The Streets of New York," *The Red Mill*

El Capitan, and *The Fortune Teller* all played in London; Herbert's *The Wizard of the Nile* even played in Vienna (in German translation). But they were not well received by European audiences accustomed to the work of home-grown practitioners who mostly did it better and certainly more to their liking. In America, moreover, the entire enterprise seemed increasingly out of touch with the nationalist bent and populist temper of a younger generation whose maturing coincided with the emergence of the United States as a world power. "American musical taste has developed to a point where it demands something that is native," Herbert declared as he proposed to change course and "write in a frank, free American style." If such a style required a native form of entertainment to contain it, however, light opera would not do, since its "European flavor," as De Wolf Hopper put it, had become a cultural liability. It was this that mitigated against the genre's further success in America, he said, and that explained, at least in part, why it would now be "all but driven from our stage by musical comedy." Hopper exaggerated, to be sure. Light opera had been undergoing a transformation of its own, and the taste for the genre in its newer forms would return with a vengeance in a few years, starting with the mania for *The Merry Widow.* But the rise of musical comedy in the meanwhile and its ensuing development into an Americanized entertainment posed a real challenge to light opera, giving theatergoers a new alternative on the musical stage immediate in its appeal and impossible to ignore.

PART TWO

INTO THE TWENTIETH CENTURY

4

THE NATIVE WIT

LITTLE JOHNNY JONES
(11/7/1904–ca. 12/1904). **Producer:** Sam H. Harris. **Book, Lyrics, Music, and Director:** George M. Cohan. **New York Run:** 52 performances. **Cast:** The Four Cohans—Helen, Jerry, George M., and Ethel Levey (Mrs. G. M. Cohan). **Songs:** "The Yankee Doodle Boy," "Give My Regards to Broadway."

FORTY-FIVE MINUTES FROM BROADWAY
(1/1/1906–3/17/1906). **Producers:** Marc Klaw and A. L. Erlanger. **Book, Lyrics, Music, and Director:** G. M. Cohan. **New York Run:** 90 performances. **Cast:** Ray Templeton, Victor Moore. **Songs:** "Mary's a Grand Old Name," "So Long, Mary."

GEORGE WASHINGTON, JR.
(2/12/1906–4/23/1906). **Producer:** Harris. **Book, Lyrics, Music, Director, and Star:** G. M. Cohan. **New York Run:** 81 performances. **Cast:** The Four Cohans. **Songs:** "You're a Grand Old Flag," "I Was Born in Virginia."

WATCH YOUR STEP
(12/8/1914–circa 6/1915). **Producer:** Charles Dillingham. **Book:** Harry B. Smith, adapted from the play Round the Clock by Augustin Daly. **Lyrics and Music:** Irving Berlin. **Director:** R. H. Burnside. **New York Run:** 175 performances. **Cast:** Irene and Vernon Castle, Frank Tinney. **Songs:** "Simple Melody," "The Syncopated Walk."

1904 view of Long Acre Square—soon to be renamed Times Square on completion of the New York Times building still under construction (center left)—with excavations for a subway train (lower right), which in time will help supplant the horse-drawn carriage as a means of transportation (lower left).

VERY GOOD EDDIE

(12/23/1915–ca. 11/1916). **Producers:** F. Ray Comstock and Elisabeth Marbury. **Book:** Guy Bolton and Philip Bartholomae, based on Bartholomae's play *Over Night*. **Lyrics:** Schuyler Greene, Herbert Reynolds, and others. **Music:** Jerome Kern. **Director:** Frank McCormack. **New York Run:** 341 performances. **Cast:** Helen Raymond, Ernest Truex, Oscar Shaw. **Songs:** "Isn't It Great to Be Married?," "Thirteen Collar," "Babes in the Wood."

OH, BOY!

(2/20/1917–3/30/1918). **Producers:** Comstock, William Elliott, and Morris Gest. **Book:** Bolton and P. G. Wodehouse. **Lyrics:** Wodehouse. **Music:** Kern. **Directors:** Robert Milton and Edward Royce. **New York Run:** 463 performances. **Cast:** Anna Wheaton, Edna May Oliver, Tom Powers. **Songs:** "Till the Clouds Roll By," "You Never Knew About Me."

LEAVE IT TO JANE

(8/28/1917–ca. 1/1918). **Producers:** Comstock, Elliott, and Gest. **Book:** Bolton and Wodehouse, based on the play *The College Widow* by George Ade. **Lyrics:** Wodehouse. **Music:** Kern. **Director:** Royce. **New York Run:** 167 performances. **Cast:** Edith Hallor, Georgia O'Ramey, Robert Pitkin. **Songs:** "The Siren's Song," "Cleopatterer," "The Crickets Are Calling."

"**M**usical comedy was of our own soil, its wit was native, its book topical, its music livelier, if cheaper [than light opera music], and it bore down heavily upon the comedy." So wrote comedian De Wolf Hopper near the end of an illustrious career that included star engagements with many of the foremost companies across the musical theater spectrum—from McCaull's in the field of light opera to Weber and Fields in the field of burlesque. As a performer, Hopper knew his subject from the inside; as a writer, he had summarized it about as well as one could in one sentence.

Musical comedy was a new, vernacular entertainment in America early in the twentieth century. As a spoken play with musical numbers inserted, it was fundamentally more relaxed than light opera: its narratives more loosely spun, its music less obviously "learned," its spirit lightweight altogether. Above all, it was modern. Its jokes were aimed at present concerns. And while its stories still focused on the social mismatch of lovers, they were up-to-the-minute confections, peopled with character types who were recognizably of the day in what they said, what they did, and what they wore. Audiences doted on its female choruses whose wardrobes set contemporary trends in fashion much as the women who wore them fostered a sleeker ideal of feminine beauty on the stage than the beefy ladies of burlesque. Its music became sleeker, too—simpler in structure, more transparent in texture, snappier in its sense of time—and as it did it both reflected and affected current tastes in popular song and dance. Like Hopper's career, then, musical comedy moved successfully between the fields of light opera and burlesque, negotiating its way between the highbrow pretensions of the one and the lowbrow vulgarities of the other.

This posed a structural problem for the new genre, as musical comedies often raised the narrative expectations of comic opera and fulfilled them in the style and spirit of variety. Kurt Gänzl has proposed the term "variety musical" to describe the kind of show such musical comedies more nearly represented: a two-act diversion in which a fairly clear storytelling trajectory in the first act was blown off course in the second by a barrage of specialty turns that made the entertainment seem more like a revue. *Watch Your Step* (1914), for example, managed to do this so well that critics were totally confused by the piece at the premiere. One called it "glorified vaudeville," another a "musical extravaganza," while the *New York Times*, which began by considering it a revue, finally conceded "so many things have been called musical comedies that 'Watch Your Step' might as well be called one."

George Ade, one of America's most popular humorists of the period, took a different tack. With a twinkle in his eye, he saw the problem of naming musical comedy more a matter of marketing than of aesthetics:

> *When the first piano was built the owner needed something to put on top of the piano, so the popular song and the light opera were invented. As the musical taste of succeeding buyers developed and improved, light opera became lighter and lighter until at last they had to weight it down to keep it on the piano. There came a time when the manufacturers were prohibited under the Pure Food Law from using the opera label. They had to call the output something or other, so they compromised on "musical comedy."*

However one understands the term or the genre it stood for, one thing is sure: There was nothing particularly American about musical comedy at the start. While the term had previously been used in isolated instances on both sides of the Atlantic, its modern usage stems from a sequence of shows produced in London around the turn of the century by George Edwardes (1855–1915). Britain's preeminent producer of musical shows at the time, Edwardes applied the musical comedy rubric to a series of lightweight, modern-dress productions starting with *A Gaiety Girl* (1893), and the immense success of his undertaking helped establish it as the future point of reference for the subject. Musical comedy thereafter became identified with the stylish farces Edwardes produced mainly at the Gaiety Theater, which housed them regularly—from *The Shop Girl* (1984) to *Our Miss Gibbs* (1909)— all the products of a house writing staff that included lyricist Adrian Ross and composers Ivan Caryll and Lionel Monckton.

That we credit a producer with the creation of musical comedy as a cultural institution is significant. It speaks to the commercial and collaborative character of musical theater as a popular medium. In that medium, the commercial production of a show normally takes priority over any abstract concept (as embodied, say, in a script or score); and it is the producer who exercises greater control over more aspects of the collaborative process that goes into the creation, performance, and dissemination of the show than anyone else. Edwardes would not have been nearly the theatrical force he was had he not sought to exploit the worth of what he had been pivotal in putting together in the first place. In short order, he exported his hits to the rest of the English-speaking world—Canada, Australia, India, the United States. Americans thus usually got to see them within a year of their London premieres (*The Shop Girl*, 1895; *A Runaway Girl*, 1898). The vogue caught on. Other producers soon followed suit, exporting other London hits in a similar vein, sometimes with smashing success. For example, *Florodora* (London, 1899; New York, 1900), with its showstopping "Sextette" (actually six women and their male counterparts: "Tell me, pretty maiden, are

Together with their suitors, six "Florodora Girls" (each 5 feet 4 inches tall and weighing 130 pounds) perform the double sextet from *Florodora*, the most popular single number from a Broadway show at the start of the twentieth century.

there any more at home like you?"), proved a sensation in New York; and *A Chinese Honeymoon* (London, 1901; New York, 1902) turned into the first great hit produced on Broadway by the Shubert brothers.

The emerging generation of American producers who shaped the course of musical comedy on this side of the Atlantic included Sam H. Harris, Charles B. Dillingham, and Charles Frohman. In power, notoriety, and longevity in the theater, however, none would rival the Shubert brothers: Lee (1875–1953), Sam (1876–1905), and Jacob J. (1880–1963). As partners, the three began taking over the management of important theaters in New York after the turn of the century. Soon they came into conflict with the Theatrical Syndicate (1896–1916), then consolidating its monopoly over legitimate theater in the United States—legitimate, as distinguished from theaters housing such entertainments as vaudeville and burlesque. A fierce war ensued for control over the American commercial stage. It lasted for more than a decade and when it was over, the Shuberts had eliminated the Syndicate as a theatrical power. "The Messrs. Shubert," as they billed themselves, then established their own monopoly with an empire of theaters in virtually every major city in the nation. For nearly half a century, Lee and J.J.—Sam died early in a train wreck—remained "America's principal *manufacturers* of theatrical productions."

Developing musical comedy as an American genre distinct from the British model involved adapting the form to suit the native wit. But bringing it into line with American ways of speech, music, movement, and manners was only partly the work of producers, not all of whom even agreed with the project—Frohman, an intense Anglophile, favored importing the genuine article from England; the Shuberts favored importing continental operettas. For audiences generally, Americanizing musical comedy depended more on the efforts of personalities working in the limelight rather than behind the scenes—performers such as George M. Cohan and Al Jolson; songsmiths such as Irving Berlin and Jerome Kern. It also had something important to do with the rise of Times Square and Tin Pan Alley and the cultural institutions they came to represent. It was the confluence of many forces in the United States from the turn of the century through the First World War that first naturalized musical comedy and made it American.

COHAN AND TIMES SQUARE

Other entertainers may have acted, sung, and danced more persuasively in the vernacular than George M. Cohan in his day. But it was his achievement to bring the vernacular style of vaudeville convincingly onto the legitimate stage and make it stick. More than anyone before him, he Americanized musical comedy in a way that put a lasting stamp on the national consciousness. Some of the five hundred songs he wrote—words and music—still have cultural resonance today ("The Yankee Doodle Boy," "Give My Regards to Broadway," "You're a Grand Old Flag"). Yet most of his songs were originally meant to be heard in the context of his work as a complete showman, for Cohan was an actor, singer, dancer, playwright, songwriter, director, producer, publisher, and theater owner all in one. Astonishingly versatile, he embodied the spirit of the great actor-managers of the nineteenth century even as he became the first all-around creator of American musical comedy in the twentieth.

The grandson of Irish immigrants, George M. Cohan (1878–1942) claimed he was born on July 4th and, whether true or not, made a point of it. More than a mere coincidence to him, it lent unassailable authority to the persona he cultivated on the stage: the cocky patriot and flag-waving song-and-dance man that, legend has it, critics hated and audiences adored. He was born into a family of vaudevillians. Barely out of his boyhood, he joined his parents, Helen and Jerry, and sister, Josephine, in a family act that toured as the Four Cohans. He also wrote some of the skits and songs. But in the hope of going beyond vaudeville and establishing himself on the legitimate stage, Cohan expanded his skits into full-length plays with songs (*The Governor's Son*, 1901; *Running for Office*, 1903). When productions of these failed to achieve his ambition, he turned to writing new plays altogether and mounting them in the heart of the Broadway that he said was "the bell I wanted to ring." Only then did Cohan begin to win the recognition he craved—as a writer (of scripts and songs), as a director, and as a star performer.

He did so most memorably with three productions: *Little Johnny Jones* (1904), *Forty-Five Minutes from Broadway* (1906), and *George Washington, Jr.* (1906). These were breezy morality plays whose stories extolled American ideals that were at once upright and down to earth. *Little Johnny Jones*, an American jockey in England, is falsely accused of throwing the Royal Derby race and, when his compatriots return home, he stays in England in order to clear his name. *Forty-Five Minutes from Broadway* takes place in the wealthy suburb of New Rochelle where a smart-alecky New Yorker falls in love with a housemaid and uncovers the will of her late employer that leaves her his estate. In *George Washington, Jr.*, the patriotic son of an unsavory American senator renounces his father's name to take the name of the father of his country and marry the American girl he loves when his father insists he marry a British aristocrat. In the era of Theodore Roosevelt and his Big Stick, ardent expressions of nationalism found resonance at home even when they verged on xenophobia. When questioned, "What makes the Americans so proud of their country?" an American in *Little Johnny Jones* replies, "*Other* countries."

Cohan sometimes called these works "plays with music," sometimes "musical plays." As plays, in fact, they resembled melodramas more than farces, and *Forty-five Minutes* even had an entire non-musical act. Cohan's output, wrote one contemporary, "is hard to classify, as it merges from the field of Drama to that of Musical Comedy, and back again." Moreover, Cohan modeled himself on Ned Harrigan and, like Harrigan, tended to conflate his work as a playwright and director. He looked to stage business, high energy, and fast pacing to offset dramaturgical defects; and he admitted as much:

> *Everything must go over with a bang. Right from the start. I don't attempt to "work up" to anything. I keep the eyes of the audience busy. And their ears. I rush characters on and off. I never permit any one actor or group of actors to remain on the stage longer than a few seconds at a time. Song must follow dance, with speed, speed, all the time speed! And no encores. No gaps. No waits. No dragging moments. No letdowns. No dull moments. The essential thing is not to give anyone a chance to get bored. . . .*
>
> *As for plot, the masses don't want it. At least, that's my dope on the matter. It's like coating bitter medicine with sugar—this business of feeding plot to an audience. And it must slide down without too much irritation. I try to unweave my plot without letting the audience know*

they're getting plot. It's sort of slipped in, unknown to them. Hand plot to an audience in a brazen fashion, and it rankles. I merely suggest, and let the audience write out the story to suit themselves.

In all, Cohan wrote scripts for over forty Broadway productions. About half consisted of plays *without* music (*Seven Keys to Baldpate*, 1913; *The Tavern*, 1929), a few of which served as the basis for his own later musicalizations (*Popularity*, 1906, became *The Man Who Owns Broadway*, 1909; *Broadway Jones*, 1912, became *Billie*, 1928, his last original musical). The other half consisted of musical plays from the start, almost all of which he directed and produced or coproduced with Sam Harris (1872–1941). The extraordinary partnership of Cohan and Harris let Cohan focus on artistic matters while Harris took care of the business. It began with *Little Johnny Jones*, and during the fifteen years it lasted, the two owned theaters together, collaborated as coproducers, and became brothers-in-law. But they split professionally over the bitter Actors' Equity strike of 1919. The Actors' Equity Association had called the strike to gain recognition from theater producers as a union and to improve the often squalid working conditions of stage performers. Equity won when it shut down half the productions on Broadway and Harris and other major producers accepted the union. Cohan opposed Equity on principle, however, and adamantly refused to acknowledge it. That left him a relatively isolated figure in the theater community. While Harris went on to produce many of the most innovative shows of the interwar period (*Of Thee I Sing*, 1931; *As Thousands Cheer*, 1933; *Lady in the Dark*, 1941), Cohan continued to work successfully on Broadway largely by repeating what he had done in the past. And as Cohan's career drew to a close, he appeared on Broadway most memorably as a performer in works not of his own making but that others now wrote, directed and produced (Eugene O'Neill's *Ah, Wilderness!*, 1934; Rodgers and Hart's *I'd Rather Be Right*, 1937).

As a performer, Cohan brought the presentational ways of vaudeville to Broadway, especially since the personalities of many of the lead male roles he created were indistinguishable from his own (Johnny Jones, George Washington, Jr.). Yet even Richard Rodgers, who saw him as "a disgruntled man with no respect for anyone's work but his own," still "had great regard for him as an actor. No matter how simple-minded or corny his shows were, he never failed to give a highly skilled, even subtle performance." And when it came to musical plays Cohan knew how to put a song across—particularly one of his own. The songs he wrote may have seemed unsophisticated to a rising generation of songwriters, and even hamstrung by Cohan's admitted inability to play anything more than "four chords on the piano in F sharp." But "though he was hardly up there with the Kerns, Berlins, or Gershwins," Rodgers allowed, "I did admire the infectious vitality of his songs." It was a vitality that electrified a Broadway in the early years of the century still largely in the thrall of Gilbert and Sullivan, their imitators, and their successors.

Consider "You're a Grand Old Flag," for instance. At a time when such issues as imperialist expansion abroad and the influx of immigrants at home divided the country, Cohan sought to tap nationalist feelings without pretense yet without offending anyone. His song addressed the flag with respect, but in colloquial terms that undercut the formal rhetoric expected of such an address. (It had none of the solemnity of the Pledge of Allegiance, for example, familiar to Americans increasingly required to recite it as a loyalty oath since Francis Bellamy first promulgated it in 1892.) Moreover, Cohan set his words to the music of a march, but undercut the martial strains with offbeat ragtime syncopations—shockingly so, in fact, by emphasizing the most inconsequential words ("home *of*," "free *and*") just when the text suggested the hymnlike climax of "The Star-Spangled Banner":

> *You're the emblem of*
> *The land I love.*
> *The home* of *the free* and *the brave.*
>
> "You're a Grand Old Flag"
> (*George Washington, Jr.*)

Inevitably, songs like this did offend many of Cohan's contemporaries. James Metcalfe, for example, condemned Cohan's "mawkish appeals to the cheapest kind of patriotism," on the one hand, and their expression, on the other, in terms of "the kind of unmetrical stuff that children compose and call poetry." Metcalfe's taste perhaps ran to something more like *The Sultan of Sulu* (1902), a musical satire of

America's "gunboat diplomacy" with music by Alfred G. Wathall and words (book and lyrics) by George Ade (1866–1944), the noted humorist, columnist, and playwright. Ade's outlook in *The Sultan* was ironic—not mawkish—and he expressed it elegantly in the metrical regularity of light verse. Here, for instance, American soldiers arrive in the Philippines almost apologizing for the enforced benefits of economic cooperation with the United States that they bring:

> *We haven't the appearance, goodness knows,*
> *Of plain commercial men;*
> *From a hasty glance, you might suppose*
> *We are fractious now and then.*
> *But though we come in warlike guise*
> *And battle-front arrayed,*
> *It's all a business enterprise;*
> *We're seeking foreign trade.*
>
> "HIKE!" (*THE SULTAN OF SULU*)

Where Cohan celebrates a feeling, Ade criticizes a policy, at least implicitly. Furthermore, the singing soldiers are not too good but too well-bred to be true. Ade's wit has a comic-opera decorum about it: It relishes the absurdity of circumlocutions with an appeal that is eminently mental. Cohan's humor, by contrast, grows out of the American vernacular: It is direct, terse, fit for the "man in the street." It also aims, as Cohan said of Harrigan's work, to "tickle the funny bone . . . [and get] to the old heartstrings at the same time." But it is not entirely mawkish. As literary critic Philip Furia reminds us, "You're a Grand Old Flag" actually exhibits "the verbal/musical wit of rhyming 'love' with a preposition ['of'] in a language in which the few other rhymes available tend to lead to sentimental clichés."

The "infectious vitality" of Cohan's songs, then, had much to do with the vernacular voice that Cohan brought with him from vaudeville to the legitimate stage. As it would prove a catalyst for change on Broadway, it also registered changes already taking place there as early as *Little Johnny Jones*. At the end of the second act, in the show's most famous scene, Johnny stands on a Southampton pier as a ship is about to leave for New York without him. He must stay behind to prove him-

self innocent of the accusation against him, and so he sings wistfully to
a friend who is preparing to board:

> *Give my regards to Broadway,*
> *Remember me to Herald Square,*
> *Tell all the gang at Forty-second Street*
> *That I will soon be there . . .*
>
> "GIVE MY REGARDS TO BROADWAY"
> (*LITTLE JOHNNY JONES*)

Entertainment and reality intersected here. Jones, the *character* singing, was in England, of course. But Cohan, the *performer* singing, was
already "there" in New York where he yearned to be. So, too, was the
"gang at Forty-second Street" which now included the audience that
sat watching *Little Johnny Jones* in the Liberty Theater, newly built on
the very street of which the show's hero sang. In fact, most buildings
on or near Forty-second Street were newly built in 1904, for the area
was in the midst of a construction boom that would last until the Great
Depression. The area was already well on its way to becoming the hub
of theatrical activity in New York and focus of the city's nightlife: in a
phrase, the "New Rialto."

Following the pattern of urban growth around the turn of the
century, New York's entertainment district had been moving steadily
northward along the diagonal that Broadway cut across midtown
Manhattan. The move began in the 1880s from Union Square (Fourteenth Street and Fourth Avenue), paused for a while at Herald Square
(Thirty-fourth Street and Sixth Avenue), and finally came to rest a
generation later at Long Acre Square (Forty-second Street and Seventh Avenue). The last was not a square at all but a commercial axis
which in time would come to stand for the commercial culture not
just of New York but of the nation. Many factors would help to bring
this about—the lure of vast real estate profits in the area; advertising
and the creation of America's first consumer culture; the growth of
mass entertainment and its gradual acceptance in the liberal Protestant community; tourism and the construction of modern transportation networks, including a major railroad terminal at Grand Central
for trains traveling to and from New York and a mass transit subway

George M. Cohan as Little Johnny Jones.

system inside the city. It was the Forty-second Street subway stop, in fact, that first bore the name "Times Square" after the newly erected tower building of the *New York Times*. The name, shortly to replace Long Acre Square, became synonymous with New York's entertainment industry and the great density of theaters and related activities stretching along Broadway from about Thirty-seventh Street to Forty-seventh Street and beyond.

Of all great Broadway showmen and women, only Cohan's statue stands in Times Square today. That seems fitting, as no single figure captures more completely the creative, performative, and entrepreneurial spirit of the district all at once. But Cohan's presence at "The Crossroads of the World" is also paradoxical. "Never was a plant more indigenous to a particular part of the earth than was George M. Cohan to the United States of his day," wrote Oscar Hammerstein II around the time of the statue's unveiling in 1958. "The whole nation was confident of its superiority, its moral virtue, its happy isolation from the intrigues of the 'old country,' from which many of our fathers and grandfathers had migrated." To say that such confidence generally eludes us today is an understatement. The very lack of it for contemporary audiences makes Cohan's work seem remote now and unrevivable under normal conditions. Yet under abnormal conditions, and for the same reason, Americans have historically turned to Cohan and his songs, especially when their sense of national purpose appeared most threatened: buying recordings of "Over There" in 1917 as America entered the Great War, flocking to the movies in 1942 to watch *Yankee Doodle Dandy* (starring James Cagney) on America's entry into World War II; even going to the theater in 1968 to see a Broadway musical called *George M!* (starring Joel Grey) at the critical turning point in America's involvement in Vietnam.

BERLIN AND TIN PAN ALLEY

The rise of Tin Pan Alley roughly coincided with the relocation of New York's entertainment district to Times Square. In the 1890s, song publishers began leaving the Union Square area to follow the northward trail of vaudeville houses, legitimate theaters, and nightlife generally.

By the next decade, the major sheet-music publishing companies were clustered around Twenty-eighth Street and Broadway (M. Witmark & Sons, Harry Von Tilzer Music Publishing Company, and so forth). In 1903, songwriter Monroe Rosenfeld dubbed this street "Tin Pan Alley," ostensibly because of the metallic din of pianos in the many offices there banging out different tunes at the same time. By then, the publishing houses of Manhattan had cornered the American song market, and it was rare for a song published elsewhere to achieve national popularity. Tin Pan Alley thus became, besides a location, a moniker for the popular music business itself. Henry Ford's newspaper alluded to the Alley as a "song trust"; and songwriter Irving Caesar even relocated it geographically as "close to the nearest buck." So the name held fast when, by the 1920s, the business had shifted its base of operations to Times Square, and then in the 1930s moved still further north to the Brill Building on Forty-ninth Street and Broadway. Since then, moreover, historians have come to use the term in an even broader sense: to refer, by extension, to the kinds of songs the business produced, their prevailing styles, and the historical period in which they dominated America's popular music (the 1890s to the 1950s). Tin Pan Alley thus applies variously to a place (or places), a business, a time, and a style (or styles).

Tin Pan Alley developed largely out of the sensibilities of minorities in the United States—many of its leading publishers and songwriters were Jewish; many of its most popular song styles were African American. But its songs were aimed at the heart of mainstream American culture. "It seems fair to generalize," wrote musicologist Charles Hamm,

> *that Tin Pan Alley songs were for white, urban, literate, middle- and upper-class Americans. They remained practically unknown to large segments of American society, including most blacks (excepting musicians and a handful of urban blacks aspiring to a life-style approaching that of whites), and the millions of poor, white, rural Americans of English, Irish, and Scottish stock clustered in the South and scattered across the lower Midwest. These two groups had their own distinctive types of music, oral-tradition music.*

The fact that Tin Pan Alley songs were, by definition, published already speaks to the nature of the public they addressed. Such songs appeared in various types—for example, novelty songs ("Take Me Out to the Ball Game"), narratives ("After the Ball"), and ballads of many kinds in which the singer represented one of the partners in a relationship between the sexes. Typically, these songs spoke in the vernacular, but not in slang; they favored sentimental expression over the maudlin kind; and their tone was sincere, but not without wit. Above all, the love they had in mind was romantic and marriage-oriented, not simply carnal; "and, of course," writes music theorist Allen Forte, "any insinuation of relations *among* the sexes was strictly verboten."

Musically and lyrically the songs followed a strophic format. At first, this consisted of several verses of an ongoing narrative each climaxing in a fixed refrain, often referred to as the chorus ("After the Ball," 1892: verse, 64 bars; chorus, 32). Later Alley songs tended to shift emphasis in favor of the chorus, paring down the verse and using it simply as a set-up for what followed ("They Didn't Believe Me," 1914: verse, 16 bars; chorus, 32). Later still, some songs eliminated the verse altogether ("Smoke Gets in Your Eyes," 1933).

The chorus thus comprised the heart of the Tin Pan Alley songs. Its form normally consisted of 32 bars of music divided equally into four sections of 8 bars each. (Though the method was imperfect, songwriters often used a letter of the alphabet as shorthand for the melodic character of each 8-bar unit: A, B, and so forth.) These sections took shape according to musically recurring patterns that tended to divide the 32 bars structurally in half—most commonly, ABAB', in which the last section began like the second but ended differently ("Till the Clouds Roll By," 1916), and ABAC, in which the last section differed throughout from what came before ("You Made Me Love You," 1913). (Recurrences of letters indicated musical similarities, not necessarily lyric ones.) Later, around the mid-1920s, another formal design found favor among songwriters and soon became the prevalent Alley song pattern: AABA ("The Man I Love," 1924). Yet many successful 32-bar songs did not fit any such schemes, though they still moved in the proportions of 8-bar sections ("All Alone," 1924).

All this made for a certain standardization in America's popular music for over half a century, and it is surely no accident that these songs were commonly referred to as "standards." Yet it also allowed for a remarkable variety within the standard conventions, especially as the different musical forms suggested corresponding narrative strategies to fit them, and as the most gifted of songwriters sensitive to such matters imaginatively rose to the occasion. Consider how verbal meanings and musical meanings confirm, contradict, or otherwise relate to each other in the choruses of two great Tin Pan Alley ballads of the period, each in a different form: "They Didn't Believe Me" (ABA'C) and "Blue Skies" (AABA).

"They Didn't Believe Me"

A	And when I told them how beautiful you are,	(4 bars)
	They didn't believe me. They didn't believe me!	(4 bars)
B	Your lips, your eyes, your cheeks, your hair,	(2 bars)
	Are in a class beyond compare.	(2 bars)
	You're the loveliest girl that one could see!	(4 bars)
A'	And when I tell them,	
	And I cert'nly am goin' to tell them,	(4 bars)
	That I'm the man whose wife one day you'll be,	(4 bars)
C	They'll never believe me. They'll never believe me!	(4 bars)
	That from this great big world you've chosen me!	(4 bars)

In this song the rough symmetry in the two halves of the musical form (AB: 16 bars; A'C: 16 bars) is mirrored in the structure of the lyric: The first half refers to the past ("And when I told them"), the second half to the future ("And when I tell them"). This effects a corresponding change in the title of the song ("They didn't believe me"/"They'll never believe me"). Yet the all-essential title line occurs in a different place in each half. By convention, the title should reappear in A' in the same spot that it appears in A—as, for instance, in this made-up lyric:

A' And when I tell them I'm going to marry you,
   They'll never believe me. They'll never believe me!

The trouble is that such a lyric would squeeze pivotally new information ("going to marry") into half a bar of music, allowing almost no time for a listener to hear it and absorb its meaning. (If the songwriters thought

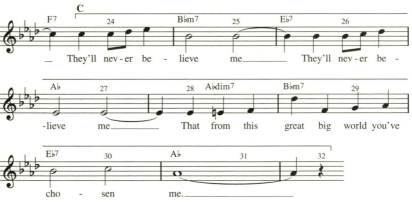

Ex. 4-1a. Jerome Kern, music, Herbert Reynolds, lyrics: "They Didn't Believe Me" mm. 1–12, *The Girl from Utah*

Ex. 4-1b. "They Didn't Believe Me" mm. 24–32

of such, they mercifully discarded it.) Instead, this information gets a line of its own, set to new music ("That I'm the man whose wife one day you'll be"). But the line is inserted just where one would expect the title to return. So thwarting formal norms here calls attention to the change in the singer, who now looks forward to getting married rather than backward to those who didn't believe him. It also dramatizes the change in the gist of the title when it returns one line later than convention dictates to start the last section of the song. This final section (labeled C for lack of a less confusing option) joins two musical ideas from different sections in the song's first half—the last 4 bars of A and the first 4 bars of B (Ex. 4-1a)—to form an unexpected yet plausible conclusion (Ex. 4-1b), in part because the three-note pickups to A and B ("And when I"/"Your lips, your") are themselves melodically the same. Embedded in the overall structure of "They Didn't Believe Me" is a marriage proposal. And with utmost economy, the songwriters work flexibly within the two-part form to clarify the progression from the singer's infatuation with his beloved to his elation over her acceptance.

By contrast, "Blue Skies" adopts an entirely different approach:

"Blue Skies"

A Blue skies
   Smiling at me,   (4 bars)
   Nothing but blue skies
   Do I see.   (4 bars)

A Bluebirds
   Singing a song,   (4 bars)
   Nothing but bluebirds
   All day long.   (4 bars)

B Never saw the sun
   Shining so bright,   (2 bars)
   Never saw things
   Going so right.   (2 bars)
   Noticing the days
   Hurrying by—   (2 bars)
   When you're in love,
   My how they fly.   (2 bars)

A Blue days,
   All of them gone—   (4 bars)
   Nothing but blue skies
   From now on.   (4 bars)

Unlike the layout of the two-part Alley song, the AABA song presents its A section three times: first, to establish a pattern; second, to confirm it through repetition; and third, to recall it by way of conclusion. The sense of recall in the last A section derives from that section's return after the intervention just before it of a contrasting B section, often called the bridge or the release. In this song, the minor-to-relative-major music of all the A sections is identical, and the image of something blue in the lyrics ties all three together verbally as well: blue skies, bluebirds, blue days. Moreover, the second A lyric reinforces the first both semantically (bluebirds signify happiness; so do blue skies) and syntactically ("blue skies" and "bluebirds" both come back in the same way in the following "nothing but" lines of each). The bridge gives the reason for such happiness: "when you're in love." Yet the final A section breaks the lyric pattern of the first two As. For "blue days" is not a happy metaphor but a sad one—which requires not a continuation of the pattern but a reversal of it to get the image in sync with the mood of the rest of the lyric: "all of them gone." Yet with "blue days" thus dispelled by the end of the first line, they cannot come back as syntactically they should in the "nothing but" line that follows. And so "blue skies" now reappear in their place, thus bringing the song home semantically and back by way of conclusion to the title. Unlike the change that occurs during the chorus of "They Didn't Believe Me," the dramatic reversal of "blue days" at the end of the song here refers back to a change in the lover's condition that took place before the chorus began (and is confirmed by the verse).

The dramatic potential inherent in these strategies makes such songs interesting from a theatrical perspective. But Tin Pan Alley songs as a rule were not theater songs. While the two song types often overlapped in form and style, they differed in function. Theater songs had to make sense according to the specific needs of a staged production, or the logic where a song fit in the progress of a story. Alley songs were more freely generic. This did not prevent them, however, from appearing on the stage as well—whether shoehorned into a story or as part of a vaudeville-type turn. Although both of the songs described above represent Alley-type ballads, the public first heard them, in fact, in theatrical settings. "They Didn't Believe Me" appeared among a handful of song interpolations that Jerome Kern provided for *The Girl from Utah* (1914) when producer Charles Frohman imported that show from London to New York. (Herbert Reynolds, who wrote the lyrics for the song, also supplied Julia Sanderson, who first sang it in the show, with appropriate changes to suit a more typically feminine orientation: "boy" for "girl," etc.) Irving Berlin wrote "Blue Skies" (words and music) for vaudevillian Belle Baker. She first sang it as the star of *Betsy* (1926), much to the dismay of Richard Rodgers and Lorenz Hart who, having written the rest of the show's score, expected the biggest song hit from the show to be theirs rather than Berlin's. (A year after its Broadway debut, "Blue Skies" also became the first song heard in a major sound film when Al Jolson sang it in *The Jazz Singer*.)

Al Jolson in his signature pose as a performer.

The theater thus served as a marketplace for Alley promoters, who competed fiercely with each other to get performers to interpolate songs they could be persuaded to like into their acts. "The real start of popularizing a song is to sell it to performers," said Charles K. Harris. "If it strikes their fancy, they will surely sing it for the public." Harris spoke from experience. He had gotten nowhere with a waltz ballad he wrote, "After the Ball," until a certain amount of cajolery, deception, and cash convinced one singer in 1892 to interpolate it into a Milwaukee production of *A Trip to Chinatown*. Its popular success there led to its inclusion as a matter of course in subsequent productions of the show and precipitated a nationwide demand for the song. It was, in fact, the unprecedented sale of some five million copies of the sheet music to "After the Ball" that revealed the commercial potential of the fledgling Tin Pan Alley industry to itself. Increasingly, sheet-music sales became the measure of a song's success, and to promote such sales it was not uncommon for a star performer identified with a song to be paid by the publisher, and (or at least) named and pictured on the cover—Marie Cahill: "Under the Bamboo Tree"; Bert Williams and George Walker: "I'm a Jonah Man"; Emma Carus: "Wait 'till the Sun Shines, Nellie"; Sophie Tucker: "Some of These Days"; and Al Jolson: "You Made Me Love You."

Al Jolson (1886–1950) was surely the singing phenomenon of the age. Born in Russia, the son of a synagogue cantor, Jolson came to the United States as a boy. While still in his teens, he sang and danced in dime museums, carnival shows, and burlesque houses. In 1908 he achieved his first major success with Lew Dockstader's Minstrels, perfecting a blackface act that would remain a trademark throughout his career. A year later he appeared in vaudeville where he came to the attention of the Shubert brothers, who hired him to open their Winter Garden Theater on Broadway. From *La Belle Paree* in 1911 until 1927 when he left Broadway for movie stardom in the first "talking picture," *The Jazz Singer*, Jolson appeared in some ten Winter Garden productions—including *The Honeymoon Express* (1913), *Robinson Crusoe, Jr.* (1916), *Sinbad* (1918), *Bombo* (1921), and *Big Boy* (1925). Most of these were lavishly mounted extravaganzas with loose-knit plots. They had serviceable scripts and music (mostly by house librettist Harold Atteridge and house composer Sigmund Romberg) though Jolson paid them little mind. "Would you rather see the rest of the show or just hear me sing?" he once asked a *Honeymoon Express* audience; and their enthusiastic response gave him license to halt the show's narrative, jump out of character, and indulge in impromptu comic bits interlarded with interpolated songs. With Jolson the unexpected became the norm. Poorly recapturable on film, live in the theater it worked magic. And to work that magic more intensely, Jolson used the ramp that the Shuberts had built out into the audience from the Winter Garden stage to get as close as possible to his public.

Jolson may have possessed a personal magnetism unparalleled among show business performers of his time. But his billing as "The World's Greatest Entertainer" was surely an exaggeration, though even the most astute of critics turned to hyperbole to describe him. Consider George Jean Nathan: "Possessed of an immensely electric personality, a rare sense of comedy, considerable histrionic ability, a most unusual music show versatility in the way of song and dance, and, above all, a gift for delivering lines for their full effect, he so far outdistances his rivals that they seem like the wrong ends of so many opera glasses." Or Robert Benchley: "The word 'personality' isn't quite strong enough for the thing that Jolson has. . . . There is something supernatural at the back of it." Or Gilbert Seldes, for whom Jolson represented "all we have of the Great God Pan" in a culture not generally given to public expression of emotion bordering on the demonic, and who thus saw in Jolson "the concentration of our national health and gaiety."

A singer's gift lay at the heart of the Jolson charisma; and at the heart of the singer, a cantorial tradition that Jolson personified on stage and screen. Irving Berlin and Eddie Cantor represented the same tradition, but they remained comedians when they sang. Jolson rather took it seriously, pushed the pathos in it, and developed a strong baritone yet unabashedly emotional vocal style—a rough male counterpart to the great female "coon shouters" of the day such as Stella Mayhew and May Irwin. No one had heard anything quite like it before on Broadway. Indeed, the emergence of the Jolson style, writes Stephen Banfield, was

arguably the single most important factor in defining the modern musical when, in tandem with and as an emotional model for the female belt, it finally managed to throw off the comedian's motley and with the help of the auditorium microphone usurped the operatic voice, hitherto the only way of singing "seriously" on the biggest scale.

Jolson's art consisted of more than plugging Tin Pan Alley songs on Broadway. For as he abandoned the scripts to his shows for an interpolated song, so he abandoned even the scripts to his songs for the sake of a high-voltage performance. We can get some idea of this from a recording Jolson made of "You Made Me Love You" shortly after inserting the song into *The Honeymoon Express.* The discrepancies between the published song (Ex. 4-2a), Joseph McCarthy (lyrics)/James Monaco (music), and Jolson's rendition of it (transposed and transcribed in Ex. 4-2b) suggest the kind of authority musical comedy stars wielded in the liberties they took—and were expected to take—with scripted material. Such liberties would hardly be considered jazz today though Jolson was considered a jazz singer at the height of the jazz craze in the 1920s. Moreover, the way we understand such liberties is further complicated today by the ideological frameworks within which critics have sought to come to terms with Jolson's practice of performing them in blackface. But even if Jolson is now only grudgingly admired as "an exploitative devotee of black art," his art is also seen as having transformed "the sound and meaning of stage entertainment" in America. And through the medium of recorded sound it remains—at once outrageous and compelling, especially when at the climax of "You Made Me Love You" Jolson sensationalizes the American craving for the insatiable, even in the matter of sex. "Give me, gimme, gimme, gimme, gimme, gimme, gimme."

"There is no question of legitimacy here," Seldes wrote in awe of Jolson on the stage. "Everything is right if it makes 'em laugh"—or weep, one might add. But it *was* legitimacy on the musical stage that concerned Irving Berlin when he made a point of claiming that the songs he wrote for *Watch Your Step* in 1914 amounted to "the first time Tin Pan Alley got into the legitimate theater." Berlin's achievement represented the first time an Alley songsmith with no connection to the stage other than as another outlet for his work provided an entire evening's worth of songs for what was ostensibly a book show, perhaps even a musical comedy.

Ex. 4-2a. James V. Monaco, music, Joseph McCarthy, lyrics: "You Made Me Love You" mm. 25–32, interpolated into *The Honeymoon Express*; **Ex. 4-2b.** "You Made Me Love You" mm. 25–32 (transposed), as recorded by Al Jolson

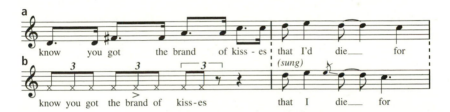

Russian-born and a cantor's son like Al Jolson, Irving Berlin (1888–1989) emigrated to New York at the age of five and grew up impoverished in the tenements of the Lower East Side. At first he sang other people's songs as a busker (street singer), as a singing waiter, and as a song plugger and boomer (singing stooge) for Harry Von Tilzer's publishing house. Then, he turned to writing songs of his own—eventually the music as well as the words—despite the fact that he had little formal education and no musical training whatsoever. With "Alexander's Ragtime Band" (1911) he achieved international success, although, ironically, the song had little to do with ragtime music. In it, in fact, Berlin redirected the culturally transgressive energies of syncopated melodies into a more respectable form of popular music acceptable to a broad sector of America's middle class. Therein lay his genius.

By 1914 Berlin had published nearly two hundred songs in a variety of styles—from ethnic and dialect numbers to opera burlesques. Yet it was chiefly for his Tin Pan Alley successes with "ragtime" songs that producer Charles Dillingham (1868–1934) hired him to write the numbers for *Watch Your Step*, "A Syncopated Musical Show in Three Acts." The show was a vehicle for the dancing Castles, Vernon (1887–1918) and Irene (1893–1969), who took advantage of the "dance craze" of the 1910s to popularize refined versions of such sexually charged ballroom items as the tango, the maxixe, and the animal-inspired grizzly bear, bunny hug, and fox trot. Models of fashion and etiquette, this attractive, modern married couple made syncopated dancing socially acceptable without

The star-studded cast of *Watch Your Step*, l. to r.: Irene Castle (as herself), Vernon Castle (Joseph Lilyburn), Frank Tinney (a Pullman Porter), Elizabeth Brice (Stella Spark), Charles King (Algy Cuffs), Sallie Fisher (Ernesta Hardacre), Harry Kelly (Ebeneezer Hardacre), and Elizabeth Murray (Birdie O'Brien).

taking all the fun out of it. The Castles' achievement in the field of popular dance thus paralleled Berlin's in the domain of popular song.

Berlin, however, saw *Watch Your Step* as an opportunity to go beyond the norms of Tin Pan Alley, and in several numbers he did. With "The Syncopated Walk" and "Ragtime Opera Medley," for example, he exceeded the constraints of the 32-bar chorus and wrote extended act finales. And with "Simple Melody" he wrote the first of his great "double songs" (later examples would include *Call Me Madam*'s "You're Just in Love," and "An Old-Fashioned Wedding" from the 1966 revival of *Annie Get Your Gun*). A double song consists of two separate songs, each expressing a different musical profile and point of view, yet so composed that both can be sung together without sacrificing the intelligibility of either. The problem as Berlin saw it was "getting two lyrics so that they didn't bump into each other"; and the solution, according to his chief arranger and musical amanuensis Helmy Kresa, was to have "one smooth melody against a rhythmic melody." In a sense, the double song in *Watch Your Step* was about the power of the double song itself. The singer of "Simple Melody," the smooth melody, longed for the genteel music of the Gilded Age ("Won't you play a simple melody/Like my mother sang to me"). The singer of "Musical Demon," the rhythmic melody, went in for ragtime ("Musical Demon, set your honey a-dreamin', Won't you play me some rag"). Musically and lyrically the two were worlds apart. But when their songs combined, the very clash between them turned into a source a delight in the fact that they even could be combined, and in the ingenuity of a mind that could imagine a musical framework capable of reconciling the melodic differences it contained.

Despite the built-in theatricality to such numbers, Berlin's *Watch Your Step* songs showed little connection to Harry B. Smith's book, which provided narrative continuity in a story of two innocents who, by running into each other in different Manhattan haunts, are repeatedly tempted to fall in love and thereby forfeit a large inheritance. Yet the show's program dubiously credited the librettist with a "Plot (if any)." And in truth, Smith deliberately minimized his book to give freer rein to Berlin's songs, the Castles' dances, and the specialty acts of the vaudeville stars who made up most of the rest of the cast. Indeed, it has been suggested the reason Dillingham bothered with a story line at all was to justify charging musical comedy ticket prices that were substantially higher than his audiences would have paid to see the same stars in vaudeville. So much for musical comedy legitimacy.

Berlin's great talent, however, did lie more in the realm of popular songs than theater scores. Prodigiously gifted and indefatigable in his work habits, he published roughly a thousand songs during his lifetime, of which an astonishingly high number were hits and many of which have since become classics. Yet he also found both a stimulus and an outlet for hundreds of his songs in theatrical settings—in some dozen major revues written between 1911 and 1942 (*Ziegfeld Follies*: 4 editions, 1911–1927; *Music Box Revues*: 4 editions, 1921–1924; *As Thousands Cheer*, 1933; *This Is the Army*, 1942); in some dozen major Hollywood film musicals written between 1929 and 1954 (*Top Hat*, 1935; *Follow the Fleet*, 1936; *Holiday Inn*, 1942; *Easter Parade*, 1948); and in the nine Broadway book shows written between 1914 and 1962 that were designated musical comedies or might be considered such (*The Cocoanuts*, 1925; *Face the Music*, 1932; *Louisiana Purchase*, 1940; *Annie Get Your Gun*, 1946; *Call Me Madam*, 1950). The compendium of songs in a Berlin musical may not always add up to a score in the strict sense, but neither can the shaping role of the theater in such songs be discounted.

Sooner or later, nearly all discussions of Irving Berlin get around to citing Jerome Kern's remark: "Irving Berlin has *no* place in American music. HE *IS* AMERICAN MUSIC." Yet Kern wrote those words in 1924, before Berlin himself had become a cultural icon or even introduced such songs as "White Christmas," "Easter Parade," or "God Bless America" into the emotional currency of the nation. The music Kern meant, of course, was that of popular song. But what was understood as a distinctly American voice in popular music at the time was usually focused on a single source, the music of African Americans—first as ragtime, then as jazz. And it was as the "King of Ragtime" that Berlin was first celebrated as a popular *American* composer in England, an image he sought to foster at home, insisting, "I'm writing American music!" Later, he modified his position by speaking of American popular song in broader cultural terms, as "the product of a sort of musical melting pot." It is in this sense that Berlin's Americanness is now more often understood. His music drew from the urban melting pot of New York, Ann Douglas said, "a knowledge of intimacy in its most pragmatic and profound meanings, a multicolored musical and linguistic palette, a keen sense of the acrobatics of which the American class system was capable, and an infallible instinct for the commercial." This embodied much of the ethos of Tin Pan Alley with which Berlin never really lost touch. His own career coincided almost exactly with its rise and fall, and no other writer was so successful both in working in Tin Pan Alley terms and in making its formulas work on Broadway and in Hollywood.

BOLTON-WODEHOUSE-KERN: THE PRINCESS THEATER

Kern's own concern, by contrast, was less with American music as such—the realm of popular song, which he conceded, above all, to Berlin—than with the realm of American theater music, which he conceded to no one. At New York's Princess Theater, in collaboration with Guy Bolton and P. G. Wodehouse, he forged a prototype of musical comedy that remained viable during the heyday of the genre in America between the two world wars.

The Princess Theater occupied a 299-seat playhouse built in 1913 in New York's new commercial theater district at West Thirty-ninth Street, just below Times Square. Its size ruled out the lavish schemes of a Shubert extravaganza or a Dillingham spectacular that set the standards in musical comedy production of the day. Nonetheless, in 1915 the Princess mounted the first of what would turn out to be a series of shows that were not just hits but landmarks in the development of American musical comedy. The idea apparently came from theatrical agent Elisabeth Marbury (1856–1933), who had played a key role in promoting the careers of the Castles in New York. She believed "that a small, intimate, clean musical comedy devoid of all vulgarity and coarseness could be made financially successful." And she proceeded to tailor to the modest dimensions of the Princess Theater a new kind of musical production that traded in intimacy, wit, and charm rather than spectacle and the more lavish accoutrements of the genre. The stage had room for no more than two sets per show and a few spots for the chorus; the pit had space for only a limited number of musicians. Moreover, to cut down on expenses, no star performers or well-known writers would be hired. Marbury made a convincing case to F. Ray Comstock, who managed the theater for the Shuberts, and for their first production, *Nobody Home*, she enlisted the talents of Jerome Kern and Guy Bolton to adapt a ten-year-old British musical, *Mr. Popple (of*

Ippleton), that had similarly tried to counter the fashion for spectacular musical comedy in England.

Jerome Kern (1885–1945), born and trained in New York, had worked early on as a song plugger for the publishing house of T. B. Harms and as a show rehearsal pianist. A songwriter with a passion for the stage, he had also spent many of his formative years mastering the (George) Edwardesian theater styles in (King) Edwardian London. Kern's early songwriting, in fact, owed much to the Gaiety Theater musicals to which he would long remain indebted. And it was in London that he met American producer Charles Frohman, who first hired Kern to compose additional songs for the European shows he was importing to New York, so legend has it, only because Frohman believed he was dealing with an Englishman.

Guy Bolton (1884–1979), an American though English-born and bred, trained in architecture before he tried his hand at playwriting. His efforts for the stage proved unsuccessful, however, until he teamed with Kern. Even then, his work on *Nobody Home* did not live up to expectations. Advertised as having a "real story and a real plot, which does not get lost during the course of the entertainment," the show fared only modestly well. But it did win praise from P. G. (Pelham Grenville) Wodehouse (1881–1975), a British humorist, columnist, author, and lyricist then living in New York and working, among other things, as a drama critic for *Vanity Fair*. In his review of the piece, he cited it (along with Victor Herbert and Henry Blossom's *The Only Girl*) as heralding a new era in which musical comedy might become "what it really ought to be— clever coherent farce, depending for its humor on a good central idea and legitimate situations, the whole peppered with attractive music." Simply writing *about* the Princess enterprise, however, proved insufficient for a man of Wodehouse's gifts. Not surprisingly, given his enthusiasm, Wodehouse would shortly be adding more than a grain of salt to it himself.

The Princess heyday was brief. Between 1915 and 1918 six musicals were produced under Princess Theater auspices. Yet not all the shows now associated with the Princess Theater style were produced at the Princess Theater itself, nor were all those that were produced there at the time written by Bolton, Wodehouse, and Kern. However inconsistent the basis for the grouping, it is the following four that are now most commonly thought of under the Princess rubric: *Very Good Eddie* (1915), *Oh, Boy!* (1917), *Leave It to Jane* (1917), and *Oh, Lady! Lady!!* (1918).

Wodehouse did not contribute to *Very Good Eddie.* That show nevertheless belongs in the company of the rest if only as the first of the series to establish the viability of the Princess approach. Thanks to its success, according to Wodehouse and Bolton, "intimate musical comedy—later to be known as the Princess Shows—became definitely a

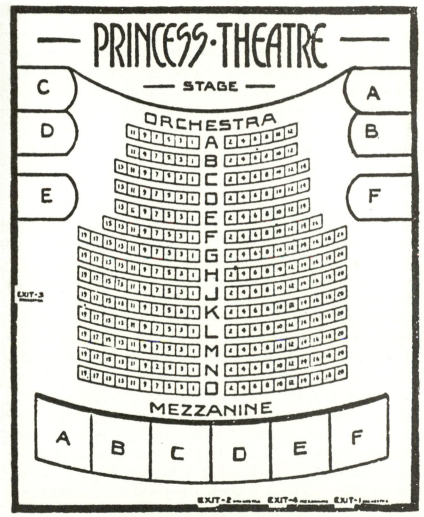

Seating diagram for the Princess Theater, whose spatial limitations both onstage and in the house (242 seats, 12 boxes) helped foster the growth of a new, intimate type of musical comedy.

New York institution." But given the more accomplished character the series took on after Wodehouse joined the Princess team in 1916, and the greater consistency of the production staff involved, it is the other three shows which together constitute "the real heart of the matter," as one critic later put it, "the mark at which any number of other composers and librettists and lyricists still are shooting."

The Princess shows mark a major shift of emphasis in the perception of what American musical comedy might be as a form of entertainment: a shift from production values to scripted ones, from a genre dominated by producers and performers to one in which writers might come to have a determining voice. The Princess writers wanted to create a more distinguished type of popular tune than that generally found in musical comedies, and a cleverer kind of script. But they also aimed to use such tunes and scripts to imbue the musical comedy undertaking itself with a sense of legitimacy derived from the spoken theater: that books might be more like plays, and that songs might relate more to their books. In the commercial arena, operetta had achieved this, too, but not in the particularly "American" way Bolton, Wodehouse, and Kern had in mind.

Bolton outlined the scenarios and Wodehouse fleshed out the dialogue for the Princess books (except for *Very Good Eddie*, for which Bolton collaborated with Philip Bartholomae who adapted his own play *Over Night*). The stories were downright silly, almost as if to divert attention from the grim news of war coming from overseas. The focus rather, Bolton said, was on "subjects and people near the audiences." The aim: to "laugh with the U.S.A. instead of at Europe, Asia and Africa in our musical comedies." In *Very Good Eddie*, for instance, two pairs of newlyweds set out for a honeymoon trip up the Hudson River and each accidentally ends up spending the night with the wrong partner. In *Oh, Boy!*, a playboy elopes with a judge's daughter and tries to win her family's approval while also keeping the marriage a secret from his Quaker aunt. In *Leave It to Jane*, a college football star falls so deeply in love with a coed at a rival college that he plays (and wins!) for the girl's school under an assumed name. In *Oh, Lady! Lady!!*, a couple puts their wedding plans on hold when the jewels of the wealthy bride-to-be are stolen and the penniless groom-to-be seems the most likely suspect. Preposterous and charming at once, the Princess plays kept to the "here" of New York and vicinity (except for *Leave It to Jane*), the "now" of the 1910s, and the farce of musical comedy.

And so the shows proved less remarkable for what they were about than how they went about it. Indeed, the Bolton-Wodehouse scripts aimed for a certain integrity at odds with the variety musical approach. The ideal libretto for Bolton involved "a 'straight' and consistent comedy [that] could stand the test of making sense, or at least coherent nonsense, as you will, without music." Even Kern agreed: "Plausibility and reason apply to musical plays as to dramas and comedies, and the sooner librettists and composers appreciate this fact the sooner will come recognition and—royalties." Critic Gilbert Seldes agreed, too, but the understanding was different:

> Each of the Princess shows had a reasonable, but not serious, plot. The advantage of a plot isn't, as one often hears, that it gives the appearance of reality to the piece, for who should expect that? There is no reason why a musical comedy should not be wholly preposterous, dramatically or psychologically, provided, like Iolanthe, it has a logic of its own. No. The advantage is that when there is a definitely perceptible structure everything else arrives with greater intensity of effect.

Everything—including, of course, the songs.

Kern's songs had an unerring sense not only of musical architecture but of musical style. By tempering the sound of English musical comedy, Kern located a musical theater voice that caught the more casual strength of American colloquial utterance without sacrificing any of its grace. The strongest harbinger of that style was "They Didn't Believe Me," the 1914 song we looked at earlier and on the basis of which Victor Herbert is said to have predicted, "That man will one day inherit my own mantle." That man had spent the previous decade, however, writing over one hundred songs for interpolation into the New York productions of musical stageworks by other composers, mostly European. ("I was a ghost for many years of English composers," he said.) It was only in the years from 1912 to 1939 that Kern would finally write most or all of the music to some thirty Broadway scores of his own. These included, after the Princess shows, *Sally* (1920), *Sunny* (1925), *Show Boat* (1927), *Sweet Adeline* (1929), *The Cat and the Fiddle* (1931), *Music in the Air* (1932), and *Roberta* (1933). He also wrote a handful of scores for London and about ten for Hollywood, including *Swing Time* (1936) and *Cover Girl* (1944). In all, Kern wrote over a thousand songs, but, unlike the case with Berlin, the greatest number of these by far were meant to be stageworthy. Kern was "a wonderful showman," Wodehouse said, "with an instinct for what was right and what wasn't, and he would never have hesitated to jettison his best melody if he thought the song did not fit."

P. G. Wodehouse, in turn, provided lyrics whose technical command, colloquial bent, and freshness of understatement perfectly matched Kern's music of the period. Wodehouse, moreover, brought a crispness of mind and lyric invention to Broadway conspicuously absent from earlier American musical comedy writing. This went beyond simply turning the blunt vernacular into a sharper instrument of wit. It had to do with a more "casual democratization of the genre." And it appears both in his use of rhyme to invigorate a cliché by pointing up the disjunction of syntax between words and music:

> *What bad luck! It's*
> *coming down in buckets*
>
>> "TILL THE CLOUDS ROLL BY" (*OH, BOY!*)

and in his abandoning rhyme altogether for the shock of a conversational phrase that undermines sentimentality:

> *I love him*
> *because he's—I don't know;*
> *because he's just my Bill.*
>
>> "BILL" ([*OH, LADY! LADY!!*] *SHOW BOAT*)

What liberated Wodehouse as a lyricist sufficiently to pursue such democratization was Kern's insistence on writing the music to the songs first. This was not the usual order of things among comic opera collaborators, especially not Gilbert and Sullivan. But it was more often than not the rule on Tin Pan Alley.

> *Jerry generally does the melody first and I put words to it. W. S.*
> *("Savoy Operas") Gilbert always said that a lyricist can't do decent*
> *stuff that way, but I don't agree with him, not as far as I'm concerned,*
> *anyway. If I write a lyric without having to fit it to a tune, I always*

make it too much like a set of light verse, much too regular in meter. I think you get the best results by giving the composer his head and having the lyricist follow him. For instance, the refrain of one of the songs in Oh, Boy *began, "If everyday you bring her diamonds and pearls on a string." I couldn't have thought of that, if I had done the lyric first, in a million years. Why, dash it, it doesn't* scan.

Finally, there was what Marbury liked to call the "Princess touch." This had to do not only with the "sense of where to stop the talking and begin the singing," but with the ability to make the transition from the one to the other with seeming effortlessness and a sense of fun at the contrivance. "Bolton and Wodehouse and Kern are my favorite indoor sport," wrote Dorothy Parker, succeeding Wodehouse as drama critic at *Vanity Fair*. "I like the way they go about a musical comedy. I like the way the action slides casually into the songs."

As an example, take the end of the first scene of *Oh, Boy!* George Budd has eloped against the wishes of his guardian aunt who is about to visit him. To pretend he is still a bachelor his wife temporarily leaves to spend the night at her mother's house. No sooner has she gone than an attractive Jacky Sampson finds refuge from a policeman in George's apartment and enlists George's help in posing as his wife when the policeman comes to inquire. Just as it becomes safe for her to leave, however, it starts to rain and George wishes to offend against neither gallanterie (by sending Jacky off in the downpour) nor propriety (by spending the night with her under the same roof). So he agrees to find other quarters for himself and let Jacky stay the night in his apartment.

That is the setup. Here, from act 1, scene 1, is the dialogue as it crosses over into the music of the verse and then the chorus of "Till the Clouds Roll By." The song became the hit of the show, and its melody has been described as "forthright, uncluttered, [and] employing a minimal number of notes, every one of which counts."

JACKY: Oh, I'm so grateful! I don't know how I can ever repay you. (*Goes toward him*)
GEORGE: (*Retreating a little*) I'd better be going now.
JACKY: You are the most resourceful man I ever knew.
GEORGE: If you want anything to eat, the kitchen is in there.

JACKY: Oh, you're too good to me. And after turning you out of your
    room so unceremoniously, too. It doesn't seem fair.
GEORGE: It's quite fair . . .

    (MUSIC CUE: INTRODUCTION: "TILL THE CLOUDS ROLL BY")

    Thank you all the same—

DUET: "TILL THE CLOUDS ROLL BY"
JACKY: I'm so sad to think that I have had to
    Drive you from your home so coolly.
GEORGE: I'd be gaining nothing by remaining—
    What would Mrs. Grundy say?
    Her conventions, kindly recollect them!
    We must please respect them duly.
JACKY: My intrusion needs explaining—(*Start rain sound effect*)
    I feel my courage waning—
GEORGE: Please, I beg don't mention it.
    I should not mind a bit
    But it has started raining.

    REFRAIN:

BOTH: [A] Oh, the rain comes a pitter, patter,
        And I'd like to be safe in bed.
      [B] Skies are weeping, while the world is sleeping,
        Thunder heaping on your/my head.
      [A] It is vain to remain and chatter
        And to wait for a clearer sky,
      [B] Helter-skelter you/I must fly for shelter
        Till the clouds roll by.

    Within less than one year, Bolton, Wodehouse, and Kern created
the three shows that mark the apex of the Princess Theater style, *Oh,
Boy!, Leave It to Jane,* and *Oh, Lady! Lady!!* Then, after 1918, the collaborators went their separate ways, working together sporadically in
the 1920s but not under Princess auspices—Bolton and Kern on *Sally;*
Kern and Wodehouse on *The Cabaret Girl* and *The Beauty Prize,* both
for London; Wodehouse and Bolton on *Oh, Kay!;* and all three once
more on *Sitting Pretty,* a failed attempt in 1924 to resuscitate the old
Princess style. Yet in one form or another, the Princess ideal prevailed:

breezily nonsensical shows with contemporary stories about upper-
and middle-class American life; shows with books that aimed to give
the nonsense a logic of its own and make it, in a word, coherent; shows
with musical numbers that came out of the mood and situations of their
books, and whose songs were in large part commensurate with the formulas of Tin Pan Alley but which represented a popular music of a
decidedly higher class. By the end of the Great War, the brief flowering
of the Princess Theater had become part of history. But because the
ethos embodied in its hit shows from 1915 to 1918 would exert a creative influence on the best of an upcoming generation of show writers,
the Princess Theater pioneered the development of a major approach
to the American musical, laying part of the foundation on which Broadway musical comedy would henceforth be built.

DIE LUSTIGE WITWE [THE MERRY WIDOW]

(Vienna, 1905). New York (10/21/1907–10/17/1908, performed in the English translation of Basil Hood and Adrian Ross). **Producer:** Henry W. Savage. **Libretto:** Viktor Léon and Leo Stein. **Music:** Franz Lehár. **Director:** George Marion. **New York Run:** 416 performances. **Cast:** Ethel Jackson, Donald Brian. **Songs:** "Vilja," "I Love You So" (The Merry Widow Waltz), "Maxim's."

NAUGHTY MARIETTA

(11/7/1910–3/4/1911). **Producer:** Oscar Hammerstein. **Book and Lyrics:** Rida Johnson Young. **Music:** Victor Herbert. **Director:** Jacques Coini. **New York Run:** 136 performances. **Cast:** Emma Trentini, Orville Harrold. **Songs:** "I'm Falling in Love with Someone," "Ah! Sweet Mystery of Life."

MAYTIME

(8/16/1917–11/19/1918). **Producers:** Messrs. Shubert [Lee and J.J.]. **Book and Lyrics:** Young [adapted from the German libretto to *Wie einst im Mai*]. **Music:** Sigmund Romberg [and Walter Kollo]. **Director:** Edward P. Temple. **New York Run:** 462 performances. **Cast:** Peggy Wood, Charles Purcell. **Songs:** "Sweethearts (Will You Remember?)," "The Road to Paradise."

ROSE-MARIE

(9/2/1924–1/16/1926). **Producer:** Arthur Hammerstein. **Book and Lyrics:** Otto Harbach and Oscar Hammerstein II. **Music:** Rudolf Friml and Herbert

---

A wedding interruption in the act 1 finale of *Show Boat*, center l. to r.: Charles Winninger (Cap'n Andy, hat in hand), Howard Marsh (Gaylord Ravenal), Norma Terris (Magnolia Hawks), Sammy White (Frank), Eva Puck (Ellie), and Edna May Oliver (Parthy Ann Hawks, pointing at Ravenal).

Stothart. **Director:** Paul Dickey. **New York Run:** 557 performances. **Cast:** Mary Ellis, Dennis King. **Songs:** "Rose-Marie," "Indian Love Call," "Totem Tom-Tom."

THE STUDENT PRINCE IN HEIDELBERG
(12/2/1924—ca. 5/18/1926). **Producers:** Messrs. Shubert. **Book and Lyrics:** Dorothy Donnelly, based on the play *Alt Heidelberg* by Wilhelm Meyer-Förster. **Music:** Romberg. **Director:** J. C. Huffman. **New York Run:** 608 performances. **Cast:** Ilse Marvenga, Howard Marsh. **Songs:** "Golden Days," "Drinking Song," "Deep in My Heart," "Serenade."

THE VAGABOND KING
(9/1/1925—12/4/1926). **Producer:** Russell Janney. **Book:** Brian Hooker, William H. Post and Janney, based on the play *If I Were King* by Justin McCarthy. **Lyrics:** Hooker. **Music:** Friml. **Director:** Max Figman. **New York Run:** 511 performances. **Cast:** Carolyn Thomson, King. **Songs:** "Song of the Vagabonds," "Some Day," "Only a Rose."

THE DESERT SONG
(11/30/1926—ca. 1/1928). **Producers:** Laurence Schwab and Frank Mandel. **Book and Lyrics:** Harbach, Hammerstein II, and Mandel. **Music:** Romberg. **Director:** Arthur Hurley. **New York Run:** 471 performances. **Cast:** Vivienne Segal, Robert Halliday, Eddie Buzzell. **Songs:** "The Riff Song," "The Desert Song (Blue Heaven)," "One Alone."

SHOW BOAT
(12/27/1927—5/4/1929). **Producer:** Florenz Ziegfeld, Jr. **Book and Lyrics:** Hammerstein II, based on the novel by Edna Ferber. **Music:** Jerome Kern. **Director:** Zeke Colvan [and Hammerstein II]. **New York Run:** 572 performances. **Cast:** Norma Terris, Helen Morgan, Marsh, Charles Winninger, Jules Bledsoe. **Songs:** "Make Believe," "Ol' Man River," "Can't Help Lovin' Dat Man," "Bill" [Broadway Revival (1946). **Additional Song:** "Nobody Else But Me"].

While musical comedy established ever firmer roots on the American stage in the early years of the twentieth century, operetta did not sit idly by. It was busy reinventing itself. Earlier, during the first phase of its history (as we saw in chapter 3), operetta was typically a sparkling, often satirical, and musically sophisticated entertainment—a comic or light opera, in fact. In this form, it first flourished in mid-nineteenth-century Paris and then developed later in distinct national schools centered mainly in London and Vienna. Yet other kinds of operetta appeared at the time as well. Johann Strauss, for instance, established a powerful model for an alternative strain with *The Gypsy Baron* (1885)—a runaway hit throughout the Austro-Hungarian Empire and a superb example of a more sentimental, romantic, and even operatic operetta. Decades later, after the turn of the century, such a model came to dominate the genre, as light opera increasingly lost touch with its lightness and shifted its focus from comedy to romance. Operettas of this newer sort did not abandon gaiety and humor, to be sure, but in them sentiment frequently held center stage. This shift in emphasis, characteristic of twentieth-century operetta altogether, marked a second broad phase in the history of the genre. Correspondingly, "operetta" took on shades of meaning in the twentieth century that often contrasted with earlier understandings of the term. One critic even went so far as to call an example of the newer type of entertainment "a rather heavy light opera."

The new-style operettas came almost entirely from Central Europe: Austria, Hungary, Germany. Their stories often took place in Central European settings as well, but in imaginary kingdoms and principalities evoked by such names as "Graustark" (from the title of George Barr McCutcheon's 1901 novel) and "Ruritania" (from the setting of Anthony Hope's 1894 novel *The Prisoner of Zenda*). Rudolf Friml, a Broadway composer of Central European origin himself, saw three ingredients as basic to the genre: "luscious melody, rousing choruses, and romantic passions." And Broadway musicals that took their measure from operetta now abounded in all of these. Melodies with a rapturous thrust informed their music, above all in love songs, which frequently appeared as waltzes and played a pivotal role in the plot (*The Merry Widow*'s "I Love You So," *Naughty Marietta*'s "I'm Falling in Love with Someone," *The Desert Song*'s "Blue Heaven"). Choruses lent local color and a stirring vocal heft to the proceedings, especially when they were all-male (*Rose-Marie*'s Royal Mounties, *The Student Prince*'s students, *The Vagabond King*'s vagabonds). And romantic passions drove the stories throughout, sometimes even to unhappy endings, with a final parting of the lovers for whom audiences had come to care (*Maytime, Blossom Time, The Student Prince*). Doomed or happy, such passions generally found expression in high histrionics of the kind one reviewer described, with reference to *The New Moon*, as "grand ululations by heroes in hand-cuffs and heroines in tears." Comic operas would not have taken such stuff seriously. Operettas did.

Dazzling, exotic, and effusive, these operettas intoxicated the first generation of theatergoers facing the twentieth century and its ills. Perhaps that was the cultural function of such works. But not everyone took kindly to the development. Karl Kraus decried it at its epicenter, in Vienna. And he blamed composer Franz Lehár (1870–1948), above all, for his role in it as the Pied Piper whose alluring operettas led audiences astray. For Lehár turned away from satire and burlesque and, most of all, the self-conscious absurdity that had earlier characterized the genre and that for Kraus constituted its quintessence. Lehár moved instead to streamline the musical form and language of operetta and to redirect its spirit toward a psychologically motivated, "rationalized" entertainment that Kraus said, "pays homage to the common sense of the traveling salesman." That stood operetta on its head as far as Kraus was concerned, and he scorned the result for the cynical commercialism he saw in it.

Yet who could deny the artistry also present in the newer operettas? Moreover, Lehár, while possibly the most responsible for the shift in priorities from satire to sentiment, was one of many gifted musicians who wrote to meet the seemingly insatiable demand for such confections: Leo Fall, Oscar Straus (no relation to Johann), Eduard Künneke, Emmerich Kálmán—even Giacomo Puccini put opera writing on hold for a while to try his hand at the genre (*La Rondine*, 1917). Operetta amounted to a business, to be sure, but also to an art—even if a limited one because it shunned the modernist concerns that haunted the operas of the period by composers from Richard Strauss (no relation to Johann either) to Alban Berg. Indeed, from a modernist perspective, with its view of history and progress intertwined, the work of Lehár and his colleagues seemed escapist, nostalgic, and historically regressive. Critics and historians have tended to bolster this view down to the present. Operetta in its twentieth-century phase has thus come to represent a cultural falling off even from the Golden Age of Johann Strauss's generation; and the onset of a Silver Age.

The Silver Age of operetta in the United States lasted roughly from the arrival of *The Merry Widow* (1907) to that of *The Great Waltz* (1934), a Viennese pastiche based on the lives and music of both Johann Strausses, father and son. Within that timespan, however, the great American contribution to the form took place in only a few years, though the cultural ripples would continue long after. Between 1924 and 1929 Broadway audiences saw an astonishingly rich output of original works of "silver" sensibilities, each running for close to a year or more. Among them were, in opening-night order, *Rose-Marie, The Student Prince, The Vagabond King, The Desert Song, Rio Rita, My Maryland, Show Boat, The Three Musketeers,* and *The New Moon.*

These shows, and shows like them that preceded and followed them on Broadway, impressed theatergoers of the age as much for their differences as their similarities. *Vagabond King* and *Student Prince* centered on aristocratic court life in times and places distant from their audiences—the one, a romance of medieval France; the other, a nineteenth-century romance that shuttled between Heidelberg and Ruritania. Other shows offered audiences more democratic vistas, or at least more familiar ones—some with women in their title roles and settings closer to home: *Rose-Marie* (Canada); *Naughty Marietta* (New Orleans); *Rio Rita* (the Tex-Mex border); all perhaps still exotic, however, from the vantage of New York. *Show Boat,* in turn, was an anomaly altogether, with its multigenerational American saga that began in the nineteenth century and ended half a century later in what was then the present. Yet all were clearly American works, created to suit the cultural conditions and commercial norms of Broadway production, distribution, and consumption. Together, they also shared a certain spirit and a set of generic conventions. With this in mind, presumably, musical theater historian Richard Traubner has suggested "the genus *Broadway operetta*" to include the various species of shows. And the suggestion is well taken, provided one takes it with an historical pinch of salt. For the nomenclature of the period did not reflect this at all. "Operetta" or its linguistic equivalent may have been the term of choice at the time in Vienna, Budapest, and Berlin. But not in New York. None of great Broadway composers working in the romantic vein—not Herbert, Friml, Romberg, or arguably Kern—called their Broadway shows operettas. They preferred "romantic comic opera" (*Eileen*), "musical play" (*Rose-Marie),* "musical romance" (*The New Moon*), and "musical adventure" (*Music in the Air*) for works we tend to label—all too quickly perhaps—with the rubric "operetta."

OPERETTA: THE SILVER AGE

The first productions in New York of *The Merry Widow* and *Naughty Marietta* clearly mark the transition from the old-style operettas on Broadway to the new. In 1907, two years after its Viennese premiere, *The Merry Widow* arrived on Broadway in a production based on George Edwardes's lightened adaptation of the piece for the London stage. Its phenomenal success unleashed a national mania for German-language operetta (in English translation) comparable to what had happened a generation earlier with its French and British counterparts. More than any other single factor, the extraordinary reception of this work precipitated a shift in American operetta priorities and secured for what became known as Viennese operetta (whether or not it originated in Vienna) a deep and influential hold on the American musical stage.

As *The Merry Widow* was based on a farce by Offenbach's librettist Henri Meilhac, it still bore ties to a comic opera tradition. (In truth, *Merry Widow* was more a transitional work than a full-blown example of the Silver Age to come.) Set in Paris and centered on a Ruritanian embassy, the story followed the ambassador's attempts to have a rich Ruritanian widow marry one of her countrymen instead of a foreign suitor who, as her husband, would withdraw her money from the national bank and thus bankrupt the country. While the libretto called for Parisian "grisettes" and hinted at an adulterous affair, it mixed passion and playfulness in a way that was teasingly suggestive without being vulgar.

Even the music teased. Franz Lehár's score for *The Merry Widow* exuded an air of sensuality so strong that the outraged Viennese theater director exclaimed when Lehár first played it for him, "That's not music!" (This was, after all, Sigmund Freud's Vienna.) And crowning the score was a waltz, simple yet haunting both in itself and in the way it functioned in the work. What most people think of as "The Merry Widow Waltz" went to the heart of the new operetta genre in its psychological use of music and movement to reveal emotional truths where words failed. Near the end of act 2, the denial of any romantic feelings between the young widow and the Ruritanian count whose relationship constitutes the focus of the work is contradicted by the music to which the two succumb in waltzing around the stage. The dance thus becomes central to telling their story. And without words to obscure the meaning of the music, the two hum its melody together as if to suggest a text best left to the imagination—a text quite unnecessary, though it is finally revealed when sung at the reprise of the waltz at the very end of the show:

> *Though I say not what I may not let you hear,*
> *Yet the swaying dance is saying, "Love me, dear!"*
> *Ev'ry touch of fingers tells me what I know,*
> *Says for you, it's true, it's true, you love me so!*

The suppressed emotional power in the combination of wordless song and dance overwhelmed audiences. One critic spoke of "the irresistible seduction of the Viennese waltz, the dance of dances that steals men's souls out by way of their toes." Here was a waltz more lilting than sweeping, one that moved with an intimacy that disarmed. And it was achieved by musical means so transparent that all could understand: a waltz whose rhythmic patterns were regular, almost predictable, and whose melody was utterly diatonic (as was the harmony but for one chord). One commentator wrote, "Listening to Offenbach or Strauss with one's eyes closed, one sometimes might have imagined oneself in an opera house; listening to Lehár, one knew one was in a theater or on a dance floor."

With its blend of wit and sensuality, its intimate use of dance, and its psychological use of music, *The Merry Widow* breathed fresh life into a moribund European operetta tradition and won a commercial success on an unprecedented international scale. On Broadway it was followed by a deluge of contemporary imports from Vienna by way of London in English translation. Among the most memorable were *A Waltz Dream*

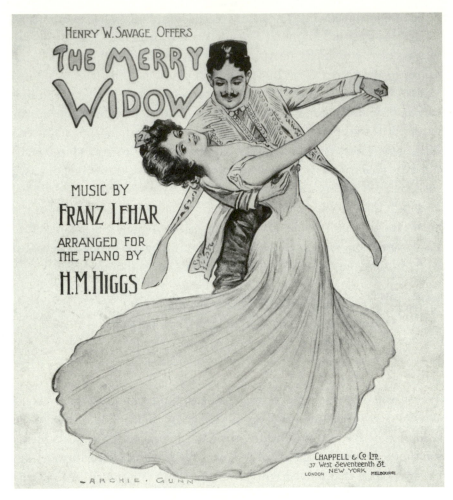

Waltzing lovers swirl across a sheet-music cover for *The Merry Widow,*
an icon of Silver Age operetta.

(Straus, 1908), *The Dollar Princess* (Fall, 1909), *The Chocolate Soldier* (Straus, 1909), and *The Count of Luxembourg* (Lehár, 1912). Through their popularity shows like these worked their way into the musical culture of metropolitan America's middle classes. Richard Rodgers remembered growing up in New York, surrounded by their music:

Both my parents were avid theatregoers, with a special passion for musicals, and since the complete vocal-piano score was always sold in the theatre lobby, Pop never failed to buy a copy. So home would come Mlle. Modiste, The Merry Widow, The Chocolate Soldier *and all the rest to go up on the piano rack. They would be played so often, both before and after dinner, that I soon knew all the songs by heart.*

Such shows also drew responses from American writers already working along similar lines or forced to shift gear to keep up with the new standard. H. B. Smith and Reginald de Koven, who had bestowed the "flattery of imitation" on Gilbert and Sullivan decades earlier, now sought to model their work on *The Merry Widow* in every important respect save one, de Koven avowed: that musical's "deftly concealed sexual interest." (It is not clear whether this reflected their own tastes or their understanding of their audiences'.) But it was Victor Herbert, already a master of the American operetta in its earlier stages, who would find the greatest immediate success in mining the new vein. His *Algeria* (1908), in fact, has been called "the first [American] operetta in the modern sense," yet it had little historical impact as it failed in its original form as well as in revision a year later. The work that did have such impact was *Naughty Marietta*, Herbert's first hit in the new style and arguably the most influential stagework of his career.

Naughty Marietta first saw life not through the usual Broadway channels, but as a production of the Manhattan Opera Company. Led by Oscar Hammerstein I (1846–1919), an enterprising German immigrant who built the first major theater in the Times Square area and who became a leading vaudeville producer and opera impresario, the company gave the American premieres of such daring works as *Elektra* and *Pelléas et Mélisande* and it even performed the scandal-ridden *Salome* when the Metropolitan Opera Company wouldn't. Hammerstein's company seriously rivaled the Metropolitan until it succumbed to pressures from the larger organization and concluded a financial deal that barred it from producing grand opera anywhere the Metropolitan operated. The ever resourceful Hammerstein then turned his attention from grand opera to light, and to Victor Herbert, the finest composer of the type in America. Thus Herbert created the first great Broadway operetta with the forces of an ex–opera company at his disposal, including the voice and the temperament of coloratura soprano Emma Trentini (1878–1959), who created the title role.

Naughty Marietta takes place in a fictitiously French New Orleans of the late eighteenth century, when the city was actually under Spanish control. Marietta is a European countess who has fled to the city in disguise to avoid a forced marriage back home. She captures the attention of the lieutenant governor's son, Étienne, who has lost interest in his mistress, Adah, a quadroon slave. But Marietta will give her heart only to the man who can complete a "dream melody," whose music haunts her in fragments. At the same time, a band of American backwoodsmen arrives in New Orleans bent on capturing a notorious pirate. The Americans are led by Dick Warrington—a model hero, democrat, and reluctant lover. By the final curtain, he has exposed the pirate as none other than Étienne in disguise; purchased Adah from Étienne and freed her; and sung Marietta's complete dream melody in full knowledge of its consequences.

In its musical scope, its melodramatic thrust, and its emphasis on romantic passion, *Naughty Marietta* set new standards for Broadway operetta. Its separate numbers proceeded in a fairly set sequence, given the

Naughty Marietta's lovers through changing times, casts, and media, l. to r.: Orville Harrold and Emma Trentini on the stage (1910); Nelson Eddy and Jeanette MacDonald on film (1935); and Alfred Drake and Patrice Munsel on television (1955).

genre's dramatic-musical conventions: a rousing male chorus with the male lead ("Tramp, Tramp, Tramp"), followed by a pert female chorus ("Taisez-Vous") and solo for the female lead ("Naughty Marietta"), then a duet for the leads ("It Never, Never Can Be Love"), followed by separate solos for the male comedian ("If I Were Anybody Else but Me") and the secondary female character ("'Neath the Southern Moon"), and so on. But as an American costume drama set in a European enclave of the New World, the show also covered a panorama of music that stretched from operatic high Cs ("Italian Street Song") and vocal ensembles ("Live for Today") to unabashedly popular songs ("The Sweet By and By") and dances ("Loves of New Orleans"). This suggested a musical gamut for American operetta that became a model for the genre. Dramatically, too, it widened the genre's gamut, infusing the farcical thrust of earlier operetta with a stark melodramatic strain. Villainy, for example, no longer simply involved the kind of mischief-making found in *Robin Hood*'s Sheriff of Nottingham: harmless and amusing. Here, in Étienne's selling of Adah, villainy resonated with a cruelty surely meant to raise hackles among audiences nurtured on egalitarian ideals.

Romance, too, covered a range from playful to serious expression. But the serious was by far the more memorable as it was central to the story. Nowhere did romance resound more passionately, in fact, than in the two instances when the dream melody ("Ah! Sweet Mystery of Life") was heard complete, and the music of *Naughty Marietta* went beyond the expressive norms of the popular stage to verge on the operatic. This happened once in the orchestra alone, in the charged musical rhetoric of the act 2 intermezzo ("*molto appassionato*" in the score). And it happened once onstage, in the finale ultimo, when, as Dick finally completed Marietta's melody, with words now as well as music, singing itself *became* the action. However contrived, without it the love story would have been left hanging. And so, while not a waltz, "Ah, Sweet Mystery" took on the pivotal dramatic function in *Marietta* that "The Merry Widow Waltz" had done in the Lehár operetta.

The song served musical as well dramatic ends. By completing in act 2 the dream-melody fragments of act 1, Herbert made the kind of connections that go beyond the separate numbers of a show and contribute to the sense of a score. Indeed, Herbert not only did his own orchestrations, he was also one of the earliest full-time Broadway composers to be concerned that the overall shape and continuity of show music amount to a score. Yet if it appears today that "bigtime American operetta, and the belief that a great musical needs great music, is his invention," it is not simply a matter of Herbert's musical ambition and ability outstripping that of his Broadway contemporaries. It is also that the best of his immediate successors in the musical theater chose to look to his work more than to any other as a model: His was the earliest product of the Broadway production system in which they worked that was worth emulating. In this sense one may speak of history bestowing Herbert's mantle on the shoulders of such composers as Sigmund Romberg, Rudolf Friml, and—the one whom Herbert predicted actually would inherit it— Jerome Kern.

ROMBERG AND FRIML

Herbert continued to cultivate the romantic side of operetta in such shows as *Sweethearts* and *Eileen*. But it was more than just the force of Herbert's example that ultimately broke the grip of musicals from Central Europe on Broadway. The Great War of 1914–18 itself played a part. America's involvement and eventual participation in the conflict precluded extending support of any kind to the enemy powers of the Triple Alliance, which included Austria-Hungary and Germany. That applied to productions in the United States of operettas originating in those countries, which would not only channel money to them in the form of royalties but also bolster their cultural standing in ways that might enhance respect for them and thus undermine morale at home. Other wars "went no deeper than the physical aspects," remarked one of President Wilson's spokesmen, "but German 'Kultur' raised issues that had to be fought out in the hearts and minds of the people as well as on the actual firing-line." The fight against German Kultur on the home front affected all walks of life. It extended to renaming hamburgers and sauerkraut "liberty sandwiches" and "liberty cabbage." People even changed their own names if they sounded Germanic. Thus Otto Hauerbach and Rudolf Friml continued working on Broadway as they had before—only now, respectively, as Ogden Hartley and Roderick Freeman.

    With the demand for "Viennese" operetta ongoing but with the supply of the real thing cut short because of the war, creation of new product now devolved onto those who could convincingly replicate it in the

United States. Musicians trained in Europe and recently immigrated to America had already written operettas for Broadway well before the commencement of hostilities. The Czech Karl Hoschna (*Madame Sherry*, 1910) and the Belgian-by-way-of-London Ivan Caryll (*The Pink Lady*, 1911), for example, had produced notable hits, though in a lighter vein. The more impassioned wing of operetta makers would come from elsewhere, however. Here it was the German-trained Victor Herbert who had led the way before the war. And he would now be followed by two sons of the Hapsburg Empire who would oversee the efflorescence of American operetta in the 1920s, Sigmund Romberg and Rudolf Friml.

Hungarian-born Sigmund Romberg (1887–1951) studied composition in Vienna and worked there as an operetta coach and accompanist before settling in the United States in 1909. Hired as a house composer by the Shubert brothers, he contributed music of all kinds to their various productions. In all, he wrote the music for over forty book shows— including adaptations of German stageworks (*The Blue Paradise*, 1915; *Maytime*, 1917; *Blossom Time*, 1921), original operettas (*The Student Prince*, 1924; *The Desert Song*, 1926; *The New Moon*, 1928), and, in later years, somewhat old-fashioned attempts at more modern musicals (*Up in Central Park*, 1945; *The Girl in Pink Tights*, 1954).

Of Romberg's most inspired work, *The Student Prince* proved to be the longest-running Broadway musical of the 1920s despite its bittersweet ending and lack of a comic subplot. Its college setting (in Heidelberg) and choral celebration of "Drink, Drink, Drink" (during Prohibition) helped to offset in part the dark romance at its core, which the waltz "Deep in My Heart" encapsulated. *The Desert Song* did have a happy ending (and a comic subplot) and a far more exuberant waltz for its lovers, "Blue Heaven." In its mastery of the genre's conventions, in fact, the show stands as a prototype of Broadway operetta of the Silver Age. It also combined the timeliness of a contemporary story and the exoticism of a North African setting in one of the most rapturous scores and finest original books of the era. Together with *The New Moon*, these shows form the foundation on which Romberg's reputation rests today, however improbable the romances at the heart of their plots: in *Student Prince*, between Karl Franz (Howard Marsh), the heir to a Ruritanian throne, and Kathie (Ilse Marvenga), a waitress in the college town where he has gone to study; in *Desert Song*, between Margot (Vivienne Segal), a Parisienne in a French outpost in Morocco, and the "Red Shadow" (Robert Halliday), leader of the Riffs fighting the French (but really the French governor of Morocco's son in disguise); and in *New Moon*, between Robert (Robert Halliday), a French aristocrat arrested in New Orleans on the eve of the French Revolution, and Marianne (Evelyn Herbert), the daughter of the owner of the ship transporting him back to France.

Yet Romberg's earlier work, if less consistently inspired, holds at least as much interest for its historical role in the transformation of European operettas into American ones. The process became a house specialty of the Shuberts', who turned it into an industry very much their own. As J.J.'s son, John, remembered it:

> *My father would buy a foreign show, in Paris or Berlin, Budapest or Vienna, and then have it adapted. You got a composer, and it didn't matter who it was in those days. Except Victor Herbert, there weren't too many greats around. My father would give the foreign piece an American adaptation—what used to be called* My Beautiful Girl in the Woods *was suddenly called* Hello, Lola! *for American consumption. There were at least twenty boys in Berlin, Vienna, Budapest, turning out the stuff once a year; my father would get somebody to doctor up the scripts and bring in a fellow from Tin Pan Alley to goose the lyrics. Then you'd add a couple of American tunes, or you'd buy a song from José Padilla in Spain and shove that in. Nobody cared. There was no author's society or Dramatists Guild, everybody got paid, though you didn't pay anybody too much money. And so, one after another, the operettas were formed.*

Blossom Time, "the most successful single production the Shuberts ever had," according to John, is also the only Shubert show of the era still licensed by the Shubert Organization. Yet it began as *Das Dreimäderlhaus (The Three Girls' House)*, a wartime sensation in Vienna and Berlin that had nothing to do with the Shuberts. Loosely based on the life of Austrian composer Franz Schubert, *Dreimäderlhaus* fairly glowed with gemütlichkeit and nostalgia, especially since its score consisted entirely of arrangements of Schubert's music beloved by German-speaking audiences.

Only after the war did the Shubert brothers buy the property and convert it into *Blossom Time*—not simply a translation of *Dreimäderl-*

haus, but a remake of it for Broadway. Where the original book ended with Schubert simply losing the girl he loved, for example, Dorothy Donnelly's libretto now had the composer dying to a chorus of singing angels. And where the original score had been judicious in its choice of musical selections, Romberg pulled out all the stops. Into the new version he inserted Schubert's "Ave Maria" and a sung rendition of the cello theme from the "Unfinished Symphony." Both melodies were better known in American culture than most of the Viennese selections originally used—so well known, in fact, they had become sonic emblems: the one representing spirituality, the other, high art. Romberg went further: He recomposed the symphony's theme into an AABA standard ("Song of Love"), and he reconfigured its rhythms and meter so as to gain a more waltzlike effect in the *Merry Widow* vein. What was left when Romberg finished with the "Unfinished" was just enough of the symphony to link it to Schubert's "melody immortal" (Donnelly's lyric) and turn it into something closer to kitsch. Other countries, too, mounted their versions of *Dreimäderlhaus* (England: *Lilac Time*; France: *Chanson d'amour*); none, however, went this far. The formula enthralled and repulsed American audiences for decades as the Shuberts continually revived the show in New York (1924, 1926, 1931, 1938, 1943) and toured with it. *Blossom Time* would also serve later generations of Broadway showmakers as both a warning and an inspiration.

The earlier *Maytime* warrants even closer comparison with its European source in considering the Americanization of operetta. *Maytime* moved through three generations of New Yorkers from 1840 to 1910. It told of the love of Ottillie van Zandt, daughter of an aristocratic family, and Richard Wayne, a laborer working for her father—an enduring love, thwarted during their lifetimes because of class differences, and realized vicariously after their deaths in the romantic union of their grandchildren (played by the same performers). It was the most popular Broadway musical of the World War I era, with an amazing run of nearly five hundred performances and in more than one theater at the same time. It was, according to Peggy Wood (1892–1978), who created the role of Ottillie, "the show the boys all asked to see before they went overseas. *Maytime,*" she said—then lending credibility to her claim—"and Al Jolson." Indeed, in pitting the cruelty of aristocratic interests against the values personified by the show's lovers—humble dignity, romantic idealism, personal sacrifice, and triumph beyond the grave—*Maytime* seems to have spoken deeply to the wartime mood, perhaps fulfilling the promise of that future for which President Wilson said Americans were fighting and dying: to make the world safe for democracy.

If it did, there is more than a touch of irony in the fact that the Shuberts modeled *Maytime* directly on an entertainment from one of the Central European powers with which America was at war. Indeed, the creators of *Maytime* had taken a Berlin-dialect farce with songs, *Wie einst im Mai*, as their source. But no one acknowledged the fact on Broadway in view of the virulent anti-German feeling at the time and a nationally endorsed policy of "100% Americanism." So while librettist Rida Johnson Young kept most of the original plot in adapting the book, she shifted the Berlin setting to New York. Romberg, however, discarded most of the original score and replaced its typically lighthearted songs with more poignant ones. Yet where the new book and score transformed the original most significantly was in the basic modality of the work: Young and Romberg converted what had been a sentimental farce with a smattering of songs into a full-fledged musical melodrama.

The term "melodrama" has sunk into disrepute through association with the crudest examples of the form: the tearjerkers of the Victorian stage, the silent movie thrillers and romances, the "soap operas" of radio and TV. Moreover, the very nature of the melodramatic undertaking seems steeped in cliché, suggested by such phrases as:

> *pursuit and capture, imprisonment and escape, false accusation, cold-blooded villain, innocence beleaguered, virtue triumphant, eternal fidelity, mysterious identity, lovers reconciled, fraudulence revealed, enemies foiled; the whole realm of adventure; the realm of mystery from the supernatural to the whodunit; the realm of vice and crime from horror to detection to reform . . . the world of shock and thrill, of what is regularly called "gripping" and "poignant."*

But melodrama is neither an eccentric nor a decadent kind of drama. It is rather "drama in its elemental form." Much as farce stands to comedy among the modes of drama that traffic in laughter, so melodrama stands with respect to tragedy among those that traffic in tears. The chief limitation to melodrama as a dramatic mode is that it simply is not mature. Nonetheless, as Eric Bentley has put it, "There is a melodrama in every tragedy, just as there is a child in every adult." It is the very "childishness" of melodrama, in fact, that connects it with farce. And much as tragedy and comedy form a meaningful pair in their own right, so do melodrama and farce, though they lack any comparably famous set of masks to fix the link in the cultural imagination. As flip sides of the same theatrical coin, melodrama and farce both ultimately turn away from reality, and in so doing, turn their backs on the possibility of tragedy and comedy as well. That the fools and knaves of farce find their natural counterparts in the heroes and villains of melodrama, in fact, can be clearly seen by comparing the act 1 confrontation scene of *Wie einst im Mai*, in which nothing seems meant to be taken seriously, and its adaptation into *Maytime*, with its almost total lack of humor.

Wie einst im Mai (1913): Act 1, Scene 17

CICERO [THE COLONEL'S NEPHEW]: Uncle, Ottillie is so nasty to me. . . . And so impolite! She got that from her bosom buddy over there, the handyman. (*Points to Fritz, who continues working*) . . .

COLONEL [VON HENKESHOVEN, RET.]: So then, my child, it's high time that this childhood friendship comes to an end. Surely I'm no snob— in fact, I quite approved when you played with the gardener's son [Fritz], and even when you two were partners at your dance lessons. But you mustn't forget that you belong to a different class, and that you are as good as promised to your cousin Cicero.

OTTILLIE [THE COLONEL'S DAUGHTER]: What? I'm to marry Cicero? (*Laughing*) Well, I thank you! I'll marry Fritz or no one!

MECHTHILDE [OTTILLIE'S GOVERNESS]: *O mon Dieu!* (*She faints*) . . .

COLONEL: What a misguided notion! My child and this fellow from the dregs of society.

CICERO: Haha! So it's a dirty handyman she wants—a good-for-nothing—a nobody!

FRITZ [THE COLONEL'S HANDYMAN]: (*Attacking Cicero*) What did ya call me? A nobody? Boy, I'm gonna let ya have it—

CICERO: (*Runs behind the Colonel*) Help, mommy! . . .

FRITZ: How'm I supposed ta keep workin' around here when this dumb snot-nose insults me?

COLONEL: (*Indignant*) How dare you use such language! Finish your work and then never let me set eyes on you again.

FRITZ: (*Upset, packing up his tools*) Aw the hell I will! And about my language, Colonel, well, that's just the way I talk. I don't mean nobody no harm. But what you just called me—that about the dregs of society—I wouldn't never have dared called you nothin' like that. I know as well as the next guy my father wasn't no commanding officer, an' I ain't no more than a handyman. But I did learn to read 'n' write.... In fact, I read once that a tailor's apprentice became a general; an' a Count became a tramp ... an' if we both have different colors in our blood, well there ain't nothin' you an' me can do about it. Maybe I woulda had blue blood if my father had drunk copying ink. (*Exits*) ...

COLONEL: What ingratitude! That's what you get from treating such people as equals. ... Go to your room, Ottillie, and stay there.

Maytime (1917): Act 1, Finale

CLAUDE [THE COLONEL'S NEPHEW]: (*Enters from house*) What's this? How dare you? ... My affianced bride in the arms of a low apprentice!

OTTILLIE [THE COLONEL'S DAUGHTER]: I'm nothing of the kind! I'll never marry you! I love Dick!

COLONEL [VAN ZANDT, AN ARISTOCRATIC MERCHANT]: What's this? What's all this?

CLAUDE: This fellow—this dependent—she was in his arms!

DICK [THE COLONEL'S MECHANIC]: Yes, she was in my arms. Where I intend to keep her! (*He puts his arms about Ottillie defiantly*)

COLONEL: You forget yourself, Dick.... There must be an end of this nonsense. You must remember your station, young man.

DICK: I'll better my station, sir! You'll see. I'll work to be worthy of her.

COLONEL: (*Sternly*) Ottillie, come to me—at once!

OTTILLIE: I love him, father. I'll never give him up!

COLONEL: You will do as I say. Understand, Richard, my daughter is not for you. And if you wish to remain in my employ, there must be no further nonsense between you.

DICK: It isn't nonsense, sir! We are no longer children. We know our minds. She belongs to me and I'll win her!

COLONEL: What! You dare defy me! Me, who have been your benefactor? Who have raised you from—

DICK: I've raised myself, sir, by hard work ...

Peggy Wood (Ottillie Van Zandt) torn between her two suitors in *Maytime*, l. to r.: Douglas Wood (Claude Van Zandt) and Charles Purcell (Richard Wayne).

COLONEL: How dare you take that tone with me. You are discharged! Go! Take your things and leave at once!

OTTILLIE: No—no, father!

DICK: You may send me away, sir, but I'll come back, and when I do it will be to claim her! . . . I'll come back your equal, Ottillie, or I'll not return at all.

COLONEL: I'm amazed at this defiance. You shall never see my daughter
    again. Go in, Ottillie, go in at once.
OTTILLIE: Dick! (*Starts*—COLONEL *stops her*) Dick. You'll come back?
DICK: Yes.
OTTILLIE: I'll be waiting, waiting always! (*Runs into house*)
DICK: You hear, sir! She'll wait! That gives a man something to work
    for! (*Exits into shop*)

By the 1920s, with the war concluded, Broadway resumed the
production of imported operettas undisguised as such. But, with few
exceptions—*Countess Maritza* (Kálmán, 1926); *Bitter Sweet* (Noël Coward, 1929)—foreign pieces were no longer as popular with American
audiences as they had been before the war. Yet there was still a demand
at home for such entertainments from several quarters, as Charles
Hamm relates:

> *recent immigrants from Europe and first- or second-generation Amer-*
> *icans enjoying a fairytale view of their ancestral culture; the upwardly*
> *mobile, who wished to associate themselves with a more sophisticated*
> *form of musical theater than the minstrel show or vaudeville, but were*
> *unwilling or unable to derive pleasure from opera in foreign lan-*
> *guages; and the urban middle class, who responded to effective and*
> *well-crafted stage pieces produced by talented writers and composers.*

Efforts to meet the situation ultimately yielded the great flowering of
Broadway operetta that began with *Rose-Marie* in 1924 and produced a
series of hits that now captivated Europe as well America. *Rose-Marie*,
for example, enjoyed unusually long runs in London (1925), Paris
(1927), Berlin (1928), and a host of other capitals. Yet *Rose-Marie* was
just the beginning of what would amount to an American invasion of
Britain and the continent, as Broadway increasingly exported its romantic musicals on a regular basis. London's Theatre Royal, Drury Lane,
for one, became a virtual outpost of Broadway as it housed *Rose-Marie*
for an astonishing 851 performances, then followed it with productions
of *The Desert Song* in 1927 (432 performances), *Show Boat* in 1928 (350),
The New Moon in 1929 (148), and *The Three Musketeers* in 1930 (240).
    Rose-Marie also marked the high point in the career of composer

Rudolf Friml (1879–1972). A native of Prague, Friml had studied composition with Antonin Dvořák and had toured Europe as a concert pianist and accompanist. Twice his tours took him to the United States, where he finally settled in 1906. In 1912, producer Arthur Hammerstein hired Friml, then still an unknown composer of concert works and salon pieces, to write the music for *The Firefly* after Victor Herbert had abandoned the project over a quarrel with the show's star. With *Firefly*'s success, Friml found a career in the theater as well as an employer in Hammerstein, who would produce half of the composer's future shows. From 1912 to 1934 Friml wrote twenty Broadway book musicals, both in a lighter style and in the heavier romantic one for which he is better known. If he proved to be a less versatile stage composer than Romberg, Friml was also musically more venturesome, and he mined a rich vein of melody that found its most popular expression in three hits of the 1920s, *Rose-Marie*, *The Vagabond King*, and *The Three Musketeers*.

The Vagabond King (1925) and *The Three Musketeers* (1928) exuded that sense of the exotic that constituted a key element of romantic operettas. Both were at once historical romances and cape-and-sword shows that took place in royal French settings. Both had also previously held the stage as spoken melodramas. The first centered on romantic-political exploits of the fifteenth-century outlaw-poet François Villon (Dennis King); the second, on romantic-political exploits of Dumas père's seventeenth-century swashbucklers and their companion D'Artagnan (Dennis King). Moreover, both reveal Friml's own nostalgic bent. "When I write music for the theatre," he said, "I like books with charm to them. And charm suggests the old things—the finest things that were done long ago."

Rose-Marie, by contrast, had an original book, a modern story, and a Canadian Rockies setting. It told of the love of miner Jim Kenyon (Dennis King) and the part-Indian singer Rose-Marie La Flamme (Mary Ellis). Her brother, however, opposes Rose-Marie's romance with Jim. He has Jim accused of murdering the Indian Black Eagle and, when Jim flees to escape the Mounties, he tries to get Rose-Marie to marry another man. Eventually, Black Eagle's unfaithful wife, Wanda, confesses to the murder. Yet not until the act 2 finale ultimo do Jim and Rose-Marie finally reunite—and to a neat reprise of the same "Indian

Love Call" that had parted them in the finale of act 1 ("When I'm calling you—oo—oo—oo—oo").

In addition to its dramatic function in the show, "Indian Love
Call" was a haunting love song in itself, and characteristic of the effusive numbers Friml composed for the principal lovers ("Rose-Marie,"
"Door of My Dreams"). So committed was Friml to this kind of writing that he tended to ignore the comedic element in romantic operetta,
as if he were convinced the genre could succeed without it. And so
it fell to Herbert Stothart (1885–1949), Arthur Hammerstein's resident music director, to write the snappier tunes like those for the secondary comic couple, Herman and Lady Jane ("Hard-Boiled Herman,"
"Why Shouldn't We?"). Friml and Stothart collaborated on still other
numbers—like "Totem Tom-Tom," the spectacular showstopper that
featured a singing murderess and the precision dancing of rows upon
rows of chorines dressed as totem poles.

Stothart wrote about half of the score, including much of the underscoring. Such music played an important dramatic role in *Rose-Marie*,
as melodies that had been sung earlier in the show reappeared at telling
moments later in purely instrumental forms. The scene of Black Eagle's
murder, for instance, was performed onstage in pantomime while syn-

A chorus line of totem-pole girls in Charles Le Maire's revue-inspired costumes for the "Totem
Tom-Tom" sequence in *Rose Marie*.

chronized in the orchestra to an underscore of mood depictions and song "impressions," "reminiscences," and "recollections" (terms used at various places in the score). Aimed at heightening an audience's responses, the effect resembled that often found in movie theaters at the time, where music accompanied the showing of silent films.

Even spoken scenes in *Rose-Marie* were underscored for emotional purposes. Consider the following excerpt from the act 1 finale, which begins with Rose-Marie learning that Jim allegedly killed Black Eagle, and ends as she lies to save him. Accompanying the action onstage, the orchestra plays fragments of three themes in quick succession, each no longer than a few seconds and instantly recognizable as a repetition or transformation of earlier music associated with another character in the show.

Spoken Onstage	Played in the Orchestra
LADY JANE: [*to Malone*] How can they say that Jim killed Black Eagle?	
ROSE-MARIE: Jim kill! Oh no! . . . (*She rushes over to* [MALONE] *and clutches his arms feverishly*) How can dis be—Jeem ees do not'ing wrong—mus' be some mistake—maybe Black Eagle try to shoot—He's bad Indian. . . . (*She buries her sobs on his shoulder . . .*)	
SERGEANT MALONE: The evidence was strong against him, besides Wanda saw him do it.	"INDIAN THEME," directly associated with Wanda, the real murderess
(*Brisk whispered orders* [*to Mounties*]) Pat—you go down to the railroad station.—Bill, you guard the hotel . . . You two wait at the gate . . .	"THE MOUNTIES," sung earlier by Malone as a vigorous march, now slowed down and harmonized ambiguously: he is torn between his affection for Jim and Rose-Marie and his duty as a Royal Mounty

ROSE-MARIE: Malone—no use to look! Jim is not here—he—he went away yes—see? He went away—(MALONE *smiles grimly . . . bows his head sadly, and turns back to his duty*)

"ROSE-MARIE," sung earlier by Jim in the major. Now played plaintively in the minor: she lies to protect the man she loves.

If all this seems no more than a poor exercise in Wagnerian leitmotifs, theatergoers of the 1920s, who undoubtedly went to silent films as well, would probably have understood such music in different terms: an extension of the "melos" techniques of nineteenth-century melodrama on the twentieth-century operetta stage. (The two, however, are not unrelated.)

Surely because of this and similar uses of continuous music in *Rose-Marie*, the program noted: "The musical numbers of this play are such an integral part of the action that we do not think we should list them as separate episodes." Yet when the show later played in London, the program bore the customary list of separate musical numbers. Someone likely had second thoughts about so blatant an expression in a musical of an almost operatic concern. One can only guess who wrote the original note. It seems more likely to have come from one of the show's dual librettists than one of its dual composers. For the one, Otto Hauerbach, now Harbach (1873–1963), was the influential book and lyric writer of over forty Broadway musicals, from 1908 to 1936, who reached the pinnacle of his career with *Rose-Marie* and for whom such integration was and would remain a major issue. And the other, Harbach's young protégé Oscar Hammerstein II, was just at the beginning of what was to be an even more influential theatrical career; and this concern with musical integration was to prove central to his life's work.

SHOW BOAT

As a nephew of the Broadway show producer Arthur Hammerstein and a grandson of the flamboyant "Father of Times Square" after whom he was named, Oscar Hammerstein II (1895–1960) was no stranger to the musical stage. As a Broadway lyricist and librettist, however,

Oscar Hammerstein II would exert a more seminal force than his fore-
bears did in the shaping of the modern American musical. He wrote
twenty-six shows in the earlier part of his career (1920–1942), many
with his mentor Harbach and in collaboration with composers such as
Youmans, Friml, Romberg, and Kern. Later, starting with *Oklahoma!*
(1943–1959), he would write nine Broadway shows in an exclusive
partnership with composer Richard Rodgers.

If a common thread links the two parts of his career, it lies in Hammerstein's view of the Broadway musical enterprise, which he described
early on not in terms of operetta so much as operatic musical comedy:

> *The history of musical comedy has passed through a variety of phases,
> but the type that persists . . . is the operetta—the musical play with
> music and plot welded together in skillful cohesion. . . . There has been
> no change in theatrical fashion so swift as that which has taken place
> since* Rose-Marie *pioneered its way to Broadway last September. Here
> was a musical show with a melodramatic plot and a cast of players
> who were called upon to actually sing the music—sing,* mind you—
> *not just talk through the lyrics and then go into their dance. . . . The
> revolution in musical-comedy vogue which* Rose-Marie *has wrought
> was not accidental. It was a carefully directed attack at the Cinderella
> show [*Irene, 1919; Sally, 1920; Little Nellie Kelly, 1922*] in favor
> of the operatic musical comedy.*

The success of *Rose-Marie* also led Hammerstein to formulate the
question that went straight to the heart of his theatrical ambition: "Is
there a form of musical play tucked away somewhere in the realm of
possibilities which could attain the heights of grand opera and still
keep sufficiently human to be entertaining?" And he came closest to
answering it in the affirmative at the time he first posed it in his partnership with Kern.

By 1925, when Jerome Kern first collaborated with Hammerstein
(and Harbach) on *Sunny*, he was secure in his reputation as a first-
rank composer of musical comedies. Kern had already written about
twenty scores for Broadway, including the celebrated series of Princess
shows. With new collaborators in Hammerstein and Harbach, however,
he would change direction, leaving behind the norms of musical comedy for a while to explore more dramatic and more musicianly ways of

structuring musicals. Building on the examples of Romberg and Friml, Kern would now work to transform the romantic operetta into a more modern stage entertainment—the most important results of the newer trend being *Show Boat* (1927), *The Cat and the Fiddle* (1931), and *Music in the Air* (1932).

While *Show Boat* has proved to have sufficient cultural clout over the years to warrant revising and reviving down to the present, the other two musicals are remembered today mainly as period pieces though in several respects they represent more fully realized works. *The Cat and the Fiddle* and *Music in the Air* not only contain some of Kern's most extraordinary inspirations, but they are musicals in which music itself becomes the focus of concern. Both rely heavily on diegetic singing and performing as well as continuity in the orchestra to further their narrative ends: They are musically integrated works in a theatrical rather than in an operatic sense. They also differ from *Show Boat* in subject and character. *The Cat and the Fiddle* takes place in Brussels and focuses on an affair between a Rumanian opera composer and an American woman who writes pop tunes. *Music in the Air* focuses on two village musicians in Bavaria whose love for one another and whose musical talent are both put to the test in the big-time professional operetta world of Munich. With such tales of contemporary romance in European settings, these shows resemble certain operettas of a decidedly modern stamp (though Kern still saw them as extensions of *Show Boat*, especially in the search evident in each for "a strong motivation for the music throughout").

But *Show Boat* was something else entirely. As its focus was dramatic, its billing as "An All-American Musical Comedy" did not do it justice. There simply was no cultural frame of reference at the time adequate to describe the piece. Its book could have been considered all-American as it encompassed a saga of three generations and five couples whose lives intersect on a floating theater on the Mississippi River. And its score was surely all-American, evoking a panorama of vernacular music in the United States from nineteenth-century minstrel shows to 1920s jazz. Yet *Show Boat* was less a musical comedy than a musical melodrama, something closer perhaps to a Broadway operetta—only one that drew deeply from the wellsprings of Broadway, on the one hand, and operetta, on the other, to transcend what till then had been understood as the limitations of both.

Based on Edna Ferber's best-selling novel of the same name, *Show Boat* begins with the arrival of Cap'n Andy's *Cotton Blossom* in Natchez in the 1880s. Wherever it docks up and down the Mississippi River, the *Cotton Blossom* offers plays onboard to entertain the townsfolk. But here the leading lady Julie La Verne (Helen Morgan) is exposed as being a light-skinned black, and as she is married to leading man Steve Baker, who is white, the couple faces arrest for consummating a mixed-race marriage, which is against the law in Mississippi. Rather than bring trouble by their continued presence on the *Cotton Blossom*, the two leading players of the troupe leave the company. They are replaced by Cap'n Andy's daughter Magnolia (Norma Terris) and a local riverboat gambler with whom she is smitten, Gaylord Ravenal (Howard Marsh). Magnolia and Gaylord eventually marry, leave the show boat, and settle in Chicago in time for the 1893 World's Fair. Yet Gaylord loses all his money gambling and, unable any longer to support his wife and daughter Kim, he deserts them in desperation. Magnolia succeeds in making her way on her own as an entertainer; and in time, Kim follows in her mother's footsteps. At the end, a chance meeting in the 1920s between Magnolia's father and Gaylord leads to a bittersweet reconciliation between the couple back in Natchez, on the deck of the *Cotton Blossom* where they first met.

Ferber's was a sober and sprawling work; Hammerstein adapted it for the stage by drastically lightening and compressing it. (Ravenal, for example, remains alive for the reconciliation at the end although he dies in the course of the novel.) The result was still uncommonly serious for a Broadway show of the period and, in the words of one reviewer, "crammed with plot." Hammerstein's adaptation bucked the prevailing practice of book writers, who created original scripts for shows or adapted lighter plays for musicalization. Some critics praised Hammerstein simply for sticking to his original source "with a fidelity unrecognized by most musical-comedy bookmakers," and "with a care seldom to be found [even] in straight dramatizations of literary works." But few critics recognized the purpose of such fidelity, though one of them noted that the liberties taken in the musical did not "twist the [original] tale nor distort its values." Indeed, the young librettist, working on his own for the first time, sought to create a new paradigm with *Show Boat*—one that might bring to the Broadway medium something of the thematic scope and narrative

Original *Show Boat* program with caricatures of all nine principal performers but only one name repeatedly featured: Ziegfeld's.

authority generally associated with the legitimate theater rather than the popular musical one.

Hammerstein did not always succeed. He raised key issues in the first act of *Show Boat*—above all, those dealing with individual responsibility and racial injustice—that he did not resolve in the second. The perennial bugbear of "second-act trouble" hounds *Show Boat* at almost every turn. The score of the second act does not attain the glory of the first. And the second-act book jumps spasmodically between 1893 and 1927, in contrast with the measured narrative of the first act. Years later, Lehman Engel took the libretto further to task: "The characters are two-dimensional, the proportions are outrageous, the plot development is predictable and corny, and the ending is unbearably sweet." But Engel's is the view of a generation already imbued with the values of Hammerstein's subsequent and admittedly finer work. In many respects Hammerstein did succeed with *Show Boat,* and perhaps nowhere better than in giving the libretto more point than that found in any of the more conventional shows of its time. Here was a romantic musical, but one which, even as it entertained, took the bloom off romance: It looked at marriages destroyed by private demons (compulsive gambling) and public ills (institutionalized racism). Most other musicals did not imagine themselves as the sort of venues for doing anything even remotely like it.

Consider *Show Boat*'s act 1 "miscegenation scene." During a rehearsal aboard the *Cotton Blossom,* Steve learns that the sheriff is about to pay the company a visit—and the reason why. Suddenly he takes out a knife. The women scream and Andy tries to intervene. But Steve persists. He cuts open Julie's finger, presses it to his lips, and sucks—then responds when the sheriff comes to arrest the couple:

STEVE BAKER: You wouldn't call a man a white man that's got negro blood in him, would you?
SHERIFF VALLON: No, I wouldn't. Not in Mississippi. One drop of nigger blood makes you a nigger in these parts.
STEVE: Well, I got more than a drop of—nigger blood in me, and that's a fact.
VALLON: You ready to swear to that in a court of law?
STEVE: I'll swear to it any place. . . . I'll do more than that. Look at all these folks here. Every one of them can swear I got nigger blood in me this minute. That's how white I am.

So grand a gesture in the name of love! One might think it sheer operetta-style bravado. Yet it differs from the bravado one finds, say, in *The Desert Song*—especially when in that show the heroine, Margot, points a gun at the outlaw, "Red Shadow," and he, counting on a certain mutual attraction, commands his men not to harm her should she kill him: "There is your pistol—and here is my heart . . ."

The histrionics in *Show Boat* are rather less self-serving. They have a moral resonance. Julie, a mulatto, has accepted an unjust racial norm by trying to "pass" for white. Her husband, Steve, a white man, resists that norm, making mockery of the miscegenation laws that uphold it by willfully becoming—by their own standard—black. Of course, Steve's love for Julie motivates his defiance rather than any desire to take arms against the institutions of bigotry as such. *Show Boat* does not advance an agenda for undoing racism; it shows the cost of racism in human terms. Its various stories thus have an investment simply in exposing the racial inequities that form the backdrop against which they unfold, one particularly meaningful to American audiences. That may be insufficient for certain critics of the piece. But the vividness of that investment gives the *Show Boat* libretto its point; and it gives the show itself its grip.

Kern was more than Hammerstein's partner in the venture. Even the idea to musicalize Ferber's novel seems to have been his, and *Show Boat* resulted in one of his most dramatically apposite scores, even if it lacks his most musically interesting songs. In fact, the range of musical styles in *Show Boat* forms part of a narrative strategy to evoke time passing through America's musical vernaculars, which the sheer sophistication of Kern's late Broadway song style would have undermined ("Smoke Gets in Your Eyes," from *Roberta*; "All the Things You Are," from *Very Warm for May*, his last Broadway show). That range extends from melodies of a bygone era, whether one of Kern's historical pastiches ("Life Upon the Wicked Stage") or an interpolation of a real song from the past ("After the Ball"); through numbers based on the blues ("Can't Help Lovin' Dat Man"), inspired by Tin Pan Alley ("Why Do I Love You?"), and even taken from a Princess show ("Bill"); up to the latest in 1920s pop ("Hey, Feller"). (Many of these numbers are actually performed in the show as songs, that is, diegetically.) Interspersed with these, on the other hand, are the clear musical hallmarks of operetta, especially in numbers for the romantic leads: a full-throated waltz, one transformed not only from a "classical" source (here, *Madama Butterfly*) but also in the manner of *Blossom Time*'s "Song of Love" ("You Are Love"); a wistful ballad, one even with a *Valse lento* middle section as in "The Merry Widow Waltz" ("Make Believe"); and throughout, an underscore of leitmotifs and song-based presentiments and reminiscences that goes far beyond *Rose-Marie* in the richness of its thematic transformations to link the show's numbers both to one another and to the narrative strands of the plot. In sum, *Show Boat*'s music combines aspects of musical comedy and operetta—even vaudeville and opera—in songs that tend to have an emotional and dramatic rightness about them as they coalesce into a score.

Perhaps the best example of the distinctive tone of that score is "Ol' Man River." For all its emotional pull this is not a love song, but rather a comment from both inside and outside the action sung by the black stevedore Joe (Jules Bledsoe, later Paul Robeson)—a work song with the dignity and power of a spiritual. (Ferber became teary-eyed when she first heard it.) Unlike most songs in the show, its thrust is also thematic: It views the fate of *Show Boat*'s characters in terms of the implacable force of nature that is the Mississippi River. And like the river itself in the story, the song engulfs the score, gathering in intensity as it moves from its first hint in the opening chorus of black dock workers loading bales of "cotton blossom" (Ex. 5-1a) to its soaring reprise at the close as Magnolia and Gaylord reunite on the *Cotton Blossom* at the same dock almost half a century later, the latter a slower, rising transformation of the former (Ex. 5-1b).

"Ol' Man River" has too much heft for a popular song. It is also musically too demanding, calling for sustained power over a wide vocal range. Yet in its simple accompaniment and pentatonic melody it avoids the rhetoric of operetta: It suggests grandeur without being grandiose. That is part of the secret of the song's success and, more generally, of Kern's musical achievement in the theater. He brought the involved styles and procedures of European light stage music into the

Ex. 5-1a. Jerome Kern, music, Oscar Hammerstein II, lyrics: "Cotton Blossom," *Show Boat*; **Ex. 5-1b.** Jerome Kern, music, Oscar Hammerstein II, lyrics: "Ol' Man River" (transposed), *Show Boat*

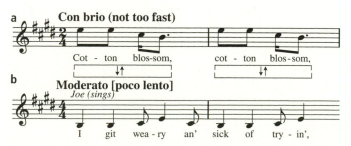

orbit of American popular song in such a way as to make them accessible to a wider audience than the one which traditionally responded to the music of Herbert, Friml, and Romberg. This fit well with Hammerstein's "operatic" approach to musical comedy. Surprisingly, it also suited the plans of a showman like Florenz Ziegfeld, who, turning his energies from revues to operettas like *Rio Rita, Rosalie*, and *The Three Musketeers*, recognized in *Show Boat* "the opportunity of my life" and successfully piloted the work to Broadway in December 1927.

The story of *Show Boat* does not end with its opening night in New York. *Show Boat* has had an extraordinary reception history and surely the longest ongoing one in the history of Broadway musicals. It is the earliest musical still regularly dusted off and performed in venues great and small across the nation. And it has enjoyed major new Broadway productions in almost every decade since its premiere (1932, Producer: Ziegfeld; 1946, Kern and Hammerstein II; 1966, Richard Rodgers; 1983, Houston Grand Opera; 1994, Livent, U.S.). It has also been altered significantly with each revival. For *Show Boat* may have originally sought to shape itself as a show organically from within, but there was not the sense about the piece (as there would be with Hammerstein's shows with Rodgers) that the form in which it first reached Broadway was somehow written in stone. On the contrary, many of *Show Boat*'s post-1927 changes, some substantial, were the handiwork of the very men who had first created the show. Arguably, such changes represent concessions by the authors rather than their intentions: They were undertaken to accommodate the needs of new performers (1928 London production), a new medium (1936 film version), new stage technologies (1946 Broadway revival). Yet given the commercial constraints of the show business that was Hammerstein's and Kern's métier, it is likely that only under the pressure of having to make such concessions in the first place would they have allowed themselves the liberty to rethink their material in ways not any less inspired than when they first broached it, or possibly with new aesthetic vistas in mind: in 1936, closer fidelity to Ferber's novel; in 1946, a post-*Carousel* ideal of the musical play. Nor, when the original creators were no longer there to exercise authorial oversight, would others hesitate to subject *Show Boat* to changes of their own—to suit later racial sensibilities (1966, Lincoln Center) and later concept-based visions of musical theater (1994, Broadway).

Miles Kreuger puts it bluntly: "The history of the American Musical Theatre, quite simply, is divided into two eras: everything before *Show Boat*, and everything after *Show Boat.*" Yet those who have chosen to configure Broadway history accordingly have not always made clear why. And those who have tried to explain it have not always given the same reasons for doing so. To some, *Show Boat* marks a turning point in the development of the Broadway musical for reasons internal to the medium: it represents the first generally successful blend of the elements of musical comedy and operetta—"the two basic forms of the American musical coaxed into one form." To others, *Show Boat* marks the Broadway musical's first bid for a legitimacy that could only come from outside the medium: both from the wider perspective of literate thought—"the first American musical that integrates the elements of a musical theater into a credible drama"—and from the broader world of social concern—"a Broadway musical [that] . . . could deal with serious issues in a suitably mature fashion." Whatever the reasons given, perhaps the most basic one came from an opening-night reviewer whose words mark a noticeable change in discourse concerning the very nature of Broadway musicals. *Show Boat*, he wrote, suggested "the tremendous possibilities of the musical comedy as an art form."

Musicals of the 1920s by and large did not share *Show Boat*'s high-mindedness. In fact, without someone like Ziegfeld at the helm to rattle the idealism of his collaborators, *Show Boat* might have failed. It succeeded, of course. But it had few predecessors to draw on and few immediate progeny to help spread the word. Broadway shows of the period were generally better characterized by their low-mindedness—Ziegfeld's included. And one can gain perhaps no clearer perspective on *Show Boat*'s accomplishment than by viewing it in the context of the many musicals produced and consumed that were more nearly representative of the pulse of Broadway at the time—now referred to as the Jazz Age.

GAY PAREE

6

A SHADOW OF VULGARITY

ZIEGFELD FOLLIES OF 1919
(6/16/1919–12/6/1919). **Producer:** Florenz Ziegfeld, Jr. **Sketches:** Dave Stamper, Gene Buck, and Rennold Wolf. **Songs:** Irving Berlin, Joseph McCarthy, and Harry Tierney, Buck and Stamper, and others. **Additional Music:** Victor Herbert. **Director:** Ned Wayburn. **New York Run:** 171 performances. **Cast:** Marilyn Miller, Eddie Cantor, Bert Williams. **Songs:** "You'd Be Surprised," "Mandy," "A Pretty Girl Is Like a Melody."

SHUFFLE ALONG
(5/23/1921–7/15/1922). **Producer:** Nikko Producing Company [John Cort, Al Mayer]. **Book:** Flournoy Miller and Aubrey Lyles. **Lyrics:** Noble Sissle. **Music:** Eubie Blake. **Director:** Walter Brooks. **New York Run:** 504 performances. **Cast:** Gertrude Saunders, Miller, Lyles, Sissle, Blake. **Songs:** "I'm Just Wild About Harry," "Love Will Find a Way," "If You've Never Been Vamped by a Brown Skin (You've Never Been Vamped At All)."

NO, NO, NANETTE
(9/16/1925–6/19/1926). **Producer:** Harry H. Frazee. **Book:** Otto Harbach and Frank Mandel, based on the play *My Lady Friends* by Mandel and Emil Nyitray. **Lyrics:** Irving Caesar and Harbach. **Music:** Vincent Youmans. **Director:** [Edward Royce] Frazee. **New York Run:** 321 performances. **Cast:** Louise Groody, Charles Winninger. **Songs:** "I Want to Be Happy," "Tea for Two."

Chorus girls flesh out the ribs of an "exotic fan" in the 1926 Shubert brothers revue *Gay Paree*.

GOOD NEWS

(9/6/1927–ca. 12/1928). **Producers:** Laurence Schwab and Mandel. **Book:** Schwab and B. G. DeSylva. **Lyrics:** DeSylva and Lew Brown. **Music:** Ray Henderson. **Director:** Edgar MacGregor. **New York Run:** 551 performances. **Cast:** Mary Lawlor, John Price Jones. **Songs:** "The Best Things in Life Are Free," "The Varsity Drag."

BLACKBIRDS OF 1928

(5/9/1928–ca. 8/1929). **Producer and Director:** Lew Leslie. **Sketches:** Leslie? **Lyrics:** Dorothy Fields. **Music:** Jimmy McHugh. **New York Run:** 518 performances. **Cast:** Adelaide Hall, Aida Ward, Bill "Bojangles" Robinson. **Songs:** "I Can't Give You Anything but Love," "Diga Diga Doo," "Doin' the New Low Down."

THE BAND WAGON

(6/3/1931–1/16/1932). **Producer:** Max Gordon. **Sketches:** George S. Kaufman and Howard Dietz. **Lyrics:** Dietz. **Music:** Arthur Schwartz. **Director:** Hassard Short. **New York Run:** 260 performances. **Cast:** Adele Astaire, Helen Broderick, Fred Astaire, Frank Morgan. **Songs:** "Dancing in the Dark," "I Love Louisa," "New Sun in the Sky."

AS THOUSANDS CHEER

(9/30/1933–9/18/1934). **Producers:** Sam H. Harris and Irving Berlin. **Sketches:** Moss Hart. **Lyrics and Music:** Berlin. **Director:** Short. **New York Run:** 400 performances. **Cast:** Marilyn Miller, Broderick, Ethel Waters, Clifton Webb. **Songs:** "Heat Wave," "Easter Parade," "Supper Time."

The term "Jazz Age" refers to the decade or so after the First World War, in which American culture underwent a seismic shift as it came to terms with the implications of modernity—and, through modernity, with itself. F. Scott Fitzgerald, the novelist who coined the term with the title to a book of short stories published in 1922, also wrote its postmortem a decade later in an essay, "Echoes of the Jazz Age." For Fitzgerald, the age began in a symbolic political moment: the May Day riots and Red Scare of 1919; and it ended similarly in an economic one: the stock market crash of October 1929. Yet the political conservatism that passed for what President Warren Harding called normalcy and the economic boom whose rashness ultimately precipitated the crash were present more or less throughout the Jazz Age. Both were essential in shaping its character from start to finish. So, too, was its cultural élan.

The United States emerged from the Great War preeminent among the Western powers, largely unscathed by the kind of spiritual exhaustion and depletion of physical resources that had devastated Europe. On the contrary, Fitzgerald wrote, "something had to be done with all the nervous energy stored up and unexpended in the War. . . . We were the most powerful nation. Who could tell us any longer what was fashionable and what was fun?" The very Europeans who had made a point of telling Americans what was fashionable in the past, in fact, now often looked to America as a source of cultural freshness and innovation. When Harold Loeb, an American magazine editor and friend of Ernest Hemingway's, went to Europe in the 1920s to gather contributions from foreign writers about the artistic conditions in each of their own cultures, he found they only wanted to talk about "New York," "skyscrapers," "advertising," "movies," and "jazz."

Jazz indeed held its own among the popular arts that contributed to the astonishing vitality of American culture during the 1920s. Yet it posed a greater challenge to long-held beliefs about the very nature of culture than the rest. A new, frenetic type of popular music—"ragtime gone daffy"—jazz emerged largely out of the experience of African Americans around the turn of the century. It even retained certain African traits as it negotiated its way into American culture back and forth across the color line. Many on both sides of the line heard the music as primitive, both in what it expressed and in how it expressed it. Furthermore, middle-class listeners, black and white, objected to the music on moral grounds. The mother of black pianist-composer Eubie Blake, for example, would not allow him to play ragtime in the house; nor to the end of his days would he allow himself to utter the word "jazz." For jazz represented "devil's music": It corrupted body and soul. "Hot" or "sweet," jazz exuded an unbridled eroticism—the very meaning of the term likely rooted in sex, understood as a transitive verb. Not simply because of its popularity was this music vulgar, but also because, as John Philip Sousa put it, it "excited the baser instincts." Commonly performed in brothels, speakeasies, dance halls, and other locales of dubious repute, the music itself picked up the taint of sex for hire, illegal booze and drugs, and criminal elements generally. Jazz came to symbolize the undoing of puritanical conventions, a potent force in the postwar breakdown of idealism and traditional values in American life. More than the music itself, "jazz" encapsulated the outright hedonism of the age. "The word jazz in its progress toward respectability," Fitzgerald explained, "has meant first sex, then dancing, then music."

Few American intellectuals of the 1920s took jazz or any of the popular arts of the period seriously. Gilbert Seldes did. "The circumstances that our popular arts are home-grown, without the prestige of Europe and of the past," he wrote, has "thrown upon them a shadow of vulgarity, as if they were the products of ignorance and intellectual bad manners." In 1924, he published *The 7 Lively Arts*, a pathbreaking collection of essays in which he hoped to dispel that shadow by countering the genteel tradition in American letters and suggesting a new way of thinking about "the vulgar arts." By "lively" arts—of which there were more than seven—he meant those "minor arts" invested with the vigor of vernacular traditions whose most characteristic stance was "high levity" rather than the "high seriousness" traditionally associated with "the great arts." "My theme was," Seldes summarized,

> that entertainment of a high order existed in places not usually associated with Art, that the place where an object was to be seen or heard had no bearing on its merits, that some of Jerome Kern's songs in the Princess shows were lovelier than any number of operatic airs and that

a comic strip printed on newspulp which would tatter and rumple in
a day might be as worthy of a second look as a considerable number of
canvasses at most of our museums.

He even tried to show that the issue of a cultural divide along high-
brow/lowbrow lines which Van Wyck Brooks had described in *Ameri-*
ca's Coming of Age was more nuanced than Brooks and others realized.
He argued that "the minor arts, those frequently called 'lowbrow,' are
not hostile to the major arts"; and that "there exists no such hostility
between two divisions of the arts which are honest—that the real opposition is between [the major and the minor arts] allied, and the polished fake." Such honesty Seldes found everywhere in the minor arts:
in jazz, in slapstick movies, in vaudeville, in popular songs, in cartoon
strips, even in musical comedy. Indeed, while Seldes could not have
foreseen the rise of the new kind of musical comedy that began shortly
after the publication of his book with such shows as *Lady, Be Good!* and
No, No, Nanette, Broadway's musical stage held a particular fascination
for him, as it did for a sizable number of theatergoers and those generally alive to developments in popular culture.

The popular culture of the 1920s overlapped to a large extent with
a developing commodity culture in which "Americans increasingly
defined themselves through items they bought on the market rather
than through inherited or workplace identities." For many, an indulgence in musicals formed part of the new patterns of consumption.
Some bought tickets to the Broadway shows; others, financially better
off, bought the land and built the theaters that housed the shows. Both
bought on an unprecedented scale. Times Square became perhaps the
most flourishing theatrical district in the world, though overextension
would lead to its precipitous collapse by the end of the decade. Close to
eighty legitimate playhouses operated during the era, each averaging
more than two hundred performances a season. Such activity reached
its peak in the 1927–28 theater season with the mounting of over 260
new productions of all kinds. Of these, though the figures vary, about
fifty were musical. Covering a variety of types, the new musical productions included, in opening night order, *Good News, My Maryland, The*
Merry Malones, Manhattan Mary, A Connecticut Yankee, Funny Face, Show
Boat, Rosalie, Rain or Shine, The Three Musketeers, and *Blackbirds of 1928*.
(There were also such holdovers from the previous season as *Scandals*

of 1926, The Desert Song, Peggy-Ann, Rio Rita, and *Hit the Deck.*) Each, moreover, ran on Broadway for at least twice the one hundred performances generally considered a profitable business venture at the time.

Many of these musical productions were operettas; most were musical comedies and revues. The three genres covered the spectrum of Broadway musical entertainment at the highest level of polish, professionalism, and financial risk. And in all three, the impact of the jazz of the age could be felt—even in operetta, where one would least expect it, though as a rule only in the comic or novelty numbers (*The Desert Song*'s "It," *Show Boat*'s "Hey, Feller"). But it left a deeper and more lasting imprint on the revue, which reached its height as a theatrical form during this period and shortly after; and on musical comedy, which now began to take on its characteristic modern shape.

REVUES: SPECTACULAR AND INTIMATE

The revue had virtually all the ingredients of musical comedy but one: plot. It cohered in other ways. A 1914 revue by George M. Cohan called *Hello, Broadway!*, for example, featured a character who appeared at various points during the performance carrying a hatbox that was supposed to contain the show's plot. When, at the end of the evening, he finally opened the box, however, it was empty. "What became of the plot?" he asked, only to receive the reply: "There never was a plot." The device, which became the talk of the theatrical season, reveals a great deal about the nature of the revue—not so much for its obvious lack of a plot but for its capacity to turn that very fact into an element of cohesion.

Commonly said to have begun with *The Passing Show* in 1894, the revue developed as a more sophisticated and unified form of variety. It presented a kaleidoscope of songs, dances, and dialogue sketches, but with the same performers reappearing in different guises throughout. (Vaudeville performers appeared only once on a given bill; revue performers constituted a company of players, each of whom played many parts.) Producers lent revues a further sense of cohesion by stamping their productions with a consistency of style, tone, and pacing: Florenz Ziegfeld's shows exuded elegance and leisure; George White's were quick and energetic.

Stage designers, too, held revues together, albeit by visual means. Hassard Short and Albert Johnson used moving turntables in *The Band Wagon* as a production motif to link the independent numbers; Ziegfeld's "Blue *Follies*" of 1915 was so called because of the dominant color scheme of its memorable decor. Stage design, in fact, became crucial to the enterprise. Musical comedies might get by with only one set per act; revues had to manage many set changes in an act without breaking the flow of a production. (Joseph Urban introduced "in-one" staging, alternating the shallow, "in-one" forestage for small scenes with the depth of the full stage space for spectacle and dance.) Often, stage designers had greater control over productions favoring song and dance than did the directors. For *Jumbo* (1935), a revuelike musical comedy, a credit line read: "Entire Production Staged by John Murray Anderson," even though George Abbott directed the dialogue scenes. Anderson made no bones about the show's priorities, as Richard Rodgers, *Jumbo*'s composer, remembered:

> [*Anderson*] *was primarily concerned with the physical aspects of the production—the scenery, lighting and costumes—and didn't really care much about the story or the way the songs fit it. I recall once just before the show's opening when he took me backstage to demonstrate the working of a huge, complicated lighting switchboard. "Each one of the lights is controlled by its own special switch," he explained. "It's all preset. All you have to do is just touch a switch and you get the exactly the lighting effect you want." Then he started to giggle. "See this little yellow one here?" he said, pointing to a tiny toggle switch at the far right of the board. "Do you know what that's for? That's for the book."*

In the absence of a book, or by downplaying the importance of one, revues tended to look to style as a form of content. Yet some revues sought greater continuity by adopting open-ended themes to link their separate parts: *Watch Your Step* had a tour-of-the-town format; *Hello, Broadway!* burlesqued Broadway hits. Thus the revue had various means for creating a coherent entertainment—only its priorities were production-based and performance-oriented rather than rooted in a script and score.

As a genre, nevertheless, the revue was caught in a structural bind. However appealing each of a show's episodes may have been on its own, it was difficult to sustain any momentum from one to the next, let alone over the length of an evening. Despite consistencies of style, staging, or theme, nothing like the storytelling trajectory of a book held things together and kept them moving forward as it did in a musical comedy. Howard Dietz, who regularly supplied revues with both lyrics and sketches, remarked on the qualitative difference in writing for the two genres:

> *Revues are difficult to do. Each scene starts from scratch and too much talent is required. The song score in a show with a plot has a thread to hold it together and the plot itself provides cues of a sentimental or comic nature; the simple declarative love song can be reprised with telling effect, whereas in a revue a reprise is just a repetition.*

This was one of the reasons for musical comedy's eclipse of the revue in the 1930s, and for Dietz as well as most of the major writers of revue material eventually to turn to plot-based musical shows.

Revues in the period between the two world wars basically came in two types. The distinction was more qualitative than quantitative: not big and small so much as what critics generally described as spectacular, on the one hand, and intimate, on the other. The spectacular revue appeared first and its heyday lasted from just before the First World War to the early years of the Depression. During this time such revues competed successfully with the nascent musical comedy form. (What they lacked in the plots that musical comedies had they made up for in other ways—especially in one ingredient that musical comedies lacked: female nudity, or its semblance.) The most durable spectacular revues reappeared annually in new editions that were similarly structured but contained new material. Like brand names, the titles of several bore the monikers of their producers as guarantors of quality, or at least stylistic continuity from one edition to the next: *Ziegfeld Follies, George White's Scandals, Earl Carroll Vanities.* Of course, not all revue producers went in for shameless self-promotion—for example, *The Passing Show* (the Shubert brothers), *Music Box Revue* (Sam Harris and Irving Berlin). But it was indeed an age in which the Broadway producer—the theatrical entrepreneur who had final say over a show not only in matters of finance but of art—was king. And the revue gave him ample opportunity to exercise both functions: As a show of high quality it could command musical comedy prices if marketed properly; as a show whose structure was segmented it required artistic intervention lest it lapse into vaudeville. At bottom, the revue may have been no more than a variety show, but it was upscale variety, shorn of the democracy of spirit implicit in vaudeville's something-for-everyone approach. Despite its trafficking in female nudity and the perceived moral laxity of the Jazz Age that condoned it, the revue was universally regarded as "high-class vaudeville." And nowhere was its class deemed higher than in the hands of its greatest practitioner, Ziegfeld himself.

The most celebrated musical producer of the age, and perhaps in the history of Broadway, Florenz Ziegfeld, Jr., remains the only Broadway impresario whose life and work both have been made the subjects of major motion pictures: *The Great Ziegfeld* (1936) and *The Ziegfeld Follies* (1946). While he produced memorable book shows (*Sally, Show Boat, Whoopee*) and several sets of revues (*Midnight Frolic, 9 O'Clock Revue*), his reputation rests mainly on twenty-one editions of *Follies*, which he produced between 1907 and 1931. With this legendary series of productions he reinvented the revue and, using it to shape American perceptions of female beauty, made it "a national institution."

At first, Ziegfeld presented a comic survey of a year's events, following the format George Lederer had established in the 1890s and that Weber and Fields later exploited in their own fashion. Ziegfeld called his first show "Follies of 1907" after a newspaper column "Follies of the Day," written by his first sketch writer Harry B. Smith. He may also have meant to evoke the sexual mystique of the Parisian *Folies-Bergère* with his title, for the emphasis of the *Follies* soon shifted toward feminine display. He did not stint on other aspects, however. He employed a greater concentration of comic headliners than could be crammed into any other kind of musical production—in the 1917 edition alone: Fanny Brice, Bert Williams, W. C. Fields, Eddie Cantor, and Will Rogers. Yet he seems to have regarded them as so many foils for the main event. Will Rogers even joked about it: to "all these beautiful girls I am the contrast. Somebody has to do something while [the] girls change clothes even if they don't have much to change."

From 1913 to 1927 the *Follies* played at the sumptuous New Amsterdam Theater on Forty-second Street. During the shows' peak years there (1915–1922), Ziegfeld secured and promoted the talents of two remarkable European artists: Joseph Urban and Lady Duff Gordon. Viennese set designer Joseph Urban (1872–1933) introduced Broadway to the "New Stagecraft" of European modernism. English costumier Lady Duff Gordon, aka "Lucile" (1863–1935), introducing live mannequins as models in her own fashion salon, inspired Ziegfeld to transform his chorus girls into "showgirls." The Ziegfeld Girl that resulted neither sang nor danced. She simply looked beautiful. She also wore beautiful clothes and moved even more beautifully as she paraded with utmost elegance to the Ziegfeld Walk, floating down staircases and ramps. No longer a chorus girl, the Ziegfeld Girl became an object of glamour: visible; desirable; and, above all, inaccessible. Irving Berlin captured her elusiveness when for the 1919 edition, often considered the pinnacle of the series, he created the song that became her anthem: "A Pretty Girl Is Like a Melody." And for the 1922 edition Ziegfeld created the motto that gave his enterprise its rationale and national resonance: "Glorifying the American Girl."

Today, such glorification appears suspect, the cautionary lessons of feminism having taught us to see public gazing at women's bodies in a different light. Ziegfeld created a "fantasy of American womanhood." As Edmund Wilson understood, the great showman

> *cunningly gauged not just the taste but also the psyche of the American male; Ziegfeld's girls have not only the Anglo-Saxon straightness— straight backs, straight brows, straight noses—but also the peculiar frigidity and purity, the frank high-school-girlishness which Americans like. He does not aim to make them . . . as sexually attractive as possible, as the Folies Bergère, for example, does. He appeals to American idealism, and then, when the male is intent on his chaste and dewy-eyed vision, he gratifies him on this plane by discreetly disrobing his goddess.*

Ziegfeld set the pace in the spectacular revue, especially in its focus on the draped and undraped female figure. Other producers sought to follow his example. The Shubert brothers mounted *The Passing Show* (twelve editions: 1912–1924) at the Winter Garden Theater to rival the *Follies*. But lacking Ziegfeld's taste and polish, they succeeded more in commercial terms than artistic ones. The Winter Garden itself had one feature, however, that distinguished their shows from the rest: a runway projecting from the stage over the orchestra pit on which "the

Dolores, surnameless supermodel (originally named Kathleen Mary Rose), struts her stuff
as the White Peacock in Ziegfeld's 1919 *Midnight Frolic*.

girls," lightly clad, would walk out into the audience. "The girls come
absolutely within your grasp," wrote one critic of a Winter Garden
production. "You could stretch forth your hand and seize 'em. Troops
of 'em, bevies of 'em, galaxies of 'em, hordes of 'em, masses come pranc-
ing across a sort of peninsula separating stage from auditorium. They
wore full evening dress modern style and slowly crossed the auditorium so you could see how full the evening dress—wasn't."

Earl Carroll (1893–1948) came perhaps closest to Ziegfeld in emphasizing male comedians and female nudity in his *Vanities* (eleven editions: 1923–1940). But he lacked Ziegfeld's class. The *Vanities* were among the bawdier of revues, featuring bananas, as burlesque comedians were called, and strippers. Carroll hired such top bananas as Joe Cook, Jimmy Savo, Jack Benny, and Milton Berle. But he seemed to have only one use for women. "Girls are a commodity the same as bananas, pork chops, or a lot in a suburban development," he once confessed, then topped himself: "They are the most fundamental of all commodities." Yet Carroll may have been outdone in vulgarity by the Shuberts, who, in another series of revues, *Artists and Models* (five editions: 1923–1930), exposed low comedy and female flesh to the limit of the law—and perhaps beyond.

George White (1890–1968) sought a greater sense of balance between "the girls" and the snappy energy and drive of 1920s dance and song in his *Scandals* (thirteen editions: 1919–1939). A former Ziegfeld hoofer himself, White left the *Follies* to stage, choreograph, and dance in his own shows. He recruited such sterling dancers as Ann Pennington, Eleanor Powell, and Ann Miller, and such top-notch singers as Harry Richman, Rudy Vallee, and Ethel Merman. He also featured the early work of such musicians as George Gershwin ("I'll Build a Stairway to Paradise," "Somebody Loves Me") and first brought the combined songwriting talents of Bud DeSylva, Lew Brown, and Ray Henderson to Broadway. The trio came up with one of the finest revue scores for the 1926 *Scandals*, in which Richman sang "Lucky Day" and Pennington introduced "Black Bottom," the dance that would outdo all others in Jazz Age popularity but the Charleston.

The *Music Box Revues* (four editions: 1921–1924) of Sam Harris and Irving Berlin were neither skin shows nor as long-lived as the others. But they were long on high-quality entertainment. Named after the thousand-seat theater that Harris and Berlin built to house them, these revues introduced the inventive staging of Hassard Short (1877–1956) to Broadway. They were also showcases for some of the finest songs of Berlin himself ("Say It with Music," "All Alone") and for the unusually clever sketches of several members of the Algonquin Hotel's notorious "Round Table," such as Robert Benchley ("The Treasurer's Report") and George S. Kaufman ("If Men Played Cards as Women Do").

In these respects, the *Music Box Revues* appear (in hindsight) as fore-

runners of the second type of revue—along with *André Charlot's Revues,*
The Garrick Gaieties, and several others. Such revues would play a more
central role on Broadway during the Great Depression, when Hollywood appropriated the spectacular revue in ways with which Broadway could not compete. Musical films, which were now equipped with
synchronized sound, presented grander spectacle, in more far-reaching
venues, and at lower prices. By contrast, Broadway revues of the newer
type were commonly described as "intimate." Often they were indeed
"little" shows that made a point of their modesty in reaction to the
all-that-money-can-buy spirit of the *Follies.* Yet others of the type had
fairly large casts and elaborate production values. Regardless of size,
intimate revues distinguished themselves as such through an aura of
connoisseurship. They addressed themselves to a more select audience,
eliminating or downplaying spectacle and flesh to concentrate on songs
of greater sophistication and sketches of more pointed humor than
before. Instead of annual editions, moreover, intimate revues tended to
appear as one-of-a-kind productions. Some of the most memorable of
these included *The Little Show* (1929), *Three's a Crowd* (1930), five separate Shubert productions at the Winter Garden—including *Life Begins
at 8:40* (1934), *At Home Abroad* (1935), and *The Show Is On* (1936)—and
the two most celebrated shows of the type *The Band Wagon* (1931) and
As Thousands Cheer (1933).

The Band Wagon (not to be confused with the 1953 MGM film,
which borrowed the title and some songs) left its mark on Broadway
history with its innovative approach to stage design. Lights from the
balcony replaced footlights, mirrors tilted on the stage, turntables set
the stage itself a-spinning. Audiences recognized the achievement from
the start, as producer Max Gordon wrote of reactions to the show's
pre-Broadway opening in Philadelphia:

> *Shouts of "Bravo" and "Encore" reverberated through the old Garrick*
> *[Theater]. Even the revolving stages won their own cheers, as they*
> *deserved. [Director Hassard] Short and [set designer Albert] John-*
> *son had integrated them into the action in all sorts of imaginative ways*
> *until they seemed to create a poetry of their own. In the [act 1] finale*
> *they turned in opposite directions, one of them bearing a carousel, while*
> *on the other the Astaires danced as they had never danced before, and*
> *the orchestra played that contagious polka, "I Love Louisa."*

Adele (1897–1981) and Fred (1899–1987) Astaire dominated the proceedings. A brother-and-sister team who had sung and danced together since their childhood days in vaudeville, the two performed separately or as a pair in most of *Band Wagon*'s musical numbers, and even in some nonmusical ones. (The show marked their last Broadway musical together: Adele married and retired from the stage; Fred went on by himself and with new partners, first on Broadway, then to more lasting acclaim in films.) Other *Band Wagon* stars included ballerina Tilly Losch (1907–1975) and comedians Helen Broderick (1891–1959) and Frank Morgan (1890–1949). Comedians, in fact, were central to the undertaking. Today, when revues amount to little more than staged portfolios of songs, it is important to remember the contributions comedians made to such shows in their heyday. If *Band Wagon* can be taken as representative, the spoken numbers that featured their work

The stars of *The Band Wagon* in the act 1 finale, l. to r.: Tillie Losch, Fred Astaire, Adele Astaire, Frank Morgan, and Helen Broderick.

took up about one-third of a revue's total running time, as the ratio of time spent on musical numbers (songs, dances, etc.) to time spent on nonmusical ones (sketches, monologues, etc.) hovered around 2:1.

The Band Wagon: Program with Running Times

5 minutes   Overture: Orchestra

ACT I (ca. 1 hour, 15 minutes):

6½   1. *Opening*, "As Others See Us"/"It Better Be Good": Company

5   2. *Song and Dance*, "Sweet Music": Fred and Adele Astaire

4¾   3. *Song and Dance*, "High and Low": John Barker, Roberta Robinson, Female Chorus

7   4. *Sketch*, "When the Rain Goes Pitter-Patter": Helen Broderick, Frank Morgan

3   5. *Ballet*, "The Flag": Tilly Losch

6¾   6. *Sketch*, "For Good Old Nectar": (with the Astaires)

4   7. *Comic Song*, "A Nice Place to Visit": Broderick

5½   8. *Song*, "Hoops": Fred and Adele Astaire

5   9. *Song and Dance*, "Confession": Chorus

10½ 10. *Sketch*, "Pride of the Claghornes": (with the Astaires)

3½   11. *Song and Dance*, "New Sun in the Sky": Fred Astaire

8   12. *Song and Monologue*, "Miserable with You": Adele Astaire, Morgan

4   13. *Song and Dance*, "I Love Louisa": Fred and Adele Astaire, Company

INTERMISSION (12 minutes)

2 minutes   Entr'acte: Orchestra

ACT II (ca. 1 hour):

1¼   1. *Sketch and Reprise*, "Again!"/"High and Low"

7   2. *Song and Ballet*, "Dancing in the Dark": Barker, Losch, Female Chorus

3   3. *Comic Song* (Quartet), "Nanette": Morgan

5½   4. *Sketch*, "The Great Warburton Mystery": (with Adele Astaire)

4   5. *Comic Song*, "Where Can He Be?": Broderick, Male Chorus

7½   6. *Ballet*, "The Beggar Waltz": Fred Astaire, Losch

6½   7. *Monologue*, "P.S.": Morgan

5   8. *Song and Dance*, "White Heat": Fred and Adele Astaire, Chorus

9½   9. *Sketch*, "Pour le Bain": (with Fred Astaire)

6   10. *Finale*: 5 Stars, Company

A single team of songwriters wrote all of *Band Wagon*'s musical numbers: lyricist Howard Dietz (1896–1983) and composer Arthur Schwartz (1900–1984). The two were the most accomplished song-writers to make their joint reputation by writing consistently for revues. Between 1929 and 1948 they wrote songs for close to a dozen such shows, including *The Little Show, Three's a Crowd, Flying Colors* (1932), *At Home Abroad*, and *Inside U.S.A.* (1948). For *The Band Wagon* they created arguably the finest revue score of the era, and in "New Sun in the Sky" one of its finest numbers. Sung and danced by Fred Astaire, the song exhibits the kind of optimism musicals cultivated during the Depression. It celebrates a newfound love, which so colors the singer's world as to make everything else in it seem new as well. That goes for new sounds, too—including such legacies of the Jazz Age as the $C^{\sharp 9}$ chord under the "new *sun*" at the start (Ex. 6-1a) and the $B^{\flat 9}$ chord at the "new *love*" of the finish (Ex. 6-1b)—both new takes on the same "blue" note ($G^{\sharp}/A^{\flat}$) in the key of F Major.

Additionally, all the sketches in the show were created by a single team of scriptwriters: Dietz and playwright George S. Kaufman (1889–1961). The consistency gave *Band Wagon* a unified tone and point of view. "No devastating wisecracks, no smutty jokes, no heavy-handed gags, and no laboriously assembled jests," wrote Brooks Atkinson of their work in the *New York Times*, "the satire is adroit, informed, and intelligent. You need not check your brains with your hat." Brains, how-ever, were only one of the anatomical parts with which the show was concerned. In one sketch, "The Pride of the Claghornes," an upstand-ing family of the Old South called off the wedding plans for their son when they learned, to their horror, that the girl he was about to marry was still a virgin. In another, "The Great Warburton Mystery," a police inspector proposed a new method of crime detection as he spoke to the guests assembled in the library of a mansion:

Ex. 6-1a. Arthur Schwartz, music, Howard Dietz, lyrics: "New Sun in the Sky" mm. 1–4, *The Band Wagon*

Ex. 6-1b. "New Sun in the Sky" mm. 29–32

INSPECTOR CARTWRIGHT: Ladies and gentlemen, no one has left this house since the murder was committed. I regret very much to inform you that the guilty person is in this room. . . . The man or woman who killed Hugh Warburton sat in this chair. No two people in the world, upon sitting in a chair, leave exactly the same impression. . . . Find the person who fits that cushion, and you will have the murderer of Hugh Warburton. . . . And now with your kind permission, ladies and gentlemen, we will proceed with the examination.

Like *The Band Wagon*, *As Thousands Cheer* sustained a unified style and point of view: Its sketches were all written by Moss Hart and all its songs by Irving Berlin. The show went beyond *Band Wagon*, however, in its search for cohesion: It invented a theme to link its sundry parts.

Taking its cue from the form and content of a newspaper, *As Thousands Cheer* played as a kind of newspaper come to life. It took current events of 1933, turned them into staged vignettes, and identified them for audiences by means of headlines. The following program illustrates, headline by headline, how each vignette functioned both as a self-contained number and as a thematic link to the rest of the revue. The stars include Ziegfeld song-and-dance protégée Marilyn Miller (1898–1936), African American singer Ethel Waters (1896–1977), deadpan comedienne Helen Broderick, and comic song-and-dance man Clifton Webb (1891–1966).

As Thousands Cheer: Program

ACT I:

1. MAN BITES DOG
>   *Opening Scene—Sketch and Chorus*: Leslie Adams, Helen Broderick, Company

2. FRANKLIN D. ROOSEVELT INAUGURATED TOMORROW
>   *Sketch*: Adams, Broderick

3. BARBARA HUTTON TO WED PRINCE MDIVANI
>   *Song*, "How's Chances?": Marilyn Miller, Clifton Webb

4. HEAT WAVE HITS NEW YORK
>   *Song and Dance*, "Heat Wave": Ethel Waters, Letitia Ide, José Limón, Charles Weidman Dancers

5. JOAN CRAWFORD TO DIVORCE DOUGLAS FAIRBANKS, JR.
>   *Sketch*: Miller, Webb, Adams

6. *MAJESTIC* SAILS AT MIDNIGHT
>   *Double Song*, "Debts"/"When the Dollar Goes to Hell": Adams, Hal Forde

7. LONELY-HEART COLUMN
>   *Song and Dance*, "Lonely Heart": Harry Stockwell, Ide, Limón, Dancers

8. WORLD'S WEALTHIEST MAN CELEBRATES 94TH BIRTHDAY
>   *Sketch*: Webb, Adams, Broderick

9. THE FUNNIES
>   *Song*, "I Couldn't Do Without the Funnies": Miller

10. "GREEN PASTURES" STARTS THIRD ROAD SEASON
>   *Scene—Sketch and Song*, "To Be or Not to Be": Waters, Hamtree Harrington

The stars of *As Thousands Cheer* in the act 1 finale, l. to r.: Marilyn Miller, Clifton Webb, and Helen Broderick.

11. ROTOGRAVURE SECTION—EASTER PARADE ON FIFTH AVENUE—1883
   Song and Dance, "Easter Parade": Miller, Webb, Company

ACT 2:
1. METROPOLITAN OPERA OPENS IN OLD-TIME SPLENDOR
   Opening Scene—Chorus and Sketch: Webb, Broderick, Miller, Adams, Company
2. UNKNOWN NEGRO LYNCHED BY FRENZIED MOB
   Song, "Supper Time": Waters
3. GANDHI STARTS NEW HUNGER STRIKE
   Sketch: Webb, Broderick
4. REVOLT IN CUBA
   Dance: Ide, Limón, Dancers
5. NOËL COWARD, NOTED PLAYWRIGHT, LEAVES FOR ENGLAND
   Sketch: Broderick, Waters, Miller, Webb

6. SOCIETY WEDDING OF THE SEASON
> *Song,* "Our Wedding Day": Miller, Webb, Company

7. ROYAL ENGAGEMENT RUMORED
> *Sketch:* Adams, Broderick, Forde, Thomas Hamilton

8. JOSEPHINE BAKER STILL THE RAGE OF PARIS
> *Scene—Sketch and Song,* "Harlem on My Mind": Waters

9. SUPREME COURT HANDS DOWN IMPORTANT DECISION
> *Finale*—Reprise, "Easter Parade": Adams
> Reprise, "Heat Wave": Waters
> Reprise, "When the Dollar Goes to Hell": Broderick
> Reprise, "How's Chances?": Miller, Webb
> *Song,* "Not for All the Rice in China": Miller, Webb, Company

Other revues, too, used themes sufficiently broad in scope to leave room for variety, yet narrow enough to give a show focus. *At Home Abroad* tied its episodes thematically to a cruise around the world; *The Show Is On* took different looks at the world of show business. But while these revues enjoyed considerable runs, such themes were no guarantee of a show's success. As ever, whether spectacular or intimate, the essential difficulty of the revue remained: to find, as Noël Coward said, "the right running order."

MUSICAL COMEDY/MUSICAL FARCE COMEDY

In theory, a musical comedy is a revue in which the "right running order" is governed by a plot. In practice, however, the principle was honored as often in the breach as in the observance. Consider a musical comedy like *Sunny,* for example, the first of the Kern-Hammerstein collaborations. Hammerstein recalled:

> *Our job was to tell a story with a cast that had been assembled as if for a revue. Charles Dillingham, the producer, had signed Cliff Edwards, who sang songs and played the ukulele and was known as Ukelele Ike. His contract required that he do his specialty between ten o'clock and ten-fifteen! So we had to construct our story in such a way that Ukelele Ike could come out and perform during that time and still not interfere with the continuity.*

Other performers required similar appeasements, including of course Marilyn Miller, the violently temperamental star for whom the show was created as a vehicle. In the end, *Sunny* proved to be a popular success, but not as the kind of plot-driven musical comedy toward which Kern had once worked in collaboration with Bolton and Wodehouse.

A decade after the Princess shows, New York audiences flocked to the musical comedies of an altogether different triumvirate: DeSylva, Brown, and Henderson. Librettist-lyricist George Gard "Bud" DeSylva (1895–1950), lyricist Lew Brown (1893–1958), and composer Ray Henderson (1896–1970) first collaborated on songs for the 1925 edition of *George White's Scandals*, then went on as a trio to write for several later editions. Their partnership lasted five years, during which they also collaborated on five book shows that constituted the most consistent string of long-running musical comedy hits of any Broadway writers of the 1920s (no small feat in light of the output of such contemporaries as the Gershwin brothers, Richard Rodgers and Lorenz Hart, and Vincent Youmans and Irving Caesar). The most popular of the DeSylva-Brown-Henderson shows included *Good News* (1927), *Hold Everything* (1928), *Follow Thru* (1929), and *Flying High* (1930).

The trio specialized in novelty ballads ("The Birth of the Blues," "You're the Cream in My Coffee") and peppy dance tunes ("The Varsity Drag," "Button Up Your Overcoat"). If such songs did not have much to say, they said what they said simply and so often that even the least attentive listeners became convinced of their rightness.

> *Oh boy! I'm lucky,*
> *I'll say I'm lucky,*
> *This is my lucky day.*

"Lucky Day" (*George White's Scandals of 1926*)

When not inserted into revues, such songs regularly found their way into topical farces whose themes capitalized on the public infatuation with sports and derring-do so characteristic of the 1920s: college football in *Good News*, prize fighting in *Hold Everything*, championship golf in *Follow Thru*, aviation in *Flying High*.

More than being literally in tune with the times, the three understood perhaps better than any showwriters of the 1920s the nature of their own limitations and those of the audiences they were writing for. Laurence Schwab, one of DeSylva's co-librettists, wrote, "Always remember that musical comedy is the entertainment for the masses. It should not be too dignified." Schwab's own librettos met the standard. Their plots involved silly blends of physical high jinks and romantic contrivance: *Good News* centered on the star player at football-mad Tait College, who needed to pass an astronomy class in order to play in the big game, and who fell in love with his tutor; *Follow Thru* centered on two lady golfers competing for a country club women's golf championship, and for the same man. But plots hardly constituted the essence of the genre. "The story is the least important part of the librettist's work," claimed Herbert Fields, another musical comedy book writer. "Rather, his work is so to handle his story that its freshness and adroitness will serve as a thin network over which to spread the laughs."

Comedy of a not too dignified kind lay at the heart of such shows, and smart librettists took pains to match their sense of humor with that of the comedians they wrote for. Much of DeSylva, Brown, and Henderson's success came from the opportunities their books provided for the antics of the great stage clowns with whom they worked: Ed Wynn (1886–1966) in *Manhattan Mary* (1927), Victor Moore (1876–1962) in *Hold Everything*, Bert Lahr (1895–1967) in *Hold Everything* and *Flying High*, Jimmy Durante (1893–1980) in *Strike Me Pink* (1933, minus DeSylva). A libretto even required a certain negative crafting in order to maintain its background status against the possibility of a comedian doing something in the foreground to tear its storytelling trajectory apart. As newspaper critic Walter Kerr later wrote, "The essential purpose of a musical-comedy book was to be interrupted. Its very quality lay in its interruptability. It wasn't supposed to *do* things, it was supposed to get out of the way of other things." Which things? First, the comedy. Then, the numbers that made the comedy musical.

The "comedy" of musical comedy gravitated toward farce—strictly speaking, not comedy at all. Farce and comedy both amuse, of course, but comedy also aims at more than amusement. Comedy resembles tragedy as a mode of dramatic representation; farce does not. Often, comedies embrace the same themes as tragedies: the passionate pursuit of love, power, wealth, ambition, etc. And, like tragedies, they deal with the conflicts and the costs in human terms of such pursuits—the pain inflicted, the pangs of conscience aroused, the lessons learned. But comedies fundamentally differ from tragedies in how they treat such themes. Comedies, if they succeed, make audiences laugh; tragedies make them feel pity, terror, and (as Aristotle put it) catharsis.

Farces, too, elicit laughter. Farce and comedy even draw from a common pool of situations and devices to drive their plots and make merry: mistaken identity, disguise (cross-dressing preferred), misunderstandings, puns, innuendo, intrigue, ribaldry, chases, doors, closets, slapstick, buffoonery of every kind. Yet comedy uses these as the means to a more reflective end, a deeper understanding of things, a larger meaning. In farce they serve no purpose greater than themselves. Without having to slow down for thought, then, farce often rushes at breakneck speed through a world of suspended morality, an innocent world in which transgressive behavior rules but no one really gets hurt (think of a Marx Brothers movie, for example). "Farce affords an escape from living, a release from the pressures of today, a regression to the irresponsibility of childhood. The comic sense, as against the farcical impulse, tries to deal with living, with the pressures of today, with the responsibilities of adulthood." And so one might consider farce, as L. J. Potts so shrewdly puts it, a

> comedy with the meaning left out; which is as much as to say, with the comedy left out. Cassell's Dictionary defines it as "a short dramatic work in which the action is trivial and the sole purpose is to excite mirth"; and this indicates the main difference between it and comedy, in which the mirth is a means to an end. Thus, though farce is not comedy, comedy can contain farce, just as wine can have bubbles, though effervescence is not a generic quality of wine.

Musical comedy farce drew its greatest strength from the performers who excelled at it. They even conditioned the writing of musical comedy books. As comedian Ethel Merman remembered it, "First a producer signed a cast; then he hired writers to rustle up some material for the cast to use. 'I've got Bert Lahr,' he'd say; 'write me a part for Bert Lahr.' Or 'I've signed Victor Moore. Get goin' buddy. Make with the Moore-type yuks.'" Thus musical comedy books functioned as blueprints: scripts, not scripture. Often, they represented little more than scenarios for funnymen who could be counted on in what they actually did onstage to keep a show going when scripts failed to amuse. And there were funnymen galore for musical comedy to call on: W. C. Fields (1879–1946) in *Poppy*

(1923), the Marx Brothers in *The Cocoanuts* (1925) and *Animal Crackers* (1928), Eddie Cantor (1892–1964) in *Whoopee* (1928), Joe Cook (1890–1959) in *Fine and Dandy* (1930). Great funnywomen were fewer in number, though Fanny Brice (1891–1951) and Beatrice Lillie (1894–1989) were outstanding among female comedians of the 1920s and 1930s to become stars of the musical stage. Their stars shone more frequently, however, in revues: Brice in the *Ziegfeld Follies* from 1910 to 1936; Lillie in *At Home Abroad* and *The Show Is On*.

Vaudeville and burlesque provided the schools for comedians to learn their craft and perfect it. In such variety-based entertainments, comedians could freely develop their delivery, timing, and bits of comic business—their shtick—outside the confines of a plot. That business became integral to their comic personas, part of what made each of them unique as clowns. But as they took such business with them into musical comedy, they often found themselves at odds with the narrative constraints of the genre. Successful librettists accommodated their writing to the styles of such performers, but given the often conflicting demands between comic stars and comic stories, what appeared onstage and on the page did not always agree. In a famous quip, George S. Kaufman once remarked to the Marx Brothers, after their performance in a show for which he had written the script, how shocked he was to have heard one of *his* lines.

The antagonism between performers and writers itself became a source of musical comedy humor. "In this show I am the plot," Ed Wynn proclaimed in *Over the Top* (1917). "You will notice the difference between my lines and the author's. Mine are very good." Even lyricists wrote with a given performer's style in mind, as Ira Gershwin did when he took his cue from the clipped syllables of comedian Walter Catlett in writing "'S Wonderful." Lyricists who failed to do so risked a performer on the warpath, seeking to replace the lyric or, better, the lyricist. Lyric discontent, for example, prompted Lahr to rewrite several of Cole Porter's lines for "It Ain't Etiquette" in *Du Barry Was a Lady* (1939). And it prompted Merman to demand that Howard Dietz be replaced as lyricist for *Sadie Thompson* (1944). When he wasn't, she simply left the show, ensuring its demise.

The difficulties faced by lyricists, however, were small when compared to those of book writers who had to structure their work around what performers could (and could not) do, and when they could (and could not) do it. (Recall the revue-like constraints under which Oscar

Hammerstein cobbled together the libretto for *Sunny*.) Even the pacing of humor in the structure of musical comedy was often revue-inspired. Guy Bolton confirmed this when he explained that his libretto for *The Ramblers* (1926) was not "just a stream of gags" for comedians Bobby Clark and Paul McCullough. It might better be described, he said, "as a series of block comedy scenes tied together by a plot. A 'block comedy scene' means one written like a revue sketch with a concentration on laughs and a final twist of 'blackout' value at the end."

The last of the DeSylva-Brown-Henderson musical comedies, *Flying High*, contained one of the most memorable of such scenes. Its blackout twist even elicited, one observer said, "the biggest single laugh in the history of the American stage"—clocked on opening night as lasting sixty-two seconds. Its success surely depended as much on the physical abilities of Bert Lahr for whom it was written as on the timeliness of the Prohibition that provided its cultural context. It remains funny nonetheless. The show's comedy centered on "Rusty" Krause (Lahr), an inept airplane mechanic who inadvertently sets a world endurance record in the air because he can't figure out how to land his plane. Rusty also happens to be rather fond of drink (when asked his nationality, he replies, "Scotch, by absorption"). Early on, Rusty has to take a physical exam to test his fitness for flying. In the doctor's office, he is whirled around in a drum cylinder to simulate the stresses of flight, and he emerges afterward utterly disoriented.

> (RUSTY *staggers out of the contraption. He takes two steps and drops to his knees. And then gets up slowly. He staggers around the stage.*)

RUSTY: Gimme a lemon and seltzer! Gimme a lemon and seltzer!

> (*The* DOCTOR *goes to his desk and gets a graduated glass for a urine sample.*)

RUSTY: Oh, there you are, bartender.
DOCTOR: (*handing him the glass*) You know what to do with that.

> (RUSTY *takes the glass, still staggering from the machine. The* DOCTOR *turns to his desk and sits with his back to the patient.* RUSTY *looks at the doctor, and then at the glass. The* DOCTOR *expects him to urinate;*

RUSTY *doesn't understand. His eyes widen in befuddlement. Suddenly, a glimmer of comprehension flashes across his face [as he remembers a flask in his pocket]. He reaches confidently into his back pocket with a quiet, knowing laugh. He takes out the flask and measures three fingers of the liquor in the glass. He staggers over to the doctor and hands it to him.)*

RUSTY: Here you are boy, that's all I can spare.

   (BLACKOUT)

That the audience did not take offense, as one of the scene's writers had feared, is a tribute to Lahr's gift as a performer and to his understanding of the farcical spirit. He explained:

> *It all reverts back to how the audience feels about you out there, if they accept you as a guy that bumbles into something—that's in the writing and in the playing. It's a matter of maintaining an air of innocence. You can do almost anything on stage, if you do it as if you haven't the slightest idea that there's anything wrong with what you're doing. Some comedians can do that particular thing, but a lot of comedians make it vulgar and dirty, and the audience won't accept it.*

When it came to musical comedy, the producer may still have been king on Broadway. Yet those directly responsible for bringing the comedy to life were surely next in line.

JAZZ-AGE "JAZZ"

If farce provided the basis for musical comedy's comedy in the Jazz Age, the basis for what made the genre musical altogether was jazz. But the jazz identified with musical comedy at the time hardly coincides with jazz as it is generally understood today. Mark Tucker, in the second edition of *The New Grove Dictionary of Music and Musicians*, describes jazz through a now seemingly fixed network of meanings: a musical tradition rooted in the practices of African Americans; a set of attitudes toward performance involving improvisation; a musical style characterized by syncopation, blues-derived elements, and a rhythmic feel for phrasing called swing. Yet the dictionary also indicates, by contrast, that "jazz in the 1920s was a fluid, unstable construct. Depending on who used the term, it could refer to Jelly Roll Morton, Vincent Lopez and his Hotel Pennsylvania orchestra, T. S. Eliot's *The Waste Land*, or George Gershwin's *Rhapsody in Blue*." In truth, if "the term 'jazz' first applied around 1916 to a rough and sexy strain of African-American music, [it] soon became synonymous with any syncopated mass-marketed popular music." Gershwin himself considered popular music of this sort to be "not Negro," as he put it, "but American." Such jazz favored a sound more "sweet" than "hot," its instrumental parts were more often arranged than improvised, and its styles and structures sprang from the Tin Pan Alley song more regularly than from blues or ragtime. Jazz in this guise shaped most of the music to Broadway's songs and dances of the period, and the distinctive sound and swing associated with it were the most salient musical features that separated musical comedy as a Broadway genre from operetta with its more "classical" bent.

Operetta songs characteristically went in for sustained melodies over a wide vocal range that assumed a singer's mastery of classical techniques of voice production, breathing, and vibrato. Musical comedy tunes, by contrast, tended to have shorter phrases that worked in a narrower vocal range, and required far less breath support from singers. They were often modeled on terse instrumental riffs and snappy dance rhythms associated with jazz. George Gershwin hailed the difference: "We are living in an age of staccato, not legato." Vincent Youmans demonstrated it. In the habit of reworking material he had originally used elsewhere, Youmans resurrected the song "My Boy and I" from *Mary Jane McKane* (1923), an unremarkable musical comedy for which he had written the songs with Herbert Stothart. Keeping the original melody virtually intact, Youmans reshaped its contours to fit a new time frame, turning what had been a graceful operetta-like waltz (Ex. 6-2a) into a jazzy duple-meter tune (Ex. 6-2b). In the process, what once had seemed leisurely now seemed rushed. (This shift may also have reflected a larger cultural condition: what many commentators of the era described as a change in the perception of time itself, the sensation of a speeding-up of experience associated with modern urban life.)

The result (with new lyrics by Otto Harbach) became the snappy title song to *No, No, Nanette* (1925). The show marked the first big musical comedy hit for composer Vincent Youmans (1898–1946), and

Ex. 6-2a. Herbert Stothart and Vincent Youmans, music, William Cary Duncan and Oscar Hammerstein II, lyrics: "My Boy and I" (transposed), *Mary Jane McKane*

My   boy   and   I   go   hand   in   hand

Ex. 6-2b. Vincent Youmans, music, Otto Harbach, lyrics, "No, No, Nanette," *No, No, Nanette*

"No,   No,   Nan - ette!"   That's   all   I   hear____

the second one for dance director Sammy Lee (1890–1968), who had choreographed Gershwin's *Lady, Be Good!* the year before. Lee was part of the Big Four group of young Broadway dance directors of the 1920s that included Seymour Felix (1892–1961), Busby Berkeley (1895–1976), and Bobby Connolly (1896–1944). His dances drew particular attention at the time as embodiments of the jazz-based spirit of the age. As one contemporary saw it:

> *The same nervous jerks, cacophonies, overwhelming rhythmical force and brutal strength that predominate in the poetry of Whitman and in the jazz of Gershwin are to be found in Sammy Lee's dances. Barbaric gestures, abrupt and pointed motions, hectic unrestraint—these things generously constitute Sammy Lee's idioms just as they must constitute every art whose mission is to interpret America. Through the dance does Sammy Lee see the jazz-crazed age and through the dance does he attempt to express it.*

Dance styles on the commercial stage in the 1920s comprised five basic types, according to Ned Wayburn (1874–1942), the most celebrated Broadway dance director of the day. These included ballet (toe dancing, classical dancing, character dancing, etc.), exhibition dancing (fox trot, one-step, waltz, etc.), acrobatic dancing (involving backbends, cartwheels, splits, etc.), tap and step dancing (buck and wing, waltz clog, soft-shoe, etc.), and, last but not least, musical comedy dancing, which, by naming the context rather than the content of a dance type, required further explanation on Wayburn's part:

Now you may think that you know just what Musical Comedy Danc-
ing is, and perhaps you do, but the name of it hardly defines it so that
it would be recognized for exactly what it is by one not thoroughly
stage-wise. . . . True Musical Comedy dancing. . . . is a cross between
the ballet and . . . tap and step or American specialty dancing. It com-
bines pretty attitudes, poses, pirouettes and the several different types of
kicking steps that are now so popular. Soft-shoe steps break into it here
and there in unexpected ways and places, adding a pleasing variety to
the menu. . . . There is no monotony, no tiresome sameness; yet the vary-
ing forms of action blend into a perfect continuity. The dance is full of
happy surprise steps, perhaps, or unexpected climaxes and variations
that arouse the interest as they quickly flash by. Often there is featured
in Musical Comedy dancing a bit of so called "character" work, which
may be anything—Bowery, Spanish, Dutch, eccentric, Hawaiian, or
any of the countless other characteristic types. Also there are touches of
dainty ballet work interspersed among the other features, at times.

No wonder Wayburn was reluctant to define it. Musical comedy
dance proved to be an umbrella term more than anything else. The
type of dance it covered typically indulged in lines of chorus girls doing
precision kicks and steps together; it also typically borrowed, incorporated, and adapted whatever it found useful in other dance types.
No, No, Nanette, for example, went from featuring ballroom exhibition
dance in one number ("You Can Dance with Any Girl"), to acrobatic
dancing in another ("Fight Over Me"), to tap in yet another ("I Want
to Be Happy"). Musical comedy dancing, then, embraced "a pleasing
variety" not only of steps but of styles. Yet, even at its best, its choreography was neither stylistically innovative nor particularly related
to the stories that it interrupted. In sum, the output of Sammy Lee, as
dance historian Frank W. D. Ries assessed it, "captures an age and a
style that made allowances for tapping chorus lines, parading showgirls, and backbending dance displays that had nothing to do with the
story at hand."

No, No, Nanette's story revolved about the young flapper of its title
and her rebellion against the constraints laid down by her guardian, a
Bible publisher who arouses the suspicion of his penny-pinching wife
by spending large sums of money on "deserving" young women. A hit
on Broadway, the show became an even greater success outside the

Louise Groody (second from right) as the quintessential flapper
in the title role of *No, No, Nanette*.

United States, the first in a string of brash American musical comedies
that would establish themselves on a truly international scale. British theatergoers had enjoyed numerous musical imports from America before *No, No, Nanette*, to be sure, the cultural barriers between
Broadway and the West End being relatively low. But local productions
of American musical comedies on the non-English-speaking stages of
Europe were virtually unknown. With *No, No, Nanette* this began to
change, despite the difficulties in capturing the essence of such entertainment in translation.

How would one translate the show's big hit song "Tea for Two," for
instance? Its lyrics were not just idiomatic but downright nonsensical
at times. In fact, lyricist Irving Caesar is said to have improvised them
as a "dummy" lyric. Written to the rhythm of Youmans's melody on
first hearing, the dummy consisted of random words and phrases chosen because they fit the music rather than made sense. The practice was
common among songwriters before easy access to portable cassettes
later in the century made it obsolete: without recourse to notation, it

gave a lyricist the right pattern of syllables and accents to work from when writing a real lyric later on if the composer wasn't there to play the music. Understandably, a dummy lyric had more rhythm and rhyme to it than reason ("Day will break and you'll awake and start to bake a sugar cake/For me to take for all the boys to see"). Yet in the end Youmans insisted on keeping the dummy, realizing perhaps that in its tit-for-tat playfulness, it came closer to the carefree spirit in the repeating riffs of his tune than any more polished use of words might have done.

Consider the opening lines of the refrain:

> *Picture you upon my knee,*
> *Just tea for two and two for tea,*
> *Just me for you and you for me alone. . . .*
>
>   "TEA FOR TWO" (*No, No, Nanette*)

The French, in translating it, took the text quite literally, keeping much of the playfulness of the original rhyme scheme but planting the seeds of logical continuity where ellipses once prevailed:

Je vous vois déjà chez nous,	*I can see you already in our home*
Buvant du thé sur mes genoux,	*Drinking tea upon my knees,*
Moi, plein d'émoi,	*I'm full of excitement*
Vous sentant toute à moi.	*Feeling you're all mine.*

The Germans in turn gave it a moral twist, turning innocence into innuendo and so rewriting the lyric that nothing of the original remained:

Wenn ein Mädel "Ja" gesagt,	*If a girl's said yes*
Bevor sie's der Mama gesagt,	*Before she's told her mother,*
Dann merkt sie bald, wer "A" gesagt,	*She soon learns that once you start*
Sagt "B".	*You wind up going all the way.*

The British, of course, required no help with the text to this or any of the show's songs. What they did need help with, however, was the music. This British reaction was atypical only insofar as it was extreme:

Saxophone players (in the limelight) worked with the energy of a savage religious festival, and when there was any chance that you might mislay the melody it was emphasised by the brass with mutes. A little of a muted trombone or trumpet is good for certain effects, but a whole melody played as if the instruments were melodious steam saws cuts into my brain and produces a mild nerve storm. The music of "No, No, Nanette" and the frenzied dancing on the stage are the epitome of modern jazzomania. If this piece be ever discovered in the far future it will be made the text for learned discourses on the nervous breakdown of the American and European nations after the great war.

No, No, Nanette epitomized "jazzomania" to Europeans at many levels of culture as well. Highbrow musicians heard its songs as markers of a lowbrow modernity: "I Want to Be Happy" appears in Ernst Krenek's opera *Jonny spielt auf* (1927); "Tea for Two" appears in Dmitri Shostakovich's ballet *The Golden Age* (1930). Some Americans, too, took it symbolically. Zelda Fitzgerald, for one, heard it as an expression of the liberated flapper lifestyle she espoused. And in Vincent Youmans's songs in particular she found the musical voice and emotional emblem of the age her husband had named.

Youmans's Broadway songwriting career lasted from 1920 to 1932, about the length of the Jazz Age itself. Though born to wealth and social privilege, Youmans led a life fraught with serious, often self-inflicted personal and professional problems. Tuberculosis finally cut his life short altogether at the age of forty-eight leaving the major promise of his talent for the musical stage largely unfulfilled. Youmans nonetheless wrote music for twelve Broadway book shows in whole or part—including other musical comedy hits besides *No, No, Nanette* (*Hit the Deck*, 1927; *Take a Chance*, 1932), operettas (*Wildflower*, 1923; *Through the Years*, 1932), and more venturesome musical plays (*Rainbow*, 1928; *Great Day*, 1929). His legacy lies in a small vein of musical gems sifted from his less than one hundred published songs. Many of these show no indebtedness even to the sweet jazz of the era ("Time on My Hands," "Through the Years"); others do—especially in the syncopated gusto of his revival tunes ("Hallelujah," "Great Day") and in the inflected chromaticism of his bluesy torch songs ("'Where Has My Hubby Gone?' Blues," "More Than You Know").

Musical comedy came to the jazz of the Jazz Age in an ethnically

London poster for the original production of *H.M.S. Pinafore*—before its
writing team became canonized as "Gilbert and Sullivan" (1878).

"Grand View of Baxter Street"
Designer Charles Witham's watercolor rendering of his backdrop for act 2,
scene 3 of Edward Harrigan's *The Leather Patch* (1886).

Early poster for the "Cohan Family"—a vaudeville foursome of mother, father, son, and daughter—plugging the talents of the children, George M. and Josie, with the parents nowhere in sight (c. 1891).

Sheet-music covers of songs from Princess Theater shows (*clockwise from top left*): *Nobody Home* (1915); *Very Good Eddie* (1915); *Oh, Lady! Lady!!* (1918); *Oh, Boy!* (1917).

a

Sketches by leading costume designers for Broadway revues: a) Lady Duff Gordon (Lucile), *Ziegfeld Follies* (1917); b) James Reynolds, *Greenwich Village Follies* (1921?); c) Romain de Tirtoff (Erté), *Music Box Revue* (1924); d) Charles Le Maire, *Greenwich Village Follies* (1926?); e) John Harkrider, *Ziegfeld Midnight Frolic* (1928).

b

c

d

e

(*Above*) Interior of the theater on board the *Cotton Blossom* in a three-dimensional model by set designer Joseph Urban for act 1, scene 6, of *Show Boat* (1927).
(*Below*) Production shot of the same scene perfomed on the stage of the Ziegfeld Theater shortly after *Show Boat*'s premiere and reproduced in the "color gravure" section of the *New York World* (1928).

Broadway songwriters enshrined on covers of *Time* magazine:
(*clockwise from upper left*) Irving Berlin (May 28, 1934);
George Gershwin (July 20, 1925); Richard Rodgers and Lorenz Hart
(September 26, 1938); Cole Porter (January 31, 1949).

"The Farmer and the Cowman" from *Oklahoma!* (1943).

more direct sense, however, with the reemergence of black musicals after a decade of their absence on Broadway. This Broadway resurgence coincided with that flourishing of African American culture farther uptown in Manhattan, the Harlem Renaissance. But the new musicals hardly fit the Renaissance agenda. (Neither did jazz, for the most part.) Such shows, performed in blackface and rooted in minstrel comedy, appeared to reinforce old racial stereotypes. To be sure, they attracted African American audiences in large numbers—some perhaps to let off steam through laughter (even if directed at themselves); some perhaps to laugh at representations on the stage of circumstances they felt they had escaped. Yet leaders of the Renaissance's "New Negro" movement had a different idea of what constituted cultural success. As they sought access to white respectability through the achievements of black artists in high artistic endeavors, they tended to dismiss such musicals for the dubious views of old-Negro life they imparted in the name of entertainment. Shows with names such as *Plantation Revue* (1923), *Dixie to Broadway* (1924), and *Lucky Sambo* (1925) only intensified the conflict.

Shuffle Along (1921) led the way, its unexpected popular success establishing the black musical as a Broadway phenomenon of the 1920s. African American poet Langston Hughes even saw it in a Renaissance context. *Shuffle Along*, he said, "gave a scintillating send-off to that Negro vogue in Manhattan, which reached its peak just before the crash of 1929. . . . It gave just the proper push—a pre-Charleston kick—to that Negro vogue of the 20's, that spread to books, African sculpture, music, and dancing." Nominally a musical comedy about a corrupt mayoral campaign in the South, *Shuffle Along* was more a grab bag of comic routines and musical numbers which its creators preferred to call a "Musical Melange." This melange—written, directed, and performed by African Americans—owed most of its appeal to the work of two teams of vaudevillians: Flournoy Miller (1887–1971) and Aubrey Lyles (1883–1932), the comic stars who expanded an old vaudeville skit without music for the book; and lyricist Noble Sissle (1889–1975) and composer Eubie Blake (1883–1983), who created the ragtime-inspired numbers. Despite a shoestring production in a run-down playhouse on Sixty-third Street, the northernmost fringe of New York's theater district, the show succeeded not only with black audiences but white audiences as well. The reason, as one critic remarked: "It was impossible to resist a jollity that the company itself appeared to experience down to

Shuffle Along chorines demonstrate perhaps why Langston Hughes said the show gave "a pre-Charleston kick" to the Harlem Renaissance.

the very marrow. . . . [They] made pep seem something different from the tame thing we know further downtown."

Shuffle Along consisted of more than just pep, however. It balanced its snappy numbers ("Bandana Days," "I'm Just Wild About Harry") with sentimental ones ("Love Will Find a Way," "I'm Craving for That Kind of Love"). And its typically boisterous humor was also self-deprecating. Consider how the comic leads broached a subject close to home:

STEVE JENKINS [FLOURNOY MILLER]: (*Hat in hand and with the characteristic pose of a politician*) (*In all seriousness*). Ladies— Gentlemenses—Peopleses—and Folkses—

SAM PECK [AUBREY LYLES]: You ain't left out nobody. I'll give you credit for dat. . . .

STEVE JENKINS: When I first entered this race for mayors of Jimtown, I had not the least redea. . . . that there was a dark horse in the race. . . . Surprised I was, I must say ver' much heap surprised I was when I found out dat dat dark horse was my own business parter . . .

SAM PECK: Well, I maght be de dark horse but you (*pointing to Steve*) ain't gwine never be no black mayor.

The show ran for some five hundred performances in New York, toured for years in white theaters across the United States, and launched the careers of such future star performers as Florence Mills (1896–1927), Paul Robeson (1898–1976), and Josephine Baker (1906–1975). Its success effectively legitimized the black musical as commercially viable entertainment in the American cultural mainstream. By the time *Shuffle Along*'s touring companies returned to New York in 1924, eight other black musicals had followed it to Broadway—among them, *Liza* (1922), *Runnin' Wild* (1923), and *The Chocolate Dandies* (1924). The new development could not be denied. Even the 1922 edition of Ziegfeld's *Follies* acknowledged it when Gilda Gray sang "It's Getting Dark on Old Broadway" and, as one commentator put it, "she was not referring to the absence of street lights."

Black musicals made their jazziest appeal to audiences by means of dance. They had recourse, in a way that comparable white musicals did not, to the full spectrum of African American vernacular movements which made "jazz rhythms visible." "I'll tell you how we changed shows," Eubie Blake recalled about the dances in *Shuffle Along*.

> *Ziegfeld, George White, the Shuberts. . . . They all had reviews with girls—beautiful girls. They walked around in beautiful clothes. The people who danced in these shows were specialties. These shows didn't have a real [dancing] chorus. These girls in beautiful costumes would just walk and kick a little. So, we came in with our show. Our girls were beautiful, and they danced!!! They danced!!! And they sang!!! Those others didn't do nothing but [he sings] "A Pretty Girl is Like a Melody . . ." and all were beautiful. But after you had seen them once, well, that's it. But our girls were—white people have a name they call dancers—hoofers—these girls DANCED!!!*

Jazz-based dancing made up the liveliest feature of the black musicals. Every show had at least one sensational production number that exploited it to the hilt—and often resurfaced in later shows, white as well as black. In *Shuffle Along*, the "Baltimore Buzz" caused such a stir that Ziegfeld hired the show's chorus girls to teach his own chorines the movements. In *Dinah* (1924), a Harlem show that never moved downtown, the "Black Bottom" so enthralled George White, he purchased it; hired DeSylva, Brown, and Henderson to write a song with its characteristic rhythms; and featured Ann Pennington dancing it on Broadway in his *Scandals of 1926*. But nothing outdid *Runnin' Wild*, which introduced the Charleston, with its flying kicks, shimmying shoulders, and that irreducible syncopation before the second beat of every bar. For the Charleston not only captivated Broadway, it soon became an international craze in its own right and surely the single most characteristic dance of the 1920s. Showstoppers all, these dance numbers called attention to themselves *as numbers*, even in their use of lyrics to instruct audiences in the right moves (Black Bottom: "clap . . . hands and do a raggedy trot") or simply to inform them about what they were watching (Charleston: "made in Carolina").

As such numbers dropped even the pretense of any connection to a plot, they were equally well suited for the purposes of revues. Indeed, the success achieved by producer Lew Leslie with the revue *Dixie to Broadway* in 1924 contributed to a trend among black shows to look to revues to showcase the musical and comedic elements that were musical comedy's most popular features while ignoring that genre's most troublesome aspect, the book. In addition, black revues that played downtown on Broadway had certain advantages over their white counterparts as they took much of their talent and material from the increasingly fashionable uptown entertainment of Harlem's cabarets. This pleased Broadway producers for whom a Harlem nightclub proved a less expensive tryout venue than a playhouse out of town. And it pleased those Broadway audiences who preferred to visit Harlem vicariously.

Lew Leslie (1886–1963) was the leading producer of such revues, the most famous of which was his *Blackbirds* (five editions: 1926–1939). They relied on the work of white writers behind the scenes and black performers up front, often of the highest caliber: Florence Mills in 1926; Ethel Waters in 1930; Lena Horne (1917–2010) in 1939. The 1928 edition, with songs by Jimmy McHugh and Dorothy Fields and dancing by the "King of Tap Dance," Bill "Bojangles" Robinson (1878–1949), became one of the longest-running of all Broadway revues and the most successful of the black musicals of the 1920s. But it was a non-Leslie show, *Hot Chocolates* (1929), in which jazz made what may have been its hottest appearance in any Broadway revue of the period—jazz, now, in all of F. Scott Fitzgerald's meanings: sex, dancing, and music. For *Hot Chocolates* was originally staged at a popular Harlem nightspot, and it did little to tone down the blue humor and erotic dancing of its floor show before moving downtown. These alone were sufficient to make the show newsworthy. Yet it also featured the songs of stride pianist "Fats" Waller and lyricist Andy Razaf ("Ain't Misbehavin'," "Black and Blue"), and the extraordinary talent of a young trumpeter who played and also sang jazz by anyone's definition, Louis Armstrong.

In the final analysis, it was really not jazz so much as jazz-inspired expression of many kinds that changed the character of Broadway in the decade or so after the Great War. However differently understood at the time, jazz became a marker—perhaps the most telling one—by which revues and musical comedies, black and white, gauged their currency and cultural relevance. "Jazz" made shows modern. But the Jazz Age ended, as Scott Fitzgerald wrote, with the stock market crash and the onset of the Great Depression. That was about the time jazz itself began to take on the qualities of a new form of expression which would become the lingua franca of American popular music in the next decade: swing. And it was about the time that Florenz Ziegfeld died; DeSylva, Brown, and Henderson abandoned Broadway for Hollywood; and Youmans's career effectively came to a close. Others would come forward to take their place, most prominent among them the Gershwin brothers, Rodgers and Hart, and Cole Porter. These writers were not new to the Great White Way, to be sure, but they would now dominate musical comedy in the 1930s. More than that, they would also transform the genre in so many ways in the next decade as to make it seem as if until now—though they had already left an indelible mark on the Broadway stage—they had only been waiting in the wings.

JEROME H. REMICK & COMPANY.

MUSIC PUB

PPER.

PRINTER

45   WHITNEY WARNER
        DETROIT   MUSIC

WHITNEY WARN
MUSIC

MUSIC PUBLISHERS.

LIPPER.

NEW YORK CLIPPER.

JEROME H. REMICK & COMPANY

WILLIA
MORR

MUSIC
PUBLISHERS

45

MUSIC
PUBLISHERS

THOMAS YO

THOMAS YOUNG JI

JEROME H. REMICK & COMPANY.
WHITNEY WARNER PUBLISHING CO

7

BROADWAY SONGBOOK

LADY, BE GOOD!
(12/1/1924–ca. 10/1925). **Producers:** Alex Aarons and Vinton Freedley. **Book:** Guy Bolton and Fred Thompson. **Lyrics:** Ira Gershwin and others. **Music:** George Gershwin. **Director:** Felix Edwards. **New York Run:** 330 performances. **Cast:** Adele Astaire, Fred Astaire, Walter Catlett. **Songs:** "Fascinating Rhythm," "Oh, Lady, Be Good," "The Man I Love" [cut in tryout].

A CONNECTICUT YANKEE
(11/3/1927–10/27/1928). **Producers:** Lew Fields and Lyle D. Andrews. **Book:** Herbert Fields, based on the Mark Twain novel *A Connecticut Yankee in King Arthur's Court*. **Lyrics:** Lorenz Hart. **Music:** Richard Rodgers. **Director:** Alexander Leftwich. **New York Run:** 418 performances. **Cast:** Constance Carpenter, William Gaxton. **Songs:** "My Heart Stood Still," "Thou Swell," "On a Desert Island with Thee" [Broadway Revival, 1943: 135 performances. **Additional Song:** "To Keep My Love Alive"].

STRIKE UP THE BAND
(1/14/1930–6/28/1930). **Producer:** Edgar Selwyn. **Book:** Morrie Ryskind, based on George S. Kaufman's 1927 libretto. **Lyrics:** I. Gershwin. **Music:** G. Gershwin. **Director:** Leftwich. **New York Run:** 191 performances. **Cast:** Blanche Ring, Bobby Clark, Paul McCullough. **Songs:** "Soon," "I've Got a Crush on You."

View of office buildings on "Tin Pan Alley," Twenty-eighth Street between Sixth and Fifth Avenues, ca. 1905: *The New York Clipper*, "sporting and theatrical" paper; Whitney Warner Music and Jerome H. Remick & Co., music publishers; and William Morris, vaudeville agent.

GIRL CRAZY

(10/14/1930–6/6/1931). **Producers:** Aarons and Freedley. **Book:** Bolton and John McGowan. **Lyrics:** I. Gershwin. **Music:** G. Gerswin. **Director:** Leftwich. **New York Run:** 272 performances. **Cast:** Ginger Rogers, Ethel Merman, Willie Howard. **Songs:** "Bidin' My Time," "Embraceable You," "I Got Rhythm," "But Not for Me."

OF THEE I SING

(12/26/1931–1/14/1933). **Producer:** Sam H. Harris. **Book:** Kaufman and Ryskind. **Lyrics:** I. Gershwin. **Music:** G. Gershwin. **Director:** Kaufman. **New York Run:** 441 performances. **Cast:** Lois Moran, Gaxton, Victor Moore. **Songs:** "Wintergreen for President," "Love Is Sweeping the Country," "Who Cares?"

ANYTHING GOES

(11/21/1934–11/16/1935). **Producer:** Freedley. **Book:** [Bolton and P. G. Wodehouse] Howard Lindsay and Russel Crouse. **Lyrics and Music:** Cole Porter. **Director:** Lindsay. **New York Run:** 420 performances. **Cast:** Ethel Merman, Bettina Hall, Gaxton, Moore. **Songs:** "I Get a Kick Out of You," "You're the Top," "Blow, Gabriel, Blow."

ON YOUR TOES

(4/11/1936–1/23/1937). **Producer:** Dwight Deere Wiman. **Book:** Rodgers, Hart, and George Abbott. **Lyrics:** Hart. **Music:** Rodgers. **Director:** Worthington Miner [Abbott]. **Choreographer:** George Balanchine. **New York Run:** 315 performances. **Cast:** Tamara Geva, Ray Bolger. **Songs:** "There's a Small Hotel" **Dances:** "Slaughter on Tenth Avenue" [Broadway Revival, 1954: 64 performances. Broadway Revival, 1983: 505 performances].

PAL JOEY

(12/25/1940–11/29/1941). **Producer and Director:** Abbott. **Book:** John O'Hara [Abbott], based on O'Hara's short stories in *The New Yorker*. **Lyrics:** Hart. **Music:** Rodgers. **New York Run:** 374 performances. **Cast:** Vivienne Segal, Leila Ernst, June Havoc, Gene Kelly. **Songs:** "I Could Write a Book," "Bewitched," "Take Him" [Broadway Revival, 1952: 542 performances].

The rise of the new-style musical comedy in the 1920s reached its zenith during the Great Depression. The climate of economic privation of the 1930s may well have been a factor in the success of a more pointed, sophisticated, and original body of work on Broadway than before. Its creators were writers of extraordinary gifts who rose to the occasion: composers such as George Gershwin, Cole Porter, and Richard Rodgers; lyricists such as Ira Gershwin, Cole Porter again, and Lorenz Hart; scriptwriters such as Herbert Fields, George Abbott, and George S. Kaufman. Not all their work was equally inspired or of equal importance to a show. But the relationship between the contributions of composers, lyricists, and librettists constitutes the better part of any history of musical comedy in the period. And so before we examine their contributions in detail, it is worth considering more generally what was understood on Broadway at the time when one spoke of writers' contributions to musical comedy in terms of "books" and "scores."

A book in Broadway jargon has come to mean the script of a show, its text. It functions as the verbal blueprint for a performance, but a performance in which music also plays an essential part. Unlike the text of a play, a book is an incomplete blueprint without a corresponding blueprint for the music. But a book is often understood to be verbally incomplete as well: It may include all the spoken words in a show but not those words that are sung. In that case, it is a book in the sense confirmed by the Broadway practice of crediting (and thus paying for) "book" and "lyrics" as separate items in a show—even if both are the work of one writer. On the other hand, if a book includes all the words in a musical—spoken, sung, or otherwise delivered—it is tantamount to a libretto: the "little book" of words (originally to an opera) whose text is regarded as a single exercise in both playwriting and versifying, even if it is the work of more than one writer.

Such variable use of "book" has clouded its meaning since around the turn of the twentieth century, when the term began to replace "libretto" on Broadway, though it meant something less than what "libretto" originally implied. Comic operas and musical comedies might both be said to have librettos, even if musical comedies really had books.

243

But the distinction was never hard and fast. Comic operas used librettists to supply both the prose of spoken dialogue and the verses that were sung. And as comic opera was a genre in which plots informed the musical numbers, this made for a high degree of verbal consistency and narrative continuity throughout. W. S. Gilbert wrote both the prose and the verse for all his operettas. H. B. Smith was a playwright and a versifier as well. So were early musical comedy writers like Ned Harrigan and George M. Cohan. But later ones like Guy Bolton or Herbert Fields specialized in prose and left the poetry to a new breed of wordsmith adept at fitting words to music in the Tin Pan Alley manner, not the other way around. Playwrights wrote books, then; versifiers wrote lyrics—a division of labor largely attributable to the influence of Tin Pan Alley as an economic force in the musical theater. Victor Herbert even attributed the decline of comic opera to the rise of theater songs tailored for independent marketability along Alley lines:

> *they must have words that are independent of the play—that is, on some general theme and attractive to the person who has not seen the play. I think that this may have had its effect in weaning us away from comic opera in which lyrics are woven into the plot and are part of it.*

The new division tended to fragment the textual consistency of a show. It also tended to reduce the cohesive force of a plot—a condition P. G. Wodehouse twitted, you may recall, when he referred to the book and its function in a musical comedy as "the stuff that keeps the numbers apart."

Favoring the work of book writers over librettists went hand in hand with favoring the work of songwriters over composers. Comic opera composers generally matched the holistic approach of their librettists by conceiving of their work in terms of scores. Sullivan wrote all his own theater music, from overture to finale ultimo, and orchestrated it all as well. So did de Koven and Herbert. But neither Friml nor Romberg did, though both surely had the necessary training. By the 1920s the Tin Pan Alleyization of Broadway was virtually complete. In operetta as well as musical comedy songwriters now held sway. Composers worked on Broadway, if at all, behind the scenes. And where they once contributed a great variety of music to a show, songwriters focused almost entirely on writing simple tunes and accompaniments in fixed musical forms. (Such was the musical state of affairs by the early 1940s that, in response to a claim that the German-born and classically trained Kurt Weill was the only composer on Broadway who still knew how to write a finale, songwriter Richard Rodgers is reported to have asked, "What's a finale?") Moreover, songwriters might consider their compositions complete not as they would actually be heard in the theater but in renditions for piano, and even then perhaps only in skeletal form—at worst, as a kind of one-finger sketch. Thus, songwriters had to rely on the skills of musical specialists to flesh out their songs. Some did so out of necessity: Irving Berlin was musically illiterate. Others did so out of choice: Cole Porter had perhaps more musical schooling than he knew what to do with but consistently deferred to the expertise of others in the hurly-burly of getting a show on its feet in time for opening night.

Among the many such specialists, Frank Saddler (1864–1921), Maurice De Packh (1896–1960), and Don Walker (1907–1989) played key roles in creating what became the characteristic sound of musical comedy in the interwar years and beyond: the wordless wit and sparkle that emanated from a theater's orchestra pit. But they remained almost totally unknown to theatergoers at the time, and are largely unknown today. The names of only two such orchestrators, perhaps the most influential of the era, have managed to rise above the obscurity of the rest: Hans Spialek (1894–1983) and Robert Russell Bennett (1894–1981). Spialek worked on over 140 productions, including many of the early Porter shows (*Anything Goes*) and most of the later ones of Rodgers and Hart (*Pal Joey*). Bennett, a composer who saw no artistic merit at all in writing Broadway music, ironically came to dominate the sound of the medium he scorned. He wrote orchestrations for some three hundred shows—including operettas (*Rose-Marie*), revues (*The Band Wagon*), and musical comedies by the best Broadway composers of the age: Kern (*Sunny*), Rodgers (*A Connecticut Yankee*), Gershwin (*Girl Crazy*), Berlin (*Face the Music*), and Porter (*Jubilee*). Both men also worked together on some of the same shows (though generally on different numbers) and with other orchestrators as well. Expert musicians of a self-effacing bent, they proved ideal collaborators, typical of a breed of musicians (including rehearsal pianists and dance and vocal arrangers) much of whose work was done under the last-minute pressures of rehearsal, and all of it out of the limelight. Moreover, their jobs regularly demanded more than just orchestration—more, that is, than simply making music written for a piano playable by a band. They bore the responsibility to make up for compositional deficiencies in the harmony or voicing of a song; to help work out the keys, introductions, and endings needed to "routine" a song into a complete musical number; and to recompose a song instrumentally for purposes of overtures, entr'actes, dance breaks, continuity, and other musical needs in the overall production of a show. The less songwriters proved to be thorough musicians, the more orchestrators were expected to be composers themselves. (Leonard Bernstein would later refer to them admiringly as "subcomposers who turn a series of songs into a unified score, who make it all sound like a 'work.'") Without diminishing the aura of originality about the contributions of the songwriters, it was the orchestrator's creative work that adapted a songwriter's music to the trajectory of a complete theater production.

In Broadway jargon a "score" has come to mean the musical counterpart of a book; and use of the term is similarly variable. In one sense, a score simply refers to a tangible document. Yet no single document generally serves as the score to a Broadway show—not one that accounts for every note played by every instrument and sung by every voice in every musical number. The orchestrators' manuscripts that serve as masterplans from which copyists extract the instrumental parts would normally be considered the full score. But this score, written in haste and geared primarily to what goes on in the pit, often fails to include all the vocal lines and lyrics that issue from the stage. These appear in what is known as the vocal score, which contains the voice parts, the texts they sing, and a piano reduction of what the orchestra plays. A vocal score is often published while the full score is not. Yet neither score gives the complete musical blueprint for a show without the other.

The term "score," however, is also used to signify something rather less tangible than a document. A score is a composition, a musical whole greater than the sum of its notes—and in a show score, greater than the sum of its songs. Yet in most musical comedies, the score (as a document) rarely sounded like a score (as a composition). Apart from obvious song reprises, the musical structure of the show was episodic with little compositional continuity from one number to the next. Even the overall key scheme to the musical numbers was not based on composers' choices so much as on performers' needs. A musical comedy score thus meant a collection of separate show numbers arranged in running order along story lines. But unlike the *narrative* thrust of a book, which could be picked up again after the digression of a musical number, no comparable *musical* thrust connected the numbers to each other once a stretch of spoken dialogue had intervened. And so it was not unusual for a musical comedy to proceed as if by inverting P. G. Wodehouse's quip—that is, as if its score functioned simply as the stuff that interrupted the book.

While a score came to mean any show-related sequence of songs on Broadway, certain songwriters took a more demanding view of the score-related aspect of their work. Not all, however, agreed on what exactly this might mean. Lorenz Hart saw it as "balancing the different musical items" in a show so that a general "musical pattern" emerged out of the sheer variety of numbers. Richard Rodgers, his songwriting partner, saw it as achieving a specific "family resemblance" so that the different numbers in a show were also discernibly alike.

Audiences, however, measured a musical comedy's success in large part by its ability to produce not memorable scores but memorable songs: hit songs. These songs, singled out for immediate applause in the theater, were often the only parts of a musical to survive the show itself. Musical comedies as such were not built to last. At once entertainments and business ventures, the shows were put together to amuse and to make money, then disposed of once a production no longer proved commercially viable. (At that point there was no practical reason to hold on to the scripts, scores, and parts needed to perform the show that had held all these materials together—nor sufficient historical awareness to seek to document the undertaking—and such items were easily scattered and frequently lost.)

Show songs, by contrast, might prove more durable: A much bigger market existed for them outside the theater than in it. Such songs were not just compatible with the popular music of the era, a great number of them actually *were* the era's popular music. As self-contained love songs for the most part, their music shared the vernacular styles and sensibilities of Tin Pan Alley, and their lyrics were sufficiently general in content to make perfect sense without reference to a book. Removed from their scores, such songs appeared in many extratheatrical venues—in clubs, where they were sung; in ballrooms, where they were danced to (often without their lyrics);

on the radio, where big bands played them in swing arrangements (sometimes even without their melodies). (The swing era, in full force by 1935, turned out to be the most popular era in jazz history partly because jazz musicians based so much of their music making directly on the pop songs of the period.) Listeners who enjoyed these songs wherever they heard them may not even have known of their theatrical origins. Moreover, show songs were still published separately as sheet music, which musically literate amateurs could buy and play for themselves. But sheet music sales, once the entertainment industry's measure of a song's success, declined by the early 1920s, and music publishers increasingly began to link their interests to the technologies of the new communications industries. By the 1930s the measure of a song's success had shifted "from print to plastic" and other sources of "mechanical royalties"—above all, phonograph recordings, radio broadcasts, and motion pictures.

The shift reflected the emergence of an American mass culture. Packaging songs in formats that reproduced them "mechanically"— no longer as blueprints for performances but as performances themselves—bypassed former presumptions of musical literacy. It made the songs accessible to a range of consumers, rich and poor, who could enjoy them now simply staying home, turning on the radio, and listening. Theater songs—and theater-related songs such as those used in the movies—could thus reach a truly mass audience for the first time. And registering the musical tastes of audiences even became a form of entertainment itself in the 1930s with the advent of *Your Hit Parade*, a weekly radio program that reputedly chose the songs it aired on the basis of a national survey of record and sheet-music sales, and which was transferred to television in the 1950s.

Beyond considerations of the reception and promotion of such songs, many of them warranted recognition for themselves: their music and their words. Indeed, recent studies of American popular song and American musical theater often converge in their assessment of the interwar years and perhaps a bit later as a "Golden Age" precisely because of the quantity of high-quality songs that the two fields shared as they never had before. While working within a formal scheme no less rigid than a sonnet's, and confined to a narrow range of subjects mostly dealing with romance, the finest songwriters of the period brought a high level of feeling, imagination, and discipline to the creation of a body of miniature compositions now widely regarded as an American vernacular art. Today, the canon that has formed around these compositions frequently goes by the name of the American Songbook. Perhaps nothing did more to fix the name and the idea in the popular mind than a series of LP recordings that began with the release of *Ella Fitzgerald Sings the Cole Porter Songbook* in 1956—a conservative move at the time, given the rising tide of rock 'n' roll. Before she finished with the project in 1964, Fitzgerald memorably sang her way through eight such songbooks, each featuring another of the golden age's songwriting masters: Rodgers and Hart, Duke Ellington, Irving Berlin, George and Ira Gershwin, Harold Arlen, Jerome Kern, and Johnny Mercer. If these albums collectively have come to represent the heart of the American Songbook, the heart of that heart rests in what might be called, in turn, the Broadway Songbook. It is no accident that the bulk of the work of most of the songwriters represented on these albums was shaped in the crucible of the theater.

While it lasted, the partnership of Broadway and Tin Pan Alley worked remarkably well. Hit songs helped to plug the shows they came from; hit shows helped to plug the songs. But relatively few writers were able to work successfully over the course of a career with one ear on the Hit Parade and the other on the stage. Designing songs to satisfy the broad demands of mass appeal, on the one hand, and the narrow constraints of theater production, on the other, involved both talent and a skill not easily acquired. A handful of songwriters nevertheless built astonishingly successful careers by making this concern central to their life's work and to what they saw as the development of musical comedy. Much of the genre's move into a position of cultural preeminence on Broadway in the 1930s is attributable to the specific achievement of such writers as the Gershwins, Porter, and Rodgers and Hart—songwriters who left their mark so deeply on the Broadway theater of their time that its musical products are more often remembered today by association with their writers' names than by the titles of the shows themselves. The sustained quality and quantity of their output (with "scores" to some fifty book shows among them produced on Broadway from 1924 to 1944) constitutes the core of any history of American musical comedy between the two world wars.

THE GERSHWINS

Jacob, the second of two sons of Morris Gershovitz, transformed himself into George Gershwin (1898–1937) by a process of self-creation that typified a whole generation born of Russian Jewish immigrants in America. George Gershwin worked his way out of poverty and into the American Dream through sheer determination and talent as a songwriter. In this he followed in the footsteps of Irving Berlin; only he went Berlin one better. "We were all pretty good songwriters," Berlin recalled shortly before his death, "but Gershwin was something else. He was a composer"—a composer, moreover, whose musical career was all the more remarkable in that the community of American composers of his day refused to recognize him as one of their own. As a composer, his was not simply "A Journey to Greatness"—the way an early biographer put it—but a journey that traveled a cultural distance greater than that traveled by any American composer before. Gershwin's music began in the marketplace of Tin Pan Alley and ended, posthumously, in the repertoire of the Metropolitan Opera Company. In between came the work for Broadway and Hollywood that also placed his music in the musical comedy mainstream.

George was an excellent pianist who realized his talent early and quit high school to work as a song plugger for Remick's publishing house on Tin Pan Alley. There, he fell under the spell of Kern's Princess Theater songs and, in a move of characteristic ambition, quit the Alley to devote himself to "production" music. "Kern was the first composer who made me conscious that popular music was of inferior quality," he said, "and that musical comedy music was made of better material." In 1919, "Swanee" (lyrics by Irving Caesar) became his first big stage hit when Al Jolson interpolated it into *Sinbad*; and Gershwin's songwriting career took off. He wrote the songs and other musical numbers for five editions of *George White's Scandals* (1920–1924) and for several musical comedies for Broadway and London's West End.

Then in 1924, Gershwin's career took a decisive turn on two fronts. That year saw the premiere of *Rhapsody in Blue*, a "jazz concerto" for piano and orchestra with which Gershwin launched a widely publicized career as a composer of orchestral music that combined American vernacular and European classical traditions. (His later concert works would include the *Piano Concerto in F*, 1925; and *An American in Paris*, 1928.) On

Broadway, Gershwin was about to launch a new career as well. But here he faced a basic problem. Hired to write the songs for what would turn out to be *Lady, Be Good!*, Gershwin told his father, "[I want to] write an absolutely new type of musical show, with modernistic words as well as modernistic tunes. But where can I find a librettist? The well-known guys want the show written their way." His father's reply: "Try Ira."

Ira Gershwin (1896–1983), though older than his brother, tended to stand in George's shadow. The brothers had quite different personalities. "If George was streamlined and propulsive, Ira was reserved and scholarly," wrote S. N. Behrman, who knew them both. "One sensed in Ira at the very center of involvement, a well of detachment. George gave you everything at once." Moreover, George's talent was for music; and Ira's for words. And like many of the great lyricists of his generation whose parents were immigrants—Lorenz Hart, E. Y. "Yip" Harburg, Howard Dietz—Ira had come to master with extraordinary wit the ways and byways of thought in a language not native to the household in which he was raised.

Ira came of age as a writer in an era not only excited by words, crossword puzzles, and new coinages, but almost drunk with a sense of inventing the native idiom afresh. From the wit expounded by the "vicious circle" of the Algonquin Hotel's Round Table to the "slanguage" of *Variety*, the weekly newspaper touted as "the Bible of the theatrical profession," there exuded a new and confident self-awareness of what H. L. Mencken now proclaimed as *The American Language*. Much of this spirit informed Ira's work as he wrote a kind of "society verse" (*vers de société*) in which he subjected humorous aperçus in the vernacular to the discipline of poetic forms. Some of his verse appeared in the "smart" periodicals and newspaper columns of the day, which, by regularly featuring such work, gave a rising generation of gifted humorists its first public exposure. Other efforts in the vein he tailored to his brother's earliest melodies, as he made his way from versifier to lyricist.

In the course of a long career as a professional lyricist, Ira was to write for many of Broadway's top musicians, both during George's lifetime (Vincent Youmans: *Two Little Girls in Blue*, 1921; Harold Arlen: *Life Begins at 8:40*), and after George's untimely death of a brain tumor at age thirty-eight (Kurt Weill: *Lady in the Dark*; Arthur Schwartz: *Park Avenue*, 1946). But it was to George and George's music that Ira seemed to respond most directly. And in a unique and particularly complementary bond that the brothers forged in collaboration with one another, they

Al Hirschfeld caricatures Ira and George Gershwin, partners in song and smoke.

created a body of extraordinary work for the Broadway stage—not to mention Hollywood, where, in 1937, for a series of movies, they reached the pinnacle of their achievement as songwriters with such songs as "They All Laughed," "They Can't Take That Away from Me," "A Foggy Day," and "Love Is Here to Stay." George "looked to Ira for guidance, for critical evaluation, for taste"; Ira looked to George for inspiration: "He was always full of new ideas, and he was so good a musician, that I could do things with lyrics that I couldn't do with just a songwriter."

Lady, Be Good! not only marked the Broadway debut of George and Ira as the songwriting team for a book show, it also heralded the arrival of fresh energy and imagination to musical comedy. "The whole thing had a new look to it, a flow, and also a new sound," recalled Fred Astaire, the star of the show. "It was slick and tongue-in-cheek, a definite departure in concept and design." The show's success helped set a standard not only for a new look and sound but also for the pacing, style, and tone of what was to become the dominant form of musical entertainment on Broadway in the next two decades. Producers Alex Aarons (1891?–1943) and Vinton Freedley (1891–1969) did not preside over the trend, yet their talent, skill, and taste as entrepreneurs did much to define such entertainment and the direction it would take. Aarons and Freedley mounted eight of the fifteen full-length musical productions the Gershwins wrote or cowrote between 1924 and 1935, the length of their joint careers on Broadway. Among these were some of the best offerings in musical comedy of the era—including *Lady, Be Good!* (1924), *Oh, Kay!* (1926), *Funny Face* (1927), and *Girl Crazy* (1930). (In 1935, the Gershwins crowned their theater collaboration—together with novelist DuBose Heyward—in an astonishing about-face from musical comedy with a three-act folk opera of deeply affecting pathos, *Porgy and Bess.*)

Of their hits in the Aarons and Freedley mold, the two most popular were *Lady, Be Good!* and *Girl Crazy. Lady, Be Good!* concerned a brother-and-sister team of vaudevillians who become ever more deeply entagled in high society as a way out of their hard luck until the heroine (Adele Astaire) saves her brother (Fred Astaire) from penury and a loveless marriage by impersonating a Mexican heiress. In *Girl Crazy*, a Manhattan playboy is sent by his father to an all-male cowboy town in Arizona to curb the affliction of the show's title; only once there he sets up a dude ranch filled with showgirls instead. The shows tempered the madcap of farce with romantic or sentimental attachments that, for want of precision, went by the name of love. But they were tempered, above all, by the Gershwins' songs, with their distinctive blend of grace and gusto.

In the showwriting partnership, George's music came first; then came Ira's words. The procedure was standard songwriting practice at the time, and because of it Ira disclaimed any connection between what he did as a "lyrist" and literature. "Since most of [my] lyrics ... were arrived at by fitting words mosaically to music already composed, any resemblance to actual poetry, living or dead, is highly improbable."

Alongside "a fondness for music [and] a feeling for rhyme," Ira felt a lyricist had to have "a sense of whimsy and humor, an eye for the balanced sentence, [and] an ear for the current phrase." He possessed these in abundance, plus a certain polish and literacy that he hid beneath terse impertinences and an impish love affair with slang: "'S wonderful! 'S marvelous. . . . 'S awful nice! 'S Paradise." Debunking formality yet eminently smart, moreover, Ira's lyrics were oblique. They moved to the contours of a fun-loving civility that both courted emotion and kept it at bay. If that saved them from becoming mawkish, it also gave the impression that the singers who sang them were more playmates than lovers. "You've made my life so glamorous,/You can't blame me for feeling amorous" was as piquant a musical comedy statement of affection as the era would afford—precisely because it never actually said "I love you."

George's music was, in his words, "full of outdoor pep." If by pep he understood what Fitzgerald called the "nervous energy" of the Jazz Age, George's pep meant "sweet" rather than "hot"—or, as he so instructed the pit band on the opening night of *Girl Crazy*, "not Harlem hot, Park Avenue hot." While many of his early songs show a rather conventional use of blue notes and syncopations ("I'll Build a Stairway to Paradise," "Sweet and Low-Down"), Gershwin soon discovered subtler and more inventive ways of developing such Jazz Age hallmarks. In the title song of *Lady, Be Good!* the blue notes are not part of the melody but the harmony. In "Fascinating Rhythm," from the same show, the phrases themselves are syncopated: a repeating melody of 7 eighth notes (6 notes + 1 rest) conflicts with the regular pulse of 8 eighth notes in every bar.

Bar 1: Fas-ci-nat-ing rhy-thm – You've
Bar 2: got me on the go – Fas-ci-
Bar 3: nat-ing rhy-thm – I'm all a
Bar 4: qui-ver.

"FASCINATING RHYTHM" (*LADY, BE GOOD!*)

Lady, Be Good! set the pace for the rest of the Aarons and Freedley shows as veritable showcases for the Gershwins: *Oh, Kay!* ("Do Do Do," "Someone to Watch Over Me"), *Funny Face* ("'S Wonderful," "My One and Only"), and *Girl Crazy*, which produced more hit songs than perhaps any of their other productions. These included "I Got Rhythm," sung by Ethel Merman in her introduction to the musical comedy stage, and "Embraceable You," one of the most exquisite ballads to come out of the Golden Age of Tin Pan Alley. The song's superb blend of wit and feeling is the result of a fine matching of musical and verbal ideas. Consider how the 3-note opening, which then repeats and expands to 7 notes, is matched by "embrace" expanding to "embraceable"; and how this is intensified by the rhyme "irreplaceable" as the melody recurs complete but at a higher level to balance off and round out the first

Ex. 7-1. George Gershwin, music, Ira Gershwin, lyrics: "Embraceable You," *Girl Crazy*

Em-brace me, My sweet em - brace - a-ble you!___

Em-brace me, You ir - re - place - a-ble you!___

eight bars (Ex. 7-1). There are few finer examples of the symbiosis of the brothers' talents.

Songs like these may account for the better part of the Gershwins' distinctive output for Broadway. But they do not account for all of it. Much of their writing in the 1930s became less concerned with creating independent show songs than theater scores in which songs played a more integral part. Three shows from their later work are of special interest for consistently moving away from the Aarons and Freedley model and toward what a newspaper at the time touted as "an entirely new [Broadway] genre." These are the musical satires *Strike Up the Band* (1927, rev. 1930), *Of Thee I Sing* (1931), and *Let 'Em Eat Cake* (1933), all with scores by the Gershwins and books by George S. Kaufman and Morrie Ryskind (1895–1985). The second of these proved a landmark in the development of Broadway musicals both for its successful marriage of verbal and musical wit, and for its rethinking of musical comedy conventions in terms of the dramatic integration of its musical parts.

Of Thee I Sing told a story that made mockery of American political institutions. Lacking a genuine political campaign issue, John P. Wintergreen (William Gaxton) runs for president on a platform to "Put Love in the White House." If elected, he will marry the winner of a nationwide beauty contest. He wins the election, but he also falls in love with his secretary, Mary Turner (Lois Moran), and marries her instead of contest winner Diana Devereaux. At a press conference following his wedding/inauguration (the same ceremony took care of both), the new president convinces everyone of the legitimacy of his action on sentimental grounds. Everyone, that is, except the French ambassador, who threatens war with the United States over the slight to the honor of Miss Devereaux, the "illegitimate daughter of an illegitimate son of an illegitimate nephew of

The highest elected office-holders in the United States as lampooned in *Of Thee I Sing*,
l. to r.: Victor Moore (Vice President Alexander Throttlebottom) and William Gaxton
(President John P. Wintergreen).

Napoleon." With the president's love life precipitating an international
crisis, his political support erodes and he faces impeachment charges.
Mary interrupts his trial to announce she is pregnant, however, and the
Senate cannot bring itself to impeach an "expectant" president. ("Posterity is just around the corner," sings the ensemble.) The revelation resolves

another impasse as well. For in the president's "delicate condition," it falls constitutionally to the vice president, Alexander Throttlebottom (Victor Moore), to save Miss Devereaux' honor by assuming those obligations the president is unable to fulfill, and the two are married.

A touch of madness inspired these proceedings, yet there was also method in it. The lead comedian, Moore, had a full-length role that was wholly part of the show rather than an excuse for interlarding it with comic bits. Here was a farce with the coherence and wit more characteristic of a stage play than of a musical comedy. Behind it lurked the brilliance of George S. Kaufman (1889–1961), journalist, playwright, play doctor, and play director. Somewhat of a curmudgeon himself, Kaufman was a master of the wisecrack, the put-down, and the riposte, and the one Round Table wit of the Algonquin circle who consistently put his humor to work on the stage. He wrote some forty-five scripts for the musical and nonmusical theaters, almost all of them in collaboration. On the legitimate stage he worked with Marc Connelly, Edna Ferber, and, most famously, Moss Hart (*You Can't Take It with You*, 1936; *The Man Who Came to Dinner*, 1939). On the musical stage his most notable collaborators included Morrie Ryskind, with whom he wrote books for *The Cocoanuts* (1925) and *Animal Crackers* (1928), both for the Marx Brothers—before their Gershwin collaborations; Moss Hart (*I'd Rather Be Right*, 1937; *Sing Out the News*, 1938), and later, behind the scenes, Abe Burrows (*Guys and Dolls*, 1950; *Silk Stockings*, 1955). In the history of Broadway musicals, few writers have created funnier librettos than Kaufman, and fewer have had his success in working in the satirical vein.

The madcap and the method of Kaufman's work with Ryskind on *Of Thee I Sing*, however, called for musical moments to match. The Gershwins rose to the occasion. Wintergreen's campaign song made mockery of political piety and dewy-eyed romance in one shot: "Of Thee I Sing, Baby." His press conference song with Mary used a love-conquers-all approach to deflect reporters' political concerns: "Who Cares?" Both numbers also became hits outside the theater, ironically as genuine love songs. But songs with no chance for Tin Pan Alley success had a freedom in the show these songs did not: to poke fun at other subjects besides love and to do so in more musical terms. They parodied birth announcements in a bounding Viennese waltz ("I'm about to be a mother"); lampooned the indistinguishability of the Supreme Court justices in the uniform steps of the whole-tone scale ("We're the one, two, three, four, five, six, seven, eight, nine Supreme Court Judges"); and travestied well-known campaign tunes outright ("Wintergreen for President!"/"Hail, Hail, the Gang's All Here"). In sum, the wit of the show was as much a product of its score as of its book.

In addition, the score extended the scope of the music beyond songs. The action itself was often sung—and no action was too trivial for singing, even the vice president's congressional roll call ("The Senator from Minnesota?"/ "Present."/ "Check!"). Moreover, as the music expanded in its storytelling function, it also expanded in form, sometimes developing entire scene finalettos to match the act finales. *Of Thee I Sing* even had a through-composed act 1 finale whose structure bore a remarkable resemblance to that of *The Mikado*. In fact, the musical abundance of the score and its direct connection to the book made this musical comedy seem more like an operetta in the vein of Offenbach and Gilbert and Sullivan—a "satirical operetta" rather than a sentimental one. *Of Thee I Sing* became a popular hit. But the use of satire at the heart of a Broadway show would shortly become an issue.

In 1932 *Of Thee I Sing* won a Pulitzer Prize for drama, the first for a Broadway musical. Yet even as the Pulitzer committee brought its national prestige to bear in recognizing the quality of the work and thus placing the musical comedy enterprise itself in a new cultural light, it misrepresented the very character of the piece it chose to honor. Since the award honored dramatic literature, the committee viewed the musical as a play—but only a play. (That placed it in competition that season with Eugene O'Neill's *Mourning Becomes Electra*.) And so it ignored the music outright. It then compounded the omission in the commission of another error in judgment: "Not only is [*Of Thee I Sing*] coherent and well knit enough to class as a play, aside from the music," the Pulitzer citation read, "but it is a biting and true satire on American politics."

Drama critic Brooks Atkinson took to the pages of the *New York Times* and took the committee to task. He praised the honorees for their success in bringing "intelligence to a form of stage writing that . . . long contented itself with hackneyed imbecility." But instead of any "biting and true satire" in what they had written, he found only "general satire and a tart version of old-line musical comedy." Indeed, the only real difference between *Of Thee I Sing* and the kind of musical comedy scripts Kaufman and Ryskind had previously written for the

Marx Brothers was the consistency with which the new show focused its cheeky irreverence on American political institutions. To historian Arthur Schlesinger, Jr.,

> *the irreverence lacked the sharp focus of really trenchant satire. This was certainly not due to a shortage of material. When "Of Thee I Sing" opened the day after Christmas 1931, there were eight million people unemployed, more than 16 percent of the labor force and twice as many as the year before. But the Depression was hardly mentioned, and then only to be dismissed: "Who cares what banks fail in Yonkers—long as you've got a kiss that conquers."*

But wasn't that the point? *Of Thee I Sing* exuded a kind of optimistic energy and confidence in America (if not in all its institutions) that would in due course be justified. Removed in spirit from any critique of Depression-era politics, *Of Thee I Sing* more closely resembled a farce with a political setting than a satire with a real political agenda. Consider the following exchange, from act 2, scene 2, between a president facing an impending impeachment trial and a bumbling vice president concerned about what to do with the executive power that will be his if the president is convicted:

THROTTLEBOTTOM: I don't know anything about being President I just found out today how to be Vice President. . . . Isn't there some book I could read?

WINTERGREEN: Sure—I'm writing one. *What Every Young President Ought to Know.*

THROTTLEBOTTOM: Has it got pictures?

WINTERGREEN: It's got everything. Tells you just what to do. Of course the first four years are easy. You don't do anything except try to get re-elected.

THROTTLEBOTTOM: That's pretty hard these days.

WINTERGREEN: The next four years you wonder why the hell you wanted to be re-elected. Then you go fishing.

THROTTLEBOTTOM: Well, couldn't I save a lot of time and go fishing right now?

WINTERGREEN: No, you got to wait until an important matter comes up and then you go fishing.

If satire and farce coincide in how they go about their business, their ends are not the same. Satire is grounded in a moral vision that farce altogether lacks. In fact, satire shapes the elements of farce into a moral pattern, seizing on comic ridicule as a weapon to expose, condemn, perhaps even reform a vice or folly. It "postulates an ideal condition of man or decency, and then despairs of it; and enjoys the despair, masochistically." Farce, by contrast, "views vice as trivial, commonplace, or frivolous, thus accepting what satire condemns. Both farce and satire perceive the distance between the world as it is and the world as it could be, but farce enjoys the world's potential for nonsense while satire yearns for the world's potential goodness." *Of Thee I Sing* simply does not meet the moral test for satire. It is so densely packed with knaves and fools and wall-to-wall nonsense that there is almost no room for goodness in at all.

Unlike *Of Thee I Sing*, the earlier *Strike Up the Band* began as a satire when it was first written in 1927, less than a decade after the end of World War I. Kaufman's script told a biting tale of a Connecticut cheese manufacturer who, to benefit his business, instigates a war with Switzerland under the cloak of patriotism (American cheese vs. Swiss cheese). The idealism of a young newspaper reporter, who risked the love of the cheese magnate's daughter to oppose the war, stood in contrast to the sanctimonious profiteering and knee-jerk patriotism Kaufman condemned. The show folded after two weeks of tryouts in Philadelphia. Scott Fitzgerald might have explained the failure one way: "It was characteristic of the Jazz Age that it had no interest in politics at all." Kaufman's celebrated dictum was perhaps more to the point: "Satire is what closes on Saturday night." Then in 1930, a show bearing the same name—and not much else—became a Broadway hit. In the interim, Morrie Ryskind had been hired to blunt the sharpness of Kaufman's book, and thus a good deal of its point. He even sweetened the nature of the war itself by changing its cause from cheese to chocolate. And so with a new and clearly happy ending, some more memorably romantic Gershwin songs ("Soon," "I've Got a Crush on You"), and the buffoonery of burlesque stars Bobby Clark and Paul McCullough to overshadow both, *Strike Up the Band* became a musical comedy hit: broadly satirical perhaps, but not strictly satire.

Both shows succeeded but in different ways: *Of Thee I Sing* never set out to be a satire in the moral sense; *Strike Up the Band* intended to, but did not end up as one. If the Jazz Age had no interest in politics, however, the generation of the Depression certainly did, and satire was one of the forms it took. Even the Marx Brothers took a shot at it, memorably, in the film *Duck Soup* (1933). Satire gave some weight to a farce much as farcical elements made satire palatable.

Yet Broadway musicals that sailed under the flag of satire had rough waters to plow regardless of their political point of view. *Knickerbocker Holiday*, by composer Kurt Weill and librettist Maxwell Anderson, began as a conservative critique of President Roosevelt's New Deal. To make sure there was no mistaking the point, Anderson published an explanation of what he called "the Politics of *Knickerbocker Holiday*" in the *New York Times*. But the collaborative pressures aimed at making a musical a success in the Broadway marketplace worked against the single-mindedness of Anderson's purpose. In the end, subjected to input of all kinds, *Knickerbocker Holiday* became something rather charming and much tamer than intended. On the other hand, *The Cradle Will Rock* maintained an uncompromising Marxist critique of American capitalism from inception to final performance. But it did so only by steering clear of both the Scylla of Broadway collaboration and the Charybdis of Broadway production. The show's book, lyrics, and music were not the work of a team, but of a single artist, Marc Blitzstein, whose idealism stayed the course. Nor was the show produced by the usual means of private enterprise but, ironically, by a publicly funded government agency, the Federal Theatre Project. On Broadway, where eventually it ran for several months, however, it garnered only what could be called a success d'estime—defined by George S. Kaufman as a success that runs out of steam.

By contrast, *Strike Up the Band* and *Of Thee I Sing*, both Broadway hits, were also forerunners of those 1930s musical comedies that embraced themes with political resonance. They differed from comparable shows of the 1920s by lampooning public affairs as much as private ones. Many were satirical; none were really satires. Some lacked the coherent focus of satire. For example, *Let 'Em Eat Cake*, a mordant sequel to *Of Thee I Sing*, lashed out in so many directions—socially up and down, politically left and right—that coauthor Ira Gershwin quipped, "If *Strike Up the Band* was a satire on War, and *Of Thee I Sing* one on Politics, *Let 'Em Eat Cake* was a satire on Practically Everything." Other shows may have had the focus but lacked the conviction: *Face the Music* began by citing real examples of corruption in the administration of New York's Mayor Jimmy Walker, and ended by forgiving the very things it had set out to satirize. In the final analysis, whether the shows touched on dubious political practices at home (*I'd Rather Be Right*; *Louisiana Purchase*) or disturbing American exploits overseas (*Hooray for What!*; *Leave it to Me*), they aimed to reassure audiences, reminding them after all that they lived, as Yip Harburg put it in *Hooray for What?*, in "God's Country": "Where smiles are broader— freedom greater,/Every man is his own dictator."

Reassurances of this sort seemed glib for the most part: Musicals that featured them rarely defined the values they celebrated, or put them to the test. (That these shows took relatively uncritical positions, in fact, undercuts the meanings that have since been ascribed to the trend in musical comedies of the Depression toward political relevance.) Neither did such shows seek to influence the making of public policy, nor were they grounded in any ideology other than what would permit conditions for the production and consumption of entertainments of their kind to prosper. ("The trouble with the country," said President Roosevelt as a character in *I'd Rather Be Right*, "is that I don't know what the trouble with the country is.") They remained farces that simply intersected with the worlds of political, social, and economic concerns.

Of these, *Of Thee I Sing* was Broadway's best example. Although a musical comedy, its script had such wit and coherence it read like a play. More to the point, the script received such a degree of respect in performance it even played like a play—actors, comedians especially, stuck to their lines. This marked a small shift of emphasis in musical comedy in favor of the text. The awarding of the Pulitzer Prize called attention to the importance of this change. And the change itself found tangible expression when *Of Thee I Sing*'s libretto was published and sold in book form—a first for an American musical comedy. Reading a musical now no longer seemed a contradiction in cultural terms. "Legitimate" playwrights might even be tempted to try their hands at a form of musical entertainment hitherto prized and despised for its mindlessness. Maxwell Anderson tried despite his sense of insecurity about the medium. Moss Hart tried despite his initial ambivalence over the less than legitimate enterprise. Indeed, established playwrights like Anderson and Hart who began scripting musicals in the 1930s helped transform the character of Broadway show making in the following decade by asserting through their musical theater work something of the authority that playwrights enjoyed on the nonmusical stage.

Where *Of Thee I Sing* least resembled a play, of course, was in its score. But even here the achievement of the Gershwin brothers would have a major impact on future developments in musical theater. For *Of Thee I Sing* stood at the creative apex as well as the chronological middle of a trio of works that challenged Broadway musical conventions by more than satirical content alone. With Ira's sly lyrics and George's jazz-based musical idioms, the scores to each of the three probed different ways of wedding the style and sensibility of musical comedy to the dramatically integrated and extended musical forms of operetta. Not always convincing in its mix of Broadway genres, the result, at its most successful in *Of Thee I Sing*, opened up a potential middle ground for musical theater by bridging categorical divisions within it. This opening laid the groundwork for a more radical probing into the mixture of forms, styles, and sensibilities that challenged entrenched divisions in American culture: the distinction between "low" and "high," and even the emerging consensus over a "middle." Despite profound differences between the themes, tone, and style of the works themselves and what they represent, the musical structures, aesthetic ambition, and imaginative leap that made a musical comedy like *Of Thee I Sing* possible were fundamentally of the same order that made conceivable the more precipitous leap to the American folk opera *Porgy and Bess* (see chapter 10).

COLE PORTER

By the 1930s, the things the Gershwin songs possessed in abundance had come to be prized generally on Broadway, in Hollywood, and on Tin Pan Alley. Polish, wit, and urbanity were now characteristic features of a song style that made New York "smartness" a national ideal. In the words of American music historian Charles Hamm, more than ever before, American popular song

> *was dominated by composers and lyricists born and trained in New York, writing songs for publishers who not only had their offices in New York, but were themselves products of the city. The style of the music and of the lyrics had become a New York style, and general attitudes as to what a song should be and where it should fit into American culture were also shaped by the climate and taste of New York.*

There was little effective cultural input from the rest of America into New York in these days, and to the extent that Tin Pan Alley songs reflected American culture in a broader sense, they did so because the rest of the country was willing to accept a uniquely urban, New York product, not because New York was absorbing elements of American culture from west of the Hudson River or south of Atlantic City. Hollywood was not a real exception to this, since it was musically a West Coast extension of New York. The songs of Kern, Gershwin, Porter, and their contemporaries were urban, sophisticated, and stylish, and they were intended for people who could be described by one or more of these adjectives—or aspired to be.

No one's songs more readily epitomized this style in the 1930s than those of Cole Porter. "Cole Porter is definitive of an era," said Johnny Mercer, a songwriter not from New York but from Savannah, Georgia, and so particularly well situated to appreciate Porter's urbanity and its cultural resonance. "He IS those years, you know? He is the style of all those shows, all that period. He represents it better than anybody else, better even than Kern or Berlin. Porter's so . . . thirties!" And so New York, Mercer might have added. But Porter, ironically, was not native to the New York style his songs epitomized. And if, as with the zeal of a convert, he learned to out–New York New Yorkers at it, the resulting tension was but one of many that characterize his work and that continue to make it a source of fascination for audiences to this day.

Cole Porter (1891–1964) was born in Indiana, wealthy, Protestant, and privileged. He attended Yale, where, to judge from his grades, he spent less time studying for classes than working on songs for football games, college shows, and a host of other undergraduate pastimes. ("In Yale," he later confessed, "I was Gilbert and Sullivan crazy.") After a year at Harvard Law School, he switched to music, pursued traditional studies in harmony and counterpoint, and in 1916 he saw his first professional musical comedy fail on Broadway. In 1917 he moved to Paris, studied composition at the Schola Cantorum, and, despite his homosexuality, married an American socialite wealthier than himself with whom he enjoyed a lifestyle of conspicuous luxury in Europe. He preferred, he said, the "rich-rich" to the unhyphenated kind.

Beneath a cultivated playboy image, however, lay a no-nonsense dedication to work. "Social in his tastes but Middle-Western-Protestant-

Puritan in the seriousness of his aspirations," Porter worked at writing songs—words and music. These were designed to amuse an international coterie of friends and celebrities who moved in his circle, and they were filled with private references and recondite allusions that rendered them virtually valueless in the more democratic marketplace of Tin Pan Alley. While many were performed during the 1920s in revues produced in London, Paris, and New York, Porter remained a kind of "gentleman-composer," in Brendan Gill's words, "seeking to avoid Broadway and yet hoping to be pursued by it." He may have counted himself among the American expatriates in postwar Paris who comprised a "lost generation." But Porter was not one of the culturally dispossessed, a lost soul in the sense of *une génération de perdus*. Rather, until he returned to Broadway in the late 1920s, he was as good as lost to his métier, part of *"une génération perdue"* in the sense Gertrude Stein apparently had in mind when she coined the phrase: someone whose professional career the war had so interrupted that, once it was over, he was too old to be apprenticed to a trade. Had he died at thirty-eight, as Gershwin did, Porter would have left a negligible Broadway legacy. At a time in life when nearly all his peers among the Golden Age's master craftsmen had already made their marks on Broadway, his musical comedy career had yet to take off.

With his return to Broadway it did take off: meteorically. From 1928 until 1944, about the time Hollywood canonized him for pop culture with a film biography (*Night and Day*, 1945), Porter created songs for a new Broadway musical comedy almost every season—fourteen altogether. And he went on to write a handful of book shows after that—including the finest theater score of his career in *Kiss Me, Kate*—though his later output was generally less inspired and less sustained. He was plagued by the permanently crippling effects of a horse-riding accident in 1937, and by the change in theatrical focus that overtook Broadway in the wake of *Oklahoma!* In a theater career that spanned nearly forty years, Porter wrote songs for numerous revues and for about twenty book shows in all. But, apart from *Kiss Me, Kate*, his best work came out of the earlier musical comedies—including *Paris*, 1928 ("Let's Do It"); *Fifty Million Frenchmen*, 1929 ("You Do Something to Me"); *Gay Divorce*, 1932 ("Night and Day"); *Jubilee*, 1935 ("Begin the Beguine," "Just One of Those Things"); *Red, Hot and Blue!*, 1936 ("It's De-Lovely"); *Leave It to Me*, 1938 ("My Heart Belongs to Daddy"); *Du*

Barry Was a Lady, 1939 ("Friendship"); *Mexican Hayride*, 1944 ("I Love You"); and, above all, *Anything Goes* (1934).

Anything Goes was originally concocted by Princess Theater veterans Guy Bolton and P. G. Wodehouse—their last joint venture as Broadway scriptwriters. It was then thoroughly overhauled by Howard Lindsay (1888–1968) and Russel Crouse (1893–1966)—their first. The story traces the screwball adventures of a lapsed evangelist, Reno Sweeney (Ethel Merman), who harbors romantic feelings for Billy Crocker (William Gaxton), although he is in love with someone else. She follows him onboard an ocean liner bound for London, where he has stowed away to prevent the girl he loves (also on board) from marrying a titled Englishman. Through a series of intrigues and with the help of a gangster, Public Enemy No. 13, who is traveling disguised as a clergyman (Victor Moore), Billy gets his girl at the end, and Reno winds up with the Englishman.

Anything Goes is the one Porter musical of the period that has survived by succeeding repeatedly in full-scale revivals in New York, albeit with revised books. Yet the original relied heavily on topical gags and plot points tailored to the talents of its stars, both typical of such shows at the time. So the book has undergone basic changes with each major new production. For all its topicality, however, *Anything Goes* can be considered as a social document of its period, perhaps less for what it touches on than for what it fails to address. The show spoofed the cultural foibles of the 1930s, but with barely a hint of the issues that informed other stageworks that came out of the Great Depression. Only in the tongue-in-cheek woes of its title song would Porter even concede that there was conceivably as much cause for alarm in the economic upheavals of the age:

> *And that gent today*
> *You gave a cent today*
> *Once had several chateaux*

as in the era's social improprieties:

> *Good authors too who once knew better words*
> *Now only use four-letter words*
> *Writing prose.*

"ANYTHING GOES" (*ANYTHING GOES*)

The revivability of *Anything Goes* rests chiefly on its score. Not only are there simply more hit tunes in it than in any other Porter work of the period, but many of them are now considered American musical comedy archetypes: the quintessential Broadway torch song ("I Get a Kick Out of You"), love ballad ("All Through the Night"), list song ("You're the Top"), title song ("Anything Goes"), and late-in-the-show showstopper ("Blow, Gabriel, Blow").

"I Get a Kick Out of You" offers a fine example of Porter's distinctive way with a theater song: It respects formal conventions but goes the extra mile with them, lyrically and musically. The main body of the song—called the *refrain* or chorus—is a classic example of the AABA format which by the 1930s had displaced the binary AB/AB' or AB/AC pattern as the preferred Tin Pan Alley archetype. (Displaced but not replaced: "You're the Top" exemplifies the older binary type.) Here, each A section details another of life's pleasures that the singer can have but doesn't want (A_1: "I get no kick from champagne"; A_2: "Some get a kick from cocaine" [I don't]; A_3: "I get no kick in a plane"). And true to form, the B section alters the pattern: musically, by changing keys (modulating to the subdominant); and lyrically, by revealing what the three As don't (that what the singer does want she can't have—the "you" of the title—and that "I Get a Kick Out of You" is, in fact, a torch song).

Porter was not given to public pronouncements about his work habits. But he once explained how he generally approached the business of songwriting:

> *First, I think of the idea and then I fit it to a title. Then, I go to work on the melody, spotting the title at certain moments in the melody, and then I write the lyric—the end first—that way, it has a strong finish. I do the lyrics like I'd do a crossword puzzle.*

Accordingly, if Porter's "idea" here is to compare love to the thrill of other "highs," he fits these together through the slang phrase that becomes his title. Then perhaps he comes up with the idea of a scalar climb for his melody. But not content simply to repeat the first A-pattern of words and music in the ensuing As, which was the Tin Pan Alley norm, Porter turns every successive A into a more intense "kick" than the last. With each new A, the number of rhymes increases,

Ex. 7-2. Cole Porter, music and lyrics: "I Get a Kick Out of You," *Anything Goes*

A¹ (mm. 5–8)

champagne: Mere al - co - (hol) does - n't thrill me at (all)

A² (mm. 21–27)

cocaine: I'm sure that (if) I had e - ven one (sniff,) it would

bore me ter - (rif) - ic' - ly too

A³ (mm. 53–59)

a plane: (Fly) - ing too (high) with some (guy) in the (sky) is (my)

(i) - dea of noth - ing to do

N.B. Because of the notation, this song is twice the usual length of a standard song:
Each section consists of 16 bars instead of 8, so the entire song is 64 bars long instead of 32.

and the melody climbs higher: in A₁ (champagne), he rhymes "alcohol" and takes the melody to B♭; in A₂ (cocaine), "sniff" gets two rhymes as the melody rises to C: in A₃ (plane), "fly" gets five rhymes as the melody goes all the way up to F (Ex. 7-2). En route to the song's "strong finish," then, Porter packs the AABA form with an intensifying wealth of details that drive home Reno's one-sided obsession.

However remarkable on their own, Porter's songs have been said to mesh awkwardly with the dialogue that surrounds them; and he himself claimed to have "no book sense" when it came to crafting librettos. There may be a grain of truth in such assertions, but neither one entirely represents the case. Consider the end of the librettists' "leadin-in" to the above song and the start of the songwriter's verse that introduces the refrain—the inevitabile "bump" in a musical comedy as it crosses over from book to score:

BILLY: You'll get a kick out of London . . .
RENO: But you won't be there.
BILLY: What difference will that make?
BILLY: Do you really want to know?
    (*She sings "I Get a Kick Out of You" and exits after song*)
    My story is much too sad to be told . . .

There is no break in logic between the spoken leadin-in and the sung verse. (Notice how nonchalantly Billy already plants the "kick" idea in the dialogue.) Yet both deliberately call attention to the change from speech to song by which that logic is articulated: "Do you really want to know?" (a sure cue for a song); "My story is much too sad to be told" (so she sings it). The song is presentational, and there is no effort wasted in pretending it is not. For Porter and most everyone involved with the medium at the time, the relationship of song to book, no matter how serious the song or the situation, was self-reflexive and often playfully ironic. At times Porter even used his verses to make sure audiences did not forget that the singers knew that they were singing—most deliciously perhaps in "It's De-lovely":

> *This verse you've started seems to me*
> *The Tin-Pantithesis of melody,*
> *So spare me, please, the pain,*
> *Just skip the damn thing and sing the refrain.*
>
>   "IT'S DE-LOVELY" (*RED, HOT AND BLUE*)

The idea of a structural "seamlessness" between a book and score goes against the grain of musical comedy.

Moreover, Porter collaborated with many of the genre's best book writers. Among them was Herbert Fields (1897–1958), a musical comedy specialist who captured the entertainment's mix of sentimentality and cynicism better than most. He was also one of the most successful writers in the business. He wrote or co-wrote books for innumerable hit shows from *Hit the Deck* in the 1920s to *Annie Get Your Gun* in the 1940s. He wrote no fewer than seven books for the team of Richard Rodgers and Lorenz Hart—*Dearest Enemy, A Connecticut Yankee*—and another seven for Porter—*Fifty Million Frenchmen, Du Barry Was a Lady*. Fields was a son of the burlesque comedian Lew Fields. (His brother Joseph and sister Dorothy also became musical comedy librettists.) Porter found this reassuring because he felt Herbert could always dip into his father's trunk for a comedy routine to rescue a show whenever book trouble occurred, as it invariably did, in the second act. (Herbert could invent such routines on his own—or with sister Dorothy. For *Something for the Boys* (1943), for example, the two contrived to have the heroine finally win the hero's heart when she guided his disabled plane to safety by picking up his radio signals on the ground through a carborundum-coated filling in her tooth.) Ultimately, musical comedy was not dramatic literature but a performative arena for Porter and his librettists: a meeting ground of actors, comedians, singers, dancers, and songs. A book simply provided the occasion; and a song served as the blueprint for a performance that was tied to the book rather than as an enhancement of the book itself.

Relying on a time-honored tradition, Porter wrote with a specific performer in mind. For Jimmy Durante (*The New Yorkers*), Bob Hope (*Red, Hot and Blue!*), Bert Lahr (*Du Barry*), Bobby Clark (*Mexican Hayride*), and the host of other great comedians who starred in his shows, Porter suited his style to what was unique in their stage personas. However different they were from one another, he distilled the idiosyncracies of each of their comic styles—from the highbrow eccentricities of Beatrice Lillie ("When I Was a Little Cuckoo," *Seven Lively Arts*, 1944) to the low-down sexuality of Sophie Tucker ("Most Gentlemen Don't Like Love," *Leave It to Me*); and from the tongue-twisting bravura of Danny Kaye ("Let's Not Talk About Love," *Let's Face It*, 1941) to the reticent impishness and vocal limitations of Victor Moore ("Be Like the Bluebird," *Anything Goes*).

Above all, and more often than any other musical comedy songwriter, Porter wrote for the comedienne who was arguably the most distinctive Broadway vocal stylist of the age, Ethel Merman (1908–1984). Starting with *Anything Goes*, he wrote five shows for her in which she not only became a musical comedy star but also forged a new leading-lady image for the genre. Earlier musical comedy stars such as Marilyn Miller had cut rather dainty figures onstage, singing with a light, operatic-style head voice that had been the prevailing vocal ideal. Merman worked both a different image and a different sound, and with sufficient pizzazz to influence an entire generation of Broadway performers. She came across as a brassy dame with a heart of gold. Her

singing seemed metallic as well: She sang with a chest-voice belt reminiscent of the coon shouters of an earlier period. Conrad Osborne, a
vocally astute opera critic, explains the belt as

> *an attempt to extend the normally "short" female chest register*
> *upward. . . . Because of the tension involved in holding the position,*
> *vocal qualities associated with relaxation (vibrato, ability to sing at*
> *less than full intensity), as well as those associated with the integrated*
> *head register it sends packing (sweetness of tone, ductility in phrasing,*
> *flexibility of movement), are closed out. There is no such thing as a*
> *quiet belt, or a beautiful one.*

Merman belted with an astonishing breath control and produced a
clarion intensity of sound without distorting the words or obscuring
the sense of her songs. Porter could not praise her gifts enough:

> *Her voice, to me, is thrilling. She has the finest enunciation of any Amer-*
> *ican singer I know. She has a sense of rhythm few can equal. And her*
> *feeling for comedy is so intuitive that she can get every value out of a line*
> *without ever overstressing a single inference. And she is so damned apt.*

Porter gave Merman practically every hit number in *Anything
Goes*—including the list song, perhaps his most characteristic specialty. List songs are ingeniously rhymed catalogues of items that may
have no particular connection to one another other than their rhymes.
Nor do they usually have any dramatic structure: one almost knows
where the lyrics will end once they've begun. The joy of such songs is
not the arrival but the clever strategies devised in getting there. "Let's
Do It," for one, is an outrageous catalogue of mating habits whose brilliance lies in the way Porter manages to make us care as much about
the list-making as about the love-making that is its subject. This may
be undramatic but it is not untheatrical, especially in the duets he wrote
for Merman in which whole choruses of list songs were be tossed back
and forth in repartee: "Friendship" (with Lahr), "It's De-lovely" (with
Hope), and "You're the Top" (with Gaxton):

> *You're the top!*
> *You're the Colosseum.*

Cole Porter and Ethel Merman rehearse *Du Barry Was a Lady.*

You're the top!
You're the Louvre Museum.
You're a melody from a symphony by Strauss,
You're a Bendel bonnet,
A Shakespeare sonnet,
You're Mickey Mouse . . .

"You're the Top" (Anything Goes)

It is not always clear in these songs whose virtuosity is really on display the performer's or the songwriter's. Yet Porter's songs assumed intelligent audiences to appreciate the virtuosity in the first place. Brimming with a wide range of cultural references, such songs flattered a listener's sense of being in the know. Other of his songs appealed to a sense of sophistication nowhere more pronounced than when they sang of sex and love, which he did not confuse with one another. Porter expanded the scope of popular songs, showing there was more to love than just romance: obsessive love ("I Get a Kick Out of You"), ambivalent love ("It's Bad for Me"), addictive love ("I've Got You Under My Skin"), love even without love at all ("Love for Sale"). And he brought his wit to bear on the subject as well. Where Irving Berlin had once naughtily suggested "Everybody's Doing It" and left it at that, Porter wrote "Let's Do It" and made sure there was no mistaking what he meant.

> *The most refined lady bugs do it*
> *When a gentleman calls.*
> *Moths in your rugs do it,*
> *What's the use of moth balls?*
>
> "LET'S DO IT" (*PARIS*)

It was Moss Hart who said, remembering when Porter's songs were new, "[they made] the majority of the songs we had been singing sound downright provincial."

Porter referred to his lyrics as "brittle, bright poesy." This suggests not the limited compass of popular song texts so much as the somewhat larger enterprise of light verse, a literary genre in which the warmth and intelligence of poetry (but not the range or density) are brought to bear on some humorous aspect of the human condition. Consider Porter, the songwriter, and W. H. Auden, the poet, in a comparable mood in the same year:

> *Is it an earthquake or simply a shock?*
> *Is it the good turtle soup or merely the mock?*
> *Is it a cocktail—this feeling of joy,*
> *Or is what I feel the real McCoy?*
> *Have I the right hunch or have I the wrong?*
> *Will it be Bach I shall hear or just a Cole Porter song?*

Is it a fancy not worth thinking of,
Or is it at long last love?

COLE PORTER, "AT LONG LAST LOVE"
(*YOU NEVER KNOW*, 1938)

Does it look like a pair of pyjamas,
Or the ham in a temperance hotel?
Does its odour remind one of llamas,
Or has it a comforting smell?
Is it prickly to touch as a hedge is,
Or soft as eiderdown fluff?
Is it sharp or quite smooth at the edges?
O tell me the truth about love.

W. H. AUDEN, FROM "TWELVE SONGS" (1938)

The similarities are extraordinary; yet the differences are no less revealing. For Porter's language is less packed than Auden's because Auden's text is self-sufficient while Porter's is incomplete without the music that gives it essential meanings not apparent from reading alone. Moreover, Porter's text was never even meant to be read: It is aimed at a theater audience—a community of listeners who have only one chance to hear it in performance—not the private world of a reader who can go back and reread at leisure. Porter chose theater as his artistic medium (though he also wrote for films and television), and his artistry must be understood in theatrical terms. But Porter's theater stands out from the rest because he saw it as a place where popular culture and elite culture could intersect—sometimes with great success (as in *Kiss Me, Kate's* juxtapositions of Broadway and Shakespeare); sometimes with no success at all (as in *Seven Lively Arts's* mix of Porter, Stravinsky, Salvador Dalí, and Benny Goodman); but mostly in bits and pieces in between.

By the standards of others working in the field, Porter may have been "ridiculously over-educated," his social and cultural horizons hopelessly elite, and his psychological disposition needlessly complicated by a dualistic mode of perception. Yet he made himself at home in what must have seemed to him the confines of Broadway's bourgeois culture; and he did so, moreover, without totally jettisoning the education, the horizons, and the disposition that distinguished his work from the rest. He may have had the most highly cultivated imagination of them all—one he might have put to finer use had, in John Updike's kind phrase, "the immeasurably wider audience for musical comedy not beckoned." But the disparity rankled the likes of Ernest Hemingway, T. W. Adorno, and other defenders of high modernism for whom Porter became an icon of the commercial culture they scorned. The work of other Broadway writers was ostensibly beneath their contempt; only *his* work seemed good enough to warrant their disdain. Not a naïf in matters of the intellect or of the heart, Cole Porter saw his talent primarily in commercial terms and gauged his ambition accordingly. With Porter, then, one was never quite sure whether he thought his songs represented the highest of lowbrow culture or the reverse, though he did leave a clue. In the world he wrote of in "At Long Last Love"—a world in which love was ambiguous if not downright deceptive, and the trash culture of mock turtle soup and used Chevrolets seemed to pass for the real thing—he placed himself quite literally amid the *colportage*. "Will it be Bach I shall hear," he asked, "or just a Cole Porter song?"

RODGERS AND HART

The partnership of Rodgers and Hart lasted for twenty-four years, longer than that of any other songwriting team of the Golden Age. The two, however, were an unlikely pair. Richard Rodgers (1902–1979) was a doctor's son, temperamental yet businesslike in his working habits, a bourgeois family man. Lorenz Hart (1895–1943) was the son of German-Jewish immigrants, a brilliant but mercurial worker, a homosexual. Their songs bore the stamp of their differences: The self-assured romanticism of Rodgers's music often seemed nothing so much as a foil for the acerbic parries of Hart's wit. But the two agreed where their collaboration most counted. "What really brought us together," Rodgers recalled of their first meeting in 1919,

> *was our mutual conviction that the musical theatre, as demonstrated by the pioneering efforts of Bolton, Wodehouse and Kern, was capable of achieving a far greater degree of artistic merit in every area than*

was apparent at the time. We had no idea exactly how it could be done, but we both knew that we had to try.

At the time, Hart, twenty-three and a Columbia University dropout, had found work adapting German operettas for the Shuberts. Rodgers, seven years his junior and with Columbia still before him, had already been exposed to Kern via *Very Good Eddie* and felt he heard in that work "the first truly American theatre music—and it pointed the way I wanted to be led." The two avoided the usual Tin Pan Alley apprenticeship and spent their first five years together writing songs mainly for charity benefits and amateur shows. Major recognition came in 1925 when their song "Manhattan" was heard in the first of *The Garrick Gaieties* revues. *Dearest Enemy*, the first of twenty-two full-length musical comedies they wrote for Broadway over the next seventeen years, soon followed.

The Broadway shows of Rodgers and Hart can be divided into two groups, separated by what Hart called "a 3½ year stretch" of working on films in Hollywood (1931–1935). Three of the twelve musicals that make up the first group were substantial hits: *The Girl Friend*, 1926 ("Blue Room"); *Peggy-Ann*, 1926 ("Where's That Rainbow?"); and the biggest of their early successes, *A Connecticut Yankee*, 1927 ("My Heart Stood Still").

All three shows had books by Herbert Fields, a fellow Columbia student who fancied his association with Rodgers and Hart as a younger, Jazz Age version of the Bolton, Wodehouse, and Kern triumvirate. Their up-to-date stories had settings close to home. In *The Girlfriend* a long Island dairy farmer wins a six-day bicycle race and the heart of the girl who helped him train for it. The heroine in *Peggy-Ann* escapes life's drudgeries in an upstate New York boardinghouse by means of dreams that ultimately lead her to reconcile differences with her boyfriend. The hero in *A Connecticut Yankee*, knocked unconscious, is transported to Arthurian England, where he is made to realize when he wakes up that he is engaged to the wrong girl, and he pursues the right one.

Field's father, who brought something of the old spirit of burlesque to the new shows, produced all three musicals. Consider *A Connecticut Yankee*, for example, based on Mark Twain's bitterly satiric novel in which the chivalric world of ancient Camelot and the contemporary world of American technology utterly destroy each other. Where

Twain not only took himself seriously but virtually paraded his indignation in the novel, the musical simply burlesqued the subject. "Fool humor it is," wrote theater reviewer Burns Mantle. "It lacks the finer touch of satire and boasts rough Broadway wit." He might have had a scene like the following in mind in which King Arthur and the Yankee "Boss" discover the king's wife and his trusted knight Launcelot in a passionate embrace:

ARTHUR: Stand forth, thou two-timer! What do ye here?
LANCELOT: Believe it or not, I'm waiting for a trolley car.
BOSS: That's not playing square with the Round Table, Lancelot.

Arthur speaks of adultery in rather colloquial terms for a king; Lancelot lies with a cliché redolent of the burlesque stage (and an anachronism to boot), and Boss reacts to both with a play on words! So much for Twain's satire—though fidelity to Twain's work here was never the intent.

Critics tired of the sophomoric humor in such juxtapositions as "thou two-timer" throughout the book. But they were delighted with its condensation into a song whose title summed up the exercise in two syllables: "Thou Swell." Indeed, the very brevity imposed by the Tin Pan Alley song form within which Rodgers and Hart worked made possible their winning blend of warmth and wit. The 32-bar song form was the basis for nearly all their work, and Hart explained how they approached its making:

> *I let Richard Rodgers get his tune first. Then I take the most distinctive melodic phrase in his tune and work on that. What I choose is not necessarily the theme or first line but the [melodic] phrase which stands out. Next I try to find the meaning of that phrase and to develop a euphonic set of words to fit it. . . . In a song of this sort the melody and the euphonics of the words themselves are really more important than the sense.*

Hart nonetheless gave his rhymes reasons. In "Here in My Arms" (*Dearest Enemy*), it was the rhythmic contour of Rodgers's melody that led Hart to a rhyme whose outrageousness he left unexplained until after it appeared:

Here in my arms it's adorable!
It's deplorable
That you were never there.

"HERE IN MY ARMS" (*DEAREST ENEMY*)

And in "The Blue Room," it was the repeated note on each downbeat of Rodgers's melody that led Hart to a triple rhyme scheme even more outrageous—and even more difficult to untwist logically in order to make it make sense:

You sew
Your trousseau,
And Robinson Crusoe
Is not so far from worldly cares
As our blue room far away upstairs.

"THE BLUE ROOM" (*THE GIRL FRIEND*)

Such musical-verbal legerdemain made these songs memorable. Indeed, much of the pleasure musical comedy audiences took in so tender a thing as a love song was to catch it in the act of "poking fun at the fun it's having." That combination of tenderness and trickery afforded one of the special pleasures of Rodgers and Hart's songs.

Later, they became less preoccupied with euphonics and cleverness and more focused on creating a sense of the character singing them. Ironies became sharper, insights more penetrating, emotions deeper, and humor more humane. But the newer development in their Broadway writing—already noticeable in songs like "You Took Advantage of Me" (*Present Arms*, 1928) and "Ten Cents a Dance" (*Simple Simon*, 1930)—was interrupted in 1931 when Rodgers and Hart fled from Broadway to Hollywood. At one time or another during the 1930s Berlin, Kern, Porter, and the Gershwins would do the same. For as the theater began to register the effects of the economic depression there was less and less work to be had in New York. Broadway was reeling from the sharpest drop in the total number of productions for a single season in its history: 233 shows in 1929–30; 187 in 1930–31. And, musicals were particularly hard-hit. Gross box office receipts that were $44,500 for the top musical for the last week in May of the 1929–30 season (*Flying High*) were $20,500 for the top musical the same week one year later (*Girl Crazy*). Hollywood offered a lucrative alternative of work in the new medium of sound film, and Rodgers and Hart took it. They chafed, however, under the limitations the studio system placed on writers who were paid only to write songs and *not* to get involved in matters of production. After three years—and the writing of several innovative film scores, such as *Love Me Tonight* (1932) and *Hallelujah, I'm a Bum* (1933)—they gladly returned to New York.

Ten new Broadway musicals make up the second group of their shows. In these George Abbott replaced Fields as the songwriters' chief collaborator—sometimes as a director and producer as well as a bookwriter. With or without Abbott, however, Rodgers and Hart now contributed to the creation of a body of work that helped move American musical comedy from its burlesque roots toward an emerging concept of musical theater. Their new shows included *Jumbo*, 1935 ("My Romance," "Little Girl Blue"); *Babes in Arms*, 1937 ("Where or When," "I Wish I Were in Love Again," "My Funny Valentine," "The Lady Is a Tramp"); *The Boys from Syracuse*, 1938 ("Falling in Love with Love," "This Can't Be Love"); *By Jupiter*, 1942 ("Wait Till You See Her"); and two that particularly expanded the scope of the musical comedy genre and have since proved revivable as well, *On Your Toes* (1936) and *Pal Joey* (1940).

On Your Toes took dancing as its theme. Its humor sprang from the juxtaposition of two dance techniques that had virtually nothing in common and that lay at opposite ends of the cultural spectrum: classical ballet ("La Princesse Zenobia") and Broadway hoofing ("On Your Toes"). The story centered on the efforts of an ex-vaudeville hoofer to reinvigorate a sagging Russian ballet company by getting it to dance a new American jazz ballet, "Slaughter on Tenth Avenue." The highlight of *On Your Toes*, in fact, was the company's performance of the ballet in fifteen minutes of pure dancing near the end of the show—an unusual way to finish a musical comedy.

But "Slaughter" itself was unusual in several respects: who danced it, who wrote the music for it, and who choreographed it. The principal dancers actually were the stars of the show, Tamara Geva and Ray Bolger, who had been chosen for their parts in *On Your Toes* precisely because they could do their own dancing. (Normally, actors and dancers were separately cast on Broadway, a practice that even *Oklahoma!*, for all its celebrated "integration" of dance in a musical, would still respect.) The music was original and expressly composed for the ballet by Richard Rodgers himself. (Normal Broadway practice was to hire a dance arranger to rework the melodies from a show's songs for the dances.) Above all, the ballet movement was not the work of a dance director, the Broadway norm at the time, but that of a classical ballet master, George Balanchine (1904–1983). Balanchine had come to New York from the Ballet Russe de Monte Carlo to form the American School of Ballet, and while he created several companies with the dancers he trained he also worked on Broadway from time to time. His talents, said Agnes de Mille, were "beyond anything Broadway had ever known"; he contributed dances to such shows as *I Married an Angel* (1938), *Cabin in the Sky* (1940), and *Where's Charley?* (1948). Balanchine not only enlarged the vocabulary of musical comedy dance, he changed the way it was understood. Beginning with *On Your Toes*, he insisted that, for what he did in a show, the usual "Dances Staged By" credit be replaced by "Choreography."

Broadway dance directors were generally not choreographers. They were more concerned with assembling steps into routines that they used to fill dance slots in a show. Earlier dance directors like David Bennett (*Rose-Marie; Sunny*) and Bobby Connolly (*Funny Face; Good News*) tended to work within the precision-dance norms of a chorus line. Others, like Sammy Lee (*No, No, Nanette; Oh, Kay!*) and Busby Berkeley (*A Connecticut Yankee; Present Arms*), might typically break the unison effect of the line for more complex production schemes. Some might even work with different emphases altogether: Seymour Felix (*Hit the Deck; Whoopee*) tied his dances to the lyrics of the songs from which their music came; Albertina Rasch (*Face the Music; Jubilee*) put her dancers en pointe, making consistent use of balletic elements in the chorus line itself.

But Balanchine choreographed. His concern was with movement, bodies, and space, not with dance steps as such. And his even greater concern was that it all be expressive. "The ballet," he observed, "has spiritual and metaphysical elements, not merely physical ones." Expressivity did not preclude humor, however. In fact, his work raised new possibilities for dance as a source of comic as well as expressive energy on the Broadway stage. In *On Your Toes*, for example, the first of Balanchine's two ballets, "La Princesse Zenobia," spoofed the Michel Fokine ballet classic

"Slaughter on Tenth Avenue" ballet from *On Your Toes*, l. to r.: Tamara Geva (Strip Tease Girl), George Church (Big Boss), and Ray Bolger (Hoofer, kneeling).

Scheherazade; the second, "Slaughter on Tenth Avenue," contrasted "elevated" European and down-to-earth American styles.

Because of its importance to the story and its position at the climax of *On Your Toes*, "Slaughter on Tenth Avenue" constituted much of the focus of the plot. But as a more or less self-contained piece set into the show, it did not really advance the plot from within. (Making the content of a ballet have direct bearing on the book of a musical was a later development, though Balanchine attempted such integration in dance sequences for subsequent Rodgers and Hart productions—"Peter's Journey" in *Babes in Arms*; "Honeymoon Ballet" in *I Married an Angel.*) *On Your Toes* served notice nonetheless that even if dance did not actually convey the narrative in a musical, it could serve as more than a decorative appendage and still be entertaining. According to de Mille, once Balanchine had earned enough money on Broadway to reconstitute a new ballet company of his own (now the New York City Ballet Company), he repudiated his commercial choreography as "ignominious and to be scorned." But the degree to which he widened the scope of musical comedy dance was no less significant for that.

Robert Alton, then among the greatest of Broadway dance directors, created the dances for *Pal Joey*; and Gene Kelly, the star of the show, performed them himself as well—everything from tap ("You Mustn't Kick It Around") to dream ballet ("Joey Looks into the Future"). But *Pal Joey* was an altogether different kind of show. In it, the kind of farcical entertainment that had for decades gone by the name of musical comedy took a decisive turn toward the real thing. If a farce can be said to be a "comedy with the meaning left out," *Pal Joey* sought to put the meaning back. That took many by surprise. On opening night, even sympathetic critics, never at a loss for words so much as concepts, could only speak of the new show as something "strangely realistic," and an occasion on which "musical comedy took a long step toward maturity."

A series of letters originally appeared in *The New Yorker* addressed to "Friend Ted" and signed "Pal Joey." Joey, a cheap nightclub performer and hustler, had no qualms about discussing sex, blackmail, and many of the other sordid details of his private life. Neither did Joey see anything wrong in what he did, nor was he smart enough to be really evil. The letters were all fictional, to be sure, the creations of novelist John O'Hara, who later asked Rodgers and Hart to musicalize "the character and the life in general" which the letters had spawned. The show that resulted centered on Joey Evans (Kelly), a punk with big ambitions as an entertainer, and two of the many women in his life. One was Linda English, an innocent as much taken *with* Joey as *by* him. The other was Vera Simpson (Vivienne Segal), a well-heeled socialite approaching middle age in whom Joey more than met his match. Indulging herself sexually with the younger man, Vera used her husband's money to set Joey up in a plush apartment and to buy him his own nightclub. She also did not hesitate to get rid of him when, under the threat of blackmail in the second act, their affair got out of hand.

VERA: I've been thinking. What if I were called away to California, or dropped dead, or something—would you be all right? I mean, for instance, would you eat?

JOEY: Honey Sug, somehow, I always eat. But what's on your mind?

VERA: Well, I think I'm going to be called away to California, or maybe drop dead.

JOEY: Come on, say it. This is the brush off. . . . You got some other guy, that's why I'm getting the brusheroo. I get it now. . . . All right— go on back to him.

VERA: I have a temper, Beauty, and I want to say a few things before I lose it.

JOEY: Lose it. It's all you got left to lose. Get out of my apartment.

VERA: Your apartment! All right. I won't even wish you all the good luck you're going to need.

Joey got his comeuppance. He lost everything he had acquired. He also learned nothing from the experience. When the final curtain came down he was literally back where he started: in front of the same pet-shop window where he had picked up Linda, looking to pick up his next "mouse." *Pal Joey* thus had "no romantic resolution, no change of heart, no happy ending—no ending at all." It was a study in cynicism as uncompromising for a Broadway musical as it was unprecedented.

That *Pal Joey* conveyed its meaning "without leaving a painful or tragic impression," however, contributed to its success not simply as a human comedy, but also an eminently musical one. Kelly explained how he actually used the musical numbers to defuse the offensiveness of the character he portrayed. He played Joey as more amoral than immoral, someone who

> *would accept his promiscuity as a matter of course, completely unaware of the hurt he was causing, and just when he was being especially offensive, I'd look at the audience, smile at them, and go into a song and dance, turning the character round, almost. I instinctively felt that this was the right approach and when [director] George Abbott did*

nothing to stop me from pursuing it, I stuck to it. But I was worried as hell at first. I said to O'Hara, "Jesus, they're going to hate me so much, I'll never get through the first act." And he said, "No, they're going to hate Joey, but they're going to like you."

The musical numbers, moreover, were particularly clever. Diegetic songs burlesqued the numbers in the tacky floorshows of the nightclubs where Joey worked: half-clad chorus girls paraded as colors, bumping and grinding their way in "That Terrific Rainbow," while in "The Flower Garden of My Heart" they impersonated posies. There were also plot-based songs with more pointedly ironic humor: The simple lyricism of "I Could Write a Book" masked Joey's attempt to seduce Linda, while in "Den of Iniquity" Joey and Vera celebrated their extramarital affair to the sophisticated strains of a gavotte.

What *Pal Joey* lacked altogether, however, what other musical comedies had in abundance: romance. Hart, Rodgers said, knew "that love was not especially devised for boy and girl idiots of fourteen and he expressed himself to that extent." Some of the partners' most original love songs, in fact, probed emotional discrepancies between the lilt of Rodgers's music and the cynicism of Hart's words. "Falling in Love With Love" did it with heartfelt earnestness:

> *Falling in love with love*
> *Is falling for make believe.*
> *Falling in love with love*
> *Is playing the fool.*

> "FALLING IN LOVE WITH LOVE"
> (*THE BOYS FROM SYRACUSE*)

"I Wish I Were in Love Again" did it with mordant wit:

> *The furtive sigh,*
> *The blackened eye,*
> *The words "I'll love you till the day I die,"*
> *The self-deception that believes the lie—*
> *I wish I were in love again.*

> "I WISH I WERE IN LOVE AGAIN"
> (*BABES IN ARMS*)

GEORGE ABBOTT

presents

"PAL JOEY"

A Gaily Sophisticated Musical Comedy

Book by JOHN O'HARA · RODGERS & HART SONGS

Dances Directed by ROBERT ALTON

WITH

VIVIENNE SEGAL   GENE KELLY
JACK DURANT   JUNE HAVOC

Scenery & Lighting by   Production Staged by   Costumes by
JO MIELZINER   GEORGE ABBOTT   JOHN KOENIG

BARRYMORE THEATRE
47th STREET WEST OF BROADWAY   MATINEES WEDNESDAY & SATURDAY

Poster for *Pal Joey* showing Gene Kelly in the title role surrounded by sixteen chorus girls.

But *Pal Joey* provided Rodgers and Hart with a character and a situation for creating one of their most extraordinary songs in the vein, "Bewitched, Bothered and Bewildered." "Here," Rodgers recalled, "we tried something that is particularly effective in comedy numbers—the contrast of a flowing, sentimental melody with words that are unsentimental and self-mocking." Sung by Vera as a knowing celebration of her sexual infatuation with Joey, "Bewitched" was a study in romance without the illusions:

> *Lost my heart, but what of it?*
> *My mistake, I agree.*
> *He's a laugh, but I love it*
> *Because the laugh's on me.*

"BEWITCHED" (*PAL JOEY*)

"Bewitched" was an emotionally ambiguous and strangely moving song for a "comedy number." Much of its haunting humor came from the new idea embodied in *Pal Joey* as to what a musical comedy might be, the kind of emotional complexity such a form of comedy might now probe. That idea bewildered many in the opening night audience, who expected an entertainment billed as a musical comedy to hew more closely to the sweet foolishnesses of the genre's past. More than bewildered, Brooks Atkinson found the lyrics to "Bewitched" "scabrous." The rest of the show disturbed him as well: "If it is possible to make an entertaining musical comedy out of an odious story, *Pal Joey* is it," he wrote; and concluded rhetorically, "Although it is expertly done, can you draw sweet water from a foul well?"

Atkinson reconsidered his opinion when, in 1952, Jule Styne and Leonard Key produced a Broadway revival of *Pal Joey* that proved to be an even greater box office draw than the original production. The show was now "a pioneer in the moving back of musical frontiers, for it tells an integrated story with a knowing point of view." The show hadn't changed between 1940 and 1952: The revival kept the original substantially intact. What had changed was the sensibility of certain theatergoers; and what had changed that sensibility most likely was the work of Rodgers and Hammerstein which had won public acceptance for more penetrating musical plays in the interim. (At the time of the revival, *South Pacific* and *The King and I* were both running on Broadway.) Rodgers and Hart did not write musical plays in the sense that we now understand the term, though they actually did write the books to several of their own shows (*Babes in Arms, I Married an Angel, By Jupiter*). Basically, they wrote scores to musical comedies some of which so stretched the limits of the genre as to seem, in hindsight, to have laid the groundwork for future developments. That future would be Rodgers's, however; not Hart's. Rodgers went on to produce an extraordinary body of work in the musical play mold; Hart succumbed to an alcoholic habit that proved fatal. After Gershwin's death and Porter's accident and seemingly diminished powers, Hart's death delivered the coup de grâce to that Golden Age of American popular song in which Broadway had so richly taken part.

About a year before Hart died, the Theater Guild approached Rodgers proposing a musical adaptation of the folk play *Green Grow the Lilacs*. Rodgers discussed it with Hart; Hart demurred. He found the material lacked wit and urbanity; in fact, it was downright corny. Culturally and geographically, moreover, it was set about as far away as one could get in the continental United States from both Hollywood and New York. So with Hart's blessing, Rodgers went ahead on the project with a new collaborator, Oscar Hammerstein II. Hart still lived to see the result: *Oklahoma!* He was present on opening night. But one can only speculate how much of his "applauding, howling with laughter, and yelling bravos" at the performance may have been tinged with the sad realization that with the success of this work, not just his partnership with Rodgers, but a whole era in American musicals had come to an end.

8

THE SCRIPT ANGLE

LADY IN THE DARK
(1/23/1941–5/30/1942). **Producer:** Sam H. Harris. **Book and Director:** Moss Hart. **Lyrics:** Ira Gershwin. **Music:** Kurt Weill. **New York Run:** 467 performances. **Cast:** Gertrude Lawrence, Danny Kaye. **Songs:** "My Ship," "The Saga of Jenny," "Tchaikowsky."

OKLAHOMA!
(3/31/1943–5/29/1948). **Producer:** The Theater Guild. **Book and Lyrics:** Oscar Hammerstein II, based on the play *Green Grow the Lilacs* by Lynn Riggs. **Music:** Richard Rodgers. **Director:** Rouben Mamoulian: **New York Run:** 2,212 performances. **Cast:** Joan Roberts, Celeste Holm, Alfred Drake, Howard Da Silva. **Songs:** "Oh What a Beautiful Mornin'," "People Will Say We're in Love," "The Surrey with the Fringe on the Top," "Oklahoma."

BLOOMER GIRL
(10/5/1944–4/27/1946). **Producer:** John C. Wilson. **Book:** Sig Herzig and Fred Saidy, based on the play by Dan and Lilith James. **Lyrics:** E. Y. Harburg. **Music:** Harold Arlen. **Director:** William Schorr. **New York Run:** 654 performances. **Cast:** Holm, Joan McCracken, David Brooks, Dooley Wilson. **Songs:** "It Was Good Enough for Grandma," "The Eagle and Me," "Right as the Rain."

Finale of *Oklahoma!* center l. to r.: Lee Dixon (Will Parker, hat in hand), Celeste Holm (Ado Annie), Alfred Drake (Curly), Joan Roberts (Laurey), Joseph Buloff (Ali Hakim, kneeling), and Betty Garde (Aunt Eller, behind wheel).

ANNIE GET YOUR GUN

(5/16/1946–2/12/1949). **Producers:** Rodgers and Hammerstein. **Book:** Herbert and Dorothy Fields, based on the life of Annie Oakley. **Lyrics and Music:** Irving Berlin. **Director:** Joshua Logan. **New York Run:** 1,147 performances. **Cast:** Ethel Merman, Ray Middleton. **Songs:** "Doin' What Comes Natur'lly," "You Can't Get a Man with a Gun," "The Girl That I Marry," "There's No Business Like Show Business," "They Say It's Wonderful."

KISS ME, KATE

(12/30/1948–7/28/1951). **Producers:** Arnold Saint Subber and Lemuel Ayers. **Book:** Sam and Bella Spewack, adapted from William Shakespeare's play *The Taming of the Shrew*. **Lyrics and Music:** Cole Porter. **Director:** John C. Wilson. **New York Run:** 1,077 performances. **Cast:** Patricia Morison, Lisa Kirk, Alfred Drake, Harold Lang. **Songs:** "So In Love," "Always True to You in My Fashion," "Why Can't You Behave?," "Brush Up Your Shakespeare," "Where Is the Life That Late I Led?"

W hen Richard Rodgers and Oscar Hammerstein II began their eighteen-year partnership as show writers in 1942, the field in which they worked was generally called musical comedy. By the time their collaboration ended with Hammerstein's death in 1960, it was more often referred to as musical theater. What brought about the change was primarily the body of work they created in the interim and the decisive influence it had on Broadway culture. In fact, their work is frequently seen in terms of a revolution in the form and function of the American musical—one that turned the book into the governing principle of a show, and one that was fought and largely won under the banner of what Hammerstein called "the musical play."

A musical *play*, originally called such to distinguish it from a musical *comedy*, was first popularized by George Edwardes, the London impresario. He used both names in the 1890s, hoping to maintain the distinctions between the two genres by housing each in a different theater. The Gaiety Theater featured musical comedies: shows with mainly farcical plots, comic characters, light singers, dancers, and elegantly dressed chorus girls. Daly's Theater presented musical plays: shows with more romantic plots, humor more the province of a comedian and a soubrette, vocalists who could hold their own in concerted finales, and chorus girls who also had to be able to sing well. In sum, musical plays were very much like romantic operettas.

The term "musical play" had thus been in circulation for about a generation when Hammerstein used it conventionally in the 1920s to describe *Rose-Marie* and *The Desert Song*. By the 1940s, however, he began to use it differently, not changing the meaning of the term so much as shifting its emphasis. As an emblem of the revolution in musical theater he wished to achieve, Hammerstein came to think of it as a *musical* play rather than a *spoken* one. The distinction was seemingly obvious, but one he saw conceptually as liberating musicals from the kind of conventions to which they were beholden in the commercial theater.

When I was very much younger, I thought that if I ever made all the money I needed out of writing musical comedy, I would then sit back

*and turn to straight dramatic plays in which I could say whatever I
wanted to say and state my reactions to the world I live in. Later on,
however, I became convinced that whatever I wanted to say could be
said in songs, [and] that I was not confined necessarily [by songs] to
trite or light subjects.*

For Richard Traubner, what Hammerstein undertook in the 1940s
amounted to no more than "a streamlined version of the 1920s romantic operetta, eliminating superfluous spectacle and novelty numbers,
adding psychology to a routinely melodramatic plot." But for Hammerstein, musical plays and "straight dramatic plays" were both plays
before they were anything else. The shift in emphasis implied a new
aesthetic program for the Broadway musical: a new type of operetta
that moved toward musical drama.

Viewed as if it actually were a play, Hammerstein's musical play
might avoid the trivial subject matter that seemed endemic to the
Broadway musical in order to address matters of substance traditionally reserved for the legitimate theater. Even to speak of "legitimate theater," however, was to engage in a dualistic discourse that had
worked to the disadvantage of musical stage productions ever since the
seventeenth century, when the term was first formally used. Originally,
legitimate simply meant "lawful": It applied to two London theaters
that had been granted exclusive royal patents (legally licensed monop-
olies) for the production of spoken drama. Further, it distinguished the
spoken plays from the offerings that got around the patents by interlarding their plays with music—thus making such offerings "illegitimate." Over time, descriptive meanings shaded into others as powerful
but less precise. By the nineteenth century, a play was considered legitimate "when the interest of the piece is mental rather than physical" or
when it had a "poetic quality or superior literary worth"; and the term
came to be widely used "by actors of the old school as a defence against
the encroachments of farce, musical comedy, and revue." By the twentieth century, a legitimate theatrical enterprise meant almost any stage
offering with cultural cachet: In one instance it was defined in American terms as "concerned with the New York commercial stage, stage
plays, or serious art; classical; semi-classical; other than popular." It is
in this context that Hammerstein seems to have viewed the musical

play as a way to maintain the musical stage as a popular medium while at the same time endowing it with some sense of that legitimacy it had been historically denied.

Nonmusical playwrights had no such cultural stigma to contend with. But few of them scripted librettos. Those who did tended to bring a sense of what was theatrically "legit" with them into the musical medium, although rarely with happy results. Laurence Stallings and Maxwell Anderson took the legitimate stage by storm in 1924 as coauthors of the powerful antiwar drama *What Price Glory?* Thereafter Stallings wrote books for two musical plays that were both commercial disasters: *Deep River* (1926) and *Rainbow* (1928). Anderson wrote books for two later collaborations with Kurt Weill that, while more successful, were not box office hits: *Knickerbocker Holiday* (1938) and *Lost in the Stars* (1949). After *Show Boat,* in fact there were no dramatically ambitious musicals that did well in commercial terms until *Lady in the Dark,* and then *Oklahoma!,* though these two shows embodied two different approaches to the musical play. Because of Hammerstein's subsequent success and influence in the theater, his notion of a musical play has since come to be accepted as definitive. His kind of musical play, however, was not the only kind to leave a mark on Broadway history. Moss Hart succeeded by taking it to mean something closer perhaps to a spoken play altogether. Bella and Sam Spewack succeeded by taking it to mean something closer perhaps to musical comedy. Yet what they all had in common as they worked in the 1940s was the tendency not just to emphasize the role of a book in the making of a Broadway show, but to elevate the book to a governing principle.

A MUSICAL PLAY

"I do not write musical comedies," replied a young Moss Hart when asked to collaborate on a new show with Irving Berlin. "I'm a playwright. I write plays—*only* plays." It was 1930, and Hart was on the verge of his first legitimate stage success as a coauthor with George S. Kaufman of *Once in a Lifetime* (a success which they surpassed with *You Can't Take It with You* in 1936, for which they won a Pulitzer Prize).

Despite his inexperience, Hart spoke from a position of strength. His attitude reflected that of the theater community at large. Hacks might write musical comedies; playwrights wrote plays.

Yet Hart soon changed his mind. There was a showman in the playwright after all, and he wrote musical comedy scripts for some of the best songwriters of the 1930s—Berlin (*Face the Music*), Porter (*Jubilee*), Rodgers and Hart (*I'd Rather Be Right*)—as well as revue sketches (*As Thousands Cheer*) and an operetta libretto (*The Great Waltz*). (Later he would write the screenplays for such successful film musicals as *Hans Christian Andersen*, 1952, and *A Star Is Born*, 1954.) But something of the playwright's attitude remained in his work for the musical stage, and it made itself felt perhaps nowhere more tellingly than in *Lady in the Dark* (1941). *Lady in the Dark* was Hart's brainchild. Based on his personal experience in psychoanalysis, he drafted a play on the subject, *I Am Listening*, as a vehicle for actress Katharine Cornell. In it a successful New York businesswoman finds herself on the verge of a nervous breakdown and undergoes psychoanalysis. She is ultimately helped in the process of self-discovery by recalling the words to a song unconsciously associated with a childhood trauma whose melody had been tormenting her as an adult.

Hart first met Kurt Weill while working on his play. Weill was a German-born and -trained composer of operas and musical theater pieces that had created sensations in Europe but were virtually unknown in the United States. Weill had made a point of collaborating with playwrights rather than librettists—Georg Kaiser and Bertolt Brecht in Germany, Paul Green and Maxwell Anderson in America. Now Hart and Weill discussed a possible collaboration. "[We] told each other vehemently why we would not write a musical comedy," Hart remembered. "Kurt Weill because he would not write the music for the regulation musical comedy book, and myself because I would not write the book for the regulation musical comedy music. . . . The tight little formula of the musical comedy stage held no interest for either of us." Weill, however, suggested a new possibility for Hart's play: "The music could describe the [heroine's] dreams." And so as *I Am Listening* evolved into *Lady in the Dark*, what had been conceived as a dramatic play with a single song in it turned into something which Hart could only later describe as a musical play: "a show in which the music carried forward the essential story and was not imposed on the architecture of the play as a rather melodious but useless addenda [*sic*]. This is an easy phrase to write but to achieve that end it was necessary to create both a new technique and a new musical form."

The "new musical form," however, involved casting the show in a way that seemed to favor the play over the music. All three men in the heroine's life were to be played by nonsingers. Even Gertrude Lawrence, who replaced Cornell in the title role, left something to be desired in the vocal department. As theater historian Foster Hirsch sums it up,

> *Gertrude Lawrence may well have been the poorest singer who ever became a major musical-theatre star. There was no song she didn't have trouble with. Her quavering voice buckled on high notes, she never landed securely on a single note, and her pitch wavered like a palm tree in a hurricane. . . . She was a legendarily poor singer— and a great performer who took command of the stage and of her audience. She was a kind of star the stage no longer produces.*

Above all, as it was produced in the theater, the "new musical form" gave no indication it even *was* a musical—at least at the start. There was no overture to set things off and no opening chorus. No singing or dancing or music of any kind. The curtain went up directly on a straight play: a realistic scene in a psychiatrist's office between Dr. Brooks and his patient, fashion magazine editor Liza Elliott (Lawrence). It was her first visit and she was there because she was panic-stricken. For the first time in her life she was unable to make important personal and professional decisions—as she would learn, she was at odds with herself as a woman who suppressed her femininity in order to succeed professionally in what was very much "a man's world." Dr. Brooks was predictably reassuring, convincing her to trust him enough to tell him of her fantasies, even to allow herself to drift off into an inner world of emotional recall. Her first thoughts were of a song she knew as a child, only she couldn't remember the words. It was the music that kept hounding her in a dream she had the night before.

LIZA: It was one of those confused, fantastic dreams. I knew the peo-
    ple—they were the people I see every day—and yet they were not

the people I knew at all. (*Her hands go to her eyes and cover them*) I can't remember it.

DR. BROOKS: How did it begin?

LIZA: With the song.

DR. BROOKS: Hum what you remember of the song. It doesn't matter about the words. Just hum the music.

(*There is a pause. Then softly,* LIZA *begins to hum the song. The lights dim. As the music swells, twelve men in faultless evening clothes, carrying lyres, march on. One carries a sign: "New York Chapter—*LIZA ELLIOTT *Admirers." It is early evening on Park Avenue*)

ALL: We come to serenade the lovely lady we adore.
She occupies the seventeenth to twenty-second floor.
Our lady so seraphic
May not be very near us,
And with the sound of traffic
She may not even hear us . . .

As Liza hummed an ambiguous melody suggesting both D minor and F major, something extraordinary happened. The stage began to revolve on turntables and the bookcase in the doctor's office split down the middle and slid apart seamlessly flowing into a projection of Liza's dream. Stage designer Harry Horner had found "so many filmic elements" in Hart's script, he designed a scheme whereby a scene might "change like a kaleidoscope, moving from one sequence to the next." And as it did, music, recitatives, songs, choruses, dances, and the panoply of visual effects all associated with a sumptuous musical production completely took over the stage. There they remained until Liza awoke again to her drab, everyday world. Then they vanished, and the spoken play resumed.

Lady in the Dark thus became musical only when the action turned patently nonrealistic. What was musical consisted of extended production numbers representing the seemingly irrational world of Liza's fantasies and dreams. These were the creations of Weill and lyricist Ira Gershwin, working on his first major show since his brother's death, and working differently than he had before. "In nine cases out of ten,"

Gertrude Lawrence (Liza Elliott) lets loose in the "Circus Dream" from *Lady in the Dark*.

Gershwin wrote to Weill, "I have written to music, or just have given a title and a couple of possible first lines." Now, however, because of the "experimental nature" of this musical play, he would provide Weill with lyrics first; Weill always worked with completed librettos. Three dream scenes ultimately made up almost the entire *Lady in the Dark* score: a "Glamour Dream" in which Liza's fantasies about living the high life are dashed; a "Wedding Dream" in which she shrinks from her impending marriage; and a "Circus Dream" in which she presents the case for *not* making up her mind ("The Saga of Jenny") and is subjected to a mock trial. Musically, these scenes were through-composed and, though different from one another, linked by melodic references to Liza's wordless song ("My Ship"). Weill dubbed them "three one-act operas of about twenty minutes' length each," though they resembled nothing so much as large-scale operetta finales. They were also specially staged: Neither by Hart, who directed his own book scenes, nor by Albertina Rasch, the choreographer in charge of the dances, but by Hassard Short, in charge of what was called "musical staging."

The alternation of book and score scenes had a trajectory. As Liza's therapy progressed, the complementary tension between the musical part of the show and the play part took on greater meaning: The discrepancy between who she was and who she wanted to be became clearer. And when at the end of the play the melody that had haunted her various dreams in fragments came back to her as "My Ship," complete with words and clearly harmonized in F major, Liza was finally able to fit the pieces of her life together and take control again. She would not give up all she had achieved professionally, but she would now share her power as a woman and an editor with the one man in her life she had come to see as her equal—though she concluded ambiguously, "Suppose we ran [the magazine] together—I might even step aside after a while if you didn't get too drunk with power."

There were clear dramaturgical grounds for keeping separate what was "musical" and what was "play" in *Lady in the Dark*, and letting the two intersect only at the end of the show through Liza's song. But the separation baffled several theater critics who on opening night mistook Hart's "musical play" for a "play with music," that is, a straight play with musical side dishes. Most critics, however, found the show excellent and understood what it represented:

> *All by itself Mr. Hart's play about a mixed-up lady editor of a fashion magazine who gets straightened out through psychoanalysis is superficial, somewhat clumsily written, and utterly uninspired in plot. But it is not meant to be taken all by itself; and with the lady's dreams set lightly to music and blown up to gorgeous spectacle, with the atmosphere of her fashion magazine lending touches of comedy, and with Gertrude Lawrence on hand to sing and dance as well as be neurotic,* Lady in the Dark *becomes very good theater.*

Perhaps it was only ancillary music that had figured in Hart's original conception, but by the time the show opened on Broadway, music had become, the playwright said, "part and parcel of the basic structure of the play. One cannot separate the play from the music, and vice versa. More than that, the music and lyrics carry the story forward dramatically and psychologically." This was a musical play, however, whose components were not integrated along the lines Rodgers and Hammerstein would shortly make popular. Rather, it was a musical play in which the book and score were mostly kept apart and juxtaposed so that they addressed each other in fresh, provocative ways. *Lady in the Dark* thus embodied a bifurcated approach to musical dramaturgy that had little immediate impact on the development of Broadway book shows, but an approach that would later gain a pervasive grip on Broadway culture in such works as *Cabaret* (1966) and *Chicago* (1975).

In the end, Hart never wrote *I Am Listening.* There was no longer any reason to do so. The theatergoing public saw in *Lady in the Dark* the result of a process Hart had undergone in private, converting his spoken play into a play that was now purposefully musical. With several later shows, the start as well as the finish of that process would be made public, as playwrights helped to musicalize plays of theirs that had already been successfully produced. Elmer Rice, for example, adapted his drama *Street Scene* (1929) for musicalization by Kurt Weill and Langston Hughes (1947); and Clifford Odets reworked his *Golden Boy* (1938)—with posthumous help from William Gibson—for a musical version by Lee Adams and Charles Strouse (1964).

A noted early example of the trend involved DuBose Heyward, who helped to convert the script he and his wife wrote for *Porgy* (1927) into the libretto for *Porgy and Bess* (1935). Of interest in this case is that both the play and the musical that came of it were produced by the same organization, the Theater Guild. For the precedent may have come to mind when the guild found itself on the verge of bankruptcy in the early 1940s and its directors, Theresa Helburn and Lawrence Langner, proposed creating a new musical from another guild-produced play in hopes that a hit show might put the organization financially back on its feet. To realize their plan, however, Helburn and Langner did an about-face now and enlisted not playwrights but *musical* playwrights to do all the adapting themselves. The guild thus came to figure importantly in the development of the modern musical play for it brought together Oscar Hammerstein II, librettist of hit operettas of the 1920s, and Richard Rodgers, composer of hit musical comedies of the 1920s and 1930s, for the writers' first full-length collaboration. The result was *Oklahoma!*, which achieved its aim and saved the guild. At the same time, not unintentionally perhaps, it achieved a lot more as well.

OKLAHOMA!: THE MUSICAL PLAY

Oklahoma! may not have been the first thoroughgoing example of the genre. But the rise of the modern musical play to a position of preeminence on the American musical stage in the post–World War II era is commonly reckoned from the night of March 31, 1943, when *Oklahoma!* opened at the St. James Theater in New York. It enjoyed a success unmatched by any prior Broadway musical, and its influence on subsequent musicals was both immediate and far-flung.

As originally produced by the Theater Guild in 1931, *Green Grow the Lilacs*, a regional play, made extensive use of traditional folksongs throughout. It depicts the life of settlers in the territory that would soon become the state of Oklahoma in 1907. Cowhand Curly McClain and farmgirl Laurey Williams, prideful and given to teasing, are in love with each other. Out of pique—and a certain fear—Laurey rejects Curly's invitation to a party and goes instead with her hired farmhand, Jeeter Fry. Jeeter, a surly character with a criminally suspicious past, is sexually attracted to Laurey. When she repulses his advances at the party, he threatens her and she fires him. Shaken, she admits her true feelings to Curly and the two marry. After the wedding, Curly and Jeeter get into a fight and Jeeter falls on his own knife and dies. Curly is arrested on his wedding night, but he breaks out of jail three nights later to be with Laurey. Easily caught, he is allowed to spend the night with his bride before returning to jail the next morning to face trial.

In preparing Riggs's play for musical treatment with broadly popular appeal, Hammerstein lightened the darker qualities of the original. He added the character of Will Parker as a comic lover for Laurey's friend Ado Annie; he subtracted a bawdy shivaree scene after Laurey and Curly's wedding; and he contrived a less ambiguously happy ending for the bride and groom to ride off on their honeymoon together. Much of the original was still retained, however, in the tale of Laurey (Joan Roberts), Curly (Alfred Drake), and Jeeter (now renamed Jud [Howard Da Silva]). Hammerstein left the onstage murder of the villain intact. Even the subplot he devised as comic relief did not go very far to counterbalance the melodramatic thrust of Riggs's plot. Hammerstein also maintained a sense of fidelity to the feeling and homespun charm of the original play right down to the folksy quirks of its characters and their ways of speech, much of which he appropriated wholesale from Riggs's dialogue. Indeed, something in the very spirit of Hammerstein's adaptations and appropriations seemed to go against the grain of a musical production aimed at Broadway.

So the show originally titled *Away We Go!* struck New York theater pundits who came to see it during out-of-town tryouts as a dubious prospect. Few saw it as accurately as *Variety*'s theater critic, who wrote:

> *Book sticks pretty close to the original, and in so doing provides a story with better-than-average tunes and terps [dances]. Through play's unorthodox opening (girls do not come on for 35 minutes), audience is made aware early that "Away" is not the conventional type of song-and-dancer. Roles are played straight rather than operetta fashion, which enhances the script angle of the production.*

Many faulted the script angle for putting the musical comedy undertaking in false perspective. A now famous catchphrase attributed to producer Michael Todd sums up their view: "No gags. No gals. No chance."

The show had plenty of humor. What it lacked were the gags, the wisecracks, the off-color jokes, the puns and double entendres, the specialty slots for a star comedian—the gamut of comic shtick that musical comedy had inherited from the burlesque stage. (When Theresa Helburn of the Theater Guild suggested Groucho Marx for the role of Ali Hakim the peddler, Rodgers and Hammerstein protested: They would have no stars in any of the roles, and certainly not one so notorious for wreaking havoc with a script!) Instead, the show's comic subplot was peopled with comic types played by more or less unknown actors: Ado Annie (Celeste Holm), a soubrette; Will Parker (Lee Dixon), a juvenile; and Ali Hakim (Joseph Buloff), a "Dutch"-style comedian with a passion for the ladies and an aversion to marrying them. And this trio, paralleling the Laurey/Curly/Jud triangle of the plot, would have jokes of its own:

HAKIM: It's a wonderful thing to be married. . . . I got a brother in Persia, got six wives.
ADO ANNIE: Six wives? All at once?

WILL: Shore. 'At's a way they do in them countries.

HAKIM: Not always. I got another brother in Persia only got one wife.
    He's a bachelor.

Not gags, then, so much as jokes that came out of script situations, a sense of fun that was true to character, and an overall geniality—indeed a pervasive good humor—constituted the "comedy" of *Oklahoma!*

Neither was *Oklahoma!* short on "gals." But the gals, too, were different. When the curtain rose, for example, they didn't greet the audience with a rousing opening number that set the scene—the musical comedy norm. There was only Aunt Eller, a middle-aged woman, who sat quietly on a porch churning butter by herself, while offstage a lone cowboy sang a ballad called "Oh, What a Beautiful Mornin'" (Ex. 8-1)—almost exactly the way the original play began. The lyrics were simple rather than smart; the music more folklike than jazzy. Even in its form the song departed from the standard AABA of show tunes in favor of the verse-refrain pattern of a folk ballad. (Rodgers's musical style had changed along with his working habits: Now he generally put notes to Hammerstein's lyrics; with Hart, he had written the music first.) As the number ended, an opening night observer recalled, "it produced a sigh from the entire house that I don't think I ever heard in the theatre. Just 'Aaaaaah!'"

"Before *Oklahoma!* came along," William Goldman generalized, "a show about Oklahoma would have begun with 'Oklahoma'"—which in this show actually turned out to be the rousing final number. Hammerstein himself once imagined how *Oklahoma!* would have begun had it been a conventional musical comedy; and, more importantly, he explained why it did not begin that way:

> *I'd have an opening chorus sung by a row of cowgirls in high boots, short skirts, bare knees and ten-gallon hats. Aunt Eller would be a musical-comedy heavy woman making wisecracks, and Ado Annie's comedy would be broader and noisier. [Yet] no matter how much the audience laughed, I'd have killed* Oklahoma! *because the rest of the story wouldn't go with that beginning. The start of your play tells audiences the kind of thing they're going to see and you mustn't mislead them.*

Ex. 8-1. Richard Rodgers, music, Oscar Hammerstein II, lyrics: "Oh, What a Beautiful Mornin'," *Oklahoma!*

The chorus girls finally did appear midway into the first act. But they showed up covered from neck to ankle in dresses that were less provocative than they were evocative of turn-of-the-century Oklahoma. Even the dancers had a different look about them, for choreographer Agnes de Mille had chosen them not on the basis of their legs or faces, she said, but based upon "talent and personality." And when they danced, they avoided the jazz-based movements of musical comedy dancing in favor of a blend of folk dancing and the abstractions of ballet and modern dance. (Only in a dream ballet that portrayed Laurey's fears did bare-shouldered dance hall girls get to indulge suggestively in a cancan. But, true to the spirit of the night-

Jud's bawdy "Postcard Girls" come to life in *Oklahoma!*'s "Dream Ballet," l. to r.: Joan McCracken, Kate Friedlich, Margit DeKova, Bobby Barrentine, and Vivian Smith.

mare in which they appeared, their bawdiness was more threatening than it was joyous.) *Oklahoma!* was not without gals, but it was distinctly not a skin show.

If *Oklahoma!* had no chance at the box office, then, it was because Rodgers and Hammerstein did not think of it as a conventional musical comedy. In a letter written just before the Broadway premiere, Hammerstein spoke of the show as "the nearest approach to *Show Boat* that the theatre has attained," and hoped "that a handful of beer-stupefied critics may not decide that we have tried to write a musical comedy and failed." Many critics did allude to musical comedy in their opening night reviews of *Oklahoma!*, but not presumably because of what they had imbibed before their theatergoing. They lacked a different cultural frame of reference in which to place the work. One called it "a little more than a musical comedy without being pretentiously so";

another even called it a "folk operetta." Hammerstein simply called it a musical play.

"There are few things in life of which I am certain," Hammerstein later wrote, "but I am sure of this one thing, that the song is the servant of the play." This amounts to his musical play credo. Applied to *Oklahoma!*, it means that songs like "Pore Jud Is Daid" and "Lonely Room" may so defy the musical and lyric conventions of Tin Pan Alley from start to finish as to make virtually no sense at all apart from the play. It also means that the play itself may not make much sense without such songs as "The Surrey with the Fringe on the Top" and "People Will Say We're in Love" (even though both songs have 32-bar refrains and Tin Pan Alley appeal). In *Oklahoma!*, Stephen Sondheim would later say, the story is "told *through* its songs, not just *with* its songs."

Musical function—not musical quantity—is the point. In terms of numbers, there were more individual songs in *Green Grow the Lilacs*, which was not a musical play, than in *Oklahoma!*, which was. Consider the musical layouts of the two works.

Green Grow the Lilacs: Musical Numbers

ACT 1

Scene 1—The Williams' farmhouses, summer morning.

"Git Along, Little Dogies" . . . . .Curly

"Green Grow the Lilacs" . . . . .Curly

Interlude: Two Folk Songs . . . . Cowboys & Girls

Scene 2—The same, showing Laurey's bedroom.

"Miner Boy" . . . . Laurey

Interlude: Four Folk Songs . . . . Martha & Girls

Scene 3—The same, showing the smokehouse.

"Sam Hall" . . . . .Curly

ACT 2

Scene 1—The porch of Old Man Peck's house, that night.

"The Little Brass Wagon". . . . . Square Dance

"The Old Chisholm Trail" . . . . Cord Elam & Crowd

"Strawberry Roan" . . . . .Banjo Player

"When I Was Young and Single" . . . . Ado Annie
"Skip to My Lou" . . . . Crowd
Interlude: Two Folk Songs . . . . Smoky & Chorus
Scene 2—The hay-field back of Williams' house, a month later.
Interlude: One Folk Song . . . . Cowboys & Girls
Scene 3—The living-room of the Williams' house, three nights later.
"Green Grow the Lilacs" . . . . Curly

Oklahoma!: Musical Numbers

ACT 1

Scene 1—The front of Laurey's farmhouse.
"Oh, What a Beautiful Mornin'" . . . . Curly
"The Surrey with the Fringe on Top. . . . .
. . . . Curly, Laurey, Aunt Eller
"Kansas City" . . . . Will, Aunt Eller & Boys
"I Cain't Say No" . . . . Ado Annie
"Many a New Day" . . . . Laurey & Girls
"It's a Scandal! It's a Outrage!" . . . .
. . . . Ali Hakim, Boys & Girls
"People Will Say We're in Love" . . . . Curly & Laurey
Scene 2—The smokehouse.
"Pore Jud Is Daid" . . . . Curly & Jud
"Lonely Room" . . . . Jud
Scene 3—A grove on Laurey's farm.
"Out of My Dreams" . . . . Laurey & Girls
"Laurey Makes Up Her Mind" . . . . . . Dream Ballet

ACT 2

Scene 1—The Skidmore ranch.
"The Farmer and the Cowman" . . Carnes & Ensemble
"All er Nuthin'" . . . . Ado Annie & Will
Scene 2—Skidmore's kitchen porch.
"People Will Say We're in Love" . . . . Curly & Laurey
Scene 3—The back of Laurey's farmhouse
"Oklahoma" . . . . Curly & Ensemble

"Oh, What a Beautiful Mornin'" . . . .
. . . . Laurey, Curly, & Ensemble

This is how Hammerstein explained the functional distinctions:

When Green Grow the Lilacs *was first produced it had songs, real American folksongs from the cow country—good ones too. They were not part of the play's texture. They were delivered incidentally, sung by the characters at a party and by a cowboy chorus to cover scenic changes. The songs we were to write [for* Oklahoma!*] had a different function. They [had to] help tell our story and delineate characters, supplementing the dialogue and seeming to be, as much as possible, a continuation of dialogue. This is, of course, true of the songs [in] any well-made musical play.*

While Hammerstein may have overstated his case, the nub of his argument rings true. In *Oklahoma!*, characters *as characters* in the play did not generally sing "songs" to each other, and certainly not to the audience of whose presence they were unaware. With a few exceptions (diegetic songs like "Oh, What a Beautiful Mornin'" and "The Farmer and the Cowman"), the characters onstage were meant to be unaware of any singing at all. And they were totally unaware of any orchestra playing. (For them the imaginary "fourth wall" of the proscenium was not only opaque but also soundproof!) Above all, the songs were of a piece with the dialogue: the lyrics continuing the dialogue without a break, and the music functioning as their emotional subtext. "The art of this thing," Hammerstein said, "is to get in and out of the numbers so smoothly that the audience isn't aware that you are jumping from dialogue to singing. The art, you understand, is not to jump but to ooze." In short, songs in *Oklahoma!* were performed representationally: They intensified thought or speech without really being songs at all. Only audiences eavesdropping on the characters through the proverbial fourth wall experienced the songs as the musical numbers they actually were.

As a musical play, then, *Oklahoma!* aimed to blur the functional distinction between spoken dialogue and musical numbers—book and score. Accordingly Hammerstein served the show as a complete librettist: He wrote both the dialogue and the lyrics. This blurring of the distinction between the two was also true of the show as it was staged by director Rouben Mamoulian (1889–1987) and choreographer Agnes de Mille (1905–1993). "To prevent a sense of shock when different elements, drama and music, come together," Mamoulian said, songs had to be performed representationally because "if [a song] were done just as a song—sung to the audience, presentational style—the play would stop." This meant the song had to be so integrated into the script as to advance the action of the play or reveal the motivation of its characters. "Integration," in fact, was the operative concept of the musical play—certainly its most invoked catchword—and Mamoulian, the concept's most ardent champion.

> [Hammerstein] wrote about me standing over him and Dick Rodgers with a club, saying: "Integrate! Integrate! Bridge, I want a bridge here!" You must remember that music, dance, and the spoken word and dramatic action are each a vital yet separate element in theater. When you go to a play, however, you miss the music. Go to a grand opera, and you miss the spoken word. . . . So you start thinking, Why not combine? Why not aim for total theater? . . . Suppose you had a dramatic scene with a rising emotion where nothing could top the spoken words except a song? Or, in dramatic action, you bring it to as big a climax as you can, which inevitably leads to a dance that lifts the whole endeavor to an even higher level. This integration of form is essential to any activity wishing to describe itself as art.

The self-conscious high point of such art in *Oklahoma!*—of the integration of drama and music, speech and song, action and dance— occurred in the dream ballet sequence that ended the first act. The action began in speech with Laurey telling her girlfriends how a whiff of some Egyptian smelling salts would help her decide who should take her to the party, Curly or Jud. The action then rose emotionally as her friends twitted her as a musical chorus ("Ol' Pharaoh's daughter won't tell you what to do/Ask your heart—whatever it tells you will be true"), and Laurey gave voice to her romantic longings in song, "Out of My Dreams." Then, as she drifted off into her dream, the action lifted dynamically into an extended ballet, "Laurey Makes Up Her Mind," revealing through dance the psychological subtext that Laurey's words alone could not articulate. "A girl has to decide which of two boys she's going to the picnic with," Agnes de Mille explained, "the man she loves or the man she's terrified of. The dance tells why she is terrified. . . . She's afraid that Jud will murder Curly." The Dream Ballet with its Freudian resonances thus became indispensable to the telling of the play. According to de Mille,

> the thing that mattered most with Oklahoma! as far as the dance was concerned was . . . the way that ballet was so enmeshed with the characters and the plot development that it could not be deleted. Everyone in the ballet was a character in the play, so that the style of the ballet was the style of the play. It was of a piece, so to speak, and the dancers were of the texture of the play and in style and in content with the rest of the play. This was new.

Oklahoma! was new in several respects, though in none perhaps so much as the skill with which it embodied key trends in the musical theater of the period and the integrity with which it gave them shape. The show jettisoned the ironic stance of musical comedy songs and dances for character-based humor and musical numbers, and it integrated such numbers into its story where comparable plays with music kept them functionally apart. Moreover, through its stunning success in doing so, *Oklahoma!* became the point of reference for a major shift in the relationship between musical and theatrical values in Broadway entertainment. Yet the show was only a beginning as its authors went on to explore the implications of that relationship in a number of other highly influential works over the next decade and a half. These works, Alan Jay Lerner later wrote, "could musically be classified as modern operetta. But the legitimacy of the books, the dramatic use of lyrics and the wedding of choreographic movement to the story produced a new form of musical theatre, which very properly was called musical play."

Oklahoma! also had another kind of significance, one that went far beyond the confines of the musical stage. *Oklahoma!* was the first musical with almost immediate national resonance as an American cultural artifact. Its success both created and fed on the very possibility that a Broadway musical could come to matter in the cultural life of the nation. It was not just that *Oklahoma!* was a more artistic show than most—a musical play—but that it dealt with American themes, that it said something about American culture and its values. It was, as Rodgers remembered it, "something that transcended theatre, music, dance or anything confined to a specific production in a specific place."

Oklahoma! marked a cultural shift away from modernity, irony, and the ethos of urban sophistication that had dominated Broadway musicals of the interwar years: the "New York style." The show celebrated the seemingly simpler values of a provincial American past, influenced by the way such values had been recast in the folkloric and populist molds of the arts of the Depression era. If these arts invested America's folkways with a monumentality aimed at the high cultural ground—Grant Wood's *American Gothic*, Roy Harris's *Folksong Symphony*—*Oklahoma!* artfully recast them in a commercial mold that made them available to the lower rungs of the middle class. The Midwestern landscapes of Wood and Thomas Hart Benton, for example, informed the *Oklahoma!* sets of Lemuel Ayers. Aaron Copland's cowboy ballets similarly served the show's dances (Rodgers and Hammerstein hired de Mille, in fact, because she had choreographed Copland's *Rodeo*). Even John Steinbeck's best-seller *The Grapes of Wrath*, which bore no direct connection to the show at all, may still have served it by way of contrast, as the novel depicted the plight of Oklahoma's farmers a generation after those depicted in *Oklahoma!*

Laurey and Curly, of course, had no way of knowing of the ravages of the Dust Bowl and the Great Depression that awaited their children—the "Okies" who would have made mockery of them singing "We know we belong to the land, And the land we belong to is grand!" But their words were not generally mocked by audiences who heard them in 1943—or after. On the contrary, Hammerstein's lyrics aroused positive and patriotic feelings among Americans at a time when World War II threatened America's very sense of national purpose. For the Oklahoma of *Oklahoma!* stood for an idealized community, one shaped by the democratic values to which Aunt Eller called attention in "The Farmer and the Cowman (Should Be Friends)":

> *I'd like to teach you all a little sayin'—*
> *And learn these words by heart the way you should:*
> *"I don't say I'm no better than anybody else,*
> *But I'll be damned if I ain't jist as good!"*

With the Depression overcome and the tide of war turning in favor of the United States and its allies in 1943, *Oklahoma!* tapped into the nationalism of wartime and an optimism that looked forward to the war's end and, more than peace, a better postwar world. Moreover, as the show ended by celebrating the promise of new beginnings—personal in the marriage of Laurey and Curly, communal in Oklahoma's preparation for statehood—it invited its audiences not just to feel with the characters onstage, but to feel good about doing so. "The audience simply knows the show makes it 'feel good,'" Rodgers said in an attempt to explain *Oklahoma!*'s popularity, "and it tells its friends to buy tickets." The example proved compelling. Musical stageworks that followed similarly sought a "feel-good" sense of communion (and its tangible rewards) by invoking regional or historical Americana: *Bloomer Girl, Dark of the Moon, Annie Get Your Gun.* But none did it with more skill, consistency, and conviction than *Oklahoma!*; and none matched its box-office success.

Indeed, *Oklahoma!* altogether redefined the parameters of the Broadway show as a commercial enterprise. It grossed a then staggering $40 million from an unprecedented five-year run on Broadway and ten-year national tour. Its songs had lucrative lives beyond the theater as well: "People Will Say We're in Love" led the Hit Parade; many came to regard "Oh, What a Beautiful Mornin'" as an American folk song; and Oklahoma adopted "Oklahoma" officially as its state song. Moreover, the entire score was absorbed into consumer culture as an idealized entity. Published in piano-vocal form, it was also issued as a "complete" set of 78 RPM recordings. Decca Records's *Oklahoma!* set, in fact, turned the "original cast album" into a mass cultural phenomenon: an indispensable tool for producers marketing a musical, and an accessible means for consumers to relive (or experience for the first time) something close to what a Broadway show really sounded like in the theater. The show's book and lyrics, too, were published and sold together for an armchair audience much in the manner of a play script. Then in 1955, with the national tour having ended, *Oklahoma!* was finally released as a major motion picture musical. Remarkably, the movie preserved the integrity of the original stagework as, contrary to previous Hollywood practice, the creators of the show themselves retained artistic control over the film adaptation. For a growing audience at home and abroad—especially in countries with little or no access to the genuine article—it was not a live performance but a film adaptation in a movie house, which provided "the first encounter" with that artifact of American culture, the Broadway musical.

LITERATE MUSICAL COMEDY

In time, Rodgers and Hammerstein made their influence felt as businessmen in the theater as well as artists. By the end of the 1940s they produced their own works. Earlier, they began their partnership as entrepreneurs by producing the works of others: plays mostly, like *I Remember Mama* (1944), and in one instance a musical, *Annie Get Your Gun*. Seemingly in the vein of *Oklahoma!* with an historical western setting, *Annie Get Your Gun* told a love story against the backdrop of America's vanishing frontier. *Annie*, however, had none of *Oklahoma!*'s aesthetic ambition. Where *Oklahoma!* used show business to celebrate America, *Annie Get Your Gun* worked more traditionally: the other way around. That made it in essence an old-style musical comedy, and the wonder is that Rodgers and Hammerstein saw fit to produce it at all. Yet having committed themselves to the project, the producers did all they could to ensure its success though it may be too much to suggest that they acted as "silent" collaborators with either Herbert and Dorothy Fields, who wrote the book, or Irving Berlin, who wrote the songs. Even musical comedies in which Rodgers and Hammerstein played no part at all showed the influence of their work—*Kiss Me, Kate,* for example. Indeed, the changes that took place on the musical stage in the 1940s under the name of the musical play affected all kinds of Broadway shows, including those that made no pretensions to the genre.

Annie Get Your Gun (1946) and *Kiss Me, Kate* (1948) were the first blockbuster hits in the wake of *Oklahoma!* to respond to the values of the musical play without abandoning the basic thrust of musical comedy. In these shows, Irving Berlin and Cole Porter made a tentative peace with "musical theater" ideals at war with the kind of musicals they had spent the better part of their professional lives creating. Since Berlin and Porter each wrote the words and the music to their songs, neither had to change collaborative habits to suit the new priority given to texts—something Ira Gershwin had to do as a lyricist, for example, and Richard Rodgers had to do as a composer. Where they did have to change was in the way they now collaborated with their librettists. As the oldest songwriting masters then still active on Broadway and understandably set in their ways, theirs were remarkable achievements. They were also limited ones. Each writer went on to create songs for three more shows before retiring from the stage—Berlin: *Miss Liberty* (1949), *Call Me Madam* (1950), *Mr. President* (1962); Porter: *Out of This World* (1950), *Can-Can* (1953), *Silk Stockings* (1955). But neither again fashioned a score so inspired or cleverly related to its book as *Annie* and *Kate*, which remain to this day the single most universally admired stageworks in their respective catalogues.

Annie Get Your Gun is a fictional tale about the real-life American sharpshooter Annie Oakley (1860–1926). It makes use of a once popular form of entertainment in America known as the Wild West Exhibition. When Buffalo Bill Cody's Wild West Show comes to her town in Ohio, Annie (Ethel Merman), a backwoods girl and an expert sharpshooter, falls in love with the show's star marksman Frank Butler (Ray Middleton). He views women in conventional terms, however, and does not exactly appreciate her talent. She knows that her romantic feelings for Frank and her sharpshooting gifts are incompatible ("You Can't Get a Man With a Gun"). But because of her extraordinary marksmanship Annie joins Buffalo Bill's troupe ("There's No Business Like Show Business"). And when a rival company places the troupe's success in jeopardy, she saves the day: The novelty of an expert female marksman turns the show into a hit, and Annie into a star. Feeling tricked by Annie, Frank puts an end to their romance, leaves the troupe, and joins the rival company. Chief Sitting Bull of Buffalo Bill's troupe now comes up with a scheme for getting Frank and Annie back together. Without her knowledge, he fixes her guns so they will misfire during a crucial shooting match between Annie and the man she still loves.

ANNIE: What's the matter with me, Papa Bull?
SITTING BULL: You do fine. Keep missing—you win. Be second best, Annie.

OVERLEAF Ray Middleton (Frank Butler) and Ethel Merman (Annie Oakley) join forces in the finale of *Annie Get Your Gun.*

ANNIE: Huh!

SITTING BULL: Remember in big tent . . . you say, "I can't get a man
    with a gun."

ANNIE: Yeh!

SITTING BULL: You get man with this gun. (*Points to sights, and winks. A
    great light dawns on* ANNIE.)

ANNIE: Why didn't I think of that!

And so Annie conspires in her own defeat on one level in order to
gain a greater victory on another: winning Frank by losing to him.

The story would have had a special resonance for audiences who
saw *Annie Get Your Gun* when it was new. A woman first assuming "a
man's role" in a crisis, then giving up her newfound equality to resume
a conventionally gendered role as second best—all this mirrored events
of the recent past in the United States. During World War II, with the
nation's industrial labor force drained by the draft of male personnel
into the armed forces, the federal government had called on the women
of America to abandon their roles as homemakers and take up many of
the jobs the men had left behind. Given the nature of the emergency
on "the home front," the government even embarked on a campaign to
change public attitudes regarding the traditional gendering of roles in
American society. This found broad support in popular culture, especially with new icons of femininity like Wonder Woman comics and
Rosie the Riveter, poster girl for the female blue-collar worker in wartime. There were also movies like *Swing-Shift Masie* and musicals like
Something for the Boys, which portrayed women working in the defense
industries in a positive light.

The most outspokenly feminist of all the hit wartime Broadway
musicals was *Bloomer Girl* (1944). The show could afford to adopt its
point of view perhaps because it avoided any direct reference to current events. A period piece like *Oklahoma!, Bloomer Girl* was overtly
political. It took place on the eve of the Civil War and featured as its
heroine a young Evelina Applegate (Celeste Holm), who joined her
suffragette aunt "Dolly" Bloomer in crusading for the abolition of
slavery and for the cause of women's rights. Parallels existed to contemporary conditions at home, to be sure, but they were oblique. Choreographer Agnes de Mille, for example, created a poignant *Civil War*

Ballet, which she described as "a serious ballet about women's emotions in war." And in a lighter vein, composer Harold Arlen and lyricist E. Y. Harburg came up with a comic song, "It Was Good Enough for Grandma," that addressed the changing societal roles of American women with a subversive charm.

Bloomer Girl enjoyed a long Broadway run of over 650 performances. But by the time it closed in 1946 conditions in the United States had changed significantly. The war had ended in 1945 and with the return of millions of servicemen, the government found itself in the position of trying to reinstate a status quo it had earlier sought to undermine. To ease the resulting job squeeze and to satisfy a general yen for stability after the disruptions of the war, it encouraged women now to leave the labor force and resume their traditional roles as wives and mothers. Again, the workings of popular culture figured in the readjustment of societal priorities, in which context *Annie Get Your Gun* takes on a sociological meaning now largely forgotten. Yet the very idea for the show originated not only with a woman, but one who also seems not to have been intent on making a social tract out of the piece at all:

> *During the war, my late husband did volunteer work down at Penn Station for Traveler's Aid, from midnight to seven a.m. And one of the ladies told him one night about a kid who'd just come in, a young soldier. Very drunk, he'd been to Coney Island and had kewpie dolls and lamps and every piece of junk you could possibly win. How come? Across his chest, he had a row of sharpshooter's medals. And as if out of the sky, from Heaven, comes this idea [into my head] . . . Annie Oakley—the sharpshooter! With Ethel Merman to play her!*

The words are those of Dorothy Fields (1905–1974), among the finest lyric writers of her generation and one of the few women in Broadway history to achieve sustained success crafting books as well as lyrics. In a profession dominated by men, she succeeded by considering herself, she said, "one of the boys." Fields began her career in the 1920s writing revue songs with composer Jimmy McHugh ("I Can't Give You Anything but Love," "On the Sunny Side of the Street"). In the 1930s she followed the drift of songwriters to Hollywood, where she provided lyrics most notably for the film songs of Jerome Kern (*Roberta*: "Lovely to Look

At"; *Swing Time*: "The Way You Look Tonight"). By the 1940s Fields returned to Broadway, where over the next several decades she contributed to the creation of a dozen book shows as coauthor (with Herbert), lyricist, or both. Her most memorable work included books for Cole Porter comedies (*Let's Face It, Mexican Hayride*), and lyrics for the theater songs of Arthur Schwartz (*A Tree Grows in Brooklyn*, 1951; *By the Beautiful Sea*, 1954) and Cy Coleman (*Sweet Charity*, 1966; *Seesaw*, 1973). She co-wrote the book for *Annie Get Your Gun* and would have written the lyrics, too, had Kern lived to write the music as planned. But when Kern died suddenly in 1945, Irving Berlin took on the *Annie* score; and Berlin would brook no one writing lyrics to his music but himself.

As it turned out, *Annie* required a kind of collaboration for which Berlin seemed ill-prepared. He was used to producing his own shows; here the producers were Rodgers and Hammerstein, and they kept a watchful eye and ear over the proceedings, and over their songwriter as well. Berlin's first idea for the show's great ballad, for example, was

> *They say that falling in love is wonderful . . .*
> *To bill and coo like a dove . . .*

"Are you sure you like that, Irving?" Hammerstein asked tactfully when he saw it. Berlin understood, went home, and rewrote the offending line with a different rhyme:

> *And with a moon up above. . . .*

The new line was no wittier than what it replaced. But it was less self-consciously contrived—without even a simile—and thus truer to the character who sang it, Annie. Berlin pursued such character-driven logic in other parts of the song as well:

> *I can't recall who said it,*
> *I know I never read it . . .*

Of course Annie couldn't have read it because, as audiences had learned from the dialogue earlier in the show, she was illiterate. Yet working like this was new for Berlin. His Broadway expertise lay mainly in writing revues; *Annie*, by contrast, represented what he called a "situation show." He even balked at first when he found himself taking lyric ideas and titles straight out of the Fields libretto. "But the songs are coming from the script," he protested to Hammerstein, who reassured him, "Where do you think the songs from *Oklahoma!* came from?" Ultimately, when Berlin realized this would be the modus operandi for the whole show, he requested a cut in his share of the profits as songwriter so that his take would be the same as that of the book writers. The gesture spoke loudly not only of Berlin's own sense of fairness but also of a general shift of priorities in the making of musicals altogether.

Ethel Merman, too, seems to have taken the book more seriously than had been her custom. While in many respects *Annie Get Your Gun* remained a gag-oriented show, she tried to play to character more than simply playing funny. One critic's remark summed it up: "She's no longer Miss Merman acting like Ethel Merman. She's Miss Merman acting like Annie Oakley." Here the input of director Joshua Logan may have been pivotal to Merman's performance. He interpreted *Annie* more in psychological than sociological terms, and insisted that the outcome of the show depended on what he called Annie's character growth. "The important character growth for Annie would come when she—who could do anything better than anyone—decided to lose the shooting contest in order to get what she really wanted, Frank." Logan built his idea on a principle of dramatic construction Maxwell Anderson had once told him was necessary for a play to become a hit.

> *A play should take its protagonist through a series of experiences which lead to a climactic moment toward the end when he* learns *something,* discovers *something about himself that he could have known all along but has been blind to. This discovery comes as such an emotionally shattering blow (and that's the key word, emotionally) that it* changes the entire course of his life—*and that change* must *be for the better. . . . For when the protagonist has this revelation, one which raises his moral stature, the audience can grow vicariously along with him. Thus people leave the theatre feeling better, healthier-minded than when they arrived.*

One is tempted to call this Anderson's *Poetics.* Logan felt it provided him with a rationale for moving *Annie Get Your Gun* away from the action-based thrust of farce and toward the character-based action of comedy. What is curious, however, is Logan's apparent need to invoke any "poetics" at all in a medium that normally prided itself on practicality. Indeed, by covering the seat-of-the-pants component in putting on a show with the dignity of a theory, Logan seemed to be making a case for a musical comedy as a more thoughtful theater piece, even a piece of legitimate theater. So it was perhaps with musicals in mind that Logan asked Anderson how far his hit-making principle applied: "You mean *any* play?"

"Any literate play," Anderson replied.

With that the playwright surely meant to limit the theatrical field. But the term "literate" would come to haunt musical comedy in the postwar period in many ways.

Eric Bentley already understood a play to be literate in a broader sense. "The fact that a play is printed," he wrote in 1946, "is sufficient warrant for judging it as literate." From such a perspective the texts to musicals now might also warrant the claim, though this had not always been the case. In the early decades of the century, the printing of show scripts was virtually unknown. At a time when musical stage offerings were commonly thought of as events, there would have been little point to publishing what P. G. Wodehouse derided as "the stuff that keeps the numbers apart." Even as attitudes began to change, in the dozen years between *Of Thee I Sing* and *Oklahoma!* only some ten Broadway librettos were published (but often in preproduction versions). Then after World War II the practice spread as publishing houses responded to the newfound prestige of musical plays and, permanently fixing their scripts in print, sold them as plays apart from their music. Such prestige was not entirely out of place. The scripts to musical plays, if never self-sufficient as plays, actually did become more playlike. Indeed, the "stuff" between their musical numbers became not only more germane to the numbers themselves but also more worthy of attention in its own right. Ultimately, several such scripts appeared in anthologies of plays, legitimate plays, as if—divorced from the formative constraints of musical production, performance, and reception—they might now be considered part of that body of humane writing generally accorded the status of literature.

Kiss Me, Kate was a likely candidate for such consideration and not simply because its script eventually found its way as a text into print. The musical was based on a play of Shakespeare's; and the show owed its success to the audience's awareness of that fact. Other musical adaptations of Shakespeare could be enjoyed without much or perhaps any detailed knowledge of their literary background—whether comic, as in *The Boys from Syracuse* (*The Comedy of Errors*), or tragic, as in *West Side Story* (*Romeo and Juliet*). *Kiss Me, Kate*, however, would be pointless without it, for the show turned to the Bard not to adapt Shakespeare but to parody him. To be sure, both adaptation and parody draw meaning from their relation to a preexisting source, and each inevitably shows likenesses to and differences from its model. But if adaptation stresses its faithfulness to the source, "parody depends upon the discord that it generates between itself and the original off which it feeds." Broadly, then, given Shakespeare's prestige as perhaps the foremost icon of high literary culture on the English-speaking stage, consider the following song from *Kate*, "Brush Up Your Shakespeare,"—sung, by a pair of lowbrows (gangsters!) bent on sexual conquest:

> *Brush up your Shakespeare,*
> *Start quoting him now.*
> *Brush up your Shakespeare*
> *And the women you will wow.*
> *With the wife of the British embessida*
> *Try a crack out of "Troilus and Cressida,"*
> *If she says she won't buy it or tike it*
> *Make her tike it, what's more, "As You Like It."*
> *If she says your behavior is heinous*
> *Kick her right in the "Coriolanus."*
> *Brush up your Shakespeare*
> *And they'll all kowtow.*

"Brush Up Your Shakespeare" (*Kiss Me, Kate*)

General parody of this sort assumed at least some familiarity with the Bard's work even as it placed its value in a less than noble light. How apt, then, the words of the critic who summarized a certain postwar ideal in musical comedy by calling *Kiss Me, Kate* on its opening night "literate without being highbrow."

"Brush Up Your Shakespeare" roamed all over the Shakespearean map, however. *Kiss Me, Kate* had a very specific Shakespearean
target: *The Taming of the Shrew.* As in the original play, the musical
Shrew was set in Renaissance Padua and it focused on the relationship of Katharine, "an irksome, brawling scold," and Petruchio, who,
despite her opposition, woos her, weds her, and ultimately earns her
love. Shakespeare's play provided the show's librettists with more than
simply an outline. Sam (1899–1971) and Bella (1899–1990) Spewack,
the husband-and-wife team who wrote the book, incorporated whole
chunks of it verbatim. Cole Porter also mined it for his score. He quar-
ried list songs directly from the text where Shakespeare supplied the
structure: "Tom, Dick, or Harry" (*Shrew*: act 2, scene 1, lines 325–78);
or the imagery: "I've Come to Wive It Wealthily in Padua" (*Shrew*:
act 1, scene 2, 68–75, 200–202). With "Where Is the Life That Late I
Led?" (*Shrew*: act 4, scene 1, 134) Porter even took Shakespeare's reference to sixteenth-century song (now lost) as the title for a new one—
one in which Petruchio finds Kate has locked him out of their bedroom
on their wedding night, and, in frustration, he recalls the love affairs
of his bachelor days. This, too, is a list song, only its music avoids the
Broadway idiom for sounds traditionally encoded as Italian—tarantella
rhythms in the refrain; mandolin thirds in the melody of the patter.
Similarly, its lyrics tend to avoid the scattershot references of musical
comedy songs in favor of consistent references to Italy's women and
cultural landmarks—some of them the same Porter had used mainly
for rhymes in list songs earlier in his career, like the Tower of Pisa in
"You're the Top":

> *You're the Nile,*
> *You're the Tow'r of Pisa,*
> *You're the smile*
> *On the Mona Lisa.*
>
> "You're the Top" (*Anything Goes*)

but now more purposefully put to work:

> *Where is Rebecca, my Becki-weckio,*
> *Again is she cruising that amusing Ponte Vecchio? . . .*

Alfred Drake (Fred Graham/Petruchio) "tames" Patricia Morison (Lilli Vanessi/Katharine)
in *Kiss Me, Kate.*

And lovely Lisa, where are you, Lisa?
You gave a new meaning to the leaning tow'r of Pisa.

"WHERE IS THE LIFE THAT I LED"
(KISS ME, KATE)

That the *Shrew* songs were so dependent on a script for their music
and lyrics marked an important departure from Porter's creative hab-

its. For he generally worked with the concrete conditions of a performance in mind even as he fitted a song to a given situation. He might
write a song to showcase a performer, for example, so that he had few
qualms about dropping it if the performer disapproved and writing a
new one in its place. When William Gaxton balked at the wide skips he
had to sing in "Easy to Love," Porter cut the song from *Anything Goes*
and replaced it with "All Through the Night," whose melody moved in
half steps. Then again, Porter might write a song to help the pace of
a given production or call attention to its look. "'My Heart Belongs
to Daddy,'" he admitted, "was written to fill in a stage wait in *Leave It
to Me*. 'I Love Paris' in *Can-Can* was written because Jo Mielziner had
designed such a beautiful set." The *Shrew* songs, however, were less
tailored to the vagaries of performance or production than to the more
abstract dictates of a given text. The Spewacks themselves were quick
to point out the change by comparing these songs with those Porter
had written to an earlier show for which they had also furnished the
book, *Leave It to Me*.

> Leave It to Me *can be called a play with music, for none of the songs
> that Cole Porter wrote for that comedy of ours advanced the story one
> iota. "My Heart Belongs to Daddy" merely repeated what Dolly had
> already told Buck Thomas [in the dialogue]: that she had to leave
> him because she listened to her heart and not her head. When it was
> sung by Mary Martin, who cared if she had already told her reasons?
> . . . But in* Kiss Me, Kate *Cole Porter's songs served the story, espe-
> cially in Shakespeare's* Shrew. . . . *When Petruchio sings "I've Come
> to Wive It Wealthily," or when Lucentio, Gremio, and Hortensio join
> with Bianca to sing "Tom, Dick, or Harry," Shakespeare's deathless
> words of plottage go into limbo. Where Porter's melodious substitution
> takes about five minutes with encores, Shakespeare takes twenty.*

A "melodious substitution" for "words of plottage." That described
how a song might function in a musical play. But it did not apply to
the whole of *Kiss Me, Kate*. For the musicalized *Shrew* constituted only
about half of the show into which it was embedded as a play within
a play. The other half took place in Baltimore and in the present. It
told the backstage story of a theater company in rehearsal for a new
musical based on *The Taming of the Shrew*. Beyond simply a framing

device, the backstage story had a life of its own that called for a plot, subplot, and even songs of its own. The subplot involved a belting ingenue, a gambling hoofer, and two gangsters who appeared backstage to make sure someone made good on the hoofer's debts. The plot focused on the turbulent relationship of the company's stars, Fred Graham (Alfred Drake [*Oklahoma!*'s Curly]) and his ex-wife, Lilli Vanessi (Patricia Morison). Though both were now romantically attached to new partners, the two were still enamored of each other, and their jealous bickering "offstage" mirrored and intruded into their "onstage" roles as Petruchio and Kate. Indeed, the ironic juxtaposition of the backstage and onstage stories throughout *Kiss Me, Kate* supplied the central element of parody in the show and the basis for its self-reflexive wit. This was the stuff of musical comedy at its most sophisticated, and here Porter was most in his element. He came up with Broadway show tunes that drew parallels to *Shrew* numbers ("Another Op'nin', Another Show," "We Open in Venice"), songs of high lyricism and operettalike charm for his stars ("So in Love," "Wunderbar"), and list songs filled with the kind of topical and unblushing references that were his specialty ("Too Darn Hot," "Always True to You in My Fashion"). *Kiss Me, Kate* thus resembled nothing so much as an old-fashioned musical comedy, except it was increasingly interrupted by scenes from a musical play version of the *Shrew* so cleverly nested into it that the two musicals became inextricably one.

One song actually served dramatically to reconcile the two parts of *Kiss Me, Kate*; and it appeared, as did "My Ship" in *Lady in the Dark*, at the end of the show. For this number alone Porter relied on Shakespeare's words almost entirely—perhaps the closest he ever came to a true collaboration with another lyricist. It was sung by Lilli, who had earlier quit the company and walked out on Fred. Now she unexpectedly returned to both during the actual performance of the *Shrew*'s final scene—entering on cue and just in time to explain her reconciliation with Fred/Petruchio in the notorious words of submission Shakespeare placed in the mouth of his heroine, "I Am Ashamed That Women Are So Simple" (*Shrew*: act 5, scene 2, 161–80). Here Lilli returned *as* Kate, and of her own free will. That made her different from the tamed virago at the end of Shakespeare's play. But that Lilli justified herself not in her own words but Shakespeare's—and with Porter's music supporting them now without a trace of irony—has left *Kiss Me, Kate* open to the criticism of sexism, if not misogyny, that has long been leveled at *The Taming of the Shrew* itself.

Throughout his career Cole Porter exhibited a certain nervousness over the books to his shows, but not because he found the social values embedded in their texts particularly disturbing. Professional competence was his concern. Rodgers and Hart had demonstrated that songwriters could successfully write their own librettos. "My great professional tragedy," as Porter put it, "is that I have to be a book hunter"—one whose quarry, moreover, was seldom choice. And so he was lucky to find in *Kiss Me, Kate* "the best musical comedy book I have ever read," which may explain in part his matching it with arguably the best set of songs for a single show he ever wrote.

Yet Porter's accomplishment was also part of a larger trend, one indebted above all to the collaborative output of Richard Rodgers and Oscar Hammerstein. "The librettos are much better," Porter said of shows generally in the 1950s, "and the scores are much closer to the librettos than they used to be. Those two made it much harder for everybody else." In effect, "those two" bridged the gap between the work of book writers and the work of playwrights (the gap Moss Hart had earlier implied was unbridgeable when as a playwright he protested—too much, as it turned out—that he did not write musical comedies). Their insistence on the cogency of a libretto, in fact, helped to turn narrative and character development into governing principles in Broadway musicals, including some of the biggest hits of the postwar era. It also served to embolden a generation of book writers to see themselves as playwrights with a mission, or at least a point of view, and thus to use their talents to address matters of some consequence. This double mandate lay at the heart of what *Kiss Me, Kate*'s librettists wryly referred to as "the New Art Form" in an essay they wrote to accompany the publication of their script:

> *You may remember that the old musical comedy consisted of a story (book), songs, dances, scenery, girls, and boys. On the other hand, the New Art Form consists of a story (book), songs, dances, scenery, girls, and boys. But there is an indefinable "something else." . . . The New Art Form require[s] a message. For instance,* Call Me Madam: *money ain't everything.* Pal Joey: *don't be a heel. These crusades, articulated for the first time in the New Art Form, have had a profound effect*

upon our society. We have a message, too. It's Shakespeare's: slap your
wife around; she'll thank you for it.

The Spewacks wrote with tongue in cheek, to be sure. Musicals
may have carried normative values but they were not apt to moral-
ize so puckishly. Beneath the Spewacks's fun, however, lay a seriousness rooted in the self-consciousness of their very act of writing about
their writing. Old musical comedies did not provide such occasions for
introspection. The scripts to shows like *Leave It to Me* remained practical, unpublished records of events defined by the specifics of a given
production. The scripts to modern shows like *Kiss Me, Kate* were published as the texts to works that superseded their events. This bespoke
a belief widely held at midcentury that something like a new art form
really was in the ascendant, and that the musical play as it was generally understood and practiced now held out the possibility for the rise
on Broadway of an indigenous and legitimate *musical* theater.

9

MUSICAL THEATER: THE NEW ART

CAROUSEL
(4/19/1945–5/24/1947). **Producer:** The Theater Guild. **Book and Lyrics:** Oscar Hammerstein II, based on the play *Liliom* by Ferenc Molnár. **Music:** Richard Rodgers. **Director:** Rouben Mamoulian. **New York Run:** 890 performances. **Cast:** Jan Clayton, Bambi Linn, John Raitt. **Songs:** "If I Loved You," "Soliloquy," "You'll Never Walk Alone."

BRIGADOON
(3/13/1947–7/31/1948). **Producer:** Cheryl Crawford. **Book and Lyrics:** Alan Jay Lerner. **Music:** Frederick Loewe. **Director:** Robert Lewis. **New York Run:** 581 performances. **Cast:** Marion Bell, David Brooks, James Mitchell. **Songs:** "Almost Like Being in Love," "The Heather on the Hill."

SOUTH PACIFIC
(4/7/1949–1/16/1954). **Producers:** Rodgers, Hammerstein, Leland Hayward, and Joshua Logan. **Book:** Hammerstein and Logan, based on *Tales of the South Pacific* by James A. Michener. **Music:** Rodgers. **Director:** Logan. **New York Run:** 1,925 performances. **Cast:** Mary Martin, Juanita Hall, Ezio Pinza. **Songs:** "Twin Soliloquies," "Some Enchanted Evening," "Bali Ha'i."

Advancing a musical play ideal, Al Hirschfeld's *My Fair Lady* logo shows George Bernard Shaw masterminding the musical based on his play from beyond the grave—with the show's living librettist, Alan Jay Lerner, nowhere in sight.

THE KING AND I

(3/29/1951–3/20/1954). **Producers:** Rodgers and Hammerstein. **Book:** Hammerstein, based on Margaret Landon's novel *Anna and the King of Siam* and the 1946 screenplay by Sally Benson and Talbot Jennings. **Music:** Rodgers. **Director:** John Van Druten. **New York Run:** 1,246 performances. **Cast:** Gertrude Lawrence, Doretta Morrow, Yul Brynner. **Songs:** "Hello, Young Lovers," "Getting to Know You," "Shall We Dance?"

MY FAIR LADY

(3/15/1956–9/29/1962). **Producer:** Herman Levin. **Book and Lyrics:** Lerner, based on George Bernard Shaw's play *Pygmalion* and the 1938 screenplay by Shaw and others. **Music:** Loewe. **Director:** Moss Hart. **New York Run:** 2,717 performances. **Cast:** Julie Andrews, Rex Harrison, Stanley Holloway. **Songs:** "The Rain in Spain," "I Could Have Danced All Night," "On the Street Where You Live," "I've Grown Accustomed to Her Face."

FIORELLO!

(11/23/1959–10/28/1961). **Producers:** Robert E. Griffith and Harold Prince. **Book:** Jerome Weidman and George Abbott, based on the life of Fiorello La Guardia. **Lyrics:** Sheldon Harnick. **Music:** Jerry Bock. **Director:** Abbott. **New York Run:** 795 performances. **Cast:** Patricia Wilson, Tom Bosley. **Songs:** "Politics and Poker," "Little Tin Box," "Till Tomorrow."

CAMELOT

(12/3/1960–1/5/1963). **Producers:** Lerner, Loewe, and Moss Hart. **Book and Lyrics:** Lerner, based on the novel *The Once and Future King* by Terence H. White. **Music:** Loewe. **Director:** Hart [Lerner]. **New York Run:** 873 performances. **Cast:** Andrews, Richard Burton, Robert Goulet. **Songs:** "Camelot," "If Ever I Would Leave You."

FIDDLER ON THE ROOF

(9/22/1964–7/2/1972). **Producer:** Prince. **Book:** Joseph Stein, based on the Tevye short stories of Sholem Aleichem. **Lyrics:** Harnick. **Music:** Bock. **Director and Choreographer:** Jerome Robbins. **New York Run:** 3,242 performances. **Cast:** Maria Karnilova, Beatrice Arthur, Zero Mostel. **Songs:** "Tradition," "If I Were a Rich Man," "Do You Love Me?" "Sunrise, Sunset."

While the impact of *Oklahoma!* was overwhelming, not every Broadway show that succeeded in its wake did so by trying to emulate it as a musical play. (It took more than a dollop of idealism to produce musical plays in what was still first and foremost a commercially speculative medium—and would very much remain so.) Theatergoers in the 1940s could choose from a variety of musical alternatives that succeeded by relying less on the cogency of scripts than on the power of performers: star-vehicle musical comedies (*Mexican Hayride*, 1944; *High Button Shoes*, 1947), "glorified" burlesques (*Follow the Girls*, 1944; *As the Girls Go*, 1948), topical revues (*Call Me Mister*, 1946; *Make Mine Manhattan*, 1948). It may seem to the selective eye of historians today that after *Oklahoma!* the heyday of such shows was over. But at the time not everyone was intimidated by the success of Rodgers and Hammerstein.

Nor did everyone buy in to the sense of cultural self-importance that accompanied their work. Indeed, Rodgers and Hammerstein pursued a different aesthetic agenda from most of their Broadway colleagues: to clear a space for themselves between high culture and low, now often mass, culture. Yet, while they hewed to a certain cultural middle ground, they faced an onslaught of criticism from defenders of both extremes. A cadre of New York theater critics, on the one hand, were determined to keep musicals in their place as lowbrow entertainment rather than theatrical art. On the other hand, a number of social critics, intent on redefining the idea of culture itself at the time, leveled scathing criticism at popular forms of culture especially those that used technological means to address a truly mass audience. This view was perhaps most forcefully expressed in the joint work of Theodor Adorno and Max Horkheimer, members of the leftist Frankfurt School who had fled Nazi Germany and were both working in the United States. With American radio, movies, magazines, and even jazz in mind, they saw mass culture as a purposefully stultifying cultural form, technologically manipulated and socially controlled. They even posited replacing the term "mass culture" with culture industry to indicate what they saw as its imposed nature from above in an industrialized society and "to exclude from the outset the interpretation . . . that it is a matter of something like a culture that arises spontaneously from the masses themselves."

Others were perhaps similarly scathing in their indictment but less monolithic in their analysis. Characterizing the postwar period, American social critic Dwight Macdonald saw America's cultural divide on three levels. In a memorable essay, "Masscult & Midcult," he described what he called Midcult as a hybrid offspring of High Culture and the mass culture he referred to, disparagingly, as Masscult. High Culture was individual, even idiosyncratic, the domain of what was historically understood as art. Masscult, by contrast, was formulaic and transparently driven by commercial interests; it was patently "non-art." But Midcult was neither, though it somehow partook of both. If anything, it was a peculiarly American form of kitsch. It could be found in Norman Rockwell's paintings, the Thornton Wilder play *Our Town*, Henry Luce's *Life* magazine, even the Revised Standard Version of the Bible (as opposed to the King James). Above all, Midcult rather than Masscult posed the greater danger to High Culture because it pretended to be what it was not—that is, it was not fine art but its debasement masquerading as the genuine article.

> *Midcult is not, as it might appear at first, a raising of the level of Masscult. It is rather a corruption of High Culture which has the enormous advantage over Masscult that . . . it is able to pass itself off as the real thing. . . . Midcult is the transition from Rodgers and Hart to Rodgers and Hammerstein, from the gay tough lyrics of* Pal Joey, *a spontaneous expression of a real place called Broadway, to the folk-fakery of* Oklahoma! *and the orotund sentimentalities of* South Pacific.

And so Rodgers and Hammerstein were drawn into the midcentury cultural debate though they were never directly part of it. In their shows more prominently than anyone's, the Broadway musical as a genre appeared as a kind of battleground between musical comedy and some higher cultural enterprise that was not exactly operetta, something perhaps on the order of opera. In their hands, then, the musical became an arena of cultural activity "striving to distance itself from its commercial roots and to redefine itself as art." Macdonald's assessment of their work, however, represented a minority view. Indeed, by carving out a new kind of niche for middlebrow culture on Broadway, Rodgers and Hammerstein became symbols in a cultural discourse in which they appeared more often as heroes than whipping boys. For every Dwight Macdonald arguing "against the American grain," as he put it, there were innumerably more voices raised proclaiming Rodgers and Hammerstein "a national institution" and their work the basis for "a vital, vibrant American art."

It was *Carousel* rather than *Oklahoma!*, however, that marked the real turning point in their cultural work. The drama critic Elliot Norton already saw its potential—and its shortcomings—during tryouts in Boston. "A perfected *Carousel*," he wrote, "containing all the emotional power of fine drama heightened by the visual and aural splendors of beautiful music and swift dancing, would come very close to being a new dramatic art form." And soon after it opened in New York, *Carousel* appeared on the cover of an issue of *Theatre Arts* magazine, which Eric Bentley called "the only theatrical magazine of repute in the English-speaking world." The entire issue, in fact, was devoted to the history of what the editors still saw fit to call American Musical Comedy. In it, the show represented the latest example of an "American theatre form" that had emerged "within the last few years, with what has seemed like suddenness." But *Carousel* contended with forces both heavier and darker than musical comedy would suggest, which prompted the editors to rethink the terms of their discussion. "Today," they concluded, "the term musical comedy is inadequate; musical theatre would be more appropriate." More than appropriate, "musical theater" would in later years displace "musical comedy" as the term of choice for the medium itself. At the time, however, the term "musical theater" commonly refered to the more circumscribed field of musical plays, a field that flourished during what Brooks Atkinson would retrospectively suggest was "the golden period between 1940 (*Pal Joey*) and 1957 (*West Side Story*)." The suggestion has since taken hold historiographically, though it is more often modified nowadays to encompass a "Golden Age" beginning with *Oklahoma!* (1943) and ending with *Fiddler on the Roof* (1964).

Unlike *Show Boat, Oklahoma!* was not an isolated phenomenon on the musical stage. It had immediate repercussions as well as long-range ones, and, however rooted in the work of others, it was clearly perceived as the start of something new. Rodgers and Hammerstein themselves followed it with a string of shows which repeated, modified, and extended the patterns of its success. In their hands musical theater came to mean ever new hybrids of high and low cultural elements such that in any single show there could be found in varying degrees the "grandeur of opera; the seriousness of 'legitimate' theater; the comedic possibilities of the variety show and vaudeville; [and] the emotionality of melodrama." Largely because of their work as creators of musical plays and eventually as heads of their own production organization, musical theater became, more than ever, a writers' medium. Rodgers and Hammerstein replaced the star system, one critic said, and became the stars themselves. For a generation they exerted an influence so powerful over Broadway that other show writers regularly measured their own success by standards the creators of *Oklahoma!*, *Carousel*, and host of other shows had set—most prominent among them, two long-standing teams: Lerner and Loewe, and Harnick and Bock. If it is now common to view as a piece historically the Broadway years that start with *Oklahoma!* and end with the acme of Harnick and Bock's achievement, *Fiddler on the Roof*, it is largely because much the finest work of the era found through the example of Rodgers and Hammerstein its own way of reconfiguring the world of musical comedy into that of musical theater.

RODGERS AND HAMMERSTEIN

Richard Rodgers and Oscar Hammerstein II wrote one movie musical together (*State Fair*, 1945), one television musical (*Cinderella*, 1957), and the nine Broadway shows on which their joint reputation mainly rests: *Oklahoma!* (1943), *Carousel* (1945), *Allegro* (1947), *South Pacific* (1949), *The King and I* (1951), *Me and Juliet* (1953), *Pipe Dream* (1955), *Flower Drum Song* (1958), and *The Sound of Music* (1959). Partly because the partners had the foresight and the clout to make sure their work would also be preserved in media more durable than live performance, their shows have demonstrated unusual staying power in popular culture. All nine stageworks can still be heard today through original cast albums that were recorded and released shortly after their premieres. All nine were also published as librettos, the first six actually printed together in a volume of the Modern Library—a collection of inexpensive editions of "The Best of The World's Best Books," by authors from Aquinas to Zola, and including no other librettos except those by Gilbert and Sullivan. Eventually, six of the shows were also converted into major Hollywood motion pictures—the last, *The Sound of Music* (1965), among the finest film musicals of its era and among the biggest box office draws.

It was for the theater that most of the Rodgers and Hammerstein shows were originally conceived, however. And it was through the devices, structures, and practices of the theater that they were first brought to life. Moreover, it is in the theatrical medium of live performance that many of them have continued to maintain their viability for more than half a century of changing taste. Of such shows, those from the first half of the partners' joint career are now widely regarded as the pinnacle of their achievement in developing the modern musical play and as the single most influential body of work on the American musical stage of the postwar period. Apart from the failed *Allegro*, they include, after *Oklahoma!*, *Carousel*, *South Pacific*, and *The King and I*.

These shows are built around social issues with love stories at their core. Unlike *Oklahoma!*, the obstacles the lovers must overcome in each lie mainly within themselves. In *Carousel*, a social misfit and ne'er-do-well kills himself while attempting a robbery and tries to redeem himself from beyond the grave through an act of love. In *South Pacific*, a navy nurse discovers that her love for an older man from another culture involves coming to terms with her own bigotry. In *The King and I*, a British schoolmistress working in Siam undermines the authority of the king who sent for her, yet for whom she comes to feel more affection than she would care to admit. These pieces are not lacking in warmth, humor, or wit. But they also explore certain richnesses of theme, complexities of character, and ambiguities of feeling more generally associated with realistic dramas than Broadway musicals. They move toward an ideal of theatrical legitimacy that leaves even *Oklahoma!* behind.

"*Oklahoma!* is about a picnic," Stephen Sondheim once said; "*Carousel* is about life and death." This remark is curt, telling, and a tad misleading. Both shows told tales in which good and evil were not to be taken lightly. But the relatively lightweight plot in *Oklahoma!* left openings for dialogue, songs, and dances that still bore the performative traces of old-style musical comedy and operetta. *Carousel*, by contrast, moved through weightier terrain, suggesting a musical heft and playlike accountability that pushed the show toward music drama. It was darker in theme than *Oklahoma!* and nearly operatic in its musical approach—a drama more keenly felt in the poetic sweep of Hammerstein's language and of Rodgers's score. The song "If I Loved You," for example, was written in the standard form of a pop ballad (AABA in 32 bars). Yet its emotional reach was anything but standard. Consider the bridge (B section), where ever searching harmonies in the orchestra convey the quality of going "round in circles" (the feeling to which the singer has just confessed) as they lift a melody from the verge of banality to a place of ineffable pathos (Ex. 9-1). Expressive intensity of this sort, built into the structure of the song rather than dependent mainly on the performer, is not characteristic of *Oklahoma!*—or most musicals of the period.

Rodgers's music in *Carousel* generally speaks in an idiom different from that of his earlier musical comedy work, and it would characterize

Ex. 9-1. Richard Rodgers, music, Oscar Hammerstein II, lyrics: "If I Loved You," *Carousel*

his approach to the musical play. Where Hart had often worked ironically to Rodgers's music, Rodgers's music responded more directly to the import of Hammerstein's words. Rodgers and Hammerstein still wrote comic songs, to be sure, but the music and the text worked together rather than at purposeful cross-purposes. Moreover, the lyricism apparent in Rodgers's earlier style now took on a more measured quality to support such genuine expressions of emotion as found in the hymn-like numbers at the heart of almost all their shows from *Carousel* ("You'll Never Walk Alone") to *The Sound of Music* ("Climb Every Mountain"). Due to their heft and technical difficulty, such songs called for "legitimate" voices. They also required acting singers, as Rodgers tailored them musically to the characters who sang them in the shows. Downplaying the more generic styles of his earlier show tunes, Rodgers now aimed to evoke in music the specific quality of each character and situation afresh, and to create a distinctive sound for each musical play to capture its spirit in a way that would make it sound wrong anywhere else. "Bali H'ai," with its exotic sensuality, is as right for *South Pacific* as it would be out place in *Oklahoma!* Here, too, the orchestra played a part. "In a great musical," said Rodgers, "the orchestrations sound the way the costumes look." And indeed, the piquant discords and lilting rhythms at the start *Carousel*, for example, not only evoke the merry-go-round and wistful atmosphere of the scene about to unfold, they established a coloration that will characterize the feel of the show itself and stamp it with a sound unlike that of any other.

For the book of *Carousel* Hammerstein took *Liliom*, a grim Hungarian fantasy play by Ferenc Molnár, and Americanized it in both setting and outlook. Relocated from Hungary to a small town in nineteenth-century New England, the show tells of the enduring love of Julie Jordan (Jan Clayton) for an abusive carnival barker, Billy Bigelow (John Raitt), his suicide following a failed attempt to steal money to provide for their unborn child ("Soliloquy"), and his ghostlike return fifteen years later at their daughter's high-school graduation to perform a selfless act of love for his wife and the child he never knew (reprise: "You'll Never Walk Alone"). *Carousel*'s hero and villain were thus one and the same: Billy had to rise above his own moral failings. And by giving him the motivation to do so—to assure his wife of the love he could not articulate while he was alive and to ensure the future happiness of his daughter—Hammerstein ended *Carousel* with a sense of hope altogether lacking in *Liliom*. Not all were convinced by the folksy graduation scene of Hammerstein's new ending. Eric Bentley saw it as "an impertinence: I refuse to be lectured by a musical comedy scriptwriter on the education of children, the nature of the good life, and the contribution of the American small town to the salvation of souls." Others, however—apparently even Molnár, who had been dead set against any musicalization of his play—felt Rodgers and Hammerstein had deepened the original with their show: "they carried into it, through the ballet . . . and in the final scene . . . a story of a father-child relationship which is not to be found in the play from which *Carousel* was fashioned." In post–World War II America, such relationships were freighted with an almost unbearable poignance. "If *Oklahoma!* developed the moral argument for sending American boys overseas," Gerald Mast has written, "*Carousel* offered consolation to those wives and mothers whose boys would only return in spirit."

Given the show's emotional compass, then, it is not surprising that music played a greater role in the telling of *Carousel* than it did in *Oklahoma!* Of all his musicals, Rodgers, said his wife, Dorothy, "was proudest of *Carousel*, because he felt it cut deeper and moved people more, and he liked the way some of the songs were not held down to 32 bars so that whole scenes were like musical plays." The prologue, with its "Carousel Waltz" playing continuously throughout, introduced the main characters, the setting, and the tone of the show entirely through music and mime, without the use of words. In another scene Billy sang a seven-minute "Soliloquy" of flexible musical ideas that reflected his changing emotions as he imagined what it would be like to be a father: It took him to a different place emotionally at the end of the number from where he was when it began. Most memorable perhaps was the "Park Bench Scene," in which Julie and Billy first came to grips with their feelings for each other. A miniature musical play in itself, it moves freely between spoken dialogue, dialogue with orchestral underscoring, and singing in various forms—reprise ("You're a Queer One, Julie Jordan"), patter ("You Couldn't Take My Money"), parlando ("When I Worked in the Mill"), arioso ("You Can't Hear a Sound"), and full-fledged song ("If I Loved You"). The entire scene thus consists of separate musical strands interwoven over the course of 23 minutes and 294 bars—not just 32—into one continuous dramatic fabric.

While *Carousel* may have been the most ambitious of Rodgers and Hammerstein's hits, with *South Pacific* and *The King and I* the partners

Jan Clayton (Julie Jordan) and John Raitt (Billy Bigelow) meet in the wordless
prologue to *Carousel.*

moved the musical play into territory no less artistic but more familiar. *South Pacific* resembled a musical comedy: It had a timely subject,
World War II; a raunchy comedian, Luther Billis; and a crew of spirited
U.S. Navy personnel playfully preoccupied with sex ("There Is Nothin'
Like a Dame," "Honey Bun"). *The King and I* resembled a comic operetta: It was set historically in an exotic locale, Bangkok in 1862, and
focused on a battle of wits between its male and female protagonists
that diverted from the underlying battle of their feelings ("A Puzzle-
ment," "Shall I Tell You What I Think of You?," "Shall We Dance?").

Yet both shows were also serious in the way *Carousel* was serious.
They were social problem plays expressed in musical terms—musical
morality plays, as it were, which effectively gave audiences permission,
as John Gassner put it, to "feel virtuous as appreciators of a humanitar-
ianism dispensed with unexacting taste and refinement." *South Pacific*
looked at the effects of racial prejudice on the lives of two Americans
serving their country overseas in wartime. Lieutenant Joseph Cable
loved a local Tonkinese girl, Liat, but could not bring himself to marry

her. Nurse Nellie Forbush (Mary Martin) harbored romantic feelings for a middle-aged Frenchman, Emile de Becque (Ezio Pinza), but was unable to accept his earlier relationship with a Polynesian woman and the interracial children he had fathered. The key indictment of their racism in the show was Cable's song "You've Got to Be Carefully Taught," which, according to James Michener, "represented why [Rodgers and Hammerstein] had wanted to do this play" in the first place. *The King and I*, in turn, looked at nondemocratic social institutions through the clash in values of two headstrong individuals. Anna Leonowens (Gertrude Lawrence), a Victorian widow, came to Siam at the request of the king in order to teach his children "what is good in Western culture." The king (Yul Brynner) was an autocrat whose adherence to polygamy, slavery, and other abhorrences to Western sensibilities prompted Anna to extend her civilizing mandate to include him as well. The king's ultimate "lesson" (and centerpiece of the show) took the form of a ballet called "The Small House of Uncle Thomas," a Siamese-style court entertainment based on *Uncle Tom's Cabin*.

In the early 1950s, while both musicals were still running on Broadway, U.S. troops were crossing the Pacific once again to fight Asian despotism, now in Korea, and there were mounting fears at home over Communist infiltration from abroad. Both shows, in fact, have often been viewed as shaped by and as shapers of American cold war sensibilities, events outside the theater rarely being unrelated to what takes place inside it. (A 1953 performance of *South Pacific* in Atlanta is even said to have prompted a bill in the Georgia legislature banning entertainments with "an underlying philosophy inspired by Moscow.") These were unmistakably "message" shows. But the messages they bore were not unmixed. Whatever ambivalences their authors harbored, they were as supportive of American institutions as they were critical of American mores. "You may call it 'bourgeois sentimentalism,' from the left, or starry-eyed liberalism, from the right, of our political spectrum," Gassner wrote, "but it is a fact that Rodgers and Hammerstein harbored a congenial viewpoint capable of sustaining a number of syncretic ideals sanctioned by World War II sentiments." Along with their artistry, achieving such an ideological consensus had much to do with their great success.

South Pacific and *The King and I* marked a significant professional departure for Rodgers and Hammerstein as well. These were the first of their creations that they produced themselves and the first they cast with star performers. For reasons of dramatic verisimilitude above all, they had cast relative unknowns as the leads in *Oklahoma!* and *Carousel*—both shows, tellingly, Theater Guild productions. By contrast, Mary Martin was already a musical comedy star and Ezio Pinza a celebrated basso at the Metropolitan Opera by the time of *South Pacific.* Gertrude Lawrence, more famous still, enjoyed an avid following on Broadway and the West End during more than two decades before *The King and I.* And yet the new shows were not exactly star vehicles. Their leading roles were such strongly written parts that others could subsequently play them with stellar success—and they did. But the move to feature star performers in them from the start clearly played to more conventional stage expectations.

Perhaps this compensated in part for the added risks the authors took in basing their shows for the first time on non-theatrical sources. *Oklahoma!* and *Carousel* had both been adapted from plays. But Rodgers and Hammerstein derived *South Pacific* from a collection of short stories; and *The King and I* from a modern novel and screen adaptation of two nineteenth-century memoirs (Anna Leonowens's *The English Governess at the Siamese Court* and *The Romance of the Harem*). Here, *South Pacific* proved particularly problematic. The nineteen stories that served as the source of the show had a single author, James Michener, but no single protagonist. Nor were they held together by anything more than "a giant operation against the Japs," Michener said, "and by the frequent reappearance of certain characters." It was only by concentrating on two of the stories—"Our Heroine" for the Nellie-Emile plot; "Fo' Dolla" for the Cable-Liat subplot—that Rodgers and Hammerstein eventually discovered how to convert Michener's gritty episodes into an evening's-length narrative with a dramatically focused and lyrical form. So close was their concentration that, together with Trude Rittmann, who wrote the incidental music, and Josh Logan, who co-wrote the book and directed, they actually located musical theater equivalents for the narrative voices normally available within short story conventions but not within the purview of realistic drama. Take, for example, an excerpt from "Our Heroine," in which Nellie becomes aware of her feelings for Emile on her first visit to his plantation home:

> *"I was looking at the cacaos," Nellie said in a sing-song kind of voice. To herself she was saying, "I shall marry this man. This shall be my*

life from now on. This hillside shall be my home. And in the after-noons he and I will sit here." Aloud she continued, "They are beauti-ful, aren't they?"

"A rugged tree," he said. "Not like coconuts. But they don't pay as well . . ."

To himself De Becque said, "This is what I have been waiting for. All the long years. Who ever thought a fresh, smiling girl like this would climb up my hill? It was worth waiting for . . ."

In the cacao pavilion the two strangers looked at one another. Each had half a smile. De Becque's gold tooth showed. Nellie's infectious grin fought for possession of her full lips. She thought that he was not an old man, and yet not a young man, either. He was a respected man, wealthy, a man with deep ideas. He was one who killed with a knife, came out for De Gaulle, and was to have led the resistance against the Japs.

"Nellie," he said quietly, scarcely audible above the lorikeets. "In the hottest months you could go to Australia." Nellie made no reply. She merely watched De Becque as he rose, crossed the silent pavilion, and bent over her. She raised her lips. Although he merely brushed her lips with his, she had the distinct impression that she had been kissed by a man, a whole man, a man worthy to be loved.

Michener writes here from several perspectives. He lets the lovers speak for themselves ("'I was looking at the cacaos'"). He reveals what they are thinking but do not say out loud ("To herself she was saying, 'I shall marry this man'"). And he articulates conditions, actions, and even unconscious feelings as an "omniscient observer" ("In the cacao pavilion the two strangers looked at one another"). Only the first of these was traditionally available to legitimate playwrights working under the constraints of stage realism. *South Pacific*'s musical playwrights, however, found ways to access the other two as well. After some dialogue in the show's opening scene, Emile turns away from Nellie to pour her a drink. Music now begins to reveal what the two are thinking as they take turns singing the same melody softly, not to each other but to themselves:

"Twin Soliloquies"

NELLIE: Wonder how I'd feel
    Living on a hillside,

> Looking on an ocean,
> Beautiful and still.
> EMILE: This is what I need,
>   This is what I've longed for,
>   Someone young and smiling
>   Climbing up my hill . . .

When they finish and move in silence toward one another, the orchestra, which had simply been accompanying them before, swells and takes over completely. It becomes the omniscient observer, articulating what Nellie and Emile are feeling as they drink together. The orchestra plays an intensified version of the "Twin Soliloquies" melody, which the score refers to as "Unspoken Thoughts." The stage directions reveal how crucial is its dramatic function:

> *As they drink, the music rises to great ecstatic heights. One is made aware that in this simple act of two people who are falling in love, each drinking brandy, there are turbulent thoughts and feelings going on in their hearts and brains.*

Thus has a literary text been made thoroughly musical-theatrical. The effect may be no match for *Tristan and Isolde*'s love draught, but the technique is distinctly Wagnerian. "This was the moment when for me the show became great," said Logan. For Leonard Bernstein the moment had implications greater still: It gave evidence that "our musical comedy has moved toward opera but *in our own way.*"

Broadway now took seriously Wagner's ideas, if not his music. Yet Wagner's *Gesamtkunstwerk* in its rejection of the opera industry and in its seamless fusion of the arts was hardly a model for the musical play, which was a commercial genre, through and through, that still went in for spoken dialogue and self-contained musical numbers. Moreover, Tristan and Isolde were nobility; Nellie and Emile, distinctly middle class. Nonetheless, musical adaptations of literary sources like *South Pacific* pointed piecemeal in the Wagnerian direction as they challenged musical playwrights to explore new capabilities of the genre each time out. Brooks Atkinson hailed this development. Show writers, he said, now "had enough vision to approach the musical stage as if it were a form of literature." Such vision, however, was often near-

Ezio Pinza (Emile de Becque) and Mary Martin (Nellie Forbush) share a drink in *South Pacific* as the orchestra conveys their "Unspoken Thoughts."

sighted and seldom far from folly. This was perhaps nowhere more the case than when legitimate playwrights took to the writing of musical librettos (Robert E. Sherwood: *Miss Liberty*, 1949; Lillian Hellman: *Candide*, 1956) and poets to the writing of lyrics (Richard Wilbur: *Candide*; W. H. Auden: *Man of La Mancha*, 1965). Literary pretension of this sort was utterly at variance with musical comedy norms. In 1929, when *A Connecticut Yankee* opened in London, a critic found ludicrous the very idea of a show that billed itself as "A Musical Adaptation of Mark Twain's 'A Yankee at the Court of King Arthur'":

> *Some musical plays from America have been so completely destitute of ideas that one is not at all surprised to discover in the latest example a frank disavowal on the author's part of any claim to originality. For, as the title boldly proclaims, Mr. Herbert Fields has turned to a quasi-classic of literature for the root-idea—and some of the incidents—of the play which came to Daly's last night.*

"Originality" here meant books that were not just newly invented, but so invented as to leave room to delight in the virtuosity of performers and other forms of self-conscious presentation endemic to the musical stage—thus making mincemeat of "literature." To this practice Hammerstein himself basically adhered in the 1920s (with the major exception of *Show Boat*). It was only later, working with Rodgers, that he consistently modified the older practice to suit a newer ideal: Representational content dictates musical form. And due mainly to the partners' unprecedented success working this way, adapted books rather than originals became not just the norm, but normative: what musicals ought to be—at least, the best of them. In fact, the Broadway community of the 1950s and 1960s often seemed beholden to an almost medieval faith in the authority of an established text to justify undertaking a new one—as if the latter were some sort of a gloss on the former. And patterns of Broadway economics and aesthetics combined to bolster the faith: Investors looked kindly on properties with built-in public recognition; writers looked kindly on properties with built-in structural supports. Librettist Alan Jay Lerner preached (and often practiced) accordingly:

> *Your chances not only of reaching production but achieving success will be inestimably enhanced if you begin with a book, a short story, a motion picture, or a play that has already been approved by public and critic alike. The value of the basic story cannot be exaggerated. . . . I can tell you the book is all-essential. It is the fountain from which all waters spring. So start off on the right foot and select a story that is all prepared for you. The translation of that story to musical form is quite complex enough. Within that frame you will find more than adequate challenge to your originality and enough on which to experiment.*

In his zeal, however, Lerner failed to mention many things: from the pinch of paying for the legal rights to someone else's work, to the pain of miscalculating a work's translatability into a medium for which it was not intended—or one's ability to do the translating. Miscalculations of this sort constituted the rule far more than the exception. Consider this sample of Broadway musical flops of the period, all adaptations of literature that bore the cultural seal of preapproval:

Sadie Thompson, 1944 (W. Somerset Maugham's "Miss Sadie Thompson" [*Rain*])

Sleepy Hollow, 1948 (Washington Irving's "The Legend of Sleepy Hollow")

The Liar, 1950 (Carlo Goldoni's *Il Bugiardo*)

Maggie, 1953 (James M. Barrie's *What Every Woman Knows*)

Shangri-La, 1956 (James Hilton's *Lost Horizon*)

First Impressions, 1959 (Jane Austen's *Pride and Prejudice*)

The Happiest Girl in the World, 1961 (Aristophanes' *Lysistrata*)

The Gay Life, 1961 (Arthur Schnitzler's *Anatol*)

Foxy, 1964 (Ben Jonson's *Volpone*)

Pickwick, 1965 (Charles Dickens's *The Pickwick Papers*)

A Time for Singing, 1966 (Richard Llewellyn's *How Green Was My Valley*)

Here's Where I Belong, 1968 (John Steinbeck's *East of Eden*)

Her First Roman, 1968 (George Bernard Shaw's *Caesar and Cleopatra*)

No one was immune from the lure of flawed assumptions, not even Rodgers and Hammerstein. The fact that all but two of their shows were adaptations was thus no guarantee of success—or of failure, for that matter. Their single greatest hit and flop of the 1950s were both adapted shows. *The Sound of Music*, based on a memoir by Maria von Trapp and its German film adaptation, ran over three years on Broadway to become the third longest-running musical in the Rodgers and Hammerstein canon. (Set in 1930s Salzburg, it told the story of Maria [Mary Martin] as she prepared to become a nun while serving as governess for the children of a widower, then fell in love and gave up her religious life to marry him, and finally escaped from Austria with her family after the *Anschluss* with Nazi Germany.) By contrast, *Pipe Dream*, based on John Steinbeck's novel *Sweet Thursday*, a sequel to his *Cannery Row*, ran just half a year, had no national tour, and remains today the least familiar of all Rodgers and Hammerstein musicals.

Yet both musicals shared a disquieting bond. For while *The Sound of Music* was remarkably well crafted and durable in its appeal, its critical reception did not match its popular success. Nor did this change after the release of the celebrated (and altered) film version in the mid-1960s (starring Julie Andrews). Critics took the piece to task for the unapologetic sentimentality of its book (by Howard Lindsay and Russel Crouse) and its score (still by Rodgers and Hammerstein). The film outraged musicologist Raymond Knapp for "the scandalous reversal of historical realities through which *The Sound of Music* manages to sell a scurrilously anti-Semitic Austria as pre-eminent among Nazi Germany's victims." But the Broadway original, too, met with critical dismay even though it had been less willing to endorse such compromises. The show was said to indulge in "the clichés of operetta"; and it seemed its authors had "succumbed to a sort of joint amnesia and forgotten everything that Broadway learned, partly under their tutelage, in the forties and fifties."

The sense of "joint amnesia" was not limited to *The Sound of Music*. It haunted the second half of the partners' career, which stands in marked contrast to the first. Early on, they had seemed almost to welcome the challenges each new musical play posed in finding a musical form uniquely suited to its play. "The very difficulties of the job we knew would lead us into unusual devices," Hammerstein said in 1945, on converting *Liliom* into *Carousel*. "We knew we wouldn't wind up with a conventional musical comedy." It is this spirit that animated the very successes from *Oklahoma!* to *The King and I* that validated their musical play ideal. But their subsequent output pleaded the case less eloquently. While "R & H" became an enterprise in the 1950s intent on producing their latest creations and overseeing the dissemination of their past hits, their newer work somehow sparkled less with the innovative genius their older work had led audiences to expect. The partners seemed less inclined toward unusual devices now than to mastering conventions, even those of their own making.

The change was poignantly brought to Hammerstein's attention by Steinbeck in 1955 as *Pipe Dream* faltered during tryouts. What stood in the way of the show's success, Steinbeck felt, was a failure to find the right musical theater equivalent for his novel: a failure of nerve on Hammerstein's part to address the sexually explicit truths in its romance between a California marine biologist and a whore. It was also a more general failure to live up to expectations and to the idea of progress that now permeated Broadway culture as much as it did the culture at large. "The show side-steps, hesitates, mish-mashes and never faces its theme," he wrote Hammerstein:

> *Sweetness, loss of toughness, lack of definition, whatever people say when they feel they are being let down . . . believe me, Oscar, this is the*

way audiences feel. What emerges now is an old-fashioned love story. And that is not good enough to people who have looked forward to this show based on you and me and Dick. You and Dick invented this form and carried it to its high point with South Pacific. *When* Oklahoma! *came out it violated every conventional rule of Musical Comedy. You were out on a limb. They loved it and were for you.* South Pacific *made a great jump ahead. But, Oscar, time has moved. The form has moved. People love* Oklahoma! *as a classic, but if you brought it in as a new show now, people would find it old-fashioned and conventional because* S.P. *and* King and I *carried it farther. . . . That's the price you have to pay for being Rodgers and Hammerstein.*

LERNER AND LOEWE

As revolutions have a way eventually of overtaking their makers, so the revolution in musical theater values that Rodgers and Hammerstein implemented in the 1940s overtook them in the following decade. Tellingly, the partners spent a year in the early 1950s trying to make a musical play out of a defiantly *un*musical play of George Bernard Shaw's, only to abandon the project after concluding it couldn't be done. The play was *Pygmalion,* which shortly thereafter Alan Lerner and Frederick Loewe would convert into *My Fair Lady,* the first show to supplant *Oklahoma!* as the longest-running musical in the history of the American stage. The show's success, however, was achieved not by turning away from the principles of Rodgers and Hammerstein so much as taking them further than Rodgers and Hammerstein themselves were willing to go. "That payment was due Dick and Oscar, there is no doubt," said Lerner. "Everyone driven towards the goal of a cohesive blending of book, words and music owes his vision and ambition to the origins they provided."

Alan Jay Lerner (1918–1986) and Frederick Loewe (1901–1988) did not inherit the mantle of Rodgers and Hammerstein; the careers of the two teams largely overlapped. Lerner and Loewe were rather the earliest show writing partners to achieve sustained success on Broadway working along the lines Rodgers and Hammerstein had established. The two began collaborating in 1942 after a chance meeting at New York's Lambs Club. Loewe had immigrated to the United States in 1924 from his native Germany, where he claimed to have been a Wunderkind, having performed as a pianist with the Berlin Symphony and composed a pop-song hit, "Katrina," while still in his teens. Since coming to America, however, his musical career had been on hold. Lerner, the younger by seventeen years, and a recent Harvard graduate, had been working as a radio scriptwriter, though his driving ambition was to write for the theater. He also proved to be a notoriously difficult collaborator, which often deeply troubled the partnership. But Loewe, who effectively retired from active work in 1960, would not again collaborate with anyone else. (They reunited briefly in the 1970s for two ill-fated projects: a staging of their Academy Award–winning 1958 film musical *Gigi*, and a new film musical, *The Little Prince*.) By contrast, Lerner was to spend forty years collaborating with many composers both during and after his career with Loewe, but with none would he write more consistently or successfully. Of the seven Broadway musicals Lerner and Loewe created together, *Paint Your Wagon* (1951) and a stage version of *Gigi* (1973) proved notable disappointments, while *Brigadoon* (1947), *My Fair Lady* (1956), and *Camelot* (1960) are generally held to constitute the heart of their work.

Lerner and Loewe created more than songs for their shows. Loewe wrote virtually all the music—from overtures to vocal and dance arrangements—and music that effectively captured the distinct local color of each show's setting: from the Scottish highlands (*Brigadoon*), to the American frontier (*Paint Your Wagon*), and beyond. Lerner was an incurable romantic—he was married eight times. Yet he wrote lyrics for characters who maintain a certain intelligence even at their most hyperbolic:

> *There's a smile on my face*
> *For the whole human race!*
> *Why, it's . . . almost like being in love!*
>
> "Almost Like Being in Love" (*Brigadoon*)

His lyrics also fit into a larger trajectory: He was "a dramatist who wrote part of his plays in rhyme." He was, in a word, a librettist, though the word put him off.

> *When I fill out a form which asks that I identify my profession I do not say I am a librettist. I say I am a "playwright-lyricist." I write every*

word that is spoken or sung from curtain up to curtain down. . . . I dis-
like the word librettist. . . . A librettist has always seemed to me someone
associated with opera and operetta and who specialized in unintelligi-
bility and anonymity. Nevertheless, that is what I am.

Brigadoon established Lerner and Loewe as a major team of show writers and as masters of the new style of integrated musical play. An historical fantasy set in a modern frame, the show told of two New Yorkers on a
trip to Scotland who stumble up on an eighteenth-century village, Brigadoon, that miraculously comes to life for one day every hundred years. On
that day, one of them falls in love with a girl from Brigadoon, who cannot
return with him to New York since no one from the village can ever leave
it. Ultimately, his love proves so strong that he chooses to stay with her
when the village disappears for the next hundred years. Like *Oklahoma!*
and *Carousel, Brigadoon* pitted a primary love plot that was serious ("From
This Day On") against an amorous subplot that was not ("The Love of
My Life"), and tied the musical together with the choreography of Agnes
de Mille ("Sword Dance," "Funeral Dance"). "For once," wrote Brooks
Atkinson, "the modest label 'musical play' has a precise meaning. For it
is impossible to say where the music and dancing leave off and the story
begins in this beautifully orchestrated Scottish idyll."

Brigadoon was not an adaptation, however. Lerner admitted that up
until then, "I was determined to write musicals with original stories,
that is to say not based on other plays, novels or short stories." Nonetheless, there was some flap over whether he had relied on an unac-
knowledged literary source for *Brigadoon.* Whether he had or hadn't
was less interesting than the fact that it mattered both to him and to
the critics. More interesting still, Lerner's views on the subject subsequently underwent a change so complete that, by the time of *My Fair
Lady,* in the words of one pundit, he would not *adapt* the material on
which the show was based so much as *adopt* it.

Shaw's *Pygmalion* was not a romance but a comedy of ideas: a satire, playful in manner and serious in aim. As it served Shaw's social
philosophy in writing it to ridicule England's class system, he utterly
reworked the ancient Greek legend of the sculptor Pygmalion, whose
love for the statue of a woman he created had moved the gods to bring
it to life. But Shaw was not content with supernatural intervention in
bringing the legend up to date (1912). He invented a professor of pho-

netics, Henry Higgins, who wins a bet that he can take a poor Cockney girl, Eliza Doolittle, and pass her off in society as a duchess simply by teaching her to speak correctly.

The Cinderella theme and the dramatic climax of Eliza's test performance in society seemed almost made for a Broadway musical. But what stymied Lerner with *Pygmalion* at first was his belief that there were "certain rules for the construction of a musical that the play seemed incapable of obeying." *Pygmalion* was too rooted in British culture and sensibilities for Broadway audiences. Its approach was quintessentially cerebral rather than emotional. And its structure as a drawing-room comedy left no room for scenes in which choruses might sing and dance; no room for a subplot with a secondary love story; no room even for a primary love story when it came down to it. "*Pygmalion* had one story and one story only," Lerner despaired. "It was most definitely a non-love story and how, may I ask, does one write a non-love song?"

What broke the impasse for Lerner was the realization that if dramatic content truly dictated musical form, then, like the mountain and Mohammed, the musical play might come to *Pygmalion* where *Pygmalion* would not come to the musical play. The upshot of this insight amounted to no less than a decisive departure from the particular practices—but not from the general ideals—of Rodgers, Hammerstein, and *Brigadoon*.

> By 1954 it no longer seemed essential that a musical have a subplot, nor that there be an ever-present ensemble filling the air with high C's and flying limbs. In other words, some of the obstacles that had stood in the way of converting Pygmalion into a musical had simply been removed by a changing style. . . . It now seemed feasible to preserve the text as much as possible without the addition of a secondary love story or choreographic integration. What was essential was that every song and every addition to the play not violate the wit and intelligence of Shaw's work. He was an ideal "collaborator" because there was so much oblique and unstated emotion that could be dramatized in music and lyrics.

Lerner and Loewe closely followed the screenplay Shaw provided for the 1938 film version in which he (together with Gabriel Pascal, Anthony Asquith, and others) opened up the play by inserting scenes

"The Rain in Spain" jota from *My Fair Lady*, l. to r.: Robert Coote (Colonel Pickering, the bull), Julie Andrews (Eliza Doolittle), and Rex Harrison (Henry Higgins, the matador).

only implied in the original. The showmen then sought out whatever emotion was implied in the text for musicalization. One song, "Why Can't the English?," revealed not just Higgins's passion for language but his petulance; another, "Wouldn't It Be Loverly?," expressed not only Eliza's socioeconomic deprivation but her neediness. They even created numbers where the text implied no emotion at all, like the dreary speech exercise "The Rain in Spain Stays Mainly in the Plain," which they musicalized at the end of an exhausting sequence when Eliza finally got it right. "It's not a great piece of music, nor a great lyric," Lerner admitted. But it did precisely what a great theater song in its context had to do: "catch the drama at the hilltops, where it could ascend no further without the wings of music and lyrics, at the same time remaining faithful to the spirit of the Irish Pope."

On the other hand, Lerner and Loewe were also keenly aware of Shaw's prose and its intoxicating, almost musical power. They were determined to stretch the limits of a musical book as far as they could to preserve *Pygmalion*'s text—to keep "as much of Shaw's dialogue as possible, which would automatically mean there would be more dialogue

than in any other musical to date." That entailed casting the male lead in
My Fair Lady primarily on the basis of an actor's ability to handle Shaw's
dialogue rather than sing or dance. It meant writing songs not only with
lyrics to approximate the dialogue but with tunes of a suitable vocal modesty for an actor to negotiate. And it involved joining book to music in so
unobtrusive a fashion that an actor might talk his way from dialogue into
song and back again, thereby obscuring the distinction between the two
and eliminating the sense of separable musical numbers from the show
altogether ("I'm an Ordinary Man"). The purpose in all this was not to
minimize the role of music in a musical play so much as to maximize the
play—a tendency which became all the more pronounced when playwright Moss Hart joined the creative team not only to direct the show
but also to "guide" (Lerner's word) some of its writing.

A famous nonsinging actor, Rex Harrison, played the male protagonist. (The precedent would be repeated with Louis Jourdan in the
film *Gigi* and Richard Burton as *Camelot*'s King Arthur, though, in the
absence of Shaw's prose, with less point.) This was appropriate, for
Henry Higgins was no typical musical hero, but rather complicated, cultivated, and verbally articulate to a fault. In fact, *Pygmalion* was largely
about articulateness; and if all the talk pushed the music to one side, it
also provided ample room for real acting where it might not have been
expected. "Although musical dramas are generally reckoned as coarser
in characterization than spoken dramas," read Brooks Atkinson's review
of Harrison's performance, "it is likely that Professor Higgins will never
again be as perfectly portrayed on either the musical or dramatic stage."

Harrison rather acted than sang Higgins's musical numbers. This,
too, was appropriate, for his songs resembled monologues to be rhythmically intoned. In contrast, stood the full-throated numbers given to
Eliza (Julie Andrews, who had the voice to do justice to "I Could Have
Danced All Night") and to her fatuous suitor Freddy (John Michael
King, who sang what became the show's pop standard, "On the Street
Where You Live"). If Higgins's numbers were not exactly patter
songs, their lines were still nimble and musically set to coincide with
how they might be spoken, and the brittle virtuosity of their texts
owed much to the tradition of English writers for the lyric stage from
W. S. Gilbert to Noël Coward. "In this genre, it is of no earthly use to
be able to sing and not perform a song," wrote Eric Bentley, "while if
you can perform a song, without being able to sing it, all criticism of

your musicianship is beside the point. Mr. Harrison speaks and acts his songs admirably."

Shaw's creation thus determined its own adaptation in ways that went beyond the mediating norms of musicals altogether. Broadway caricaturist Al Hirschfeld captured the spirit of the Irishman's posthumous control over the proceedings in a cartoon taken up as *My Fair Lady*'s logo. It depicted the deceased playwright as a godlike puppeteer in heaven, pulling the strings of Higgins/Harrison on earth, who, as a puppeteer in turn, pulled the strings of Eliza/Andrews. Hirschfeld's visual wit called attention to the parallel between the occasion and the subject of *Pygmalion*'s transformation—and to the ethos of *My Fair Lady* as a musical play that was so playlike it seemed to have bypassed adaptation entirely. This was really Shaw's *My Fair Lady* after all, it implied.

But of course it was Lerner and Loewe's. Indeed, the ultimate genius of the show lay in its inspired departures from Shaw's work as much as in the celebrated fidelities to it. And where the show most pointedly parted company with Shaw was at the end, which John Gassner decried as "the mineral oil of the musical's dénouement." At *Pygmalion*'s final curtain Eliza simply declares her independence from Higgins and leaves. But *My Fair Lady* goes on from there and, doing so, proves ultimately *not* to be "a British political comedy about the economic [consequences] of language but an American musical comedy about love's triumph over the obstacles of social class." In the new ending (modeled directly on the ending of the Pascal-Asquith film), Eliza's very leaving motivates Higgins to launch into the "non-love song" that Lerner had sought. The song is one of self-discovery whose music spells out just how far the misogynist has traveled emotionally since the show began—Eliza having subtly transformed him as a sentient being while he was busy transforming her as a social one. Higgins now not only reprises the quick 8-note motto with which he had protested "But let a woman in your life" in act 1 (Ex. 9-2a), he audibly reshapes it, transforming it into the broad 8-note admission of emotional dependence "I've Grown Accustomed to Her Face" (Ex. 9-2b). Then, shockingly, Eliza returns to his home of her own accord so that, as the final curtain falls, Eliza and Higgins are alone together onstage while the orchestra, *molto maestoso*, reprises the music to "I Could Have Danced All Night," the song in which she first gave voice to unnamed feelings of elation that somehow involved him.

Ex. 9-2a. Frederick Loewe, music, Alan Jay Lerner, lyrics: "I'm an Ordinary Man," *My Fair Lady*

Ex. 9-2b. Frederick Loewe, music, Alan Jay Lerner, lyrics: "I've Grown Accustomed to Her Face," *My Fair Lady*

And so romance resounds unmistakably at the end of the musical. But Shaw left explicit instructions to avoid even the hint of such an entanglement. So irked was he by actors who had sought to improve his work in this regard that he wrote an epilogue to *Pygmalion* in which he railed against "the ready-mades and reach-me-downs of the rag-shop in which Romance keeps its stock of 'happy endings' to misfit all stories." If anyone at all, Shaw peevishly insisted, Eliza ends up not with Higgins but with Freddy. To which Lerner replied by way of a note to the published libretto, "Shaw and Heaven forgive me!—I am not certain he is right." Lerner's tact was well gauged. He did not have to insist he was certain Shaw was wrong. *My Fair Lady* did it for him.

Camelot was "a further development of a growing form," even "an advance" over *My Fair Lady*—or so it seemed to T. H. White, whose novel *The Once and Future King* formed the basis of the show. But *Camelot* was also a more compromised piece of work, despite the return of most of *My Fair Lady*'s production team, from director Moss Hart on down. The musical, about the medieval King Arthur (Richard Burton) and his mythical rule in Camelot, was not a historical romance. On the contrary, it told how Arthur's efforts to replace chivalry with a new order of civility, the Round Table, were destroyed by the adultery of his wife Guenevere (Julie Andrews) with his most trusted knight, Lancelot (Robert Goulet). Loewe had his misgivings, since he felt cuckoldry was a subject better suited to comedy. Yet *"Camelot* is a musical tragedy, not a musical comedy," White insisted. Lerner, he said, had "introduced a moral problem, almost as if he were Ibsen." Between these two extremes the show never found its focus. Moreover, it lost what integrity it had when tryout audiences in Boston disapproved of Guenevere's betrayal of her husband, and Lerner obliged them by changing the queen's relationship with Lancelot into an unconsummated one. "The theatre is a practical affair," after all, White concluded; and "well, Alan Lerner was writing a *musical*, not wholly an Ibsen tragedy."

Yet *Camelot* did turn into an emblem of tragedy after it closed. Though its ostensible subject was the Matter of Britain, Americans came to associate the doomed idealism of Arthur's rule with that of the young John F. Kennedy, whose presidency, roughly coinciding with the show's Broadway run (1960–1963), was brutally cut short by assassination. Within weeks of the president's death, his widow was quoted in the pages of *Life*, America's favorite magazine:

> *When Jack quoted something, it was usually classical, but I'm so ashamed of myself—all I keep thinking of is this line from a musical comedy. At night before we'd go to sleep, Jack liked to play some records; and the song he loved most came at the very end of this record. The lines he loved to hear were:*

> > *Don't let it be forgot*
> > *That once there was a spot*
> > *For one brief shining moment that was known*
> > *As Camelot.*

From then on, invoking Camelot became one way for Americans to remember the Kennedy years that had now passed into history—perhaps even a way of remembering altogether, as one writer put it, for "a country that somehow couldn't get over thinking of itself as a Broadway show with a noble message and a bittersweet ending."

For some, *Camelot* also became an emblem of the fate of the musical

play itself, the dissolution of its romantic ethos and the culture of consensus that supported it.

> *Perhaps Lerner and Loewe's* Camelot *was more prescient than it*
> *seemed as it began the era of the 1960s. The dying King Arthur may,*
> *at the end of* Camelot, *optimistically urge a young boy to recount the*
> *glories of his kingdom (read* America*) to keep its vision alive. But*
> *the tale the musical tells is one where Camelot begins as a heaven on*
> *earth, only to become eventually ruined through conflict, treachery, and*
> *a breakdown of trust and loyalty—a destruction primarily wrought*
> *by romantic love itself. The musical would go on in America, but now*
> *it would be reshaped by a more changing and problematic American*
> *world than Broadway had hitherto envisioned.*

Camelot, too, marked the end of the career of Moss Hart, who died
within a year of the premiere, and of the collaboration of Lerner and
Loewe. Lerner would go on to collaborate with others—e.g., Burton
Lane (*On a Clear Day You Can See Forever*, 1965; *Carmelina*, 1979) and
Leonard Bernstein (*1600 Pennsylvania Avenue*, 1976)—but never again
to such memorable effect or with such success. At about the same time,
the death of Hammerstein in 1960 had forced Rodgers for his subsequent shows to write lyrics himself (*No Strings*, 1962) or find new
partners, among them the finest of a younger generation of lyricists—
Stephen Sondheim (*Do I Hear a Waltz?*, 1965) and Sheldon Harnick
(*Rex*, 1976)—but again without great success. In different ways, however, Sondheim and Harnick would succeed on their own. Sondheim as
both lyricist and composer eventually spearheaded a movement away
from the musical play aesthetic altogether, while Harnick, forming a
partnership with composer Jerry Bock, became part of perhaps the last
major creative team to work significantly under its spell.

HARNICK AND BOCK

Before the two met in 1956, the careers of Sheldon Harnick (b. 1924)
and Jerry Bock (b. 1928) ran a parallel course. Separately, each had
worked on musical productions in midwestern colleges (Harnick:
Northwestern University; Bock: University of Wisconsin); served

apprenticeships writing shows for northeastern summer resorts (Harnick: Green Mansions, NY; Bock: Camp Tamiment, PA); and earned his first credits on Broadway with songs for revues (Harnick: *New Faces of 1952*; Bock: *Catch a Star!*, 1955). Then, for a dozen years that stretched over the decade of the 1960s, they combined their talents in the creation of seven Broadway shows: *The Body Beautiful* (1958), *Fiorello!* (1959), *Tenderloin* (1960), *She Loves Me* (1963), *Fiddler on the Roof* (1964), *The Apple Tree* (1966)—actually three one-acters—and *The Rothschilds* (1970). *Fiorello!*, *She Loves Me*, and *Fiddler* are their most highly regarded works.

Harnick and Bock were songwriters through and through. Where Rodgers and Hammerstein and Lerner and Loewe normally wrote their own books as well as songs, Harnick and Bock did not (except for *The Apple Tree*). Yet their songs were no less the creations of musical playwrights; indeed, perhaps even more so. When asked the inevitable question of songwriters, "What comes first, the words or the music?" their response was: "The book." Harnick and Bock created theater songs that not only began in books but remained deeply enmeshed in them. Unlike the songs of the earlier teams, theirs did not generally achieve commercial popularity apart from the shows they were designed to serve.

To be sure, their songs performed the now standard functions of songs in musical plays, which Harnick summarized as follows: "to continue the flow of the story, to provide insight into character, to heighten climactic moments, or to enrich the feeling of time and place." But they often did so with music that was less self-contained or with lyrics that were more specific than would allow them to stand readily on their own as songs (like *South Pacific*'s "Some Enchanted Evening" or *My Fair Lady*'s "On the Street Where You Live") whatever the kind of show Harnick and Bock were writing. *Fiorello!*, for example, an energetic musical comedy in a satirical and romantic vein, depicted the early career of New York politician Fiorello La Guardia (Tom Bosley), later to become one of the city's best-loved mayors. Its most characteristic songs, however, were not really songs so much as musical scenes that, at their most thematic, took gentle swipes at both ends of the viable spectrum of New York politics: at Democrats corrupt with power ("Little Tin Box") and at Republicans cynical without it ("Politics and Poker"). *She Loves Me*, an intimate romantic comedy, involved the employees in a perfume shop in prewar Budapest. Its finest musical moments were less fixed-form songs than extended soliloquies in which the heroine (Barbara Cook) expressed her growing affection for her anonymous pen pal ("Will He Like Me?," "Ice Cream"); at the show's end she learned he was the co-worker with whom she had been bickering all along. And *Fiddler on the Roof,* a musical play, dealt with the erosion of traditional values in a poor Russian-Jewish village at the turn of the twentieth century. At its musical core were concerted numbers for its community ("Tradition") and monologues for its protagonist, Tevye the milkman (Zero Mostel), though these seemed more like one-way dialogues with himself, or God, or the audience ("If I Were a Rich Man"). These shows had their share of traditional songs, too. But it was characteristic of the musicals of Harnick and Bock holding sway over the 1960s that the musical-dramatic center of interest in them shifted from the song to the scene.

It is difficult therefore to extract a Harnick and Bock song and expect it to make perfect sense out of context. Consider this duet between Tevye and his wife:

TEVYE: *Do you love me?*
GOLDE: *Do I what!*
TEVYE: *Do you love me?*
GOLDE: *Do I love you?*
　　　　With our daughters getting married
　　　　And this trouble in the town,
　　　　You're upset, you're worn out,
　　　　Go inside, go lie down.
　　　　Maybe it's indigestion.
TEYVE: *Golde, I'm asking you a question—*
　　　　Do you love me? . . .
GOLDE: *I'm your wife.*
TEYVE: *I know—*
　　　　But do you love me?
GOLDE: *Do I love him?*
　　　　For twenty-five years I've lived with him,
　　　　Fought with him, starved with him.
　　　　Twenty-five years my bed is his.
　　　　If that's not love, what is?
TEYVE: *Then you love me?*

GOLDE: *I suppose I do.*
TEYVE: *And I suppose I love you, too.*
BOTH: *It doesn't change a thing,*
       But even so,
       After twenty-five years,
       It's nice to know.

"Do You Love Me?" (*Fiddler on the Roof*)

The words are clearly patterned here, yet they have more the ring of conversation about them than they do the stylized shapes and rhymes of conventional lyrics. Moreover, to understand what the words mean requires some knowledge of the situation that occasions them: the naïveté of the two characters; the insularity of their culture; the references to daughters and a troubled town—in short, the dramatic context of the show itself. Tevye's and Golde's marriage twenty-five years earlier had been arranged by a matchmaker, the custom in the shtetl of Anatevka, where they live. It is only now, however, when one of their daughters breaks the custom to choose a husband for herself because she already loves him, that the older couple pause for the first time to consider them-selves in terms of their affection for one another too. The awkwardness of the moment is very funny and very touching for an audience inured by the norms of modernity to the idea of marrying for love. But the intel-ligibility of "Do You Love Me?" is limited outside of *Fiddler on the Roof* precisely because the number is so thorough an example of musical-play songwriting.

Fiddler is not a conventional musical play, however—at least not on the Hammerstein model. It has no plot to speak of. Instead there are three subplots, one apiece for Tevye's three oldest daughters, and all focused on the escalating challenge each girl poses to her father's authority and to her community's customs and beliefs by how she mar-ries. Tzeitel marries a man she chooses in disregard of a matchmaker; Hodel marries without her father's permission; Chava marries outside her faith. Tevye agonizes only to accommodate himself to his daughters in every case but the last. Customs can be bent; abandoning Judaism is unforgivable—though even here there is a grudging hint of reconcili-ation at the close.

The book took its material from selected short stories by Sholem

Zero Mostel (Tevye) talks to God (and the audience) in *Fiddler on the Roof*.

Aleichem, the author whose work more than anyone's effectively turned Yiddish from the linguistic opprobrium of a "jargon" into a respected literary vehicle. It was adapted and masterfully put together by Joseph Stein (b. 1912), a specialist in turning modern literary classics into musical librettos: Sean O'Casey's *Juno and the Paycock* (*Juno*, 1959, score by Marc Blitzstein); Eugene O'Neill's *Ah, Wilderness!* (*Take Me Along*, 1959, score by Bob Merrill); Nikos Kazantzakis's *Zorba the*

Greek (*Zorba*, 1968, score by John Kander and Fred Ebb). But while Tevye may have been Aleichem's mouthpiece in these stories, *Fiddler's* story was not exactly his. Jerome Robbins, the show's director, insisted that the writers find a different kind of trajectory for the Aleichem material. If the musical was to have more than limited ethnic appeal, he maintained, its focus had to be less on the individual narratives than on an underlying theme that tied them together. He prodded Stein to make that theme *Fiddler's* real story:

> DRAMATIZE STORY OF TEVYE AS THAT OF A MAN IN THE STATE OF TRANSITION. *This is the story we are telling; without it our show is just a touching narrative Jewish* Cavalcade. *There is a much more vital, immediate and universal one to tell, i.e., the changing of the times . . . and the conflicts and tensions made by these changes. Tevye's conflicts, his attempts to keep his traditions and still follow his heart are* MISSING. . . . *The audience must be strongly directed to Tevye's ambivalences and struggles, and you must dramatize the tension of his struggle to keep his traditions while being assailed by outside forces* THAT ARE PROJECTED IN TERMS OF HIS DAUGHTERS AND THEIR SUITORS

Stein obliged. The confrontation of traditional communities with modernity remained a theme to which he was repeatedly drawn, from his first Broadway book (*Plain and Fancy*, 1955) to his last (*Rags*, 1986). He set Tevye's episodes against the impending threat of a pogrom, and in the prologue to act 1 had him explain with his opening words both the theme and its connection to the title of the show (inspired by a Marc Chagall painting):

> *The exterior of* TEVYE'S *house. A* FIDDLER *is seated on the roof, playing.* TEVYE *is outside the house.*

> TEVYE: A fiddler on the roof. Sounds crazy, no? But in our little village of Anatevka, you might say every one of us is a fiddler on the roof, trying to scratch out a pleasant, simple tune without breaking his neck. It isn't easy. You may ask, why do we stay up here if it's so dangerous? We stay because Anatevka is our home. And how do we keep our balance? That I can tell you in a word—tradition!

"Tradition," the musical scene that followed, became at once the opening number and through line of the show, the thematic core around which the action revolved and its meaning coalesced. For Tevye, tradition bound the Jews together "in the circle of our little village," and tradition both distinguished them from and bound them to the Russians: "They make a much bigger circle." Through circles the idea of tradition took physical form onstage and shaped the show's production concept. The Anatevka set turned on a revolving platform. The people in it moved in folklike circle patterns of dance. And even when they sang of the community ties and family roles that kept them together—papas, mamas, sons, daughters—they did so in the circular manner of rounds. Only with the expulsion of the Jews from Anatevka was the circle pattern broken. The symbolism was clear as friends and neighbors now dispersed at the end of the show to find new homes elsewhere, Tevye and his family setting off, significantly, for America—on an implied journey from exclusion to acceptance.

Fiddler on the Roof had astonishingly wide cultural resonance despite what some feared would be "too Jewish" a show to play outside New York. That it negotiated deftly between the particularity of its subject and the universality of its theme accounts in large measure for its success. It broke all previous records for a musical's length-of-run on Broadway and proved a worldwide hit as well. Foreign audiences apparently had little trouble identifying with the plight of people in a traditional society undergoing the stresses of modernization. Stein even recalled the show's Tokyo producer once asking him whether they actually understood *Fiddler on the Roof* in America. "I said, 'What do you mean?' He said, 'It's so Japanese!'"

But emphasizing the universality of *Fiddler* tends to mask the particular power of the show in Broadway culture—the culture from which it sprang and for which it was intended. For the translation of Aleichem material into a stageworthy experience for an American showgoing public at the time involved a translation in meaning central to the experience itself. Simply put, Broadway's Tevye is no longer Aleichem's. In Aleichem, Tevye defends the values of the world he believes in but is powerless to prevent from coming apart; and he ends up a man crushed by the weight of his experiences. But in the musical, Tevye emerges as a defender of change, a legitimizer of Jewish adaptability to ideals of progress and individual rights which are fundamentally neither Russian nor Jewish—but American. "Whatever the success of 'Fiddler on the Roof,'" Cynthia Ozick has written, "its chief nontheatrical accomplishment has been to reduce the reputation of a literary master to the very thing he repudiated." In effect, *Fiddler* turns Tevye into a "Jewish Pilgrim," escaping from the religious persecution of the Old World to an implied haven in the New, where Aleichem saw America not as a promised land for Jews but a place of exile. Aleichem's stories thus become the occasion for something they never were nor were meant to be: not simply a Broadway musical as such, but one validating the experience of Jewish assimilation into the mainstream of American life.

It comes as no surprise that *Fiddler*'s creators were themselves mostly of Jewish origin—Harnick, Bock, Stein, Robbins, producer Hal Prince, etc. Nor is it surprising to learn that there was a large Jewish component to the audience that saw the show during its eight-year Broadway run. Yet both of these conditions would not have been much different in the case of most Broadway shows and their audiences at the time. Not only were Jews as a group involved in virtually all aspects of Broadway show business—creating, producing, disseminating, and consuming shows—but Broadway culture itself was regularly perceived as somehow Jewish in character. Indeed, the "disproportionate" Jewish presence in, on, and around Broadway altogether became a topic of interest in many discussions of twentieth-century American popular culture. Those who were so singled out did not necessarily identify themselves as Jews—though most perhaps did. Rather, they were perceived as Jews—even though some were not.

What does come as a surprise in the case of *Fiddler*, however, is the intensity of "Jewishness" expressed—positively, seriously, openly—in the forum of a Broadway show that became a smash hit; this in light of the history of antisemitism in America and its particular virulence during the interwar years and after. Remarkably, *Fiddler* made thematic the Jewish presence that comparable earlier hit shows had either eliminated from their texts (*Liliom*'s Wolf Beifeld, a Jew, became, in *Carousel*, the puritanic Enoch Snow) or taken the caution to encode, usually comically, as subtexts (Yiddish character actor Joseph Buloff created the role of *Oklahoma!*'s "Persian" peddler). Self-censoring of this sort stemmed in large part from the anxieties of many Jews over their place as outsiders, not in Broadway's culture but in American life. Only the changed discourse about Jewishness in postwar America, which shifted in focus from race to religion and ethnicity, and the more liberal climate of the 1960s, made possible a show like *Fiddler* and its success. Time would diminish the particularity of that success. For *Fiddler's* poignance ultimately derived from its author's sense of bidding farewell to a world most of them did not really know, but most of their parents did: the shtetl culture annihilated by the Second World War. That had special resonance in the 1960s for audiences who no longer shared the values of that culture but who could still be made to feel that those values were meaningful.

There is yet another tradition to which *Fiddler* relates as a farewell. With *Fiddler on the Roof,* Alan Lerner maintained, "the *belle époque* of the musical theatre came to an end"—the Golden Age that began with *Oklahoma!* For Lerner it was the last great expression of the kind of musical theater he had helped create: that of the integrated musical play most consistently and successfully represented by the work of Rodgers and Hammerstein, Loewe and himself, and now Harnick and Bock. Yet *Fiddler* brought with it a new sense not only of how to integrate a book and a score but of how to proceed from the one to the other in putting a show on its feet. It represented a new fluidity of movement, production, and design all accountable to the vision of a master stager— here, Jerome Robbins, whose last full Broadway musical it was. In this respect, *Fiddler* can be seen as the harbinger of a coming shift of focus in musical theater from a writers' medium to one for stagers.

Lerner's view has become the more prevalent, however. Nowadays, *Fiddler on the Roof* tends to be seen as a retrospective achievement, a culmination of things past and passing on Broadway in the 1960s, including Lerner's own best work—even a summing up of possibilities engendered by the musical play as a legitimate art form in the balancing of all its elements. Indeed, it ultimately kept its balance as a musical play by negotiating deftly between the twin competing tendencies that underlay the very structure of the genre. One pulled the musical play toward musical comedy. The other pulled it toward opera, as we shall see.

Winter
Garden

PLAYBILL

a weekly magazine for theatregoers

WEST SIDE STORY

10

OPERA, IN OUR OWN WAY

PORGY AND BESS
(10/10/1935–1/25/1936). **Producer:** The Theater Guild. **Book:** DuBose Hey-ward, based on the play *Porgy* by DuBose and Dorothy Heyward. **Lyrics:** D. Heyward and Ira Gershwin. **Music:** George Gershwin. **Director:** Rouben Mamoulian. **New York Run:** 124 performances. **Cast:** Anne Wiggins Brown, Todd Duncan, Warren Coleman. **Songs:** "Summertime," "Bess, You Is My Woman Now," "It Ain't Necessarily So."

CARMEN JONES
(12/2/1943–2/10/1945). **Producer:** Billy Rose. **Book and Lyrics:** Oscar Hammerstein II, based on the libretto by Henri Meilhac and Ludovic Halévy to the opera *Carmen*. **Music:** Georges Bizet. **Directors:** Charles Friedman and Hassard Short. **New York Run:** 502 performances. **Cast:** Muriel Smith/Muriel Rahn (alternating). **Songs:** "Dat's Love" (Habañera), "Stan' Up an' Fight!" (Toreador Song).

STREET SCENE
(1/9/1947–5/17/1947). **Producers:** Dwight Deere Wiman and The Play-wrights' Company. **Book:** Elmer Rice, based on the play by Rice. **Lyrics:** Rice and Langston Hughes. **Music:** Kurt Weill. **Director:** Friedman. **New York Run:** 148 performances. **Cast:** Polyna Stoska, Anne Jeffreys, Brian Sullivan, Norman Cordon. **Songs:** "Somehow I Never Could Believe," "Remember That I Care," "Lonely House."

Removing the mystique surrounding opera, ballet, and Shakespeare at a stroke, the *West Side Story Playbill* cover shows Carol Lawrence (Maria) and Larry Kert (Tony) in modern dress running joyfully down a New York City street, garbage cans and all.

THE CONSUL

(3/15/1950–11/4/1950). **Producers:** Chandler Cowles and Efrem Zimbalist, Jr. **Book, Score, and Director:** Gian Carlo Menotti. **New York Run:** 269 performances. **Cast:** Patricia Neway, Marie Powers, Cornell MacNeil. **Musical Numbers:** "To This We've Come," "Now, O Lips, Say Good-bye."

WEST SIDE STORY

(9/26/1957–6/27/1959). **Producers:** Robert E. Griffth and Harold Prince. **Book:** Arthur Laurents, based on William Shakespeare's play *Romeo and Juliet.* **Lyrics:** Stephen Sondheim. **Music:** Leonard Bernstein. **Director and Choreographer:** Jerome Robbins. **New York Run:** 734 performances. **Cast:** Carol Lawrence, Chita Rivera, Larry Kert. **Songs:** "Something's Coming," "Maria," "Tonight," "America" [Musical Numbers: "Prologue," "The Dance at the Gym"].

As the musical play established itself in American popular culture, it also created a favorable environment for even more ambitious undertakings. *Carousel* hinted at new directions with its dark story and extended musical scenes. So did *South Pacific* in the vocal sound and artistry required of its male lead, bass Ezio Pinza. But such hints were like the tip of an iceberg. Few saw them as clearly at the time as Herbert Graf, a stage director trained in Europe and working at the Metropolitan Opera, who surveyed the Broadway scene from a privileged point of view: the outsider's. "To an American," Graf wrote in 1951,

> *"Broadway" means the legitimate theater and musical plays. It does not include the Metropolitan Opera. . . . But "Broadway" has its own opera. Not the pretentious grand opera of the European tradition, associated with the Met, but a sort of American folk opera. The word* opera, *though, is often avoided on the programs and a variety of ruses are used to disguise the actual nature of the offerings. To such an extent is Broadway afraid of losing its audience if it appears to go "highbrow." Or, more accurately perhaps, to such an extent has the conception of opera as an import, remote from life, and sung in a foreign tongue alienated a large segment of the American public. . . .*
>
> *If opera is to enter the American scene "through the back door of Broadway," as Hammerstein thought, he and Rodgers have done a great deal toward getting it through the portals. But they have taken care to be sure nobody would notice that precisely this was happening.*

Rodgers and Hammerstein had indeed been reconfiguring the parameters of musical comedy in the 1940s. But their commercial instincts helped them to steer clear of anything pretentious, highbrow, or remote that might have sunk their shows as Broadway ventures by turning them into "more" than musical plays. If at times their musicals seemed operatic, "opera" never arose in them as an issue.

Frank Loesser set out to follow a similar course in the 1950s with *The Most Happy Fella*. The show marked a major stretch for him in its departures from the kind of musical comedy songwriting at which he had earlier proved himself master (*Where's Charley?*, 1948; *Guys and Dolls*, 1950). The new show, an adaptation of Sidney Howard's 1924 Pulitzer Prize–winning melodrama *They Knew What They Wanted*, told a sentimental story of a middle-aged winegrower in Napa, California; his attempt to win himself a young mail-order bride; and the anguished complications that arise when, lacking confidence in himself, he sends her a photo of the handsome young foreman on his farm as if it were his own, and she believes the foreman to be the man she'll marry when they first meet. Loesser himself adapted the book of the show as he wrote the score—one of the few in the annals of Broadway to write book, lyrics, and music. Yet in doing so, he felt compelled to take the Rodgers and Hammerstein model a step further. "The purpose of this show is to portray emotional expression, as the play calls for it, through songs," he said; then dropped the other shoe: "I tried to emotionalize everything." He told so much of the story through songs and other musical numbers, in fact, that it took three acts (instead of the usual two) to get it all on a Broadway stage, and three LP discs (instead of the usual one) to get it all onto an original cast recording. In this musical, spoken dialogue was no longer of prime importance. So little room was left for plain talking that the few lines of spoken dialogue in the show were simply printed in the piano-vocal score in the empty spaces between the notes. All this was evidence not of a dissatisfaction with the aesthetic norms of the postwar musical play so much as of a musical ambition altogether uncommon in the commercial theater.

The ambition was not only Loesser's. There were suggestions of it in the work of other Broadway songwriters, too—Harold Rome, for example, whose writing for *Fanny* (1954) showed a greater musical range and emotional reach than could be found in his earlier work for revues (*Call Me Mister*, 1946) and musical comedy (*Wish You Were Here*, 1952); and Harold Arlen, who expanded his music for the show *St. Louis Woman* (1946) into what he would later call a blues opera, *Free and Easy* (1959). Moreover, classically trained composers with an affinity for the stage such as Kurt Weill, Marc Blitzstein, and Leonard Bernstein had been moving in the same general direction—seeking to mine "that vast, unexploited field between grand opera and musical comedy," as Weill had put it, and come up with "a musical play of operatic proportions." Even the most acclaimed opera composer in America working in the grand European tradition at the time, Gian Carlo Menotti, had his works produced not at the Metropolitan Opera but on Broadway.

Thus it appeared at midcentury as if there were a movement afoot to create serious music drama in the United States but by less than serious means—by flouting the cultural assumptions associated with the undertaking. A small but astonishingly gifted group of artists created works that treated weighty themes on the legitimate stage with music of such technical virtuosity and emotional power it could only be described as operatic. Yet at the same time they parted company with the conventions of grand opera in their pursuit of a more populist ideal: the choice of contemporary and American subjects; the adoption of vernacular musical idioms and closed musical forms; the use of spoken dialogue at times, instead of sung recitative; the preference for unadorned singing, realistic acting, and dramatically focused staging; the acceptance of the collaborative norms and commercial constraints of production on a Broadway stage.

There were repeated attempts to create stageworks with some or even all of these features. But it would be difficult to speak of them as a movement since there were so few. Moreover, each piece remained virtually one of a kind, with few shared sensibilities among those who created them. "I have an absolute loathing for musical comedy," Menotti confessed. "I hate musicals, especially those with operatic pretensions." Yet he made an exception in the case of *West Side Story*, though Leonard Bernstein ironically was constrained in writing the music for that show by collaborators who hated opera. "I am depressed," Bernstein wrote during rehearsals. "All the aspects of the score I like best—the big, poetic parts—get criticized as 'operatic'— and there's a concerted move to chuck them." Indeed, if there were any doubts where the weight of Broadway opinion stood in the matter, the show's book writer, Arthur Laurents, cleared them up in no uncertain terms: "I'm not writing any fucking libretto for any goddamned Bernstein opera!"

Small wonder, then, that the more musicals approached the operatic, the more they avoided "the O word." "I am not calling my work an opera," Kurt Weill said of *Street Scene*. "I would rather term it a dramatic musical." Loesser was more coy: "There has been some discussion of the fact that I have called *The Most Happy Fella* a musical. That's exactly what it is. It's not a play with music; it's not an opera. . . . It's a musical—with a lot of music." Tacit agreement on what *not* to call the phenomenon came easily: It was the musical that dare not speak its name. A consensus on what to call it was another matter. Bernstein, for example, went to lengths to describe Marc Blitzstein's *Regina* simply as a "work," before allowing,

> *I suppose that I should have just relaxed once or twice and said "opera"; just come right out and said it. But the particular stigma which has attached itself to this term in America has prevented me— and, I should guess, the producers of* Regina *as well—from frankly using it. American composers are constantly on the search for a substitute word which can describe the Broadway equivalent of what was once known as opera, and which excludes the forms we know so well as "musical comedy" and "revue." . . . "Music-drama" is ruled out because of its immediate Wagnerian connotations. "Musical drama" is all right, but awfully close to Wagner. "Musical play" has served nobly and well until now, most recently in the case of* South Pacific; *but* Regina *is a far more ambitious undertaking, containing more music, more kinds of music, more complicated music, and more unconventional music than* South Pacific.

It was Weill who apparently first used the term "Broadway opera" with regularity to describe some of his musicals of the later 1940s. While ambiguous and of limited applicability, the term remains useful nonetheless in reference not only to Weill's output at the time but also to a broad spectrum of highly original work from around the middle of the twentieth century that has no more suitable generic designation. At one end of that spectrum there were romantic melodramas in the tradition of the postwar musical play. Shows such as *Fanny* and *The Most Happy Fella were* musical plays, in fact, only with greater opportunities not just for musical numbers but for more *musical* musical numbers, and sometimes for opera singers in key roles as well—Ezio Pinza in *Fanny*, Robert Weede in *Fella*. Despite the greater musical ambitions of such shows, however, they generally adhered to the spirit of the Rodgers and Hammerstein undertakings, if not to all the conventions. At the other end of the spectrum there were works of an altogether different kind: stark, all-sung dramas in the European operatic tradition. These were operas in every respect, though sung in English, staged with an emphasis on dramatic values, and produced for open runs in commercial theaters—Menotti's *The Consul* and *The Saint of Bleecker Street*, for example. There stood between these two types a handful of realistic stagepieces all the more fascinating perhaps for being neither quite musical plays nor operas conventionally understood. Each of them saw the issues of generic propriety and venue embedded in the idea of "Broadway opera" in a different and quite original way. And each correspondingly referred to its undertaking by a different name: folk opera (*Porgy and Bess*), musical drama (*Regina*), dramatic musical (*Street Scene*), musical tragedy (*Lost in the Stars*), even tragic musical comedy (*West Side Story*).

The spectrum was generally continuous. For the sake of clarity, however, the following lists gather representative examples of the more operatic of its ventures into two related groups. While only a few such ventures can be considered small in terms of forces (*The Medium* calls for five singers, a mime, and an orchestra of fourteen), most were purposefully plain in spirit rather than grand in the operatic sense. Anticipated by the creation of *Porgy and Bess* in the mid-1930s, these works constituted a brief flowering of American stageworks that challenged many of the most cherished notions associated with opera as a highbrow enterprise. Together, they represent a peculiarly American midcentury cultural project: to create an essentially dramatic yet musically enriched kind of Broadway undertaking akin to opera—"opera," as Bernstein would put it, "but *in our own way*."

Opera on Broadway   **Broadway Opera**

Carmen Jones (1943)   *Porgy and Bess* (1935/1942)
The Medium (1947)   *Street Scene* (1947)
The Consul (1950)   *Lost in the Stars* (1949)
The Saint of Bleecker Street (1954) *Regina* (1949/1953)
Trouble in Tahiti (1955)   *West Side Story* (1957)
Maria Golovin (1958)

OPERA ON BROADWAY

As a catchall term "opera" encompasses sung theater pieces of many kinds. Some operas are funny (*The Marriage of Figaro; The Barber of Seville*). Some are filled with talk (*The Magic Flute; Fidelio*). Some are folklike and in popular styles (*Der Freischütz; The Bartered Bride*). Some are even originally in English (*Dido and Aeneas; Peter Grimes*). But most are none of these. The operas that make up the bulk of the standard repertory today tend to be quite different. Not funny, talky, folklike, or in English, they are rather serious in tone and subject, for the most part sung throughout, and both written and performed in cultivated musical styles and foreign languages. No surprise, then, opera is not a favorite of the general theatergoing public in the United States.

It was not always so. Through the early nineteenth century, opera was a commercial enterprise widely available in America—a form of popular culture presented in English by numbers of touring companies and often reconfigured to suit local tastes. (Henry Bishop, for example, "Englished" even Mozart's *Don Giovanni* so that, as *The Libertine*, it could be performed not only in English but with the more complex numbers simplified and the recitatives spoken rather than sung.) It was only later in the century that American urban elites developed institutions to select and present opera as something distinct from commercial entertainments. The move, part of a larger cultural effort that led, especially after Wagner, to a legitimating ideology, split the world of musical theater into light and heavy parts, devaluing the very conventions through which opera had become popular. It also led to an established canon of operas of the "better" kind and appropriate venues for their presentation: "the standard repertory." The process itself represented a general shift in values that affected theater, dance, and other forms of expressive culture. All were gradually distanced from commercial concerns, raised to a position of high culture, and enshrined there as if that had always been their place. As sociologist Paul DiMaggio reminds us:

> even though systems of cultural classification present themselves as based on natural and enduring judgments of value, they are products of human action, continually subject to accretion and erosion, selec-

*tion and change. In each case, some combination of patrons and art-
ists created boundaries that polarized what had been a continuum of
aesthetic practice.*

The formation of the Metropolitan Opera Company in 1883 was
part of this boundary-setting process; and as the Metropolitan has
become the nation's biggest, costliest, and oldest surviving operatic
institution, it has assumed an emblematic position in the history of
opera in the United States. The newly moneyed class of New Yorkers
who created the Metropolitan saw in opera an expression of high culture—indeed, "the great vessel of social salvation" that Henry James
called it. Yet not until the Metropolitan removed itself from the marketplace entirely did it consolidate its position as an institution at the
acme of cultural prestige. This it did in the 1930s, when, financially
strapped during the Depression, it restructured itself as the Metropolitan Opera Association and became a trustee-governed not-for-profit
enterprise. It thus took on the character of a benevolent association
with a cultural mission of educating and improving audiences. Doing
so, it gained a form of "cultural capital" whose benefits can be gleaned
from Virgil Thomson's response to the suggestion of the Metropolitan's general manager in 1951 that the company return to a more commercially oriented course:

> *Some member of the Metropolitan board should explain to the general
> manager that the Metropolitan Opera Association is not engaged in
> show business, that it is a nonprofit society vowed to the advancement
> of musical art and of public taste, that this purpose has been recog-
> nized by the state of New York as justifying an exemption from real
> estate taxation and recently by the federal government as justifying
> exemption from the amusements tax. Gifts to the Metropolitan, more-
> over, can be deducted from anybody's taxable income up to fifteen per-
> cent. Such privileges are not granted to the amusement trades.*

The amusement trades, by contrast, encompassed a whole range of
entertainment and lighter fare that included musicals. As such, musicals had no access to the subsidies and tax exemptions that companies
like the Metropolitan had; and without the benefits of *cultural* capital, they had to scramble for the real thing. For them the box office

represented the bottom line and, at the top, the lines of authority ran to and from producers. They were the ones ultimately responsible for financing such speculative ventures, coordinating their operation and production, and dealing with the consequences of their success—or failure. Producers had no choice but to be hard-nosed about what they produced, as a poor choice could put them out of business. Profits alone meant staying alive, and while opera was a feather in anyone's cap, its status in the marketplace was at best shaky. Oscar Hammerstein II summed it up, and as a grandson of one of New York's greatest opera impresarios, he had grounds for knowing. "Opera was a way people lost money." Producers usually shunned it, or, if they did finance an opera, rarely stood behind it when something more lucrative beckoned. In 1958, David Merrick closed Menotti's *Maria Golovin* after only five performances allegedly to make way for *La Plume de Ma Tante*, a revue that subsequently ran on Broadway for over two years.

Nevertheless, some producers defied the odds and undertook operatic ventures on Broadway more than once. The Playwrights Producing Company (1938–1960), a collective of playwrights (mostly Pulitzer Prize winners such as Elmer Rice, Maxwell Anderson, Robert E. Sherwood, and Sidney Howard) who bypassed the middleman to produce their own plays, produced Kurt Weill's *Street Scene* (Rice's script) and *Lost in the Stars* (Anderson's) and nearly lost their shirts. And there was Cheryl Crawford (1902–1986), an independent producer who enjoyed an operatic hit with a *Porgy and Bess* revival and endured an operatic flop with *Regina*. She defended the latter venture nonetheless on idealistic rather than fiscal grounds:

> *If you tingle with a sudden awareness of things you only dimly felt before, of evil, of compassion, so that you know more about life after such an experience, that is all I ask. I'm going to see to it that the audience sitting before* Regina *has an emotional experience they won't forget. That is theatre. That's why I'm in it. Gags and sugarstick romance have a place in a public's entertainment, but I'd like to give them something richer, truer, deeper.*

Regina was a gripping musicalization of Lillian Hellman's *The Little Foxes*, a tale of murder, greed, and sexual politics in the New South. It failed on Broadway, where it received mixed reviews. Some thought it too operatic; others found it to be "an incomplete opera . . . one that hands over the expressive obligation to mere speech whenever the composer feels inadequate to handle the dramatic line." Not content with failure in one venue, however, Marc Blitzstein revised his musical drama for subsequent production in another. With its musical focus expanded, *Regina* returned to the stage four years later, not on Broadway (which would have entailed another open run) but in repertory at the New York City Opera. In this form it has been presented in opera houses ever since.

To speak of producing a work on Broadway and in an opera house implies more than a difference in place, which might be seen as external to the work. The two venues are not interchangeable—certainly not in the way one might think of simply booking a given show into one theater if another isn't available. The difference, in fact, tends to reflect something about the work itself, something that makes it structurally suited for one venue rather than the other. There is no question, of course, that operas and musicals are both deeply collaborative artistic forms, whatever their differences in style, function, or apparatus. But the nature of collaboration in each is not the same. Opera is primarily governed by musical considerations, whereas it is a truism in musical theater that "no single medium—music, poetry, prose, dancing, acting, staging, costume and so on—has the controlling interest." This has had a defining effect on the way music relates to all other elements in the commercial musical theater—including the drama. Brooks Atkinson suggested as much in 1947 when he distinguished between two operatic works that were both playing on Broadway at the same time: "Between opera and the dramatic stage there is a difference in emphasis that keeps the two mediums fundamentally separate. . . . In *Street Scene* the music illustrates the drama. In *The Medium* the drama is the music." Atkinson did not elaborate much further, unfortunately. But what he meant perhaps relates to what musicologist Stephen Banfield has more recently explained in the following terms:

> In opera, traditionally, the music commands an exclusive viewpoint
> on the drama . . . it cannot be resisted or resist itself (which is a way
> of saying that it is not self-aware and is why it can so rarely cope
> with wit and irony). . . . In the musical, however, music—we might
> do better to call it song, so as to include the lyrics—has tradition-

ally behaved much more self-consciously and presentationally, *that is, as one mode of representation rather than its governing medium; and indeed we could say the same of dance, comic dialogue, and all the other stage topoi that make up a show. Correspondingly, music is often (though not as pervasively as in the film musical) the subject of representation on the stage; it can often not just move in and out of the drama but in and out of itself, and is more dramatically agile, perhaps therefore even more epistemologically aware (thus serving as a model of human self-knowledge), than in most opera.*

In light of the tensions between such cultural forms—the one mainly aesthetic, musically driven, and cultivated; the other commercial in focus, collaboratively structured, and vernacular—what possessed musicians to go against the cultural grain and attempt the operatic on Broadway's terms? The reasons are as varied as the results. Populist composers with European training like Weill and Blitzstein looked to Broadway to extend their reach and reinvigorate their work, even if it required them to give up some of their creative authority as composers. Unlike the hothouse atmosphere of opera houses in midcentury America with their entrenched repertoires and encrusted modes of production and performance, Broadway constituted "an active, vital part of the modern theatre" that imposed a more open, demotic set of cultural imperatives and gave access to a wider audience. On the other hand, ambitious songwriters with Broadway roots like Gershwin and Loesser looked to opera as the ultimate challenge of their métier: musical theater writ large. Even if they lacked the necessary fullness to meet all its compositional demands, opera meant a chance to explore a wider range of dramatic possibilities than Broadway normally permitted them, and to do so in essentially musical terms—a chance to write "the-musical-that-is-more-than-a-musical," and so to secure a more prestigious and lasting kind of artistic success in the theater than opera alone appeared to offer.

Complicating the issue were the appearances or near appearances of "real" operas on Broadway—operas conventionally recognized as such, like Benjamin Britten's *The Rape of Lucretia* (1948), which closed after twenty-three performances, and Igor Stravinsky's *The Rake's Progress* (1951), for which a Broadway premiere was contemplated at first until producer Billy Rose thought better of the idea and Venice's Teatro la

Fenice came up with an offer more to the composer's liking. Two such Broadway productions, however, *Carmen Jones* (1943) and *The Consul* (1950), enjoyed significant runs, though neither was without its problems where Broadway opera was concerned.

Carmen Jones was the brainchild of Oscar Hammerstein II who referred to it as "a musical play, based on an opera." That made it perhaps the closest Hammerstein would come to realizing a musical theater ideal he had voiced as early as 1925:

> *Is there a form of musical play tucked away somewhere in the realm of possibilities which could attain the heights of grand opera and still keep sufficiently human to be entertaining? . . . I have an extravagant theory that little light opera, a healthy youth all alive and ambitious, can be so developed that he can come in at the back door and give his big brother, grand opera, a stiff battle for artistic honors.*

Carmen Jones, however, was more than the musical play Hammerstein claimed it was. Although updated and Americanized from its original setting in nineteenth-century Spain, it was rather more like *Carmen* "Englished." More than simply "based on an opera," it *was* an opera, and an internationally loved classic at that—*Carmen* (1875)—but with the original French translated into an American vernacular, the recitatives spoken instead of sung, and the orchestration reduced for a band of thirty-three players. Hammerstein hewed as close to the original opera as he thought he could get away with on Broadway. Georges Bizet's original version of *Carmen*, for example, also had spoken dialogue, though shortly after the composer's death Ernest Guiraud set the dialogue to music, thus converting *Carmen* into a grand opera, in which form it established itself internationally. Moreover, Hammerstein kept the score of Bizet's *Carmen* virtually intact. Even Hammerstein's aims in the undertaking resembled Bizet's. Hammerstein sought to turn the Broadway musical into an operatic musical comedy with his version of *Carmen*; Bizet proposed "to change the *genre* of *opéra-comique*" with his.

The Opéra-Comique, a theater in nineteenth-century Paris, presented bourgeois family-oriented entertainments of the same name— typically with moral plots, edifying characters, and happy endings. Into this world *Carmen* scandalously intruded. The opera told a tale of sexual passion between a Spanish army officer and a gypsy. Its characters represented an underclass of soldiers, gypsies, smugglers, and factory workers. And it ended with the murder of the gypsy by her lover and his arrest by the police. In short, *Carmen* violated the basic conventions of its genre: It was a realistic, even tragic opéra comique. And yet conventionally humorous and sentimental episodes relieved some of its starkness. Moreover the music was so immediately graspable and informed by such a wealth of folkloric and vernacular styles that the opera has since become a favorite of lowbrows and highbrows alike. "Its story and catchy, familiar music make it available to a mass audience, while its status within the [operatic] canon confers cultural prestige upon its fans: it serves as a 'hook' for attracting listeners to the pleasures of 'high art.'"

Carmen was thus an inspired choice for a Broadway-bound operatic project. Yet Hammerstein also aimed to make its production as an opera unique by mounting it not just *on* Broadway but on Broadway's terms. That meant removing what he called the "opera-house barnacles" that encrusted its performances elsewhere and impeded its intelligibility. He derided the general practice of producing operas according to a high cultural ideal that tended to make audiences "feel out of things," and he proposed to replace that ideal with another more focused on the audience. With *Carmen Jones*, then, Hammerstein aimed to bring *Carmen* into line with the ethos of the commercial musical theater, where

> *the lines of authority run from the audience to the creators, not the other way around: the audience authorises what "works" by applauding, laughing, buying tickets, writing rave reviews, telling their friends; there is little or no sense in which the composer, or any of the other creators, is given license to educate or improve the audience or even instil a vision.*

Hammerstein took some of that license nonetheless: He preserved the original as much as he felt he could even as he adapted it for a public mostly unaccustomed to opera. He transplanted *Carmen* into a contemporary American setting, peopled it with an all-black cast, and hired actors who looked their parts and also acted as well as sang. Carmen, a gypsy in the original opera, was a social outcast; in Hammerstein's version, Carmen, an African American, was similarly marginalized. Further, he restored the spoken dialogue of the opéra comique original (at a time when the all-sung grand opera version was almost everywhere preferred), and he translated the libretto not simply into English but into the kind of English he insisted on if opera was ever to be popular: "singable, understandable, and dramatic." We can see what Hammerstein had in mind by comparing *Carmen*'s "Habañera" in the standard English translation of the opera from which he worked and the lyric he wrote to replace it in *Carmen Jones*. Hammerstein's dialect here may seem in questionable taste though he used dialect elsewhere in this period: *Oklahoma!, Carousel, South Pacific, The King and I*—in the first two, at least, not to designate ethnic outsiders. In this context, however, it does make abundantly clear the kind of "barnacles" of language he took pains to remove.

Carmen: "Habañera"	*Carmen Jones*: "Dat's Love"
Naught avails,	*One man gives me his diamon' stud*
* neither threat nor prayer,*	
One speaks me fair,	*An' I won' give him a cigarette.*
* the other sighs,*	
'Tis the other that I prefer,	*One man treats me like I was mud*
Tho' mute, his heart	*An' all I got dat man c'n get.*
* to mine replies.*	
—TRANSL.	—TRANSL.
DR. THEODORE BAKER	OSCAR HAMMERSTEIN II

Finally, there was a practical side to *Carmen Jones*'s success: It was splendidly produced by Broadway showman Billy Rose and ticketed at "popular prices"—from $1.20 to $3.60. That placed it in between the ticket price scale for the productions of *Carmen* during the same season at the Metropolitan ($1.20 to $6.60) and at the New York City Opera ($.90 to $2.40).

Night after night for over a year, *Carmen Jones* offered spectators an operatic experience in a Broadway theater. Its commercial success showed it was possible to "naturalize" an opera in terms an American audience of nondevotees could appreciate. But *Carmen Jones* was neither

Muriel Smith sings "Dat's Love" as Carmen in *Carmen Jones,* a role she alternated on Broadway with Muriel Rahn due to its operatic vocal demands.

a new nor a native work. Even major opera houses in the United States at the time rarely produced new American operas. The Metropolitan Opera, for example, produced only four such pieces in the quarter century ending in 1966, when the company relocated to Lincoln Center (Menotti's *The Island God,* 1942; Bernard Rogers's *The Warrior,* 1947; Samuel Barber's *Vanessa,* 1958, and *Antony and Cleopatra,* 1966). New works and native works both fared better at the New York City Opera during the same period. The City Opera had been formed in 1944 as a civic opera company in a New Deal spirit: to attract a broader audience, to encourage more young American singers, to mount more operas in English. The company even devoted three seasons entirely to contemporary American operas, which it presented between 1958 and 1960 with a grant from the Ford Foundation. Several of the operas produced in those seasons had previously run the risk of open runs in Broadway theaters (Blitzstein's *Regina* and *The Cradle Will Rock*; Weill's *Lost in the Stars* and *Street Scene*; Bernstein's *Trouble in Tahiti*; Menotti's *The*

Medium, The Consul, and *Maria Golovin*). And so one might call all of these Broadway operas—except for the Menotti works.

Italian-born Gian Carlo Menotti (1911–2007) came to the United States while still in his teens to study composition at Philadelphia's Curtis Institute of Music. He established himself in America as both a librettist and a composer of operas that were intensely theatrical, lyrically focused, and written largely in a sometimes dissonant yet tonal musical idiom. Throughout his career, traditional opera houses regularly produced his works. But some of his most acclaimed works premiered in startlingly different venues—on the radio (*The Old Maid and the Thief,* 1939) and on television (*Amahl and the Night Visitors,* 1951). Others enjoyed productions, unconventionally, on Broadway (*The Medium* and *The Telephone* [a double bill], *The Consul, The Saint of Bleecker Street, Maria Golovin*). Menotti may have composed his operas in a conservative idiom by concert standards, but he tended to produce them in innovative ways.

The Consul (1950) was Menotti's first full-length opera and possibly his finest work. As an opera on Broadway, it won both a Pulitzer Prize for music and the New York Drama Critics' Circle Award for best musical play. A cold war drama set in a contemporary European police state, *The Consul* focuses on the plight of Magda Sorel (Patricia Neway), the wife of a freedom fighter wanted by the secret police. Hounded by the authorities and unable to get a passport to leave the country, she ultimately kills herself. Throughout, both in the subject and in its treatment, the spirit of Italian *verismo* pervades the piece. The wonder remains why Menotti produced the work on Broadway at all rather than in an opera house. Years later he explained:

> *People have said that I wrote operas for Broadway, and that is untrue. I simply wanted to experiment and see if operas could be taken out of the opera house and run the way plays run—with consecutive performances—and be accepted by a so-called non-operatic audience. It so happened that I found two producers who were equally interested in this experiment and we found a theater on Broadway. But it had nothing to do with Broadway per se. . . . I wanted to prove that opera, if presented with the care and love for details with which a play is presented, could find a new audience and even pay for itself, and no longer depend on subsidization. All of this I think I proved with* The Medium *and* The Consul.

An unflinching high modernist composer like Pierre Boulez would in due course recommend blowing up the opera houses as the most elegant solution to what he saw as "the opera problem"—the irrelevance of opera to contemporary life. Menotti practiced a less violent form of cultural renewal: mounting operas on Broadway. But his operas, while commercially produced on Broadway, were clearly not *of* Broadway. He conceived them not in terms of songs or separate musical numbers (as Gershwin ultimately did even with *Porgy and Bess*) but as through-composed music dramas. And he made almost no concession to a Broadway style or an American vernacular in language, movement, or music (not even in *The Saint of Bleecker Street*, with its explicitly New York setting). Private commissions, moreover, made possible the creation and mounting of several of them rather than the uncertainties of venture capitalism. And with Menotti himself writing the librettos and scores to all his operas and also supervising their staging, they revealed little of the collaborative ethos associated with Broadway musical productions. *The Consul*, along with Menotti's four other operas produced on Broadway between 1947 and 1958, might serve as illustrations of what Broadway operas generally were not.

Perhaps *Carmen Jones* came closer to the mark. But it was an anomaly: Its approach defied generalization. Other Broadway ventures that Americanized the librettos or updated the productions of familiar operas while retaining their original scores proved commercial disasters (*Once Over Lightly* [*The Barber of Seville*], 1942; *My Darlin' Aida* [*Aida*], 1952; Baz Luhrmann's *La Bohème*, 2002). However, several later shows ostensibly modeled on familiar operas became hits when they freely parodied the original librettos and virtually ignored the scores (*Miss Saigon* [*Madama Butterfly*], 1991; *Rent* [*La Bohème*], 1996; Elton John and Tim Rice's *Aida*, 2000). Yet *Carmen Jones* remains important as much for its own triumph over cultural odds as for its broader impact on the history of Broadway shows. For its success as a realistic opera in musical comedy form followed on the heels of *Porgy and Bess*'s similar success the previous season. Such back-to-back hits suggested that the approach was viable; they helped frame the ambitions of a few artists in the commercial theater at the time who wished to imbue Broadway musical productions with operatic sensibilities—not simply to reproduce an opera on Broadway, as Hammerstein had done, but to reinvent opera afresh on Broadway's terms.

BROADWAY OPERA

Two works perhaps epitomize the hybrid concept of Broadway opera and its cultural trajectory. One is *Porgy and Bess* (1935), whose music was written by a Broadway songwriter moving "up" in the cultural hierarchy to opera. The other is *Street Scene* (1947), whose music was written by a European-trained opera composer moving "down" to Broadway.

Porgy and Bess anticipates by more than a decade the comparable works of Weill, Blitzstein, Loesser, and Bernstein. As the folk opera that George Gershwin composed and saw to its premiere in the mid-1930s, it is not really part of the Broadway-opera development of the 1940s and 1950s—not, say, a "Broadway opera" before the fact. Yet the cultural impact it had after Gershwin's death places its reception squarely in the history of that development. More importantly, *Porgy and Bess* is perhaps the earliest and most distinguished example of the general trend: the indispensable example of a Broadway opera of any kind. By writing it (and reinventing himself as a composer yet again), Gershwin effectively created a new ideal of opera in America. For Gershwin saw *Porgy and Bess* in terms his contemporaries saw as paradoxical. It was "an opera for the theatre"—one, that is, not for the opera house but of, by, and for Broadway, and above all entertaining. "The reason I did not submit this work to the usual sponsors of opera in America was that I hoped to have developed something in American music that would appeal to the many rather than to the cultured few. It was my idea that opera should be entertaining." Moreover, it was an opera that was self-possessedly American even as it was all-sung in the grand European fashion—one whose democracy of spirit was compositionally everywhere to be felt: in its folkloric materials, its vernacular idioms, its very use of songs. "It is true that I have written songs for 'Porgy and Bess' [because] . . . without songs it could be neither of the theatre nor entertaining." No one in the United States had ever grappled with opera on quite these terms before. Indeed, "The real drama of the piece," said Virgil Thomson with grudging perception at the Broadway premiere, "is the spectacle of Gershwin wrestling with his medium."

The overt drama of the piece lay elsewhere, of course: in *Porgy*, a play of 1927 by DuBose and Dorothy Heyward that DuBose converted into a libretto, together with lyricist Ira Gershwin. It took place in Cat-fish Row, a black ghetto in Charleston, South Carolina, and it told of an impossible love between Porgy (Todd Duncan), a crippled beggar, and Bess (Anne Wiggins Brown), the prostitute whom he shelters when her lover, Crown, goes into hiding after murdering a man. The play, grim in its realism, was not without hope, humor, and an abiding sense of strength in the poverty-stricken black community it depicted. Ger-shwin felt particularly drawn to this community through his involve-ment in the culture of African Americans, and as a pianist and composer whose music was deeply touched by the spirit and artistic traditions of ragtime, spirituals, blues, and jazz. These he brought to bear in fill-ing the three-act musical canvas of *Porgy and Bess* with an astonish-ing range of songs: from those with the folklike resonance of lullabies, banjo tunes, and street cries ("Summertime," "I Got Plenty o' Nuthin'," "Strawberry") to those shaped more directly in a Broadway idiom ("It Ain't Necessarily So," "A Redheaded Woman," "There's a Boat Dat's Leavin' Soon for New York"). There were operatic-style ensembles as well in the form of duets ("Bess, You Is My Woman Now," "What

Todd Duncan (Porgy) and Ann Wiggins Brown (Bess) look on (seated lower right) as the rest of Catfish Row celebrates in *Porgy and Bess*.

You Want Wid Bess?") and a trio ("Bess, Oh Where's My Bess?"). And there were outpourings of all kinds of choral expression from the black community itself: at work and play ("It Take a Long Pull," "I Ain' Got No Shame"), and in contemplation and prayer ("Gone, Gone, Gone," "O Doctor Jesus").

Gershwin sought to weave the separate songs, ensembles, and choruses together into a single composition for the stage mainly by two means. One was an orchestral underscore of reminiscences and leitmotifs similar to that found in operettas like *Rose-Marie* or *Show Boat*, only now nonstop and in Gershwin's own orchestrations. The other was the use of recitative, virtually unheard of in the musical theater. Gershwin's collaborators had advised against vocal declamation in principle—against singing the dialogue of the play rather than just its lyrics. But Gershwin felt that recitative was essential to "operatic form," and so to the sense of creating something of artistic permanence that otherwise eluded him on Broadway. This required of him as a composer to break the songwriting habit of writing music before knowing the words to be sung. And it required his audience to break its theatergoing habit of listening for the prosaic in a musical production to be spoken. Gershwin had already indulged the practice in *Of Thee I Sing,* for example, though the appearance of recitative in that work had been sporadic and meant to spoof operatic convention. Here its appearance was both pervasive and serious; and if the results sometimes proved awkward, Gershwin's recitative at its best could still be as full of feeling as any song—and far more economical. Consider this passage from the picnic scene in which Crown confronts Bess. Torn between her lust for him and her love for Porgy, she pleads with him to let her return to Porgy by using a rhythmically flexible declamatory vocal line that rises melodically through a single chord, interval by interval, to the top of her range and to the brink of despair (Ex. 10-1). Such "musical prose" allowed Gershwin to tell more than a continuously musical story. It enabled him to create a musical world whole, uninterrupted (except for the white intruders into that world, who, as intruders, talked), and often deeply affecting.

From the start, however, it was not clear whether all this added up to the folk opera Gershwin hoped *Porgy and Bess* would be. The production was a Theater Guild revival of the play *Porgy* that the Guild had produced eight seasons earlier. Now, however, the play was sung from start to finish. Uncertain about where the new work belonged in

Ex. 10-1. George Gershwin, music, Ira Gershwin and DuBose and Dorothy Heyward, words:
"It's like dis, Crown," *Porgy and Bess*

the cultural scheme of things, therefore, the *New York Times* took the extraordinary step of sending both a drama and a music critic to cover the opening, and publishing their reviews side by side the next day. Drama critics, who normally covered musicals, tended to view opera as a debased form of drama; music critics, who normally covered operas, tended to view musicals as a debased form of opera. And indeed, Brooks Atkinson liked the songs in *Porgy and Bess* well enough but chafed at the work's recourse to recitative: "Why commonplace remarks that carry no emotion have to be made in a chanting monotone is a problem [I] cannot fathom. Turning 'Porgy' into an opera has resulted in a deluge of casual remarks that have to be thoughtfully intoned and that amazingly impede the action." On the other hand, music critic Olin Downes chafed at the work's recourse to songs, for they amounted to the kind of "sheer Broadway entertainment" that another music critic, Lawrence Gilman, saw as "a blemish on its musical integrity . . . sure-fire rubbish." Whether as a musical with recitatives or an opera with songs, then, *Porgy and Bess* was a generic contradiction in terms. "I don't mind [Gershwin's] being a light composer and I don't mind his trying to be a serious one," said Virgil Thomson with patronizing precision. "But I do mind his falling between two stools."

If *Porgy and Bess* was thus compromised in the realm of opera, it was no less troubled where its folk element was concerned. For the work was focused on an impoverished black community in the American south, and so it was performed by blacks, but created by whites—middle-class northern whites mostly—for audiences largely like themselves. *Porgy and Bess* seemed racially conflicted, if not an act of cultural exploitation, however well intentioned its creators. In the fervent years of civil rights activism in the 1960s it would become an emblem, "the most perfect symbol of the Negro creative artist's cultural denial, degradation, exclusion, exploitation and acceptance of white paternalism. . . . Negroes had no part in writing, directing, producing, or staging this folk-opera about Negroes."

But even in a less heated climate it was clear that some of the work's power was diminished through its evocation of racial stereotypes and the lack of authenticity in its representation of black culture. It amounted, in a word, to "fakelore," and perhaps nowhere more blatantly than in the religious irreverences of Ira Gershwin's rhymes for "It Ain't Necessarily So," a song in which the dope peddlar Sportin' Life stepped completely out of character to sound just like Dorothy Parker. (Twitting stories from the Bible, Sportin' Life sang of Jonah and the whale, for example: "He made his home in / Dat fish's abdomen." Here was the entertainment Gershwin said his opera had to have, a musical comedy moment that distinguished *Porgy and Bess* from the operatic stereotype. But it portrayed a stereotype of a different kind, one that was hardly true to the spirit of the folk culture the show purported to represent.

As "crooked folklore and halfway opera" (in Virgil Thomson's words), *Porgy and Bess* failed in its 1935 New York premiere, though the Broadway run was followed by a national tour. In 1942, however, Cheryl Crawford's revival production on Broadway brought the work commercial success by downplaying its operatic ambition: It reduced the size of its cast, chorus, and orchestra; and it reduced its running time by cutting some of the numbers and replacing most of the recitatives with spoken dialogue. By converting *Porgy and Bess* in effect into a musical play, the revival sharpened the intelligibility of the drama and clarified its musical profile, giving the whole a crisper sense of pace and direction for an audience more attuned to Broadway than to operatic norms. In this "streamlined" form, Gershwin's folk opera began to establish itself in the American theater in the 1940s and in America culture at large. In the 1950s, a new revival of the piece restored much of the original's operatic dimensions and became a cultural weapon in the cold war through a U.S. State Department–sponsored tour of Europe in 1952 and, later, a booking in the capital of the Soviet Union itself. This production, with a young Leontyne Price as one of the alternating Besses, ran on Broadway for over three hundred performances in 1953. *Porgy and Bess* also entered the mainstream of American popular culture at the time in other forms—in a full-length 3-LP Columbia recording, in an MGM Hollywood film adaptation, and in numerous jazz versions of its numbers (of which the 1958 Gil Evans–Miles Davis collaboration is the most celebrated).

More recently, in versions still closer to the original with all or almost all of its music restored, *Porgy and Bess* has established itself in the opera houses of the United States and of the world—the Houston Grand Opera Company brought its production to Broadway in 1976; and in 1985 the Metropolitan Opera produced it for the first time, fifty years after its premiere. It is tempting to celebrate this turn of events as a final vindication of *Porgy and Bess* as a work of art: to view it and indeed Gershwin's career in terms of a narrative of cultural ascent, with many detours en route, from Broadway to the Metropolitan. But such a view risks selling *Porgy and Bess* short by underestimating the uniqueness of the work itself and of its cultural achievement. While it may not fit easily into the institutional structures of Broadway, neither does it comfortably fit those of the Metropolitan. Indeed, opera house productions have tended to distort the work by adapting it to their own conventions, as its particular ethos and idiom are not easily acquired by companies whose expertise lies in the interpretation of European masterworks of the past. And so questions not only of style and performance practice but of the meaning of the piece and its cultural position as an opera remain far from settled.

As it turns out, a staunch advocate for removing the recitatives from *Porgy and Bess* was Kurt Weill; and he advised Crawford about her production that turned the piece into a posthumous hit, in part, by going against Gershwin's own wishes in this regard. Weill may thus have taken courage as well as pleasure from the success of this production. Besides vindicating *Porgy and Bess* (and emboldening Oscar Hammerstein to proceed with his adaptation of *Carmen* along similar lines), it established a precedent for the general viability of producing quality work of operatic ambition on Broadway's terms—including Weill's own.

Kurt Weill (1900–1950), born and musically educated in Germany, developed a major reputation as a composer of concert works, operas, and musical theater pieces. Though he began composing in a modernist idiom, during the 1920s his music began to embrace more accessible musical styles and especially popular-song types that addressed a broader public. Among his most acclaimed stageworks that show the trend were *The Threepenny Opera* (1928) and *The Rise and Fall of the City of Mahagonny* (1930), both to texts by playwright Bertolt Brecht. When the Nazi regime put a halt to his career in Germany, he fled to France, then England. In 1935 he emigrated to the United States, where he wrote not for opera houses but for the commercial theater. He felt this was the most suitable outlet in America for his talent and ambition. "I want to use whatever gifts I have for practical purposes," he said, "not waste them on things which have no life, or which have to be kept alive by artificial means. That's why I've made the theater which exists without benefit of subsidy my life work." The eight musicals he wrote for Broadway include *Johnny Johnson* (1936), *Knickerbocker Holiday* (1938), *Lady in the Dark* (1941), *One Touch of Venus* (1943), *The Firebrand of Florence* (1945), *Street Scene* (1947), *Love Life* (1948), and *Lost in the Stars* (1949). Characteristically, these works combined Weill's social concerns with a search for ever new forms of musical theater that in effect stretched "Broadway's modest tolerance for innovation to the breaking point," said theater critic Michael Feingold. He enumerated:

*a satirical operetta about the corruption of democracy (*Knicker-bocker Holiday*); a psychological-realist spoken drama interrupted by three one-act surrealist operas (*Lady in the Dark*); a musical bur-lesque on modern art's dilemma of self-awareness (*One Touch of Venus*); a pageant of American history, told vaudeville style, as the story of one marriage's failure (*Love Life*); a naturalistic social drama transmuted to Puccinian heights (*Street Scene*); a choral cantata, its sections alternating with narrative scenes, on the tragedy of racism (*Lost in the Stars*).*

Street Scene, Weill's self-styled Broadway opera, depicted the squalor of tenement life and the passions, frustrations, and violence of its working-class population, much like *Porgy and Bess*. But it took place in New York City and dealt with the sense of individual isolation among a diversity of white ethnic groups. Based on a 1929 play by Elmer Rice, who adapted his work for the libretto, *Street Scene* told of the loveless mar-

Norman Cordon (Frank Maurrant) points a gun at his neighbors in *Street Scene* in an effort to escape after murdering his wife.

riage of Frank and Anna Maurrant, an Irish-Catholic couple, her marital infidelity, and eventual murder by her jealous husband. It also told of their daughter Rose, her feelings for Sam Kaplan, a Jew of Eastern European origins who hoped to marry her, and her ultimate parting from him to seek a better life elsewhere. The production sought to avoid the fast-paced variety and visual splendor of musicals in favor of a measured pace and an intensity of focus more at home in classical tragedy. It all took place on a single set, in front of the tenement where the principals lived. It observed the Aristotelian unities of time, place, and action. And of its pacing a critic remarked, "There seems to be something almost Greek in the slow preparation for tragedy and then the sudden, swift catastrophe."

Indeed, there was pathos and catastrophe, even death in *Street Scene*. But there was no tragedy in the strict sense. Like *The Most Happy Fella* and *Porgy and Bess, Street Scene* adapted its material from a melodrama of the American realist school of the 1920s. The very project of creating "Broadway opera" seemed so rooted in earlier American melodramas of social concern that, even if a given source was not particularly American, realistic, or working class in its original form, it almost had to become so to qualify—the case of *Romeo and Juliet* and its conversion to *West Side Story*. Only *Lost in the Stars* was actually billed "a musical tragedy," perhaps because it posed questions of moral value and religious belief as well as social inequity. A collaboration of Weill and Maxwell Anderson, *Lost in the Stars* was based on a novel about racially troubled South Africa that examined a black pastor's loss of faith in God and his struggle to find meaning in his son's trial and execution for the murder of a white man who, ironically, had championed the rights of blacks. Given the musical's literary source (Alan Paton's *Cry the Beloved Country*), its foreign focus, and its unabashed bid for tragic elevation, it was an exception among Broadway operas.

Structurally, *Street Scene* was a kind of number opera in which the dialogue was spoken or underscored rather than sung.

> *The great challenge for me was to find a form which transfers the realism of the action to the music. The result is something entirely new and probably the most "modern" form of musical theater, since it applies to the technique of opera without ever falling into the artificiality of opera. It is a type of "number opera," but the spoken dialogue between the musical numbers is "through-composed" [underscored?]*

like recitative, so that the dialogue melts into the musical numbers and creates a unity of drama and music.

The numbers themselves, however, were stylistically disparate. Some were through-composed and classically sung in the manner of an operatic aria ("Somehow I Never Could Believe"), an ensemble ("There'll Be Trouble"), or a choral scene ("The Woman Who Lived Up There"). Others were very much in a popular mold—a jitterbug tune ("Moon Faced, Starry Eyed"), a Rodgers and Hammerstein charm song ("Wrapped in a Ribbon and Tied in a Bow"), a blues ("I Got a Marble and a Star").

Weill even attempted a hybrid of the two approaches in what he felt was the show's theme song, "Lonely House." For the song as such was a standard AABA ballad, but Weill called it an arioso, perhaps because of its exquisitely evocative lead-in or because the ongoing musical connections in the instrumental accompaniment made it seem more through-composed. What went on in Weill's orchestra, in fact, is of special interest throughout the work. (Weill was possessed of such musical literacy and sense of compositional craft as to insist on writing—besides the vocal music, of course—his own instrumental music and orchestrations. This was at odds with the practice of most Broadway songwriters, who were not technically up to the task or did not see it as part of their job.) Weill's orchestra does more than just accompany singers. It also acts as an independent voice in its own right—not only to underscore the dialogue but also to underscore the numbers as they are sung. Consider how the orchestra envelops Sam and Rose at the climax of their duet "Remember That I Care" (Ex. 10-2). While the lovers hold on to their highest notes, it is the orchestra that sings out a wordless reprise of the melody they sang at the start of the duet as they remembered the words of Whitman's "When Lilacs Last in the Dooryard Bloom'd" ("In the dooryard fronting an old farmhouse. . .").

It is not easy to reconcile the enormous range of musical styles and gestures in *Street Scene*—from Wagner to the blues. Earlier, George Gershwin had been taken to task as a theater composer for comparable mixtures of styles and levels of culture. Now it was Weill's turn, only with Weill the criticism was often additionally freighted by the implication that he should have known better. Gershwin, by comparison, seemed an American cultural naïf whose musical genius and ambition had somehow pointed him in the direction of high art. He fit

Ex. 10-2. Kurt Weill, music, Langston Hughes, lyrics (Walt Whitman, poetry): "Remember That I Care," *Street Scene*

*Quoted from "When Lilacs Last in the Dooryard Bloom'd" by Walt Whitman.

the image of those Jazz Age celebrities who were sort of "'high low-brows,' to use [Charlie] Chaplin's phrase about himself, eager to capture mass acceptance and elite adulation in a single stroke." Weill was a different kind of artist, more technically schooled and culturally self-aware. He had also come to reject the elitist stance of modernism and dedicate his genius to a more populist ideal—to become, as it were, a low highbrow. That has made him a particularly problematic figure in Broadway musical history: a composer regularly working in a métier that in the 1940s rather called for songwriters, though the distinction was far from absolute. Weill was thus viewed as a misfit on both sides of the aisle. Alec Wilder, defending American popular song, faulted him as a songwriter for managinging only "the astute imitation without the quality of self-involvement." Theodor Adorno, defending Eurocentric high culture, faulted him as a composer who "talked as if concession to the commercial field were no concession, but only a pure test of 'skill' which made everything possible," and whose profile as a composer was therefore "scarcely touched by the concept of a composer as such."

Weill saw his Broadway involvement in other terms. Late in his career, he explained his artistic stance in a letter responding to criticism from an American colleague:

> *What you call corn . . . is really a part of life in our time (and probably in other times too)—and life is what I am interested in as the basis of musical expression. My teacher [Ferruccio] Busoni, at the end of his life, hammered into me one basic truth which [he] had arrived at after 50 years of pure aestheticism:—the fear of triviality is the greatest handicap for the modern artist, it is the main reason why "modern music" got more and more removed from reality, from life, from the real emotions of people in our time. I lost this fear through years of working in the theatre, and in doing so, my whole aspect towards musical composition changed. Instead of worrying about the material of music, the theory behind it, the opinion of other musicians, my main concern is to find the purest expression in music for what I want to say . . . regardless of the style I am writing in.*

As a Broadway opera, then *Street Scene* risked the trivial for a higher goal. On Broadway it did not succeed commercially, though it received

much critical admiration. For all its stature, it lacked the kind of immediacy that ultimately made for the success of *Porgy and Bess*. Nor has
it gained much of a Broadway following since its premiere, despite the
efforts of several more recent listeners to hear precisely what modernist critics once heard as faults in Weill's music as the virtues of "a post-
modernist before his time." Ironically, the considerable afterlife *Street
Scene* has enjoyed has been in opera houses, not commercial theaters. In
this, however, its fate has been no different from that of *Porgy and Bess*
and virtually all Broadway operas—except *West Side Story*.

WEST SIDE STORY

In 1956, when television was in its infancy and the medium still regarded
in many quarters as a potential uplifter of mass culture, Broadway opera
entered the cultural mainstream as a topic of conversation on a TV show
that focused on the arts. The show was *Omnibus*, the subject was American Musical Comedy, and the speaker was Leonard Bernstein. Bernstein, a young American musician and media personality, had an uncanny
ability to explain cultural issues in a way that made them come alive
for a middlebrow audience. With consummate charm (and determinis-
tic determination), Bernstein treated his subject as one worthy of serious attention. He surveyed the history of musical comedy in America in
terms that hovered somewhere between Hammerstein and Hegel. With
Hammerstein, he saw the increasing integration of book and score in
Broadway shows as progress. "The whole growth of our musical comedy can be seen through the growth of integration," he told his audience. "We have made astonishing progress." With Hegel, furthermore,
he saw such progress to be mandated by history: "For the last fifteen
years, we have been enjoying the greatest period our musical theater has
ever known." Then, after enumerating the shows from those years that
he already called classics—*Pal Joey*; *Oklahoma!*; *Annie Get Your Gun*; *Kiss
Me, Kate*; *South Pacific*; *Guys and Dolls*—he went on to predict:

> *We are in a historical position now similar to that of the popular
> musical theater in Germany just before Mozart came along. In 1750,
> the big attraction was what they called the* Singspiel, *which was the*
> Annie Get Your Gun *of its day, star comic and all. This popular*

form took the leap to a work of art through the genius of Mozart. After all, The Magic Flute *is a* Singspiel; *only it's by Mozart. We are in the same position; all we need is for our Mozart to come along. If and when he does . . . what we'll get will be a new form. . . . And this . . . can happen any second. It's almost as though it is our moment in history, as if there is a historical necessity that gives us such a wealth of creative talent at this precise time.*

If the Mozartean comparison seems strained, it is probably because Bernstein had other than disinterested reasons for making it. Two readily come to mind: one in response to the recent past; the other, in anticipation of the immediate future. For Bernstein likely wished to counter those who had recently denied it was even feasible for musicals to move in an operatic direction. Cecil Smith had done so, on the one hand, to preserve what he saw as the integrity of musical comedy:

There is a widespread belief today that . . . in a few more years [musical comedy] will grow right into American opera. This strikes me as a misinterpretation of the facts in the first place, and as an undesirable hope in the second. . . . A musical comedy does not exist for the same purpose as an opera, nor, essentially, does it employ comparable musical or plot materials.

On the other hand, Joseph Kerman had done so to preserve what he saw as the integrity of opera:

Musical comedy . . . might [theoretically] serve as a proving-ground for art, just as opera buffa *did in the eighteenth century; but in over a hundred years operetta and musical comedy have come forth with not a single serious dramatist: only Auber and Offenbach, Suppé and Johann Strauss, Sullivan, Sigmund Romberg, Gershwin, and Kurt Weill. It seems to be no longer possible, as it was for Verdi, to evolve drama by fifty years of strenuous experiment in the theater. It is always possible to have the instant intuition of drama, like Mozart; but not probable.*

So while the odds of a new Mozart appearing on Broadway in 1956 were low, the cultural stakes seemed sufficiently high to warrant invoking the precedent of the eighteenth-century wunderkind on television. But there was surely another reason for the Mozartean comparison. For what was actually about to come along at the time were the Broadway openings of two musicals by Bernstein himself: *Candide* in December, and *West Side Story*, the following fall. Neither quite turned out to be American Musical Comedy's answer to *The Magic Flute*. But, in comic and in tragic ways respectively, they had a decided effect on enlarging the possibilities of the genre.

Leonard Bernstein (1918–1990), American born and American trained, became an instant celebrity in 1943 when on short notice he replaced the ailing conductor Bruno Walter in a concert with the New York Philharmonic Orchestra that was broadcast over radio nationwide. A composer as well, Bernstein wrote concert works of a vernacular bent and a variety of theater pieces, which often cut across the boundaries of genre. Five were Broadway shows: *On the Town* (1944), *Wonderful Town* (1953), *Candide* (1956), *West Side Story* (1957), and *1600 Pennsylvania Avenue* (1976). Yet his first success as a composer for the stage was with a jazz-style ballet, *Fancy Free* (1944), written for choreographer Jerome Robbins and premiered by the Ballet Theatre. Its scenario about three sailors on twenty-four hours' shore leave in New York became the basis for the musical comedy *On The Town*; Betty Comden and Adolph Green worked up the book, Bernstein created a new score, Robbins new dances, and director George Abbott put it all together and brought it to Broad-

Leonard Bernstein blurring the boundaries between educator and entertainer as he surveys the history of "American Musical Comedy" on national television in 1956.

way. *On the Town* was a hit. But it aroused the displeasure of conductor Serge Koussevitzky, who saw it as a blot on his protégé's developing career as a classical musician; and Bernstein abandoned Broadway until after Koussevitzky's death in 1951.

Bernstein's theater-based writing of the 1950s moved in several directions as he pursued a divided career as a conductor and a composer. If there is a single thread that unites at least some of his output of the period, it might be a desire to compose "one real moving American opera," he said, "that any American can understand (and one that is, notwithstanding, a serious musical work)." *Trouble in Tahiti* (1952), a one-act opera about marital malaise in suburbia, briefly played on Broadway in 1955, and Bernstein later incorporated it into a full-length opera, *A Quiet Place* (1983–84). *Wonderful Town* was a musical comedy that reunited the *On the Town* collaborators in a star vehicle for Rosalind Russell. *Candide,* a comic operetta, drew serious parallels between Voltaire's fictive Westphalia and Senator Joseph McCarthy's all too real America. Then came *West Side Story*, Bernstein's finest stage work, which, as one critic would write, "has joined the company of *Porgy and Bess* (and perhaps *Show Boat*) as a classic of American musical theater—a term indicating that vaguely defined area between musical comedy and opera, which is not operetta, either."

West Side Story brought four extraordinary creative talents together: Broadway veterans Robbins and Bernstein; playwright Arthur Laurents, writing his first Broadway libretto; and Stephen Sondheim, writing his first Broadway lyrics. They created a Broadway opera that mixed the aestheticism of *Carmen Jones* with the naturalism of *Street Scene. West Side Story* appropriated the substance of a European classic even as it updated and Americanized it, yet changed its meaning utterly by replacing the courtly society of the original with a contemporary world rent by urban anxiety, underclass rivalry, and ethnic hatred.

The classic was *Romeo and Juliet,* Shakespeare's drama of love, family feuds, and killing and counterkilling. The new work shifted the setting of the original to the United States, and the focus to the social ills underlying the teenage gang warfare making headlines at the time. Yet unspoken parallels to Shakespeare abounded throughout *West Side Story*. The Montagues and Capulets of Renaissance Verona became

New York street gangs, "American" Jets and Puerto Rican Sharks; Romeo became the American Tony; Juliet, the Puerto Rican Maria. The ball where the lovers first meet became a dance in the gymnasium of a settlement house; the lovers' balcony scene took place on a tenement fire escape; their wedding, in a dress shop.

On the other hand, *West Side Story* included elements of social satire that had nothing at all to do with Shakespeare—especially in songs like "America":

> *Immigrant goes to America,*
> *Lots of hellos in America;*
> *Nobody knows in America*
> *Puerto Rico's in America.*

In addition, the changes in the outcome of the plot had much to do with the liberal outlook and reformist zeal of the show's creators. Tony, like Romeo, lay dead at the end of *West Side Story*; but Maria, unlike Juliet, remained alive to address the social condition that destroyed her love by confronting both gangs directly and effecting a reconciliation between them. "*West Side Story* is conceived as a social document," wrote Norris Houghton, "*Romeo and Juliet* as a *Liebestod*. Consequently, it becomes important to the contemporary play's message that a resolution of the gang warfare be effected, not as a postscript [as in Shakespeare], but by the hand of one of the play's protagonists."

Such seriousness of subject demanded a seriousness of form that seemed well beyond musical comedy's reach. One critic wondered "whether it [was] a legitimate subject at all for the shallow treatment required of a Broadway song-and-dance show, or whether, on the other hand, the whole thing [was] either an example of social irresponsibility or merely an exhibition of bad taste." Indeed, some specifically raised ethnic objections to *West Side Story* and its portrayal of Hispanics and Latino culture altogether. Yet Robbins saw the show's value in other terms. "For me," he said,

> *what was important about* West Side Story *was in our* aspiration. *I wanted to find out at that time how far we, as "long-haired artists," could go in bringing our crafts and talents to a musical. Why did we*

have to do it separately and elsewhere? Why did Lenny have to write
an opera, Arthur a play, me a ballet? Why couldn't we, in aspiration,
try to bring our deepest talents together to the commercial theater in
this work? That was the true gesture of the show.

Laurents wrote a drama that moved swiftly and not without humor toward its tragic end. It was muscular and unusually lean even for a libretto. For Shakespeare's characters were inescapably verbal creatures, while *West Side Story*'s teen-age toughs were hard-pressed to put their feelings into words. Laurents gave them a jargon of their own, but their instinctive mode of communicating was less verbal than it was geared to the senses and above all physical. So it was natural for movement, gesture, and body language to take over much of the narrative thrust of *West Side Story*—for "the ballet [to] convey the things Mr. Laurents is inhibited from saying because the characters are so inarticulate." The premise played stunningly into the hands of those of Laurents's collaborators who were responsible for creating everything essential to the show but the words.

Bernstein wrote a score that caught the teenagers' alienation and restlessness in a musical language of angular melodies, dissonant harmonies, and cross-rhythms. It was a language new to Broadway and he filtered it through a variety of contemporary styles—from neoclassic Stravinsky ("A Boy Like That") to Latin ("The Dance at the Gym") to modern jazz ("Cool")—but in ways still accessible to listeners more attuned to the traditional sounds of show music. Bernstein also used a number of devices to bring some unity to that variety of styles. One was a three-note idea, formed by a tritone and a half step, which he thought of as the kernel of *West Side Story* "in that the three notes pervade the whole piece, inverted, done backwards," etc. The three notes forged a seminal link, for example, between Tony's two songs "Something's Coming" and "Maria." In the first, a song about unspecified anticipation, the kernel (D-G♯-A) is first sung to the words "Who knows?" (Ex. 10-3a). In the second, sung two scenes later, Tony discovers what he was anticipating in the feelings aroused by a girl he has just met, and the kernel (E♭-A-B♭) now reshapes itself around the name he has overheard her being called: "Ma-ri-a" (Ex. 10-3b).

Bernstein further unified his score by continuing where most Broadway composers normally left off and writing his own dance

Ex. 10-3a. Leonard Bernstein, music, Stephen Sondheim, lyrics: "Something's Coming" (transposed), *West Side Story*

Ex. 10-3b. Leonard Bernstein, music, Stephen Sondheim, lyrics: "Maria," *West Side Story*

music. And with five ballets and several smaller choreographed numbers in the show, there was much dance music to write. Robbins had conceived *West Side Story* in the spirit of a ballet—one with a story, dialogue, and songs—a *ballet d'action*. In addition, Robbins presided over the execution of *West Side Story* as both the choreographer of the show and its director—not unprecedented on Broadway but uncommon. Robbins's double function had far-flung consequences. In hiring performers, for example, he did not cast separately for actors, a singing chorus, and a chorus of dancers, as was customary, but for dancers who could do it all: dance, sing, and act. This enabled him to realize a production concept that blurred the boundaries between what was acted and what was danced so that the narrative of the show might proceed by moving freely between musical and non-musical staging. Everything was so fluidly staged and in such a constant a state of stylized motion, in fact, that there were few clearly defined moments in *West Side Story* when physical action could be said to stop and danced movement to begin.

Robbins told *West Side Story* with a kind of cinematic fluidity in moving from one type of representation to another that was new in the theater. The show might move in traditional fashion from dialogue to song to dance ("America," "Cool"). Yet it could also skip the song and go from dialogue to dance directly ("The Rumble," "Taunting Scene"). Or it might use dance to replace dialogue and song altogether, as it did at the start of the show. (In an early draft, the prologue had words where now it has none.) "The opening is musical: half-danced, half-

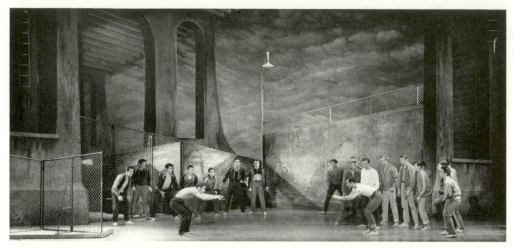

"The Rumble" from *West Side Story*, l. to r.: Ken LeRoy (Bernardo, in front of the Sharks) and Mickey Calin (Riff, in front of the Jets) confront each other with knives drawn.

mimed," the script now reads. "It is primarily a condensation of the growing rivalry between two teen-age gangs." Thus, before an intelligible sentence had been uttered onstage, or a phrase of music sung, dance conveyed the show's dramatic action with Robbins's choreography stylizing streetwise moves and gestures to show the rivalry develop. At the start, a calm nervousness prevails: fingers snap, "backs rise into arches that would make alley-cats envious, [and] stealthy feet slip sideways into circling pools of hostility." By the finish, the stage is overwhelmed by a riot of bodies in a balletic free-for-all that can be stopped only by the arrival of the police—which then leads into dialogue and then into song. And so the show proceeded throughout, in ever shifting balances and combinations of theatricalizing modes: ballet, film, play, musical comedy, opera.

What all this amounted to, Bernstein said, was "a musical that tells a tragic story in musical-comedy terms, using only musical-comedy techniques, never falling into the 'operatic' trap." But there was no denying the times when *West Side Story* was deeply operatic, and thrillingly so: in Tony's ecstatic repetitions of "Maria" as the orchestra played the melody; in the dramatic profile of the vocal polyphony of the "Tonight" quintet; in the Maria-Anita duet with its luminous transformation of Maria's response in "A Boy Like That" into "I Have a Love." What Bernstein disdained by "operatic" then, probably had to do with classical voice production or the use of recitatives, which were both scrupulously avoided in the show. "Lenny never wanted it sung like an opera," recalled Carol Lawrence, who created the role of Maria. "He would always say: 'Sing it from your heart. I don't *want* pear-shaped tones.'" Moreover, he not only avoided setting dialogue as recitative, he also knew when not to set a lyric to music—even one meant for the dramatic climax of the show where music was most expected. This happened with a dummy lyric Laurents had written for Maria to sing as a "mad aria" over Tony's body. "It cries out for music," said Bernstein.

> *I tried to set it very bitterly, understated, swift. I tried giving all the material to the orchestra and having her sing an* obbligato *through-out. I tried a version that sounded just like a Puccini aria, which we really did not need. I never got past six bars with it. I never had an experience like that. Everything sounded wrong. [And so] I made a difficult, painful but surgically clean decision not to set it at all.*

Maria's riveting monologue before the final curtain is thus spoken rather than sung—a clear demonstration, said Stephen Banfield, of "the dramatic potency and rightness of music's self-denial in this genre that is not opera."

West Side Story was to have an enormous impact on the subsequent development of Broadway musicals—so much so, in fact, that it has been seen as beginning "a new age in the theater." But as a Broadway opera, its success came not a moment too soon. By the time of the show's conversion into an Academy Award–winning film in 1961, the wind had gone out of the sails of any project to create American opera anew on Broadway's terms. What had once seemed a consensus, even if a fragile one, now foundered and came apart. Weill was dead. Arlen, Rome, and Loesser all gained success on Broadway by lowering their sights to less ambitious musical ventures (respectively: *Jamaica*, 1957; *Destry Rides Again*, 1959; and *How to Succeed in Business Without Really Trying*, 1961). Blitzstein, Menotti, and Bernstein all turned away from Broadway altogether. Blitzstein, after repeated Broadway failures (*Reuben, Reuben*, 1955; *Juno*, 1959), accepted a commission from the Metropolitan for an opera, which he left unfinished at his death in 1964; Menotti returned to the opera house milieu of his origins (Opéra-Comique, Paris: *The Last Savage*, 1963; New York City Opera: *The Most Important Man*, 1971); and Bernstein devoted himself primarily to a career in conducting. It was almost as if Bernstein sensed that with *West Side Story* he had gone as far as he could to coax a "popular form"—as he once described the achievement of *The Magic Flute*—into taking "the leap to a work of art." Now it was for others to follow his example. "I felt there would then be a whole succession of young composers who would take the next step, and the next," he recalled years later. "This, to my regret, has not really happened."

Developments since the 1970s suggest otherwise. The success on Broadway of British rock operas (*Jesus Christ Superstar*, 1971; *Evita*, 1979; *Tommy*, 1993) or other all-sung or nearly-so musicals (*Les Misérables*, 1987; *The Phantom of the Opera*, 1988; *Miss Saigon*, 1991), and the adoption by opera companies worldwide of works originally created for the Broadway stage (*Porgy and Bess, Street Scene*, even *West Side Story*, which in 2003 was performed at Milan's La Scala)—all indicate that "we may have arrived today at one of those grand shifts in cultural perceptions that put out the door the assumptions of one era while bringing in others that seem quite contrary or at least wholly new." Yet such a cultural shift—one that now goes by the name of postmodernism—took place too late to affect the creation of Broadway opera as the American project it was conceived to be in the postwar period. Historically, *West Side Story* was the end of the line: the last critically acclaimed and commercially successful example of an extraordinary but marginal development in the tradition of *Porgy and Bess*.

And there was no overlooking the marginality of Broadway operas in the cultural mainstream of the period, even if such works were too extraordinary to ignore as cultural achievements. The center clearly lay elsewhere, and it was recognized and endorsed in 1958 by the American Theatre Wing in its choice for the Antoinette Perry "Tony" Awards. Alan Jay Lerner put the choice in context:

> *When spring came and the sound of the Tony was heard in the land,*
> The Music Man *and not* West Side Story *won the Award for Best*

Musical. As an indication of the slow appreciation of Bernstein's score, Meredith Willson also won the Award for Best Composer. Even the Drama Critics crowned The Music Man *as Best Musical.*

Lerner's implied criticism, however, was beside the point. The postwar years were more centrally defined in Broadway culture not by *West Side Story* and perhaps *Street Scene* or even *Lost in the Stars*, but by *Annie Get Your Gun*; *Finian's Rainbow*; *Kiss Me, Kate*; *Guys and Dolls*; *Wonderful Town*; *The Pajama Game*; *Bells Are Ringing*; *The Music Man*; *Gypsy*— not, that is, by a prestigious *tragic* musical comedy or two but by an embarrassing wealth of comic ones.

11

The Great American Showshop

FINIAN'S RAINBOW
(1/10/1947–10/2/1948). **Producers:** Lee Sabinson and William R. Katzell. **Book:** E. Y. Harburg and Fred Saidy. **Lyrics:** Harburg. **Music:** Burton Lane. **Director:** Bretaigne Windust. **New York Run:** 725 performances. **Cast:** Ella Logan, Albert Sharpe, David Wayne. **Songs:** "How Are Things in Glocca Mora?," "Old Devil Moon," "Necessity."

GUYS AND DOLLS
(11/24/1950–11/28/1953). **Producers:** Cy Feuer and Ernest Martin. **Book:** Abe Burrows [Jo Swerling], based on short stories by Damon Runyon. **Lyrics and Music:** Frank Loesser. **Director:** George S. Kaufman. **New York Run:** 1,200 performances. **Cast:** Vivian Blaine, Isabel Bigley, Robert Alda, Stubby Kaye. **Songs:** "Fugue for Tinhorns," "Adelaide's Lament," "Sue Me," "Luck Be a Lady."

THE PAJAMA GAME
(5/13/1954–11/26/1956). **Producers:** Frederick Brisson, Robert E. Griffith and Harold Prince. **Book:** George Abbott and Richard Bissell, based on Bissell's novel *7½ Cents*. **Songs:** Richard Adler and Jerry Ross. **Directors:** Abbott and Jerome Robbins. **New York Run:** 1,063 performances. **Cast:** Janis Paige, Carol Haney, John Raitt, Eddie Foy, Jr. **Songs:** "Racing With the Clock," "Hey, There," "Steam Heat," "Hernando's Hideaway."

George Abbott, the dean of American musical comedy, observes a rehearsal from the dark of the house.

CANDIDE

(12/1/1956–2/2/1957). **Producers:** Ethel Linder Reiner and Lester Osterman, Jr. **Book:** Lillian Hellman, based on the novel by Voltaire. **Lyrics:** Richard Wilbur, John Latouche and Dorothy Parker. **Music:** Leonard Bernstein. **Director:** Tyrone Guthrie. **New York Run:** 73 performances. **Cast:** Barbara Cook, Irra Petina, Robert Rounseville, Max Adrian. **Songs:** "The Best of All Possible Worlds," "Glitter and Be Gay," "Make Our Garden Grow."

THE MUSIC MAN

(12/19/1957–4/15/1961). **Producers:** Kermit Bloomgarden, Herbert Greene, and Frank [Loesser] Productions. **Book:** Meredith Willson [Franklin Lacey], suggested by Willson's memoir *And There I Stood with My Piccolo*. **Lyrics and Music:** Willson. **Director:** Morton Da Costa. **New York Run:** 1,375 performances. **Cast:** Cook, Robert Preston. **Songs:** "Ya Got Trouble," "Goodnight My Someone," "Seventy-Six Trombones."

GYPSY

(5/21/1959–3/25/1961). **Producers:** David Merrick and Leland Heyward. **Book:** Arthur Laurents, suggested by the memoirs of Gypsy Rose Lee. **Lyrics:** Stephen Sondheim. **Music:** Jule Styne. **Director and Choreographer:** Robbins. **New York Run:** 702 performances. **Cast:** Ethel Merman, Sandra Church, Jack Klugman. **Songs:** "Small World," "Everything's Coming Up Roses," "Rose's Turn."

HOW TO SUCCEED IN BUSINESS WITHOUT REALLY TRYING

(10/14/1961–3/6/1965). **Producers:** Feuer, Martin, and Frank Productions. **Book:** Burrows, Jack Weinstock and Willie Gilbert, based on the novel by Shepherd Mead. **Lyrics and Music:** Loesser. **Director:** Burrows. **New York Run:** 1,417 performances. **Cast:** Bonnie Scott, Robert Morse. **Songs:** "I Believe in You," "The Company Way."

Musical comedy made a startling comeback in the post–World War II period. It had never really left the Broadway stage; but the popularity of more serious musical plays had challenged its status as the dominant form of musical theater entertainment. In an effort to regain center stage, or at least something of its former hold on the public, musical comedy redefined itself as a genre in the postwar years. But in doing so, it took on aspects of a more sober kind of entertainment than it had before the war.

George S. Kaufman, humorist, wit, and farcical playwright extraordinaire, deplored this turn of events. In a tongue-in-cheek essay published in 1957 in the *New York Times*, he described what he saw as a genre war, "Musical Comedy—or Musical Serious?":

> *A funny thing happened to a musical comedy on its way to the theatre the other night. It met a joke. Then, before it realized the audacity of such behavior, it took it along to the theatre, and presently there it was in the show.*
>
> *Well, sir, the audience was pretty surprised. . . . Conditioned to musical versions of O'Neill* [New Girl in Town] *and to teen-agers fighting each other with switch-blade knives—and killing the hero, to boot* [West Side Story]*—they were naturally taken aback. Most of them, embarrassed, had the good taste to look the other way and pretend it never had happened. Quite a number broke down and cried, having grown accustomed to crying at musical comedies in recent seasons.*
>
> *But a few people with long memories had the temerity to laugh. Admittedly, they didn't feel comfortable about it. Laughing at a musical comedy!—whoever heard of such a thing?*

At stake was more than a matter of whether a genre that prized laughter was compatible with one hell-bent for catharsis. For it was not clear that there was a place for musical comedy at all in the new "musical theater." Or if there was, what kind of shape it would have to take. Or whether it was even possible to reconcile the presentational bent

"Musical Comedy—or Musical Serious?": The dilemma as Al Hirschfeld saw it in 1957.

of musical comedy and the representational stance of the musical play when the former was preoccupied with exposing what the latter was at pains to conceal: the artifice of the musical stage. Yet musical comedy did not simply pack it up after *Oklahoma!* On the contrary, it made its comeback by accepting in a most pragmatic fashion many of the values that *Oklahoma!* and its progeny had come to represent.

As it thus became harder to distinguish between musical comedies and musical plays, the word "musical" gained currency in the nominative form, a practical if inelegant way to avoid even the need for distinguishing between the two. This did not mean that the different forms of entertainment now subsumed by the term "musical" (shorn of its adjectival past) had necessarily disappeared. It meant only that they were more difficult to detect. For the shadow cast by *Oklahoma!* served to complicate musical comedy as a genre—punctutating its upbeat ironies from time to time with more serious concerns, disturbing its surface glitter with more emotional grip, turning its very enterprise as a diversion into a more legitimate theatrical endeavor.

The two genres remained distinct in matters of style, tone, spirit, and purpose. Musical plays put a premium on stories of dramatic weight and performers who could convey that weight through "legitimate" singing. They also chose subjects and settings remote from their audiences in time, or place, or both. This gave them free rein to create scores that evoked their periods and locales while freeing them from any need to entertain their audiences directly by invoking the popular music of day. Musical comedies, by contrast, told lightweight tales that did not require the services of singers with classical training: Crooners and belters did fine. As exuberant and energetic entertainments, they put a premium on dancing and big production numbers. They also connected more directly to audiences who saw something of themselves and their culture represented on the stage: They had the look and feel and the sound of middle-class America of the time. Indeed, their songs and dances were in the styles of the popular music one might hear at any time on the Hit Parade; and their orchestrations conveyed the feel-good ease of a swing band (reeds, brass, and rhythm sections) but with greater flexibility and with strings (though fewer than found in the pits of musical plays). Perhaps no single musical piece more brilliantly captured the sound of postwar musical comedy than the Overture to *Gypsy* (orchestrated by Sid Ramin and "Red" Ginzler), which elicited a response unlike anything one would expect from an audience at a musical play. As the show's composer, Jule Styne, remembered it, "All I know is that when the trumpet player started playing that strip music, the audience went crazy. We were a hit even before the curtain went up."

In matters of structure, on the other hand, the two genres were almost indistinguishable. Both generally followed a two-act format (the first act always longer than the second), and both gave their greatest structural weight to the numbers that appeared at three crucial points in a show: the act 1 opening, the act 1 curtain, and the act 2 finale. The opening number functioned as an ice breaker; it set the terms of expectation for the show to come ("Comedy Tonight," *A Funny Thing Happened on the Way to the Forum*). Often it also constituted the establishing number that defined the show's time, place, characters, and relationships ("Runyonland," *Guys and Dolls*). The act 1 curtain number involved some unanticipated or intensified complication to the plot just before intermission, which, if handled well, brought audiences back after the intermission to find out how it would be resolved ("Hey There" reprise, *The Pajama Game*). The act 2 finale not only resolved the main conflict but, at its best, also summed up the special meaning of the show ("Minuet in G," out of tune and barely recognizable, *The Music Man*). This was sometimes preceded or even replaced by an "eleven o'clock number" (coined presumably when Broadway shows began at 8:40), a solo and all-out showstopper for the star minutes before the final curtain ("Rose's Turn," *Gypsy*).

The rest of the songs in a show fleshed out this structural frame. They can be classified in one of two ways, though the two are not mutually exclusive: according to a song's musical-lyric character, and according to a song's function in the show. In the anatomy of show songs, the musical-lyric character types include ballads ("The Party's Over," *Bells Are Ringing*), rhythm songs ("Luck Be a Lady," *Guys and Dolls*), charm songs ("Happy to Keep His Dinner Warm," *How to Succeed in Business Without Really Trying*), and comedy songs ("Doin' What Comes Natur'lly," *Annie Get Your Gun*). In the physiology of show songs, director-choreographer Bob Fosse distinguished three further types, which he named according to their function: "I Am Songs," which define character and situation ("I Believe in You," *How to Succeed in Business Without Really Trying*); "I Want Songs," which drive the plot ("Whatever Lola Wants," *Damn Yankees*); and "New Songs," which constitute special material or novelty numbers suited to the strengths of particular performers ("Trouble," *The Music Man*'s great patter song). Such was the structural layout of both musical comedies and musical plays in the postwar period.

Perhaps most telling in the rapprochement between the two genres at the time were the many ways in which musical comedy came to qualify the notion of comedy itself. For the comedy of the genre was now more often driven by character, or motivated by plot, or tempered by wisdom; not an exercise in humor for its own sake. And so musical comedy contained less caricature or satire without a humanizing cause ("Sue Me," *Guys and Dolls*; "Free," *A Funny Thing Happened on the Way to the Forum*), less self-conscious parody or cleverness without a sincere apology for it at the end ("I Am Ashamed That Women Are So Simple," *Kiss Me, Kate*; "Make Our Garden Grow," *Candide*), and less ribaldry or guileless fun without a swipe at social or psychological meaning ("When the Idle Poor Become the Idle Rich," *Finian's Rainbow*; "Let Me Entertain You," *Gypsy*). Musical comedy retained enough of the rowdy spirit and presentational self-awareness that characterized the genre in the first place. The brilliance of its postwar comeback rested on its ability to take from the musical play whatever it needed to survive outside the conditions of the pre-*Oklahoma!* Eden it had once inhabited.

The term "postwar" here applies roughly to the quarter-century that began toward the close of World War II in the 1940s and ended in the 1960s in the quagmire of Vietnam. This period saw the rise of two superpowers locked in an ongoing battle of diplomacy and global confrontation known as the cold war. Soviet Russia headed a communist Eastern bloc of nations; the United States led a largely capitalist and democratic West. While the West held the advantage, the power of the United States rested on more than military might alone. It was the richest country in the world, and the most successful in the manufacture, marketing, and export not only of its products but of its consumer culture. By the 1950s "Made in USA," stated or understood, had become an internationally recognized cachet that was sought in connection with American goods of all sorts, from basic needs to luxury items.

That included musicals, as these were now increasingly regarded as well-made artifacts for a kind of connoisseurship. They were also exemplars of American values and even deployed by the U.S. State Department as cultural weapons in the cold war. In 1958, performances of *Carousel* and *Wonderful Town* appeared along with more traditional examples of American culture and technology as part of the U.S. exhibit at the World's Fair in Brussels, Belgium. Yet Europeans themselves were now also embracing such shows on their own terms. Between the German-language premieres of *Küss mich, Kätchen* in 1955 (Frankfurt/M.) and *My Fair Lady* in 1961 (Berlin), a whole epoch for the Broadway musical in Germany is said to have begun. "By the dawn of the 1950s," wrote a European observer, "America had thoroughly taken over the position previously held in turn by France, by Britain, and by Austria as the epicenter of the world's musical theater—as the creative source from which the bulk of shows that entertained musical-theatergoers around the world flowed." The focus of that epicenter was Broadway, with its musical production industry in high gear, its output of quality goods steady, and the outlook for its future strong. No critic risked being misunderstood if he reviewed the opening of a new Broadway hit at the time not just as an accomplishment in its own right but as a "milestone in the upward and onward course of the great American showshop."

Musicals also loomed larger than ever in American culture at home. Performances of Broadway shows reached national audiences now not only on tour and on film, but on television. Televised revivals were regularly broadcast in the 1950s as "spectaculars" to millions of viewers from coast to coast (*Lady in the Dark* [1954], *One Touch of Venus* [1955], *Annie Get Your Gun* [1957]), some even with their original stars (*Peter Pan* [1955]; *Kiss Me, Kate* [1958]; *Wonderful Town* [1958]). New musicals were also created expressly for TV by writers with Broadway credentials: Sammy Cahn and James Van Heusen's *Our Town* (1955), starring Frank Sinatra; Arthur Schwartz and Maxwell Anderson's *High Tor* (1956), starring Bing Crosby; and Rodgers and Hammerstein's much anticipated *Cinderella* (1957), in which Julie Andrews starred and which an estimated 107 million people watched. Television even memorably boosted a running Broadway production when, in 1961, the *Camelot* cast performed some of the musical's numbers on prime-time's *The Ed Sullivan Show* and turned what had been a faltering Broadway show into a hit almost overnight.

Ethel Merman, too, appeared in a TV spectacular of *Anything Goes* (1954), though by then she had been moving away from the kind of shows in which she had starred some two decades before. Her remarkable Broadway career spanned both the prewar and postwar eras, and in the latter she became perhaps *the* Broadway diva of the age. Merman can be said to have symbolically opened and closed the postwar era by starring in its first and last musical comedy blockbusters: she played Annie when *Annie Get Your Gun* opened in 1946, and Dolly when *Hello, Dolly!* closed in 1970 (she did not create the role, though it was originally offered to her). In between, she created what was surely the greatest musical comedy heroine of the period, Mama Rose in *Gypsy*, a role that required her to act, and to do so in a show that was as much a musical play as it was a musical comedy.

If Merman successfully made the transition, however, Bert Lahr did not. He, too, was a brilliant star whose musical stage career spanned both eras. But his career ended in 1964 with a flop, *Foxy*. According to Larry Blyden, his young co-star, Lahr's personal success as the star of *Foxy* hastened the failure of the show. Indeed, Blyden discovered in working with Lahr the habits of mind that made it next to impossible for the older comedian to adapt to the newer constraints of the musical comedy medium:

Sometimes he would abandon the play completely for a funny line. He came up with dozens. They get laughs; God knows, they get laughs, but in a sense that is abandoning the play; the action is arrested to accommodate the laugh—that is an anachronism . . .

He said to me, "Well, in this sketch we should do so and so . . ." Well, it is not a sketch. It's a book musical. There are scenes connected to each other. In a sketch you go from one laugh to another, then blackout. In his mind Foxy *was a sketch . . .*

He said to me, "Look, kid, I'm making them throw out the end of the show, because I'm not strong at the finish, and I gotta be strong at the finish. If they end the show the way it is, it's going to be your show. It's not going to be your show, it's going to be mine." Direct quote. Verbatim. Never forgot it. It was a thought I'd never heard expressed in the theater. It takes your breath away. By becoming completely his show, Foxy *was damaged.*

The era nonetheless created musical comedy stars of its own—among singers: Mary Martin (1913–1990), Barbara Cook (b. 1927), Julie Andrews (b. 1935), Alfred Drake (1914–1992), and John Raitt (1917–2005); among dancers: Gwen Verdon (1925–2000) and Chita Rivera (b. 1933); among comedians: Nancy Walker (1921–1992), Carol Channing (b. 1921), Phil Silvers (1911–1985), and Zero Mostel (1915–1977). To succeed, however, such stars had to balance their own strengths and weaknesses as performers with the demands now made on them by musical comedies that genuinely depended on books. On the other hand, endemic to musical comedy was the possibility of a star stopping a show with a performance that undermined the narrative progress that a book sought to promote. To be sure, it was a rare occurrence; but when it happened it was like a force of nature, not to be ignored. Producer Cy Feuer recalled such a moment when an unknown dancer named Gwen Verdon stopped the premiere of *Can-Can.*

It was in New York, at the opening on May 7 [1953], that she stopped the show. I had never before seen a show truly stopped. . . . This was a star emerging, recognized fully by the audience. It is a pretty impressive thing, when the audience takes over and refuses to allow the performance to continue. The audience outburst came after Gwen's Apache routine in the second act. They rose from their seats and applauded and cheered with such determination that it left the actors for the coming scene standing there, unable to continue the show. The set had already changed. Gwen was in her dressing room getting into her next costume, but the crowd wanted her back for a bow. And they wouldn't stop. I was out front and recognized that this was not going to subside, so I went backstage and dragged Gwen back to the stage. She was in her dressing gown. She didn't want to come. I insisted. And so she finally came, clutching her gown, grinning awkwardly, standing there while this appreciation washed over her. And the show was stopped while the audience, just for fun, continued applauding. They took over the show.

Gwen Verdon (Claudine) shows her bloomers in *Can-Can*.

Among the great writers of postwar musical comedies there were almost no exclusive, long-standing partnerships as there had been before the war. Shifting alliances among collaborators were more characteristic of the age. Yet certain patterns emerged: here, a nexus of writers who preferred working together, even if only off and on; there, a nexus of writers who directly supported each others' work. The creative efforts of four such collaborative networks resulted in the most important musical comedies of the period. The first group consisted of those who worked with George Abbott, the oldest practicing master of the form. The second group comprised writers and composers such as "Yip" Harburg, Fred Saidy, Harold Arlen, and Burton Lane, most of whom returned from years of Hollywood employment to realize their finest work on Broadway. The third interconnected group was made up of talents such as Frank Loesser, Meredith Willson, Richard Adler, and Jerry Ross, all new to Broadway, whose total output was small. The fourth such group also consisted of Broadway newcomers whose output however was prodigious: Betty Comden, Adolph Green, and Jule Styne. Except perhaps for Styne, Comden and Green, and the indefatigable Abbott, then, one searches in vain through the musical comedies of the postwar era for the kind of stylistic consistency, productive longevity, and sustained success that characterized the best in musical comedy writing before World War II. On the contrary, despite a fairly stable system of values, it is the genre's surprising variety of styles and approaches and a certain unpredictability of subject and authorship that better seem to capture the spirit of musical comedy of the age.

THE ABBOTT TOUCH

While Rodgers and Hammerstein presided over the development of the musical play, George Abbott (1887–1995) was the dominant force behind American musical comedy. A protean Broadway figure who kept on working until he died at the age of 107, Abbott was an actor, director, author, producer, and play doctor with a knack for turning a faulty script into a hit show. Over a career of more than eighty years, Abbott participated in more than a hundred productions on Broadway and off, more than a quarter of which were musicals. His earliest successes were straight plays (*Chicago*, 1926; *Twentieth Century*, 1932;

Three Men on a Horse, 1935). Later, he ventured into musical productions, working on a series of shows with Rodgers and Hart (*Jumbo*, 1935; *On Your Toes*, 1936; *The Boys from Syracuse*, 1938; *Pal Joey*, 1940). Then, for something like thirty years, there was never a season without at least one Abbott show on Broadway, and sometimes two or three. Abbott preferred to work with young, unknown talent: "Besides saving money, it saves wear and tear on the nervous system." So as he masterminded more than a dozen musical hits from the 1940s to the 1960s, he taught his approach to the craft of musical comedy making to many of the best new talents in the field. The following roster of authors, songwriters, stagers, performers, and entrepreneurs who first made their Broadway mark in Abbott shows reads like a *Who's Who in Musicals* of the age. It attests to the centrality of Abbott's influence, his genius for recognizing new talent, and his ability to nurture those in the developmental stages of their careers and shepherd them through their first Broadway success.

> *Best Foot Forward* (1941): Hugh Martin and Ralph Blane, composer-lyricist team; Nancy Walker, comedian;
>
> *On the Town* (1944): Jerome Robbins, choreographer; Leonard Bernstein, composer; Betty Comden and Adolph Green, librettist-lyricist team; Oliver Smith, producer;
>
> *High Button Shoes* (1947): Jule Styne, composer; Sammy Cahn, lyricist; Phil Silvers, comedian;
>
> *Where's Charley?* (1948): Frank Loesser, composer-lyricist; Cy Feuer and Ernest Martin, producers;
>
> *The Pajama Game* (1954): Bob Fosse, choreographer; Richard Adler and Jerry Ross, composer-lyricist team; Harold Prince and Robert Griffith, producers;
>
> *New Girl in Town* (1957): Bob Merrill, composer-lyricist;
>
> *Fiorello!* (1959): Sheldon Harnick, lyricist; Jerry Bock, composer; Jerome Weidman, librettist;
>
> *A Funny Thing Happened on the Way to the Forum* (1962): Stephen Sondheim, composer-lyricist; Burt Shevelove and Larry Gelbart, librettists;
>
> *Flora, the Red Menace* (1965): John Kander, composer; Fred Ebb, lyricist; Liza Minnelli, actress.

Abbott was both a playwright and a director in the line of George S. Kaufman and Moss Hart. His concern for dramatic integrity in a musical show—connecting gags to humor, humor to character, and character to plot—had less to do with the influence of Rodgers and Hammerstein than with his own experience on the nonmusical stage. A playwrighting student of George Pierce Baker, Abbott shaped librettos into well-made plays, streamlined in action and logical (rather than psychological) in motivation. As director, he became famous for his "Abbott touch," which usually referred to a clarity in staging, boldness in presentation, and crispness in performance that gave the sense of wasting no time in going after what was emotionally "honest" and "real" (words that loomed large in his personal lexicon). He summed up his work with a laconic irony characteristic of the man: "I helped bring plot and common sense into the musical." He did so, moreover, as a director-playwright whose work often had the effect of erasing distinctions between a performance and its text.

> *"Exactly what is the Abbott touch?" an interviewer asked me the other day. "I make them say their final syllables," I answered. A joke, but with much sense to it. . . . If I were to give a serious answer to the question about my method, I would say that the quality which I impart to a show that may make it seem different is taste. By taste I mean artistic judgment—the decision as to just how much to do or not to do, at what point to leave one scene and get into another. . . . The director must always function to some extent as a collaborator. Sometimes he is one, of course; and in many cases he is one in fact even though he receives no program credit for his work. But outside of these instances in which he collaborates in the actual writing, he is always an influence upon the shape of the play. He influences what is put in and what is taken out.*

Eminently practical in his approach to the Broadway musical, Abbott aimed, above all, at making hits. If for Abbott the box office was the final arbiter of success, then the longest running of his many hit shows, *The Pajama Game*, heads the list.

The Pajama Game was a typical Abbott show: a fast-paced farce with a sentimental core and a harmless nod in the direction of social realism.

Indeed, it was archetypical in its conventional treatment of an unconventional subject. The subject: the battle between capital and labor. The treatment: a romantic comedy formula with a new twist. In a midwestern pajama factory whose workers are overworked, BOY (the new foreman [played by John Raitt]) MEETS GIRL (the union shop steward [played by Janis Paige]); BOY FIRES GIRL (for her part in a factory slowdown to demand a 7½-cent wage increase); BOY REHIRES GIRL (after he settles a strike by discovering the boss has secretly added the increase to the books already and has kept the money for himself)—AND MARRIES HER.

Abbott, who directed the show, also co-wrote the script with Richard Bissell, author of the novel *7½ Cents* on which the musical was based. (Abbott supplied the comic subplot and the other musical comedy conventions missing from Bissell's book.) Bissell would later turn his *Pajama Game* experience into another humorous novel, *Say, Darling*, a roman à clef that spoofed the making of the show and caricatured everyone connected with it. In this excerpt, Bissell, newly arrived in New York, phones his wife back in Indiana to report on the efforts of director Richard Hackett (Abbott) and producers Sam Snow (Hal Prince) and Ted Crosby (Bob Griffith) to get him to turn his novel into a libretto:

> *"Lunch like I said at Schrafft's. Blah blah blah we think your book is terrific, fresh, captivating, different, and literate."*
>
> *"What's that last?"*
>
> *"Literate. They are all the time saying 'literate.' That's the new word down here. Opposite of ill-literate, get it? Very powerful word down here."*
>
> *"'Literate.' Okay. Go on."*
>
> *"After lunch we went up to the office and I met Richard Hackett. He's about six feet I guess, looks taller. . . . We talked for a while about the 'property.' . . . then they . . . shoved me over to the theater and plunked me into the front row of* Can-Can *for the matinee. Pretty crummy show but very high underpants content."*
>
> *". . . Zoom! [Back] up to the office. Hackett says, 'How'd you like it? Think you can write a musical now?' 'No,' I said. 'I can't write gags.' 'Hmmmm,' says Hackett. 'Sure you can write gags,' says Sam. 'Your book is funny as hell.' 'No,' Hackett says, 'you can't write gags.'*

'Well, maybe not gags,' says Sam. 'But you've got something better than gags,' says Hackett. 'That's right,' Sam says. 'You've got an individual style,' Hackett says. 'Your people are real people not cardboard cutouts,' Crosby says. 'We want a literate script,' Sam says. 'Humor from within,' Crosby says. 'All right, boys,' Hackett says, 'hold everything. I knocked out a rough scenario this afternoon. Suppose I give Mr. Jordan [Bissell] an outline of the first scene and some nice clean sheets of paper and a lovely pencil and leave him in sublime isolation for an hour or two and see what happens.'"

For all the caricature, however, the show-biz buzzwords were no exaggeration. "Gags" and "cardboard cutout" people were out. "Literate scripts" about "real people" with "humor from within" were in. The world of musical comedy had indeed changed. Even the stars now served the story; and the story left no room for interpolated specialties as it might have done a generation earlier. At least such were the musical comedy ideals in the wake of *Oklahoma!*, even when shows fell short

"Steam Heat" from *The Pajama Game*, l. to r.: Buzz Miller (Second Helper), Carol Haney (Gladys), and Peter Gennaro (Worker).

of them. And *Pajama Game* did fall short, for example, when what one critic called "an animated cartoon named Carol Haney" (rather than a real person) led a trio of dancers in the "Steam Heat" number that stopped the show; or when its humor came from without as comedian Eddie Foy, Jr., the pajama factory's efficiency expert, cavorted about the stage with his shirt cuff caught in the zipper of his pants.

What *Pajama Game* did have in abundance was the Abbott touch, which meant "skillful playcrafting and synoptic songs" that arrived at just the right moment in the plot and told the audience just what it needed to know. Take the first three numbers, for instance. "Racing with the Clock," THE ESTABLISHING NUMBER at the top of the show, established the work routine in the pajama factory, the boss's refusal to grant his employees a pay raise, and the arrival of the new foreman. "A New Town Is a Blue Town," the hero's I AM SONG defined the foreman, his loneliness in the new job, and his resolve to stick with it. "I'm Not at All in Love," the heroine's I AM (NOT) SONG, defined the union shop steward, the vulnerability beneath her toughness, and her denial of the obvious after her first clash with the foreman. *Pajama Game* was a musical of transparent clarity: clean, straightforward storytelling, and sheer fun.

Unfortunately, its Broadway opening in May 1954 took place in the middle of the U.S. Army–McCarthy hearings in Congress—at a time of cold war hysteria, when alleged Communist infiltration into all walks of American life was an issue of national import. And in the intimidating climate of the era now associated with the name of Senator Joseph McCarthy, *Pajama Game*'s focus on organized labor in a clash between management and workers in the garment industry aroused political suspicion in certain quarters sufficient to discourage writers from working on the project and to prevent backers from investing in it. According to Abbott, everyone saw the show as "a propaganda pitch either for management or for labor. None of them could seem to get our idea of poking fun at the whole thing, with no propaganda either way."

Pajama Game was almost militantly apolitical, as were all of Abbott's shows—even *Fiorello!*, whose very subject was politics, and *Flora*, whose subject was still more inflammatory: "the Red Menace." Beneath the comic surface of *Pajama Game*, in fact, there was no serious intent of any kind, and certainly no satire. To make sure there was no mistaking this, Abbott began the show's proceedings with comedian Eddie Foy, Jr., addressing the audience directly:

> *This is a very serious drama. It's kind of a problem play. It's about Capital and Labor. I wouldn't bother to make such a point of all this except later on, if you happen to see a lot of naked women being chased through the woods, I don't want you to get the wrong impression. This play is full of symbolism.*

Furthermore, Abbott resolved the proceedings by means of a plot contrivance at the final curtain rather than on the basis of a worldview: It was not the structural workings of a capitalist system that stood in the way of everyone's happiness at the Sleep-Tite Pajama Factory, but the greed of one redeemable boss. Yet the Abbott touch ultimately rested on a worldview of its own, one that an astute reviewer summed up with reference to *Pajama Game*, though it is applicable to almost all of Abbott's ventures on the musical stage: "Which side is the show on in the battle between capital and labor? The audience's!"

HARBURG'S CIRCLE

Satire involved going against audience sensibilities in some respect; if not, what was the point? But that was risky business where crowd-pleasers were concerned. Most shows avoided genuine satire even when they were mildly satiric. Among musicals with cold war relevance, for example, *Silk Stockings* took easy swipes at Soviet Communism; and *Call Me Madam* had harmless fun with European views of "the ugly American"—one of its songs, "They Like Ike," even providing Dwight Eisenhower's successful run for the White House in 1952 with its campaign slogan.

On occasion musicals did take more pointed aim: at political smugness in "The Country's in the Very Best of Hands" (*Li'l Abner*); at corporate conformity in "The Company Way" (*How to Succeed in Business Without Really Trying*); at social meliorism in "Gee, Officer Krupke" (a comic song in *West Side Story*). But few shows ever called on satire consistently to address the most basic conditions of American life. *Flahooley*, for one, took America's political and economic systems to task.

Finian's Rainbow, for another, took on its class and racist institutions as well. And *Bloomer Girl* added the inequities of gender to the slate of satirical reforms a musical might address. All three were characteristic of the work of E. Y. Harburg, who took his satire as seriously as Broadway would allow.

Edgar "Yip" Harburg (1896–1981) had pursued a successful business career before entering the songwriting profession after he was financially ruined in the stock market crash of 1929. He saw the Great Depression as an enforced liberation from the life of money-making, which he said he hated. A lyricist with a pronounced social conscience, Harburg came to view songwriting less as a profession than a mission:

> *Words make you think a thought. Music makes you feel a feeling. A song makes you feel a thought. . . . A song can degrade your culture, debase your language; can pollute your air and poison your taste or it can clear your thoughts and refurbish your spirit. It is the pulse of a nation's heart, the fever chart of its health. Are we at peace? Are we in trouble? Are we floundering? Do we feel beautiful? Do we feel ugly? Are we hysterical? Violent? Listen to our songs.*

Harburg achieved early success in his new career by writing the words for a revue song that became a Depression anthem, "Brother, Can You Spare a Dime?" (*Americana*, 1932). Yet he wrote romantic lyrics for other interpolated theater songs and revues as well ("It's Only a Paper Moon," "April in Paris"). He also worked in Hollywood, most notably with Harold Arlen, with whom he wrote the score for *The Wizard of Oz* (1939) and additional songs for the film version of *Cabin in the Sky* (1943; the original Broadway score of 1940 was by Vernon Duke and John Latouche). Then, in the anti-Communist wave that swept the country in the late 1940s, he was blacklisted by the movie industry. In the 1950s he could not find work in radio, television, or films.

Broadway, however, continued to furnish Harburg with a professional outlet for his work. There in the 1940s and 1950s he moved toward a new kind of musical comedy, one that aimed to bring to the satirical whimsy of political shows like *Of Thee I Sing* the moral investment of Rodgers and Hammerstein's musical plays. In all, Harburg wrote the lyrics for eight Broadway book shows, four of which were commercially successful: *Hooray for What!* (1937), *Bloomer Girl* (1944), *Finian's Rainbow* (1947), and *Jamaica* (1957). Additionally, he was at times involved in playwriting, directing, producing, and, most often, generating the concepts that motivated his shows.

Yet he was above all a Broadway showman who chose to collaborate, albeit with a small circle of colleagues. He worked with librettist Fred Saidy (1907–1982) on all four of his shows of the 1940s and 1950s, developing stories with timely social themes: women's rights and black emancipation in a Civil War setting (*Bloomer Girl*, produced toward the end of the liberal Roosevelt coalition); racism and capitalism in a modern-day fable of the South (*Finian's Rainbow*, produced at the start of the cold war); corporate culture and political persecution in a contemporary toy factory (*Flahooley*, 1951, produced at the crest of McCarthyism); colonialism and the impact of commercialism on a Caribbean island (*Jamaica*—though here the satire of the Harburg-Saidy book was diluted by producer David Merrick, who turned the show into a showcase for Lena Horne). Among the composers in his circle, were Sammy Fain and Jule Styne; but Harold Arlen (1905–1986) was most often Harburg's choice. A superb songwriter who had a disappointing theater career, Arlen wrote the songs for seven Broadway book shows, most successfully with Harburg (*Hooray for What!*, *Bloomer Girl*, *Jamaica*), yet also notably with Truman Capote (*House of Flowers*, 1954) and Johnny Mercer (*St. Louis Woman*, 1946, and *Saratoga*, 1959). It was with composer Burton Lane (1912–1997), however, that Harburg and his collaborators found their greatest success in the theater, creating in *Finian's Rainbow* the show of the age that most deftly reconciled the competing claims of satire and musical comedy.

Perhaps because it suggested that the capitalist system was the structural basis for the inequities of wealth, class, and race in the United States, *Finian's Rainbow* has been called "a socialist analysis in the form of the American musical." It was indeed charmingly seditious: a mixture of "fairly batty fantasy with fairly purposeful satire," told in two interlocking fables. One dealt with the show's hero, Finian McLonergan, and his quirky view of capitalist economics. A poor Irishman, Finian unleashes three wishes when he steals a pot of gold from the leprechaun Og and, with Og in hot pursuit, travels from Ireland to Missitucky, USA, to bury it underground so it might grow like the gold at Fort Knox. The other fable dealt with the show's villain, Sena-

tor Billboard Rawkins (named for two notoriously bigoted congressmen of the era, Theodore G. Bilbo and John Rankin), and his quirky
view of social justice. Though an unflinching racist, Rawkins undergoes a change of heart when one of the pot-of-gold wishes miraculously turns him into a black man and he learns how it feels to live
under his own Jim Crow laws. (Practicing what it preached, *Finian's*

Confronting racism in his own way in *Finian's Rainbow*, l. to r.: David Wayne (Og) tries magic to
exorcise the bigotry of Robert Pitkin (Billboard Rawkins).

Rainbow had an integrated cast of black and white performers singing and dancing together throughout.)

The naïve charm of such quirkiness was shrewdly meant to ease the sting of satire. Here innocence was not the thing satirized but the means of satire itself. "We really tried to imagine: How would we present the racial problem to a child?," Harburg explained. "In *Finian's* it's all presented through the eyes of a leprechaun—through a completely unbiased and child mind which can't understand all this human foolishness about the color of a man's skin making such a difference." The strategy proved crucial to the show's success.

Equally crucial to *Finian's* success were the songs. Lane's music, at once infectious and inventive ("Old Devil Moon"), evoked the stylistic strains of the book: Irish ("How Are Things in Glocca Mora?"), gospel ("The Begat"), country ("On That Great Come and Get It Day"). Lane also knew when to take a backseat to the lyrics and when to match wits with Harburg. He wrote a guileless waltz for the virtuoso wordplay of "When I'm Not Near the Girl I Love (I Love the Girl I'm Near)." In this song the leprechaun, confused by the onset of human emotions, admits his lascivious delight in discovering the tug of temptation. Yet even when his melody does nothing more than repeat three notes over and over to mirror the recurring sounds of his words, Lane gives the harmony a chromatic descent that drives the phrase with as much musical point as the delicious point Harburg makes in his handling of the lyrics: "When I can't fondle the hand I'm fond of/I fondle the hand at hand."

Finian's Rainbow was a rarity: a musical comedy with a critical point of view—a serious one, moreover, made all the more palatable by means of fantasy, humor, and wit as well as song and dance. That compromised the piece for theater critic Louis Kronenberger who, taking naïveté for cuteness, felt it exuded the "sense of people who are running away from the standard Broadway scene but continually sneaking back for another glimpse of it." Yet perhaps the ultimate intelligence of the show lay in its very balancing act: its ability to indict systemic ills and all the while entertain.

This was not the case with *Flahooley*, which used a similar combination of fantasy and satire but failed on Broadway four years later. A sense of propaganda in that show tended to outweigh the whimsy of Harburg's satire on corporate greed and political repression that took the form of McCarthy-like witch hunts and loyalty oaths. Perhaps Harburg's laughter had become haunted by a certain self-consciousness since he himself had fallen victim to the anti-Communist fever that had gripped the nation in the interim. In this he would not be alone.

Musical comedy practitioners outside the Harburg circle found their careers in jeopardy as well, and Broadway became a politically more nervous place in the 1950s. On separate occasions, for example, Abe Burrows and Jerome Robbins were summoned to testify about their past leftist associations before the House Committee on Un-American Activities (HUAC). Under pressure at their respective hearings, each surrendered the names of former associates. Their compliance may have severely strained their personal relationships with many in the Broadway community. But it is difficult to determine how or even whether it affected the nature of their Broadway work. Their immediately subsequent shows (Burrows: *Can-Can, Silk Stockings*; Robbins: *Peter Pan, Bells Are Ringing*) were no less apolitical or supportive of American politics than their earlier shows (*Guys and Dolls* and *Call Me Madam*, respectively) had been.

By contrast, the summons to testify before HUAC had a galvanizing effect on playwright Lillian Hellman. She determined to turn her experience into a form of protest accessible to a Broadway audience. It was her idea to make a musical using *Candide*, Voltaire's eighteenth-century satire on the Catholic Church and the followers of Leibnitz's theory of optimism, to indict the culture of intimidation and complacency she found in twentieth-century America. While the result differed greatly from the postwar musical comedies in style and spirit, it shared the Harburg shows' deep and abiding bent for genuine satire. According to Leonard Bernstein, who wrote the score for the show, the satirical targets of Hellman's script were "puritanical snobbery, phony moralism, inquisitorial attacks on the individual, brave-new-world optimism, essential superiority." But the real focus of her critique seems to have been McCarthyism itself. In an act of subtle defiance at her HUAC hearing, she caused a letter she had sent the committee chairman to be read into the record. An early draft of *Candide* referred to this now-famous letter, when, before a hearing of the Holy Inquisition in the show, a prisoner was granted permission to read aloud the following prepared statement:

> *Though I honor this court*
> *And approve of its aims,*

I must draw the line
At the naming of names.

These lines were expunged from the final script, however, and many similarly pointed political references in dialogue and lyrics were cut, pruned, or blunted in acts of self-censorship before the show ever opened. To compare an early lyric for the start of the Inquisition scene with the one that replaced it when the show reached Broadway in 1956, for instance, is to hear the point of satire blunted into silliness.

Original Version	**Broadway Version**
What a day, what a day,	*Look at this, look at that.*
For an auto-da-fě!	*What a pretty new hat!*
What a sunny summer sky!	*But the price is much too high.*
Big and small, one and all	*Here be wine! Here be spice!*
Will be itching to buy,	*Worth at least twice the price.*
Everyone in town is coming down,	*But we haven't any money,*
So raise the prices high!	*So there's nothing we can buy!*

With the loss of its satirical focus, the troubles at the heart of *Candide* became all too apparent. It lacked a dramatic trajectory, the sense of a story going somewhere. Taking its cue from Voltaire's picaresque novella, the musical unfolded as a series of vignettes. It traced Candide's episodic journey from naïve belief in "The Best of All Possible Worlds" to despair, and ended with his rejection of the affairs of the world to devote himself and his beloved Cunegonde to "Make Our Garden Grow." The show also lacked a consistency of tone, taste, and approach. *Candide* was "an uneasy mix," said Jonathan Miller, who directed a later production of it for the Scottish Opera.

I don't know why [Voltaire's play] was chosen in the first place. I think
it perhaps has to do with that awe-struck thing that Americans have
for European culture. But they couldn't resist turning it into a vaude-
ville, and it is filled with the most appalling pieces of kitschy vulgar-
ity. . . . For example, "What a Day, What a Day for an Auto-da-fě"
is a wonderful piece of music, but it is absolutely scandalous to have
it in the middle of something which is actually to do with burning

people to death. And it is not only filled with questionable moral taste, it is also filled with pieces of real Broadway shallowness—it's real garment-trade stuff.

Candide flopped on Broadway, though, unlike *Flahooley*, it was a flop that refused to die. This was mainly because of its astonishing score. Its lyrics crackled with the corrosive wit of writers John Latouche, Richard Wilbur, and Dorothy Parker. And its music showed Bernstein at his ebullient best—the score among the most brilliant ever composed for the American commercial stage, and so effective in purely musical terms that its overture has become a concert-hall staple. Freed from its book, in fact, *Candide*'s score took on a life of its own, especially through sales of its original cast album, which continued to fuel interest in the work long after it had closed. Then in 1974, with a new book and a new production concept, Harold Prince overhauled the show for Broadway and turned it into a popular success. But as this version tended to favor the production elements and undercut the power of the score, it was succeeded by numerous reincarnations, each emphasizing the music in a different way—the New York City Opera version (1982), the Scottish Opera version (1988), the London Symphony Orchestra concert version (1989, rev. 1993).

It would be misleading therefore to speak of *Candide* today in any one definitive form. Yet already in its original form, *Candide* was an anomaly on Broadway, billed not as a musical comedy but "A Comic Operetta based on Voltaire's satire." Bernstein took it largely as an occasion to spoof the forms, styles, and postures of nineteenth-century light and lyric opera. It brimmed with echoes of Gilbert and Sullivan ("Dear Boy," cut in 1956, reinstated in 1982), Strauss-like waltzes that suggested both Richard and Johann II ("Paris Waltz Scene"), and a coloratura showpiece that reminded listeners of the "Jewel Song" in Gounod's *Faust* ("Glitter and Be Gay"). Thus, while it contained moments of pathos and emotional power ("It Must Be So," "Make Our Garden Grow"), *Candide* was, more than anything, a "Valentine card," Bernstein said, to European music.

Parody, pastiche, and caricature were not the stuff of satire, however. Not in any but the most general sense of the word, which is not the sense Hellman had in mind. On the other hand, Hellman was a novice where musical comedy was concerned. Distinguished though she was for powerful work in the legitimate theater (*The Children's Hour, The Little Foxes, The Autumn Garden*), she very probably approached the commercial musical medium with unrealistic expectations. Something similar may have been true of Sir Tyrone Guthrie, the eminent British director who, directing his first Broadway musical, cut the HUAC satire from the Inquisition scene that lay at the heart of Hellman's vision for the show. "You've sold out," she cried. "You're a whore." But Guthrie saw *Candide*'s failure as a generic fault. "This was no medium," he wrote of Broadway musicals generally after *Candide*'s closing, "for hard-hitting argument, shrewd, humorous characterization, the slow revelation of true values and the exposure of false ones." Musical comedy was no medium for satire.

A LOESSER ORBIT

Neither was musical comedy a medium for comedy in any but the broadest sense. George Abbott's shows, the emblems of musical comedy success in the postwar era, pointed rather toward farce with their emphasis on externally motivated action. That a show's plot might hinge, by contrast, on the internally motivated action of its characters—should hinge, in fact—was a tenet of the musical play. But it was a tenet whose growing acceptance in Broadway culture now had the effect of complicating musical comedies. Abbott was not comfortable with such psychologizing. When an actor asked him in rehearsal what the motivation for his character was, Abbott is said to have replied, "Your paycheck." It is in the work of others that one finds approaches closer to the new comedic ideals of portraying "real people" and deriving their "humor from within" on the musical stage. Newcomers to Broadway after the war in particular provided several examples of hit shows that attempted to move from caricature to character in musical comedy—from farce to comedy itself—or at least to play with the ambiguity between them.

Foremost among them was Frank Loesser (1910–1969), one of the most original songwriters and dynamic theatrical figures of the postwar generation. Primarily a lyricist, Loesser developed his talent for theater and musical composition late in his career. Not that he had lacked the opportunity earlier. As a boy, he simply refused the musical training that would have been his for the asking at home: His father was a German-born teacher of classical piano, his older half-brother, Arthur, a noted concert pianist. But Loesser rebelled. He favored popular music and rejected the high Germanic culture his family prized. His anti-elite rebellion led him to embrace the very popular culture that they disdained. Where they were genteel, he would be tough, streetwise, even foul-mouthed—an anti-intellectual intellectual. He dropped out of college and eventually found work as a lyricist, first on Tin Pan Alley, then in Hollywood, where he wrote lyrics for the songs of such composers as Burton Lane, Arthur Schwartz, and Jule Styne. In time, he wrote his own music as well, and won an Academy Award for "Baby, It's Cold Outside" (1948), a song whose comic dialogue format showed theatrical flair. Loesser then shifted the focus of his songwriting to Broadway, where he saw five musicals produced: *Where's Charley?* (1948), *Guys and Dolls* (1950), *The Most Happy Fella* (1956), *Greenwillow* (1960), and *How to Succeed in Business Without Really Trying* (1961). *How to Succeed* won a Pulitzer Prize. But *Guys and Dolls*, Eric Bentley said, "is a special case. Possibly it is the best of all American musical comedies."

Billed "A Musical Fable of Broadway," *Guys and Dolls* brought to life a whole world: the Broadway world of Damon Runyon. Runyon, one of New York's leading journalists between the wars, wrote short stories with surprise endings set in a Times Square underworld of disreputable characters—hoodlums, street toughs, and hangers-on—who spoke in an unforgettable patois of great refinement riddled with slang. What delighted on the page was hard to capture on the stage, however, and when an early book for the show proved unworkable, producers Cy Feuer (1911–2006) and Ernest Martin (1920–1995) enlisted humorist Abe Burrows (1910–1985) to create a new one. Guided in his first Broadway assignment by the hand of the show's director, George S. Kaufman, Burrows wrote a superb script. It found stageworthy equivalents for the Runyon style "without the savage undertow of most of his stories—more Runyonesque than Runyonese." And it fit amazingly well with Loesser's score, which was retained from the earlier book. Burrows explained:

> *Frank Loesser's fourteen songs were all great, and the libretto had to be written so that the story would lead into each of them. Later on, the critics spoke of the show as "integrated." The word* integration *usu-*

ally means that the composer has written songs that follow the story line gracefully. Well, we accomplished that but we did it in reverse. Most of the scenes I wrote blended into songs that were already written.

However Burrows got there, he created in *Guys and Dolls* as close to a masterpiece of musical comedy writing as Broadway is likely to produce. The following shows a scene-by-scene breakdown of the Burrows book and a synopsis of the Runyon story on which that book was chiefly based. To align the two where they agree is to see at a glance what is more revealing: how much they disagree—how much, that is, the libretto had to invent or flesh out from hints in other Runyon stories in order to satisfy the technical requirements and aesthetic constraints of postwar musical comedy practiced at the highest levels of Broadway craft and art. So solid is the structure that there is constant variety in the alternation of "in-one" scenes played by a few characters in front of a curtain (while the next scene is set up behind) and full-stage scenes for the big numbers. And so fine is the storytelling that there is virtual equality between the plot involving Sky's dating Sarah (based directly on Runyon's "The Idyll of Miss Sarah Brown") and the subplot involving Nathan's conflicting addictions: gambling and Miss Adelaide (only suggested by Runyon's "Pick the Winner").

The Idyll of Miss Sarah Brown	*Guys and Dolls*
	ACT ONE
Sky Masterson, a gambler addicted to playing long shots, is smitten by mission worker Sarah Brown when he first sees her preaching on a Broadway street corner.	1: Broadway ("RUNYONLAND" PANTOMIME; "FUGUE FOR TINHORNS") Salvation Army worker Sarah Brown invites sinners to repent and come to a mission prayer meeting ("FOLLOW THE FOLD"). Nathan Detroit needs $1000 for a place to hold his crap game ("THE OLDEST ESTABLISHED"). He bets fellow gambler Sky Masterson the money he needs that Sky cannot take Sarah on a date to Havana.

Sky contributes generously to the mission's collection box. Sarah expresses her concern to him over how few souls the mission seems to be saving. Sky tries to figure out some way of helping her.

2: Interior, Save-a-Soul Mission. Sarah's mission has been failing in its task to convert sinners. Sky makes a deal with Sarah to guarantee one dozen sinners at the mission's prayer meeting if she will have dinner with him in Havana. She refuses ("I'LL KNOW").

3: A Phone Booth. Unless Nathan can come up with $1000 right away he will have no place to hold his crap game that night.

4: The Hot Box Nightclub ("A BUSHEL AND A PECK"). Miss Adelaide, a showgirl, has been engaged to Nathan for fourteen years. Though he loves her, Nathan manages to foil her efforts to get him to give up gambling and marry her ("ADELAIDE'S LAMENT").

5: A Street Off Broadway. Sarah's mission band passes with Sky following. Some of the gamblers fear Adelaide is distracting Nathan from the game. They muse over how guys turn foolish for the love of dolls ("GUYS AND DOLLS").

6: Mission Exterior. Sky learns the mission will be closed unless there are sinners at the upcoming prayer meeting. He reminds Sarah of his offer.

7: A Street Off Broadway. As a cover for the suspicious goings on in preparation for the crap game, Nathan promises Adelaide he will elope with her that night. But when Nathan sees the mission band pass by without Sky or Sarah, he figures he has lost his bet.

8: El Café Cubano ("HAVANA" DANCE). Sky and Sarah relax in each other's company. He orders drinks and she gets drunk for the first time in her life.

9: Outside El Café Cubano. Sarah wants to remain in Havana ("IF I WERE A BELL"). Sky confesses he only took her there because of the bet and he resolves to take her back to New York.

Sarah finds out Sky is a professional gambler and that his interest in the mission has less to do with repenting than with Sarah's good looks. She informs him that the mission will no longer accept his ill-gotten gains. This puts an end to his attentions.

10: Exterior of the Mission. On returning from Havana, Sky and Sarah declare their love for each other ("MY TIME OF DAY"; "I'VE NEVER BEEN IN LOVE BEFORE"). They are interrupted by a police raid on the mission, where, in desperation, Nathan has held his crap game while the mission workers were out all night recruiting sinners for the coming night's prayer meeting. Sky is as surprised as Sarah by all this, but she believes he deliberately set her up and breaks with him.

ACT TWO

1: The Hot Box Nightclub ("TAKE BACK YOUR MINK"). Adelaide is all set to elope, but finds herself stood up by Nathan because of his crap game ("ADELAIDE'S LAMENT," REPRISE).

2: 48th Street. Sarah is comforted by a fellow mission worker ("MORE I CANNOT WISH YOU"). Sky informs her that he still intends to make good on his part of the deal.

Brandy Bottle Bates says he cannot win a crap game bet to save his soul. Sky takes him up the idea. If Sky wins, Bates has to join Sarah's mission. As Sky loses thirteen times in a row he suspects Bates's dice are loaded and is about to draw his gun when Sarah walks in. Angry with Sky for what he is trying to do for her, she bets him for his own soul, rolls Bates's dice and wins.

3. Crap Game in the Sewer ("THE CRAP-SHOOTERS DANCE"). Sky gives Nathan $1000, telling his friend that he lost the bet on Sarah. Sky bets the other gamblers that if he wins the game they have to attend the prayer meeting at the mission that night ("LUCK, BE A LADY").

4: A Street Off Broadway. Nathan tells Adelaide he has to put off eloping with her that night because he has to attend a prayer meeting. She is convinced he is lying ("SUE ME").

Sarah calls Sky a fool. And Sky, having in the course of his travels read his share of Gideon Bibles, quotes St. Paul: "If any man among you seemeth to be wise in this world, let him become a fool, that he may be wise." Sky tells Sarah he loves her.

5: Interior, Save-a-Soul Mission. Sky, having won the crap game, delivers the gamblers and leaves. They participate in the meeting ("SIT DOWN, YOU'RE ROCKIN' THE BOAT"). The mission is saved. Thinking to protect Sky, Sarah lies to the police about the raid of the night before. Nathan tells Sarah what Sky had told him about the Havana bet. She realizes Sky has lied to protect her, as she just did to protect him.

6: Near Times Square. Sarah informs Adelaide that Nathan told her the truth: he really was at the prayer meeting. Exasperated, the two dolls resolve to marry their guys now—and reform them later ("MARRY THE MAN TODAY").

Sky marries Sarah and joins the mission. He lets her brag about how she won his soul, never letting on that the dice, with which she won, were loaded.

7: Broadway. Sky has married Sarah and become part of the mission. Nathan has landed a steady job and heads for the mission with Adelaide to be married ("GUYS AND DOLLS," REPRISE").

Character songs dominated the show, the funniest of them based on incongruities of style. "I don't invent languages," Loesser proclaimed. "I make use of them." He meant an ironic use of the meanings encoded in the languages in which he wrote—musical as well as verbal. "I want to combine some things that are said to have certain rules and some that are said to have certain other rules," he said. Thus, for example, three lowlifes give conflicting tips for betting on the horses, only they

Crap game in the sewer scene from *Guys and Dolls*, third from l. to r.: Stubby Kaye (Nicely-Nicely Johnson), B. S. Pulley (Big Jule, standing), Robert Alda (Sky Masterson, rolling dice), Johnny Silver (Benny Southstreet), and Sam Levene (Nathan Detroit, in striped suit).

do so to the devices of counterpoint, which suggests musical learning and respectability ("Fugue for Tinhorns"). Or a chorus of gamblers sings of an illegal crap game in terms of close a cappella harmonies that evoke an aura of hymns and alma maters ("The Oldest Established"). Loesser virtually exults in the clash of lowbrow content and highbrow form—the use of learned, elevated, or pious musical styles to house ignoble sentiments. Yet the point does not come off as ludicrous or arch because it is not made at the expense of the characters involved. What seems funny to the audience does not seem so to those onstage. On the contrary, "to their way of thinking, the *Guys and Dolls* males aren't loafers, but are in a business: crap-shooting is the thing they do, just as selling is the thing a bond salesman does." Loesser's songs simply extended the cultural incongruities of the Runyon style itself into the musical domain. And so if "the essence of Guys and Dolls," according to Burrows, "was that these bums act like they were written by Noël

Coward," then those critics were on the mark who spoke of the show as a Broadway *Beggar's Opera*.

It was in "Adelaide's Lament," however, that Loesser's feeling for character emerged with greatest humor and affection. As originally conceived, Adelaide (Vivian Blaine) was a stripper with an occupational ailment: Each time she undressed in the drafty nightclubs where she plied her trade she caught a cold. But Loesser was convinced that "no performer of any stature would really strip in front of a Broadway audience." He gave Adelaide greater respectability by turning her into a "showgirl." More inspired still, he switched the cause of her ailments from an external to an internal one: Her colds were now the psychosomatic expressions of a fourteen-year despondency over Nathan's not marrying her. He reasoned that "if Adelaide's colds were made a disease with an emotional basis, relating to her love life and thereby becoming a story point, the comedy could be carried along for more than just one joke." "Adelaide's Lament" imbues what was little more

Ex. 11-1. Frank Loesser, music and lyrics: "Adelaide's Lament," *Guys and Dolls*

than a cartoon figure with a certain humanity: It lends her "humor from within." Moreover, it does so with touchingly funny incongruities of its own. As a duet for one performer, it switches back and forth: from the book Adelaide reads out loud ("The av'rage unmarried female . . .") to her interpretation of it ("In other words . . ."); from the book's psycho-analytic jargon to her Runyonesque argot; and from recitative-like sing-ing to nightclub swinging in G♭ Major (Ex. 11-1).

How to Succeed in Business Without Really Trying reunited Loesser with the *Guys and Dolls* team of Burrows, Feuer, and Martin a decade later. Yet while the earlier show was a romantic musical comedy, *How to Succeed* was a cynical one—a musical cartoon, that made its points at the expense of all the characters in it, who remained somehow likable nonetheless. Its story took place at the World Wide Wicket Company and followed the irresistible rise of J. Pierrepont Finch (Robert Morse) up the corporate ladder from window washer to chairman of the board. En route, it poked fun at Finch and exposed the backstabbing ways of American corporate culture that made possible his success. Even the love interest in the show proved suspect:

ROSEMARY: Darling, I don't care if you work in the mail room, or you're chairman of the board, or you're President of the United States, I love you.
FINCH: Say that again.
ROSEMARY: I love you.
FINCH: No, before that.

Songs were intrinsic to the show's satirical agenda. So instead of garnering sympathy for the characters who sang them in the manner of *Guys and Dolls*, they served as transparent attempts to hide their characters' faults. In business affairs, they served to further servility ("The Company Way"), hypocrisy ("Brotherhood of Man"), and deceit ("Grand Old Ivy"). In affairs of the heart, they cloaked narcissim ("I Believe in You"), masochism ("Happy to Keep His Dinner Warm"), and venality ("Love From a Heart of Gold"). Thus *How to Succeed* was as consistent at being "amusingly mean," in Burrows's words, as its char-acters remained one-dimensional. At the end Finch was the same rogue he was at the start, but as played with such innocuous boyish charm by Robert Morse, the audience invariably forgave his sins.

Perhaps there was a bit of Finch in Loesser himself. If nothing else, he proved to be a shrewd businessman in his own right. He acquired Music Theater International, produced his last two shows, and formed his own publishing company, Frank Music Corporation. Through Frank Music he also developed and promoted the careers of other show writers, exerting a direct influence on their work. Several who thus entered the Loesser orbit had a major impact on Broadway. Among them were Richard Adler (b. 1921) and Jerry Ross (1926–1955), a team of pop songwriters who had back-to-back hits with the only Broadway shows they were to write together, as Ross died of a lung ailment at age twenty-nine: *The Pajama Game* and *Damn Yankees*. And there was Meredith Willson (1902–1984), a concert composer and novelty song-writer who wrote three Broadway musicals—*The Music Man* (1957), *The Unsinkable Molly Brown* (1960), and *Here's Love* (1963)—and created a classic with the book and score for the first.

Willson was a schooled musician who had already achieved wide recognition for his work in radio, film, and television before writing *The Music Man*. The show was based on Willson's boyhood experiences in Iowa before the First World War, and it evokes a nostalgic world of Americana, from parlor songs to Sousa marches to barbershop quartets. The title refers to Harold Hill (Robert Preston), who is as much the villain of the piece as its hero. Hill is an itinerant swindler who arrives in a town, cons its citizens to invest in setting up a boys' band to improve their community, and then runs off with their money. Before he can leave River City, however, the town's skeptical librarian, Marian Paroo (Barbara Cook), gets wise to his scam. She also falls in love with him, and reforms him. She realizes that, without his intending to, he has brought a fresh sense of life to a joyless, closed-minded Iowa community. He has taught it that music can be heard in all things if only one really listens: in the rhythm of shop-talking salesmen ("Rock Island"); in the staccato of gossiping women ("Pick-a-little, Talk-a-little"); even in the excruciating wrong notes played by the boys' band that materializes at the final curtain ("Minuet in G").

Music also serves other purposes in *The Music Man*. Harold Hill uses it to mask his deceptions, seducing the townspeople in rhythm to a mock evangelical harangue ("Trouble"), and later diverting their suspicions with oily-smooth barbershop chords ("Sincere"). Meredith Willson, for his part, uses music to disclose the hidden affinities of his main characters, which motivates the outcome of the show. He explained,

> *Marian was lonesome and lovelorn underneath her stand-offishness. Wasn't Harold lonesome too, despite his flamboyance and girl-in-every-town behavior? Maybe it would be interesting if these two could subtly convey to the audience this characteristic they had in common by separate renderings of the same song—a march for him, a ballad waltz for her.*

Marian's waltz, "Goodnight, My Someone" (Ex. 11-2a), and Harold's march, "Seventy-six Trombones" (Ex. 11-2b), are melodically and harmonically really the same song. But their tempo and character are so different—the one, a lilting ballad; the other, a rousing rhythm song—that the coincidence usually goes unnoticed when they are first sung in the show. The connection is dramatized at the show's climax, however, when Marian and Harold reprise their respective songs by alternating phrases and, at the moment they realize their feelings for each other, exchanging them outright. It is he who now sings the waltz; and she, the march. For the first time in his life, this "Music Man" is mesmerized by someone else's music, and he takes it as a sure sign of love. This is the musical comedy paradigm waged in essentially musical terms.

Ex. 11-2a. Meredith Willson, music and lyrics: "Goodnight, My Someone," *The Music Man*

Ex. 11-2b. Meredith Willson, music and lyrics: "Seventy-six Trombones," *The Music Man*

But that such use of music is meant to make the conversion of a scoundrel plausible to an audience willing to suspend disbelief is both the ultimate illusion of this show and the animating genius of the genre itself: "the idea of the musical as a con game."

COMDEN AND GREEN—AND STYNE

Unlike musical comedies with regional settings (the Iowa of *The Music Man*, *Pajama Game*'s Indiana, even the "Missitucky" of *Finian's Rainbow*), the shows of Betty Comden and Adolph Green took place in an idealized New York—or if not, at least were informed from top to bottom by a New York sensibility. More consistently than anyone else, the two collaborators spent their careers together in the theater making explicit both the Broadway showmanship and the New York style it represented that lay at the heart of American musical comedy. They made no bones about their bias. In fact, they trumpeted their agenda as early as the opening number of their first Broadway show, when three sailors (Green among them) arrived onstage to announce what they would do with twenty-four hours' shore leave:

> *We've got one day here, and not another minute*
> *To see the famous sights;*
> *We'll find the romance and danger waiting in it*
> *Beneath the Broadway lights;*
> *But we've hair on our chest, so what we like the best*
> *Are the nights—*
> *Sights, lights, nights.*
> *New York, New York, a helluva town,*
> *The Bronx is up but the Battery's down,*
> *And people ride in a hole in the ground;*
> *New York, New York, it's a helluva town!*
>
> "NEW YORK, NEW YORK," (ON THE TOWN)

In that spirit Comden and Green began on Broadway and in that spirit they continued to work together throughout a collaboration that was to last more than fifty years, the longest exclusive creative partnership in the history of the American theater—perhaps because they were not married to each other. Shortly after Green's death, Mayor Michael Bloomberg even proclaimed an Adolph Green Day in New York, saying of the partners,

> *They captured our city's unique variety, flavor, and idiosyncracies with scenes in the Brooklyn Navy Yard with Manhattan's skyline, Coney Island, Carnegie Hall, taxis, Greenwich Village, Grand Central Station, Sutton Place, and the streets. They conveyed the wonder of new arrivals, and the eccentricities of some residents (not us), and summed it all up in "New York, New York," our unofficial city anthem.*

Betty Comden (1917–2006) and Adolph Green (1915–2002), both native New Yorkers, first joined forces in 1939 in a Greenwich Village nightclub to perform their own satiric material. Eventually they performed on Broadway, playing key roles in their first musical, *On the Town,* and starring together at the height of their careers in a show of their own, *A Party with Comden and Green.* Indeed, the fact that they were performers may have even accounted for a certain theatrical flair in their written work. But they made their marks in the entertainment world as writers. They wrote the screenplays for several memorable musical films (*Singin' in the Rain,* 1952; *The Band Wagon,* 1953). And they wrote lyrics and/or books for seventeen Broadway shows. They collaborated on eight shows with composer Jule Styne (*Bells Are Ringing,* 1956; *Do Re Mi,* 1960: book, Garson Kanin; *Subways Are for Sleeping,* 1961); and they also collaborated with Leonard Bernstein (*On the Town*; *Wonderful Town*: book, Joseph Fields and Jerome Chodorov), Charles Strouse (*Applause,* 1970: lyrics, Lee Adams), and Cy Coleman (*On the Twentieth Century,* 1978; *The Will Rogers Follies,* 1991: book, Peter Stone). Stone once described how they worked together:

> *The form and structure came from Betty, so did the style and sensibility. Then what, you might ask, did Adolph do? The answer is: the madness. The sheer, outlandish, surreal, weird, goofy, uniquely Adolphian madness. This was a marriage between Dorothy Parker and all five of the Marx Brothers rolled into one.*

It may have been just this combination of wit and madness that David Merrick had in mind when he drafted Comden and Green to

write the book for a musical comedy based on the memoirs of burlesque stripper Gypsy Rose Lee. But *Gypsy*, as the show would be called,
turned out to be a very different kind of musical, with a different kind
of madness to it—and without Comden and Green.

David Merrick (1911–2000), one of the theater's most powerful
impresarios, exemplified a distinct type of Broadway showman, the
"tyrannical producer who ruled by gut instinct and took sole responsibility for financing, mounting and promoting a production." Merrick
combined those qualities that marked him for success in his profession, as Dick Schaap put it: "the delicacy of the Marquis de Sade, the
humanity of Attila the Hun, the generosity of Ebenezer Scrooge, and
the sophisticated taste of Yogi Berra." Something of a Phineas T. Barnum as well, Merrick shamelessly manipulated his image as Broadway's "Abominable Showman" to benefit his productions. The musical
Subways Are for Sleeping, for example, opened to sufficiently bad reviews
in 1961 for most producers to have closed it on the spot. Not Merrick.
Instead, he ran an ad with rave reviews for the show from seven men
he found in the telephone book who had identical names to those of the
seven drama critics who had panned it. Photos of Merrick's "critics"
accompanied their statements in the ad, so hardly anyone was taken in
by the ruse. But the notoriety the ad generated gained publicity for the
show itself and helped keep it running on Broadway for half a year.

More than conniving to salvage flops, Merrick schemed to make
hits—and in that department he was no man's fool. His record remains
unsurpassed in the annals of the New York stage when it comes to
productivity and profitability. In a high-risk industry where only 20
to 25 percent of musicals return their investment during their Broadway runs, Merrick's hit percentage was about 55–60 percent for all his
shows. His musical hits include *Fanny* (1954), *Jamaica* (1957), *Gypsy*
(1959), *Irma La Douce* (1960), *Carnival* (1961), *Oliver!* (1963), *Hello,
Dolly!* (1964), *I Do! I Do!* (1966), *Promises, Promises* (1968), *Sugar* (1972),
and *42nd Street* (1980). *42nd Street* and *Hello, Dolly!* were the most profitable of these; *Gypsy*, however, was the most distinguished.

The task of writing the book for *Gypsy* finally fell to Arthur Laurents (b. 1918) when Comden and Green abandoned the project. That
changed the nature of the undertaking. Although Laurents had written
the libretto for *West Side Story*, he was primarily a playwright (*Home
of the Brave*, 1945; *The Time of the Cuckoo*, 1952), and the book he came

7 OUT OF 7 ARE ECSTATICALLY UNANIMOUS ABOUT SUBWAYS ARE FOR SLEEPING

HOWARD TAUBMAN .... "ONE OF THE FEW GREAT MUSICAL COMEDIES OF THE LAST THIRTY YEARS, ONE OF THE BEST OF OUR TIME. It lends lustre to this or any other Broadway season."

WALTER KERR .... "WHAT A SHOW! WHAT A HIT! WHAT A SOLID HIT! If you want to be overjoyed, spend an evening with 'Subways Are For Sleeping.' A triumph."

JOHN CHAPMAN .... "NO DOUBT ABOUT IT. 'SUBWAYS ARE FOR SLEEPING' IS THE BEST MUSICAL OF THE CENTURY. Consider yourself lucky if you can buy or steal a ticket for 'Subways Are For Sleeping' over the next few years."

JOHN McCLAIN .... "A FABULOUS MUSICAL. I LOVE IT. Sooner or later, every one will have to see 'Subways Are For Sleeping'."

RICHARD WATTS .... "A KNOCKOUT, FROM START TO FINISH. THE MUSICAL YOU'VE BEEN WAITING FOR. IT DESERVES TO RUN FOR A DECADE."

NORMAN NADEL .... "A WHOPPING HIT. RUN, DON'T WALK TO THE ST. JAMES THEATRE. It's in that rare class of great musicals. Quite simply, it has everything."

ROBERT COLEMAN .... "A GREAT MUSICAL. ALL THE INGREDIENTS ARE THERE. As fine a piece of work as our stage can be asked to give us."

Evgs. Mon. thru Thurs. Orch. $8.60, Mezz. $6.90, Balc. $5.75, 4.80; 2nd Balc. $3.60. Fri. & Sat. Evgs.: Orch. $9.40, Mezz. $7.50, Balc. $6.90, 5.75, 4.80, 2nd Balc. $3.60. Wed. Mat: Orch. $4.80, Mezz. $4.10, Balc. $4.05, 3.60, 2nd Balc. $3.00. Sat. Mat: Orch. $5.50, Mezz. $4.80, Balc. $4.30, 3.60, 2nd Balc. $3.00.

MAIL ORDERS FILLED THRU JAN. 1963

ST. JAMES THEATRE 44th St., W. of B'way

The David Merrick hoax as it appeared in the *New York Herald-Tribune* in 1961; only the pictures reveal the identities of the ad's amateur reviewers, who happened to have the same names as the foremost professional theater critics in New York at the time.

up with seemed both serious and strong enough on its own that the show's lyricist, Stephen Sondheim, thought it *could* be a play. Laurents disagreed.

> *Not the way I wrote it. It's too big. The characters are overblown, the strokes are too bold and too broad. . . . There are fireworks in a scene with about two lines and they are screaming and yelling at each other. Music allows you that style. The absence of music doesn't. [Moreover,] a musical needs construction. . . . Probably more than a play because you must construct things to build to a song. Every line must make its point or you don't have it. A musical calls for the most economical writing there is in the theater . . . [so] the characters tend to be thin unless they are filled out by the songs they sing.*

In one critical respect, however, *Gypsy* did resemble a play. Laurents changed the focus in telling the story of Gypsy Rose Lee so there would be more point to it than simply tracing the life of a famous stripper. He made the central figure not Gypsy but her mother, Rose, a woman whose story could be dramatized because she had something important to learn: In Laurents's words, "if you try to live your children's lives, you'll destroy yourself."

The title *Gypsy* is misleading, therefore, but the story is clear. During the 1920s, Rose, the mother of June and Louise, dreams of making June a vaudeville star ("Let Me Entertain You"). To realize that dream Rose enlists the help of Herbie, a former theater agent, who falls in love with her ("Small World"). Rose, however, is consumed by an ambition that is suffocating her daughters and destroying her relationship with Herbie. When June elopes with a dancer to get away from her mother, Rose is crushed but undaunted and transfers her hopes for June to Louise ("Everything's Coming Up Roses"). In time, Herbie realizes Rose will never marry him and leaves. And Louise, who has been working as a burlesque stripper ("You Gotta Have a Gimmick"), eventually becomes a Minsky headliner under the name Gypsy Rose Lee—without her mother's help. Abandoned by June, Herbie, and Louise, Rose explodes in frustration and resentment, suffering a nervous breakdown alone on the stage of an empty theater that she believes is filled with an audience cheering her on to perform as if she herself now were the star ("Rose's Turn").

This was hardly material for a musical comedy. If anything, it was better suited to a musical play. Yet the worlds of vaudeville and burlesque in which it took place did much to shape it as a show along musical comedy lines. "What made *Gypsy* a break with the past," Alan Jay Lerner said, "was that where previously musical plays were written in the post-*Oklahoma!* modern operetta style, *Gypsy* told a realistic and emotional story to the beat of the musical and lyrical language of pure musical comedy." *Gypsy* moved, in other words, to the vernacular wit and boldness of Sondheim's lyrics and the music of Jule Styne.

Jule Styne (1905–1994), perhaps the last of the great Tin Pan Alley–based Broadway composers, grew up as a classical piano prodigy in Chicago and played in dance bands on the city's South Side when the area became a haven for jazz in the 1920s. Later he worked in New York and Hollywood as a vocal coach and a pop song composer. He wrote songs for over forty films, many of which, especially those written for Frank Sinatra, dominated the Hit Parades of the 1940s ("Saturday Night Is the Loneliest Night of the Week," "I Fall in Love Too Easily"). His chief collaborator was lyricist Sammy Cahn and with Cahn he also wrote his first stageworks, though for the better part of his theater career Styne worked with others. Of some twenty Broadway shows for which Styne supplied the music, the most successful—apart from *Gypsy* and the Comden and Green shows—include *High Button Shoes* (1947: lyrics, Cahn), *Gentlemen Prefer Blondes* (1949: lyrics, Leo Robin/rev. as *Lorelei*, 1974: lyrics, Comden and Green), *Funny Girl* (1964: lyrics, Bob Merrill), and *Sugar* (1972: lyrics, Merrill). Many of these served as vehicles for female musical comedy stars, and Styne had a knack for tailoring his songs so well to the voices of those who sang them that over time his songs became their vocal signatures: Carol Channing's "Diamonds Are a Girl's Best Friend" (*Gentlemen Prefer Blondes*); Judy Holliday's "The Party's Over" (*Bells Are Ringing*); Barbra Streisand's "People" (*Funny Girl*).

In a sense, *Gypsy* too was a star vehicle, but one in which the cultural stakes were higher. Ethel Merman was at once the star of the show and the most acclaimed musical comedy star of the age. And a song like "Everything's Coming Up Roses," even as it became a signature for her, became an emblem of American musical comedy itself.

Consider the line "Gonna have the whole world on a plate!" As Stephen Banfield saw it:

> *It's colloquial, it's ungrammatical, it's picturesque and it's pure New York—rarely can the meaning of the Big Apple have been put into fewer words. And it's not just rhetoric. Opera can deal with rhetoric, but it can almost never cope with verbal wit. It's that quality of wit, surely, that makes the musical such an indigenous achievement—that Rose can couch such sublime ambition in such vernacular terms.*

Here altogther was the spirit of postwar musical comedy in a nutshell.

Gypsy broadened the dramatic scope of musical comedy. It turned the conventions of the genre into the stuff of drama. In it, the archetypes of light entertainment came to serve the subtext of a dark libretto. "Small World" was the LOVE BALLAD indispensable to any musical of the period (it even achieved Hit Parade status outside the show as such). But it was also Rose's way of using romance to seduce Herbie into handling her daughters' act. "All I Need Is the Girl" was the big DANCE NUMBER. But it also foreshadowed June's escape from Rose by eloping with a dancer who needed a girl for his act. "You Gotta Have a Gimmick" was the NOVELTY SONG, here an introduction to the seedy world of no-talent burlesque. But it also set up the motivation for Louise to consider not only taking her clothes off in public but making a gimmick of her very reluctance to do so—that is, inventing the ultimate tease in Gypsy Rose Lee's strip.

Even the conventional modes of musical comedy stardom served the structural nodes of the drama, at once presenting Merman without neglecting to represent Rose. Merman's GRAND ENTRANCE—yelling "Sing out, Louise!" to her daughter onstage as she stormed down the aisle from the back of the house—established with one stroke the character of this most outrageous of stage mothers. Merman's knock-'em-dead ACT 1 CURTAIN, "Everything's Coming Up Roses," revealed a desperate Rose rationalizing her use of one daughter to replace the other. And "Rose's Turn," Merman's over-the-top ELEVEN O'CLOCK SHOWSTOPPER, enacted Rose's final breakdown.

"Rose's Turn," the climax of *Gypsy,* served as the linchpin in its

dramatic structure and the moment toward which the rest of the evening had been building. As a musical mad scene, it burst the seams
of self-contained song to become an extended soliloquy made of distorted fragments of songs already heard in the show. This number,
too, was double-edged. Others had had their chance; it was now Rose's

Ethel Merman (Mama Rose) in *Gypsy,* belting "lyrics over the footlights like a baseball coach
belting flies to an outfield."

turn to do what she always wanted to do for herself. And it was Rose's turn in the vaudeville sense: her number, her moment in the spotlight, her showstopping star performance. To remain true to her character, however, Merman's performance had to be a showstopper that did *not* stop the show. For stopping a show breaks more than the continuity in the ongoing illusion of a separate reality onstage. It breaks the illusion itself. In a conventional musical comedy this is often part of the fun—something the audience milked on the opening night of *Can-Can* when Gwen Verdon had to return to the stage to acknowledge its applause, no longer in character but as herself. *Gypsy*, however, was no conventional musical comedy, and maintaining the illusion was crucial to the show.

For this reason, Sondheim urged Styne not to put a big final ending on "Rose's Turn," which would have encouraged applause, but to have the music simply trail off into the final dialogue. "To have a mad scene and then have a bow," he said, "violated everything that I thought I had learned from Oscar Hammerstein, who taught me to be true to the character and true to the situation." Yet Hammerstein himself thought otherwise when he saw the result during *Gypsy's* Philadelphia tryout. Merman needed a real ending on the number, he insisted. Sondheim asked why.

> *Because the audience is so anxious to applaud her that they are not listening to the scene that follows. Since the scene that follows is what the entire play is about, if you want them to listen, you must let them release themselves. And that's what the applause is for. I know it's dishonest, but* please, *fellows, put a big ending on that number if you want the rest of the play to play. Or bring the curtain down there. You have to choose one of those two things.*

The big ending went in, and "Rose's Turn" predictably stopped the show.

But the performance history of the number continues. In 1974 Laurents directed a revival of *Gypsy*, starring Angela Lansbury, in which by slightly changing the staging of "Rose's Turn" he found a way to encourage applause without violating the representational premise of the show. It now became the portrayal of a showstopper as well as an indulgence in the real thing. Now after Rose finished the number she acknowledged the audience's applause by bowing—the only time in the show she did so. Yet once the audience's applause had died down, Rose continued to bow—in dead silence—to the applause which only she could hear in her head and to which, as the audience now came to realize with a shock, she had been bowing all along. Rose had gone mad. And so, even as the audience's applause had stopped the show, it had unwittingly contributed to furthering the illusion the show had created.

Gypsy defied the stereotype: a musical comedy with a meaning; a musical comedy with a mad scene; a musical comedy that let audiences think they had stopped the show, then let them know they hadn't; a musical comedy George S. Kaufman might have called musical serious. Sondheim sought to put the show's last scene, with its poignant accommodation between Gypsy and Rose, into perspective:

> *In* My Fair Lady *[you] are told that you, too, can be the belle of the ball even if you aren't educated. . . .* The Sound of Music *says you can eat your cake and have it—you can get away from the Nazis, marry the man of your choice, without compromising your religious goodness.* Hello, Dolly! *says that a loud, middle-aged lady can get the man she wants. Now that may sound cynical, but those are fairy stories . . .* Gypsy *says something [different and] fairly hard to take: that every child eventually has to become responsible for his parents. That you outgrow your parents and then eventually they become your responsibility . . . they become your children. It's something that everybody knows but no one likes to think about a lot. . . . The last scene is what the play is about—the unpleasant truth of it. I think it's quite moving. But it's not very cheerful.*

Combining the traditions of musical comedy and the musical play, *Gypsy* brought together the two main divisions of the Great American Showshop, that part of the United States entertainment industry that turned out Broadway shows. It did so at one of the last moments historically when the showshop's output was still broadly perceived as headed on an "upward and onward course." At the start of the 1960s, middle-class urban Americans for the most part still considered Broadway musicals part of the cultural mainstream and their artistic possibilities almost limitless. That perception would not hold. Popular culture in the United States was changing; and so was Broadway. Outside the theater, a cultural revolution had been fomenting that found its symbol now in something called rock 'n' roll, a music that would soon dislodge Tin Pan Alley from its position at the center of American entertainment. Inside the theater, a revolution that had long been gestating beyond the orbit of Times Square now organized itself as a movement to challenge the centrality of that very orbit under the banner of "Off Broadway." Everywhere, it seemed, a seismic shift in cultural sensibility was under way.

PART THREE

TOWARD THE NEW MILLENNIUM

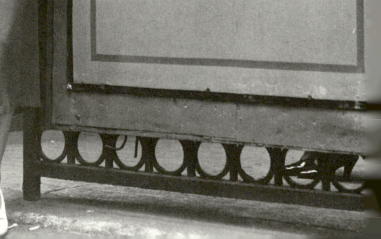

12

AWAY FROM BROADWAY

THE CRADLE WILL ROCK
(6/16/1937–7/1/1937). **Producers:** WPA Federal Theater Project 891 [John Houseman]. Broadway (1/3/1938–4/9/1938). **Producers:** Sam H. Grisman and The Mercury Theater. **Book, Lyrics, and Music:** Marc Blitzstein. **Director:** Orson Welles. **New York Run:** 127 performances. **Cast:** Olive Stanton, Howard Da Silva, Will Greer. **Songs:** "Nickel Under the Foot," "Art for Art's Sake," "Croon-Spoon."

PINS AND NEEDLES
(11/27/1937–6/22/1940). **Producer:** Labor Stage, Inc. [Louis Schaffer]. **Sketches:** Charles Friedman, Arnold B. Horwitt, Blitzstein, and others. **Lyrics and Music:** Harold J. Rome. **Director:** Friedman. **New York Run:** 1,108 performances. **Cast:** Amateur actors from the International Ladies' Garment Workers' Union. **Songs:** "Social Significance," "One Big Union for Two."

DIE DREIGROSCHENOPER [THE THREEPENNY OPERA]
(Berlin, 1928). New York (3/10/1954–5/30/1954; 9/20/1954–12/17/1961, performed in an English adaptation by Blitzstein). **Producers:** Carmen Capalbo and Stanley Chase. **Book and Lyrics:** Bertolt Brecht, based on *The Beggar's Opera* by John Gay. **Music:** Kurt Weill. **Director:** Capalbo. **New York Run:** 2,707 performances. **Cast:** Lotte Lenya, Jo Sullivan, Beatrice Arthur, Scott Merrill. **Songs:** "The Ballad of Mack the Knife," "Pirate Jenny," "Tango Ballad."

Olive Stanton (Moll) looks at a poster for the forthcoming production in which she would make history as the first to rise and perform unexpectedly from the audience on opening night.

THE GOLDEN APPLE

(3/11/1954–circa. 4/1954). **Producers:** The Phoenix Theater [T. Edward Hambleton and Norris Houghton]. Broadway (4/20/1954–8/7/1954). **Producers:** Phoenix, Alfred de Liagre, Jr., and Roger L. Stevens. **Book and Lyrics:** John Latouche, based on *The Iliad* and *The Odyssey* of Homer. **Music:** Jerome Moross. **Director:** Norman Lloyd. **New York Run:** 173 performances. **Cast:** Priscilla Gillette, Kaye Ballard, Stephen Douglass, Jack Whiting. **Songs:** "Lazy Afternoon," "It's the Going Home Together," "Windflowers."

THE FANTASTICKS

(5/3/1960–1/13/2002). **Producer:** Lore Noto. **Book and Lyrics:** Tom Jones, based on the play *Les Romanesques* by Edmond Rostand. **Music:** Harvey Schmidt. **Director:** Word Baker. **New York Run:** 17,162 performances. **Cast:** Rita Gardner, Jerry Orbach, Kenneth Nelson. **Songs:** "Try to Remember," "Soon It's Gonna Rain," "Much More."

MAN OF LA MANCHA

(11/22/1965–3/18/1968). **Producers:** ANTA-Goodspeed, Albert W. Selden, and Hal James. Broadway (3/20/1968–6/26/1971). **Producers:** Selden and James. **Book:** Dale Wasserman, suggested by the life of Miguel de Cervantes and his novel *Don Quixote de la Mancha.* **Lyrics:** Joe Darion. **Music:** Mitch Leigh. **Director:** Albert Marre. **New York Run:** 2,328 performances. **Cast:** Joan Diener, Richard Kiley, Irving Jacobson. **Songs:** "The Impossible Dream," "Dulcinea."

HAIR

(10/29/1967–12/10/1967). **Producer:** New York Shakespeare Festival [Joseph Papp]. **Director:** Gerald Freedman. Broadway (4/29/1968–7/1/1972). **Producer:** Michael Butler. **Director:** Tom O'Horgan. **Book and Lyrics:** Gerome Ragni and James Rado. **Music:** Galt MacDermot. **New York Run:** 1,836 performances. **Cast:** Rado, Ragni. **Songs:** "Aquarius," "Let the Sunshine In," "Frank Mills," "I Got Life."

For those who view the theater in ideological terms, Broadway and Off Broadway belong to separate—perhaps even parallel—universes. Yet it is not out of keeping with a history of the Broadway musical to pause at this point to survey what some writers have called the Off Broadway musical. Not to do so, in fact, would be to overlook the remarkable postwar production of Off Broadway musicals as a development in its own right. And it would be to overlook the impact that this development has had in turn on the Broadway musical itself, complicating the very concept. In theory, Broadway and Off Broadway may well represent parallel universes. In practice, however, the history of their relationship has shown them to be not so parallel that they can't intersect.

For much of the twentieth century, professional theater in the United States was the virtual monopoly of Broadway: a place, a business, a profession, a state of mind. Geographically, Broadway formed the spine of New York's theater district, whose heart was Times Square. Financially, Broadway implied a way of doing business by making substantial investments in high-risk ventures that were produced for long runs in big proscenium houses and that yielded one of two possible results: a hit or a flop. Professionally, Broadway meant meeting big-time standards: exacting, competitive, and self-regulated, but also monitored at one end by unions that required membership for Broadway employment (above all, Actors' Equity Association) and at the other end by newspapers that reviewed only Broadway-level work (above all, the *New York Times*). Psychologically, Broadway signified glamour and the prize: the golden apple of the Big Apple, plus the ballyhoo—that glorious but evanescent sense of life at the top in the American theater.

Broadway was exclusive, and exclusionary; and therefore limited. It did not extend to theatrical activity that took place in relative obscurity outside the Times Square district; or that was primarily motivated by noncommercial concerns; or whose standards were amateur or semiprofessional; or whose values deviated significantly from the cultural mainstream. Yet an abundance of theatrical activity did not fit the Broadway template. And such artistry often took place almost within earshot of Broadway, to say nothing of the nation at large. In New York it found a consistent home in and near Greenwich Village, a haven for artists, bohemians, and "nonconformists" of many kinds well to the south of the commercial hub of Times Square. (The names of shows, such as *The Grand Street Follies*, and the names of theaters, such as the Sullivan Street Playhouse, sometimes flaunted the location.) Financially, it was undertaken by theater companies and cooperatives that were organized as repertory or resident ensembles, or that were financed on a nonprofit basis through subscriptions, contributions, and private or publicly funded grants. Professionally, it employed the talents of unknowns, amateurs, and union members alike, who often performed in small low-rent spaces with or without a proscenium stage. And psychologically, what it lacked in glamour it made up for in a spirit of adventure, a feeling of community, and a sense of mission that inspired the production of neglected classics or new works slated for neglect because of their controversial content or experimental form. Such activity grew out of a perceived need to develop alternatives to the ways of Broadway that were based on what theatrical producer Norris Houghton called "the twin concepts of the decentralization and decommercialization of the American theatre."

The remarkable growth of alternatives on a permanent basis after World War II led to public recognition of the legitimacy of a non-Broadway theater movement now officially called Off Broadway, though the term had been loosely applied since the 1930s. Broadway preferred to see Off Broadway chiefly in terms of geography and theater size: as a minor-league version of itself. Jule Styne even hailed as "the best thing ever done off Broadway" *Once Upon a Mattress*, a Broadway show in every respect save for the Lower East Side location of the Phoenix Theater, where it was first produced in New York. (*Once Upon a Mattress* moved to Broadway within months of its Off Broadway premiere.) Off Broadway, as Styne saw it, was simply "a showcase for new talent . . . a fertile farm system for the big Broadway arena." Those who saw Off Broadway as somehow different in kind from Broadway were only "damaging the theater as an institution."

But the term "Off Broadway" also came to stand for the different kind of theater that was presented "off" Broadway, and for the cultural movement that this kind of theater represented. Indeed, the idea of "the theater as an institution" was at odds with the very spirit of Off Broadway ventures that saw themselves as filling a need for noninstitutional alternatives. Off Broadway one could mount works—even feel free to fail in the attempt—without incurring prohibitive expenses. Off Broadway unknowns had the opportunity to perform. Off Broadway theater was more accessible to those on limited budgets simply because tickets were cheaper. The week *Once Upon a Mattress* moved to Broadway in November 1959 the show raised its top ticket price by $2. Elsewhere, the difference was even more pronounced. To have seen *Gypsy* or *Fiorello!* from the best seat in the house on Saturday night that week would have cost $9.40; to have done the same at an Off Broadway hit such as *Little Mary Sunshine* or *The Threepenny Opera* would have cost only $4.95.

Director Alan Schneider (*Waiting for Godot*, 1956; *Who's Afraid of Virginia Woolf?*, 1962) preferred to understand Off Broadway in the second sense. "Off Broadway is only partly geographical and physical," he said. "Mostly it's psychological. It's a way of looking at theater." For him Off Broadway represented a cultural space "in which to experiment, to work on plays with serious themes, plays that may have somewhat strange form or content, plays with limited audience appeal"—plays, in other words, that might never find their way onto the Broadway stage. Broadway was not necessarily the goal of Off Broadway. On the contrary, said Schneider,

> The idea of working Off Broadway came to me as a salvation and an answer when I was at an absolute dead end on Broadway. . . . I never went to Off Broadway to be discovered; I had been discovered. I went there in order to work with better material under more creative conditions. I was subsidizing my opportunity to do that by being willing to work for twenty-five to fifty dollars a week. I think that often we forget that people do work Off Broadway not just to go on to something else but because the opportunities there, both artistically and personally, are more satisfying.

At its core, Off Broadway provided a place for theater folk who might or might not want to go on to something else, and for audiences seeking exposure to the kinds of theater they could not get anywhere else.

The term "Off Broadway" originally referred only to a place in New York, but then also to the movement of the 1940s and 1950s that flourished in that location and that first broke the Broadway monopoly as a professionally recognized form of alternative theater. Yet we might also use the term more broadly to designate the alternative theater of any epoch, before and after, and in any of its many forms. The term might thus apply to the "art theater" or "little theater" movement of the World War I era; or to the political New Theater of the 1930s. Or it might also pertain to the great expansion beyond New York and the national organization of regional theaters in the 1960s; or to the rise in the same decade in New York of the aptly named Off-Off Broadway movement.

Musicals, however, were not high on anyone's list of Off Broadway priorities. They were more costly to mount than straight plays and seldom as serious. Yet musical productions came to figure significantly in almost all of the Off Broadway movements. *Johnny Johnson*, *Pins and Needles*, and *The Cradle Will Rock* gave voice to the New Theater sensibility of the Depression. *The Threepenny Opera*, *The Golden Apple*, and *The Fantasticks* played key roles in Off Broadway's post–World War II Renaissance. *Man of La Mancha*, *Hair*, and *Godspell* emerged from the regional theater and Off-Off Broadway movements in the 1960s. But just how each of these musicals came to figure in the larger history of Off Broadway is sufficiently different in each case to defy generalization. Perhaps it is this that ties such disparate works together and gives them a certain concinnity. Not that they all flouted the Broadway production system and its tendency to homogenize, for in the final analysis few of them did. But rather that, while mainstream shows made their peace with the Broadway system from the start, each of these shows developed another kind of ambivalent relationship to it, negotiating its own terms with it and provoking part of a complex of interactions that would lead to a redefinition of Broadway itself by century's end.

EARLY ALTERNATIVE MUSICALS

Perhaps the earliest Off Broadway prototype of importance was the art theater movement that developed in the United States around the time of the First World War. The movement, part of a larger cultural rebellion against the genteel inheritance of the Gilded Age, sought expression in literary realism, social criticism, and artistic experimentation. As the iconoclastic spirit swept the theater, it infected performers, writers, designers, and directors who were dissatisfied with the standard plays and musicals of the commercial stage. Inspired by European models and drawing on a tradition of parlor theatricals and thespian societies in the United States, they formed companies of their own with the aim of creating a new American dramatic art. Typically, they set up in small, low-rent theaters where they mounted productions of new one-act plays. Performers and playwrights were usually part of a repertory company and were seldom paid, while audiences consisted mostly of annual subscribers who often had a hand in choosing what was performed. Little theater is said to have begun with the founding in 1912 of the Toy Theater in Boston and the Little Theater in Chicago. The movement spread quickly, especially in the Midwest—a Little Theater in Indianapolis (1915); an Arts and Crafts Theater in Detroit (1916). By the time of America's entry into World War I, there were over fifty comparable little theaters all over the United States.

New York became the center of America's experimental theater with the creation of three little-theater companies: the Provincetown Players (1916–1929), the Washington Square Players (1915–1918), and the Neighborhood Playhouse (1915–1927). Each set up shop in Manhattan well to the south of the midtown theater district: the Provincetown and Washington Square Players in Greenwich Village, the Neighborhood Playhouse on the Lower East Side. Each had its own agenda. The Provincetown Players, dominated by idealists like George Cram Cook and playwrights like Eugene O'Neill, experimented with new and revolutionary forms of drama as a way "to encourage the writing of American plays of real artistic, literary and dramatic—as opposed to Broadway—merit." The Washington Square Players had a broader outlook. Led by Lawrence Langner and modeled on Chicago's Little Theater, they rejected commercial standards in order to give actors, designers, and playwrights greater freedom in producing European as well as American plays of distinction. The Neighborhood Playhouse served as a community theater for the Lower East Side immigrant population and as a forum for raising standards in American theater at large. It mounted original plays based on folk and religious themes as well as contemporary European dramas by such playwrights as Anton Chekhov and Bernard Shaw.

None of these groups staged musical productions as such. As little theaters, they lacked the resources; as art theaters, they lacked the interest. Typically not modernist, iconoclastic, or high-minded, musicals represented almost everything the art theater was not. They belonged, in a word, uptown. In fact, when the first notable downtown musicals appeared Off Broadway, they took the form of "little" revues. These were simpler to assemble than book shows, and could accommodate a variety of subjects, some aimed directly at Off Broadway clientele, others at a wider theatergoing public. Three series proved memorable: *Greenwich Village Follies* (eight editions: 1919–1928), *The Grand Street Follies* (six editions: 1924–1929), and *Garrick Gaieties* (three editions: 1925–1930).

In 1919 producer-director John Murray Anderson (1886–1954) staged the first of his revue series at the Greenwich Village Theater, to whose intimate setting he brought a cabaretlike chic. The revues were small in size but big in aspiration, and he called them *Greenwich Village Follies* much to the chagrin of Florenz Ziegfeld, who felt he had exclusive right to the "Follies" title. Ziegfeld had cause for concern. It cost him $175,000 to produce his 1919 *Follies* on Broadway; Anderson only $35,000 to produce his (though this was a staggering sum by Off Broadway standards). In addition, Anderson featured "girls" and such Ziegfeld performers as singer Bessie McCoy Davis and bandleader Ted Lewis. After six weeks Anderson even took his *Follies* uptown, and by 1921 he had relocated permanently to Broadway. There his revues distinguished themselves from the competition by their use of bohemian motifs, new stagecraft design, and a production style he referred to as "simplicity itself." Among the notable painters, costumiers, and stage designers who contributed to that much-vaunted simplicity were Reginald Marsh, Lady Duff Gordon, James Reynolds, and Erté.

The Grand Street Follies, originally mounted on the small stage of the Neighborhood Playhouse, were inexpensive revues that eventually found their way to Broadway as well. What they lacked in staging they made up in wit and sharp burlesques of the major dramas of the day ("They Knew What They Wanted Under the Elms," "Strange Inner Feud," "What Price Morning-Glories"). They were among the earliest sustained examples of an intimate revue style that would captivate Broadway in the 1930s, and their success, though modest, gave added impetus to the efforts of other revues that had moved away from the spectacles then prevalent on Broadway—Raymond Hitchcock's *Hitchy-Koo* (1917–1920), and *André Charlot's Revue* (1924–1926), a British import that introduced the extraordinary foursome of Noël Coward, Beatrice Lillie, Gertrude Lawrence, and Jack Buchanan to the American stage.

The Theater Guild produced *Garrick Gaieties* at its Garrick Theater (formerly Harrigan's Theater). An outgrowth of the Washing-

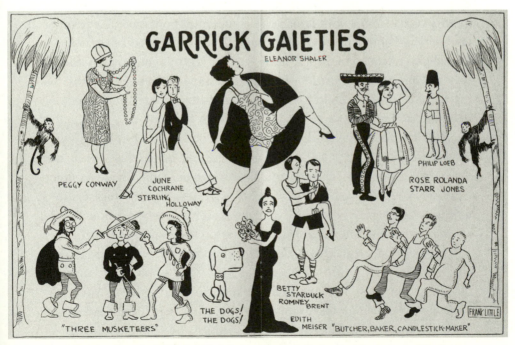

Caricatures from the 1925 *Garrick Gaieties* program, including June Cochrane and Sterling Holloway as they perform "Manhattan."

ton Square Players, the Theater Guild was founded in 1918 for the purpose of mounting full-scale Broadway productions of modern dramas of distinction that might not otherwise have reached the commercial mainstream. Averaging six productions a season, the guild succeeded by circumventing the traditional norms of Broadway production: It was supported by public subscription, run by a committee directorship, and dedicated to furthering the art of the legitimate stage. The Theater Guild became the first commercially successful art theater company in America. It premiered distinguished American dramas (Sidney Howard's *They Knew What They Wanted*, 1924; Eugene O'Neill's *Strange Interlude*, 1928; Maxwell Anderson's *Both Your Houses*, 1933—all Pulitzer Prize winners) and later helped in the creation of works of dramatic distinction on the musical stage (*Porgy and Bess, Oklahoma!, Carousel*). It also sponsored a series of *Garrick Gaieties* revues that were put together by the Guild's Junior Players, which included the then-unknown talents of Libby Holman, Edith Meiser, and Herbert Fields. In their emphasis on literate humor and satiric wit, these shows too were forerunners of the intimate revue. But what distinguished them from other revues of the type was the quality of the songs with which the equally unknown writing team of Rodgers and Hart outfitted almost all of the first two editions. *Garrick Gaieties*, in effect, established Rodgers and Hart as much as the other way around, for the critical attention the shows received brought the team out of professional obscurity and put their songs on the map of popular culture ("Manhattan," "Mountain Greenery").

As a rule, little revues had little choice but to develop those qualities with which the better-endowed revues of Broadway would not or could not compete: the charm and intimacy of small-scale production; the youthful verve of undiscovered talent; a bent for scripted urbanity and wit. Even John Murray Anderson, whose shows were strong on production values, still attributed their success to the ways in which they diverged from Broadway norms: They were "an agreeable potpourri of youth, style and distinction—something entirely different from the kind of heavy-handed extravaganzas that Mr. Ziegfeld produced up on Broadway." It was perhaps for the freshness of such features that Off Broadway revues of the 1920s succeeded in the cultural mainstream and helped pave the way for those Broadway revues of the 1930s that would strive to capture something of the spirit of the little revues on the great stages of the commercial theater.

The peak years of the so-called intimate Broadway revue coincided with the onset of the Depression and lasted roughly from *The Little Show* (1929) to *The Show Is On* (1936). While such shows still emphasized elegant and innovative approaches to stage design, they were generally pitched at a more sophisticated audience than their lavish counterparts had been. It was of *The Band Wagon*, you may recall, that Brooks Atkinson had famously remarked, "You need not check your brains with your hat." Yet this greatest of the intimate Broadway revues, which opened in 1931 at the nadir of the Depression, took no measure of the scope of what was happening outside the theater. Other revues of the era, however, did find places for sobering moments of reflection on timely themes: the bitter effects of unemployment in "Brother, Can You Spare a Dime?" (*Americana*) or of racial murder in "Supper Time" (*As Thousands Cheer*). But even these were no more than foils for the main thrust of the shows in which they appeared. ("Supper Time"—described by its black performer Ethel Waters as "a dirge [that] told the story of a colored woman preparing the evening meal for her husband who had been lynched"—met with serious opposition from several quarters and might well have been cut from its show had not Irving Berlin, who wrote the song, also been the show's coproducer.)

A different situation prevailed Off Broadway. Much of the noncommercial theater was gripped by a fervor that grew out of the most pressing concerns of the period: the devastation of the Great Depression at home and the rise and spread of fascism abroad. The New Theater of the 1930s was above all a theater of ideas that developed in response to these concerns. It was associated with spoken plays and new to the extent that it departed from the psychological focus in American drama to concentrate on the external world of social forces and political events. While New Theater was not rooted in any specific ideology, the groups that took part in it generally represented a spectrum of the political left, from New Deal liberalism to Marxism and Soviet-style Communism. The more extreme groups that took to the amateur stage in the early 1930s to advocate social revolution often did so by using Soviet agitprop (agitation and propaganda) techniques: "direct appeal to the audience, choral effects, political slogans, nonillusory setting and staging, episodic structure, type characters." Later in the decade, along with a relaxation in Marxist ideology and the embrace of a more broad-based Popular Front, such groups sought to rouse American workers to the class struggle by mounting less severe amateur musical productions, especially revues (*Big Boycott of 1938*, *We Beg to Differ*, *Pink Slips on Parade*).

While the political radicalism of such revues kept them from the Broadway stage, *Parade* (1935) proved a notable exception since the largely nonpartisan Theater Guild produced it. The work mainly of sketch writers Paul Peters and George Sklar and songwriter Jerome Moross, it was billed as "a revue with a definite idea and not just a potpourri of songs and sketches about sex and love and the moon above." The "definite idea" involved a satiric approach to contemporary issues from a strongly left-wing perspective. The show took the form of a series of mordant sketches on socially relevant themes: "Home of the Brave" transplanted Nazi racial policy to the New World as scalping squadrons of Native Americans terrorized Americans of European ancestry; "The Dead Cow" showed a starving Depression family reduced to eating what was left of its furniture. And it included songs that utterly ridiculed critics of leftist causes: "The Tabloid Reds"; "Send for the Militia." Perceived as unrelentingly propagandistic, the show failed to find an audience and quickly disappeared. But if *Parade* had no real impact on Broadway or its culture, there were two subsequent musicals which came out of left field, so to speak, that did. One was *Pins and Needles* (1937), a union amateur show which would run longer than any musical that had preceded it. The other was *The Cradle Will Rock* (1937), a theater project of the WPA, which became the first musical whose premiere made the front page of the *New York Times*.

Pins and Needles was so named because of its origin as an in-house, morale-boosting entertainment for members of the International Ladies' Garment Workers' Union. As the show came to the attention of a growing circle of admirers outside the ILGWU, however, the original weekend performances of *Pins and Needles* turned into a regular run. Eventually, the revue went into three editions to keep up with the current events it spoofed, moved to Broadway, and tallied a record-setting 1,108 performances before it closed in 1940.

Much of its charm derived from its homemade feeling and freshness as an amateur undertaking. It was mounted at the 299-seat Labor Stage (formerly the Princess Theater). Charles Friedman directed it, he acknowledged, "in the tradition of the intimate music halls such as the Grand Street Follies." The orchestra consisted of two pianos, one of which was played by the show's songwriter, Harold Rome (1908–1993). And the cast was drawn from the ILGWU rank and file—garment workers and amateur actors all, who became professionals on joining Actors' Equity only after the fact. (In a contretemps worthy of a comic sketch in the show, since Actors' Equity was affiliated with the AFL and the ILGWU belonged to the CIO, the cast members refused to pay double union dues.) The whole production might thus have been another "little" revue. But as it was intended as "a weekend ILGWU educational activity" sponsored by the Union's Cultural Division, it was also "new": its material was mainly social and political in nature, and presented from a working-class point of view.

By the time it opened, New Theater had largely abandoned agit-prop and the class struggle and redefined the mission of the leftist stage in terms of a "struggle against war, fascism, and censorship." The show took swipes at all three targets in sketch and song: the pacifist poses of heads of state ("Four Little Angels of Peace"), Mussolini's campaign for an Italian population boom, congressional interference in the Federal Theater Project ("FTP Plowed Under"). In this the revue resembled *Parade*, though its satiric bent was more genially inclined. Where it most differed from *Parade*, however, was in the ability to turn its humor back on itself. For *Pins and Needles* also took swipes at the kinds of things it might have been expected to defend, excuse, or ignore had it been simply a propaganda piece and nothing more: union rivalry between the AFL and CIO ("Papa Lewis, Mama Green"), proletarian agitprop dramas ("The Little Red Schoolhouse"), a working-class equivalent of "Easter Parade" ("Sunday in the Park"). Even its love songs revealed a pro-labor bias that was winningly self-mocking ("It's Better with a Union Man," "One Big Union for Two," "Social Significance"). Indeed, the last of these seemed to mock *Parade*'s own rejection of songs about "sex and love and the moon above," for in it Rome "brought off the trick of making fun, not only of love songs, but of the overwrought seriousness of individuals who have no time for them."

We're tired of moon songs
Of star and of June songs
They simply make us nap.
And ditties romantic
Drive us nearly frantic
We think they're full of pap. . . .

Sing us a song with Social Significance
All other tunes are taboo.
We want a ditty with heat in it,
Appealing with feeling and meat in it.
Sing us a song with Social Significance
Or you can sing till you're blue.
Let meaning shine from ev'ry line
Or we won't love you.

"SOCIAL SIGNIFICANCE" (*PINS AND NEEDLES*)

That diluted the satire of the show for many left-wing critics, who balked at working-class actors performing on behalf of middle-class values. America's Communist Party newspaper *The Daily Worker* condemned the Labor Stage itself for "going out of its way to deride . . . the very sources from which it evolved." Even the music failed to pass social muster. For Rome, who wrote both words and music, worked entirely in the pop song idioms of the day; these were held to be creations of a manipulative culture industry and "repressive *per se*" by Theodor Adorno, who thus concluded, "Those who ask for a song of social significance ask for it through a medium which deprives it of social significance." Right-wing critics, on the other hand, condemned *Pins and Needles* with less subtlety. The Daughters of the American Revolution found it "so profane, so Communistic and so broad in its implications as to make it unfit for any child to see and to make an adult ashamed to be in its audience." (The Daughters themselves became the butt of satire in the 1939 version of the show when, in a sketch called "The Red Mikado," they sang: "Three little D.A.R.s are we/Full to the brim with bigotry.") Attacked from the left and from the right, *Pins and Needles* situated itself somewhere in the cultural middle, though clearly to the left of center. It was even given as a command performance in the Roosevelt White House. In short, it succeeded where *Parade* had failed. And with its success Harold Rome found a mainstream outlet for his work in subsequent Broadway revues (*Sing Out the News*, 1938; *Call Me Mister*, 1946) and book shows (*Wish You Were Here*, 1952; *Fanny*, 1954; *I Can Get It for You Wholesale*, 1962).

By contrast, little of the work of *Parade*'s chief songwriter Jerome Moross ever appeared on Broadway, and never seemed at home there when it did (*Ballet Ballads; The Golden Apple*). His idea of musical theater diverged radically from the norms of the commercial stage, and he articulated the differences in 1935 when he took to the pages of *New Theatre* magazine to expose the limitations of Broadway musicals and outline a vision of musical theater that was "new" not only in content but in form:

> *The constant interruption of the story to allow for the music and dancing in [musical comedy] and the disconnected vaudeville quality of the [revue] are equally bad for the expression of a unified political and social point of view. . . . [Even] the elaborateness of dancing and costuming, which are so essential a part of the revue form as presented on Broadway, are unnecessary if the piece has anything to say. . . .*
>
> *The revolutionary revue should, if possible, combine both musical comedy and revue forms, telling an important story in swift-moving five-minute blackouts, revue fashion. . . . I envision a new revue in America, a swift and vital form rising above flippancies, the music being more than the banalities of Tin Pan Alley, the lyrics achieving the worth of a Gilbert or a Brecht, the sketches using the blackout technic not for bathroom humor, but for terse dramatic punches.*

Moross was not alone in calling for a stage form rooted in the vernacular traditions of musicals, yet gounded dramatically in the socially conscious theater of the day. At least something of the spirit of this "revolutionary revue," as he called it, could be found at the time in productions of the Theater Union and the Group Theater. In 1935, the Theater Union (1933–1937), America's leading socialist theater, produced a dramatization of Maxim Gorky's *Mother* by Bertolt Brecht (music by Hanns Eisler) in English translation. In 1936, *Johnny Johnson*, a pacifist play by Paul Green (music by Kurt Weill), was produced by the Group Theater (1931–1941), an organization founded as an offshoot of the Theater Guild by Harold Clurman, Lee Strasberg, and Cheryl Crawford, which would become the most influential alternative company of the 1930s. Both productions involved plays of serious social and political import, and both made use of songs in vernacular idioms.

And both were outright failures. The Group Theater modeled itself on Constantin Stanislavski's Moscow Art Theater and it was steeped in the conventions of stage realism. Strasberg, who admitted viewing *Johnny Johnson* more as a play than a musical, directed the work from a realistic bias, a decision he later came to regret: It did not allow for the kinds of theatricality that a musical production invariably demands. The Theater Union for its part erred similarly with *Mother*. One of the board members considered it an "Eisler operetta" and the company revised Brecht's script to make the work more emotional, inconsistently applying the nonillusionist techniques demanded by Brecht's "epic theater" style, in which the very use of music was meant to call attention to the artifice of the stage. Brecht, in New York for the production, voiced his distress at the realism accorded his work with characteristic bluntness: *"Das ist Scheisse."*

The one stagework of the period that achieved a degree of popular success and actually came closest to realizing Moross's ideal was *The Cradle Will Rock*. It began significantly as a production of the Federal Theater Project (1935–1939), one of five Arts Projects that formed part of the New Deal's mammoth Works Progress Administration, whose mission it was to put the country's unemployed back to work. More than simply a relief agency, WPA became a symbol of the social revolution implicit in the New Deal itself; its architect, Harry Hopkins, saw the WPA Arts Projects in particular as engines of the "democratization of culture." The Federal Theater Project involved the most ambitious effort ever undertaken by the federal government to produce theater in America, and it brought professional performers to many American audiences who had never before experienced commercial theater. Of some twelve hundred productions that it mounted, more than fifty were musical—among them, the first performance of an eighteenth-century piece, the earliest known American ballad opera, *The Disap-*

pointment (1937), and the premiere of a New Theater–style revue, *Sing for Your Supper* (1939).

From its inception, however, the Federal Theater Project was hounded by controversy in Washington, where many congressmen saw it as the first step toward a nationally subsidized theater. The New York City unit proved an especial bone of contention as it used government funds to mount politically provocative works and to employ workers who were reputedly Marxist or outspoken left-wing sympathizers. None of this could be denied (only its relevance to the mission of the WPA could be questioned). Even Harold Clurman of the Group Theater was frank to admit that, in the late 1930s, "some of the fire that appeared extinguished in organizations like the Group and the Theatre Union had gone into various elements of the Federal Theatre Project (reactionary Congressmen were able to see it) [and] productions like *The Cradle Will Rock* were its new manifestation."

Marc Blitzstein (1905–1964) joined the Communist Party in the mid-1930s, though members of Congress would surely not have known this at the time. (He admitted it to a congressional committee only later, in the 1950s.) Yet there was no doubt about the nature of his political leanings in 1936 when in five weeks he wrote the book, music, and lyrics for *The Cradle Will Rock*, as he said, "at white heat." This was Blitzstein's first mature stagepiece, and a curious one for a composer who had begun his career as a student of Nadia Boulanger in Paris and Arnold Schoenberg in Berlin, writing concert works imbued with the art-for-art's-sake ethos of high modernism. But Blitzstein had come to change his view of the artist's place in society and of the social function of art. And this precipitated a change of focus in his work from the concert hall to the theater and to a more accessible musical style open to vernacular idioms, such as the workers'-song style Hanns Eisler had used in *Mother* and the popular-song style Kurt Weill had used in *Johnny Johnson*.

Federal Theater Project director Hallie Flanagan undertook to produce *The Cradle Will Rock* as soon as Blitzstein auditioned it for her. "It took no wizardry," she said, "to see that this was not a play set to music, nor music illustrated by actors, but music + play equaling something new and better than either." Blitzstein's self-styled "play in music" was the first American musical of note to show the influence of "epic theater" at a time when neither Brecht's plays nor his theories were yet familiar in the United States. *Cradle* was even dedicated "To Bert Brecht," and for good reason. The German playwright had given Blitzstein the idea for the piece during his American visit in 1935 after the composer showed him some sketches for a prostitute's song, "Nickel Under the Foot." Brecht suggested making the song the centerpiece of an entire show and its central metaphor: "To literal prostitution," he said, "you must add figurative prostitution—the sell-out of one's talent and dignity to the powers that be."

The Cradle Will Rock was thus a Marxist allegory. Blitzstein set it to music that ranged from the Tin Pan Alley pop style he caricatured ("Croon-Spoon," Honolulu") to the proletarian mass–song style he managed to invest with warmth ("Nickel Under the Foot," "Joe Worker"). In cartoonlike stereotypes, the show pitted the struggle of steelworkers to form a Union in Steeltown, USA, against a Liberty Committee of the town's leading citizens marshaled to suppress the workers' efforts. The action did not take place linearly, but in independent episodes and flashback scenes. Each of these varied the theme of "figurative prostitution" in songs showing one member of the Liberty Committee after another compromising himself under pressure from the steel company's ruthless owner, Mr. Mister. Editor Daily undermined "The Freedom of the Press" he sang of by allowing his paper unjustly to discredit the Union; Yasha and Dauber, a violinist and a painter, debased their "Art for Art's Sake" credo selling their talents to the highest bidder; and there were similar sellouts by representatives of the medical establishment, Dr. Specialist, the academy, President Prexy, and the church, Reverend Salvation.

Opposing Mr. Mister and his crew was Larry Foreman, Steeltown's leader in the struggle for Union recognition. As *Cradle*'s hero, he embodied the alternative ideal to the forces of reaction, an ideal that found its most defiant expression in the show's title song. This was a marchlike anthem in the proletarian-song style of the agitprop theater, a style Harold Rome deliberately avoided in keeping with the tongue-in-cheek spirit of *Pins and Needles*. But Blitzstein was in dead earnest here, embracing a host of musical dislocations not for the sake of humor, but to make ominous his warning of the revolutionary winds of change that would soon rock the cradle of capitalist power. And by its emphatic ending, cutting off before reaching any musically

Ex. 12-1. Marc Blitzstein, music and lyrics: "The Cradle Will Rock," *The Cradle Will Rock*

"safe" conclusion, the song was surely meant to rattle the listener as well (Ex. 12-1).

Marc Blitzstein consciously simplified his art for political ends and made it accessible to a broad theatergoing public. But there were other things about *Cradle* that militated against its success in the cultural mainstream: It was polemical; it was didactic; and it came down on the "wrong" side of the political spectrum. "If the standard Broadway musical plugs ... the folklore of capitalism,'" wrote Virgil Thomson,

"this play with (or 'in') music recites with passion and piety the mythology of the labor movement."

That mythology sparked a controversy that went beyond the confines of the stage. For *Cradle* seemed nothing short of political dynamite
at the time of its premiere on June 16, 1937. A look at the headlines
that day was enough to confirm the timeliness of the Federal Theater's undertaking. With labor violence in Chicago and steel strikes
in Youngstown, Ohio, and Johnstown, Pennsylvania, the goings-on in
"Steeltown, USA," were likely to raise questions as to which indeed was
the stranger, truth or fiction. Moreover, with the Federal Theater itself
under political fire in Washington and facing severe cutbacks in funding,
official word went out to all project directors to postpone the opening of
all new productions. Flanagan saw the move as "censorship under a different guise," and with no guarantee that *Cradle* would ever be allowed
to open, producer John Houseman and director Orson Welles determined to proceed with the work as planned. On the day of the scheduled
premiere at the Maxine Elliott Theater, government officials interceded,
padlocked the theater, and confiscated the scenery, costumes, and props.
Another available house, the Venice Theater twenty blocks away, was
located only at the last minute. Under circumstances that have become
the stuff of legend, the first-night audience waiting outside the locked
theater marched en masse to the new one, where *The Cradle Will Rock*
had its world premiere—without orchestra, costumes, scenery, or performers. Alone onstage, Blitzstein began playing his score on a gutted
piano, prepared to perform the parts himself. Then, starting with Olive
Stanton, several of the actors in street clothes joined him, singing and
speaking their parts from where they sat or stood in the audience—
the regulations of their own union, Actors' Equity, barring them from
appearing on any stage but the one contracted for by their employer,
the Federal Theater. According to Lehman Engel, the conductor of the
show, who now had no orchestra to conduct,

> *With Orson's scenery—realistic, heavy, and cumbersome—no longer
> a participant, and with the audience relying on its own imagination,
> the show was better. . . . Duets were sung by actors seated on opposite
> sides of the theater. . . . Marc supplied the missing roles. Everything
> actually gained in this kind of presentation.*

"Art for Art's Sake" from *The Cradle Will Rock* in the Mercury Theater's "oratorio version," with the cast all seated onstage when not performing in a scene. Standing center l. to r.: Peggy Coudray (Mrs. Mister), Edward Fuller (Yasha), and John Hoysradt (Dauber), with composer-librettist Marc Blitzstein seated at the piano.

The performance had itself turned into the kind of act of defiance that the piece was about. Outside the theater, *Cradle* became a cause célèbre. In a rare move, the *New York Times* featured the show's premiere on its front page ("STEEL STRIKE OPERA IS PUT OFF BY WPA") amid the news of actual rioting and steel strikes abroad in the land ("JOHNSTOWN MAYOR APPEALS TO [PRESIDENT] ROOSEVELT TO INTERVENE"). Inside the theater, the work proved electrifying. Through the impromptu responses of those involved to the extraordinary circumstances of the premiere, *Cradle* had found perhaps its most appropriate production style by eliminating all traces of the stage illusionism that had been planned for it. Houseman and Welles acknowledged this when they made their break with the Federal Theater over *Cradle* to form a theater company of their own. When their Mercury Theater (1937–1939) produced *Cradle* on Broadway a few months later, they jettisoned their original staging scheme along with Blitzstein's orchestrations and incorporated the piano and most of the non-illusory aspects of production that were discovered by accident, as it were, on *Cradle*'s opening night. Most subsequent productions of the piece have done the same.

The Broadway run of *Cradle* was short, ending early in 1938. Congress abolished the Federal Theater Project altogether in 1939. The New Theater movement itself was on the wane. And Blitzstein, who went on to compose several more overtly political pieces (*I've Got the Tune*, 1937; *No for an Answer*, 1941), eventually turned his attention to the commercial stage and its broader audience. Yet even there he sought to expand the scope of musical theater, refashioning legitimate dramas of social conscience into haunting Broadway musical dramas, but without Broadway success (*Regina*, 1949; *Juno*, 1959). It was with a different kind of refashioning that Blitzstein was to receive his greatest recognition in the musical theater: his translation/adaptation of *The Threepenny Opera*. Yet that work no longer reflected the climate of the dissident theater of the 1930s, but rather that of the alternative theater of the 1950s which would become known as Off Broadway.

THE OFF BROADWAY RENAISSANCE

When Burns Mantle first used the term "Off Broadway" for the 1934–35 season in his annual summaries of the New York stage, he meant little more than a scattering of theatrical activities that were mostly semiprofessional and generally ignored by the press and the public. A discernible Off Broadway movement as such began only after the Second World War; and it was distinct from what had preceded it. The Art Theater movement had been a rebellion led by artists and intellectuals against the commercial theater. New Theater had been a rebellion against society led by theater professionals. Off Broadway saw young professionals rebelling against a theater system that gave them virtually no chance to work. Their revolt tended to be less purely artistic or social in motivation than professional; and their attitudes toward Broadway also more ambivalent.

Off Broadway described more than a postwar resurgence of

alternative theater in New York, with its epicenter still in Green-wich Village. (The bohemian ambience there continued to provide a cultural draw for offbeat plays, unknown talent, and adventurous audiences.) Off Broadway now established a more widespread and lasting alternative to Broadway than before, one conscious of itself as "Off Broadway" and effectively organized as a broad movement. A 1949 agreement concluded between Actors' Equity and five Green-wich Village theaters newly formed into an Off Broadway Theater League made the term legally precise in its application to geogra-phy and theater size. The contract granted professional status to Off Broadway, allowing Equity members to appear with nonunion members under certain conditions for the first time. It was valid everywhere except "in any theatre located in the area bounded by Fifth and Ninth Avenue, 56th and 34th Streets, in the City of New York." And it applied to theaters of no more than 299 seats. (Reor-ganized in 1959 as the League of Off Broadway Theaters and Pro-ducers [now The Off Broadway League], the League's contractual terms now apply "Off Broadway" to theaters of between 100 and 499 seats, some even located in the Broadway theater district.)

Recognition by Actors' Equity may have turned Off Broadway into a professional enterprise. But it could not confer the sense of legitimacy needed for Off Broadway to establish itself artistically as well. Such cultural recognition came in 1952, when Circle in the Square revived Tennessee Williams's *Summer and Smoke*, which had failed earlier on Broadway. Though a non-Broadway production, it was now covered by the *New York Times* and favorably reviewed by Brooks Atkinson:

> *When "Summer and Smoke" was put on at [Broadway's] Music Box in 1948 it looked a little detached, perhaps because the production was too intricate or because the theatre was too large. [Off Broadway's] Circle in the Square is an arena style playhouse for a small audience and a simple production, and "Summer and Smoke" comes alive in that environment.*

At the Music Box Theater, a standard Broadway house with a pro-scenium stage, the audience sat directly in front of the stage, which is the norm in all such theaters. Circle in the Square was housed in a former nightclub whose circular dance floor had been converted into a "thrust" stage with audiences surrounding the playing area on three sides. In this space, the straight crossings and diagonals that characterized the traditional blocking and movement of the proscenium stage would have proved stultifying. Director José Quintero replaced these with a more circular approach to staging that brought audiences into the play in a new way. "One of the direct legacies of Off-Broadway was the discovery that theatre could happen in unconventional spaces," said theater historian Gerald Berkowitz, "and Quintero's insights into how such spaces could reshape acting and production styles were seminal." Atkinson's review was also pivotal. The recognition of Quintero's work by theater officialdom legitimized Off Broadway for an informed set of theatergoers and with *Summer and Smoke* gave Off Broadway its first smash hit.

Over the next decade, Off Broadway became the concept now understood by the name. It meant performers exploring new acting methods and getting a professional start (Geraldine Page, Colleen Dewhurst, Jason Robards, James Earl Jones). It meant theater professionals of all kinds experimenting with unfamiliar production styles and rehearsal techniques (the Living Theater's production of *The Connection*, 1959; Gene Frankel's direction of *The Blacks*, 1961). It meant audiences discovering unusual new plays (Samuel Beckett's *Endgame*, 1958; Edward Albee's *The Zoo Story*, 1960) and recovering what had been lost or overlooked in older plays through new productions (O'Neill's *The Iceman Cometh*, 1956; Pirandello's *Six Characters in Search of an Author*, 1963). It meant professionals and audiences alike cultivating an alternative sensibility altogether for theater in New York.

A growing interest in the work of Bertolt Brecht led to several Off Broadway productions that encouraged a sense of cultural discovery and recovery all at once (the Experimental Theater's *Galileo*, 1947; the Phoenix Theater's *The Good Woman of Setzuan*, 1956; the Living Theater's *In the Jungle of Cities*, 1961; ANTA's *Brecht on Brecht*, 1962). Yet nothing called attention to Brecht's work in quite the way that *The Threepenny Opera* did—as much for musical reasons, however, as theatrical ones. Indeed, *The Threepenny Opera* would be to Off Broadway's musical theater what *Summer and Smoke* had been to the Off Broadway movement as a whole. More than that, the Off Broadway openings on successive nights in 1954 of *The Threepenny Opera* and *The Golden Apple* suggested, at least for the moment, that audiences might now have to look beyond Broadway entirely to find the best in musical theater in New York. Again Brooks Atkinson:

> *Only a few years ago the musical play was the most progressive art form in the uptown theatre. Nothing has collapsed with such dismal equanimity. . . . The brains, taste and inventiveness of the musical theatre have moved off-Broadway. . . . Off-Broadway houses are currently presenting the most talented and most original musical plays of the season. "The Threepenny Opera," by Kurt Weill and Bert Brecht, is taxing the seating capacity of the miniature Theatre de Lys in Christopher Street. "The Golden Apple," by John Latouche and Jerome Moross, has introduced the phenomenon of the perpendicular playgoer to the Phoenix Theatre in Second Avenue. . . . By now thousands of theatregoers have found their way safely to Second Avenue and Twelfth Street and gotten home again without losing either their dignity or their way.*

The success of *Threepenny* may have established the cultural validity of a major Off Broadway musical undertaking. But it did not establish the prototype of an "Off Broadway musical" comparable in any way to a Broadway one. The work was sui generis: It was simply the first of a number of memorable musicals whose importance involved an Off Broadway production or creation on Off Broadway's terms. Foremost among them were *The Threepenny Opera, The Golden Apple,* and *The Fantasticks* (1960).

Like *Summer and Smoke, The Threepenny Opera* was a breakthrough: a successful Off Broadway production of a stagework that had previously failed on Broadway. It achieved both critical and popular success in a way no theatergoer could mistake. *Threepenny* ran longer than any musical production up to that time, on Broadway or off. For some the idea of Off Broadway as a venue for a long-running musical hit was certainly bizarre. And even more so as the production spawned another Off Broadway first: a best-selling original cast album. Yet these may also have served to mollify the image of Greenwich Village as an inhospitable place for Broadway audiences, and thus to have helped alter the demographics of New York theater by contributing to the popularity and growth of Off Broadway itself. By 1961, when *Threepenny* closed, the number of Off Broadway theaters had increased from seven at the time of its opening to thirty-eight, and there were more productions of all kinds of plays Off Broadway than on.

What made *The Threepenny Opera* an "Off-Broadway musical" was more than just its location. It was different from the usual Broadway offerings in character, method, and intent: sardonic where they were cheerful, didactic where they aimed to entertain, shot through with a subversive streak where they rather upheld the status quo. Premiered in Berlin as *Die Dreigroschenoper* in 1928, it was the creation of poet-playwright Bertolt Brecht (1898–1956) and composer Kurt Weill. Brecht, a Marxist, and Weill, a Jew, were part of a migration of artists and intellectuals from Germany to America in the Nazi era, yet once in the United States, they had minimal contact with one another. Weill had a successful career in Broadway musicals, which Brecht vilified generically as "empty entertainment." (Brecht remarked, "the Broadway musical which, thanks to certain fiercely competing groups composed of speculators, popular stars, good scene designers, bad composers, witty if second-rate songwriters, inspired costumiers, and truly modern dance directors, has become the authentic expression of all that is American." It was not meant as praise.) Weill became an American citizen; Brecht did not. On the contrary, in 1947 Brecht appeared before the House Committee on Un-American Activities and returned shortly thereafter to what had become Communist East Berlin, unregenerate in his un-Americanism.

Ultimately, *Die Dreigroschenoper* was not really a musical at all but rather a kind of play-with-songs in the ballad opera tradition. Adapted directly from John Gay's *The Beggar's Opera*, it told essentially Gay's story of topsy-turvy morality centered on the criminal Macheath, his foul dealings in London's underworld, and his reprieve at the last minute at the gallows. But Brecht gave his parody of the eighteenth-century classic a twentieth-century twist. Where Gay's satire had originally been leveled at English politics, Brecht's was more broadly aimed as an anticapitalist critique of middle-class mores altogether. "The play," he said, "showed the close relationship between the emotional life of the bourgeois and that of the criminal world."

Right from the start, however, audiences were drawn to the work for its renegade appeal. *Dreigroschenoper* seemed to shock and please at the same time, if not actually to please by shocking. Instead of castigating those whose injustices were the targets of its criticism, its villains came across as enviable, and, said Elias Canetti, "everything was glorified that one would otherwise shamefully conceal." Moreover, Weill's score captured the contradiction in an original style that traded on the banalities of popular music while subverting them through unexpected dissonances, awkward phrases, and jazz-style orchestrations that were at once captivating and off-putting. The tension underlies the "Tango Ballad" duet between the whore Jenny and Macheath ("Zuhälterballade"), which speaks in the crudest of terms of Jenny's aborted pregnancy, even though Brecht considered it "the tenderest and most moving love-song in the play." Just what did Brecht mean by this? "The charm of the piece," as Weill put it, "rests precisely in the fact that a rather risqué text . . . is set to music in a gentle, pleasant way." Fraught with ambiguity, the number was often taken by audiences for the thing it seemed to satirize. It was emblematic of the whole.

This was no doubt contrary to Brecht's intentions. He had been developing a new dramaturgical form, epic theater, of which he saw *Dreigroschenoper* as the first successful demonstration. According to theater historian Jonas Barish, Brecht's epic theater presented "not a slice of life but an artfully composed fiction, designed to teach us certain momentous truths about our lives and to challenge us to change them." It was moral in purpose, didactic in method, and out to supplant "dramatic" theater by subverting the Aristotelian unities and the devices of theatrical illusion conducive for an audience so to abandon itself emotionally in a play as to miss its ideological content.

This subversion was to be accomplished through a "de-familiarizing" process Brecht called *Verfremdung*, sometimes translated as "distancing" or "alienation." Its most potent agent was the "Song" (Weill and Brecht both preferred the English term since it was free of the historically highbrow associations that clung to the German word *Lied*). Indeed, epic theater's "most striking innovation," he said, "lay in the strict separation of the music from all the other elements of entertainment offered." Unlike the integrated song ideal of the Romantic musical stage, epic theater songs were *not* to emerge from within the action or emotion of a play, but to stand outside it, as it were, often even commenting on it. Such songs, he elaborated, *were not organic consequences of the whole, but stood in contradiction to it; they broke up the flow of the play and its incidents, they prevented empathy, they acted as a cold douche for those whose sympathies were becoming involved. . . . The play [had] a double nature. Instruction and entertainment [were made to] conflict openly.*

The very titles of songs signaled their distance from the play. Depersonalized, factual, and descriptive, some *Dreigroschen* titles were generic ("Love Song," "Jealousy Duet"); others were specific but speculative ("On the Uncertainty of Human Conditions," "Ballad About the Question: 'What Keeps a Man Alive?'"). Even the staging of the songs was meant to disrupt any sense of sympathetic connection they might have to the play: lights flooded the stage whenever songs appeared, placards were lowered with the song titles on them, actors deliberately altered their delivery style from speech. Nonetheless, almost despite all the devices of *Verfremdung*, a song such as "Tango Ballad" was still strangely moving. And there were many others like it in the score.

All this was alien to the sensibility of the Broadway musical of the period: the intellectual energy, the emotional complexity, the moral underlay. So it is not surprising *The Threepenny Opera* failed dismally when it was first produced in English on Broadway in 1933. Moreover, Weill, who once in America discouraged performances of his European works, would not consider another production of the piece until he heard Marc Blitzstein's translation of the one song "Pirate Jenny" in 1950 and asked Blitzstein to go ahead with the rest. Blitzstein's adaptation, set in 1870s New York and completed after Weill's death, premiered in a concert version at Brandeis University led by Leonard Bernstein. It became the basis for the production that established the work on the English-speaking stage.

At least as important to *Threepenny*'s belated success in English was the Off Broadway setting. It allowed for novice producers like Carmen Capalbo and Stanley Chase to undertake the work, and to do so in a spirit of fidelity to the original. This was lacking in productions of *Threepenny* that had been proposed by Billy Rose, Roger Stevens, and other "big-name producers [who] either didn't understand it," in the estimation of Weill's widow, Lotte Lenya, "or thought they should

Lotte Lenya (Jenny) sings "Pirate Jenny" in the Greenwich Village production
of *The Threepenny Opera.*

rewrite it" to suit Broadway tastes. Thus the 299-seat Theatre de Lys
came to house a production in which

> *the open Brecht epic form carried its own commentary on the narrow,*
> *realistic, Ibsenesque psychological drama [that dominated Broad-*
> *way] of the 1940's and 1950's. The sets were nonrealistic. Entrances*
> *were made down the aisle. Actors occasionally addressed the audience*
> *directly from the thrust stage. Songs were sung straight out.*

In other respects, however, this *Threepenny* did not differ substantially from a Broadway production, with its attendant commercial
concerns. It was a professional undertaking that, by the authorita-

tive participation of Lenya kept in touch with the work's original performance style, then still largely unfamiliar on the American stage. (Lenya played the whore Jenny, the role she had created in 1928; for her performance she won a Tony Award—the only time Broadway conferred this honor on an Off Broadway performance.) The production was also commercially organized, capitalized by private investors at under $9,000—minuscule in Broadway terms; astronomical for Off Broadway—and with gross receipts totaling nearly $3 million. It even released an original-cast album just as if it were a Broadway show; and "The Ballad of Mack the Knife" became one of the biggest hit singles of the era, recorded by numerous pop and jazz vocalists from Bobby Darin to Louis Armstrong. As an enterprise, the *Threepenny* production thus pointed in a direction that Off Broadway itself was to take as it became "not so much an alternative to Broadway as an alternative version of it." Yet *Threepenny* proved that distinguished if controversial musicals not only could succeed without Broadway's elaborate production values, but that there was also a place Off Broadway to develop what was uniquely theirs.

A similar ambivalence marked the productions of the Phoenix Theater, formed by Norris Houghton and T. Edward Hambleton in 1953 as a nonprofit company offering noncommercial plays. But Phoenix's investment in the alternative theater movement was somewhat different: It was committed "to release actors, directors, playwrights and designers from the pressures forced on them by the hit-or-flop pattern of Broadway [and] to provide for the public a playhouse within the means of everyone." Over some two decades of activity it came to occupy, as Stuart Little put it,

> *an anomalous position somewhere between Broadway and off-Broadway in size, somewhere between New York and regional theater in sophistication, somewhere between the commercial and the art theater in audience appeal, [and] somewhere between the contemporary theater and the classic in the thrust of its programming.*

While its staple was spoken drama, the Phoenix occasionally produced new musicals whose scope mirrored the company's eclecticism. *Sandhog* (1954—book and lyrics: Waldo Salt; music: Earl Robinson), for example, was a stark, socially conscious musical play based on a Theodore Dreiser story about the men who risked their lives to build the first tunnel under the Hudson River in the 1880s. *Once Upon a Mattress* (1959—book: Jay Thompson, Marshall Barer, and Dean Fuller; lyrics: Barer; music: Mary Rodgers) was a musical spoof of "The Princess and the Pea" starring Carol Burnett, which in short order moved to Broadway. Culturally somewhere in between was Phoenix's most important musical undertaking, *The Golden Apple*. Though conceived for production on a Broadway scale, *Golden Apple* had been repeatedly turned down by commercial producers as being "too special for Broadway." As the show tried to say something knowing about American values by parodying *The Iliad* and *The Odyssey* in nonstop songs and dances, the producers were quite right—and the creators knew it. When one suggested, "You might say that it's a philosophical musical comedy," the other enjoined, "Oh, no, don't say that. Nobody'll come to see it." Nor were the two helped in their cause by their less than impressive Broadway credentials. Librettist-lyricist John Latouche (1917–1956) had written lyrics for everything from operettas to star-vehicle musical comedies without great success. Composer Jerome Moross (1913–1983) had written ballet music, film scores, and a symphony, but songs for only one Broadway revue: the infamous *Parade*. Yet *The Golden Apple* was one of the most original, witty, and affecting of all American musicals, and one which the Phoenix was uniquely positioned to produce.

The show took its narrative mostly from *The Odyssey*, using the episodes as a frame for a more modern story and theme but with overt Homeric parallels. Latouche elaborated:

> *I set out to tell the stories of Ulysses and Penelope, Paris and Helen, as they would have happened in America. It was to be no adaptation of Homeric grandeurs, but a comic reflection of classical influence on the way we think nowadays. Therefore any myths we might use were to arise out of our native songs, dances, jokes and ideas.*
>
> *For example, Ulysses was to be a veteran returning home to Penelope after a hitch in the Spanish-American War. Helen was to be a farmer's daughter, and Paris a traveling salesman.*

Out of the epic source material Latouche shaped a mock epic that was serious in theme: "Ulysses' search for a set of stable values in the frenetic process of change" as the United States entered the twentieth century. And "to bypass the heaviness that threatened such a theme, and to give it a general rather than a private meaning," he said, "we agreed to describe that search in terms of the popular songs and dances of the period—waltzes, ragtime, blues, vaudeville turns, etc." Thus, Ulysses's wanderings through the corrupting enticements of modern America became so many musical acts in a revue: Mayor Hector called on the citizens of his metropolis to undo Ulysses and his men in a soft-shoe number ("People Like You and Like Me"); the Sirens lured victims to their doom as hula girls in a Hawaiian dance ("Goona Goona Goona Lagoon"); Scylla and Charybdis, a pair of stock brokers, ruined those who took their advice in a comic routine modeled on the vaudeville team of Gallagher and Shean. However heavy the theme, its musical embodiment was light.

Similar pastiches of song types from the vernacular heritage of the musical stage served to turn Greek myths into bits of Americana throughout the show. And between these numbers, sung patter took the place of spoken dialogue. Everything in the show therefore was musi-calized, yet there was little about *The Golden Apple* that had the feel of a traditional opera. Instead, it seemed to use the forms of opera and ballet as vehicles for musical comedy, abandoning the sobriety associated with such genres for the sake of nonillusionist whimsy. A character like Paris, for example, fully danced his role throughout without so much as uttering a sound, while a prop like the figurehead on Ulysses's ship actually came to life and sang. Songs, too, often exhibited a playful-ness that kept them emotionally apart from the action even as they, in point of fact, served it. This held true whether such songs were meant to provoke thought, as in Ulysses's limerick recounting of the Spanish-American War:

> *Wherever we went they loved us*
> *So dazzled were they with our charms*
> *The folks in them lands*
> *Ate right out of our hands*
> *But why did they chew off the arms?*

"It Was a Glad Adventure"
(*The Golden Apple*)

or to appeal to the senses, as in Helen's lyrical seduction of Paris:

> *It's a lazy afternoon*
> *And the beetle bugs are zoomin*
> *And the tulip trees are bloomin*
> *And there's not another human*
> > *In view*
> > *But us two.*

"Lazy Afternoon" (*The Golden Apple*)

The Golden Apple was an original attempt to reconcile opera's musical continuity and seriousness of theme with the comedic spirit and performance traditions of the popular musical stage. It was perhaps too original in its mix of genres to become a popular success. While it garnered critical acclaim, including the New York Drama Critics' Circle Award, a commercial run on Broadway following its Off Broadway premiere proved disappointing. It seemed that *Golden Apple* needed the conditions characteristic of both environments to thrive. For if its special kind of originality marked the work as Off Broadway in spirit, the kind of production required to do it justice was very much *of* Broadway: ten principal parts cast by legitimate voice type, a singing chorus, a dancing chorus, a twenty-piece orchestra, and six full stage sets. *On* Broadway the work seemed to belong *Off*; and vice versa.

With a seating capacity of twelve hundred, the Phoenix was surely the largest of Off Broadway's theaters. Its size served to raise Broadway expectations even though a musical was more apt to succeed Off Broadway by developing a small production style that appeared as an outgrowth of a performance rather than a limitation placed on it. Many Off Broadway musicals based their success on production styles that delighted audiences by purposefully subverting Broadway norms. Revivals, pastiches, and retrospective revues all thrived in modest Off Broadway productions, and even new musicals were winningly tailored to the diminished conditions of Off Broadway. A version of *Leave It to Jane* (1959), for example, "revived" the Bolton-Wodehouse-Kern hit of 1917 with such intimacy, charm, and freshness as to spark further Off roadway mountings of musical comedy classics (*Oh, Kay!* 1926/rev. 1960; *Anything Goes*, 1934/rev. 1962; *The Boys from Syracuse*, 1938/rev.

1963). An Off Broadway revival of *The Boy Friend* (1958), a 1953 British parody of 1920s musical comedies, inspired the creation of other full-length pastiches Off Broadway that affectionately miniaturized what had once been larger-than-life entertainments (*Little Mary Sunshine*, 1959: 1920s operettas; *Dames at Sea*, 1968: 1930s Hollywood musicals; *Grease*, 1972: 1950s rock 'n' roll movies). *A Party with Comden and Green* (1958), a performed "portfolio" of the partners' own material, led to more Off Broadway cabaret-style revues that entertained with overviews of the output of other songwriters (*The World of Kurt Weill*, 1963; *The Decline and Fall of the Entire World as Seen Through the Eyes of Cole Porter*, 1965; *Jacques Brel Is Alive and Well and Living in Paris*, 1968). And even Off Broadway musicals that were newly written scored their biggest successes in terms of the modest production styles through which they were created (*You're a Good Man, Charlie Brown*, 1967; *Your Own Thing*, 1968; *Godspell*, 1971). The earliest successful example of the trend among new shows was *The Fantasticks*, and it proved so successful it became the longest-running theatrical production in the history of the American stage.

But *The Fantasticks* was never meant to be small. On the contrary, the pair of unknown and inexperienced writers who created it, librettist Tom Jones (b. 1928) and composer Harvey Schmidt (b. 1929), had set out to convert a charming nineteenth-century French play, *Les Romanesques*, into a full-scale Broadway show by working in the grand style of Rodgers and Hammerstein, with a cast of forty-five and, as Schmidt put it, "a Rudolf Friml–type chorus." After years of work on it, the project had gotten nowhere: It kept collapsing under its own weight. Only the chance to see their musical produced as a one-acter under the drastically reduced conditions of a summer theater at Barnard College in New York prompted the writers to rethink the material from an entirely different angle. "It was suddenly fun, after working on it so big," Schmidt recalled, "to do it as tiny as we could." Together with director Word Baker (1923–1995), they began whittling their show down to the bare essentials that ultimately made for its success.

In its finished form, *The Fantasticks* was launched at Off Broadway's Sullivan Street Playhouse, an arena-style theater with a closer than intimate playing space and a seating capacity of about 150. Schmidt later acknowledged,

The original company of *The Fantasticks*, l. to r.: Jerry Orbach (El Gallo, the Narrator), Rita Gardner (Luisa), Kenneth Nelson (Matt), George Curley (Mortimer, in top hat), Hugh Thomas (Bellamy), and William Larson (Hucklebee).

A lot of what is now considered to be the "style" of The Fantasticks *had to do with the limitations of that theater. We didn't want that theater. It was the only one we could get, and although the show was already leaning in a certain direction, the restrictions of the space carried it even further.*

Shrinking to the dimensions of its non-Broadway home, *Fantasticks* undertook what no standard Broadway show would have brooked: a theater style out of a minimum of production values. "We decided to have the little play," Jones recalled,

> *acted out on a simple platform stage by a small band of actors in the manner of a commedia dell'arte troupe. More than that, we decided to make our musical a celebration of the presentational stage devices which were, at that time, almost totally absent from the American the-atre. We decided to have a Narrator who could speak directly to the audience, setting the scenes and explaining the story and moving us forward whenever necessary, dispensing with the "realistic" exposi-tion and time-consuming realism of the modern stage. We decided to utilize the "Invisible" Prop Man from the Chinese theatre to assist in creating scenic effects by such simple suggestions as holding up a cardboard moon or sprinkling confetti to evoke the image of rain or snow. We decided to keep the musicians in full view. We decided to have direct address to the audience. And we decided to have the whole thing written in verse. In other words, our concept was to put actors on a simple platform and, with the use of presentational stage devices* and the imagination of the audience, *to see if we could tell a story of growing up that would touch people.*

The show now featured a cast of nine (later eight) on a platform and a bare stage with no proscenium to separate spectators from the players. Audiences were asked to conspire with the actors by using the mind's eye to transform what was not present onstage (but suggested) into what was. In the absence of any scenery, they were encouraged to develop a sense of double vision: to take the contents of a prop box both for the props they were and for the make-believe items the actors indi-cated them to be—a stick for a wall; a cardboard circle for the moon; confetti (if white) for rain, (if green) for a forest, and (if multicolored) for the magic of the transformation process itself that descended on the house during the overture with the first throwing.

The show called upon the mind's ear, too. Where Broadway musi-cals were apt to overwhelm audiences with belted songs and brassy orchestrations, *The Fantasticks* was low key. It had only a piano and a harp for an orchestra, and its songs rather tended to beckon ("Soon It's Gonna Rain," "They Were You"). "Try to Remember," for example, sung by the Narrator (Jerry Orbach), invited "the audience back to a more romantic time" to the lilt of a waltz with circular chord progressions and a melody of folklike simplicity. "The proper words and music," said Jones, "can evoke a spectacle in the mind that's so much more satisfying than anything the most skillful scenic designer could possibly devise."

Cast entirely with unknown performers, *The Fantasticks* are two rebellious adolescents, Luisa (Rita Gardner) and Matt (Kenneth Nelson), who live in a world of fantasy and whose love for one another thrives on the apparent opposition of their fathers to it. In secret, however, the fathers have actually prearranged their children's marriage and built a wall to keep them apart, applying reverse psychology to get Luisa and Matt to want what the fathers want them to want ("children, I guess, must get their own way/The minute that you say no"). Yet after Luisa and Matt are finally united and they learn the truth about their parents' collusion, the pain of disillusion sets in, their love withers, and they part. Only with the onset of genuine adversity does their love blossom anew, and the two eventually find their separate ways toward some sense of maturity, and each other.

A fable about the fear of growing up and leaving home, the show is presented, as one critic decried, "without irony or reflectiveness, without a sense of history or of contemporary life, as though the fable embodies a set of timeless values." Yet a large part of its appeal lies in its whimsical universality, its very fabulousness, the indulgence in fantasy that makes "fantastics" not only of its lovers but of its audience as well—any audience. Without establishing a clear sense of time or place or even meaning, *The Fantasticks* leaves more to the imagination than it gives, turning its theme about the nature of illusion and reality into the method for staging the show. The effect is fragile and not easily duplicated in a theater lacking the physical intimacy of the Playhouse on Sullivan Street where *Fantasticks* wove its spell for forty-two years (its longevity immeasurably boosted by such factors as a small cast, low operating costs, and a 150-seat capacity). Yet while the show's creators wisely resisted efforts to move the original production to larger quarters, the show has succeeded in other venues over the years: some

200 professional productions in the United States and Canada alone; nearly 7,000 amateur ones; a 1964 TV special with Bert Lahr and Stanley Holloway as the fathers; and foreign productions in Latin America, Europe, Africa, and Asia—even in a 3,500-seat theater in the People's Republic of China. Simple to produce and universal in appeal, *The Fantasticks* proved to be "the first truly international American musical, playing in countries that still hadn't seen *Oklahoma!*"

The Fantasticks was small in every way. Its inordinate success helped establish the viability of small musicals much as it helped establish Off Broadway itself as a privileged place for their production. Off Broadway subsequently became a haven for the creation of small musicals, chamber musicals, and mini-musicals of all kinds. These were not always less broadly extroverted in character than their Broadway counterparts, as *The Fantasticks* was, but they were physically reduced in ways that often furthered innovation. Small casts, for example (*You're a Good Man, Charlie Brown*: six; *Dames at Sea*: seven), might function in unusual ways: all principals (*Your Own Thing*; *Dames at Sea*), all chorus (*Hair*; *Godspell*), or a combination of the two.

Many such shows eventually moved to Broadway with resounding success. And Broadway even produced relatively modest musicals of its own: some of an introverted bent with a minimum of dance and spectacle (*She Loves Me*; 1776); some with severely reduced casts (*Stop the World—I Want to Get Off*; *I Do! I Do!*, with only two: Mary Martin and Robert Preston). There were even times during the 1960s when the Broadway and Off Broadway theaters began to resemble one another. Broadway featured the new work of performers, directors, and writers whose careers had been launched or first succeeded Off Broadway. Schmidt and Jones themselves went on from *The Fantasticks* to write for Broadway—even David Merrick productions (*110 in the Shade*, 1963; *I Do! I Do!*, 1966)—though their approach seemed more at home in the Off Broadway milieu to which they subsequently returned (*Colette*, 1970; *Philemon*, 1975). And Off Broadway became a victim of its own success, having now to deal with economic and professional pressures that tended to drive up costs and alter the scope and expectations of its very enterprise: to limit the bold experimentation and spontaneity, the feeling of being "in" on something new and different that had been so much part of its raison d'être.

FARTHER "OFF" AND COMING BACK

"Off Broadway was originally established as an alternative theatre for serious works of art," wrote Robert Brustein in the early 1960s. Thus, he went on, "the accumulation of musicals in the minority theatre is a depressing sign of commercial accommodation." Blanket scorn for musicals was nothing new among intellectuals; what was new was the Off Broadway setting. Yet Off Broadway musicals only tended to reflect the development of Off Broadway itself. There was a distinction, for example, between the aesthetic project of a *Sandhog* or a *Golden Apple* earlier in the 1950s and the newfound commercial appeal in such spoofs as *Once Upon a Mattress* and *Little Mary Sunshine* later in the decade. Moreover, musicals made up but a fraction of the Off Broadway scene that was Brustein's real concern. By the 1960s, in the face of spiraling costs and mounting commercial pressures, Greenwich Village producers across the board had grown artistically cautious. "Off Broadway is turning into a conservative institution," Brustein lamented:

> *The rise in ticket prices and production costs, the employment of high-salaried actors from the commercial stage, the burgeoning of new high-rent theatres, the marked increase in press-agentry and advertising—all these tokens, along with a general decline in the quality of Off Broadway fare, suggest that powerful economic pressures are putting the squeeze on Off Broadway's aesthetic freedom.*

Two new developments in particular rose to challenge Off Broadway at the forefront of the search for alternative theater in America: the expansion of organized regional theater across the United States and the rise of an Off-Off Broadway movement in New York. Neither was musical in focus. Yet both inevitably produced new musicals, some even to leave a mark on the national culture by means of substantial runs that they would eventually enjoy, of all places, *on* Broadway. Indeed, the establishment of a more ambiguous and even mutual relationship between Broadway and non-Broadway theater rather than an adversarial one became a major factor in producing musicals in the 1970s. Perhaps nothing called attention to this so dramatically as the arrival on Broadway in the watershed year of 1968 of both *Man of La Man-*

cha (originally from Connecticut's Goodspeed Opera House) and *Hair* (originally from the New York Shakespeare Festival).

With the regional movement, the decentralizing spirit of Off Broadway in the postwar era took off from New York altogether to establish community-based, professional, nonprofit theater companies throughout the United States. Most regional companies began as amateur groups intent on producing classic plays and contemporary dramas. They became professional as their performers signed union contracts with Actors' Equity. And they acquired nonprofit status by organizing themselves financially so that any net earnings were not distributed among shareholders but were returned to the companies to be used for the purposes for which they were established. There was no requirement that "nonprofits" actually had to lose money, though most did. They had to supplement subscriptions with outside financial support, which they received on a national scale starting in the late 1950s in private grants, principally from the Ford and Rockefeller Foundations, and after 1966 also in public funds allocated by Congress through its creation of the National Endowment for the Arts.

These companies, growing out of local conditions and serving mainly local needs, came to be known as regional or resident theaters. "I prefer the word resident to regional because this system was originally intended as an alternative to Broadway, not as a provincial tributary," wrote Brustein, who became founding director of a major resident company in 1979, the American Repertory Theater in Cambridge, Massachusetts.

> *This movement wished to decentralize American theater in the belief that it was unhealthy to originate so much stage activity in one cultural capital (New York). It sought partial subsidy in an effort to free the theater from undue dependence on the timidity of the box office. And it wished to consolidate itself out of a conviction that permanent ensembles of actors, directors, designers and administrative staff, preserving the classical repertory and developing new plays, created a potentially more enduring theatrical art than pickup casts assembled for a single show and dominated by star personalities. . . .*
>
> *Perhaps its most radical idea was that theater could develop the talents of artists and the imagination of audiences, not just be a source of profit and deals for backers, producers and agents.*

The impetus for the development grew largely out of the work of Margo Jones, the visionary director who founded America's first resident nonprofit professional repertory theater in Dallas (Theater '47, 1947) and whose 1951 book advocating arena staging, *Theatre-in-the-Round*, became a virtual bible for the movement. Directors in other cities followed with similar companies of their own: Nina Vance in Houston (Alley Theater, 1947), Zelda Fichandler in Washington (Arena Stage, 1950), Herbert Blau and Jules Irving in San Francisco (Actors' Workshop, 1952). Then in the 1960s, these scattered developments began to coalesce into a full-fledged movement. Landmarks in this development included the establishment in 1961 of Theater Communications Group, a national service organization to promote not-for-profit professional theater in America; the founding in 1963 of the Guthrie Theater in Minneapolis, the sole major resident theater actually to choose its city rather than to have evolved out of one; and the forming in 1965 of the League of Resident Theaters (LORT), a trade organization to negotiate contracts between nonprofit regional companies and the Actors' Equity Association.

Resident musical theaters, by contrast, were somewhat different in spirit. They had established themselves earlier in the form of repertory companies offering limited engagements of classic operettas and related musical stageworks. The most famous of those that are still in operation are the St. Louis Municipal Opera (opened in 1919 with *Robin Hood*) and the Los Angeles and San Francisco Civic Light Operas (opened in 1938 with *Blossom Time*). While these companies have specialized in operetta revivals, they have not neglected to develop new musicals as well. The Civic Light Opera originated a number of musicals of note—some of which went on to Broadway (the Mark Charlap–Carolyn Leigh, Styne-Comden-and-Green *Peter Pan*, 1954; several collaborations of Robert Wright and George Forrest: *Song of Norway*, 1944; *Kismet*, 1953; *At the Grand*, 1958/rev. *Grand Hotel*, 1989), others of which did not make the journey (*Zenda*, 1963, with a Vernon Duke–Martin Charnin score; Meredith Willson's *1491*, 1969; Stephen Schwartz's *The Baker's Wife*, 1976).

The opening of the Goodspeed Opera House in East Haddam, Connecticut, in 1963 gave a major boost to professional nonprofit resident repertory companies more interested in mounting musicals than operettas. Set in a restored Victorian building, "the theatre itself is a band-box," as Dale Wasserman described it, "the seats arranged squarely around a nearly wingless stage. Patrons sitting on the sides must twist around to see the performance. It's worth it, for the sound is crystal-line and the intimacy inspiring." Goodspeed, which opened with a new production of the Princess Theater classic *Oh, Lady! Lady!!,* claimed to be "the only theatre in America entirely dedicated to the preservation of the heritage of the American musical and the development of new works to add to the repertoire." It has produced well over one hundred American musicals since then, both revivals of vintage shows (*Very Good Eddie,* 1915/rev. 1975; *Going Up,* 1917/rev. 1976; *Whoopee,* 1928/rev. 1979) and premieres of new works (*Man of La Mancha,* 1964; *Shenandoah,* 1974; *Annie,* 1976). All six of these productions transferred to Broadway, part of a growing trend toward regional-to-Broadway transfers in the 1970s. Even resident companies not particularly partial to musical theater developed new "Broadway" shows: the Guthrie Theater (*Cyrano,* 1973); the Arena Stage (*Raisin,* 1973); even Brustein's own American Repertory Theater (*Big River,* 1984). Broadway, once virtually the sole source of new musicals, now often took on the aspect of a showcase for musicals originating elsewhere.

The fact that a musical originated in a resident theater, then, did not necessarily say much about the kind of show it was. It was not unusual for nonprofit companies to develop new musicals with an eventual Broadway run in mind. Nor was it uncommon for commercial producers to turn regional productions into out-of-town tryouts for New York. Above all, it was not clear what, if anything, distinguished a regional musical from the Broadway kind—other than economics. Yet for a variety of reasons, many such musicals were not typical Broadway shows. *Raisin* hewed closely to Lorraine Hansberry's *A Raisin in the Sun,* addressing questions of African American identity and ambition whose answers were not flattering to a Broadway audience. *Big River* brought *Huckleberry Finn* to life on the stage through a range of country music styles appropriate to the subject but strange-sounding in a Broadway house. *Man of La Mancha* presented interlocking stories of Cervantes and Don Quixote by means of a theatricalism designed for a thrust stage rather than a Broadway proscenium. Such shows were all atypical; but each in a different way. Taken as a group, there was nothing consistently "regional" about them save for their provenance.

Man of La Mancha was the first musical to originate at the Goodspeed Opera House, the creation mostly of musical theater novices: librettist Dale Wasserman (1914–2008), lyricist Joe Darion (1911–2001), and composer Mitch Leigh (b. 1928). It was also the first Goodspeed production to transfer to New York, where it played at the ANTA Washington Square Theater in Greenwich Village. "This is an all-Broadway production with an all-Broadway cast," a critic remarked, "and it is [not on Broadway] for one reason only—it had to have a thrust stage and the ANTA was the only such theater available." He may have put the cart before the horse. As Dale Wasserman remembered it:

> On Broadway there was no theatre available for an oddball musical with a production budget of $200,000, which is why, in desperation, we accepted an equally oddball theatre that was available only because no one wanted it. . . . There were good reasons no one wanted it. More of a shed than a theatre, it had no proscenium. No curtain. No flyloft. No provision for scenery and no proper stage. Nor was there an orchestra pit; forced to improvise, we split our orchestra (as we'd done in East Haddam) into two units, stashed in the wings 50 feet apart, an arrangement that drove the conductor dangerously close to a mental breakdown but later garnered praise for the production's "stereophonic effects."

The net effect was a practical imperative to approach the musical stage in new ways. Theater critic Martin Gottfried summarized some of them:

> Scenery is ruled out, and so is absolute realism. Choreography must be in patterns viewable from all angles. And most seriously, the structure of the book must be designed so that the drama is played for depth rather than width. The great problem is that there is no tradition from which to have learned. It is all new ground.

Making a virtue of necessity, set and lighting designer Howard Bay (1912–1986) and director Albert Marre (b. 1925) came up with inventive ways of telling the story of *Man of La Mancha* in terms of a thrust-stage unit set. The show told two interrelated stories. The first, historical and grimly realistic, dealt with sixteenth-century author

Howard Bay's dramatic set design for *Man of La Mancha* calls attention to the movable drawbridge and the arena-style stage.

Miguel de Cervantes and the terror of his imprisonment and impending trial before the Spanish Inquisition. It took place on a dimly lit stage with an enormous drawbridge lowered into the prison as new prisoners entered to await trial and old ones left to face it. The second story, fantastical and hopeful, revolved around Don Quixote, a visionary character of Cervantes's invention whose exploits the author enacted before his fellow prisoners. This was more brightly lit, more given to lively movement, and more open, to allow the prisoners as well to take part in enacting Don Quixote's adventures. The title *Man of La Mancha* then referred to Cervantes *and* Quixote (both played by Richard Kiley); and the musical unfolded by juxtaposing the "real" story of the first, which was not sung, and the "imagined" story of the second, which was. In order not to break the spell created by balancing the one against the other, moreover, the whole thing was performed—in defiance of Broadway norms—without an intermission.

This was no musical play in the traditional sense. While it dealt with one of the canonical texts of Western literature, *El ingenioso hidalgo Don Quixote de la Mancha*, it was less a musical dramatization *of* than *about* Cervantes's novel. Unlike *Oliver!*—an adaptation of *Oliver Twist* with Dickens nowhere in sight—*Man of La Mancha* dramatized the relationship between the author and his fictional alter ego to get at a meaning that had to do with the need for idealism in the face of a brutish reality. Wasserman summed it up in words: "illusion as man's strongest spiritual need, the most meaningful function of his imagination." The production staff went him one better, going beyond the power of words to theatricalize the meaning in terms of the limitations of their "oddball theatre." As the contrast between the darkness of reality and the light of imagination played out on the same unit set, the audience's imagination needed to soar along with Cervantes's as the one was unforgettably transformed into the other:

> *The suspended stage platform, jutting out into the banked, semi-circular auditorium, was tilted toward the audience. Behind it towered a huge staircase suspended whenever necessary to provide a link between the outer world and the dungeon into which Cervantes and his servant have been thrown. . . . The transformation of Cervantes into Don Quixote and his servant into Sancho Panza was done simply with makeup kits in full view of the audience, and their subsequent horseback ride was accomplished on two wooden frames attached to two dancers wearing horse head masks.*

In the cultural climate of the 1960s, the musical's message found resonance. "They're not just watching a play," said Marre of *Man of La*

Mancha's audiences, "they're having a religious experience." Even those who never saw the show could not have escaped its reach, for its musical centerpiece, "The Quest" (often called "The Impossible Dream"), was virtually everywhere to be heard. The song was among the last of American theater songs to permeate America's popular culture. As an inspirational number adaptable to almost any occasion (and with no lack of causes to be taken up in the 1960s), it caught the spirit of self-righteous idealism abroad in the land.

> *To dream the impossible dream,*
> *To fight the unbeatable foe,*
> *To bear with unbearable sorrow,*
> *To run where the brave dare not go . . .*
>
> *This is my Quest, to follow that star,*
> *No matter how hopeless, no matter how far,*
> *To fight for the right without question or pause,*
> *To be willing to march into hell for a heavenly cause!*
> *And I know, if I'll only be true to this glorious quest,*
> *That my heart will lie peaceful and calm when I'm laid to my rest . . .*
>
> "THE QUEST," JOE DARION (*MAN OF LA MANCHA*)

Compare this lyric, however, with one that it replaced. The earlier version was written by poet W. H. Auden—improbable as it seems, the original "lyricist" for the show.

> *Once the voice has quietly spoken, every knight must ride alone*
> *On the quest appointed him into the unknown*
> *One to seek the healing waters, one the dark tower to assail,*
> *One to find the lost princess, one to find the grail . . .*
>
> *Though I miss my goal and perish, unmarked in the wilderness,*
> *May my courage be the more, as my hope grows less.*
> *No man can command his future; maybe, I am doomed to fail;*
> *Others will come after me till the right prevail.*
>
> "SONG OF THE QUEST," W. H. AUDEN
> (UNUSED IN *MAN OF LA MANCHA*)

Both "Quest" lyrics responded to Wasserman's notes of intention for a motto song for Don Quixote. The original went in for poetry unleavened by the dictates of popular song; the replacement went in for lyrics unleavened by the unpredictable turns of poetry. Great theater songs generally strike a balance between these two tones. What was troubling here was the purity of each lyric: a sign of the widening gap between pop and literate cultures that a powerful strain in postwar show writing had tried to hold together.

Broadway culture found itself in a state of transition in the mid-1960s. The direction of shows to come may not yet have been clear, though the defining emphasis on production values in *Man of La Mancha* was indicative. Moreover, such powerful figures as Gower Champion in *Hello, Dolly!*, Bob Fosse in *Sweet Charity*, and Harold Prince in *Cabaret* were already working toward a new ideal in which stage directors would assume the creative authority previously held by writers. With an erosion in literate sensibility taking place, even the best Broadway showmakers no longer seemed convinced that their work should be approached, in Brooks Atkinson's telling phrase, "as if it were a form of literature." In some quarters the feeling went further: a loss of faith in even the value of literate culture. This appeared pervasive, in fact, not so much in the Broadway theater at the time but in the theater now being called Off-Off Broadway.

Named, it is said, in 1960 by critic Jerry Tallmer of the *Village Voice*, Off-Off Broadway grew out of Off Broadway as a kind of second-generation alternative theater movement in New York. The term "Off-Off Broadway" reflected the activism and the irony of those who saw Off Broadway now becoming more and more a Broadway-like institution. In its artistic daring and shoestring economics, the new development resembled Off Broadway in its youth a decade earlier. But it also differed in several key respects, not the least being the blanket disdain with which it held middle-class institutions and values and stigmatized them as "The Establishment." As William Goldman contrasted the two in his 1969 book *The Season*,

> *Off-Broadway tended to be traditional: Broadway for a highly selective audience. Off-off is revolutionary; it wants to change theatre from a spectator sport to almost a participation sport. Off-Broadway was basically European: Genet, Chekhov, Brecht were the real strength of*

the operation; off-off is totally and completely American, in style, con-
tent, you name it. Off-Broadway was serious and solemn; off-off is
serious and basically comic in outlook. Off-Broadway was primar-
ily revivals; off-off, and this is crucial, is new plays, mostly short, by
American writers. And finally, if one can really generalize and say
that the acting style of off-Broadway was basically [the Stanislavski]
Method, then the acting style of off-off is basically improvisational.

For Actors' Equity, however, the real distinctions were legal and
contractual. Off-Off Broadway performances consisted mostly of
"showcases"—basically "self-subsidized auditions"—that were governed by Showcase Codes permitting actors to appear without sal-
ary in noncontractual theaters of not more than ninety-nine seats.
In truth, Off-Off Broadway took place wherever necessity dictated or
convenience allowed: in playhouses, to be sure, but also coffeehouses,
churches, and lofts. Coffeehouse Caffe Cino, the cradle of the movement, provided the first home of *Dames at Sea* (1966), a spoof of the
Gold Diggers movies, starring a then unknown Bernadette Peters. Judson Memorial Church housed the Judson Poets' Theater, where Rev.
Al Carmines (1936–2005) mixed the pulpit and the stage to create a
new genre of "wickedly delightful and loose-jointed" chamber musicals,
including *Home Movies* (1964), *In Circles* (1967), *Promenade* (1965/rev.
1969), and *The Faggot* (1973). A loft served as the venue for Café La
MaMa (later, La MaMa Experimental Theater Club), which was run by
the indefatigable Ellen Stewart (b. 1920) and became the most fecund
artistic center of the movement. La MaMa nurtured such diverse talents as Tom O'Horgan (director of *Hair*), Elizabeth Swados (composer
of *Runaways*), and author John-Michael Tebelak, whose *Godspell* (1971)
La MaMa first produced in New York—before Stephen Schwartz's
songs transformed the piece into a full-fledged musical.

Some Off-Off Broadway companies sought to develop new forms of
theater to attain new levels of consciousness among audiences and performers. To that end several questioned textual authority and the primacy of scripts in the playmaking process. The Living Theater and the
Open Theater, for example, put their faith in a workshop approach that
relied on group improvisation and the collective input of all involved to
create theatricalized experiences rather than fixed works as such. "De-
emphasis of text, exploration of nonverbal and nonrational communi-

"Runyonland"
Designer Jo Mielziner's rendering of his backdrop for the opening scene of *Guys and Dolls* (1950).

"The Dance at the Gym" from *West Side Story* (1957).

"Willkommen, bienvenue, welcome" to the Kit Kat Klub in *Cabaret* (1966).

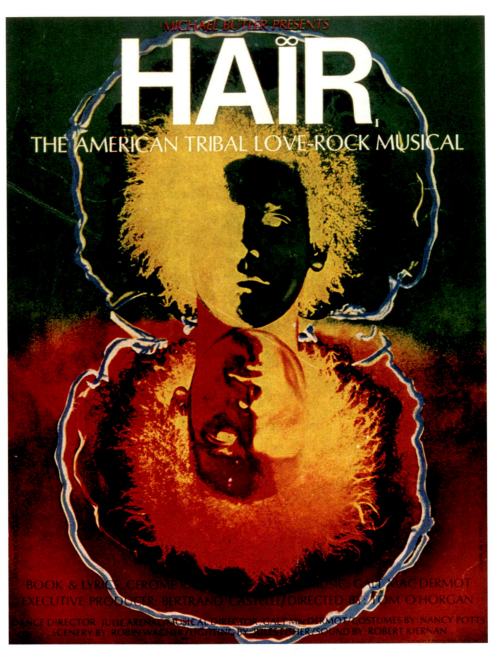

Poster for *Hair* ablaze in psychedelic colors (1968).

Costumes for *Chicago*'s female chorus—from page to stage: (*above*) as sketched by designer Patricia Zipprodt; (*below*) as worn by Bob Fosse's dancers (1975).

Seurat freezes his finished painting as a *tableau vivant* in the act 1
finale of *Sunday in the Park with George* (1984).

Gondola ride on a candlelit lagoon beneath the Paris Opera House in *The Phantom of the Opera* (1988).

The cast of *Rent* celebrates "La Vie Boheme" (1996).

cation, attempts to break down the barriers between play and audience, and open utilization of the technology and artifice of theatre"—all characterized the work of these groups. Out of the hotbed of such Off-Off Broadway activity *Hair* emerged.

As a generation of post–World War II baby boomers grew to maturity in the late 1960s, it formed a youth culture aware of itself as such and of the power that its sheer numbers represented. The boomers' identification with a lifestyle distinct from, often even opposed to that of their parents fueled much of the social turbulence of the period. Many of the young embraced the hedonism of drugs and the mores of the sexual revolution. At the same time many devoted themselves to social and political causes, promoting civil rights at home, protesting the war in Vietnam. *Hair* began in the Open Theater's Workshop, the conception of two actors who, if not exactly part of the under-thirty generation, were at least close to it in spirit: Gerome Ragni (1935–1991) and James Rado (b. 1932). They hoped to capture the unfettered energy of the youth movement in copious sketches they wrote for their show and in lyrics to songs for which composer Galt MacDermot (b. 1928) eventually wrote the music. Their title referred to the hippie counterculture for which long hair, on males especially, represented a transgressive badge of membership since short hair was the social norm.

Producer Joseph Papp was looking for plays that, he said, "have some passionate statement to make that is commensurate with the times we are living in," and he chose *Hair* for the inaugural production in 1967 of his New York Shakespeare Festival in its new home at the Public Theater in lower Manhattan's East Village. Gerald Freedman, the theater's artistic director, however, was "taken aback by the lack of form and lack of credible writing ability. It had practically no scenes or anything you could call an event. It had so many musical numbers that you couldn't separate out what you wanted the audience to remember. And they kept bringing in rewrites every day." In Freedman's hands, the material took shape as a modest antiwar musical focused on an East Village hippie who has been drafted, spends his last hours as a civilian with his friends, and ultimately goes off to fight and presumably die in Vietnam.

Hair met with an enthusiastic response at the Public Theater. But as it had been booked for a limited engagement with other produc-

Hair, The American Tribal Love-Rock Musical on Broadway, foreground l. to r.: Steve Gamet (Member of the Tribe), Steve Curry (Woof, "59"), Shelley Plimpton (Crissy, on mattress), and Hiram Keller (Member of the Tribe).

tions scheduled to follow, it had to close after eight weeks. It next made a brief appearance at a discotheque; and subsequently reappeared at the Biltmore Theater—on Broadway. Unlike *Man of La Mancha*, which had relocated to a Broadway house the month before with some minor adjustments to suit the new proscenium setting, *Hair* had been thoroughly overhauled for the occasion: rewritten, recast, restaffed, and restaged. Chiefly responsible for the change was La MaMa director Tom O'Horgan (1924–2009). He used the production, or so it seemed, to violate as many of the norms of Broadway showmaking as he could. He threw out the old script and any sense of plot, which he replaced with a near-continuous sequence of musical numbers. These he staged inventively—sometimes shockingly—bringing the modes of Off-Off Broadway experimentation to Broadway and sensationalizing them. The in-your-face performance environment with actors mingling with the audience; the anti-illusionist devices, such as performers using hand-held microphones when they sang; the free flow of profanity throughout, and, in an infamous moment at the end of the first act, full frontal nudity— all served to assault establishment senses and sensibilities. Freedman thought O'Horgan had turned *Hair* into a "freak show"; and when Robert Brustein called O'Horgan "the Busby Berkeley of Off Off-Broadway," he did not mean it as a compliment. In a real sense *Hair* had been turned inside out. The hippies "at the Public were hippies because they opposed the war. At the Biltmore, they opposed the war because they were hippies." But the new production seemed so innocent and like such a breath of fresh air on Broadway that audiences there, and then audiences everywhere, simply could not get enough.

On Broadway, *Hair* made a necessary connection between the unconventional hippie lifestyle that had become its subject and the unconventional theater forms of Off-Off Broadway. This "American Tribal Love-Rock Musical" was now performed as if it were improvised, so the authors fittingly called their book a "non-book" (and critics in the same spirit referred to the dances as "non-dances"). Without a book and without dances, as one of the cast put it, "the music said it all." While the music seemed fresh and ingratiating, it "said it all" in a rock idiom, a clear departure from the traditional musical language of Broadway. For rock was the popular music of the youth movement. Its lyrics favored counterculture values and challenged establishment stands on issues of the day. Its music—typically loud (electric amplification), raw (metallic timbres), and unrelenting (fast, driving rhythms)— drove a stylistic wedge between generations. Broadway partisans decried it as a music whose stylistic inflexibility made it inherently "non-theatrical"—though, in truth, it was a music that redefined theatricality on its own terms.

Unbeholden to the structure of a book and loosed from the stylistic moorings of conventional show music, *Hair*'s songs were not the usual theater songs. Their subjects reflected a spectrum of themes mostly ignored by musicals, from the cosmic and spiritual ("The Age of Aquarius," "Good Morning, Starshine") to the worldly: praising drugs ("Walking in Space") and sex ("Sodomy"), opposing racism ("Colored Spade") and the Vietnam War ("Three-Five-Zero-Zero"). Their music drew on a range of popular contemporary styles, some representative of the voices of social groups generally excluded from the urban, white, middle-class cultures that were the mainstays of Broadway: rhythm-and-blues ("Easy to Be Hard"), Motown and soul ("White Boys/Black Boys"), country and western ("Don't Put It Down"). And their lyrics spoke with a bluntness meant to be taken for sincerity precisely because it cut through the artifices of theater songs. As a love song, "Frank Mills," ditched the overt poetic trappings of lyrics in favor of prose:

> *I met a boy called Frank Mills*
> *On September twelfth right here in front of the Waverly*
> *But unfortunately I lost his address.*

Other numbers rejected discursive logic entirely. "I Got Life" an anatomical celebration, reduced its language to a four-word mantra ("I got my ———" [fill in the blank]) and its music to a few blues-based chords, giving new (minimalist) meaning to the concept of a list song (Ex. 12-2).

Hair captured the spirit of a moment in American social history. O'Horgan saw it as a "once in a lifetime" opportunity to create "a theater form whose demeanor, language, clothing, dance, and even its name accurately describe a social epoch in full explosion." *Hair* itself did not survive that epoch. (A 1977 Broadway revival lasted one month, though a 2009 revival currently on Broadway suggests a hitherto unsuspected vitality in the show itself.) But its influence has unquestionably persisted, and for that *Hair* has come to be viewed as a watershed in the history of American musicals. It opened up Broadway theater music to contemporary styles. It discarded a plot and replaced it with an almost uninterrupted sequence of songs. It brought both spectator and spectacle together in a total performance environment. It challenged the very notion of a musical as a fixed work by allowing for changes from pro-

Ex. 12-2. Galt MacDermot, music, James Rado and Gerome Ragni, lyrics: "I Got Life," *Hair*

duction to production and from one performance to the next. "If *Hair* does not represent a revolution in musicals," wrote Robert Brustein, "it does point the way toward such a revolution: it will be very hard, in the future, to compose a Richard Rodgers–type work with quite the same confidence and equanimity as before." The revolution was not long in coming, and *Hair* can be seen as a bellwether for some of its key developments: the rock musical with spoken dialogue (*Godspell, Grease*); the rock opera without (*Jesus Christ Superstar, Evita*); the environmentally staged musical (*Candide* revival, *Cats*); the plotless ensemble musical (*A Chorus Line, Working*). All these shows could trace lineage to *Hair* in one way or another, and like *Hair*, all had Broadway runs though none was of Broadway origin.

Indeed, on the basis of its experience with *Hair*, the New York Shakespeare Festival, which first produced the show, became the most successful not-for-profit theater company in the United States. The Festival had been founded as a workshop in a Lower East Side church in 1954 by Joseph Papp (1921–1991), who has been described as "the American theatre's nearest approach to a Diaghilev, a workaholic totally dedicated to his theatre and as skilled in raising money and manipulating civic authorities as he was in spotting and supporting artistic talent in others." Under Papp's stewardship beginning in the 1970s, the festival pursued a pattern of transferring original musicals it had successfully developed downtown to Broadway and, if they proved to be hits, to the nation at large: *Two Gentlemen of Verona* (1971), *A Chorus Line* (1975), *The Mystery of Edwin Drood* (1985). It also used its enormous profits from such ventures to subsidize more experimental musical productions which never left the Public Theater or which transferred to Broadway and flopped: *For Colored Girls Who Have Considered Suicide/When the Rainbow Is Enuf* (1976), *Runaways* (1978), *The Umbrellas of Cherbourg* (1979).

If, by such activity, the Shakespeare Festival effectively blurred distinctions between New York's commercial and noncommercial theaters, it was not alone in doing so. *Grease* (1972), *Ain't Misbehavin'*, (1978), and *The Best Little Whorehouse in Texas* (1978) were all Off Broadway or Off-Off Broadway transfers to Broadway that turned into runaway hits. Not only were theatrical productions drawn into the Broadway orbit, but in a symbolic move uptown in 1972, Circle in the Square took advantage of new contractual possibilities and relocated from Greenwich Village to Broadway and Forty-ninth Street. By the mid-1970s a Theater Row project was under way to convert rundown buildings into small playhouses on the far west spur of Forty-second Street, which gave Off Broadway and Off-Off Broadway theaters a presence within blocks of the Broadway theater district. The blurring of the lines did not stop there. For as non-Broadway companies were moving geographically into the Broadway area, several were also redefining themselves professionally to move "up" in the theatrical hierarchy along similar lines. Theater historian Gerald Berkowitz described the trend:

> *A successful Off Off-Broadway production could become Off-Broadway literally overnight, by moving to a larger theatre and paying everyone more. The Off Off-Broadway Circle Repertory Company officially became an Off-Broadway company in 1976, and the Off-Broadway Roundabout Theatre Company declared itself a Broadway operation in 1990 (primarily to make its shows eligible for Tony awards) simply by signing the appropriate union contracts. In each case, most of their subscribers could be excused for hardly noticing.*

Historically, the Off Broadway initiative had shown a genius for reinventing itself: as art theater, New Theater, regional theater, and so on. But it could not reinvent itself as an alternative theater in perpetuity, though it would have had to do so in order to exist apart from Broadway, staving off the pressures of professionalism and commercialism that inevitably accompany success. By the 1970s, the sheer scope of its success made it seem as if an important part of the non-Broadway theater were returning to the very condition of Broadway from which it had declared its independence a generation earlier. Only Broadway had not stood still in the interim. For one thing it had changed in its financial character, as it often became too expensive to function independently without access to the cheaper ways of its "off"-Broadway counterparts in New York, in the nation, and even overseas. And it had changed in its aesthetic outlook as well. As Berkowitz aptly summed it up: "It was not so much that Off-Broadway, having had its experimental fling, had retreated back into the theatrical mainstream. Rather, the mainstream had been altered and expanded so that artists and sensibilities that had once been peripheral now made up a significant part of the center."

13

THE METAPHOR ANGLE

CABARET

(11/20/1966–9/6/1969). **Producer and Director:** Harold Prince. **Book:** Joe Masteroff, based on *The Berlin Stories* of Christopher Isherwood and the play *I Am a Camera* by John Van Druten. **Lyrics:** Fred Ebb. **Music:** John Kander. **New York Run:** 1,165 performances. **Cast:** Jill Haworth, Lotte Lenya, Joel Grey. **Songs:** "Willkommen," "If You Could See Her," "What Would You Do?," "Cabaret."

COMPANY

(4/26/1970–1/1/1972). **Producer and Director:** Prince. **Book:** George Furth. **Lyrics and Music:** Stephen Sondheim. **New York Run:** 706 performances. **Cast:** Elaine Stritch, Dean Jones. **Songs:** "Sorry-Grateful," "Side by Side by Side," "Barcelona," "Being Alive."

FOLLIES

(4/4/1971–7/1/1972). **Producer:** Prince. **Book:** James Goldman. **Lyrics and Music:** Sondheim. **Directors:** Prince and Michael Bennett. **New York Run:** 522 performances. **Cast:** Alexis Smith, Dorothy Collins, Gene Nelson, John McMartin. **Songs:** "The Road You Didn't Take," "Losing My Mind," "Who's That Woman?"

The set and staging help capture the concept behind *Company* as Larry Kert (Bobby) stands isolated from the very people whose company he keeps.

SUNDAY IN THE PARK WITH GEORGE

(5/2/1984–10/13/1985). **Producers:** [Playwrights Horizons] Shubert Organization and Emanuel Azenberg. **Book and Director:** James Lapine. **Lyrics and Music:** Sondheim. **New York Run:** 604 performances. **Cast:** Bernadette Peters, Mandy Patinkin. **Songs:** "Finishing the Hat," "Sunday," "Putting It Together," "Children and Art."

ASSASSINS

(12/18/1990–2/16/1991). **Producer:** Playwrights Horizons. **Book:** John Weidman, based on an idea by Charles Gilbert, Jr. **Lyrics and Music:** Sondheim. **Director:** Jerry Zaks. **New York Run** [Off Broadway]: 73 performances. **Cast:** Terrence Mann, Jonathan Hadary, Victor Garber. **Songs:** "Everybody's Got the Right (to Be Happy)," "Another National Anthem."

When *Man of La Mancha* and *Hair* moved from non-Broadway venues to Broadway in 1968, they entered into an arena of both complacency and ferment. The year before, theater critic Martin Gottfried had resorted to the polarizing rhetoric of the day to describe Broadway's condition in his book *A Theater Divided*. Musical theater, he wrote, consisted of "right-wing musicals" and "left-wing musicals." The "right-wing" comprised George Abbott–style musical comedies and Rodgers and Hammerstein–style musical plays. Both were types of book shows structured around a story in which characters usually burst into song and dance at emotional high points to further the narrative. Such shows had flourished in the 1940s and 1950s; now they seemed old-fashioned. The future, he claimed, belonged to the "left-wing," where musicals grew out of "a conception that is musically theatrical . . . as opposed to a literary idea." The following year, Gottfried judiciously dropped the political jargon when he repeated his position in a review of *Zorba*: "The crucial problem of modern musicals [is] the battle of the book: how to replace the idea of a story (or find a new way to tell it). . . . Conception is the big word here—it is what is coming to replace the idea of a 'book.'" And by the early 1970s, Gottfried was insisting on another term entirely for the kind of undertaking he so admired:

> Follies *is* a concept musical, *a show whose music, lyrics, dance, stage movement and dialogue are woven through each other in the creation of a tapestry-like theme (rather than in support of a plot). This has been a conscious development in a line of musicals that began with* West Side Story.

If Gottfried did not coin the term "concept musical," he was certainly instrumental in popularizing it early on. It quickly became a Broadway buzzword. But what did it mean? Stephen Sondheim, who had written the *Follies* score, derided its use: "'Concept' is this decade's vogue word, just as 'integrated' was the vogue theatrical word of the '40s." Worse yet, he denied its significance. "Every show has a con-

cept," Sondheim said. "What [critics] think they mean by concept is
directorial style, but, in fact, [the term] has no meaning. It came into
being around the time of *Company* because they didn't know how to
describe a plotless piece." Concept musical was indeed "a critics' term,"
but not merely so. Nor was it devoid of meaning. On the contrary, perhaps it had too many meanings. Sondheim's own objections implied as
much when he spoke of it from two perspectives. One had to do with
the emergent condition of the musical theater as a director's theater.
The other involved an approach to the theme and structure of a musical that made it seem like a plotless piece.

The term "concept" has long been used in the theater to describe
a unifying approach to the many elements of a production, a governing idea without which a production might lack focus. A concept may
precede the writing of a script or it may bring a certain stylistic consistency to bear on a given reading of a script. Whose reading? Nowadays, clearly the director's—though the emergence of the independent
director in the modern sense, one who is neither also an actor nor an
author, is largely a twentieth-century phenomenon. (Before, the authority for such readings was often vested in the playwrights themselves or
the performers.) Today, as Stephen Banfield puts it, "the director decides
what the play is 'about' and seeks to have this reflected or stated in all
the disciplines and elements of production." Thus one speaks of Tom
O'Horgan's *Hair* as distinguished from Gerald Freedman's, or Harold
Prince's *Cabaret* in contrast to Bob Fosse's.

This marked a significant shift in priorities from those of the postwar musical stage, generally thought of as a writers' theater. One speaks
of "Rodgers and Hammerstein's *Oklahoma!*," for instance, and in terms
of artistic priority, *Oklahoma!* "belonged" to Rodgers and Hammerstein
before it belonged to anyone else. The contributions of everyone else,
in fact—director Rouben Mamoulian, choreographer Agnes de Mille,
set designer Lemuel Ayers, and all the others whose involvement in the
show was indispensable to its success—essentially came afterwards,
aesthetically and chronologically. But this is not the case with shows
like *West Side Story* or *Cabaret*, both of them forerunners of the concept
musical that would flourish in the 1970s. Here artistic priority belongs
less to the writers than to Jerome Robbins and Harold Prince, respectively, the directors who not only directed these shows but conceived

them. Their point of departure was not an existing script to be realized onstage so much as a vision or stage idea that in turn helped shape the script's development.

Indeed, the emergence of the concept musical, and with it the rise to positions of creative authority of directors skilled in the ways of theatricality unique to the musical stage, paralleled the general decline of the literary (and literate) book as the animating force in a Broadway show. By the 1970s talk of "a Prince show," "a Fosse show," a "Bennett show" was so common, no one could deny who occupied the driver's seat. On Broadway the director even came to be regarded much as French film theorists had come to regard the movie director (not the writer of the screenplay) a film's real auteur—the author in the literal generative sense. And as the concept musical registered the most distinctive new theatrical sensibility to emerge in the aftermath of the musical play, so the script angle now had to widen to encompass the directors' metaphoric production schemes, or give way to them altogether.

Which brings us to the second of Sondheim's points. "If the script is not preexistent but can be fashioned as the discussion of a topic," Banfield writes, "'concept musical' can come to indicate a show in which 'linear' plot is abandoned or downgraded in favor of vignettes; it becomes a multiple perspective on a subject, like cubist painting or sculpture." The rise of the modern concept musical parallels the decline of narrative as the focus of a show. In *West Side Story*, the narrative and the concept work hand in hand as partners. In *Cabaret*, the narrative and the concept are separated from one another and compete. In *Company*, the narrative yields to the concept altogether—and in the absence of a narrative, the concept becomes what the show is about.

Rather than following a story from a single point of view, then, many concept shows focus on a particular issue or thematic idea and examine it from a variety of perspectives. But by celebrating the variety in the focus, such shows often amount to revues in disguise. *Company* looks at marriage from several different points of view, no one of which prevails. *A Chorus Line* looks at the audition process through the eyes of a number of different auditioners, no one of whom dominates. The effect is kaleidoscopic: It gives the sense of circling around a subject rather than moving forward along a story line. Yet concept shows often pursue a larger trajectory toward some kind of denouement. In *Company*, a bachelor is somehow motivated by what he sees in the people around him to make a commitment to share his life with someone at the end. In *A Chorus Line*, the auditioners finally find out whether or not they make the grade. In a sense, such shows can be seen as plotted. If we can distinguish between a plot and a story—"plot implies a specific chart of events; story implies the tale that is told"—then these shows might be said to have plots without stories. Years earlier, Alan Jay Lerner had driven the point home when he referred to *Love Life*, for which he wrote the book and lyrics, in paradoxical terms. It was, he said, "a vaudeville with a plot."

The concept musical departed from prevailing Broadway practices as early as the 1940s in some shows now seen as precursors of the genre—*Call Me Mister* (1946), a revue whose separate sketches and musical numbers revolved about a central theme; *Allegro* (1947), a story show with a nonrealistic Greek chorus setting scenes and revealing what the characters cannot say; *Love Life* (1948), a 150-year chronicle of a nonaging family interrupted by vaudeville-style numbers commenting between the scenes. For Hal Prince the last two were more than precursors. "*Love Life* and *Allegro* were the first concept musicals," he declared. "Subconsciously, when I first saw them, I noted that they were shows driven by concepts. They didn't work, though I was too young at the time to realize that." Perhaps he learned from these shows when he eventually came to the realization. For Prince would spend much of his career in the theater seeking ways not only of making shows that were driven by concepts, but also making them work. Sondheim, for his part, would acknowledge outright in later years, the ongoing influence of *Allegro* on his work.

> *Right away I accepted the idea of telling stories in space, of skipping time and using gimmicks like the Greek chorus. All the stuff that's in* Allegro, *of somebody playing with the idea of theatre, Pirandello-ish almost. . . . I'm drawn to experiment . . . I realize that I am trying to recreate* Allegro *all the time.*

Liberated from the need to tell a story, the concept musical freely rediscovered the inherent theatricality of the musical medium and used that very theatricality to generate a new kind of show. For their purposes, creators of such shows looked less to literary sources than their predecessors who had adapted plays (*Carousel; Street Scene*), screenplays (*Fanny; Silk Stockings*), novels (*Camelot, Oliver!* [*Twist*]), and short stories (*South Pacific, Guys and Dolls*). Even if based on literary texts concept musicals were not really conceived in the spirit of textual adaptations at all. Many looked directly to diverse forms of musical theater presentation, often for the purpose of exploring the very meanings through which they had been culturally constructed as "shows"—that is, as forms of display: commedia dell'arte (*Pippin*), revue (*Follies*), circus (*Barnum*), cabaret (*Cabaret*), vaudeville (*Chicago*), burlesque (*Grind*), the Broadway musical itself (*A Chorus Line*). This resulted in a self-reflexive, postliterate musical theater whose chief architects were not usually writers but stage directors—artists in their own right to be sure, but practitioners of what Aristotle, for one, deemed a lesser art.

In sum, the term "concept musical" commonly refers to a show with "a multiple perspective and a coherently packaged topic." It locates itself as a genre therefore somewhere between the anarchy of plotlessness and the tyranny of directorial style. From the tension between these two, moreover, it seeks to extract new cultural meanings out of old theatrical forms—to "deconstruct the traditional Broadway musical (both structurally and thematically) to reconstitute it in a modernist form." And it seeks to accomplish this without losing sight, above all, of its function to entertain.

Sondheim is ultimately right when he says, "Every show has a concept"—even *Oklahoma!* It is the particular concept of the new type of musical, however, that makes it different from other kinds of shows. Gerald Mast has put it well:

> *Although concept musical has become the accepted term, it assumes an opposite—a "realist musical" or "story musical"—as if that opposite were not itself a concept. This older concept, which can be traced from opera to Oscar Hammerstein, reconciled the irreconcilable—internal psychology and singing. . . . Only the vitality of musicals built on this concept hid its paradox for over three decades: that a realistic musical is an oxymoron. To sing thoughts and feelings is necessarily to stylize them. With the steady contraction of new shows within the old con-*

*cept, the few writers, producers, and directors who stuck with musi-
cals turned to explore the very paradoxes and contradictions in the
old concept. . . . Like the modernist move toward self-consciousness
in every twentieth-century art, the concept musical explored itself—
its forms, its traditions, its variants, its conventions of credibility and
style. Songs became less psychological expressions of specific characters
than metaphoric comments on personal belief, social custom, or musical tradition. "Modernist musical" or "musical metaphor" describes
the new concept better than "concept musical," which simply changed
concepts to fit the new cultural times.*

CABARET AND THE CONCEPT MUSICAL

No one has been more central to the development of the concept musical than Harold Prince (b. 1928). As a director (and often producer), he
has masterminded the creation of a greater, more consistent body of
distinguished work in pursuit of the ideal than anyone else. He developed this ideal into a distinctive genre, tentatively separating out production concepts from their narratives at first (*Cabaret, Zorba*), then
boldly integrating them in a series of shows with Stephen Sondheim in
which any narratives there were came to serve the conceptual thrust of
the production itself (*Company, Follies*).

Prince was trained by two staging masters who imbued him with a
clear sense of the fundamentals of the métier. "A musical has an arc," he
said, "which only the director is in charge of: I learned about that arc
from George Abbott and Jerome Robbins." Beginning his Broadway
career as Abbott's assistant stage manager, Prince rose in the ranks
to produce seven Abbott shows, including such hits as *Pajama Game,
Damn Yankees, Fiorello!,* and *Forum.* With Robbins he worked on nine
shows, and he produced such landmarks as *West Side Story* and *Fiddler
on the Roof,* which exerted decisive influences on his career through
their sobering themes and fluid approaches to the stage.

Thus far Hal Prince has directed some twenty original musicals
on Broadway, most of which he also produced. He first established his
reputation as a director with a series of eight shows that premiered
between 1966 and 1981 and which, despite the highly innovative nature

of many, were developed through traditional Broadway channels. He created the last six together with Sondheim; the first two with John Kander and Fred Ebb. Of these *Cabaret* was the first: the breakthrough musical in terms of Prince's directorial career and the development of the overtly metaphoric kind of show with which he would afterward be associated, the modern concept musical.

For *Cabaret* (1966) Prince brought together librettist Joe Master-off (b. 1919), composer John Kander (b. 1927), and lyricist Fred Ebb (1928–2004). Masteroff's brief Broadway career effectively ended with the show. But it was just the beginning for the team of Kander and Ebb. Prince had produced the songwriters' first Broadway collaboration the year before, *Flora, the Red Menace*. But *Cabaret* gave them their first Broadway hit, which cemented a songwriting partnership that would last for over forty years. In all, Kander and Ebb created the scores for twelve Broadway shows, of which the longest running were *Cabaret, Zorba* (1968), *Chicago* (1975), *Woman of the Year* (1981), and *Kiss of the Spider Woman* (1993). As personalities, the two presented a study in contrasts: "Kander, the unflappable Midwesterner, mild-mannered and buoyantly optimistic, and Ebb, the acerbic New Yorker who wears his wit and insecurities on his sleeve." As songwriters for the theater, however, they spoke as one. Typically, they blended verbal clichés and musical pastiches into songs that, in the right context, could be double-edged and thus appear fresh. Prince described the Kander and Ebb style as "accessible (and, yes, quintessentially Broadway show business)."

What ended up as *Cabaret* began as a conventional book show, adapted largely from a 1951 hit play, *I Am a Camera*, which John Van Druten had written, based on Christopher Isherwood's *Berlin Stories* (*The Last of Mr. Norris, Goodbye to Berlin*). The musical took place in Weimar Germany circa 1930. It told the story of Cliff Bradshaw (Bert Convy), an American novelist looking for something to write about in Berlin and finding it in Sally Bowles (Jill Haworth), an English girl singing in a sleazy club and enjoying the city's sexually permissive lifestyle. The show also had a subplot in the middle-aged romance between Fräulein Schneider (Lotte Lenya), the German landlady of the boardinghouse where Cliff lived, and Herr Schultz (Jack Gilford), the Jewish grocer to whom she was engaged. Neither story ended happily. Cliff and Sally's affair broke up when she aborted the child they were about to have. Schneider and Schultz's engagement broke up over her fears of being married to a Jew in an increasingly anti-semitic Germany. Despite the darkness of the stories, however, the show remained true to the traditional structure of a musical play. The Sally-Cliff plot had its book songs ("Perfectly Marvelous," "Why Should I Wake Up?"), and the Schneider-Schultz subplot had its book songs ("Pineapple Song," "Married"). Had that been all there was to the show, Martin Gottfried might well have called it a right-wing musical.

He didn't. He called it "partly left-wing" because something quite remarkable intervened to change the show by the time it opened. Scattered throughout the musical now were nightclub numbers that were not part of Sally's act in the Kit Kat Klub where she worked, and not justifiable in terms of any of the book scenes. The numbers, wholly grotesque in character, emanated from no definable place except what the singer of the first of them, "Willkommen," kept referring to as a "cabaret." And the singer! Here was one of the musical theater's most unforgettable characters: an effeminate Master of Ceremonies (Joel Grey), garishly whitefaced, lipsticked, and rouged, who broke the fourth-wall illusion of the rest of the show and played directly to the audience with unabashed theatricality often described as camp. His numbers were by far the evening's most entertaining, but they seemed to have nothing to do with anything else. "We had two shows—my book, and Joel [Grey]'s fifteen minutes [of cabaret numbers]," said Joe Masteroff. "It never occurred to me that when you put the two shows together you would have a new kind of musical, but Hal knew."

Somewhere between the first draft of the projected Isherwood musical and opening night of *Cabaret* three years later, the emphasis of the show had shifted fundamentally: from simply telling a story to developing a metaphoric approach to convey a theme. Kander acknowledged the source: "*Cabaret* evolved from Hal Prince's concept." The emcee's cabaret act with its arch humor, ambiguous sexuality, and increasingly menacing routines had become the conceptual spine of the show. For it was part of Prince's idea to make "the life of the cabaret," he said, "a metaphor for Germany"—an outrageously theatricalized metaphor that would put the small, personal problems of Isherwood's characters in a larger historical context. Thus the emcee's song-and-dance numbers stood self-consciously on the "outside": They popped up unpredictably to interrupt the narrative, play for applause, and vanish so that the narrative might continue. But they placed a chilling political, social, and moral frame around the tales that were going on inside. The stage thus spun about two foci: the real world of Sally Bowles and her friends, and the surreal limbo of the German state of mind on the eve of the Nazi rise to power. In the way the one related to the other the meaning of *Cabaret* emerged.

Joel Grey (Master of Ceremonies) in *Cabaret.*

Consider, for example, the dramatic context for the song "If You Could See Her (Through My Eyes)." Fräulein Schneider arrives at Herr Schultz's grocery shop in act 2 to break off their wedding engagement. Schultz just about manages to convince her that her fears of Nazi persecution are groundless, when suddenly,

(*A brick crashes through the window.* FRÄULEIN SCHNEIDER *and* HERR
    SCHULTZ *jump up*)

FRÄULEIN SCHNEIDER: You see? You see!
SCHULTZ: It is nothing! Children on their way to school! Mischievous
    children! Nothing more! I assure you! (HERR SCHULTZ *runs out. We
    see him outside the broken window, looking for the culprit and question-
    ing the onlookers. No one seems to have seen anything.* HERR SCHULTZ
    comes back in) Schoolchildren. Young—full of mischief. You un-
    derstand?
FRÄULEIN SCHNEIDER: (*Slowly—thoughtfully*) I understand.

Lights fade

The EMCEE *enters, walking hand-in-hand with a gorilla. The gorilla is really rather attractive—as gorillas go. She wears a chic little skirt and carries a handbag.*

EMCEE: (*Singing*)

> *I know what you're thinking—*
> *You wonder why I chose her*
> *Out of all the ladies in the world . . .*
>
> *If you could see her through my eyes,*
> *You wouldn't wonder at all.*
> *If you could see her through my eyes,*
> *I guarantee you would fall (like I did) . . .*
>
> *I understand your objection,*
> *I grant you the problem's not small.*
> *But if you could see her through my eyes,*
> *She wouldn't look Jewish at all.*

Blackout

"IF YOU COULD SEE HER (THROUGH MY EYES)"

(*CABARET*)

Though a bit bizarre, the number seems no more than a diversion, a silly vaudeville routine—until the final line. The offense gives point to what otherwise might have been a harmless burlesque. But the song is far from harmless; or it is about as harmless as the "mischievous children" Schultz imagines in refusing to accept the unthinkable. Its closing line stings with the impact of the brick that went through the window of his shop.

"The song was to end that way," Kander explained, "to have you laughing and then catch your breath, to make you the audience realize how easily you could fall into a trap of prejudice." The number clearly played on audiences' conflicting feelings: fun, and guilt at having had the fun. For the song was isolated and yet strategically placed. It entertained as it pointed up the meaning of the scene the audience had just witnessed. Rather than expressing a feeling, however, it presented an attitude, and it did so in the telltale manner of what are usually referred to as comment songs:

> *musical sequences, vocal or choreographic, which do not advance action or express character directly (as per the dictum of the Rodgers and Hammerstein "integrated" musical), but comment from odd angles to create a musical profile having more to do with tone and point than emotion and character.*

The carnivalesque music, too, marked "If You Could See Her" as a comment song. With its bouncy rhythms and stepwise wheedling tune, it differed in style and spirit from the more traditionally lyrical book songs in the show.

The relationship of "If You Could See Her" to the scene that preceded it represents *Cabaret* in a nutshell. Other emcee numbers worked similarly. After a scene in which Sally moved in with Cliff, the emcee appeared with two girls saying, "Everybody in Berlin has a perfectly marvelous roommate. Some people have two people!," and he proceeded to sing "Two Ladies" in praise of promiscuity and lesbianism. After a scene in which Cliff arranged to earn money by becoming an unwitting courier for the Nazis, the emcee popped up saying, "There's more than one way to make money," and made his way through a cadre of girls singing "The Money Song" in praise of prostitution. Moreover, each song was more alarming than the last. For the cabaret numbers traveled along an arc that showed how the real world of the musical play gradually succumbed to the ever darkening metaphor world of the emcee—promiscuity, prostitution, antisemitism, Nazism. (Prince: "If you have Nazis from the start where does the show have to go? You've given everything away.")

This Broadway show systematically took time out from telling its story to seduce and disturb an audience through its very use of musical numbers. Prince meant to turn *Cabaret* into "a parable of contemporary morality," he said, and for all the showbiz pizzazz of it he was in earnest. "What attracted the authors and me was the parallel between the spiritual bankruptcy of Germany in the 1920s and our country in the 1960s." To drive home the parallel, set designer Boris Aronson created a large mirror backdrop so that those looking at the curtainless stage as they entered New York's Broadhurst Theater would see themselves as the patrons of the Kit Kat Klub. The very act of watching the show reminded the audience of its own escape from the concerns of the turbulent outside world of the late 1960s by sitting in a theater. For theater scholar John Shout, the show invariably left audiences in a moral bind:

> As they laughed at the M.C. and revelled, somewhat hiply, in his depravities, they presumably indicted themselves as part of the decay. A new Catch-22 was in operation: those whom the production had successfully wooed and were in attendance were convicted of neglecting what they should have been doing instead of being there.

Aronson not only came up with the basic visual metaphor for *Cabaret*'s concept in the onstage mirror, his design of the stage space itself was essential to Prince's nonverbal articulation of meaning in the show. Indeed, Aronson's work as a stage designer became indispensable to Prince's whole conceptual approach, and Aronson would design Prince's next five productions. A native Russian, Boris Aronson (1900–1980) had firsthand experience of the avant-garde theater movements of Vsevolod Meyerhold and Alexander Tairov, which were virtually unknown in the America to which he immigrated in the 1920s. His best work of the 1930s involved designs for New York's Yiddish Theater and for the Group Theater, whose principal designer, Mordecai Gorelik, was to become a major influence with his theory that stage setting should be a visual metaphor for the meaning of a play. In the 1940s Aronson designed a few notable musicals for Broadway (*Cabin in the Sky*; *Love Life*). But it was not until Aronson's contributions to *Fiddler on the Roof* and *Cabaret* that Prince came to realize the designer's functional importance to the success of a show. Prince recalled,

> With Abbott, I did the scenery. He didn't care about it—he didn't even have lighting—he just wanted to know where the doors were going to be. He'd arrive the first day of rehearsal and be shown the scenery. Boris made it clear to me just how advisable it could be to start the design of a show at the moment it was being written—when there

was nothing on paper except an idea. Some designers are authors—Boris was an author.

For the *Cabaret* production, Prince and Aronson split the stage into two sharply divided areas. One area represented the real world of the book scenes, upstage. The other, "the Limbo Area," represented the metaphoric world in which the emcee held sway, downstage. To keep the two areas separate throughout the show, they built a curtain of footlights six feet back from the edge of the stage which came on only when the emcee performed and thus obliterated the real world behind. One time only in the show were the two areas connected, and with a symbolism intended to be devastating. At the climax of *Cabaret*, Cliff left Berlin while Sally chose to stay. As a sign of her giving in to the gathering darkness of Nazism, she began to sing the show's title song with its seductive "come to the cabaret" refrain upstage as if it were part of her act in the Kit Kat Klub. But as she sang, Prince said, she "lost track of her audience, broke down, and for the first time in the evening, stepped across the footlights into the Limbo Area, and the audience understood."

Or so Prince would have hoped. But the number cut two ways. While it had a chilling conceptual function in the show, the song "Cabaret" itself was a showstopper, a rousing eleven o'clock number that exuded a theatricalism all its own. "It's certainly possible to interpret the song as a negative statement," said Masteroff of its function in the story, "but in performance the song really takes over and becomes a celebration." While meant to condemn fascism without being didactic, "Cabaret" entertained sufficiently to make fascism covertly alluring. The very project of *Cabaret*—indeed of the concept musical as a metaphor—was not only double-edged, but dangerously so. It could easily be misunderstood—and it often was.

For his "cabaret" metaphor, Prince drew on major European sources that affected the theatricalist climate of the early 1960s. Most influential perhaps were the Brecht-Weill comment songs in *The Threepenny Opera*, which ended its astonishing Off Broadway run in 1961. That show marked a major breakthrough in the American reception of Brecht as a playwright and theorist, and it popularized an approach to theater he had developed earlier in Germany that worked both inside and outside the frame of a play. It combined story and comment by means of songs that did not grow organically out of the story but, as Brecht said, "stood in contradiction of it." Other influences came from elsewhere, and they included the juxtapositions of fantasy and reality in the Theatre Workshop production of *Oh, What a Lovely War!*, which British director Joan Littlewood brought to the United States in 1964, and the constructivist production techniques of Vsevolod Meyerhold, which Prince saw on a visit to Moscow in 1966. Thus *Cabaret* was receptive to an altogether different kind of energy from that which the mainstream of Broadway musicals had been tapping. Yet even as the show reflected such influences, it was still very much shaped by Prince in Broadway terms. The real significance of the piece, according to Walter Kerr, was that it

> *opened the door—partway, at least—to a fresh notion of the bizarre, crackling, harsh and yet beguiling uses that can still be made of song and dance. Instead of putting the narrative first and the singers and dancers wherever a small corner could be found for them, it popped the clowns and the gartered girls directly into our faces, making them, in effect, a brightly glazed window . . . through which we could perceive the people and the emotional patterns of the plot.*

Later on, *Cabaret* would be used by other directors to open the door even further. For a 1972 film version, Bob Fosse cut almost all of *Cabaret*'s story-based musical numbers and kept only the comment numbers performed in the cabaret. For a 1998 staged revival, Sam Mendes and Rob Marshall had the entire show mounted in a real nightclub. Prince, however, took a greater interest in applying the conceptual discoveries of *Cabaret* to his next show, *Zorba*. Working again with Kander and Ebb, he used a Greek chorus as a framing device to tell the story of Nikos Kazantzakis's novel *Zorba the Greek*. But where *Cabaret* had succeeded two years before, *Zorba* failed. Moreover, as concept musicals, both shows still had only gone "partway." Entering into a new creative partnership with songwriter Stephen Sondheim, Prince would now determine whether a show could be made to go the distance.

PRINCE, SONDHEIM & CO.

Stephen Sondheim (b. 1930) began his extraordinary career in musical theater as a protégé of Oscar Hammerstein II, who instilled in the fledgling composer-lyricist the values of a musical playwright. "Oscar taught me that a song should be like a little one-act play, with an exposition, a development, and a conclusion; at the end of the song the character should have moved to a different position from where he was emotionally at the beginning." Sondheim has collaborated on sixteen original Broadway musicals to date. He worked early on as a lyricist for Leonard Bernstein (*West Side Story*), for Jule Styne (*Gypsy*), and for Richard Rodgers (*Do I Hear a Waltz?*, 1965). But the earliest shows for which he wrote the complete scores were the successful *A Funny Thing Happened on the Way to the Forum* (1962) and the failed *Anyone Can Whistle* (1964). In 1969 he began an eleven-year collaboration with Hal Prince, creating scores for what would become the most challenging, innovative, and probing body of Broadway musicals of the era: *Company* (1970), *Follies* (1971), *A Little Night Music* (1973), *Pacific Overtures* (1976), *Sweeney Todd, the Demon Barber of Fleet Street* (1979), and *Merrily We Roll Along* (1981). (Prince also produced a song anthology *Side by Side by Sondheim* on Broadway in 1977.) In these works Sondheim emerged not only as a brilliant composer-lyricist in his own right but as the leading musical dramatist in the American theater of his generation.

Prince and Sondheim have much in common. "We have the same point of view although we're abrasive with each other," said Sondheim. "We see the large and small parts exactly the same, but it's the middle ground where we disagree violently and it causes a lot of good work to be done." Foster Hirsch also sees differences in temperament between them that have proved productive as well:

> *Prince galloping ahead while Sondheim holds tightly onto the reins; Prince the affable public-relations man, glibly articulating concepts and trajectories, Sondheim leery of publicity; Prince relishing the activity of the rehearsal process, Sondheim disliking it: out of the fusion of their temperamental dissimilarities they have become modernism's answer to Rodgers and Hammerstein—the makers of the self-reflexive musical.*

Their first two collaborations, *Company* and *Follies*, set the pace. *Company*, a landmark in the development of American musical theater, did away with storytelling as its governing principle. "Up until *Company* most musicals, if not all musicals, had plots," said Sondheim. "Up until *Company*, I thought that musicals had to have very strong plots. One of the things that fascinated me about the challenge of the show was to see if a musical could be done without one. . . . The problem was to find the form for it." The idea for the form came from Prince, who whittled down and refocused eleven one-act plays by George Furth until he found an underlying theme. "I thought, what if we could construct a musical about New York marriages and if we could create a central character to examine these marriages."

In the absence of a story line, *Company* moved as a set of variations on a theme. Much of its comic spirit and formal looseness resembled the thematic revues of an earlier generation. But where such revues had been externally motivated (newspaper headlines: *As Thousands Cheer*; a world tour: *At Home Abroad*), *Company* looked inward. Through its sketches it depicted the psychological dynamics and emotional ambivalences in the love lives of five upper-middle-class couples all living in 1970s Manhattan, and a thirty-five-year old bachelor, Robert (Dean Jones), and his three girlfriends. Presented in no apparent order and interlocked in kaleidoscopic fashion, their vignettes reflected a common involvement with Robert, the enigmatic still-point at the center of the show. Robert's friends claimed to wish to see him married, though they doted on the kind of company he provided in his unmarried state. And he seemed content simply to observe the amorous foibles of the friends who were also his company in turn (as well as the "company" performing the show). *Company* did not develop so much as accumulate. At the end, Robert emerges from his cocoon of detachment to seek emotional fulfillment by committing himself to another human being ("Being Alive").

The plotless form that *Company* took as a concept musical came out of the show's content as an ongoing discussion about the nature of love and marriage. Neither celebrating marriage nor disparaging it (as some felt), *Company* took a hard, sometimes agonizing look at the difficulties of being married and at the difficulties of being single, "the total possibility and impossibility of relationships." Beneath the funny surface with its multiple perspectives on marriage, however, lurked a sobering and unifying darkness. It was "the secret metaphor," Sondheim said, "that nobody knows except the authors . . . a comparison between a contemporary marriage and the island of Manhattan." A sense of depersonalization and loneliness thus pervades the show. "Chekhov once said: 'If you're afraid of loneliness, don't marry,'" Sondheim explained. "Most succinct. In the deepest sense, that's what *Company* is about."

Boris Aronson's unit set reconceived the metaphor in spatial terms and made it visible. For the apartments in the Manhattan highrises where each of the married couples lived he created a Plexiglas jungle gym with an elevator down the middle and platforms isolated at different levels on the sides. The five couples occupied their own levels, oblivious of each other's presence. Beyond visually embodying the sense of the show, Aronson's construction served Sondheim as an inspiration for the score. "The opening number of *Company*," he said, "is about the set." The other numbers in the show, no less compellingly thematic, revealed Sondheim's astonishing range and penetration. "You Could Drive a Person Crazy," sung by Robert's three very frustrated girlfriends, shimmered with fun, wit, and wordsmithery of a kind seldom heard on Broadway since the great lyricists of the 1920s and 1930s:

> *When a person's personality is personable,*
> *He shouldn't oughta sit like a lump.*
> *It's harder than a matador coercin' a bull*
> *To try to get you off-a your rump.*

"You Could Drive a Person Crazy"
(*Company*)

In "Sorry-Grateful," on the other hand, the attempt by some husbands to articulate the ambivalences of marriage yielded a searing honesty that did not settle for easy answers:

> *You're sorry-grateful,*
> *Regretful-happy.*

Why look for answers where none occur?
You always are what you always were,
Which has nothing to do with,
All to do with her.

"SORRY-GRATEFUL" (*COMPANY*)

Above all in *Company*, Sondheim explored the new uses for songs that concept musicals made possible. He explained:

> *It was new for me because we realized early on that the kind of song that would not work in the show was the Rodgers and Hammerstein kind of song in which the characters reach a certain point and then sing their emotions, because George [Furth] writes the kind of people who do not sing. To spend time exploring the characters was wrong because they were primarily presented in vignettes, and as soon as you'd try to expand them with song it would be a mistake. All the songs had to be used . . . in a Brechtian way as comment and counterpoint.*

Instead of following past practice and gradually building up to a musical number as the emotional climax of a scene, a song in *Company* often came as a surprise. It might precede a scene ("Getting Married Today"); or punctuate it in pieces ("The Little Things You Do Together"); or frame it ("Another Hundred People"); or freeze it entirely ("You Could Drive a Person Crazy"); or involve no discernible scene at all ("Side by Side by Side"). In its function, then, a song might become

> *commentative (or editorial, if you like), illustrative, connective, a punctuation device or be used for exposition, or contrapuntally, or even—and this would ordinarily be anathema in the dramatic form—serve as breather. In short . . . song [could] once again exist for itself and still, instead of detracting from from the aesthetic design and integrity of the whole, complement it.*

In its content, too, a *Company* song could delve into the ambiguities and psychological complexities of its theme since it was freed of the need to advance a plot. "There are, of course, plots," Prince said, "but they are subtextual and grow out of subconscious behavior, psychological stresses, inadvertent revelations." These were the emotional arenas where *Company*'s characters struggled to come to terms in song with not always recognized feelings of hostility ("The Ladies Who Lunch"), ambivalence ("Sorry-Grateful"), vulnerability ("Being Alive"), and confusion ("Someone Is Waiting"). "Barcelona," for example, was a two-character musical playlet in song that explored what might have seemed a romantic situation were it not for the degree of its psychological nuance. In fact, it turned out to be the very antithesis of a love duet, though sung together in bed by Robert and April, the airline stewardess with whom he has just spent the night:

Company: Act 2, Scene 2

(The lights come up on the bedroom as before. ROBERT *has his hand over his eyes; both he and* APRIL *are completely exhausted. The alarm clock goes off.* APRIL *shuts off the clock and turns on a light. She begins gathering her clothes. They sing)*

ROBERT:	APRIL:
Whatcha thinking?	Barcelona.
. . . oh . . .	Flight Eighteen.
Stay a minute.	I would like to.
. . . So? . . .	Don't be mean.
Stay a minute.	No, I can't.
Yes, you can.	No, I can't.
Where you going?	Barcelona—
So you said—	And Madrid—
Bon voyage—	On a Boeing.
Good night.	You're angry.
No.	I've got to—
Right.	Report to—
Go.	That's not to
	Say
	That if I had my way . . .
	Oh well, I guess, okay.
What?	I'll stay.

But . . .
(*As she snuggles down*)
Oh, God!

Blackout

"BARCELONA" (*COMPANY*)

"Barcelona" shines with a new kind of Broadway sophistication: It reveals as much by what it doesn't say as by what it does. The words are banal phrases tossed back and forth, not the usual stuff of theater lyrics. And there is less of Broadway in the music than there is of the monochromatic idiom of an Erik Satie. Simply put, "Barcelona" lacks Broadway's markers of verbal eloquence and a hummable tune. Its melody rather clings to the utterances of two characters who, avoiding the traditional symmetries of song, express themselves awkwardly, as they might in real life—hemming, hawing, repeating themselves, interrupting each other. For Robert doesn't really mean what he sings; except for his final remark, he merely observes the social graces. Indeed, his insisting three times in the middle of the number that April is "a very special girl" to him when he can't even remember her name—he calls her June—is but the tip of an emotional iceberg. Submerged beneath lies a subtext of feeling, or of the absence of feeling, that is the key to Sondheim's musical dramaturgy here and elsewhere in his work. He explains:

> *What [subtext] means simply is, give the actor something to act. . . . A playwright when he writes a scene always gives some subtext, or it's a very shallow scene. Well, that happens with lyrics. They may be very good, but if they're just on the surface, if there's no pull, there's a kind of deadness on the stage. . . .*
>
> *There's a song in* Follies *called "The Road You Didn't Take" which on the surface is a man saying, "Oh, I never look back on the past, I mean, my goodness, it just wouldn't be worth it." He's doing it to con himself as well as the lady he is with; in point of fact, he is ripped to shreds internally. Now, the actor has the ripped-to-shreds [feeling] that he can play. There's also a stabbing dissonance in the music, a note in the music that tells you, the audience, that something is not quite kosher about what this guy is saying.*

Follies is virtually *all* subtext as a show. It is, said Sondheim, "about a party and nothing happens in it at all, except people say hello and have a few drinks and go home. That's the entire plot." Something does happen in the show, of course, only what it is goes on beneath the plot. Two married couples and once close friends meet again after thirty years at a 1971 reunion. They are now quite different people. Sally and Buddy Plummer (Dorothy Collins, Gene Nelson) lead nondescript suburban lives in Phoenix. Phyllis and Ben Stone (Alexis Smith, John McMartin) are New Yorkers, urban and urbane. We come to learn, however, that Buddy is a womanizer; Sally believes she is still in love with Ben, as she had been thirty years earlier; and Ben and Phyllis have a loveless marriage. *Follies* probes their follies—their foolishness, their madness—as they deceive themselves and each other about the anguished reality of their present by idealizing their past. Yet the pressure of the reunion forces them to face feelings long suppressed, and in an emotional climax in which Ben suffers a nervous breakdown, the couples finally come to more realistic terms with themselves.

The reunion itself, however, gives the telling of such personal follies scope. For the party is being thrown for performers who appeared decades earlier in the Weissman Follies, a Ziegfeld-style revue. This one-time get-together takes place on the stage of the very theater where they used to perform, which is now slated for demolition. Sally and Phyllis had been roommates who danced together in the Follies; Buddy and Ben were college pals who dated the girls. For the two couples the stage now becomes an arena for painful confrontations between the past and the present, and their self-delusions are shown to be made of the same stuff as the illusions the Follies themselves once fostered as a form of entertainment. The theatrical "Follies" thus becomes a cultural metaphor for the follies of living unrealistically in the past. The show, *Follies*, embodies both the theatrical and the metaphorical implications of the term.

In its staging, *Follies* drew on the new wave of nonnarrative films of the 1960s and on the surreal imagery in particular in the work of film director Federico Fellini. The show moved "cinematically" with past and present happening at the same time. Alongside the two middle-aged couples, their thirty-year-younger selves appeared at the reunion, shadowing them and confronting them at almost every turn. Michael

Bennett, codirector with Prince as well as the show's choreographer, caught the haunting sense of distance crossed by the passage of time in the single most celebrated visual metaphor of the show. As the aging chorines at the reunion somewhat awkwardly join together to try to re-create a mirror dance they used to perform ("Who's That Woman?"), a pale chorus of beautiful young dancers from out of nowhere joins them in a mirror of its own—the ghostlike memories of the girls they once were, dancing perfectly as they once danced.

What Prince, Bennett, and Aronson created with movement, mirrors, and other visual effects to relate past and present, Sondheim paralleled with echoes of bygone musical styles. His twenty-one-song score was deliberately "schizophrenic": About one third were book songs, the rest constituted a pastiche of theater song styles of the 1920s and 1930s. But it was a pastiche that engaged in a tug-of-war between outright nostalgia for the musical tropes of the Golden Age of theater songs and skepticism over the past they represented. Given this ambivalence, *Follies* differed emotionally from the one-dimensional revivals of older shows that fed a burgeoning nostalgia craze on Broadway at the time (*No, No, Nanette*, 1925/rev. 1971; *Irene*, 1919/rev. 1973). *Follies* was not a nostalgia show so much as a show *about* nostalgia. And so it was crucial, Prince said, that the work should attempt to be "traditional and accurate in all ways but one. Sets, costumes, music, movement; all this is faithful to the past. What's different and unusual about it is the content, what it's all about."

Nowhere did this double-edged quality work more pointedly than in the Ziegfeld-Follies fantasy that climaxed the show ("Loveland"): a follies within *Follies*. Coming at the height of the emotional turmoil of the two couples, "Loveland" portrayed a Follies of the mind that broke sharply with reality. It ran as a continuous twenty-minute sequence of musical numbers whose forms and styles all echoed the song tropes of Broadway's past, but whose content echoed the deeply troubling prob-lems of the present that each of the protagonists had expressed earlier in the show. Buddy's earlier book song "The Right Girl" finds a parallel in Buddy's performance now as a burlesque funnyman ("The God-Why-Don't-You-Love-Me (-Oh-You-Do?-I'll-See-You-Later) Blues"). Sally's earlier song "In Buddy's Eyes" is now paralleled as she sings a torch song, Helen Morgan–style ("Losing My Mind"). Phyllis's "Could I Leave You?" is paralleled as she delivers a honky-tonk ballad ostensibly in a Cole Porter vein ("The Story of Lucy and Jessie"). And Ben's "The

"Who's That Woman?," the mirror dance from *Follies*, foreground l. to r.: Sheila Smith (Meredith Lane), Ethel Barrymore Colt (Christine Donovan), Alexis Smith (Phyllis Rogers Stone), Dorothy Collins (Sally Durant Plummer), Helon Blount (Deedee West), and Yvonne De Carlo (Carlotta Campion).

Road You Didn't Take" is paralleled as he goes into a debonair Fred Astaire routine ("Live, Laugh, Love"). An especially poignant example within "Loveland" of a traditional form losing its traditional content is provided by Sally's torch song, which, so reminiscent of Gershwin's "The Man I Love," differs utterly from its model in meaning. Where the Gershwin song posits a singer who looks promisingly to a romantic future with her "Prince Charming" (Ex. 13-1a), Sally can only look back on a nonexistent past with hers (Ex. 13-1b). Musically, too, the nearly identical melodic motifs ("The Man I Love"; "I dim the lights") repeat obsessively in both songs, but over a falling chromatic line in the one and a rising one in the other.

Follies was a musical about the death of a kind of innocence that musicals once represented in American culture. But as a show that pointed out the hollowness of Broadway nostalgia during a craze for the revival of shows that capitalized on it, it did not succeed at the box office. Moreover, amid the ironies, ambivalences, and subtexts of the show, its emotional allegiances were not always clear to audiences. Its self-reflexive concept used traditional Broadway musical means to undermine traditional Broadway musical ends. Yet at the same time the

Ex. 13-1a. George Gershwin, music, Ira Gershwin, lyrics: "The Man I Love," cut from *Lady, Be Good*

Ex. 13-1b. Stephen Sondheim, music and lyrics: "Losing My Mind," *Follies*

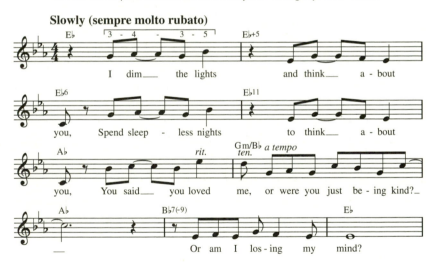

show furthered those ends by entertaining mightily en route. As a theatrical event, in fact, *Follies* celebrated the very tradition it dissected. It is this paradox which many found emotionally confusing, and which lies at the heart of the bittersweet brilliance of the piece and of the Prince-Sondheim collaborations in general. Foster Hirsch elaborates:

Despite the attack on sentimental cliché that has informed almost all of their shows, underneath the cool surfaces of their work, the uplift and romanticism that supplied the motor for the old-fashioned musicals struggle to be released. It is the resulting conflicts between modern ambivalence, irony, skepticism, and self-reflexiveness on the one hand and show business schmaltz on the other that give their work its distinctive sweet and sour pungency.

This pungency characterized their subsequent shows as well, though they strove not to repeat themselves in form or content. The variety was remarkable. Some of their later work abandoned the overt "concepts" and contemporary American concerns of their first two shows for period pieces that moved more traditionally along narrative lines. *A Little Night Music* was a comedy of manners, love, and foolishness, set in turn-of-the-twentieth-century Sweden, and based on Ingmar Bergman's film *Smiles of a Summer Night.* For this Sondheim wrote an operettalike score in which all the numbers were in some form of triple or compound time. *Sweeney Todd,* "A Musical Thriller," was a nineteenth-century British melodrama in which a half-crazed barber takes revenge for injustices done him by murdering his victims and using their corpses to fill meat pies. Here Sondheim's score was almost entirely through-sung, "not because I wanted to do an opera, but because I realized that the only way to sustain tension was to use music continually, not to let the heat out, so that even if they're talking, there's music going on in the pit." Other Prince-Sondheim shows pursued more abstractly conceptual paths: *Pacific Overtures* traced the Westernization of Japan through a panoramic scrapbook of Japanese-American relations from 1853 to the present. With almost all the roles in the show played by men, Sondheim and Prince mixed Kabuki and Broadway musical theaters in an evocative blend of Eastern and Western styles of music and performance. And *Merrily We Roll Along,* based on an unsuccessful play by Kaufman and Hart, followed the breakup of a three-way friendship over twenty-five years—but moving backwards in time, from the compromises of middle age to the idealism of youth. Here the score consisted of musical connections that worked backwards and forwards, even songs whose reprises came chronologically (for the audience) "before" the songs themselves. The show was a failure, however, and a stunning disappointment to Prince and Sondheim. With it their collaboration came to an end (though it was revived briefly in 2003 when the two worked together on *Bounce*, a show that played in Chicago and Washington, then, revised as *Road Show* and directed by John Doyle, had a short Off Broadway run in 2008).

If signs of the differences between Prince and Sondheim haunted *Merrily We Roll Along*, they could be found in their earlier collaborations as well. (Sondheim's score for *Sweeney Todd*, for example, focused on a tale of personal wrong and revenge; Prince's concept theatricalized the dehumanizing effects of the Industrial Revolution, and he built an enormous iron foundry onstage to dwarf the human story.) Yet the achievement of the two together far outweighed in significance any tension between them that had not been integrated into their previous work. No body of work of Broadway origin, in fact, would be more esteemed by the post–Rodgers and Hammerstein generation than what Prince and Sondheim created between *Company* and *Merrily We Roll Along*. It was at once a brilliantly conceived extension of Broadway musical traditions and a thoroughgoing challenge to them from within.

It also proved highly influential despite its failure to produce a single Broadway blockbuster. It gave the director and his production staff new and central roles to play not simply in the staging of Broadway musicals but in their creation. It reconfigured the musical itself into a self-reflexive medium that used theatrical metaphors and production concepts to examine themes of social and cultural import. It developed such metaphors and concepts by blending book, music, and movement in ways that obliterated traditional distinctions between them. And in doing so, it mustered the resources of the stage and the trappings of show business not only to amuse, but also to disturb habits of thought and feeling and thus provoke the very audiences that came to their work expecting solely to be entertained. Ultimately, it served notice that nothing in a musical could be presumed "innocent" any longer since the medium itself now aspired to self-awareness, that is, to "something reasonably adult that works on at least more than one level . . . an entertainment, but with a subversive edge." Sondheim hoped, as he once said of *Company*, that audiences "would sit for two hours screaming their heads off with laughter and then go home and not be able to sleep."

The Prince-Sondheim collaborations effected a Broadway revolution in the best of Broadway traditions: out of bold ad hoc responses to new and problematic material, not on the basis of any theoretical precepts. But the freshness that animated the approach proved difficult to maintain over time. When *Company* first appeared in 1970, it excited a new sense of possibility for the musical. It seemed "like a new animal, requiring a total brain adjustment," Michael Bennett said. But by the time *Merrily* appeared roughly a decade later, the excitement had abated. Walter Kerr attributed the new show's failure largely to Prince and Sondheim returning yet again to "the one thing they seem determined to sell: disenchantment" so characteristic of their previous work. "The insistence on a single theme, a single attitude, is becoming monotous," he wrote, though, to put his words in context, he had liked none of the partners' previous work. Finally, he urged "the collaborators to stop parroting themselves and take fresh stock of their imaginative energies." They took fresh stock now; but separately.

SONDHEIM AFTER PRINCE

If the frustration over *Merrily* precipitated the unraveling of the partnership of Prince and Sondheim, it also marked a significant turning away from Broadway by two masters of the Broadway métier. While both had previously enjoyed a certain privilege working in the commercial arena, Broadway's changing financial and institutional structures could no longer provide adequate room for the development of their innovative work. "Until *Merrily We Roll Along*," Prince acknowledged, "I really had what amounted to my own production team. I had my own design staff and a loyal group of investors. We were like a repertory company that just happened to be located on Broadway instead of the regional theatre." After parting from Sondheim, Prince continued to work through Broadway channels. But failing on Broadway again with two conceptually based pieces (*A Doll's Life*, 1982; *Grind*, 1985), he sought and found success by developing musicals outside the United States—notably in London (following the earlier success of *Evita* in 1978 with *Phantom of the Opera* in 1986) and in Toronto (*Kiss of the Spider Woman*, 1992)—before bringing them to Broadway. Sondheim in turn, without Prince, turned to Off Broadway and regional theater to create his later work.

Sondheim's major post-Prince Broadway musicals include *Sunday in the Park with George* (1984), *Into the Woods* (1987), *Assassins* (1991/2004), and *Passion* (1994). These shows, while often more overtly emotional than his earlier ones, also revel less in the trappings of "show business schmaltz." This tends to make them at once more direct in their appeal and more abstract in their conceptual approach. *Sunday* imagines the wider world suggested by a famous painting by Georges Seurat in order to explore the nature of artistic creation and its human costs. *Into the Woods* interweaves the stories of familiar fairy tale characters (Cinderella, Little Red Riding Hood, Rapunzel) to pose questions about communal responsibility and individual morality. *Assassins* plays havoc with history by bringing together the killers and would-be killers of America's presidents to examine the nightmare side of the American Dream. *Passion* probes the mysteries of love and obsession as a young man is emotionally drawn away from one woman who is sexually desirable toward another who is plain and dying. *Passion* is so preoccupied with introspection and death, in fact, it quite loses touch with the spirit of what a Broadway show was once assumed to be: "a noisy vulgar, bumptious exhibition of our appetite for life." For critic John Lahr, this show represents nothing less than "the dead end to which Sondheim, in his perverse brilliance, has brought the American musical"—a heavy burden for anyone to bear, even hyperbolically.

Between them, *Sunday* and *Assassins* reflect the range of demands Sondheim's more recent musicals make on audiences. They also reflect the range of responses these shows have elicited and through which they have been culturally understood. Only *Sunday* of all the Sondheim shows won a Pulitzer Prize for drama, which it received during its Broadway run. Only *Assassins* of all the Sondheim shows premiered on Broadway to win a Tony Award not as a new musical but as a revival. Presumably, in the thirteen years between the show's Off Broadway premiere and its first Broadway appearance, the several productions of it in England and elsewhere in America argued for *Assassins*'s meeting Tony eligibility rules as a stagework already deemed a "classic or in the historical or popular repertoire."

Sunday in the Park with George marked a turning point for Sondheim on several fronts. It introduced him to new collaborators and a new way of working in the theater. Foremost among these collaborators was James Lapine (b. 1949), the writer-director with whom he created

Sunday, Woods, Passion and a 1985 revision of *Merrily We Roll Along* (for the La Jolla Playhouse). Sondheim's previous librettists had generally been close to him in age or older—George Furth (1932–2008), *Company, Merrily*; James Goldman (1927–1998), *Follies*; Hugh Wheeler (1912–1987), *Night Music, Sweeney Todd*. This was also true of Hal Prince; but not of Lapine. Sondheim compared the two:

> *The main difference between Jim and Hal is generational. So not only are the methodologies different, but also the temperaments. Hal is my age, we've had a more than thirty-five-year collaboration, and it's something of a marriage. Hal is ebullient, outgoing. Jim is twenty years younger and quiet, soft-spoken. He comes from an off-Broadway background where there is a different way of working and there's more of a community feeling; everybody feels much more like a family— closer, actually, to the experience you have in a school play.*

Significantly, Off Broadway shaped Lapine's theatrical outlook. He first achieved recognition for his work at the New York Shakespeare Festival, where he directed numerous plays, including his own (*Twelve Dreams*, 1978; *Table Settings*, 1980). He then found success directing his first musical (*March of the Falsettos*, 1981) at Playwrights Horizons, another nonprofit company, where his contact with André Bishop would prove of lasting importance. Bishop, as artistic director of Playwrights Horizons and later of Lincoln Center Theater, would play a key role in providing the Off Broadway umbrella for the readings, workshops, and subscription productions through which Sondheim—with and later without Lapine—now approached the creation of his shows.

Lapine, a playwright as well as a director, saw theater from a different angle of vision than the script angle. "I was a photographer and a designer and I just never went to the theater until the late Seventies. And I was more into the avant-garde stuff . . . the visual theater, not stuff that was reliant on a text." Yet his kind of "visual theater," already noticeable in *Sunday in the Park with George*, did not resemble that of, say, *Einstein on the Beach* (1976), the sensational "opera" by Philip Glass and Robert Wilson in which music and images altogether displaced the central role traditionally played by verbal discourse and its meanings. *Sunday* still relied essentially on words, spoken and sung. But its use of a painting rather than a text as the engine for the show reflected a major shift in values on the late twentieth-century musical stage. Sond-heim spoke of how he and Lapine moved from the canvas that they chose to the stage:

> *We realized that the painting was the setting of a play. All the people in that painting . . . when you start speculating on why none of them are looking at each other . . . and maybe there's a reason for that . . . maybe someone was having an affair with another one, or one was related to someone else. And then Jim said, "Of course, the main char-acter's missing." And I said, "Who?" And he said, "The artist." And once he said that, I knew there was a real play there.*

Sunday in the Park with George is a two-act work of fiction though it is grounded in historical fact. It tries to come to grips with an art-ist and his art, viewing each in terms of the other. The art here is *A Sunday Afternoon on the Island of La Grande Jatte*, at once a mounu-mental painting and a monument of nineteenth-century French post-Impressionism: It makes brilliant use of a novel technique of dot-like brushstrokes to depict a once popular recreation spot near Paris. The artist is named George—there is a George in act 1 and a George in act 2, but they are not the same man (though both are played by the same actor). Act 1 takes place in mid-1880s Paris and focuses on the historical Georges Seurat, the painter whose masterpiece visu-ally and thematically dominates the show. Seurat (Mandy Patinkin) is portrayed as a modernist artist through and through. Uncompro-mising in his commitment to art, he removes himself from everyday concerns and neglects the needs of Dot (Bernadette Peters), his mis-tress and the mother of his child. In a moving coup de théâtre at the end of the act, he completes his painting as the separate figures and objects in it, having appeared earlier only isolated and in fragments, all come together to take their final places on the canvas of the stage. Dot, however, though still very much in love with George, decides to move on with her life, marry someone else, and emigrate with him and her child to America.

Act 2 labors under a disadvantage: What theatrical experience could equal the stunning realization of the painting at the conclusion of act 1? As if it were another show, in fact, act 2 takes place one hun-dred years later in New York. It, too, features an artist George, who is presumably the great-grandson of Seurat and Dot. But this George is so caught up in the trendy world of high culture that he has lost touch with his art. At the end of the show he pays a visit to the island of La Grande Jatte itself where Seurat once painted, and where Dot now mystically reappears to inspire him to connect with the past and regain his creativity. *Sunday* thus leaves off on a reassuring note. Moreover, its views of art—of transcendence, inspiration, and artistic genius—are all by now traditional in the extreme. "In philosophy of art, generally, I'm a conservative," says Sondheim. "My beliefs are conservative, but my work is not." What makes *Sunday* difficult, then, is not what it says so much as how it says it. It is not a narrative piece. Its two acts have little to do with one another in time, place, and action. What links them is a theme that works self-referentially as it examines the nature of the creative process itself. That makes *Sunday* a modernist work, indeed a "concept" musical in which meaning is produced "not in a representational correspondence with the world but as a consciously critical engagement with reality that addresses where reality and representation meet."

Sondheim's score makes few concessions in style to Broadway or to popular music generally. Instead, it favors a kind of minimalism of rhythmically detached or repetitive musical ideas that suggest Seurat's pointillist brushstrokes in sound. Its structure is equally demanding. *Sunday*'s most important musical connections occur in sections over large spans of time, and even across the acts. Moreover, when numbers do recur they are not simply reprised but rather reimagined in new contexts—and at times barely recognizable. In "Finishing the Hat" (act 1), for example, Seurat sings wistfully of the personal price he pays as an artist, having to distance himself from Dot and from the everyday world in order to create a work of art (Ex. 13-2a). In "Putting It Together" (act 2), Seurat's great-grandson sings acerbically of the price he pays as an artist, having to neglect his art to devote himself to the everyday politics of the art world in order to succeed (Ex. 13-2b). The two numbers are more than ironically related. For all their differences—in placement and character, in text and tone, in tempo and articulation, in meaning—their melodic contours are the same ("fini-shing the hat"/"put-ting it to-[ge]-ther"). Such correspondences may be essential to make sense of *Sunday*'s musico-dramatic discourse. Indeed, they ground the show and imbue it with an astonishing consis-

tency. But they are difficult for many Broadway theatergoers to hear—
and for at least one Broadway performer as well: the one who first sang
them. Sondheim relates:

> *Mandy had been in the show about a year-and-a-half, and we were*
> *having a farewell party. I don't know what it was that I said, but he*
> *replied: "What do you mean they're the same tune?" I said: "Mandy,*
> *you've been singing it for a year and a half. You didn't know that*
> *'Finishing the Hat' and 'Putting it Together' are the same tune?"*
> *And he looked at me as if I had taken his Christmas away.*

Assassins, by contrast, reverses the relationship. *How* it says what it
says is accessible, often funny, and always tuneful. *What* it says, however, is terrifying. Without stars or a story, the show takes shape as a
revue. Its book, by *Pacific Overtures* librettist John Weidman (b. 1946),
consists of trenchant sketches, some of which are hilarious. And its
score consists of songs which, taken as a whole, form a patchwork of
American musical vernaculars that fall easily on the ears: bluegrass
("The Ballad of Booth"), a Sousa march ("How I Saved Roosevelt"),
a hoedown ("The Ballad of Czolgosz"), a cakewalk ("The Ballad of
Guiteau"), a barbershop quartet ("Gun Song"). Yet everything else
about the songs—from who sings them to why—is horrific. *Assassins*
is no ordinary revue. Its humor is ultimately grim, and its songs are
deceptively pleasant. It is, in fact, a concept musical that takes a deeply

Ex. 13-2a. Stephen Sondheim, music and lyrics: "Finishing the Hat," *Sunday in the Park with George*

Ex. 13-2b. Stephen Sondheim, music and lyrics: "Putting It Together," *Sunday in the Park with George*

ironic stance with regard to the conventions of the musical in order to take a critical look at underlying beliefs in an "American way of life" that most Americans hold dear. Shockingly, it subverts cultural expectations. It not only humanizes the villains of American history (rather than the heroes), it takes them seriously. Weidman elucidates:

> *Thirteen people have tried to kill the President of the United States. Four have succeeded. These murderers and would-be murderers are generally dismissed as maniacs and misfits who have little in common with the rest of us.* Assassins *suggests otherwise.* Assassins *suggests that while these individuals are, to say the least, peculiar—taken as a group they are peculiarly* American. *And that behind the variety of motives which they articulated for their murderous outbursts, they share a common purpose: a desperate desire to reconcile intolerable feelings of impotence with an inflamed and malignant sense of entitlement. Why do these dreadful events happen* here, *with such horrifying frequency, and in such an appallingly similar fashion?* Assassins *suggests it is because we live in a country whose most cherished national myths, at least as currently propagated, encourage us to believe that in America our dreams not only* can *come true, but* should *come true, and if they don't someone or something is to blame.*

Assassins asks deeply disquieting questions. It looks at the American Dream through the eyes of those who responded pathologically when they felt it had failed them—from John Wilkes Booth, who shot Lincoln in 1865, to Lee Harvey Oswald, who shot Kennedy in 1963, and beyond. To clarify the "common purpose" it posits between its killers and would-be killers, the show rearranges American history. But the show also implies certain shared values not only between the men and women portrayed onstage, but between them and those sitting in the audience. The very premise of the show is threatening, if not morally repugnant. *Assassins* is anything but a feel-good show. Nor does it offer comfort at the end, where it fails to deliver any traditional emotional "payoff." The last song simply reprises the first without drawing a conclusion—the idea being, according to Sondheim,

> *not to make a sort of moral point of view at the end. If one attempted to draw a moral it would either be simple-minded and banal and sen-*

The company of *Assassins* forms not a chorus line so much as a police lineup, l. to r.: Annie Golden (Lynette "Squeaky" Fromme), Jonathan Hadary (Charles Guiteau), Debra Monk (Sara Jane Moore), Terrence Mann (Leon Czolgosz), Victor Garber (John Wilkes Booth), Lee Wilkof (Samuel Byck), Eddie Korbich (Giuseppe Zangara), Greg Germann (John Hinckley), and William Parry (Proprietor of a shooting gallery).

tentious or it would be smug and I think undeserved on our part. . . . [The show should end rather] on a note of extreme sadness—sadness for the people, sadness for the situation, and sadness for any set of circumstances that invites or promotes or encourages the kind of horrifying acts that these people did.

Compounding the inherent difficulties of the show, there have been external obstacles to *Assassins*'s success that have haunted its most important productions in New York. Its 1991 Off Broadway premiere coincided with the Persian Gulf War. A decade later, slated for its first Broadway production by the Roundabout Theater Company, it was blown off course by the devastation of 9/11 and its aftermath. The authors' rationale for postponing the Broadway production revealed much about the sensitive nature of the show itself:

> Assassins *is a show which asks audiences to think critically about various aspects of the American experience. In light of Tuesday's murderous assault on our nation and on the most fundamental things in which we believe, we . . . believe this is not an appropriate time to present a show which makes such a demand.*

Theatergoers of a conservative bent may have been forgiven for wondering at the time whether *any* time was appropriate. Or for wondering the same perhaps with respect to other Sondheim shows as well. In fact, except for *Forum, Company,* and *A Little Night Music*—none them blockbusters—Sondheim musicals have failed to find an audience sufficient to pass the Broadway acid test: Can a show can run long enough to recoup its investment? This makes Sondheim perhaps the first major figure in the history of Broadway musicals to have made a career predominantly on flops.

The term "flops" in this context is somewhat misleading, however. If success is counted in box-office receipts, then most of Sondheim's shows technically flopped on Broadway when they were new. But they were not flops in a simple sense: shows that lost money, closed, and disappeared. Because of the compelling originality and high artistic quality of Sondheim's output, most of his shows have had vigorous Broadway afterlives, especially in England and in the regional theaters of the United States. Moreover, by now a new Broadway generation has grown up that never saw the originals, and sufficient time has passed for the majority of the shows to have returned to New York in new productions to play Broadway a second time as revivals. Of course, Sondheim's oeuvre may not yet constitute a canon of classic musicals. Yet the Kennedy Center in Washington, D.C., did much to move public perception in that direction when in 2002 it produced an extraordinary season of six of his shows in repertory, from *Company* to *Passion* (see p. 552). In Sondheim's case, then, the hit/flop dichotomy so ingrained in Broadway thinking demands a more nuanced approach. If for the most part his shows may not have been Broadway hits, they may have proved themselves not exactly flops either.

Repertoire or canon? Poster depicting the shows (and an event) produced as part of the Kennedy Center's 2002 Sondheim Celebration, l. to r., top: *Pacific Overtures*, Frank Rich's interview with Sondheim (pencil), *Company*; center: *A Little Night Music*, *Passion*, *Sunday in the Park with George*; bottom: *Sweeney Todd*, *Merrily We Roll Along*, *Into the Woods, Jr.* (an abridged version of *Into the Woods* for middle-school-aged performers).

Thus Sondheim's work endures despite the formidable demands it poses and its lack of major commercial success. That durability is based on a quality of work and of mind unequaled by anyone presently working in the field of commercial musical theater. From the consummate detail of his songs to the broad moral vision of his shows, Sondheim has set a new standard not only for the Broadway musical but for what a Broadway musical might mean. No comparable writer of the past generation has been able consistently to marry words and music to match his in sheer craft, wit, dramatic incisiveness, and psychological penetration. Nor has anyone's achievement in the medium been more widely recognized, if not always entirely appreciated. He has accrued Tonys for Best Broadway Musical (*Company, Follies, Night Music, Sweeney Todd, Into the Woods, Passion*), Grammys for Best Show Album (*Company, Night Music, Sweeney Todd, Sunday, Into the Woods, Passion*), even an Oscar for Best Song in a Film ("Sooner or Later" from *Dick Tracy*, 1990)—awards that are now endemic to the entertainment industry and generally considered its pinnacles of recognition. At the same time he has been singled out for distinctions more intellectual or purely artistic in kind, and extraordinary for someone in the business of writing Broadway shows: election to the American Academy and Institute of Arts and Letters (1983), appointment as first Visiting Professor of Contemporary Theatre at Oxford University (1990), bestowal of a National Medal of Arts from the National Endowment for the Arts (1997). Sondheim's output has even become the subject of dissertations, monographs, and essays pouring forth from the very academic community that once regarded the musical itself as unproblematically middlebrow, thus neither sufficiently low sociologically nor sufficiently high aesthetically to engage the sustained attention of first-rate critical minds. If this has changed, it is Sondheim's work that has perhaps proved most persuasive in altering perceptions, in effect, repositioning the musical on the cultural spectrum between amusement and art.

Such is the legacy of the concept musical as, through the metaphor angle, it has opened up Broadway showmaking to modernist perspectives during its quarter-century heyday from *Cabaret* to *Assassins*. But there is a troubling dimension to so remarkable an achievement. Embracing such overtly self-conscious forms of artistic expression, the musical—or at least a significant segment of Broadway musical activity—may be losing its ability to engage a broader public. The musical may simply be losing touch with what has made it a popular and commercially viable entertainment in the past. Here, more than anyone else's, Sondheim's shows have become emblems— even inspirations to a new generation of writers with less direct ties to Broadway traditions than his. At times such shows suggest, through their example, that the musical may be in the process of transforming itself beyond recognition. And this has led to a reevaluation not only of the proper cultural place conceptually for such creations, but of the proper venue for producing them, which may no longer be on Broadway—or on Broadway's terms. David Walsh and Len Platt, two British cultural and social critics, see this as a problem and, while they frame it in European terms, their concerns have broader relevance:

> In many ways, Sondheim's effect on the musical has been to create a musical for connoisseurs, and this may not be so problematic in itself. What does become problematic for the form of the musical pioneered by Sondheim (which is very rich in an aesthetic sense) is if it becomes, as is often the case with Sondheim's musicals in Europe, a musical to be found only in state-subsidized theaters and opera houses and not in commercial theater. Historically the musical has been produced by commercial theater. It may be a tribute to the musical as a form to find itself in the cultural realm of state-subsidized art, but this distances it from popular culture. It is given, through such theatrical institutionalization, the characteristics of "high" culture. Neither popular culture nor the musical could be seen to gain from this in the end, because it would encourage an artifice that loses contact with the organic. More specifically, the musical may lose its ability to entertain.

To entertain means simply to hold one's attention. But the word can be used in seemingly conflicting ways: on the one hand, to amuse or to divert; on the other, to consider or to contemplate, as to entertain an idea. The writers here clearly have amusement in mind. Their concern may be warranted. Certain stageworks now call themselves musicals in which the entertainment factor long associated with musicals has been reduced or virtually eliminated: *Caroline, or Change* (2004) reserves it mainly for a radio and laundry appliances that happen to sing; *Marie Christine* (1999) tells a new and yet no less bleak version of the story of *Medea*. If such works can be said to entertain, they come down more nearly on the side of contemplation than amusement.

But neither of these pieces is a concept musical—and tellingly so. For the brilliance of the concept musical at its best lies in its very ability to entertain in both senses of the word at once. And this holds true in large measure even of Sondheim's musicals for connoisseurs, wherever they happen to be performed. They regularly refer to nearly all the elements of entertainment traditionally found in musicals save perhaps for dance, which figures less insistently in Sondheim's shows apart from his collaborations in the early 1970s with choreographer Michael Bennett. Dance would figure centrally in the development of a different kind of concept musical, however, and Bennett himself would play a key role in that development. Bennett saw dance, in fact, as the quintessence of the musical, and he would join the efforts of other key figures from the world of Broadway dance to reconceptualize the concept musical and turn the idea of a director's theater altogether into that of a choreographer's.

14

A DANCING PLACE

ALLEGRO

(10/10/1947–7/10/1948). **Producer:** The Theater Guild. **Book and Lyrics:** Oscar Hammerstein II. **Music:** Richard Rodgers. **Director and Choreographer:** Agnes de Mille. **New York Run:** 315 performances. **Cast:** Lisa Kirk, John Battles. **Songs:** "A Fellow Needs a Girl," "The Gentleman Is a Dope."

HELLO, DOLLY!

(1/16/1964–12/27/1970). **Producer:** David Merrick. **Book:** Michael Stewart, suggested by Thornton Wilder's play *The Matchmaker*. **Lyrics and Music:** Jerry Herman. **Director and Choreographer:** Gower Champion. **New York Run:** 2,844 performances. **Cast:** Carol Channing, David Burns. **Songs:** "Before the Parade Passes By," "Hello, Dolly!"

CHICAGO

(6/3/1975–8/27/1977). **Producers:** Robert Fryer and James Cresson. **Book:** Fred Ebb and Bob Fosse, derived from the play *Chicago* by Maurine Dallas Watkins. **Lyrics:** Ebb. **Music:** John Kander. **Director and Choreographer:** Fosse. **New York Run:** 923 performances. **Cast:** Gwen Verdon, Chita Rivera, Jerry Orbach. **Songs:** "All That Jazz," "Razzle Dazzle," "Nowadays."

Jerome Robbins (in black), choreographer, director, and conceiver of *West Side Story*, dances with the cast in rehearsal.

A CHORUS LINE

(7/25/1975–4/28/1990). **Producer:** Joseph Papp. **Book:** James Kirkwood and Nicholas Dante. **Lyrics:** Edward Kleban. **Music:** Marvin Hamlisch. **Director and Choreographer:** Michael Bennett. **New York Run:** 6,137 performances. **Cast:** Donna McKechnie, Priscilla Lopez, Sammy Williams. **Songs:** "I Hope I Get It," "At the Ballet," "Nothing," "One," "What I Did for Love."

GRAND HOTEL

(11/12/1989–4/25/1992). **Producers:** Paramount Pictures Corporation, Jujamcyn Theaters, Martin Richards, Mary Lea Johnson, and others. **Book:** Luther Davis, based on the Vicki Baum novel *Grand Hotel* (*Menschen im Hotel*) and the 1932 screenplay by Baum and others. **Songs:** Robert Wright, George Forrest, and Maury Yeston. **Additional Music:** Wally Harper. **Director and Choreographer:** Tommy Tune. **New York Run:** 1,017 performances. **Cast:** Karen Akers, David Carroll, Michael Jeter. **Songs:** "We'll Take a Glass Together."

T he work of Harold Prince played a pivotal role in transforming the musical theater of the last third of the twentieth century into a director's theater. But Prince himself was something of an anomaly among the influential show directors of the age. He was *not* a choreographer at a time when a big Broadway hit with a distinctive look and flow to it was usually the creation of a director who was. In fact, the longest-running American blockbusters of the era were almost all the products of directors who had risen from the ranks of choreographers: *Fiddler on the Roof,* Jerome Robbins; *Hello, Dolly!* and *42nd Street,* Gower Champion; *A Chorus Line,* Michael Bennett.

These shows exuded a new sense of what was physically possible on the musical stage. They were shaped by directors who saw performance and spectatorship through the lens of dance. Their approach to dancing may have differed: Robbins came from the ballet; Champion had been a hoofer; Bennett began as a Broadway gypsy. But they were driven by a common ideal in which a Broadway show might now be more integrated through its movement and visual design than through its scripted material. The ideal attracted other dance-trained directors as well, Bob Fosse and Tommy Tune being the most successful among them. And together, for more than a generation—roughly from the opening of *West Side Story* (1957) to the closing of *A Chorus Line* (1990) and beyond—such dancers/stagers helped reinvent the musical genre by merging the functions of a choreographer with those of a director. This new kind of musical extended "dance sensibility into realms beyond dancing" and it bore the unmistakable stamp of a new kind of creator: a choreographer-director, or director-choreographer—in effect, a superdirector. This development did not happen overnight. It was decades in the making. To appreciate how it came about, one needs to delve into Broadway history a bit to trace the evolution of show dancing and the ways the choreographers of shows have gone about their business.

It took most of the first half of the twentieth century to develop a characteristic Broadway dance style of some distinction. In the first three decades of the century, Broadway dance was robust but rudimentary, its basic vocabulary limited to steps and movements derived largely from social, stage, and jazz-based dance styles of the period. These were arranged into fairly standardized routines for production numbers, which ranged from tap to class acts—those with top hat and tails. Frequently, the routines involved precision-dancing kick lines of all-girl troupes of the kind that John Tiller (1854–1925) famously brought to Broadway from England during the First World War. The girls generally were poorly paid and had little professional ability as dancers. But then, the dances they danced functioned simply as embellishments to a show, exciting for audiences to watch perhaps for their feminine delights and rhythmic charms, but offering only a limited idea of what choreography could do. Those who created the dances and drilled the girls in them were not considered choreographers at all, in fact. They were the show's dance directors. And as they did not work equally well in all styles of movement and dance idioms, they tended to specialize. A Broadway show might thus credit contributions from several dance directors in a single production: one for overall supervision, the rest for special numbers or for bringing in their own dancers for a particular sequence. Director Hassard Short "staged" Marilyn Miller's *Sunny* in 1925; Julian Mitchell received credit for supervising the dances, along with Dave Bennett "for his tap numbers, John Tiller for his precision lines (called 'Marilyn Miller Cocktails'), Alexis Kosloff for the ballet sequences, and Fred Astaire for his work on the social-dance routines for Miller."

Such practices continued well into the 1930s and beyond. But by then, forms of concert dance were making inroads on the commercial stage and changing the outlook there for both the dancers and the dance. Chester Hale and Albertina Rasch led notable Broadway troupes in a blend of show-style movement and ballet, or "toe-dancing." But it was Ballet Russe choreographer George Balanchine who gave the strongest impetus to the growth of ballet on Broadway when he settled in New York in 1933. Until he formed his own company in 1948, Balanchine not only created numerous show ballets (*On Your Toes, I Married an Angel*), he also famously demanded that such commercial work be recognized as "choreography"—and got his way (see chapter 7, p. 280). Modern dance, too, was taking root in American soil at the same time, most influentially through the work of Ruth St. Denis and Ted Shawn and their Denishawn Dance Company. Of their students, Doris Humphrey worked regularly on the commercial stage both independently and together with Charles Weidman, another Denishawn graduate and Broadway's most successful early modern dance choreographer (*As Thousands Cheer, I'd Rather Be Right*).

The development of a distinctive form of modern Broadway dance resulted from the convergence of these two quite separate traditions: "one the earlier-day Broadway musical, which purveyed popular entertainment that was vibrant but limited in its horizons; the other the newly introduced forms of ballet and modern dance, which for its small but ardent following had connotations of 'high' art and spiritual ennoblement." But dances of any kind, cultivated or vernacular, served a limited function in the structure of a Broadway show. Their appearances were discrete, not ongoing; their purposes energizing, not narrative.

In the Broadway chain of command, a dance director was almost always subordinate to a stage director. The stage director often managed an entire production but mainly worked with the actors on whom a show focused. He motivated them as individual characters, coached them in delivering lines, and gave them their blocking—that is, the arrangement of the actors' stage movements. He also worked without music. (Rouben Mamoulian was an exceptional director, so musical he even staged the songs in his shows. Director George S. Kaufman, on the other hand, seems to have had no use for music whatsoever.) The dance director, by contrast, worked with an ensemble of dancers, both nameless and voiceless as they were meant only to be seen—and then often simply as visual ornaments to songs. For the dance director, however, music was indispensable in creating "the composition, steps, movement, and dynamics that constitute a dance"—that is, in creating the more stylized movement patterns of choreography.

The director and the dance directors or choreographers tended to work separately until late in the rehearsal process of a show. Their functions differed, and so did their priorities. "A choreographer is never afraid to move you around, while most directors have their mind on keeping you where you will be heard," Gwen Verdon remarked. As a star dancer and actress combined, Verdon had much experience of both. She also had her preference. "Choreographers have a greater sense of the visual, the composition of a scene, the look of a scene. You don't have to depend on words all the time." Words, however, were the stock in trade of directors who, like George Abbott, were frequently at a loss in dealing with dancers altogether: "They live in their own world," he said. "They talk to the rest of us, they sometimes marry us, but at the same time they shut us out. We can never learn to speak their language unless we become one of them. We call them gypsies—and they call themselves that." Less musical than choreographers as a rule and virtual aliens in the galaxy of dance, directors had to work within their more earthbound limitations. "My strong suit is with text," Hal Prince confessed. "If I were a choreographer and I got into trouble, I'd probably rush right down to my feet to solve the problem. I can't do that. [I rush] to my head, to the words."

In general, the division of labor between a director and a choreographer reflected the textual division of a show into a book and a score. A book required blocking; a score, choreography. Yet a score typically called for other modes of stage demeanor as well: song, mime, stage movement—indeed, for a range of physical activities that, while neither quite blocking nor choreography, could bridge the gap of stylization between them. This was elusively referred to as *musical staging*, and it involved "moving singers, dancers, and actors around the stage in a musical number." Falling between the jurisdictional cracks, it might be entrusted to a director, to a choreographer, or even to a third-party specialist. *Lady in the Dark*, which was almost a spoken play but for three long and richly musicalized dream sequences, actually made use of all three. During rehearsals, Moss Hart directed the play in one Broadway theater, Albertina Rasch choreographed the dream dances in another, and Hassard Short staged the rest of the musical dream scenes in yet a third.

Under the rallying cry of "integration" in the 1940s, however, writers who sought a closer blend between a show's book and score were apt to work with stagers who might match their efforts. In directing *Carousel*, for example, Rouben Mamoulian asked his actors not to break character as they switched from speaking lines to singing lyrics. A song was to further the narrative, he said; it *must give a feeling of dialogue to music. And the same thing is true of the element of speech. The nearer it comes to a song the more rhythmic the speech becomes. And the movement must all be rhythmic too. Realistic movement would be terrible in this musical. What you finally have is a balance or a blend of rhythms, but all so sustained that it seems perfectly natural.*

This approach made it less clear where a stage director's responsibilities left off and those of a dance director began. The ambiguity led to certain turf wars. Mamoulian clashed with choreographer Agnes de Mille over *Carousel*'s "Prologue," in fact. As this exquisite number took the place of an overture, it was musical. But it was also staged though nothing in it was sung, or spoken, or danced. "This scene is set to the music of a waltz suite," reads the script. "The only sound comes from the orchestra pit. The pantomimic action is synchronized to the music, but it is in no sense a ballet treatment." Since musical staging was thus called for, the two directors entered into an uneasy truce to achieve it.

By the start of the 1950s a choreographer would take over such musical staging entirely, as Michael Kidd did when he directed the "Runyonland" opening of *Guys and Dolls*. Yet Kidd did not direct the show; George S. Kaufman did. Only later in the decade would a choreographer succeed in staging a show from start to finish, thereby helping to create a new type of musical altogether. Such was Jerome Robbins's achievement in *West Side Story*, and with that show the age of the choreographer-director or director-choreographer is commonly said to have begun. Both designations, however, suggest that the functions on either side of their hyphens existed in equal measure. This was true in theory perhaps, but not in practice. Because of the highly specialized disciplines involved in dance, making a musical a more physical experience throughout was a task that fell more naturally to stagers who began as choreographers and then assumed the authority of directors—not the other way around.

THE BALLET-DIRECTORS: DE MILLE AND ROBBINS

Had Rodgers and Hammerstein's *Allegro* succeeded at its premiere, the age of the choreographer-director might have begun a decade sooner than it did. For the authors assigned all the staging in that show to one person, as if to avoid the recurrence of a *Carousel*-like conflict. Their decision to do so was as extraordinary as was their choice of Agnes de Mille (1905–1993) to do it. De Mille was not a director but a choreographer; furthermore, as a woman, she took on what many still thought of as a man's job. Her formative influences as a choreographer did not come from Broadway at all but from modern dance and classical ballet: In the 1930s she became part of Martha Graham's circle in New York; in London, she worked with Marie Rambert and Antony Tudor. Her return to the United States coincided with Lucia Chase's founding of Ballet Theatre (later American Ballet Theatre), and de Mille created some of her most important pieces for the company (*Three Virgins and a Devil*, 1941; *Fall River Legend*, 1948). But it was her cowboy ballet for the Ballet Russe, *Rodeo* (1942), that called her work to the attention of Rodgers and Hammerstein and led to the first in a string of musical hits that she choreographed for Broadway in the 1940s: *Oklahoma!, One Touch of Venus, Bloomer Girl, Carousel, Brigadoon.* In these works de Mille transformed the function of Broadway dance with unprecedented single-mindedness. She took what had often been no more than a side show, a divertissement, and made it central to the narrative structure of a show: a kinetic means of exploring character and driving home a story. De Mille had thus become a commanding figure on Broadway by the time of *Allegro* in 1947. And given the pedigree of its collaborators, the show seemed destined for success.

But *Allegro*, no ordinary musical, was fraught with problems from the start. Hammerstein's prior shows with Rodgers had been adaptations; here he wrote an original. It traced the life of a man from his birth in a small Midwest town to age thirty-five, when he turned away from a failed marriage and a promising medical career in a Chicago hospital to return to his roots and ultimate fulfillment as a country doctor. The play was sprawling and not a little didactic. A Greek-style chorus, placed in an abstract stage set, told a good part of the story. If, in part at least, *Allegro* may be considered a concept musical before the fact, central to its concept was the work of scenic designer Jo Mielziner (1901–1975). He designed the show to play on an open stage; and he used screen projections to define locales, and treadmills to eliminate set changes so that scenes might flow seamlessly from one into the next. This left the stage free to accommodate the comings and goings of eighteen actors, a chorus of twenty-two dancers, and a singing chorus of thirty-eight. De Mille kept this enormous apparatus of people and devices afloat by bringing a choreographer's instinct, imagination, and technique to bear in shaping it dramatically. But the material never quite came into focus, and the task of getting it on its feet proved overwhelming. Three weeks before *Allegro*'s opening out of town, Hammerstein stepped in to direct his book scenes, as did Rodgers to stage his musical numbers. De Mille, left with only the dances to choreograph, still retained her credit as the show's director. *Allegro* did not succeed, yet her contribution may well have been the most cogent of the undertaking. "For those of us who believe that the salvation of the [musical] theatre depends upon its abandonment of the effort to keep up with the fancy literary set and its acknowledgement of its humble origin in the dithyramb," wrote *New York Times* dance critic John Martin, "Miss de Mille . . . succeeded in giving form and substance to material with little of either to boast of."

De Mille would continue on into the 1960s choreographing eight more musicals; even the most popular of these (*Paint Your Wagon, 110 in the Shade*) failed to match her earlier successes. James Mitchell, one of her lead dancers, described what he felt were her shortcomings:

> *She had a limited vocabulary and wasn't interested, for instance, in jazz. She didn't like anything abstract, didn't know what it was. There was no moving forward into new areas of dance or explorations of new kinds of movement. She didn't catch up with what was happening, and so other choreographers rode over her.*

Nonetheless, de Mille's sensational successes of the 1940s altered the very purpose of show dancing, and the innovative role she played in *Allegro* inspired a breed of young dancers, almost all now classically trained, to become Broadway choreographers or even choreographer-directors—Michael Kidd (1915–2007), Peter Gennaro (1919–2000), Onna White (1922–2005), Herbert Ross (1927–2001), Joe Layton (1931–1995), and Ron Field (1934–1989). Indeed, those choreographers who turned to directing in the 1950s tended to approach the stage with a sense of invention that stamped otherwise conventional book shows with a memorable theatrical energy, image, and style. But for the most part, they continued to work piecemeal, directing book scenes as one thing and musical numbers as another.

Michael Kidd's work offers a good example. Over more than four decades, Kidd choreographed, directed, and choreographed-directed seventeen Broadway shows. Early in his career he had been a featured dancer with Ballet Theatre, where he danced in works by Fokine and Tudor as well as Robbins and de Mille. In the late 1940s he became a choreographer himself, making his mark both on Broadway (*Finian's Rainbow, Love Life, Guys and Dolls, Can-Can*) and in Hollywood (*The Band Wagon*, 1953; *Seven Brides for Seven Brothers*, 1954). Then in the

"Sadie Hawkins Day Ballet" from *Li'l Abner*, l. to r.: Tina Louise (Appassionata von Climax, standing), Edie Adams (Daisy Mae, jumping), and Peter Palmer (Li'l Abner, flying).

late 1950s he emerged as a choreographer-director with such musicals as *Li'l Abner* and *Destry Rides Again*. Typically, his choreography invested Broadway dancing with a power and athleticism that called upon the gymnastic abilities of his male dancers in particular. Yet as his dances were conceived as set pieces, it is difficult to detect any functional difference between those he created for shows which he did not direct ("The Crapshooters' Dance," *Guys and Dolls*) and those for shows which he did ("The Whip Dance," *Destry*). Only on occasion are there hints of the dual roles of choreographer and director coming together to suggest a larger whole—the fluidity of the "Runyonland" sequence with which the Times Square milieu comes to life in *Guys and Dolls*; the kinetic buildup of *Li'l Abner*'s first act climaxing in the "Sadie Hawkins Day Ballet." But that is about as far as it went.

Jerome Robbins (1918–1998) changed the matter decisively when he succeeded in merging the roles of choreographer and director to effect a seamlessness of style and movement throughout a show. He became the complete choreographer-director first with *Peter Pan* and then masterfully with *West Side Story*. But Robbins approached Broadway dance itself from a rare perspective. He was one of the foremost choreographers in twentieth-century ballet, along with such masters of the form as Michel Fokine, George Balanchine, Antony Tudor, and Frederick Ashton. That he also spent from 1944 to 1964 creating new and even innovative works for Broadway must be understood in the broader context of his sixty-year professional engagement with a variety of forms of dance and theatrical expression.

Robbins worked early on as a Broadway gypsy until he was accepted as a dancer by Ballet Theatre in 1940 and in time created his first major ballet, *Fancy Free*, for the company. In 1948 he joined Balanchine's newly formed New York City Ballet, where he danced, choreographed (*The Cage*, 1951; *The Concert*, 1956), and soon became associate artistic director. He left to form his own dance company, Ballets: USA (1958–1961), then also directed plays and headed his own American Lab (1966–1968), where he aimed to "make theater pieces the way I make ballets." But he returned to the City Ballet in 1969 as a choreographer (*Dances at a Gathering*, 1969; *Watermill*, 1972) and eventually as co-ballet master in chief with Peter Martins.

While his involvement with cultivated dance provides the one continuous thread in his career, Robbins also worked commercially in television, film, and, above all, on Broadway where he is credited with contributions to fifteen book shows. In addition, he was among the most savvy of show doctors (uncredited but usually well compensated) coming into rehearsals when the musicals of others were in trouble, diagnosing the ailment, and prescribing the cure—*Wonderful Town, Silk Stockings, A Funny Thing Happened on the Way to the Forum.* Robbins's intervention in *Forum*'s opening number, for example, is a now well-known instance of his doctoring to salvage an otherwise fine show that wasn't working during its tryout in Washington, D.C. What ended with Sondheim writing a raucous new song for the opening number, "Comedy Tonight," and Robbins staging it, began quite differently. In Robbins's words:

> *That was someone not thinking deeply enough about what they were doing. [Forum] started out with sort of a nice ballad, "Love Is in the Air." And then very slowly [as the show progressed] the humor started to work in. I said, "I think that's all wrong and I think it is for this reason: you've got to tell the audience what this show is about. You've got to make them understand this is a comedy [right from the start]. Let them get used to the fun of it. They're ready. They'll laugh at anything. And then you'll be on the right track." So, they did that, and it worked. Then the whole show began to switch.*

Robbins made his earliest mark as a Broadway choreographer in *On the Town, Billion Dollar Baby, High Button Shoes, Call Me Madam,* and *The King and I.* Memorable here were his extended dance sequences that told stories with utmost wit and poignance—but still as set pieces within their shows ("Mack Sennett Ballet," *High Button Shoes;* "The Small House of Uncle Thomas," *The King and I*). In 1954 Robbins moved into directing with conspicuous success in *The Pajama Game* (codirected with George Abbott); then both choreographed and directed *Peter Pan* and *Bells Are Ringing* (co-choreographed with Bob Fosse); and established himself finally as the consummate choreographer-director with *West Side Story* (co-choreographed with Peter Gennaro), *Gypsy,* and *Fiddler on the Roof.*

With his first foray into musical comedy, *On the Town,* Robbins stretched the scope of Broadway dance: The show derived not from any literary source but from his *Fancy Free* ballet scenario. "My feeling was that 'On the Town' had been planned, worked out, and delivered in a ballet key," said critic Louis Biancolli, who referred to the show as a "ballet comedy."

> By that I mean the sense of kinetic action is felt even where ballet isn't the featured factor. Dialogue and song often appear geared to a dynamic pattern, as if any moment things will blaze again into dance. . . . [Ballet] is as much embedded in the fabric as the music—maybe more so. Ordinarily, in a standard musical, you're not surprised when talk suddenly modulates to song. Anyone can break out singing in a nostalgic monologue or romantic duet, and you feel that's the way it should be. Song becomes a kind of a heightened speech—set by the mood and surroundings. In "One the Town" you feel that way about the dance.

The piece was still very much a book show, however, and Robbins, used to the norms of ballet, was unprepared to put dance into a non-dance context.

> On the Town . . . was very dancy, with a lot of musical numbers, and when they went on the stage, a lot of them didn't work. That was a shock to me. It was the first time I learned the lesson that one's work in a musical is not alone on the stage—what comes right before and after it can affect it. A dance may be absolutely wonderful, but it may not go at all because of the way the audience is at that point. . . .
>
> The master of it all was Mr. Abbott. . . . He stepped right in, took my second-act ballet—which I thought was terrific, I still believe in the conception of it—cut it right down the middle and put a scene in between the halves. The ballet was a dream image of what Coney Island was going to be like, and then the reality of it. I wanted to contrast them, but he said, "No, we have to cut this."

Collaborating with Abbott on half a dozen shows over the next decade, Robbins learned the director's craft from one of its ablest practitioners. He also explored "what the difference was in the source of expression for acting as opposed to dancing" at the Actors Studio, and used the Method acting technique taught there in his subsequent work both in ballet and on Broadway.

All this came together with telling effect in *West Side Story*—the musical, as de Mille saw it, in which Robbins "realized the potentialities of an effort that I began in *Allegro*." Like *Allegro*, *West Side Story* had its "Entire Production Directed and Choreographed" by one person—so ran the credit. But the later show no longer noticeably separated actors and singers from dancers. Its chorus was now made up of individual characters each of whom had to act and sing as well as dance. Robbins even shaped his dances around the characters' natural movements so as to eliminate any break between blocking and choreography. Thus dancing in *West Side Story* was no longer physically separable from the rest of the production as the show moved with kinetic fluency from one scene to the next. In a nondance scene, for example, Maria tries on the new party dress she will wear at a dance that evening, her first dance in America since coming to New York from Puerto Rico. As she whirls ecstatically around the room in it, colored streamers descend, the room slides off, and other girls whirl onstage who are already jitterbugging in the next scene, the dance at the gym. "In an instant," said critic Frank Rich, Robbins "simultaneously raised the heroine's emotional pitch, advanced the plot, and changed the set without ever interrupting the continuous flow of dance."

West Side Story had an additional credit that distinguished it from *Allegro*: It was "Based on a Conception" of the same person who choreographed-directed it. Not just the production but the composition, too, was now subject to the stager's supervision: Robbins was collaborator in chief right from the start. Indeed, the deliberately skeletal libretto and the heightened musical staging needed to flesh it out were so much of a piece it was almost impossible to imagine a different production of *West Side Story* without losing the essence of the work. Robbins was a musical playwright, in effect, by other than scripted means. And with his double program credit he claimed the authority of a staging author in the show, if not quite to shape his own material, then at least so thoroughly to reshape the material of others that it became his own.

By the time of *Fiddler on the Roof,* Robbins had become the seminal force in designing a musical and a master overseer in getting it to work from every angle. "He drove everybody crazy because he had a vision that extended down to the littlest brushstroke in the scenery and the triangle part in the orchestra," said Sheldon Harnick. Robbins's vision and his relentlessness in its pursuit made the show:

> *He was like the world's greatest district attorney, asking us question after question, probing—"What's the show about?"—and not being satisfied with the glib answers we were giving. We kept saying, "Well, it's about a dairy farmer and his daughters and trying to find husbands for them," and he kept saying things like, "Yeah, but that's 'Previous Adventures of the Goldberg Family,'" and he didn't want to do that. I don't know who finally made the discovery that the show was really about the disintegration of a whole way of life, but I do remember that it was a surprise to all of us. And once we found that*

"Bottle Dance" from *Fiddler on the Roof*.

out—which was pretty exciting—Robbins said, "Well, if it's a show about tradition and its dissolution, then the audience should be told what that tradition is." He wondered how we could do it succinctly. Then he suggested that we create a song that would be a tapestry against which the whole show would play. So we wrote "Tradition" because he insisted on it.

"Tradition" became *Fiddler*'s spine—the opening number and conceptual through-line of the show. "Once Robbins got the handle that the show was about the dissolution of traditions," said Jerry Bock, "then, in his mind, in some way every scene had to deal with that. The score we had written suddenly was no longer appropriate . . . we had to rewrite nine songs because . . . his idea of what the book was changed." Yet given the conceptual focus of his vision, Robbins never lost sight of the narrative thrust of the piece. *Fiddler* struck a fine balance between the book-based past of Broadway musicals of the postwar era and their concept-oriented future. Robbins himself went no further and effectively retired from Broadway musicals with the show.

Fiddler holds a historically pivotal position on other grounds as well. "Before it, the best choreographers might also direct. After it, the best directors were (except Hal Prince) choreographers"—and the most powerful. They became the new authors, indeed the auteurs of musical theater. Inspired by Robbins's example not only as a choreographer-director but as "the musical's commander-in-chief," they now collaborated with the writers of a show from its inception rather than wait until the rehearsal period to stage what the writers had already written. Thus they turned their backs on veterans like Richard Rodgers who insisted "the director is not a creator: he can suggest additions and changes which then require the approval of the writers." They were directors who came to exercise the power of creators; but their creations were not primarily texts. The most determined among them even effected a revolution in musical theater no less profound in its way than Rodgers's own with Hammerstein. They did so largely by standing the world of Rodgers and Hammerstein on its head: They often looked first to musical staging concepts as the basis for new shows, and only then to the work of writers—if at all.

THE HOOFER-DIRECTORS: CHAMPION AND FOSSE

"After the initial three, Robbins, Kidd, and me, the two choreographers to make the biggest impact on the Broadway scene have been Robert Fosse and Gower Champion." So wrote Agnes de Mille in 1980, and she was on the mark. Yet Fosse and Champion made their impact not only later but from another perspective. While the initial three were all trained in classical ballet, the later two were more at home in the American vernacular. Trained as commercial dancers, they approached terpsichore not through the ethos of the concert stage but through the norms of show business. Theirs was a world of song-and-dancemen and women, "terpers," "hoofers"—a more limited world perhaps, but sufficiently wide nevertheless to encompass a diversity of styles. Champion gravitated to the elegance of the ballroom and the supper club; Fosse, to the sleaze of strip-joints and burlesque.

Yet each forged a personal style out of a variety of sources, indebted above all to the pioneering work of Jack Cole (1911–1974), who developed the jazz dance idiom that has become the dominant look of and technique for dancing in a Broadway show. A former Denishawn dancer, Cole choreographed ten book musicals between 1943 and 1965. Merging classical technique with isolations, acrobatic falls, and knee slides, he created a personal, vital, and sexually charged idiom that combined ballet, jazz, and ethnic styles: Brazilian (*Magdalena*, 1948); Middle Eastern and Indian (*Kismet*); Afro-Cuban (*Jamaica*); Spanish (*Man of La Mancha*). If today his name is less familiar to audiences than Robbins's or de Mille's, his approach lives on in the work of virtually every major choreographer active on Broadway since the 1950s. Cole was, de Mille said, "the first commercial choreographer to put a lasting stamp on the national style."

That style stamped the work of Champion and Fosse as well. But each of them also developed into a major choreographer-director, which Cole never did (his few Broadway forays into the terrain were outright failures). During the 1960s and 1970s, then, these two sought ways to stretch their styles over the course of an evening's-length entertainment. But where de Mille and Robbins drew on their ballet backgrounds to create a sense of movement uniquely suited to a particular show, Champion and Fosse each developed a personal idiom that was more immediately recognizable from one show to the next. In their best work as choreographer-directors, nonetheless, they succeeded in turning style itself into the cohesive force of a show—above all, in *Hello, Dolly!* and *Chicago*, respectively.

Early in his career Gower Champion (1920–1980) established a national following through his television and film appearances as half of a popular dance team with his wife Marge. On Broadway he danced, choreographed, and directed in the 1940s and 1950s, mostly in revues, then came into his own in the 1960s as a superstager of book musicals. Among the hits of the nine original shows for which he is credited as choreographer-director are the earliest—*Bye Bye Birdie* (1960), *Carnival* (1961), *Hello, Dolly!* (1964), *I Do! I Do!* (1966)—and the last, *42nd Street* (1980). While no two of these shows had scores by the same writers, almost all had books by Michael Stewart (1929–1987). And for each Champion characteristically devised tableaux, choreographed movement, and stage design, and he made such elements thematic. *Birdie*, for example, was a cartoon of midcentury American foibles centered on the teenage mania over a rock-'n'-roll idol. For the show's "The Telephone Hour" sequence, Champion built an enormous honeycomb set and placed a solitary teenager on the phone in each of the cells. It made a vivid stage picture as they sang and danced together that also caught the teenagers' isolation, connected as they were to one another only by their phones. For *Carnival*, a more poignant piece about a traveling circus troupe, Champion made thematic use of a "unit set": On a bare stage at the opening the troupe set up its tent, filled it with life during the course of the show, and took it down at the end.

By the time of *Hello, Dolly!*, Champion's stage design went so far as to require restructuring the very theater in which the show was performed. "When I'm considering a show, I usually get a visual picture of something in my mind. In *Dolly!* it was the wrap around the orchestra." This involved extending the stage out with a runway between the orchestra and the audience—a scheme producer David Merrick rejected out of hand. Besides the added cost up front, it would eliminate a hundred of the choicest, most expensive seats in the house. Merrick not only held the purse strings, he famously terrorized those he hired for his shows. But in the ensuing clash of wills, Champion prevailed, certain indication of his growing power in the theater: He would be the first choreographer-director to receive star billing over the title of a show. (While Merrick was often called Broadway's "abominable showman," Champion, it was said, was its "Presbyterian Hitler.") This reflected the status now accorded to stagers in general, and institutionalized when in 1959 they formed their own union, the Society of Stage Directors and Choreographers, which gained contractual recognition in 1962 from the League of American Theaters and Producers (now The Broadway League).

Hello, Dolly! was an entertainment package conceived and produced by Merrick, who years before had produced the play on which it was based, Thornton Wilder's *The Matchmaker*. A farce set in 1890s New York, the play revolved around a fun-loving, meddlesome widow Dolly Gallagher Levi (Carol Channing) whose outrageous connivings as a marriage broker result in her bringing three young couples together and snaring a churlish "half-a-millionaire" (David Burns) for herself. Stewart deftly fit the play to musical comedy norms, deleting the low farce elements of the original and delivering its comedic highs to song and dance. The songs by Jerry Herman (b. 1933) were skillful showtune evocations of a bygone age. Herman, who would go on to create several notable Broadway scores (*Mame*, 1966; *Mack and Mabel*, 1974; *La Cage aux Folles*, 1983), wrote with an idealized past in mind of which he apparently still sees himself as the avatar. He describes himself without irony as "Mr. Show Business, the razzmatazz musical-comedy writer, a cheerful man whose life is dedicated to making people smile and feel good and leave the theater humming a showtune." And in the mid-1960s *Dolly!*'s title song had many across the nation humming it who had never even seen the show. (Not only did it become a pop standard in its own right, especially as recorded by Louis Armstrong, but the Democratic Party adapted and adopted it for the 1964 presidential campaign of Lyndon Johnson.)

The song is unremarkable, however, save for its observing the right conventions to convey the sense of a song anyone raised in the sound-world of Tin Pan Alley might have heard before (Ex. 14-1). (A plagiarism suit against its composer was settled out of court, with the plaintiff reputedly receiving $275,000.) As a theater song, it lacks a distinct dramatic profile of its own, which is perhaps its cardinal virtue in the show: It provides the occasion for something else. Indeed, what

Ex. 14-1. Jerry Herman, music and lyrics: "Hello, Dolly!," *Hello, Dolly!*

survives of *Hello, Dolly!* as a scripted piece of work gives less an indication of what made the show the unprecedented hit it became than what vanished with its Broadway production: the larger-than-life portrayal of star comedienne Carol Channing (and her several replacements by larger-than-life stars of the past, including Ginger Rogers, Pearl Bailey, and Ethel Merman); the sumptuous sets of Oliver Smith suggesting turn-of-the-century rotogravures theatrically come to life; and the Gower Champion touch from start to finish.

The song "Hello, Dolly!," in fact, was the first thing Champion worked on in rehearsal and, once he decided how to stage it, it became the touchstone for the rest of the show. Carol Channing recalled:

> *At first, he wanted* Dolly *to be an intimate musical. He said, "You must start rehearsing with the 'Hello, Dolly' number. If I were Josh Logan, we'd start with the dialogue, and we'd all be on our books for the first two weeks, until we had the lines learned. I can't do that. As soon as I know how you all sing and dance, then I know your characters." . . . We spent the first two weeks on the "Dolly" number. He wanted it to be little. Then he moved the waiters in, and the cooks, and everybody in the Harmonia Gardens, and it got bigger and bigger. Then he said, "I think we should make the steps higher." And he would run around to the back of the theatre and say, "Spread out more" and run back again. He would look and say, "I can't get it big enough. These boys are too dinky—get bigger boys next to her." Then he'd say, "Gee, now we've got it." It was getting mammoth, and he realized, "I haven't got an intimate show here." That's how Gower got his level.*

In context, "Hello, Dolly!" appears in act 2 as Dolly is about to wreak supreme havoc in the name of matchmaking. She has arranged for several rendezvous at cross-purposes to take place at the same time in the Harmonia Gardens, a once-favorite restaurant to which she is returning after an absence of many years. The scene begins with a "Waiters' Gallop," a split-second choreographic tour de force with waiters and busboys performing the "lightning service" for which the restaurant is famous—as Walter Kerr described it, "racing through a silverware concerto in which chairs float about, shish-kebab skewers duel one another, and stacks of jellied dishes change hands in the night. The moment peace is restored, a pair of curtains part and [Dolly] comes down a long stairway, red [dress] on red [carpeting], to begin the evening's title song." First sung by Dolly as she makes her grand entrance, the song turns into the waiters' 32-bar salute to Dolly's feeling, as she says, "back home where I belong." It is heard five times all told (in a variety of tempos, keys,

"Waiters' Gallop" from *Hello, Dolly!*

and song and dance combinations) without stopping until Dolly and the waiters have leaped and high-kicked it cakewalk-style across the brightly lit runaway in front of the orchestra, finishing almost in the laps of the audience.

Little in postwar musical comedy surpassed the sheer exuberance of this showstopper. But for those who approached musicals seeking dramatic causes for their effects, it seemed prodigal to lavish so much on a moment of so little import to the plot. "It's a moment of extraordinary theatrical artifice," wrote one critic, "in that it evokes an emotion for which there has been absolutely no preparation." The lack, not an oversight, was inherent in Champion's approach to the musical medium. Wilder, said librettist Peter Stone, distilled the essence of his play in the conversations at the tables in the restaurant. But "Gower put a curtain around the tables and staged a big splashy number, the waiters' dance. David Hartman was the head waiter. You could hardly miss him and the other dancers running around with trays. All you missed were matters of the utmost consequence—happening off-set behind a curtain."

Stone saw clearly into the heart of the matter; all he missed, however, was the point. As a play, *The Matchmaker* unfolded in dramatic time; it worked its way from start to finish through the linear trajectories of the spoken word. *Dolly!* was not only a musical, by contrast, but one which figuratively winked at the audience from time to time to indicate it was aware of itself as such. It did not necessarily dispense with *Matchmaker*'s trajectories. Rather, it paid lip service to them as it condensed them in order to revel in another sense of time: a musical time, as it were, that more often than not proved dramatically static. In directing a musical comedy rather than a play, then, Champion treated the whole musical sequence leading up to and including "Hello, Dolly!" as if this were a matter of the utmost consequence as well. And given the premium that a musical comedy traditionally placed on the visual and aural energy of a number unfolding in musical time, it was. If it also seemed dramatically unmotivated, audiences generally knew well enough not to mind or even to care. On the contrary, highlighting the interplay between the very differences in time was part of what musical comedy was all about; and Champion's gift for staging such artifice, here and throughout the show, ultimately made *Hello, Dolly!* the extraordinary hit it turned out to be. Not until his 1980 reworking for Broadway of the 1933 Busby Berkeley film *42nd Street* would he again achieve a success comparable to *Dolly!*'s—a success of which he never learned. Champion died on the day the show opened in New York. Merrick, however, kept the news secret until after the performance, when he stopped the curtain calls to announce it from the stage. (Whether or not it was intended, Merrick's action won him a new publicity: The next day his photo appeared in a front-page story in the *New York Times*. Merrick would not get such coverage again until his own death in 2000.)

The success of choreographic direction gave a new boost to the notion of integration in a musical—only this time, not from the script angle so much as out of concern for the totality of a live performance. "Musicals are more of a piece now, not scenes directed by one man and dance numbers staged by another," said Bob Fosse, Champion's younger contemporary. "The ideal is to make the movement consistent throughout, make the actors' movements blend with the dance movements." That ideal in time became the very substance of Fosse's shows as he increasingly approached musical staging not as a means but as an end in itself. Fosse in fact thrived on extremes, even to the point of self-destruction. His, however, was but an extreme case of the general trend.

That Bob Fosse (1927–1987) began dancing professionally as a teenage hoofer in Chicago strip houses comes as no surprise. The distinctive idiom he would develop as a choreographer was an erotically charged one derived from what E. L. Doctorow called "the galvanism of burlesque's bump and grind that he distributed throughout the body in a kind of satire of our sexual nature." Fosse characteristically used dance to bait and wink at his audiences at once, as he worked in the theater within and against the conventions of musical comedy. His Broadway career lasted from 1954 to 1986 and can be understood in two phases. The first marks his development as a choreographer, collaborating with Abbott and Robbins on such shows as *The Pajama Game, Damn Yankees, Bells Are Ringing,* and *New Girl in Town.* The second phase marks his mature work as a choreographer-director, and it includes *Sweet Charity, Pippin, Chicago,* and *Dancin'.* (It also includes some of his most powerful output as a director of films in which music and dance are central: *Sweet Charity,* 1969; *Cabaret,* 1972; *All That Jazz,* 1979.)

Pajama Game was Fosse's first assignment as the choreographer of a musical comedy, and in "Steam Heat" a trio of dancers in black derby hats, memorably introduced his hunched-over, hip-swiveling, finger-snapping style to Broadway (see p. 423). Admittedly a sensation, the number was of no relevance at all to the plot; and to allay Abbott's fears, Robbins agreed to step in and choreograph himself if in rehearsals Fosse's musical staging proved inadequate to the book. Thus when Fosse simply let the cast stand and sing the first big vocal number, "7 ½ cents," Robbins stepped in. Rather than arousing animosity, what followed earned Robbins this tribute from his younger colleague:

> *I think I learned more in a couple of hours watching him stage than I had learned previously in my whole life. . . . He was very sweet about it and as he did the number he would consult with me and ask me what I thought. (I had no opinion at all I was in such awe of the man.) And in two hours he staged this song absolutely brilliantly. And I am so glad. I think it was a turning point in my career as a choreographer. I get the idea now and I see what you can do and what should be done and how to go about it and everything, and it's been something that's been of value to me for the rest of my career.*

With *Redhead* (1959—book: Herbert and Dorothy Fields; lyrics: Dorothy Fields; music: Albert Hague), Fosse moved into directing at the insistence of Gwen Verdon, the show's star, in whom he found an ideal collaborator in many ways onstage and off; they were married during the show's run. His next major career move, *Sweet Charity* (1966—book: Neil Simon [and Fosse]; lyrics: Dorothy Fields; music: Cy Coleman), was the first musical Bob Fosse conceived, choreographed, and directed. Here the eroticism of Fosse's signature style emerged in full force—"Big Spender," for example, occasioned the now classic image of taxi dancers lined up at a railing behind the footlights, waiting for customers and eyeing the audience, each in a differently suggestive pose. *Charity* was also pivotal in separating Fosse's earlier shows, with their reliance on book-based narratives, from his later ones, centered on concepts in which dance, rather than supporting a story, became "the medium and the main event." To ensure that such concepts would succeed, moreover, Fosse now extended the scope of superdirecting into the realm of authorship. With *Pippin* (1972—book: Roger O. Hirson [and Fosse]; lyrics and music; Stephen Schwartz), he barred the show's writers from rehearsals as he overhauled their material. With *Chicago* (1975—book: Fred Ebb and Fosse; Lyrics: Ebb; music: John Kander), he received program credit as co-writer of the script. With *Dancin'* (1978), he did away with scripted material entirely—and received unofficial credit of another kind in an opening-night telegram from Alan Jay Lerner: "You finally did it. You got rid of the author."

During Fosse's temporary leave from Broadway after *Charity* he became a film director. His superb adaptation of *Cabaret* put him directly in touch with the concept musical development of Hal Prince. But he utterly reworked the original for the film, dropping the show's book songs and confining virtually all the musical numbers to the Berlin cabaret, where they could be "justified" as part of the entertainment. Doing so, Fosse not only espoused the premises of screen realism but also sharpened the conceptual focus of *Cabaret*, separating the plot from the concept and using musical performance itself to underscore the latter. "I wanted to keep it pure," he said.

In a series of vignettes, *Pippin* centered on the search by Charlemagne's son for some meaning in life. Songwriter Stephen Schwartz (b. 1948) had written and mounted the innocent piece as a student at Carnegie Mellon University, then innocently thought he might do on Broadway what he had done in college. Fosse had other ideas. In his hands, said producer Stuart Ostrow, "the tone of the musical changed—from a sincere, naïve, morality play to an anachronistic, cynical burlesque." Fosse sought to impose coherence on the material by means of a production concept: a magic show performed by a Leading Player (Ben Vereen) and his troupe of commedia dell'arte players, who now presented Pippin's story to the audience and interrupted it at intervals. Schwartz, Ostrow reported, "thought his CMU baby was being perverted into a Broadway whore." Yet it was Fosse's showmanship and flimflam inventiveness more than anything that turned *Pippin* into a Broadway hit. (For the Australian and Mexican productions Schwartz went back to his original concept, and the show failed.)

With *Chicago* Fosse more convincingly meshed storytelling with a conceptual use of the musical stage. Based on the real-life acquittal in 1924 of two Chicago murderesses, the story was originally the work of Maurine Watkins, who converted her wry coverage of the two cases as a

A performing duo of murderesses in *Chicago*, l. to r.: Chita Rivera (Velma Kelly) and Gwen Verdon (Roxie Hart).

reporter for the *Chicago Tribune* into a Broadway comedy hit in 1926. In Fosse's version, set in 1920s Chicago, Roxie Hart (Gwen Verdon) has an extramarital affair and murders her lover; manipulates her husband, the law, and the press to get herself acquitted; then trades on her newfound notoriety to become a vaudeville celebrity in an act with fellow murderess Velma Kelly (Chita Rivera). Into this narrative Fosse folded his concept: a vaudeville show whose separate song-and-dance routines were performed by the actual characters in the story but played presentationally to the audience as the story unfolded. Such "acts" were cynically double-edged: As each act parodied the style of a famous vaudeville star of the 1920s, its contents provided another bitterly ironic revelation of the plot. "When You're Good to Mama" played on the sexual innuendo of a Sophie Tucker song, but a prison matron sang it, soliciting bribes in return for jailhouse favors. "Mister Cellophane" echoed the vulnerability of Bert Williams's "Nobody," but Roxie's cuckolded husband sang it as he was duped by her lawyer. "Me and My Baby" evoked marital bliss Eddie Cantor–style, only it was about the pregnancy Roxie feigned in order to gain sympathy on the witness stand. That nothing in this "Musical Vaudeville" could be taken at face value was both the method of the show and its message. In "Razzle Dazzle" Roxie's lawyer (Jerry Orbach) summarized it with appropriate crudeness:

> *Give 'em the old razzle-dazzle: razzle dazzle 'em.*
> *Give 'em an act with lots of flash in it*
> *And the reaction will be passionate.*
> *Give 'em the old hocus-pocus: bead and feather 'em.*
> *How can they see with sequins in their eyes?*
> *What if your hinges all are rusting?*
> *What if, in fact, you're just disgusting?*
> *Razzle dazzle 'em, and they'll never catch wise!*
>
> "RAZZLE DAZZLE" (*CHICAGO*)

Fosse's approach clearly took its cue from *Cabaret*. But Fosse's vision in *Chicago* was more unremittingly bleak. Drawing parallels between Roxie's duplicity and the corruption of national life that the Watergate scandal had recently disclosed, *Chicago* found morally tainted everything it touched, and finished by implicating show business itself in the morass. As a celebration of showmanship and cynicism, "Razzle Dazzle" became the ambivalent emblem not just of *Chicago* or even the Broadway musical culture it represented but of Fosse himself and his role in it. Ostrow, who knew him well, remarked,

> *If Bob Fosse ever needed a theme song it would have been "Razzle Dazzle," because the dialogue he and Fred Ebb wrote for the character of the show-biz lawyer, Billy Flynn, came straight from his crooked heart. Bobby told me he thought of himself as "a fraud with a couple of good dance steps." He was a genius, of course, and died much too soon, leaving a creative musical theatre legacy second only to Jerome Robbins. I once wrote a line for Bob Fosse in the movie* All That Jazz, *which he loved: "I always look for the worst in people, and usually find it." His tragedy was wanting to believe it.*

Dancin', by contrast, was Fosse's purest work, its morality liberated from the spoken word. "Most stories in musicals are only long cues to the next number," he said. In *Dancin'* he did away with them altogether. What remained was a kinetic tour de force that asserted the independence of Broadway dance not only from the cohesive constraints of narrative but from the collaborative process itself. With no book to speak of and a score that was a compendium of already well-known musical numbers, *Dancin'* was less a Broadway musical than a vernacular ballet concert. An anthology of original Fosse dances, it resembled a series of showstoppers without a show to stop. Drama critics balked. Dance, Walter Kerr remarked,

> *can stand by itself when it aspires to, and achieves, the interior integrity, the long spiritual spine, of ballet. But this is mainly* show *dancing, these are the steps that have distinguished and/or set fire to "Sweet Charity" and "Cabaret" and "Pippin."* . . . *At their best they are not intended for independent statement; they are decorative, illustrative, meant for reinforcing something else. They want a book, if only a book to fight with.*

To be sure, *Dancin'* proved a dead-end as far as the book musical was concerned. Yet that limitation proved no obstacle to its commercial success—or to the later success of shows by others similarly made of virtually nothing but dance: *Stomp* (1994, choreography: Luke Cresswell and Steve McNicholas), *Bring in 'Da Noise/Bring in 'Da Funk* (1996, choreography: Savion Glover) *Contact* (2000, choreography: Susan Stroman), *Movin' Out* (2002, choreography: Twyla Tharp). First-rate dance shows all, these were essentially nonverbal revues to which foreign tourists flocked by way of catching a musical in New York without the barriers of language to contend with (though increasingly Broadway spectacles with doggerel or words of minor import served a similar purpose). They were also immensely popular with domestic audiences—as much an indication perhaps of the waning of literate culture in the commercial theater as of the rise of a sense that theater dance had now come into its own.

Signs of growing awareness of a distinctive heritage of dance in America abounded in the cultural mainstream of the period, and that included Broadway. In 1975, choreographer Lee Becker Theodore (1933–1987), who had created the role of Anybodys in *West Side Story*, founded the American Dance Machine. Created as a "living archive" of American theater dance, the company reconstructed major dances from shows of the past, preserved them in notation and on videotape, and performed them in concerts of all-Broadway dances divorced from the shows for which they were created. The company saw its mission as custodial rather than commercial. Nonetheless, Theodore supervised a Broadway mounting of *The American Dance Machine* (1978), in which a company of sixteen dancers re-created memorable show numbers originally choreographed by Agnes de Mille, Bob Fosse, Joe Layton, Michael Kidd, Onna White, and many others. Its run was short, but its spirit may have contributed to the later creation of such multimillion-dollar retrospectives as *Jerome Robbins' Broadway* (1989) and *Fosse: A Celebration in Song and Dance* (1999), both of which played on Broadway for extended runs. The first of these, actually supervised by Robbins, marked the choreographer's return to Broadway after a twenty-five-year absence to re-create his finest show dances (mostly from the memories of their original performers) and, in effect, preserve them along with the legacy of his concert ballets. The second, undertaken after Fosse's death, was the brainchild of choreographer-director Ann Reinking, codirector Richard Maltby, Jr., and co-choreographer Chet Walker. Such retrospectives had something of arty self-consciousness about them, yet each ran for several seasons on the Great White Way. Covering between them more than four decades of the work of stagers whose choreography changed what American musicals did and how they did it, the two shows served to remind contemporary audiences that Broadway was once indeed a dancing place.

A CHORUS LINE AND AFTER

The diminished value that superdirectors placed on the role of writers in creating musicals paralleled a rise in the importance they attached to the contributions of designers. Teams of set designers, lighting designers, and costume designers all reflected the new emphasis on conceptual staging of the 1970s and 1980s. They shaped the stage space to create a distinctive look that suited the overall style of a director, the metaphoric trajectory of a show, and the practical needs of a performance. As they played a key role in taking the ideas of the superdirectors and bringing them visually to life onstage, designers helped define the character of the musical theater of the era. Superdirectors, for their part, once they had found designers compatible with their approach, tended to hold on to them from one show to the next, ensuring consistency in their work where they felt it counted most. From *Pippin* to the end of his career, Fosse's Broadway production staff largely stayed the same: Tony Walton (b. 1934) handled the sets; Jules Fisher (b. 1937), the lighting; Patricia Zipprodt (1925–1999), the costumes. Writers now might come and go; designers endured.

The same was largely true of the few shows Michael Bennett (1943–1987) created as a superstager before he died of AIDS in his early forties. Bennett, a dancer ambitious in the extreme and a deeply intuitive creator, had a meteoric Broadway career. In less than a decade and a half, the Buffalo-born high-school dropout rose from dancing as a teenage gypsy for Michael Kidd (*Subways Are for Sleeping*; *Here's Love*) to masterminding the creation of a Pulitzer Prize–winning musical (*A Chorus Line*). In addition to Bennett's directing straight plays and doctoring the troubled shows of others, his musical staging credits include ten Broadway productions from 1966 to 1981. The first five of them he choreographed, among them *Promises, Promises* (1968), *Coco* (1969), and *Company* (1970). The other five he choreographed and also directed: *Follies* (1971, codirected with Hal Prince), *Seesaw* (1973), *A Chorus Line* (1975), *Ballroom* (1978), and *Dreamgirls* (1981). On each of the shows over which he exercised total control as choreographer-director, Bennett typically worked with a different team of writers: *Seesaw* (book: Michael Stewart and Bennett; lyrics: Dorothy Fields; music: Cy Coleman); *A Chorus Line* (book: James Kirkwood, Nicholas Dante; lyrics: Edward Kleban; music: Marvin Hamlisch); *Ballroom* (book: Jerome Kass; lyrics: Marilyn and Alan Bergman; music: Billy Goldenberg); *Dreamgirls* (book and lyrics: Tom Eyen; music: Henry Krieger). But his design team (save for *Seesaw*) remained unchanged: Robin Wagner (b. 1933), sets; Tharon Musser (1925–2009), lighting; Theoni Aldredge (b. 1932), costumes.

For Bennett the script was much the variable and the staging the constant. The essence of musical theater lay in its evanescence.

Bennett's work brought a cinematic fluidity of movement to the staging of a show, in which he sought to ground his choreography in the dramatic motivation of the characters. This made his dances different from show to show, and it distinguished his work from that of a superdirector like Fosse. "Michael Bennett was a great theatre man, but can you say what his style was?," a Fosse dancer once asked rhetorically. "You can look at a piece of [Fosse's] work, and there's no doubt that it's Fosse. What Martha Graham did for modern dance and Balanchine did for ballet, Fosse did for musical comedy." But one might continue in the vein: What Fosse did for musical comedy, Bennett, following Jerome Robbins, did for musical theater. Indeed, Bennett's chief concern was to motivate stage movement dramatically—"to choreograph the characters," as he put it—even if the characters couldn't dance. He choreographed *Company*, which was not a particularly dance-driven show. Its cast consisted almost entirely of actors, one of whom recalled,

> *The fact that we were not dancers was a great credit to Michael— because he looked at us and said, "How am I going to use these people?" The first thing he said in rehearsals was that he didn't want us to do dancing. Pretend we're in the PTA talent show. He said, "Don't worry about it, I only want you to move the way the character would move, to make the person watching forget he's watching an actor."*

At his best, Bennett surprised his audiences by drawing fresh, unexpected meanings from the conventional vocabulary of Broadway dance. *Company's* "Side by Side by Side," for example, was a song-and-dance routine for Bobby and the married couples who made up his circle of friends. In their company, however, Bobby, a bachelor, seemed out of place—two's company, three's a crowd—always the extra "by side." At the climax of the number, Bobby and his friends formed an old-fashioned cakewalk line, with each of the couples taking a tap-dance break together, the one partner pointing to the other to join in during the musical spots where Bobby had previously sung his "by side"s. When it came his turn for the break, Bobby started the tap dance like the couples who had preceded him. But when he gestured to his partner—there was no one. In that one gesture Bennett not only made musical theater tradition double back on itself. He caught what the show was about—at once by means of and at the expense of the dance. "That was emotional," said Arthur Laurents, who found the rest of *Company* cold but warmed to this moment in the show for the way it captured the poignancy of Bobby's loneliness. "It was visual, it was theater, it was what musical theater should be."

A Chorus Line, however, towers over the rest of Bennett's accomplishments through its then unprecedented Broadway run as well as its national and international acclaim. Yet it is also his single finest piece of work, the one in which he genuinely succeeded like no stager before or since in making dance "the essence of the Broadway musical," which he maintained dance was *by nature*. *A Chorus Line*, a show in some sense *about* dance, was also choreographed in almost every detail as if it *were* a dance. Even its existence as a musical stemmed from the very process by which choreographers choreograph: much of it was fixed in rehearsal before it was ever written down. In this, little in recent Broadway history suggests the break with the past that *A Chorus Line* represents.

A Chorus Line sprang unconventionally not from scripted material but from several all-night sessions Bennett taped in which a group of Broadway gypsies talked openly about why each of them had become chorus dancers in the first place. In a kind of group therapy, they explored their motives for pursuing careers that were so highly competitive, short-lived, self-effacing, low-paying, and fraught with physical and emotional risk. To hone this raw material into a theater project, producer Joseph Papp offered Bennett financial support and the Off Broadway workshop setting of his New York Shakespeare Festival. Papp thus gave Bennett something he had not known before, an alternative to the usual pressures of time and money under which Broadway shows were put together.

> *I was used to having five weeks of rehearsal, four days of tech[nical rehearsals], two weeks out-of-town, you move to New York, have previews and open. . . . All I was doing was looking at the clock and thinking, "Do I dare try this? What if I'm wrong? I've just wasted three days of rehearsal." . . .*

Workshops give you the opportunity to test material on actors, to try things out. They give the writers time, without being under the pressure of being in a hotel room in Boston, out of town with a deadline and $4 million on their back. [A] workshop allows you to be wrong, then fix it.

Unfettered by normal Broadway constraints, Bennett found a new freedom to create. Rather than staging a show already written, Bennett used the workshop situation to approach *A Chorus Line* by putting it together as a choreographer might put a dance together and bring it to life: on its feet. Without benefit of a book or score, he began with little more than a few ideas, a drummer, and some dancers with whom he would work out his ideas in a practice room, by trial and error, over the course of months. (Many of the dancers had been among those who first told their stories on Bennett's tapes—some would even be part of the original cast, though the characters they would eventually portray onstage were not themselves by and large but composites of the originals.) The real writing of the book and score came later, mainly as a result of the workshop process rather than the other way around— and significantly it represented the work of relative novices or hitherto unsuccessful writers for the stage: book writers James Kirkwood (1924–1989) and Nicholas Dante (1942–1991), lyricist Edward Kleban

ABOVE: The company of *A Chorus Line* as random auditioners at the show's beginning.
OVERLEAF: The same company transformed into a chorus line at the show's end.

(1939–1987), and composer Marvin Hamlisch (b. 1944). Improvisation and the collaborative input of actors, stagers, and writers had been typical of Off-Off Broadway groups such as Joseph Chaikin's Open Theater. And among musicals that made an impact on the Broadway mainstream these techniques had previously been used in the making of *Hair*, which, not coincidentally, had also begun life at the Shakespeare Festival.

What came out of this process was a musical largely about the process itself, a stagework at once conceptual and emotional, metaphoric and realistic. Its concept was rooted in the self-reflexive involvement of an audience watching an actual show taking shape about a fictive show taking shape. More than simply telling a backstage story, this musical moved in ways that made it "hot" in Bennett's lexicon rather than "cool—its essential energy was presentational rather than representational. Its dramatic premise was the final chorus audition for a new Broadway musical. The cast appeared as auditioners in rehearsal clothes and on an empty stage. As part of the audition, besides dancing, they had to tell the director something about themselves. And as the voice of the director came from the back of the theater in which the audience sat, the auditioners presented themselves to the audience as well as to him.

In separate vignettes, then, the dancers emerged as individuals from the chorus, as they stepped forward to divulge intensely personal confidences. Some were traditional solos about untraditional subjects: Cassie (Donna McKechnie) sang and danced "The Music and the Mirror" to reveal she was a former star in desperate need of work and trying to return to the chorus to get it; Paul (Sammy Lee) simply spoke at length about coming to terms with his homosexuality and sense of manhood. Others were ensembles or spliced montages of music, movement, and dialogue in a seamless joining of scenes and songs: "At the Ballet," about the needs of three dancers to escape from unhappy lives at home; "Hello 12, Hello 13, Hello Love," about the funny, embarrassing, and touching experiences of puberty. Through them all, each applicant took on a distinct personality.

Two memorable chorus numbers thematically framed the vignettes. In the show's opener, the dancers expressed their anxiety and their need to land the jobs for which they were auditioning. They did so first

Ex. 14-2. Marvin Hamlisch, music, Edward Kleban, lyrics: "One" mm. 9–20, *A Chorus Line*

as a group ("I Hope I Get It"), then as a solo ("Who Am I Anyway?") as they lined up in their motley rehearsal clothes with their resume pictures symbolically held up in front of their faces. In the finale, "One," their collective wish came true as they donned identical costumes and joined in a step-and-kick chorus, performing the showstopper from the new musical for which they had auditioned. "One" not only fulfilled the aspirations of the dancers onstage. It also satisfied the expectations of the audience, which invariably cheered and shouted its approval as it got to see the all-out production number that had been rehearsed during the audition now finally performed as it was meant to be (only without the star who was its "One," the point being that anyone could be plugged in as the star).

"One" did not exactly make for a happy ending, however. The music had already made this clear. For the expression of vulnerability in the opening number was moving in a way that the exuberance of the finale was not. Indeed, the lyrical, wide-open melody leaps of "Who Am I Anyway?" contrasted with the tight intervals, mechanical rhythms, and unprepared clash of keys (G minor, F♯ minor, E♭ minor) that gave a sense of heartlessness beneath the pizzazz of "One" (Ex. 14-2).

There was method in this. Kleban sought to explain why "One" may have seemed rather like "Hello, Dolly!" deconstructed:

"One" was a craft-technique challenge, in that it was a song that was supposed to have been "written" by somebody. It's not someone singing their true feelings. It's something that some songwriter—the composer of the score of the show for which they're auditioning—has written, and yet it has to have a subtext about other things in the play. To get all specific meaning out of it so that it can seem to have all kinds of other meanings is one of the harder tasks. You have to prune out any possible specificity, keep it very plain, like it's almost a Jerry Herman song, but it isn't quite. . . . To say nothing is always harder than to say something.

Despite the exhilaration with which "One" finally brought together the actual chorus line that *A Chorus Line* had so painstakingly spent the evening taking apart, Bennett viewed it as "a comment on the audience, as well as on the state of dancing in musical-comedy theater." For the dances Broadway audiences seemed most to delight in were hollow exercises in routines, while choreography, he insisted, "is not about steps, just steps, in terms of shows. . . . It's got to have a point of view. It's got to be about something." "One" may have seemed like a sequence of musical comedy routines, but it was informed by a dramatic subtext that went to the heart of the meaning of the show:

We've been given insight into the assembling of the very different personalities which make up the line, [yet] without the final anonymity of the line the story would lose its poignancy. We see only for a moment that the dancers have souls, that they are human; then they return to their roles of faceless entertainers doing the job they love and we expect.

Like many a conceptual piece, *A Chorus Line* ended with an old-fashioned production number transformed into something contemporary by its ambivalent pull. Yet it was still a funny and blatantly emotional show throughout—not as cynical as *Chicago* nor as hermetic as *Follies*. In fact, its depiction of gifted yet otherwise seemingly ordinary people putting themselves "on the line" to get work had remarkably broad appeal. Shortly after its East Village opening, the musical moved to Broadway, where it ran for fifteen years, generated national and international touring companies, and grossed over $280,000,000. It also netted some $38,000,000 for Papp's not-for-profit Shakespeare Festival, the income forming the basis for an endowment the Festival used to produce dozens of new pieces—which Papp compared to the state subsidies that theaters received in Europe.

His point did not go unnoticed in the New York private sector. In fact, *A Chorus Line* proved a landmark, it won broad acceptance for "workshopping" new shows, and it popularized the concept musical. Nor was Papp's the only workshop in town. Jerome Robbins's American Theater Laboratory had explored similar possibilities in the late 1960s under a grant from the National Endowment for the Arts, but without practical results. Then, in 1973, Stuart Ostrow negotiated the first workshop agreement with Actors' Equity Association and formed a Musical Theater Lab of his own. Working in the basement of St. Clement's Church, the lab produced twenty-six experimental musicals, starting with *The Robber Bridegroom*. Ostrow described the operation:

> *These "gypsy run-throughs" were rehearsed with Actors' Equity Association members (at a sixth of weekly union scale salary) for four weeks, and performed five times over an additional two-week period, with six days of rewriting time after the second performance. No reviews were permitted. They were performed with no scenery, no lighting, in rehearsal clothes, with makeshift props, and were accompanied by one piano. This was done for several reasons—to emphasize improving the material more than presenting a finished production, and to allow no limitations as to size of cast and style of production. When Michael Bennett came to St. Clement's, he thought he was in heaven. The realization of rehearsing and performing a new musical inexpensively was just what he had needed in order to implement his concept of a musical about Broadway gypsy-dancers.*

He referred, of course, to *A Chorus Line*. But it wasn't until later, once *A Chorus Line*'s profits vindicated the process that had created the piece, that producers came to accept the workshop as a viable alternative to the costlier ways of Broadway preproduction. After *Chorus Line*, many of Broadway's most original musical offerings enjoyed workshop origins. Among them were Bennett's own two subsequent shows which he workshopped at 890 Broadway, a building on East Nineteenth Street he bought with his newfound wealth and converted into an arts center. The first of these was the short-lived *Ballroom*, a "cool" show about a dance hall in the Bronx and a middle-aged widow who seeks romance there—the songs and dances were representational, thus beholden to the book. The second was *Dreamgirls*, a "hot" show (and a presentational hit) about the rise of a black vocal trio in the exploitative world of show business that was told through a nearly constant flow of music, movement, and stage design.

Following Bennett's last Broadway show, however, the heat in the superstager movement itself began to cool. Other choreographer-directors appeared in the 1980s and 1990s to be sure, but their shows generally lacked the near demonic intensity and thoroughgoing inventiveness that had made the stagework of their predecessors so astonishing. Major choreographers from outside the orbit of Broadway dance, for example, tried their hands at directing musicals with varying degrees of success: Twyla Tharp (*Singin' in the Rain*, 1985); Peter Martins (*Song and Dance*, 1985, codirected with Richard Maltby, Jr.); Mark Morris (*The Capeman*, 1998, though Morris was ultimately replaced by director Jerry Zaks and choreographer Joey McKneely, both uncredited). For more sustained work in the medium, however, Broadway looked to its own—and consistently now to women as well, notably Graciela Daniele (b. 1939) and Susan Stroman (b. 1954). The Argentinian-born Daniele, who was Bennett's dance assistant on *Follies* and Fosse's on *Chicago*, first gained attention with her choreography for New York Shakespeare Festival productions in the early 1980s. She then conceived, choreographed, and directed her own first production at INTAR Hispanic American Arts Center (*Tango Apasionado*, 1987), and went on to distinguish herself as choreographer-director of unusual musicals both Off Broadway and on (*Once on This Island*, 1990; *Marie Christine*, 1999). The work of Susan Stroman, on the other hand, sits well in the mainstream. She has emerged as perhaps the brightest star in the Broadway dance firmament with her Tony Award–winning choreography (*Crazy for You*, 1992; *Show Boat*, 1994) and choreography and direction (*The Producers*, 2001).

Of all new musical stagers toward century's end, however, surely no one laid stronger claim to the mantle of the great superdirectors of the past than Tommy Tune (b. 1939). Tune, a Bennett protégé and a gangling six-foot-six-inch dancer, drew attention for his boyish charm, above all with incongruously smaller partners such as the four-foot-ten-inch Baayork Lee (*Seesaw:* "It's Not Where You Start") and the five-foot-six-inch Twiggy (*My One and Only:* "'S Wonderful"). While he continued to perform, he forged an extraordinary career choreographing, directing, and ultimately choreographing and directing a string of Broadway hits that included *The Best Little Whorehouse in Texas* (1978, codirected with Peter Masterson), *Nine* (1982), *My One and Only* (1983, co-choreographed-directed with Thommie Walsh), *Grand Hotel* (1989), and *The Will Rogers Follies* (1991). While Tune's work often proceeded along musical comedy lines, he continued the development of the concept musical through a concern for total staging, movement, and dance, in shows such as *Nine* (book: Arthur Kopit; lyrics and music: Maury Yeston) and *Grand Hotel* (book: Luther Davis; lyrics and music: Robert Wright, George Forrest, and Maury Yeston), perhaps his single most inspired work to date.

With *Grand Hotel,* Tune took a failed attempt of some thirty years before to convert Vicki Baum's novel into a musical and turned it into a hit, replacing the linear approach of the earlier version with a conceptual one. The show now revolved like a kaleidoscope around Baum's six principal characters and the dark secrets each tries to hide as their lives intertwine by happenstance in an elegant hotel in 1928 Berlin. Tune's balletic concept required a nearly continuous musical score to connect the mosaic of tales as he wove a dense polyphony of choreographed movement through a unit set suggesting the interior spaces of the Grand Hotel itself. As a result, the entire show, raved one critic, "is like one great musical scene—but so pictorially musical that production becomes inseparable from composition." Not all reviewers raved, however. Indeed, warned Michael Feingold, when it came to *Grand Hotel,* production *was* the composition:

> In earlier times, if a new musical came along with a great score (or even a few great songs), a workable book, and a brilliant performer or two, that would be enough to make it a success. Today . . . what a musical needs to be a hit is a production that gives the impression of having [these elements]. The image, or more precisely the marketing of the image, is everything. If we leave the performances out of consideration for a moment (because it is very well performed), Grand Hotel has nothing that would make people want to see it. Its book

is shoddy; its music and lyrics are triteness. But Grand Hotel *has, in its jumbled-up ragbag of tired theatrical tricks, one hit Tune, first name Tommy. Under his direction, the old hash is made to sizzle as though it had new flavors, the dead conventions are shoved out onstage to dance and grin as if they were still alive. Even the fact of all the deadness and triteness in the material is toyed with, as a way to give the production the substance the work doesn't inherently have: in lieu of passion, or meaning, or music, an "evocation of a vanished era" or some such half-thought for the half-educated.*

While after *Grand Hotel* Tune could still put together a hit with his masterful staging of *Will Rogers Follies,* its success as a show was hollow—"smoke and mirrors," as he once said of his work on *Nine,* "to divert the viewer from the fact that it lacked a plot." Thereafter, his career took a sharply downward turn from which it has yet to recover. By the mid-1990s, Tune despaired not only over his own work but over the future of the whole development of shows masterminded by dance-trained directors. "There aren't many of us doing them now," he said. "Michael Bennett is dead. Bob Fosse is dead. Joe Layton is dead. Gower Champion is dead. The director/choreographer is dead."

If Tune's conclusion was arguable, the mood it registered rang true. Broadway no longer teemed with the kind of innovative and influential work it had produced for decades, ever since Jerome Robbins first confounded all expectations for movement and dance on the commercial stage. Beginning in the 1950s and 1960s, Robbins had brought a depth of choreographic technique and imagination to an unprecedented breadth of vision for the Broadway musical genre. The vocabulary and invention of Champion, Fosse, Bennett, Tune, and others who succeeded him as the choreographic authors of Broadway shows may have been more limited—and perhaps their vision was as well. But as a group their work was sufficiently brilliant in its own right to transform the American song-and-dance show of the 1960s, 1970s, and 1980s into a more pointedly visual, continuously musical, and thoroughly kinetic form of entertainment.

What sorely weakened this development, however, was not only the deaths of so many of the most gifted Broadway dancers, choreographers, and choreographer-directors in the 1980s. It was also the emergence in that decade of a rival phenomenon that was heralded by the advent of *Cats*—a show that would in time surpass even *A Chorus Line* as Broadway's longest-running musical. *Cats*, too, was practically an all-dance piece, and it is perhaps telling that the sole member of its creative team with any firsthand experience creating Broadway shows was its choreographer and associate director, Gillian Lynne. *Cats* surely would have been unthinkable without the collective achievement of the American superstagers whose work preceded it. But as an altogether different type of entertainment, *Cats* was the first in a series of block-busters originating in London rather than New York, and designed for a global audience. *Cats* was thus the harbinger of a new kind of show that raised the question altogether of what one meant now when one spoke of a Broadway musical.

15

DISTANCING EFFECTS

JESUS CHRIST SUPERSTAR

(10/12/1971–6/30/1973). **Producer:** Robert Stigwood. **Book:** 1970 LP concept album, suggested in part by Fulton J. Sheen's *Life of Christ*. **Lyrics:** Tim Rice. **Music:** Andrew Lloyd Webber. **Director:** Tom O'Horgan. **New York Run:** 720 performances. **Cast:** Yvonne Elliman, Jeff Fenholt, Ben Vereen. **Songs:** "I Don't Know How to Love Him," "Everything's Alright," "Superstar."

EVITA

(London, 1978). New York (9/25/1979–6/26/1983). **Producer:** Stigwood. **Book:** 1976 LP concept album, suggested in part by Mary Main's biography *The Woman with the Whip*. **Lyrics:** Rice. **Music:** Lloyd Webber. **Director:** Harold Prince. **New York Run:** 1,567 performances. **Cast:** Patti LuPone, Mandy Patinkin, Bob Gunton. **Songs:** "Don't Cry for Me, Argentina," "Another Suitcase in Another Hall."

CATS

(London, 1981). New York (10/7/1982–9/10/2000). **Producers:** Cameron Mackintosh, David Geffen, Really Useful Theatre Co., and Shubert Organization. **Book:** Based on selected poems in T. S. Eliot's *Old Possum's Book of Practical Cats*. **Lyrics:** Eliot, Trevor Nunn and Richard Stilgoe. **Music:** Lloyd Webber. **Directors:** Nunn and Gillian Lynne. **New York Run:** 7,485 performances. **Cast:** Betty Buckley, Terrence Mann, Ken Page. **Song:** "Memory."

The high-tech ascent on a rubber tire in the finale of *Cats*, l. to r.: Ken Page (Old Deuteronomy) and Betty Buckley (Grizabella).

LES MISÉRABLES

(Paris, 1980; London, 1985). New York (3/12/1987–5/18/2003). **Producer:** Mackintosh. **Book:** Based on the novel *Les Misérables* by Victor Hugo. **French Lyrics:** Alain Boublil and Jean-Marc Natel (English Translation: Herbert Kretzmer and James Fenton). **Music:** Claude-Michel Schönberg. **Directors and Adapters:** Nunn and John Caird. **New York Run:** 6,680 performances. **Cast:** Judy Kuhn, Colm Wilkinson, Mann. **Songs:** "On My Own," "Do You Hear the People Sing?," "Bring Him Home."

THE PHANTOM OF THE OPERA

(London, 1986). New York (1/26/1988–). **Producers:** Mackintosh and Really Useful Theatre Co. **Book:** Stilgoe and Lloyd Webber, based on the novel by Gaston Leroux. **Lyrics:** Charles Hart and Stilgoe. **Music:** Lloyd Webber. **Director:** Prince. **New York Run:** 9,290+ performances. **Cast:** Sarah Brightman, Michael Crawford. **Songs:** "The Music of the Night," "All I Ask of You," "Angel of Music."

BEAUTY AND THE BEAST

(4/18/1994–7/29/2007). **Producer:** Walt Disney Productions. **Book:** Linda Woolverton, adapted from the 1991 Disney screenplay. **Lyrics:** Howard Ashman and Rice. **Music:** Alan Menken. **Director:** Robert Jess Roth. **New York Run:** 5,461 performances. **Cast:** Susan Egan, Beth Fowler, Mann, Burke Moses. **Songs:** "Be Our Guest," "Beauty and the Beast."

THE PRODUCERS

(4/19/2001–4/22/2007). **Producers:** Rocco Landesman, SFX Theatrical Group, The Frankel-Baruch-Viertel-Routh Group, and others. **Book:** Mel Brooks and Thomas Meehan, adapted from the 1968 screenplay. **Lyrics and Music:** Brooks. **Director and Choreographer:** Susan Stroman. **New York Run:** 2,502 performances. **Cast:** Nathan Lane, Matthew Broderick. **Song:** "Springtime for Hitler."

"**O**h, please," says Bebe, one of the characters trying out for the proverbial new show within the show *A Chorus Line.* "I don't wanna hear about how Broadway's dying. 'Cause I just got here." Bebe's grit captures the sprit of the new generation of performers depicted in *A Chorus Line*'s fictional world. Her words also catch this concept musical doing what concept musicals typically do: teasing out the relationship between representation and reality.

The sense that Broadway was dying was no fiction outside the Shubert Theater on Forty-fourth Street, where *A Chorus Line* ran from 1975 to 1990 in the heart of New York's theater district. Many factors contributed to that perception. The post–World War II flight of America's urban middle classes to the suburbs and the deterioration of the inner cities loomed large among them. By the 1960s, the area synonymous with commercial theater in New York City had turned into a much publicized symbol of urban decline. Forty-second Street between Seventh and Eighth Avenues, once the shining epicenter of the Times Square district, now took on the character of "the worst block in town." The Great White Way became a hotbed of rival diversions as financially strapped playhouses in the neighborhood now competed with massage parlors, "porn" shops, and houses of prostitution. (A few Broadway producers even tried to rival such rivals by mounting low-budget "adult" musicals that traded in outright nudity and simulated sex acts of various persuasions—most notably *Oh! Calcutta!* [1971] and *Let My People Come* [1976].) The situation was not entirely new. "The white-light theater district of Times Square had coexisted since the nineteenth century with a thriving red-light district," only now it bore the added stigma of what the police called "the Dangerous Deuce"—a place of crime, drugs, violence, and a strong undercurrent of racial and ethnic tension. Business interests tried to improve the district since the situation there discouraged theater-seeking tourists and middle-class patrons generally. But when, in the mid-1970s, an economic recession brought the city itself to the brink of bankruptcy, public and private investors put major plans for the "urban renewal" of the Times Square area on hold—indefinitely.

The theater business had internal problems to face as well. Financing a Broadway show has always been a high-risk venture. (For most of the past half century, some 75 percent of all musicals have failed to return their investments during their Broadway runs.) Now, it became prohibitive as well. The cost of producing musicals in the 1980s skyrocketed far beyond the general rate of inflation. To mount *Follies* on Broadway in 1971 had required a then staggering $750,000. A decade later, according to one estimate, "You couldn't even touch it for less than $5 million." In the 1980s major shows had to run two or more years on Broadway simply to break even. Partly to blame were unions protecting blue-collar jobs, white-collar guilds insisting on bigger pieces of the pie, directors clamoring for state-of-the-art stage technologies, and producers demanding costly forms of advertising to stay competitive (*Pippin*, the first show to advertise on TV, extended its Broadway run thereby). But steeply rising costs also had to do with a change in the structure of doing business on Broadway as productions decreased in number, attendance declined, and theaters went dark.

The ethos of rugged individualism, once prevalent in the theater business, seemed a thing of the past. Corporations now replaced the David Merricks and other strong-willed producers who once presided over the making of shows. The new model consisted of a corporate troika, which spread executive responsibilities among an artistic director, a general manager, and various multiproducers. This last group, dominated by business-oriented investors, now joined up with theater owners who went back to the older practice of also producing shows in order to fill their own theaters. (Such owners included the Shubert Organization: 17 theaters, the Nederlander Organization: 9, and Jujamcyn Theaters: 5—the three together owning and/or operating some 90 percent of Broadway's legitimate houses.) The new scheme developed in response to the new pressures on show production. Yet corporate inefficiency often contributed to the very costs the new structure was meant to contain. In addition, with new productions increasingly driven by business concerns, producers were less inclined to take chances not only financially but artistically as well—especially where new talent was concerned. Stephen Schwartz, after an extraordinary Broadway debut writing songs for three hits in the early 1970s (*Godspell*, *Pippin*, *The Magic Show*), decried the situation he found later in the decade, as his Broadway career went into a holding pattern from which it would not fully recover until *Wicked* (2003), nearly thirty years later:

> *Anyone who has tried recently to do a Broadway musical knows why you can't do one. There are no producers. The theatre owners have taken over, and it doesn't work the same way with people who are essentially businessmen. It's not that people in the Shubert Organization lack artistic judgment. What they lack is artistic passion!*

If things looked bleak on the production side of the theater ledger, on the consumption side they appeared no less grim. Escalating ticket prices tended to reduce Broadway attendance, and an ever widening "generation gap" threatened to diminish the audience for musicals altogether. As the population to whom musicals traditionally mattered most aged, the baby boomers who came of age in the 1960s and 1970s showed little interest in Broadway shows. The new generation preferred rock music and its attendant forms. Yet, despite attempts to create viable rock-based musicals, only *Hair* succeeded in such a way as to bridge the generation gap and run on Broadway for over four years (1968–1972). The show proved an anomaly, however, even for its creators. While it propelled them to the forefront of the commercial musical stage, they had only checkered Broadway careers thereafter and never again achieved anything even approaching *Hair's* success.

The more durable voices of the generation of songwriters that established itself with a body of Broadway work in the 1960s and 1970s belonged to such showmen as John Kander, Fred Ebb, Cy Coleman, Stephen Sondheim, and Jerry Herman. They were all clearly "over thirty" and thus held suspect by a generation that preferred to put its trust in the hands of those whose age fell below that benchmark. The mistrust of the young proved well founded. Little in the work of these writers showed the influence of rock or the rock-related vernaculars with which those under thirty identified. In fact, as the pop music industry became ever more youth oriented, Broadway musicals tended to become rather more "supremely adult" (as an observer described one of Sondheim's shows). The schism hardened along ideological lines. "When popular music stopped caring about theater music," said Kander, "people who wrote for the theater stopped writing for the market."

In losing touch with the market, however, Broadway effectively ceased to matter in the mainstream of popular culture. The new condition left room for show makers to experiment with the stage musical medium more than they had before, and several of their finest efforts resulted in shows that were dark, introspective, and not necessarily commercially viable. Some key musicals of the 1970s took the musical itself for subject matter, as much to indulge in the familiar modes of show business as to challenge its myths and their place in American culture. Many viewed such metamusicals, with their self-reflexive bent, as a sign of the medium's exhaustion; others saw vitality in the ability of show makers so to deconstruct the medium as to make entertainment out of what it no longer was. Frank Rich wrote of *Follies*, for example:

> *It is easy to avoid* Follies *on the grounds that it is, after all, a Broadway musical—and, given what Broadway musicals have come to mean, such a bias is understandable. But that is precisely why you should see it, for* Follies *is a musical about the death of the musical and everything musicals represented for the people who saw and enjoyed them when such entertainment flourished in this country.*

Even *A Chorus Line*, despite the show's unprecedented success at the time, came to be seen as an emblem of the Broadway musical in its terminal state. Michael Feingold wrote:

> *Leaving aside the economic and social causes, Broadway died (and it has died—what we have left is a mumble) because its practitioners started believing their own myths. The joy of appearing on The Great White Way, the splendor of having your name up in lights, the excitement, the struggle, the sense of belonging among the insiders, all started out as frank hokum—and, like the artists, the public knew that the myth was half to be taken seriously, like all good hokum. . . . A* Chorus Line *is a show about the kids and the myth. It never questions the assumptions of the myth, which is a major drawback, but its creators have taken pains to be accurate to the lives of the people who worship at the shrine of Broadway, with the result that the show is built around a very hard kernel of truth and genuine feeling. It's perfect, too, that A* Chorus Line *should be created at the Public Theatre, on public money, as living proof that the entrepreneurial side of*

Broadway can no more be depended upon these days than the artistic side. A Chorus Line *is, in effect, the last Broadway musical.*

And, in a sense, it was. By the time *A Chorus Line* closed in 1990, alternatives had emerged in the theater that no longer took for granted traditional notions of either Broadway or the musical. Several developments, unforeseeable at the time the show had opened fifteen years before, had begun to reshape the medium in the interim; they would continue to do so as the century drew to a close. One involved a seeming invasion of Broadway starting in the 1970s with the successes of Tim Rice and Andrew Lloyd Webber in bringing a new kind of musical from England to America, the rock opera. Another involved a further English development, the megamusical, and the use of it by producer Cameron Mackintosh in the 1980s to transform what had been an American preserve into a transnational one. A third involved an ongoing trend to turn the live musical theater into a medium increasingly mediated by technology—a trend emblematically associated with the Walt Disney Corporation and its role in the 1990s in the growth of movicals. More directly perhaps than other trends of the age, they set the terms for the state of the art in musical theater as the end of the millennium approached. But there was a disturbing aspect to them as well. More than simply the latest developments in the history of an ongoing Broadway tradition, it seemed to many that these developments represented the effects of an ever more distancing movement away from that tradition altogether.

RICE, LLOYD WEBBER, AND ROCK OPERA

The catchphrase "British invasion," coined following the Beatles' first American tour in 1964, referred to the inroads of British rock groups into the pop music market of the United States—the homeland, after all, of rock 'n' roll. Some two decades later, the phrase circulated afresh when an influx of high-profile musicals from London laid siege to the market in Broadway musicals. Earlier, musicals from England had successfully played Broadway in more or less peaceful coexistence with local offerings. Much of the past appeal of such shows drew on the authenticity of their very Englishness. And so the Broadway community did not see them as undermining local cultural interests or posing an economic threat, and certainly not as raising the aesthetic specter of war. Now, however, they seemed to be engaged in all of the above. Moreover, the new shows became a cause for nationalist resentment on both sides of the Atlantic: for the perceived invasion from Europe, and for the ungracious reception accorded it in America. At the Broadway opening of *Chess* in 1988, Frank Rich published a negative review and, after a brief run, the show closed. Presumably, since *Chess* had already succeeded in London (though in a different form), Björn Ulvaeus, one of its three European creators, saw fit to attack the messenger rather than the message. Rich, he said, perhaps "felt that the musical is an American invention and the Europeans should stay out of here." Any protectionist sentiment in America, however, grew in proportion to the London-based musicals that succeeded on Broadway, not those that failed. Yet, indeed, the cumulative effect of all such shows—hits and flops alike—did amount to a perceived invasion, as, from the late 1970s through the 1990s, they kept coming from London in waves of high-tech extravaganzas that overwhelmed all other Broadway productions of the period. More than simply challenging America's postwar rule over the English-speaking musical stage, this "British invasion" implied a sustained assault on the institution of Broadway itself.

Britannia had for centuries ruled the waves, of course, and in doing so, had also dominated the Atlantic trade where musicals were concerned. In the eighteenth century, England's musical theater had been virtually synonymous with America's. It remained the preeminent influence on the American stage throughout the nineteenth century as well, nowhere more durably so than through the works of Gilbert and Sullivan. Not until the waning of Edwardian musical comedy around the time of the First World War did England begin to cede its preeminence on the English-speaking musical stage to the United States. Thereafter, musicals by several of Britain's foremost writers, such as Ivor Novello and Vivian Ellis, never even crossed the Atlantic. Moreover, the musicals of their more celebrated colleague Noël Coward that did make the crossing (*Bitter Sweet*, 1929; *Set to Music*, 1939) did not win the acclaim in New York accorded to his nonmusical plays and other theatrical activities. Only after World War II, as London's West End succumbed paradoxically to what the

English perceived as an "American invasion" of musical shows, did British musicals begin to capture the interest of Broadway audiences with some consistency again (*The Boy Friend*, 1954; *Irma La Douce*, 1960; *Stop the World—I Want to Get Off*, 1962; *Half a Sixpence*, 1965). By far the most successful of these was *Oliver!* (London, 1960/New York, 1963). For that show Lionel Bart (1930–1999) created both book and score by adapting Dickens's *Oliver Twist* as a musical play in the manner of Rodgers and Hammerstein. Bart made the most of the English character of the piece, to be sure, especially in its nineteenth-century London settings. He even tinged its musical detail with colors from English folk song ("Where Is Love?") and the music hall ("Consider Yourself"). But the show's overall sensibility and scene-to-song form depended largely on the models of *Oklahoma!* and its Broadway progeny. In this Bart was not alone among English show-writers of the period. "Before *Cats*," said Leslie Bricusse, co-author of *Stop the World*, "to achieve international success, you had to Americanize yourself—whether consciously or not."

The work of Tim Rice (b. 1944) and Andrew Lloyd Webber (b. 1948) proved the exception that proved the rule. Like many aspiring British writers for the stage at the time, the two began collaborating using *Oliver!* as a model. But their dissatisfaction with the approach and a willingness to look elsewhere soon set their work apart. "What Tim and I wanted to do," said the composer, "was to create a different sort of English stage musical, instead of aping Broadway badly." Something "more like *Hair* than *Oklahoma!*," said the lyricist. If the partners did not turn out to be quite the "saviours of the modern musical" that an enthusiast would later call them, they seemed at least "the men who would bring Broadway up to date."

Both staunchly English and middle-class, Tim Rice and Andrew Lloyd Webber had otherwise little in common. Rice was tall, relaxed, extroverted; Lloyd Webber small, intense, and rather shy. Rice, a would-be rock singer, worked in the recording industry and wanted to write pop singles. Lloyd Webber, a son of the director of the London College of Music, liked popular and classical music well enough but really wanted to write shows. "The combination of Andrew's being an expert and very much steeped in theatre from an early age, and my being more interested in rock music and records," said Rice, "that com-

bination of ignorance and experience probably helped us to be origi-
nal." Rice had a flair for writing lyrics that were wry, edgy, and current.
Lloyd Webber had a gift for composing romantic melodies in a blend
of pop and classical styles. Together they wrote three hit shows: *Jesus
Christ Superstar* (1971), *Evita* (London, 1978/New York, 1979), and
Joseph and the Amazing Technicolor Dreamcoat, a fifteen-minute cantata
(London, 1968) gradually expanded over the years into a full-length
Broadway production (1982).

As the first major stage hits of the team of Rice and Lloyd Webber,
Superstar and *Evita* together posed a consistent alternative to Broadway sensibilities in content, style, and form. Although English in origin, these shows rejected identifiably English subjects and themes for
tales of more universal resonance and even mythic proportions. They
also musicalized such tales in a variety of styles that included songs
in a rock idiom. Furthermore, they were staged with a minimum of
dialogue in moving from one song to the next, thus virtually eliminating the distinction in a musical between the book and the score.
Challenging basic assumptions about the medium on several fronts at
once, *Superstar* and *Evita* amounted to the first postwar British hits to
establish a new template for success in musical theater.

By their very choice of subjects, the young writers set themselves
apart. Jesus of Nazareth's last days on earth and death by crucifixion
seemed not the most likely stuff for a musical show. Neither did the life
of so ruthless a woman as María Eva Duarte de Perón (aka "Evita"),
who engineered her rise from poverty to the height of national power
and world acclaim as the wife of Argentinian dictator Juan Perón. *Evita*
and *Superstar* were emphatically not musical biographies in the mold of
Funny Girl (Fanny Brice) or *Fiorello!* (La Guardia). Rather than stress
the true-to-life qualities of their subjects, these shows focused on what
was larger-than-life about them. They used their subjects to explore
ambivalences in the use of political and religious power, questioning
the costs of superstardom to the superstars themselves and to the
masses in their thrall.

As they did so, moreover, the shows raised questions of propriety,
not just in making entertainment out of such material in the first place,
but in portraying their subjects in human terms when the one was central to the religious beliefs of most English-speaking audiences, and
many still adored the other (some even as a saint) decades after she had

left the political arena. Consider how in *Superstar*, for example, Herod debunks the very idea of Jesus's divinity in song:

> *So you are the Christ, you're the great Jesus Christ*
> *Prove to me that you're no fool—walk across my swimming pool.*

"KING HEROD'S SONG"
(*JESUS CHRIST SUPERSTAR*)

The view expressed was scandalously Herod's, of course, and played for laughs; surely no one was meant to take it seriously. But many did as the show itself seemed to support such skepticism throughout. As if advancing a revisionist gospel, it glossed over the resurrection and presented Jesus as a neurotic, self-doubting, historical figure rather than a divine one. No less an authority than the progressive Dean of St. Paul's Cathedral in London stepped in to argue that *Jesus Christ Superstar* was no blasphemy. In a jacket note to the original record-ing, Fr. Sullivan asked listeners shocked by what they heard to "listen to it and think again. It is a desperate cry. Who are you Jesus Christ? is the urgent enquiry, and a very proper one at that." With Chris-tian revivalism afoot at the time and particularly strong in the United States, how refreshing to find a member of the clergy interceding on behalf of a musical. And—in light of clerical objections to musicals going back at least to *The Black Crook*—how ironic. (Even seeming blasphemies from entertainers could have serious consequences. In 1966, John Lennon triggered a massive backlash against the Beatles in the United States when he said, a bit indelicately perhaps, he thought they had become "more popular than Jesus.") Whatever the effect of Fr. Sullivan's words, *Superstar* succeeded. It did so in part because its very depiction of Jesus as a psychologically vulnerable human being gave the familiar title character a defamiliarizing edge that fascinated audiences. Yet in the face of what many still saw as sacrilege, protest-ers took to the streets to demonstrate against the piece when it was staged in New York. Years later, *Evita* proved similarly controversial, only this time protesters took to the streets to decry what they saw as that show's glorification of fascism.

The use of rock in both shows gave rise to protests as well, no less vehement in their way, though considerably less physical. Conservative theatergoers found rock disturbing on several grounds: the raucous sound, the rebellious spirit, the restrictive style in a dramatic setting. "Born of a marriage of lower-class American black and white musics," rock referred to a grassroots populism in sound that came to dominate America's commercial music industry in the 1960s. The clangor of electric keyboards, drums, and guitars; the thumping of a motor-driven beat; the drone effects of a few recycling chords; the sheer loudness of electrically amplified sounds—all these made up rock's instrumental profile. On the vocal side, rock songs typically embraced syncopated, speech-inflected melodies, which singers sang in a gritty style or screamed with strong nasal resonance. In brief, rock amounted to a wholesale rejection of the more polished Tin Pan Alley style that had for decades dominated urban taste in America and served as a model for the musical stage.

There was also more to the music than met the ear. It had a strong ideological component: rock symbolized change—social, political, generational. Associated with the emergence of a youth culture in rebellion in the 1960s, rock derived much of its emblematic power from its status as an outsider genre. The lyrics of rock songs regularly defied establishment values in their frank espousal of civil-rights and antiwar activism, and their even franker advocacy of drugs and sex. The music of rock songs throbbed with raw energy and a blatant emotionalism that scorned middle-class decorum with a let-it-all-hang-out appeal to unbridled freedom of expression. To the under-thirty generation rock represented authenticity of a kind show music could not begin to approach. Rock made the very urbanity that Broadway took as a sign of taste and civility seem vapid, irrelevant, and downright phony.

Only with the triumph of *Hair* in the 1967–68 season did rock finally make a major breakthrough into the theatrical mainstream. Then, for the next decade or so, the theater community could be heard speaking of rock musicals—and for a variety of reasons. *Hair* and *Your Own Thing* actually defined themselves as such. *Jesus Christ Superstar* and *The Who's Tommy* were originally marketed as rock albums. Other shows, even as they embraced the ideology of Broadway more than that of rock, sang in the common language of pop/rock sensibilities (*Godspell*), or borrowed from older rock 'n' roll idioms (*Grease*), or simply made use of related musical vernaculars not much heard on Broadway before the 1970s: gospel (*Purlie*, 1970), soul (*The Wiz*, 1975), country (*The Best Little Whorehouse in Texas*), Motown (*Dreamgirls*). These shows, taken as a whole, gave evidence of the inroads of rock musicals of all kinds into Broadway's musical-theater culture. Most of those mentioned became hits; some, like *Grease*, even turned into Broadway blockbusters. Yet most also turned out to be flukes, the work of promising writers who may have begun their careers with a Broadway bang but rarely succeeded on Broadway a second time—Jim Jacobs, Warren Casey, Gary Geld, Peter Udell, Charlie Smalls, Carol Hall, Tom Eyen, Henry Krieger. Even some of *Hair's* creators, Galt MacDermot and Gerome Ragni, in trying for a comparable success, succeeded only in shortening their Broadway careers with such costly failures as *Dude* (1972) and *Via Galactica* (1972, without Ragni). The work of all these writers may not have been theatrically strong enough to sustain careers on Broadway over time without the hands of others more savvy in the ways of the commercial stage consistently to guide them.

A cabal of theater critics felt the reasons ran deeper. They dismissed rock itself as incompatible with the needs of music for the stage. (Rockers, rock fans, and the rock press proved no less combative when it came to what they viewed as Broadway's basic commercialism and the creative constraints of its collaborative ways.) Rock "couldn't be used in a play context," said one, "for its unmodifiable sound quality can't express mood or establish tone." Another concluded that, given its "restricted melody and repetitive style," rock ultimately revealed itself as "orgiastic, rather than dramatic." If such arguments were not unassailable, the misgivings they expressed were not unfounded. *Jesus Christ Superstar* especially seemed to go all-out in its embrace of rock, and hard rock at that. In "Gethsemane," for example, Jesus bargained with God by repeating a syncopated riff over and over and over ("I'd have to know . . .") as his voice rose in 2-bar spurts ultimately to shout and scream in its highest register (Ex. 15-1). Pushing the chest voice ever higher and louder in the manner of rock vocalists, Jesus worked the passage into a state of frenzy only to arrive climactically at virtually the same lyric and musical idea with which he began ("Why should I die?").

Rock, however, was but one of many styles in Lloyd Webber's musical arsenal. In fact, at the beginning and the end of "Gethsemane," as Jesus first questioned then resigned himself to his fate, the song moved with a sustained, almost classical lyricism that belied the hard rock idiom in the middle. Perhaps the real drama of the number lay in the juxtaposition of its conflicting styles.

Ex. 15-1. Andrew Lloyd Webber, music, Tim Rice, lyrics: "Gethsemane (I Only Want to Say),"
Jesus Christ Superstar

Such eclecticism characterized the show in its embrace of everything from a country-style ballad, on the one hand ("I Don't Know How to Love Him"), to the vanguard of modern concert music, on the other ("Crucifixion"). It would become a hallmark of Lloyd Webber's musical language generally, exceeding the limited repertoire of styles traditionally associated with show music. The composer espoused an inclusive musical aesthetic, one more culturally ambitious and more demotic in spirit than Broadway audiences had been accustomed to accept.

But Lloyd Webber's musical eclecticism also stemmed in part from the fact that both shows began not as shows at all but as LP concept albums. Because these recordings contained only separate song tracks, when they were staged, both *Superstar* and *Evita* lacked spoken dialogue: They consisted entirely of back-to-back musical numbers. They were thus said to be "through-composed," which really meant, quipped Arthur Laurents, "sung . . . *incessantly*." More than simply rock musicals, then, these were rock operas—a neologism regularly applied to both shows if only by default: less for the ever-presence of music in them than for the ever-absence of a book.

The Who, a British rock band, had earlier promoted the idea of rock opera in connection with their 1969 recording of *Tommy*, a concept album in which an implied story linked the separate song tracks. The Who then exploited the theatrical potential of their album by performing it live, in concert form, on the road. Neither taking their rock opera too seriously nor poking such obvious fun at it that those who wanted to take it seriously couldn't, they had the cheek to book themselves into the least likely of rock venues when they got to New York: the Metropolitan Opera House. Rock made opera accessible; opera gave rock cachet. Yet opera also made rock now seem to be chasing after the very culture it had been born to rebel against: as if Beethoven came back to sing "Roll Over, Chuck Berry!" (Over time, the ironies compounded. In the several versions of *Tommy*—as a record, a concert, and later a film—the title remained and the Who took part. But when at long last it became a Broadway musical in 1993, *The Who's Tommy* reversed the matter: The presence of the Who in the title now served to call attention to their absence in the performance. Writers of Broadway shows as a rule did not also perform in them. But for rock fans the idea was absurd. What was the point of *Tommy*, after all, *without* The Who?)

The ambiguities of rock opera proved useful, nevertheless. What meant one thing to rockers like the Who meant something quite different to Andrew Lloyd Webber, a nonrocker whose tastes ran closer to the operatic mainstream. "I have always felt that staging continuous music as opposed to a music piece with dialogue is the key to musicals," he said. "I want to make musicals a continuous musical event like opera." Perhaps he later realized his ambition with *The Phantom of the Opera.* But at this point in his career his "musical events" resembled operas less than they did staged song cycles for a cast of singers: *Superstar* and *Evita* used their lyrics to tell their stories rather than to dramatize them. Thus they remained true to their origins in LP recordings of numbers that were then staged as an afterthought, as it were, without narrative links from one to the next. Such recordings had implications that went beyond the dramaturgy of the musical stage. They reversed not just the marketing strategies of musicals but their cultural priorities as well. If recording a show in the past had been a way of preserving what had clearly been a theatrical occasion, with these shows a generation unschooled in the ways of Broadway now came to the theater to "see what it perceived as a rock concert of a favorite album."

Theatricalizing these recordings fell squarely on the shoulders of directors who had to invent what such albums lacked. Both directors were American. Tom O'Horgan imbued *Superstar* with an outrageous opulence that sensationalized the piece, much as he had done with *Hair* three years before. Hal Prince, by contrast, approached *Evita* more thematically. Acknowledging that he was staging a "revue-with-an-umbrella for a story," he took each of the album's songs and developed a striking visual metaphor to make it stageworthy and turn it into a scene. "The Art of the Possible," for example, became a game of musical chairs among Argentina's military to show Juan Perón's rise to power. "Goodnight and Thank You" used a revolving door through which Eva reappeared better dressed each time to show her rise in society by means of increasingly rich lovers. And tying it all altogether, Prince filled the stage with pageantry and the machinery of politics—banners, microphones, spotlights—ultimately to manipulate his public much as Evita herself had once manipulated hers.

The Broadway success of *Evita* demonstrated that *Jesus Christ Superstar* was not an isolated phenomenon, either in its approach to musical theater or in its cultural resonance. Through their joint success in the

The cast of *Evita* proclaims "A New Argentina," center l. to r.: Patti LuPone (Eva Perón),
Bob Gunton (Juan Perón), and Mandy Patinkin (Che).

1970s, in fact, the two shows set the stage for a more intensive British campaign to corner the market in new musicals during the 1980s. Thus the invasion of Broadway broadened and deepened into what seemed more like an occupation in the next decade. Rice and Lloyd Webber would continue to take part in it as well—but no longer as a team.

MACKINTOSH AND THE MEGAMUSICAL

With *Evita* the partnership of Tim Rice and Andrew Lloyd Webber effectively came to an end. If not quite the enfants terribles of the 1970s, the rebel collaborators now took separate paths to fame and fortune—and into the English establishment: Sir Tim was knighted in 1994; Sir Andrew was knighted in 1992, then made a lord in 1997. Rice went on to work with several different composers as he provided lyrics, notably for *Chess* (London, 1986/New York, 1988, Benny

Andersson and Björn Ulvaeus) and such Disney sponsored shows as *Beauty and the Beast* (1994, Alan Menken), *The Lion King* (1997, Elton John), and *Aïda* (2000, John). Lloyd Webber, for his part, emerged as a businessman in his own right and a showman extraordinaire. He took The Really Useful Company, which he had formed earlier to produce his own work, and expanded it into an international conglomerate and the co-owner of the largest theater chain in London. He also became an artistic force to reckon with in the theater. Teaming up with ever new lyricists, he wrote the music for roughly a dozen London shows, most of which he eventually produced or coproduced himself on Broadway, where some met with unprecedented success: *Cats* (1981/1982, T. S. Eliot), *Song & Dance* (1982/1985, Don Black), *Starlight Express* (1984/1987, Richard Stilgoe), *The Phantom of the Opera* (1986/1988, Charles Hart and Stilgoe), *Aspects of Love* (1989/1990, Black and Hart), *Sunset Boulevard* (1993/1994, Black and Christopher Hampton), *By Jeeves* (1996/2001, Alan Ayckbourn), and *The Woman in White* (2004/2005, David Zippel).

In *Cats*, his first show without Rice, Lloyd Webber helped spark a trend for so-called megamusicals, as he built on his earlier innovations with Rice and took them to another level. Like *Cats*, the great megamusicals of the 1980s all came out of London. They included *Starlight Express, Chess, Les Misérables, The Phantom of the Opera*, and *Miss Saigon*, among others (not all of them by Lloyd Webber). Such shows often resembled rock operas in the underlying earnestness with which they took up sweeping tales of lofty import and grand emotions—or those that at least aspired to such. Their music showed rock opera leanings as well, though, without the influence of Rice, the rock element diminished. They still featured ambitious scores in a variety of styles in which the characters sang almost everything, including the dialogue, and the orchestra seldom stopped playing. Where such shows most differed from their predecessors, however, was in their approach to staging. Eye-popping scenic spectacle, elaborate sets and lighting schemes, high-tech wizardry, an architectural use of theater space, sheer grandeur of scale—all these together helped to justify the new prefix and to turn "megamusical" into an acceptable Broadway buzzword by the end of the 1980s.

Not all of Lloyd Webber's post-Rice shows were megamusicals, of course. Yet *Cats* and *The Phantom of the Opera* certainly fit the description.

And as these shows turned into the supreme successes of Lloyd Webber's career, they make a compelling case for the viability of the genre they have come to represent. The two shows in effect redefined the parameters of a musical's success in global terms and, doing so, they also redefined much of what is now internationally understood as musical theater.

Significantly, Lloyd Webber's most important collaborator on these shows was no longer his librettist, whoever it now happened to be. Instead, it was his producer, Cameron Mackintosh (b. 1946), an entrepreneur who before *Cats* had only a spotty track record. In fact, Mackintosh's earlier hits included only a small revue of songs by an American writer then little known in England, *Side by Side by Sondheim* (1976/1977), and English revivals of *Oliver!*, *My Fair Lady*, and *Oklahoma!* Yet under Mackintosh's command in the 1980s the British invasion would shift into high gear. Through the astonishing triumph of four megamusicals whose successes he engineered, Mackintosh consolidated a basic shift in theatrical relations between London and New York, the West End now becoming as much a source for Broadway as a reflection of it. These shows made Mackintosh the single most powerful theater producer of the age, and a very wealthy man. They include, besides *Cats* and *Phantom, Les Misérables* (Paris, 1980/London, 1985/New York, 1987) and *Miss Saigon* (London, 1989/New York, 1991). And as the first three of these also currently hold the record as the three longest-running musicals of any kind in Broadway history, they proved themselves "mega" in yet another sense of the word.

Cats was a revue with virtually no umbrella to cover its musical numbers. Lloyd Webber simply chose poems from a collection of light verse by T. S. Eliot, detailing the idiosyncrasies of different kinds of cats, and set them to music in a pastiche of styles from rock to the Pucciniesque. Eliot, the great modernist poet who had died in 1965, was in no position to object. Moreover, his widow approved. She even provided access to an unpublished poem, which inspired the show's great power ballad, "Memory." The immense popularity of "Memory" outside the theater, following "I Don't Know How to Love Him" (*Superstar*) and "Don't Cry for Me, Argentina" (*Evita*), confirmed Lloyd Webber as the sole composer of the era consistently capable of writing show songs of sufficiently broad appeal to become top-selling singles on their own.

But the genius of the piece went beyond its score. Mackintosh assembled a production team in whose hands the show became, he said, "an experience rather than just another musical." Director Trevor Nunn (b. 1940), scenic and costume designer John Napier (b. 1944), and choreographer and codirector Gillian Lynne (b. 1927) turned *Cats* into a veritable pageant. They not only costumed the actors to look like cats, they also created an environment for them to cavort in as cats. They converted the theater space into a junkyard 3½ times life-size, with man-made rubbish scaled to the size of the actor-cats and strewn about without distinction between the stage and the auditorium. That placed the audience eye to eye with the kitties it had come to watch from the safety of the house, and it whimsically obliged the audience to experience *Cats* from the cats' perspective. The cats even mingled with the spectators; and in London's New London Theater, where the show premiered, the stage itself revolved—and so did a section of the auditorium where the spectators sat. ("Latecomers not admitted while auditorium is in motion" ran one publicity line.) But for the seats of the theater being bolted to the floor of the house, *Cats* aspired to nothing perhaps so much as a theme-park ride. "It's based on the same basic, unspoken contract as Disneyland," said Nunn of his next Lloyd Webber collaboration, *Starlight Express*, though he might as well have been talking about this one. "Here is my money, hit me with the experience."

What hit the Broadway community hardest about the experience was the spirit of mass culture that informed it. Although the show originally traded on the cachet of the poems of T. S. Eliot, *Cats* tweaked its whiskers at any literary approach to the stage. Its appeal was unabashedly physical, even thrilling in its sense of fun. It drew on the allure of theme parks with their wraparound environments, daredevil simulations, and high-tech special effects. The climax of the show consisted of a mystical ascent to cat heaven on a huge rubber tire that rose like a spaceship twelve feet above the stage. The effect, together with others, cost $2.5 million to accommodate, by means of gutting and rebuilding New York's Winter Garden Theater. Spectacular coups de théâtre of this sort became megamusical emblems in the hands of Mackintosh and company: *Phantom*'s chandelier crashing down over the heads of the audience; a helicopter landing and taking off again in *Miss Saigon*. But it was *Cats* that set the pace, changing the look and texture of a Broadway show by the boldness of its physical design and an emphatic engagement with technology.

Such overwhelming sights were matched, moreover, by overwhelming sounds that rivaled FM and CD in quality and movie theaters and rock arenas in volume. Here, too, technology worked its powers to transform the experience of musical theater. While the practice of concealing microphones onstage to ensure acoustic balance went back at least to the 1940s, it took the impact of *Promises, Promises* (1968) and *Jesus Christ Superstar* (1971) to promote the overt miking of singers and instrumentalists as something desirable. *Cats* went further still. Every one of its performers now wore a wireless radio mike, which allowed each of them a new freedom of movement. It also gave their voices a certain disembodied presence, as if the cats were all lip-synching to prerecorded songs when they were actually singing. The sounds they made no longer reached the audience directly. A new kind of theater technician controlled them: a sound designer, who digitally amplified, equalized, compressed, and otherwise manipulated them on a soundboard before sending them via loudspeakers throughout the house. This new system of sound delivery, now the norm in the musical theater, enabled a genre like the rock musical to thrive in a way that would not have been possible earlier. But it also changed the relationship between performers who no longer needed to project their voices to be heard, and audiences who no longer needed to make the effort to listen in order to hear what was performed. It compromised, or at least complicated the Broadway musical as a "live" experience.

Thus was the sensationalism of nineteenth-century extravaganza refitted for an electronic age—and a global audience. *Cats* asked "nothing of [its] audience beyond attendance on a certain night," remarked English critic Sheridan Morley, "No language problem for tourists, no demands of a shared heritage or education, no cultural barriers to be stormed." Perhaps that was the basis for its seemingly inexhaustible popularity—virtually everywhere (London, New York, in franchise around the world) and for all time (to quote its own publicity, "Now and Forever").

By contrast, *The Phantom of the Opera*, a lurid melodrama with a romance at its core, took a rather different approach to the musical stage. Based on a Gothic novel set in nineteenth-century France, the show told the backstage story of an opera composer (Michael Crawford) who wears a mask to hide a facial deformity; of his thwarted passion for the soprano Christine (Sarah Brightman), who loves another man; and of his reign of terror inside the Paris Opera House in order to have his way—above all, with Christine. Building on the underlying sexual tension of the plot, *Phantom* knowingly moved back and forth between romance and horror, kitsch and camp, without settling comfortably in any single vein. Lloyd Webber called the novel "a piece of hokum." It also describes the show.

But inspired hokum—particularly in the hands of director Harold Prince and stage designer Maria Björnson (1949–2002). The staging fairly reveled in an almost baroque sense of astonishment, nowhere more so than in the sensuous spectacle of scenes that brought the Paris Opera to life in all its glory: inside the house, with its sweeping staircase; on the roof overlooking the City of Light, where Christine met her lover Raoul at night; even below the basement, as the Phantom rowed Christine in a gondola to his hiding place on the other side of a subterranean lagoon exquisitely lit by hundreds of candles. The music, too, evoked the richness of a repertoire once actually heard at the house—sometimes simply to burlesque the artifice of opera ("Hannibal," "Il Muto"), yet at other times quite genuinely to enlist the genre's heightened emotionalism in the service of the romantic plot ("The Music of the Night," "All I Ask of You"). The through-sung score and lush orchestrations, the rhapsodic lyricism of the show's many ballads, and the legitimate singing required to do them justice—all gave clear indication that with *Phantom* Lloyd Webber wished to move away from rock opera toward something closer to the "real thing."

Others, too, sought to fashion heartfelt stageworks approaching "the grandeur of opera in popular garb"—works often dubbed pop operas, or, more archly, poperettas. The most successful at it were lyricist Alain Boublil (b. 1941) and composer Claude-Michel Schönberg (b. 1944), two Frenchmen with close ties to the pop recording industry in France. Boublil saw *Jesus Christ Superstar* in its original stage form in New York and found in it his inspiration. He admired the monumental subject, the pop-infused song style, the through-sung structure. And he hoped to create something comparable in Gallic terms, even though French audiences did not take kindly to Broadway-style musical shows—notoriously so, almost as a matter of national pride. Together, Boublil and Schönberg wrote *La Révolution Française* (1973), based on that defining epochal moment in the history of France (and indeed the West); and *Les Misérables* (1980), based on a monumental literary classic familiar to readers wherever French culture held sway. They produced each as concept record album first, then staged it as a spectacle (in the French sense of the word) in Paris's Palais des Sports. The second of these caught the attention of Cameron Mackintosh. He waxed enthusiastic on hearing the recording and proposed to convert *Les Misérables* into an entertainment more suited to English-speaking audiences. Mustering the forces of London's Royal Shakespeare Company under the direction of Trevor Nunn and John Caird, Mackintosh oversaw its remake into the show now affectionately known the world over as "*Les Miz.*" The triumph of *Les Miz* in global terms, in fact, and of *Miss Saigon* by the same writers four years later, effectively transformed the British invasionary force into a multinational coalition.

In order to arrive at *Les Miz*, Mackintosh and company had to do more than translate *Les Misérables* into English. They had to transform a particularly Gallic form of entertainment into something closer to an Anglo-American musical. The French creators, assuming their audiences already knew the story, had presented scenes from the novel in a series of tableaux rather than a fully developed narrative. The English collaborators could not make the same assumption. They had to rework the material to make the narrative clearer, adding a prologue and fleshing out character. They even introduced an ongoing theme of religious belief that required Boublil and Schönberg to create new songs to express its various perspectives (e.g., the hero's selfless prayer to a redeeming God, "Bring Him Home"; the belief of the hero's nemesis in a righteous God who metes out justice, "Stars"). In its new incarnation, the show became not only the most successful megamusical of the 1980s, but the single most successful musical of all time. Perhaps the surest confirmation of how supremely well the Englishmen accomplished their conversion came in 1991 when, after almost universal success elsewhere, *Les Miz* finally opened in Paris—retranslated into French—and failed.

Les Misérables, the musical, adapted and compressed the sweep of Victor Hugo's magisterial novel of the same name (loosely translated, "The Downtrodden"). As an epic, the show had to balance a multiplicity of themes as it dramatized them: above all, a story of love requited, an outcry against social injustice, and a search for spiritual redemption. It took three hours to convey all this on the stage. Over the course of seventeen years, from 1815 to 1832, the show traced the sufferings of Jean Valjean (Colm Wilkinson), an ex-convict and parole jumper—his relentless pursuit by Javert (Terrence Mann), the honor-bound policeman whose life Valjean ultimately saves; his devotion to the orphan girl Cosette (Judy Kuhn), whom he raises as his daughter; her love in turn for Marius, a student involved in an ill-fated Paris uprising brutally suppressed by army troops. Yet, as many of the plot connections became lost in the interlocking welter of details, and as the show contained almost no spoken dialogue to help sort them out, the success of *Les Miz* depended less on the narrative as such than on the power of projecting the narrative thrust in sounds and sights.

The score followed the sprawl of Hugo's melodrama through a fluid soundscape of recurring numbers. Yet, unlike reprises of songs for a dramatic point in a more traditional show, musical self-references here at times took on lives of their own. The score proved remarkable nonetheless for the immediacy of its characterizations and the variety of its expressive purposes and musical shapes. It moved between reverence ("Bring Him Home") and vulgarity ("Master of the House"); public outcry ("Do You Hear the People Sing?") and private confession ("On My Own"); the simplicity of a nursery rhyme ("Castle on a Cloud") and the complexity of an operatic finale ("One Day More"). At its most ambitious, the score even suggested the kind of emotional heft one expects of opera rather than of musicals—perhaps more than suggested, as a comparison

Ex. 15-2a. Claude-Michel Schonberg, music, Herbert Kretzmer and Alain Boublil, lyrics: "Bring Him Home," *Les Misérables*

Ex. 15-2b. Giacomo Puccini, music: "Humming Chorus" (transposed), *Madama Butterfly*

of the music to "Bring Him Home" (Ex. 15-2a) and that of the Humming Chorus in Puccini's *Madama Butterfly* (Ex. 15-2b) itself suggests.

As he had done with *Cats*, John Napier brought his environmental approach to the staging of the show. "My starting point was the centre of the play's biggest moment, the barricade," he said. "Once that was solved everything else fell into place. The barricade could split, lift, and revolve, and was a mass of *objets trouvés* which the actors picked up from time to time and used." Indeed, the scenic design interpreted the plot through stage pictures extraordinarily vivid in their impact and sufficiently unambiguous in their meaning to bypass the need for words altogether—the massacre of students barricaded in the streets of Paris; Valjean's escape with a wounded Marius through the sewers below; Javert's suicidal leap into the Seine. Many left the theater overwhelmed by the power of such depictions and, as these served to suggest Hugo's indictment of social injustice and Valjean's moral ascent, even uplifted by the experience. Others found it stultifying. For them, *Les Miz* and shows

Michael Maguire (Enjolras) mounts the barricades in a doomed attempt at revolution in *Les Misérables*.

like it succeeded all too easily by eliciting responses from audiences that were often unmotivated by dramatic development—ready-made rather than earned. "They give the impression, rather than the reality, of feeling," wrote Richard Eyre and Nicholas Wright, "like Victorians scattering water on letters to look as if they'd been written in tears."

In a similar vein, *Miss Saigon* gave Boublil and Schönberg the opportunity to revisit *Madama Butterfly*, this time not to seek inspiration in Puccini's score but to sensationalize the plot. An Anglo-French venture now from its inception, *Miss Saigon* turned the very intimate story of the original into a monumental one. It updated the turn-of-the-century tale of an American serviceman in the Far East and the Asian girl who bears his child alone after he returns to the United States, and placed it in the brutalizing context of the Vietnam War and its aftermath. This Mackintosh venture, too, proved to be an enormous hit. Yet the megamusicals that followed it to Broadway with comparable designs on the Gothic and melodramatic literature of the nineteenth century—many of them now Anglo-American ventures—proved less successful or even flops (*Jekyll & Hyde*, 1997; *Jane Eyre*, 2000; *Dracula, The Musical*, 2004).

What has defined the megamusical, however, has not been its content but rather "its replacement of content by a form in which spectacle and sound are constitutive of its nature." Due to its mass appeal, overriding the boundaries of language, this form has lent itself to a commercial trajectory of global proportions, which no one has pursued with greater aplomb than Cameron Mackintosh. In an age of increasing rule by committee, Mackintosh has approached the business of making musicals as the man-in-charge of an enterprise that systematically encompasses everything from financing and production to marketing and distribution. First, Mackintosh joined the forces of London's commercial and subsidized theaters to produce heavily capitalized shows at about one third the cost of production in New York, then tested these in front of British audiences to minimize the risks in positioning them for Broadway. The approach would surely not have worked the other way around, had he started in New York. For between London and New York—outposts of what can be viewed as a single English-speaking culture—lies an ocean of differences in norms and expectations when it comes to the theater. Nunn elaborated:

In New York the commercial theatre . . . is the sole form of theatre that reaches a large public. . . . In London the scene is dominated by government-subsidised theatre. . . . Therefore the London theatre is fundamentally more experimental and less traditional than the Broadway stage. . . . A theatre business that has only smash or flop categories is problematic for investors, because if the critical judgements of journalists go against, there is no management skill or expression of faith that can alter the doom of the stricken show. So not surprisingly, nobody wants to back a high-risk enterprise; if it had been necessary to originate Cats *in America, it might not have got off the ground.*

Next, after shepherding the creation of his shows and masterminding their production, Mackintosh embarked on aggressive marketing campaigns to promote them, hoping to ensure their public success whatever their critical reception. To judge by the nature of the publicity generated, a Mackintosh show was no longer just a show but an event, commercially hyped by saturating the media with all kinds of artifacts and ads reminding the public of its importance. Typically, Mackintosh anchored his campaigns in the use of logos, all the more effective in their instant recognizability as pictures without any need for words: *Cats*'s twin green eyes; *Phantom*'s mask and rose; *Les Miz*'s Cosette and flag; *Miss Saigon*'s helicopter and sun. (By removing language entirely as a marketing factor, such images were perfectly designed to fit the global trajectory of the Mackintosh enterprise.) In sum, Mackintosh managed to create and maintain a must-see aura about his shows that kept audiences coming to them despite often negative reviews. He made his shows, in a phrase, critic proof.

Finally, instead of selling his rights to foreign buyers as British producers had previously done, Mackintosh retained control over his shows, re-producing them around the globe with notorious "breath for breath" fidelity to the original. Thus the roles in his musicals have tended to stamp the actors who perform them more than the actors have put their stamp on the roles. In fact, the standardized product and interchangeability of performers necessary to transport it anywhere in the world have come to characterize the megamusical in Mackintosh's hands as much as the spectacular use of state-of-the-art technology to create virtual environments on the stage. The Mack-

Official logos for the four megahits Cameron Mackintosh produced:
(a) *Cats*; (b) *Les Misérables*; (c) *The Phantom of the Opera*; (d) *Miss Saigon*.

intosh model, however, has not proved easy to follow. Others who have pursued similar approaches in musicals have generally failed to recoup the staggering costs of their Broadway investments—the case, for example, with *Chess* ($6 million), *Carrie* (1988, $8 million), and even such Lloyd Webber shows as *Starlight Express* ($8 million), *Aspects of Love* ($8.5 million), and *Sunset Boulevard* ($13 million). Mackintosh, by contrast, has consistently succeeded to recoup—*Cats* ($4 million), *Les Miz* ($4.5 million), *Phantom* ($8 million), *Miss Saigon* ($10 million)—and then gone on to reap hitherto unimaginable profits with runs that have lasted from ten to more than twenty years on Broadway alone.

No one ever expected the British invasion to turn into the long-term occupation of Broadway that it did, starting in the 1980s. Yet by the early years of the twenty-first century that occupation seemed largely to have spent its force: the "forever" of most of the Mackintosh megahits turned into "now," and "then" with their Broadway closings. Some of the later work of Lloyd Webber (*Whistle Down the Wind*, *The Beautiful Game*) and Boublil and Schönberg (*Martin Guerre*) did not even make it to New York—though probably because the relatively modest reception of such shows in London's West End precluded positioning them for a shot at Broadway. It seems unlikely that high-profile musicals would succeed elsewhere and bypass New York. Even in a globalizing age, when it comes to musicals, the Broadway cachet is still considered at least an economic plus. "I think you can have a huge hit in London, and you can have great successes that go around the world," said Mackintosh. "But in the musical theater, that hit needs to also be a hit on Broadway, and that is what dictates it on its final journey around the world." Mackintosh's emphatic "also" speaks volumes, however. The great influx of European megamusicals on Broadway may be over. But the revolution that influx sparked is ongoing. And in its wake, the most fundamental cultural assumptions about the Broadway musical—ones concerning its origin, its identity, even its ownership—can no longer be taken for granted. As musical theater scholar John Snelson sees it:

> *A musical no longer has to be, or aspire to be, American. In itself, this is a significant redefinition of the "Broadway musical," moving it toward a global art form, with expressions of national identity becoming more a localized coloring than an essential element of the musical's identity.*

DISNEY AND THE MOVICAL

The prospect of a future of Broadwayless Broadway musicals irked not only showgoers with a keen attachment to Broadway's past but also show makers with a stake in renewing it. Thus for many, the big news of the 1990s was the rise of entertainment conglomerates on this side of the Atlantic seeking to produce shows that might rival the British megahits—even on their own turf. But the rise of such conglomerates proved troubling as well. Their success would so profoundly corporatize Broadway as to alter the way it went about both the business and the art of making musicals. Among them were the now defunct Live Entertainment (Livent), Inc. (*Kiss of the Spider Woman, Ragtime*), and SFX (now Clear Channel) Entertainment (*The Producers, Hairspray*). Even the most formidable of all entertainment conglomerates, the Disney Corporation, entered the Broadway arena it had previously scorned. Named for Walt Disney (1901–1966), the legendary graphic artist and entrepreneur who created Mickey Mouse and founded Disneyland, the Disney Corporation had no intention of giving up its base of operations in the motion picture industry. It simply sought a new market for its wares. So the company with "the biggest marquee name, the deepest pockets and, in truth, the most skill" in the entertainment industry now saw fit to extend the franchise to include—along with movies, videos, theme parks, ice shows, T-shirts, and lunch boxes—an outpost of the Magic Kingdom on the Great White Way. In 1994 it formed Walt Disney Theatrical Productions. Here Cameron Mackintosh saw his own influence at work:

> *I think that extraordinary sequence of British shows, starting with* Cats *and then* Les Miz, Phantom, *followed by* Saigon, *completely rebuilt the road. . . . [These shows] helped Broadway become this huge financial machine. Before Andrew [Lloyd Webber] and I had these kind of worldwide successes, companies like Disney weren't interested in coming into the theater. Disney thought the theater was small beer, but then suddenly people said, "These shows made how much?"*

In a sense, Broadway had already piqued Disney's interest before 1994, since the company had been hiring songwriters with strong musical theater credentials to create the scores for its latest crop of animated films—Howard Ashman, Alan Menken, Tim Rice, Stephen Schwartz. These animated features reanimated Disney's fortunes in the 1990s when, starting with *The Little Mermaid* (1989), they turned into huge box office hits. Their success as a group, in fact, sent shock waves through the company. Could the same entertainments that proved such hits as films also draw a family audience previously untapped to the theater—the live theater? There was little precedent to go by. Others had already converted popular comic strips into stage musicals with great success (*Li'l Abner*, *You're a Good Man, Charlie Brown*; *Annie*). On the other hand, those who had converted successful film musicals into comparable works for the stage had generally failed (*Gigi*; *Seven Brides for Seven Brothers*; *Singin' in the Rain*). Yet no one had ever made a Broadway musical out of a feature-length musical cartoon. Disney took up the challenge. The company marshalled its considerable forces to convert the most popular of its animated films into the costliest productions ever mounted on Broadway—the first alone estimated at $15 million. The gamble paid off. To the dismay of a Broadway theater community ever wary of outsiders (foreign or domestic), the first two Disney megamusicals turned into megahits: *Beauty and the Beast* (Hollywood, 1991/Broadway, 1994) and *The Lion King* (1994/1997). They set the pace; more in the same vein followed: *Tarzan* (2006) *Mary Poppins* (2006), *The Little Mermaid* (2008).

Beauty and the Beast took its cue from a centuries-old fairly tale of the same name. It told of a girl whose love for a hideous creature ultimately breaks the spell cast on it and transforms the beast back into the handsome prince it once was. The original story was both dark at its core and sexually charged. For the screen version, Disney utterly tamed its sexuality and lightened its spirit with gags, songs, and the company's specialty: turning animated animals and objects into peoplelike characters. For the live version, Disney followed the film while adding more songs ("If I Can't Love Her," "Home"), expanding production numbers ("Be My Guest"), and, taking a cue perhaps from its own theme park attractions, devising special effects even more special live than on the screen (the beast's high-tech metamorphosis into a prince at the climax of the show). The new extravaganza succeeded with children of all ages, including children who had children of their own. But theater critics gave it only mixed reviews. "At its campy, shameless best," wrote one, "the Broadway *Beauty* brings to mind Busby Berkeley movies, Radio City Music Hall spectacles, the Ziegfeld *Follies* and Fourth of July at Disney World. . . . The one thing this riot of color and noise does not bring to mind is the modern Broadway musical."

Disney responded by approaching its next screen-to-stage musical adaptation with greater theatrical resolve. To direct *Beauty*, Disney had looked to its own. To direct *The Lion King*, Disney now went

Actor-puppets bring African animals to life in Julie Taymor's staging of "The Circle of Life" from *The Lion King*.

outside the company and hired Off Broadway's Julie Taymor (b. 1953). She brought her own vision to what was, in essence, a coming-of-age parable set among animals of the African plain. Instead of simply staging the film she theatricalized it. She emphasized the Africanness of the setting in sight and sound, and brought the animated animals to life with a stunning sense of what makes live theater different from other kinds of entertainment. She called on ancient rituals and non-Western theater forms, adapting such devices as Indonesian puppetry and African masks and headdresses to suggest the animals portrayed onstage while at the same time revealing the actors who portrayed them. Thus *Lion King* drew on the imagination of its audience, as the show celebrated the make-believe of stage enactment rather than hiding such make-believe for the sake of realistic illusion. "I think *The Lion King* bridges the divide between Broadway and avant-garde theater," said Taymor. But bridging the divide was not the same as overcoming it, as critic John Lahr was quick to point out. "You have this kind of schizophrenic experience where you're imposing onto very standard Disney material a very exotic sound and look—it has the look and feel of the avant-garde but the heart of a Hollywood production."

The Lion King triumphed nevertheless. Its success, this time both critical and popular, confirmed that Disney was on Broadway to stay—and not only as a producer of shows. Disney had become a theater owner as well, having invested heavily in the New Amsterdam Theater, where *The Lion King* played. This once sumptuous playhouse on Forty-second Street, home to Ziegfeld's *Follies* in the 1920s, had deteriorated during the Depression, then served as a movie house, and finally fallen into disuse. Disney, looking for a Broadway home of its own in the mid-1990s, saw an opportunity and seized it. Through a favorable financial arrangement with the City of New York, the company acquired an exclusive forty-nine-year lease for the New Amsterdam and spent some $6 million to renovate it, restoring the theater "interpretively" to its former glory and to active use.

The move benefited not only Disney. It had a catalytic effect on the fortunes of the theater district as a whole. With the scuttling of the "urban renewal" project that would have "saved" Times Square by building new office towers and incorporating it into the business district, Disney's investment became a rallying point for saving Times Square under a wholly different rubric: historic preservation. Disney's commitment to keep the district a middle-class entertainment zone spurred others to invest in theater restorations (the Republic Theater, restored as the New Victory, 1995; the Lyric and the Apollo Theaters, combined and restored as the Ford Center, 1998 [now the Hilton]). And it encouraged corporate investment in other forms of amusement there as well (AMC Entertainment's multiscreen movie complex; Madame Tussaud's Wax Museum). It even became a rallying point for cleaning up the district altogether—with the concerted help of New York's police force.

Surely it would be too much to claim, as Alexander Reichl does, that, "with its sparkling image of wholesome Americana, Disney's presence alone would symbolize the conquest of Forty-second Street by the forces of good over evil." Yet the turnaround was as undeniable as was Disney's role in it. Where crime and sleaze once held sway, families with children could now be seen fearlessly taking to the streets to see a Disney show, at a Disney theater, en route to the Disney retail store next door. Disney's name, in fact, became synonymous with the conversion of Times Square into "a romantically idealized tourist version of its former self." All it lacked was the particularity of place—that place inscribed in American popular culture by George M. Cohan and peopled by the denizens of *Guys and Dolls*. Less local in character now—less idiosyncratically "New York"—the world of Broadway reflected more than ever the values of a transnational mass culture that was corporate-owned, corporate-run, and corporate-mediated.

Broadway may well have been the last major sector of the American entertainment industry to become corporatized—decades after the movie industry, the television industry, and the recording industry had all gone that route. As a result, musicals too became part of that business synergy, whereby companies seek profits not just by selling a given product outright but also by integrating it into a network of related products that help sell each other. Broadway shows now regularly came packaged with show-based T-shirts and other merchandise sold not only in stores (where one might expect to find them) but in the lobbies of the theaters where the shows depicted on the T-shirts were playing. More significantly, Broadway shows themselves now often originated as synergistic repackagings of other forms of entertainment. Concept record albums, when repackaged for the stage, had radically transformed musical theater in the 1970s and 1980s as rock operas and megamusicals. Now movies similarly made their presence felt—a tendency noticeable earlier, but given an enormous boost by Disney's move to Broadway in the 1990s. A neat aphorism summed up the state of affairs: "The film sells the musical; the musical sells the film; both sell related merchandise; producers profit from all sales."

Before long other film studios followed the Disney model: They set up their own theater production divisions to convert their properties into stage shows. MGM On Stage, for example, produced Broadway musical versions of *Dirty Rotten Scondrels* in 2005 and *Legally Blonde* in 2007; and in 2008 DreamWorks Theatricals took on the Disney Company directly when it made its Broadway debut with the converted animation *Shrek The Musical*. So pervasive would this screen-to-stage practice become that it seemed only a matter of time before some wit would call the shows that exemplified it movicals. But Broadway had long been in the business of turning nonmusical movies into musicals and staging them. Previously, however, showmakers looked to films as simply one of several sources of

material, and not the most important. They also approached films somewhat in the spirit of literary properties, screenplays with visual enhance-
ments—the case, for example, with *The King and I* and *My Fair Lady.*
They even gave their musicals different names from those of the films
that inspired them, not in an effort to hide their sources, but to establish
their independence from them *as shows*—artistically (because they genuinely sought to adapt such sources to the musical form in order to reveal
new meanings in them) and, perhaps more to the point, commercially (to
distinguish between competing products).

By contrast, showmakers nowadays turn to Hollywood on a regular
basis. And they place a greater emphasis on remaining faithful to the
visual aspects, the performative qualities, indeed the whole aura of the
original films in their adaptations. (In a dazzling display of sheer scenic
ingenuity, *Sunset Boulevard*, the musical, even staged the film's famous
frontal shot of the hero's corpse as seen from the bottom of the pool in
which it floated facedown.) In converting such films into staged musical properties, therefore, they tend to keep the same name—and thus
to keep the synergy between the two in the public eye. "If you liked the
movie," they imply, "now you can also see it live." The following list
demonstrates the trend: It contains two groups of titles of some representative Broadway musicals derived from films, paired with the titles
of the films from which they derived. The two groups of ten shows
cover roughly comparable spans of time (1953–1973, 1982–2008) but
separated by about thirty years:

Hazel Flagg, 1953 (*Nothing Sacred,* 1937)
Silk Stockings, 1955 (*Ninotchka,* 1939)
Oh Captain!, 1958 (*The Captain's Paradise,* 1953)
Donnybrook!, 1961 (*The Quiet Man,* 1952)
Here's Love, 1963 (*Miracle on 34th Street,* 1947)
Sweet Charity, 1966 (*Nights of Cabiria,* 1957)
Promises, Promises, 1968 (*The Apartment,* 1960)
Applause, 1970 (*All About Eve,* 1950)
Sugar, 1972 (*Some Like It Hot,* 1959)
A Little Night Music, 1973 (*Smiles of a Summer Night,* 1955)

Nine, 1982 (*8½,* 1963)
Little Shop of Horrors, 1982 (*Little Shop of Horrors,* 1960)

La Cage aux Folles, 1983 (*La Cage aux Folles,* 1978)

Passion, 1994 (*Passione d'Amore,* 1981)

Sunset Boulevard, 1994 (*Sunset Boulevard,* 1950)

Big, 1996 (*Big,* 1988)

The Full Monty, 2000 (*The Full Monty,* 1997)

Hairspray, 2002 (*Hairspray,* 1988)

Monty Python's Spamalot, 2005 (*Monty Python and the Holy Grail,* 1975)

Billy Elliot, 2008 (*Billy Elliot,* 2000)

Not all the shows in the second group were undertaken in the same spirit, however. The creators of *Nine* and *Passion* sought to make their stories meaningful in different ways from their filmic sources; the creators of *Sunset Boulevard* and *Spamalot* seemed more interested in reproducing their sources as closely as possible on stage.

An even more telling picture of the new synergy between Broadway and Hollywood emerges when one looks at films already held to be musicals, or that featured strong musical components, before their conversion into musicals for the stage. Here the new development involves not simply an intensification of an existing trend, but the reversal of one. From the rise of talking films in the 1920s until the 1970s when the practice no longer proved profitable, Hollywood adapted successful Broadway musicals for the screen as a matter of course. Now, the traffic tends to flow in the opposite direction. Largely because of the studios' stockpiles of musical film properties and the potential profits of a live musical megahit in the global marketplace, Hollywood is more likely to encourage Broadway to adapt a once popular screen musical for the stage. *42nd Street* (1980) may have led the way by dint of its megasuccess on Broadway in the 1980s. But Disney provided the great impetus here because of its consistency in institutionalizing the trend and of its doing so within its own corporate structure. Apart from the Disney shows with their specialized focus, representative examples of musical-to-musical adaptations that began on the screen include: *Seven Brides for Seven Brothers* (1982 [1954]), *Singin' in the Rain* (1985 [1952]), *Meet Me in St. Louis* (1989 [1944]), *Victor/Victoria* (1995 [1982]), *State Fair* (1996 [1945]), *High Society* (1998 [1956]), *Footloose* (1998 [1984]), *Saturday Night Fever* (1999 [1977]), *The Producers* (2001 [1968]), and *Thoroughly Modern Millie* (2002 [1967]).

All these retained their original titles. Still, most of them failed on Broadway or proved only modestly successful. Few could offer the sense of continuity from one medium to the other that *Victor/Victoria* did: Julie Andrews starred in both. Barring that, such live musicals often had to compete with charismatic performers caught in a larger-than-life perfection on the screen that was infinitely repeatable. (Think of Gene Kelly's "Singin' in the Rain" sequence, or Judy Garland's "Trolley Song" in *Meet Me in St. Louis*.) Movicals, by keeping the titles of their film sources, might attract a certain pre-sold audience to the theater. But those that could not memorably distance themselves on the stage from such ever-present models on the screen tended to come off, ironically, as poor shadows of the originals.

After *42nd Street*, *The Producers* has proved the most successful of these musicals to date. Based on the cult film of Mel Brooks, the show alights on its comic premise by standing the most cherished of Broadway's creeds on its head: In a business where everybody hopes for a hit, two producers aim to make their fortunes by creating a flop. Max Bialystock (Nathan Lane) and Leo Bloom (Matthew Broderick), the rascals in question, have concocted an illegal producing scheme to get rich by overselling shares in a new musical so awful in all respects it is guaranteed to fail. They reason that once the show fails, their backers will no longer expect returns and the IRS will no longer be interested, so they can pocket the excess investments and run off to South America. Problems arise, however, when, after all their efforts, they find the opening-night audience hilariously enjoying their show as a deliberate spoof of itself; and their sure-fire flop turns into a hit. ("Where did we go right?" they lament in song.) For the stage version, Brooks wrote sixteen new songs to add to his two from the film. He also rewrote his screenplay with librettist Tom Meehan, adding and dropping scenes, and framing the whole with a new beginning and ending. In this form, as a stage musical, *The Producers* ran on Broadway for six years and won twelve Tonys, breaking the record for the number of such awards accumulated by a single show.

The success of the musical, in turn, prompted the making of a new film in 2005, also called *The Producers*—this one, a film musical version of the stage musical version of the original film. The new film, too, underwent marked changes, this time from its Broadway source. But as Susan Stroman directed both musical versions, and as Lane and Broderick also starred in both, the more meaningful differences now had to do with the nature of the media involved. At the top of the stage version, for example, Max sings "The King of Broadway." It introduces him to the audience as a once successful producer who now stands in front of the Shubert Theater, where his latest show has just bombed on its opening night. Stroman cut the song from the movie version and gave her reasons:

> *I did shoot a production number called "King of Broadway" that introduced Max Bialystock [as a great theater impresario wearing his tuxedo and cape on opening night—as he did in the stage version]. But when I edited it [for the film] it seemed as if we were repeating information. It was emotionally a hard decision to cut it. It had become a well-known song in the theater community. But in the theater, the audience sees everything in a wide shot. In film, the close-up of the camera gives you information immediately. I found that we were duplicating details. It ultimately was better to see Max in his disheveled form in his messy office at the top [of the film], and follow his journey from that state rather than seeing him in his opening night outfit [as in the stage version]. . . . [In the film] you can see from his office, the different posters, and the props from his various shows, [Max] was once a great impresario; and he wants to be on top again.*

This change, one of countless others, epitomizes the differences between a live entertainment form and one shaped by technology. Such differences effectively undid all but those shows that succeeded in their transformation from screen to stage because they knew enough to accommodate them.

Hard on the heels of the motion picture industry in that network of entertainments for which Broadway now serves as a conduit came the music industry—those businesses that produce, record, publish, market, distribute, and broadcast popular songs. Before the 1960s ascent of rock, Broadway shows regularly supplied this industry with songs that became hit Top-40 singles. Today, the reverse holds true: Pop hit singles form the basis of many Broadway shows, as if in homage to the music industry itself.

The early years of the twenty-first century have seen a trend in so-called jukebox musicals. These shows search the back-catalogues of singer/songwriters or vocal groups with proven mass appeal and repackage their recorded songs live for the stage. Nothing necessarily holds the songs together other than their association with the vocalists who once recorded them. Nor are any of the songs theater songs, which usually aim for something other than instant appeal or universal applicability. Theater songs do theater work: They express the thoughts and feelings not of their writers but of the characters who sing them, and they relate to other singing characters in the course of a sequence of events acted out on a stage. The songs used in jukebox musicals, by contrast, were created—if not entirely for the jukebox— at least for more general purposes. And so to provide such songs with a sense of theatrical occasion, some jukebox shows invent new plots to accommodate them: *Mamma Mia!* (2001, ABBA) tells the story of a girl who, raised by a single mother, reads her mother's diary to find out who her father might be, and invites the three candidates to her wedding; *Movin' Out* (2002, Billy Joel) uses dance to tell the tales of five teenagers from Hicksville, Long Island, whose lives are drastically altered by the Vietnam War. Other jukebox shows work biographically; they are about the performers whose songs make up the scores: *The Boy from Oz* (2003), Peter Allen; *Jersey Boys* (2005), Frankie Valli and the Four Seasons.

Critics often cite *Ain't Misbehavin'* (1978) as the jukebox musical prototype. This revue used a catalogue of period songs associated with "Fats" Waller to re-create the performance styles of black artists of the Harlem Renaissance. Critics mostly raved about this show, in fact, but dismissed almost all the shows of the catalogue type that came after. Such shows not only exuded a different spirit, they had different priorities as well: The songs came first, then came a theatrical concept. "Most of the singing scrapbooks that followed in the succeeding decades," wrote Ben Brantley, "were either antiseptic, industrial-revue-style fare (like *Smokey Joe's Cafe* [1995, Jerry Leiber and Mike Stoller]) or karaoke-ish kitsch (like *Mamma Mia!*)." *Mamma Mia!* has proved the runaway hit of the genre nonetheless, and its success has fueled the jukebox craze despite the harsh reality that most such ventures fail. In 2005, three together in one year alone lost close to $30 million: *Good*

Vibrations (The Beach Boys), *All Shook Up* (Elvis Presley), and *Lennon* (John Lennon, mostly without the Beatles).

If the subjects of jukebox shows tend to vary, their scores share a similar profile. Altogether, their songs constitute a cross-section of hit tunes selected from a significantly limited timespan: from the late 1950s to the early 1980s. Such songs reflect the popular music of the mainly white, middle-class, and aging baby-boom generation. They include a range of styles—rock 'n' roll (*All Shook Up*), country (*Ring of Fire*, 2006), bubblegum (*Mamma Mia!*)—almost any kind of song, it seems, but a theater song. This is no accident. Since the 1960s and the ensuing rift between show music and industry music, Broadway songs rarely reflected the styles of the commercial mainstream during this period. As a consequence, jukebox shows have more recently aimed to close the gap, attracting to Broadway a core audience enamored of the pop repertoire of the era who might not have gone to the theater otherwise. Taken as a group, then, these shows have enabled the commercial musical theater to find its way back into the web of popular culture from which the rise of rock had severed it. And they have enabled the music industry to work the business synergy even more blatantly than the movie industry to secure an outlet for its products on the musical stage.

In sum, the incorporation of Broadway into the network of entertainment conglomerates and the Disneyfication of the Times Square district have led to a musical theater boom of unprecedented proportions. No one talks of Broadway dying any longer. But the optimism accompanying any sense of renewal is not unalloyed. "Everyone's really happy that there's so much work right now," says Steve Swenson, a Broadway stage electrician and lighting designer. "The problem is that there's so much crap being staged that it's sort of hard to care much about the work you get, once you get it." While perhaps needlessly dismissive, Swenson clearly sums up the sense of paradox, dilemma, and even impasse that has come to pervade Broadway musical culture. The recent boom rests on a significant transformation in Broadway musicals to accommodate it—a transformation that began in the 1970s, continues to the present, and serves to complicate any simpler, if idealized notion of the genre. Nowadays, one has to balance conflicting senses of what one actually means by Broadway: on one hand, the epicenter of the art and commerce of the American musical theater; on the other, an outpost for the most successful musicals of all time, which are neither American nor even Broadway-based at all. And one has to balance conflicting senses of what one means by the musical itself: on one hand, a live art form which remains essentially "uncompromised by the distancing tool of technology"; on the other, a mass cultural phenomenon, corporate controlled and technologically mediated at every turn. It is this very complexity that has dislodged us culturally from entertaining whatever more comfortable ideas of the Broadway musical we might once have harbored. And it amounts to perhaps the most disturbing of all distancing effects.

16

ANOTHER BROADWAY ...
ANOTHER SHOW ...

JELLY'S LAST JAM
(4/26/1992–9/5/1993). **Producers:** Margo Lion and Pamela Koslow-Hines. **Book and Director:** George C. Wolfe. **Lyrics:** Susan Birkenhead. **Music:** Jelly Roll Morton and Luther Henderson. **New York Run:** 569 performances. **Cast:** Tonya Pinkins, Gregory Hines, Savion Glover, Keith David. **Song:** "Dr. Jazz."

FALSETTOS
(4/29/1992–6/27/1993). **Producers:** Barry and Fran Weissler. **Book:** William Finn and James Lapine. **Lyrics and Music:** Finn. **Director:** Lapine. **New York Run:** 486 performances. **Cast:** Barbara Walsh, Michael Rupert, Stephen Bogardus, Chip Zien. **Songs:** "Four Jews in a Room Bitching," "I Never Wanted to Love You," "Everyone Hates His Parents," "Unlikely Lovers."

FLOYD COLLINS
(2/9/1996–3/24/1996). **Producer:** Playwrights Horizons. **Book, Lyrics, and Director:** Tina Landau. **Lyrics and Music:** Adam Guettel. **New York Run** [Off Broadway]: 25 performances. **Cast:** Cass Morgan, Theresa McCarthy, Christopher Innvar, Jason Danieley. **Songs:** "The Call," "The Riddle Song," "How Glory Goes."

View of Times Square by night at the end of the millennium.

RENT

(4/29/1996−9/7/2008). **Producers:** Jeffrey Seller, Kevin McCollum, Alan S. Gordon, and New York Theater Workshop. **Book, Lyrics, and Music:** Jonathan Larson, based on a concept of Billy Aronson. **Director:** Michael Greif. **New York Run:** 5,123 performances. **Cast:** Daphne Rubin-Vega, Idina Menzel, Adam Pascal, Anthony Rapp. **Songs:** "One Song Glory," "La Vie Bohème," "Seasons of Love."

HEDWIG AND THE ANGRY INCH

(2/14/1998−4/9/2000). **Producers:** Peter Askin, Susann Brinkley, and James B. Freydberg. **Book:** John Cameron Mitchell. **Lyrics and Music:** Stephen Trask. **Director:** Askin. **New York Run** [Off Broadway]: 857 performances. **Cast:** Miriam Schor, Mitchell, Trask. **Songs:** "The Origin of Love," "Wig in a Box."

PARADE

(12/17/1998−2/28/1999). **Producer:** Lincoln Center Theater. **Book:** Alfred Uhry. **Lyrics and Music:** Jason Robert Brown. **Director:** Harold Prince. **New York Run:** 85 performances. **Cast:** Carolee Carmello, Brent Carver. **Songs:** "You Don't Know This Man," "Come Up to My Office," "It's Hard to Speak My Heart."

A final chapter ought to conclude. This one remains somewhat inconclusive, however, not only because important shows will still be written, performed, and appreciated after this book has gone to press, but also because of the uncertain status of the Broadway musical itself at the turn of the millennium. Indeed, by the 1990s the new Broadway had emerged in full force and it had a transforming effect on musical theater. Many in the theater community greeted the development with mixed feelings. Some chose not to greet it at all. Rather than facing the present situation, they found more appealing alternatives looking to the past, or to the future. Neither of these options was easily accessible. The past had already come and gone; the future was still up for grabs. But these appeared attractive precisely because they could be idealized. In the haze between memory and fantasy, both became fields of ideological construction. Looking backward, one might construct a usable past for lovers of the old-style Broadway musical and locate its commercial application in the revival of classic shows for a new mass audience. Looking forward, one might construct a usable future especially for an upcoming generation of show writers who reject the idea of the musical mainly as a commercial enterprise, and hope to raise the aesthetic bar on what a musical might be by questioning the traditional boundaries of the genre. Whether either represented a realistic option for the musical theater mainstream remains questionable. Both, however, led to some of the most memorable musical theater ventures of the *fin de millennium.*

REVIVALS

As if paralleling the British invasion in another dimension, an ongoing movement mushroomed in the 1980s and 1990s, filling the stages of Broadway with proven imports not from another place but from another time. For decades prior, a small number of older shows had been dusted off and overhauled to run commercially as revivals alongside new Broadway productions. Now that movement reached critical mass. Revivals proliferated. Today's Broadway has become so haunted by yesterday's that historicism itself seems to play a role in determining the current repertoire of Broadway offerings. Since the 1990s, when revivals of old Broadway musicals began to outnumber productions of new ones, America's musical theater appears to have entered a moment in its history when the "pastness" of its past has even come to trouble its present.

The American Theatre Wing took note of this state of affairs, established a new Tony Award category to recognize it; and formulated a new definition to determine eligibility for it:

> A "Revival" shall be any production in an eligible Broadway theatre of a play or musical that . . . is deemed a "classic" or in the historical or popular repertoire . . . [or that] was previously presented professionally . . . in substantially the same form [anywhere in Manhattan; or, after the 1946–47 season when Off Broadway was defined, in an eligible Broadway theatre] and that has not had a professional performance in the Borough of Manhattan at any time during the three years immediately preceding the Eligibility Date.

This definition considers only external aspects of a revival, which it views in two ways. One concerns the cultural consensus about a show: Is it in some sense a classic? The other concerns the where-and-when details of its production: Has it been absent from Broadway for at least three years? But what really matters is the inner spirit that animates a revival, and this eludes a simple definition. There is no single approach to the revival of any work but rather a spectrum of approaches that range from curatorship to revisionism. One might distinguish among three such approaches, each with its own purpose in reviving an old show. The first would be to set the historical record straight by preserving the original material or restoring it to its condition at the time of its Broadway premiere (the archival-based Angel/EMI recordings conducted by John McGlinn, such as Show Boat [1988] and Brigadoon [1992]; the historically reconstructed "Encores!" productions that began in 1994 with Fiorello!, Allegro, and Lady in the Dark). The second, to respect the original material for what it is, but to modify it to make it more accessible to a new audience (On Your Toes, 1983, with small changes; Show Boat, 1994, with large ones). And the third, to view the material as a stimulus to the imagination of showmakers, thus to use it as a springboard for "reinventing" the original, perhaps even altering its meaning in the process (the "revisal" *Crazy for You,* 1992; the radically reconceived *Cabaret,* 1998).

Revivals are nothing new, of course. In the eighteenth and nineteenth centuries, stock companies regularly offered seasons of plays that audiences already knew and took delight in seeing again. Later, even as the stock system gave way to theatrical combinations and productions came to focus on long runs of single shows, producers still sought to re-produce an old piece from time to time in hopes of turning a once bankable property into a cash cow. (Think of the irrepressible *Black Crook*s of the nineteenth century, or the tatterdemalion *Blossom Times* and *Student Prince*s of the 1930s and 1940s that might have lent new meaning to the phrase *"déjà vu* all over again" had it yet been coined.) But the current trend goes beyond the perennial exercises in caution of audiences choosing a show based on name recognition, or producers investing in that illusory safe bet. It rests also on the cultural capital that has accrued to a certain repertoire of musicals in the recent past.

The success of the new-style musical plays that set the pace in musicals during the post–World War II period led to a general shift of emphasis in musical theater: from the ephemeral productions of shows as star-based performances to the elevation of their scripted materials as durable "works," even works of art. A new respect for the libretto grounded the shift, and the regular publication of librettos helped spread the sense of a show as a work in its own right. The shift had a practical side as well. To cover rising production costs in the 1940s, producers generally opted for longer runs rather than higher ticket prices. But, faced with the possibility of a run of many years, stars no longer readily signed run-of-the-show contracts. (This had earlier been the practice when shows could run less than a year and still recoup their investments.) Thus, to continue to attract an audience during a show's run after its stars had been replaced, producers needed to create an aura about the show itself as an artistic entity that ultimately transcended its stars—stars no longer for whom the show had been created, but who simply created its lead roles. All this was perhaps nowhere more powerfully embodied than in *Oklahoma!* and Rodgers and Hammerstein's ensuing hits in which the leads were replaced many times during their lengthy runs.

Even the development of the long-playing disc (LP) by Columbia Records in 1948 gave a boost to this shift in sensibilities. Holding up to thirty minutes of music per side, a single LP could now contain the essential score to a new show—all its basic musical numbers— in one original cast album. By reading the published libretto to fill in the gaps between the separate cuts on an LP, listeners could now get a fairly accurate sense of a show as a durable work divorced from the ephemera of its production values. And with the realization that older musicals, too, could now be recorded in the same way (only with studio casts), two men began applying something of the post-*Oklahoma!* sensibility to pre-*Oklahoma!* shows. In a landmark collaboration, Columbia Records executive Goddard Lieberson (1911–1977) and Broadway conductor Lehman Engel (1910–1982) produced a series of LP recordings of scores to such previously unrecorded shows as *Pal Joey, Babes in Arms, The Boys from Syracuse, Girl Crazy, Oh, Kay!,* as well as the most complete recordings of *Porgy and Bess* and *Show Boat* up to the mid-1950s. Their *Pal Joey* LP proved such a revelation that it led to the successful Broadway revival of the show in 1952 starring the record's Joey, Harold Lang.

Still, it was the post-*Oklahoma!* musicals that argued loudest for the shift, and Engel himself eventually provided a theoretical scaffolding for it. In his 1967 book *The American Musical Theater,* he derived what he called "working principles . . . imposed by the nature of the genre" from about a dozen post-*Oklahoma!* shows. These shows he considered "models of excellence" in themselves as well as avatars of the American musical theater "in its most complete and mature state." Viewing the genre through the lens of the libretto, however, Engel came up with a reductive reading of musical theater history. His canon of shows has provided a ready template for later accounts that have stuck to his premise but tinkered with some of the details: While they have changed some of the shows Engel took as models, they continue to view the medium itself canonically. Such thinking has fostered a climate in which producers now market shows in the canon (or those that can be made to appear as such) as classics, worthy of placing before the public in rotating perpetuity—as revivals. The idea is hardly new. As early as 1956, Lieberson argued in the pages of the *New York Times* that "the time is now ripe for . . . a musical repertory theatre," and for its "first imaginary season" he drew up a list, based more on scores than librettos, of what he called "The Ten Musicals Most Worth Preserving": in chronological order, *Naughty Marietta; Show Boat; Girl Crazy; Pal Joey; Oklahoma!; Annie Get Your Gun; Street Scene; Kiss Me, Kate; Guys and Dolls;* and *My Fair Lady.*

There is no indication that Lieberson had Broadway itself in mind for his musical repertory theater. Such wishful thinking, in fact, went against the grain of commercial musical theater of the postwar period. Producing Broadway musicals then meant creating new ones—an assumption that virtually precluded the mounting of revivals altogether. Fourteen of the twenty theater seasons that span the 1950s and 1960s saw no Broadway revivals at all; of the rest, only one season had more than one or two (1951–52 saw five). To see first-rate professional revivals on a steady basis within at least earshot of Broadway, one had to visit the New York City Center Light Opera Company on Fifty-fifth Street. There, between 1954 and 1968, Jean Dalrymple (1902–1998) staged vintage musicals for limited engagements each spring. There was also the Music Theater of Lincoln Center, where, between 1964 and 1969, Richard Rodgers mounted limited runs of older shows in the belief that "the need to preserve and recreate the great works of our musical theater is of equal importance to preserving and recreating the masterpieces of the concert hall and the opera house." (Most of the shows he revived there were his own.) Because of the nature of the companies that produced them, however, such revivals did not qualify for consideration as part of the Broadway production system.

Nowadays they do. What has changed is not the shows themselves but the growing consensus on our view of them—their increased cultural prestige and ensuing bankability as moneymakers. By the end of the twentieth century old shows were being successfully produced as commercial ventures for open runs on Broadway as a matter of course. To be sure, their number has varied from season to season, and more have been flops than hits. But their sheer presence in the commercial arena has had a culturally transforming effect. In addition to touring companies, summer stock, community theaters, and all the other institutions that have traditionally preserved musicals by re-creating them as part of the larger "post-Broadway" subculture, there is now—paradoxically—Broadway itself. The phenomenon of revivals is not new, then, but their pervasiveness is. And so is the sense that, in keeping alive a national cultural treasure that would otherwise be lost, it *should* be so.

A 1971 production of *No, No, Nanette* precipitated the trend by turning that show into an unexpected Broadway hit again almost half a century after its premiere. Advertised now as "The New 1925 Musical," *Nanette* was commonly said to have succeeded in revival by riding a wave of nostalgia. If so, such nostalgia was for a past less real than imagined. The new *Nanette* had altered the original's book and score significantly; and the big-name old-timers brought in to lend the new production an air of old-fashioned authenticity—Busby Berkeley, Ruby Keeler—had had nothing at all to do with the original.

But it was not the show that was the real object of nostalgia so much as the ethos the show represented. Just when Broadway seemed to have succumbed to the idea that musicals at their best were "musicals with something to say," here was a show that harked back to a time when musicals were content simply to be musicals. *Nanette* was a musical comedy of unalloyed joy, in an age that tended to disdain such things. As Burt Shevelove, the revival's librettist-director, told the cast at the start of rehearsals:

> *The world today is not a pretty place. It is filled with terrible news every day of Vietnam, campus riots, pollution, crime, inflation. The audiences that will come to see our show will have heard enough— much too much—about all those things. We must take their minds off those problems and make them concerned only with this: Will Nanette, this innocent little child, get her wish and spend a weekend in Atlantic City? Nothing else, nothing else at all, is important. This warm, sunny, lovely little show must be our valentine to the audience.*

Similar attempts at such valentines soon followed *Nanette* to Broadway, though none proved as successful: *Irene* (1973/1919), *Good News* (1974/1927), *Very Good Eddie* (1975/1915), *Whoopee* (1979/1928). These were musical comedies of the 1910s and 1920s whose original productions lay safely beyond the living memory of all but the most veteran theatergoers of the 1970s. Revivals were thus free to reinvent or simply alter the originals to suit the different expectations of new audiences. At times such alterations went so far as to result in the creation of new shows altogether. Often humorously called revisals, these shows clearly distinguished themselves from revivals by changing their titles: *Funny Face* (1927) thus became *My One and Only* (1983);

Girl Crazy (1930) became *Crazy for You* (1992). No longer considered to be in "substantially the same form" as their originals, both these shows received Tony Award nominations in the category of Best Musical rather than Best Musical Revival. (*Crazy for You* won.)

By contrast, a different spirit governed revivals of shows that had been created later in the century. Artists and entrepreneurs approached the reproductions of such shows as *Gypsy* (1974/1959), *The King and I* (1977/1951), *Peter Pan* (1979/1954), and *Oklahoma!* (1979/1943) as literal reproductions aimed at keeping the originals intact with a minimum of changes. The 1983 revival of *On Your Toes* even involved the hands-on collaboration of key creators of the 1936 original: George Abbott revised his book for the occasion and redirected the new production; Hans Spialek supervised the restoration of his orchestrations. John Mauceri, musical director of the new production, expressed the hope that the commercial and artistic success of so historically self-conscious an enterprise would mark "the beginning of a new attitude toward our 'Old' shows":

> *To take the curse off "Old" shows, producers traditionally rewrite and update, rearrange and reorchestrate. When* No! No! Nanette! *came to Broadway in 1971, it was called "The New 1925 Musical," and in 1983,* My One and Only *was advertised as "The New Gershwin Musical." The 1983 production of Rodgers and Hart's* On Your Toes, *however, is definitely the old* On Your Toes *from 1936. . . . We have come to realize that something new will never come along to replace Rodgers and Hart, Gershwin, Porter and Berlin. The half-century that has passed since the 1930's has minimized the "dated" qualities of the great shows and has taught us to treasure the American musical theater heritage.*

Despite the multiple approaches, if Broadway revivals have anything in common, it is the requirement that, as commercial ventures, they bring something new to the undertaking lest they seem dated. On the other hand, if they bring too much of something new, they run the countervailing risk of misrepresenting the very shows they claim to revive by reinventing them. Revivals that depart radically from their sources are often touted as "reinventions," a term usually meant to elicit a positive response. But the reaction of theater critic Mark Steyn to a reinvented *Show Boat* in 1994 was not positive at all. And he knew where to point the finger of blame: "Before *Show Boat*, we had star vehicles; after *Show Boat*, we had shows; now, even the greatest show is no more than a star vehicle for the director."

The director, Harold Prince, took full responsibility for reshaping this ultra classic of American musicals. He also took the extraordinary step of using the playbill (normally reserved for credits, bios, and ads) to defend on theoretical grounds what he had done. In effect, Prince made the revival enterprise itself an issue. He began by undermining the textual authority of the first production of *Show Boat* in 1927, spreading such authority out among so many texts as to weaken the hold of any one. Indeed, since the show's original creators had never established a "definitive" text for the show, Prince felt free to draw on any aspect of the numerous versions of *Show Boat* that they themselves had produced. ("This version of *Show Boat*," he wrote, "is culled from the original 1927 production, the subsequent London script [1928], the 1946 B'way revival and the 1936 film.") With such freedom, Prince went on to change the "arc of the show," as he put it, bringing a wholly new vision to the project in order to address some of the major problems that have hounded the piece almost since its inception. These included the following:

> *dramatic structure:* "to replace the conventional and irrelevant second-act opener at the Chicago World's Fair, returning instead to our principal story";
>
> *stagecraft:* to take "advantage of modern techniques to create montages that integrate a leap of years, restore serious incidents and clarify plot and character motivations";
>
> *social sensibility:* "to eliminate any inadvertent stereotype in the original material, dialogue which may seem 'Uncle Tom' today";
>
> *aesthetic scope:* to restore "some of the most beautiful material" originally cut, like "Mis'ry's Comin' Aroun'," "because they thought it was too serious *for a musical.*"

Such reasoning revealed less about *Show Boat* itself perhaps than its reception—about taking material for a show created for an audience early on in the twentieth century and adjusting it to the beliefs of what a musical at the end of the twentieth century could be, or even should be. Above all, Prince articulated a view of musical theater as a fluid and fundamentally reinterpretable medium that proved itself in the very act of revival.

The investment of major talent and resources in reinterpreting old musicals through new productions of all kinds became a fact of life in the 1990s. And when revivals of *Guys and Dolls* (1992), *Grease* (1994), and *Chicago* (1996) became long-running Broadway hits in their own right, the re-production of such pieces took on a level of importance comparable to the production of new ones. If only on economic grounds, the Broadway community could no longer ignore the new reality. For the first time since 1947, when the American Theatre Wing first bestowed Tony Awards to recognize "distinguished achievement in the theater," it instituted a category for musical revivals in 1994. *Carousel* won the first time around, followed in subsequent years by *Show Boat, The King and I, Chicago, Cabaret, Annie Get Your Gun*, and, in 2000, *Kiss Me, Kate*, a revival of the first musical ever to win the Tony in its original Broadway production more than half a century earlier.

The retrospective turn in American musicals also permeated beyond Broadway. Even British invaders have succumbed to the trend. Cameron Mackintosh, for example, in conjunction with the Royal National Theatre, produced revivals of *Carousel* (London, 1992/New York, 1994) and *Oklahoma!* (London, 1998/New York, 2002), which changed our understanding of these works by darkening them. And the 1990s saw American repertory companies offering more revivals of Broadway musicals in their seasons of straight plays. Some of the more memorable of these played on Broadway for open runs—as did New York's Roundabout Theater Company's production of *Cabaret* (1998, itself an adaptation of a 1993 London revival), which differed so markedly from the original Broadway show that it sparked sufficient interest to run twice as long on Broadway as *Cabaret* did when it was new.

The 1990s, too, saw the rise of repertory companies dedicated to producing "concert stagings" of notable "shows from America's past which may never see the light of day [again] as full productions." Such revivals—often performed with script in hand, without elaborate sets or costumes, and for runs of only a week or so—have proved popular, especially among audiences who enjoy mixing their theatergoing with a sense of connoisseurship. Along with the sheer pleasure of recovering past shows in less than formal settings, audiences have embraced these minimal productions almost as if in reaction to the cult of megamusicals and the cultural dumbing-down that such entertainments have come to represent. In 1989, director Ian Marshall Fisher inaugurated a popular series of such shoestring revivals in London called Discover the Lost Musicals. San Francisco followed in 1993 with its series 42nd Street Moon. In 1994, City Center's director Judith Daykin began an Encores!: Great American Musicals in Concert series, which became a showcase for stagers and performers who conspired to stretch the idea of a simple "concert staging" to its limits. With an emphasis on scores and with books pared down to essentials, these productions have succeeded through a winning combination of "the quintessential New York interests in historic preservation and high-stepping pizzazz." Since then, other cities across the nation have started similar series of their own: Los Angeles, Reprise! (1997); Washington, D.C., Words and Music (1998); Chicago, Ovations! (2000); Boston, American Classics (2000).

In addition, the recording and publishing industries have been busy producing tangible artifacts in support of the revivalist cause and its retrospective culture. Original cast albums long out of print are now available on CD re-releases, new releases abound of studio cast "restorations" as well as "original cast" revivals (including many of the Roundabout Theater and Encores! productions). Even television, videos, and films have gotten into the business of both documenting performances of classic works (Glyndebourne Festival's *Porgy and Bess*, 1993) and mythologizing them (Tim Robbins's *Cradle Will Rock*, 1999). Furthermore, Broadway's past has become the subject of increasing numbers of publications of all kinds: from articles in fan magazines (*Show Music*), scholarly journals (*Studies in Musical Theatre*), and the organs of research centers and performance rights organizations (*Kurt Weill Newsletter*) to the sustained investigations of reference books (Gerald Bordman's *American Musical Theatre: A Chronicle*, now in several editions), critical monographs (the "Yale Broadway Masters" series, begun in 2003 with Geoffrey Block's *Richard Rodgers*), and histories like the one you hold in your hands—all engaged in examining an area of cultural activity once consigned to the margins of serious concern.

What has given a larger sense of legitimacy to these developments is the belief in a historical Golden Age from which Broadway has for decades been moving ever farther away. "Every so often there is a flow-ering of a particular art form in a specific time and place . . . then it goes somewhere else," said Kitty Carlisle Hart, once a musical per-former herself and former chair of the New York State Council on the Arts. "We had our flowering with the American musical theater." The nature of this flowering may be ill-defined, but the view expressed is widely held. So, too, is the sense of valedictory. Ever since 1967, when Brooks Atkinson first spoke retrospectively, even nostalgically, of a "golden period between 1940 (*Pal Joey*) and 1957 (*West Side Story*)," there has been an ever growing acceptance of the idea that an extraor-dinary moment in American cultural history has come and gone—that, as Atkinson put it, "the days of consistent high endeavor on the musical stage are over and that the Broadway stage has reverted to the kind of hackwork which was acceptable until *Show Boat* broke the mold." That there has also been significantly much more than hackwork on Broad-way since 1957 is unarguable. The consistency of such work over the past half century remains the question.

Belief in a historical Golden Age inevitably invites unflattering comparisons with the current one. This represents a seismic shift in perspective from the way things looked at the height of the Golden Age itself. In 1950, when Cecil Smith published the first compre-hensive study of what he called *Musical Comedy in America*, he gave voice to the then prevailing notion that the history of his subject con-stituted a "steady progress . . . toward general artistic excellence." Smith thus looked forward to what the future held for musicals; for us, more than half a century later, that future seems less assured. Indeed, the present condition of America's musical theater is under-stood far less often nowadays as a prelude to future achievements than as a postlude to what has already been achieved. To cite the title of a recent comprehensive study by way of example, the history of the medium is now told, more often than not, in terms of *The Rise and Fall of the Broadway Musical*.

What has already been achieved is not to be denied. The finest shows of the past have indeed transformed the dazzling ephemera of the musical stage into more durable items, many still capable of hold-ing an audience and thus worthy of being revived, whatever it takes to get them back on their feet. But while belief in a Golden Age has been the ideological underpinning for resuscitating part of the Broadway repertoire and awakening new audiences to old excellences, it has also tended to diminish the value of newer work. There is a danger, "a downside to Broadway's obsession with looking back," the *New York Times* critic Anthony Tommasini recently warned. For Broadway's resources are not unlimited, and

> *the effort, talent and, especially, money that go into revivals decreases the potential resources for new material. . . . If audiences will turn up for a familiar old show, why should investors take a risk on something new? The more successful the revival movement becomes, the more this supposed celebration of the American musical's past will wind up stifling its future.*

The point was not lost on Stephen Sondheim. "Revivals encourage more revivals," he remarked. "Like kudzu, they are choking out new shows."

ANTIMUSICALS

The turn of the twenty-first century teemed with new shows nonetheless—though perhaps not the kind that Sondheim had in mind. The return of big-time musical comedy dominated the news on Broadway in the form of shows with a solid, old-fashioned mix of nonsense, prurience, and pizzazz. *The Producers, Hairspray*, and *Monty Python's Spamalot* headed the list, enjoying substantial money-making runs in the Times Square arena. (Not coincidentally, all were also based on successful films.) Shows unwilling or unable to swim in this cultural mainstream, however, have been hard-pressed to find a niche for themselves on the Great White Way. In recent decades, more thoughtful or literate musicals, or simply original shows of distinction of a more intimate, provocative, or idiosyncratic kind, have rarely received commercial productions. These were most likely the new shows Sondheim spoke of; and there were plenty of them clamoring to be seen and heard—including one of his own: *Assassins*. The show opened Off Broadway at Playwrights Horizons in 1991 and, while produced elsewhere in the interim, it remained a non-Broadway item until the Roundabout Theater mounted it thirteen years later. (By contrast, Broadway saw *Sunday*

in the Park with George within a year of its premiere at the same Playwrights Horizons venue in 1983.) *Assassins*'s deeply subversive spirit
might have accounted for the delay. "As [*Assassins*] attempts to rewrite
American history," Frank Rich wrote, "so the composer audaciously
attempts to rewrite the history of American music. This is an antimusical about anti-heroes [and] every song upends a traditional native
form." As a major theaterpiece by Stephen Sondheim, however factious,
Assassins eventually did make its way onto the Broadway stage.

Works of comparable ambition by other writers have rarely been
that fortunate. Rather than despair at the situation, however, some, like
upcoming show writer Kirsten Childs, view it with a certain defensive
optimism:

> *I'm mainly hopeful because the alternative is unacceptable. But also
> because I see a lot of new work that's interesting . . . by writers who
> are unafraid to try new approaches to musical theater form and by
> writers who are unashamedly embracing traditional musical theater to
> explore new themes. . . . Because of them and others yet to come, musi-
> cal theater will continue to flourish. Maybe it'll take a while before a
> lot of Broadway producers take the kinds of chances on new shows that
> they used to. Or maybe those days are gone for good. That just means
> that Broadway's not going to be where you go to see great, interesting,
> cutting-edge musical theater. I think everybody's pretty much made
> their peace with that.*

Childs speaks for an emerging generation of show writers who
see the world of musicals divided into unequal parts that exist almost
irreconcilably at odds with one another: musical theater, concerned
more with the art of the musical business; and the Broadway musical, more focused on the business of the musical art. For Rodgers and
Hammerstein and their contemporaries in the middle of the twentieth
century, popularity and artistic success constituted a single package,
the result of an ideal negotiation between musical theater and Broadway shows that could work to the benefit of both. Today many view
the relationship between the two in more antagonistic terms. "A musical doesn't have to be popular to be artistically valuable," said Wiley
Hausam, former associate producer of musical theater at the New York
Shakespeare Festival. "If it aspires to be art today, it's probably more

likely to achieve this status if it *isn't* popular." Hausam speaks on behalf of writers who tend to see themselves as the heirs of Prince and Sondheim. Their shows collectively represent "an American landscape that is almost the polar opposite of Rodgers and Hammerstein's." Such shows for him are no longer musicals in the traditional sense at all, but "anti-musicals." The term unfortunately implies a normative idea of what musicals are or ought to be. But it is also arresting. Rich used it to describe *Assassins's* subversive strategy. Hausam uses it to define a genre. Antimusicals, he said,

> confound the expectations, responses and needs of the Broadway musical audience. They have dispensed almost entirely with the two most cherished conventions of the form: Song (simple in its traditional structure and therefore memorable) and the Happy Ending. Next, entertainment has been made secondary to the political concerns that were the heart of the not-for-profit theaters in the 1980s and 1990s—especially the politics of race, sexual preference and gender. Finally, the mythology of the American Dream, which was merely questioned by Prince and Sondheim, has been indicted by his new generation. Consequently, the work is ironic, skeptical and sometimes disenchanted and disbelieving. When it's funny, it's biting. It leaves teeth marks. Obviously, this is no way to be popular.

As an outsider genre, then, antimusicals seem to relish the adversarial position. They avoid happy endings, indict the American Dream, and engage in the socially sensitive issues of "identity politics," that is, "political claims made or resisted in terms of group-based identities, such as race, ethnicity, religion, gender, sexual orientation, and disability." While the rationale for this may not be clear, Hausam's summary remains a useful guide to the contours of an arena of activity little known to those whose love of musicals does not take them much beyond the Times Square domain. The following is a sample of non-Broadway antimusicals that have received considerable critical attention.

Hello Again (1993, book, lyrics, music: Michael John LaChiusa)
Floyd Collins (1996, book, lyrics: Tina Landau; music, lyrics: Adam Guettel)

Violet (1997, book, lyrics: Brian Crawley; music Jeanine Tesori)

A New Brain (1998, book: James Lapine; lyrics, music: William Finn)

Dream True (1999, book, lyrics: Tina Landau; music, lyrics: Ricky Ian Gordon)

Running Man (1999, book, lyrics: Cornelius Eady; music: Diedre Murray)

The Last Five Years (2002, book, lyrics, music: Jason Robert Brown)

Typically, these shows were produced in New York by Off Broadway or Off-Off Broadway companies, and they each ran for about a hundred performances or less. A few comparable shows, however, have sparked sufficient interest to defy this pattern and reach a wider audience. *Jelly's Last Jam* and *Falsettos*, for example, though they too originated Off Broadway, garnered both critical accolades and respectable Broadway runs. And while *Hedwig and the Angry Inch* never moved to Broadway, it played Off Broadway for more than two years and became a film in 2001. Conveniently, these three shows also illustrate the different types of identity politics that Hausam describes as characteristically informing the subjects of antimusicals: *Jelly* exemplifies the politics of race; *Falsettos*, of sexual preference; and *Hedwig*, of gender.

As a show in a century-long tradition of all-black Broadway musicals, *Jelly's Last Jam* (1992) traces its ancestry back to *Shuffle Along, In Dahomey*, and *A Trip to Coontown*. It resembles none of these, however. It has more in common with such confrontational black revues of the 1970s as *Ain't Supposed to Die a Natural Death* (1971; book, lyrics, music: Melvin Van Peebles) and *Don't Bother Me, I Can't Cope* (1972; book, lyrics, music: Vicki Grant). Indeed, while it is a show about, and mostly by, African Americans, *Jelly's Last Jam* seeks to avoid the very things its playwright-director, George C. Wolfe (b. 1954), abhorred: first, the "mindless giddiness" endemic to musicals generally; second, the "cultural strip-mining" endemic to black musicals in particular. Early black musicals, said Wolfe, "required 'energy' and 'vitality' and a false kind of sex appeal. But nothing really edgy, and nothing really dangerous. *Jelly's Last Jam* required an attitude and a sexuality and a presence and a dynamic that I don't think is often asked of black artists in the musical theatre. Particularly in all-black shows."

Jelly's Last Jam traced the flamboyant career of one of New

Orleans' greatest musicians, Ferdinand "Jellyroll" Morton (Gregory Hines)—pimp, pianist, composer, and self-styled inventor of jazz. Morton's music, arranged by Luther Henderson (and with lyrics by Susan Birkenhead), formed the basis for the songs and dances in the show. Yet the piece did not simply showcase Morton's work—as *Ain't Misbehavin'* (1978) did Fats Waller's, or *Sophisticated Ladies* (1981) did Duke Ellington's. Instead, the show had an underlying seriousness of purpose that its punning title masked. It took as its premise the occasion of Morton's death to look back over the course of his life. In that context, "Jelly's last jam" referred to Morton's Last Judgment, which hit a divine snag over the musician's lifelong denial of his relationship to African American culture. Morton, a light-skinned Creole of Color, not only saw his roots as lying in French culture but also "really . . . didn't like Negroes," as his wife once delicately put it. The show then examined the ambiguities of racial identity while indicting the immorality of racism within the larger African American community itself. But it did so problematically, making race the determining factor in the construction of cultural value, and of the history of

Two tap-dance generations meet in "The Whole World's Waitin' to Sing Your Song" from *Jelly's Last Jam*, l. to r.: Savion Glover (Young Jelly) and Gregory Hines (Jelly Roll Morton).

jazz. Thus Morton's music was truly jazz to the extent that it turned away from Creole sensibilities to draw from the musical wellsprings of dark-skinned Negroes—Negroes whose cultural worth he denied. That made the show not just "edgy" but contentious—a celebration of the black musical tradition whose conventions it undermined: a black antimusical.

With a similar sophistication, Wolfe went on to probe the history of African Americans by means of black improvisational dance in *Bring in 'Da Noise/Bring in 'Da Funk* (1996), a tap-dance-based theater piece he conceived and directed, and which Savion Glover (b. 1973) choreographed. Wolfe explained the title:

> *The words "Noise" and "Funk" work in tandem with one another. Noise is the outlet, the release, the expression of self. Savion Glover dancing, or Michael Jordan on the courts, or some sixteen-year-old kid doing spoken word poetry—they are each bringing in 'da Noise. And Funk is the texture, the history, the grit and grease that's churning underneath. For example, if Bessie Smith singing the blues is her bringing in 'da Noise, then slavery, lynchings, lost love and oh, say, collard greens are some of the textures that make up 'da Funk that's underneath.*

In terms of importance, 'da Noise outweighed 'da Funk in early black shows; Wolfe's musicals have sought to bring the two into a strikingly new kind of equilibrium.

Jelly's Last Jam played a key role in the ongoing history of the black musical, an established show type; *Falsettos* (1992) played a key role in the development of a new one: the "gay musical." Gay musicals made homosexuality their theme and placed it at center stage. Earlier shows, if they touched on the subject at all, did so only obliquely. Indeed, homosexuality had long been part of the subtext of theater life, its issues largely closeted in the theater as elsewhere in American life because of religious, legal, and social sanctions against its expression in any form. Nonetheless, the arts, the theater, and the musical theater in particular remained more open than most sectors of national life to a significant gay presence. Many of the most distinguished theatrical creators and performers were themselves homosexual or comfortable with the ways of the gay subculture that influenced the shaping of sensibilities both onstage and in the audience. The cultivation of socially marginal modes of presentation on the stage—campy, androgynous, transvestite (in drag)—suggested as much. So did the ways certain devotees in the audience drew coded meanings from musicals that others did not, especially from so-called diva musicals built around larger-than-life female stars whose performances transgressed prevailing norms of femininity—Ethel Merman, Carol Channing.

It was during the 1970s, amid increasing activism and public awareness in the wake of the 1969 riots at the Stonewall Inn, a popular gay bar in Greenwich Village, that "the gay subtext started to become the text in some shows." Musicals such as *Coco, Applause, Seesaw,* and *A Chorus Line* included memorable gay characters, though none in lead roles and all still portrayed somehow as sexless, ashamed, or the butt of humor. With the success of *La Cage aux Folles* as a Broadway show in 1983 this changed significantly. Adapted from a French farce by librettist Harvey Fierstein (b. 1952), songwriter Jerry Herman, and director Arthur Laurents, *La Cage aux Folles* took place in and around the drag nightclub in Saint-Tropez whose name gave the musical its title. The show presented the club's owner, Georges (Gene Barry), and the club's transvestite star performer, Albin (George Hearn), as a homosexual couple. The two were also the stars of the show. *La Cage* became the first Broadway musical to feature a gay relationship between its lead characters, to dignify that relationship, and to go on to become a blockbuster hit. As Fierstein, a gay playwright and performer himself, inimitably put it:

> *Gay sensibility was always in the theater. But whether we got seen by large groups of people or not, there's a difference. This is America, and unless you can make money it don't count. So* La Cage aux Folles: *hardly the first gay musical on Broadway, but the first gay musical to make money. And that's what makes it count!*

Whether or not the first show of its kind, *La Cage* was clearly a gay musical, not a gay antimusical. It succeeded with mainstream audiences largely because of its skill in balancing two conflicting impulses: the show's desire to out the traditional Broadway musical, and "its eagerness to be merely a 'gay version' of it." On the one hand, *La Cage* ended its first act with a defiant "I Am What I Am," a song sufficiently political in its thrust to be taken up as a gay anthem outside the theater. Sung by Albin in the context of the show, the song, said Jerry Herman, expressed the feelings of "a gay man who finds pride by challenging his own son's bigotry toward homosexuals." On the other hand, *La Cage* had virtually all the hallmarks of a conventional musical comedy: the sentimentality, the production numbers, the show tunes (even "I Am What I Am" boiled down essentially to an AABA number in 32 bars), and the happy ending—only its lovers were middle-aged, domesticated, and both male. For one British wit, *La Cage* amounted to "just another warm-hearted, conventional Jerry Herman musical, only this time, as if recognizing that Dolly [Carol Channing] and Mame [Angela Lansbury] and the other caricature broads had been drag queens all along, the big lady on the staircase was a guy in a frock."

By contrast, *Falsettos* confounded conventional musical expectations. As a two-act chamber musical without production numbers, show tunes, or a happy ending, it represented more nearly a gay antimusical. Unlike *La Cage aux Folles*, moreover, *Falsettos* presented homosexuality not as a cause to defend but as a fact of life to be dealt with. The show's gay protagonist, Marvin (Michael Rupert), appeared as one of five characters in act 1, all of them—heterosexual and homosexual—flawed. The others included Marvin's ex-wife, Trina, who later married his psychiatrist, Mendel; Marvin's preteen son, Jason, who feared becoming gay like his father; and Marvin's same-sex lover, Whizzer, surely the least neurotic character of the bunch. (Act 2 introduced Charlotte and Cordelia, a lesbian couple who lived next door.) At the middle of this group stood Marvin, charming, articulate, funny; also childish and impossibly self-absorbed. Enmeshed in a network of dysfunctional relationships, he wished to hold on to all of them as his one big happy family. The multiple conflicts that this caused became occasions for exploring the show's theme: "what manliness is," regardless of one's age or sexuality. The song "March of the Falsettos" spoke centrally to that concern. In this all-male quartet, the three men actually sang falsetto, joining Jason in his high-pitched boyish register, to ask who was "man enough" to march from the childishnesses of both childhood (Jason) and adulthood (Marvin, Mendel, Whizzer) toward that implicit deepening, physical and psychological, that would come with maturity. *Falsettos* showed them making this journey.

The company of *Falsettoland*, l. to r.: Danny Gerard (Jason), Lonny Price (Mendel), Faith Prince (Trina), Michael Rupert (Marvin), Stephen Bogardus (Whizzer), Janet Metz (Cordelia), and Heather MacRae (Dr. Charlotte).

The creation of songwriter-librettist William Finn (b. 1952) and librettist-director James Lapine, *Falsettos* told its story entirely through songs instead of the spoken scenes of a play. Such songs revealed Finn's acerbic originality and idiosyncratic humor already in some of their titles: "Four Jews in a Room Bitching," "Everyone Hates His Parents." They also tended to avoid the 8-bar symmetries (4 + 4) of standard show tunes. The melody of "I Never Wanted to Love You," for example, consists of 12 bars grouped irregularly (5 + 2 + 5): 5 bars (1 bar pickup + 4) delivered almost angrily in quick notes, 2 bars of transition, and 5 bars (4 + 1 bar overlap) of sustained notes sung to warmer confessions of feeling (Ex. 16-1). In context, the song works as a complete musical scene in which one character after another gets to sing the melody to someone else as each of Marvin's relationships dissolves.

Whizzer's ironic mention of death in the song as he leaves Marvin at the end of act 1 has a special poignance. For at the start of act 2, Marvin and Whizzer will reunite on better terms, then part for-

Ex. 16-1. William Finn, music and lyrics: "I Never Wanted to Love You," *Falsettos*

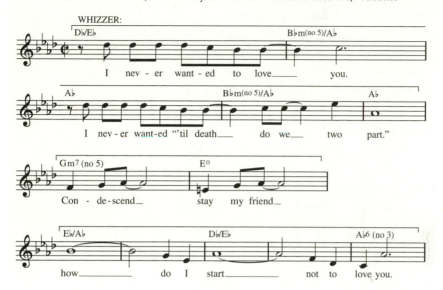

ever when Whizzer himself dies at the end of the show. Yet, curiously, the two acts—the high-voltage energy of the first; the heartbreak of the second—were not really planned to fit together as a single show. Over a period of a dozen years, in fact, Finn wrote three different one-act musicals about Marvin, each of them first produced separately Off Broadway at Playwrights Horizons as a self-contained work: *In Trousers* (1979), *March of the Falsettos* (1981), and *Falsettoland* (1990). Only later did Finn and Lapine turn the last two one-acters into the two halves of *Falsettos*, though, after finishing *March of the Falsettos*, the collaborators were not quite sure how to proceed. "History gave us an inevitable next step to write about," said Playwrights Horizons artistic director André Bishop: "AIDS and its horrifying impact on the lives of gay men in the 1980s and beyond." That became the focus of the last part of the trilogy, as Whizzer's dying of AIDS led to a genuine coming together of Marvin's extended family and to Jason's rising to the occasion to become a man. *Falsettos* thus remains a most unconventional show: in content, more like a play altogether than a musical; in form, all sung, but not in the least operatic.

More unconventional still, *Hedwig and the Angry Inch* (1998) took the form of a rock club act that told the story of its transsexual star—

an unusual story to say the least for a musical of any kind. To escape from communist East Berlin in 1988, Hansel Schmidt underwent a sex-change operation and married an American GI. The botched operation, however, left him sexually neither male nor female, with only a fleshy "angry inch," and confused about his/her gender identity. In America, divorced, and now as Hedwig rather than Hansel, she became the androgynous singer in a rock band called The Angry Inch. In "The Origin of Love" (Hedwig's version of Aristophanes' myth in Plato's *Symposium*), she sang that love involved completing one's self by reuniting with the other half from whom one had originally been separated by the gods. Hedwig felt she found that soulmate in a teenager; she named him Tommy Gnosis and taught him the ways of rock 'n' roll. But Tommy rejected her. She remained, in her words, "the internationally ignored song stylist" while he eventually became a "well-known rock icon." Yet the ambiguous ending of the show suggested a reconciliation between the two as Hedwig stripped herself emotionally as well as of most of her clothes to reveal a male torso, possibly that of her other half, Tommy.

If the subject of gender identity marked *Hedwig* as a postmodern musical, so did the form in which the show took shape. Instead of assigning roles to different players to act out Hedwig's story, Hedwig told it to the audience herself in seemingly improvised banter in between the songs that constituted her act in a tacky rock club or drag bar setting. She told her tale with wit and humor. And from time to time, she would launch into a song, drawing on a range of styles from rock power ballads ("The Origin of Love," "Wig in a Box") to punk and grunge anthems ("The Angry Inch," "Exquisite Corpse"). In this form, *Hedwig* resulted in one of the better realizations of the rock musical that had troubled musical theatergoers ever since the success of *Hair* some thirty years before. *Hedwig and the Angry Inch* succeeded, not by integrating the divergent traditions of rock and musical theater so much as allowing them to coexist.

John Cameron Mitchell (b. 1963), who created the *Hedwig* script, also played Hedwig. Stephen Trask (b. 1965), who created the *Hedwig* songs, played lead guitar in the show's onstage band. *Hedwig* thus preserved something of that sense of a performer's authenticity of self-expression so rooted in the ideology of rock and contrary to the practices of musical theater. (Unlike rock's singer/songwriters,

The mainstays of *Hedwig and the Angry Inch*, l. to r.: Stephen Trask (composer of the show and bandleader of The Angry Inch) and John Cameron Mitchell (Hedwig).

creators of musicals are usually not the best people to perform what they create.) Even Mitchell's performance of Hedwig suggested less the role playing of the musical stage than the androgynous theatricality of the glam rock star. Indeed, *Hedwig* gave a new twist to the diva musical altogether. It turned from the traditional divas of Broadway's gay culture to embrace the ambiguities in the gender-bending personas of those glam rock performers who, starting in the 1970s, sought to replace the staunchly masculinist ideals of earlier rock icons. As John Clum has written,

> *Rock and roll, traditionally testosterone music, has been stirring up the gender issue for years from chic bisexuality (Mick Jagger, David Bowie, Michael Stipe), to glitzy homosexuality (Peter Allen, Elton John, now sanctified by Disney), to various forms of drag. More than Broadway, which has religiously maintained the trappings and traps of heterosexual romance even to tell gay stories [as in* La Cage aux Folles*], rock has offered liberation from the notion of natural formulations of gender and sexuality. By merging the traditions of musical theater with those of rock-and-roll performance,* Hedwig and the Angry Inch *has found a more liberating stance in which gender and sexuality remain mysteries both poignant and comic.*

Antimusicals, then, are shows that in one way or another go against the Broadway grain. Positioning themselves as anti-Broadway musicals, they explore social concerns, or political issues, or artistic forms of marginal interest to the entertainment industry since these seem to lie outside the comfort zone of mainstream audiences who would probably not go to them in sufficient numbers to justify costly Broadway productions. Even such shows as *Jelly's Last Jam, Falsettos*, and *Hedwig*, which registered extraordinary successes for antimusicals, have proved neither broadly popular nor populist. At their best, however, such shows have widened the scope of musical theater, each in its own way. But to do so, they have had to thrive on the self-satisfying joy of taking risks just when "risk-free" ventures in the form of revivals, movicals, and catalogue shows have become the new corporate ideal on Broadway.

SONDHEIM'S CHILDREN

Writing history is a messy undertaking. To write a history of Broadway musicals by reducing the story to a strict linear narrative would do a disservice both to Broadway musicals and to the historical undertaking itself. Yet simply to record the mess as one finds it, on the other hand, would be not to write a history at all but a chronicle. Working between these two extremes—of conceptually determining or even schematizing information, and of conceptual laxity in organizing it—I have sought to shape this history throughout in ever-shifting combinations of data and ideas as these correspond to changing cultural pressures over time, as best I understand them.

The current Broadway situation is no exception. As we move further into the new millennium, Broadway seems more intent than ever on producing new shows based on proven older forms of entertainment—whether recordings, films, or remakes of Broadway shows themselves. But by no means does this constitute the whole picture. Broadway still has a place for new shows of a dramatic bent that adapt their material from literary sources, as was once the norm. *Wicked* (2003—book: Winnie Holzman; songs: Stephen Schwartz), *The Color Purple* (2005—book: Marsha Norman; songs: Brenda Russell, Allee Willis, Stephen Bray), and *Spring Awakening* (2006—book and lyrics: Steven Sater; music: Duncan Sheik) come to mind as recent examples. *Wicked* puts a revisionist spin on L. Frank Baum's classic *The Wonderful Wizard of Oz*. It tells its tale now from the villain's point of view, as it traces the growing friendship between the Wicked Witch (Idina Menzel) and the Good Witch (Kristin Chenoweth) well before Dorothy arrives in Oz. *The Color Purple* takes its cue from Alice Walker's Pulitzer Prize–winning novel about a poor black woman in rural Georgia, Celie (LaChanze), who overcomes a past of abuse and unendurable hardships to find her own identity and love. And *Spring Awakening* draws on a nineteenth-century German play by Frank Wedekind, *Frühlings Erwachen*, as it follows a group of teenagers trapped in a repressive society and struggling to come to terms with their newfound sexual feelings.

By way of contrast, moreover, Broadway also has a place for new musicals with original tales to tell and fresh ways of telling them—especially small, edgy, comic shows with a knowing, self-reflexive bent. Here, *Urinetown* (2001—book and lyrics: Greg Kotis; music and lyrics: Mark Hollmann), *Avenue Q* (2003—book: Jeff Whitty; songs: Robert Lopez, Jeff Marx), and *The Drowsy Chaperone* (2006—book: Bob Martin, Don McKeller; songs: Lisa Lambert, Greg Morrison) can serve as examples. As a political satire that never takes itself too seriously, *Urinetown* takes place in a police state in which the scarcity of water precludes the use of private bathrooms. All citizens, therefore, must use "pay-to-pee" public toilets or pay the ultimate penalty. *Avenue Q* amuses as a kind of *Sesame Street* for adults. It uses the devices of children's TV (including singing puppets) to address the not-always-cheery concerns of a group of twenty- and thirty-something friends. *The Drowsy Chaperone* puts an ironic frame around nostalgia. When a show fanatic listens to a recording of a beloved old musical, he imagines that it actually comes to life. And as the audience watches it play itself out in his drab apartment—cliché by glamorous cliché—he slyly comments on the proceedings.

And yet, for all the variety that Broadway offers, perhaps the most promising voices in musical theater today seem to be coming from elsewhere—from a younger generation of show writers for whom, more than anyone's, the work of Stephen Sondheim has become the touchstone. They have come of age imbued with Sondheim's idealism but still working in his shadow. That few of their shows ever get Broadway productions is not only because Sondheim's work has raised the bar of expectation so exactly high, however. Broadway itself has become far too expensive a place to afford the kind of in-house apprenticeships by which new talent used to learn the ins and outs of the musical entertainment trade. Nor can Broadway any longer afford to provide the traditional outlets for their fledgling work. How, then, do young show writers learn their craft (beyond simply writing and rewriting on their own)? How do they survive while they hone it (without necessarily waiting on tables)? How does their work get to be seen and heard (outside the partisan circle of family and friends)?

For more than a generation, the most durable of institutions for training new show writers has been the BMI Musical Theater Workshop, now named for Lehman Engel, the Broadway composer, conductor, and author who created it in New York in 1961. Ever since, the workshop has held classes for promising lyricists, librettists, and composers to learn the principles and practice the craft of show writing. Engel's curriculum for first-year songwriters, for example, required them to spot a potential musical moment in a spoken play and to create a particular type of song for it: a ballad for *A Streetcar Named Desire*, a charm song for *The Member of the Wedding*, a comedy song for *The Moon Is Blue*, a musical scene for *Death of a Salesman*. Engel and the class critiqued the results. Surviving that, songwriters could then undertake projects of their own choosing. Best known of the workshop's songwriting alumni are Edward

Kleban (1939–1987): *A Chorus Line, A Class Act* (2001); Maury Yeston (b. 1945): *Nine, Titanic* (1997); Alan Menken (b. 1949): *Little Shop of Horrors, Beauty and the Beast*; and such teams as Lynn Ahrens (b. 1948) and Stephen Flaherty (b. 1960): *Once on This Island* (1990), *Ragtime* (1998); Robert Lopez (b. 1975) and Jeff Marx (b. 1970): *Avenue Q*; and Brian Yorkey (b. 1970) and Tom Kitt (b. 1974): *Next to Normal* (2009)—this last show, originally a ten-minute workshop project about a woman undergoing electroconvulsive therapy for a severe mental disorder, is among the most provocatively moving and successfully original musicals to reach Broadway in the first decade of the new millennium. BMI eventually set up branches elsewhere as well (Toronto, Nashville, Los Angeles), and it inspired other organizations to form workshops of their own (The ASCAP Foundation/Disney Musical Theater Workshop, New York and Los Angeles; New Tuners Theater, Chicago; Mercury Workshop, London). Similar programs have even appeared in the formerly disinterested halls of academe. In 1981, New York University became the first school in the nation to offer a Graduate Musical Theater Writing Program at its Tisch School of the Arts.

But it has required other approaches to address the practical concerns and professional needs of fledgling show writers. One has involved establishing grants and cash awards to support the most promising in the early stages of their careers (the Gilman and Gonzalez-Falla Foundation Musical Theater Award; Richard Rodgers New Horizons Award; Kleban Prize for Musical Theater). Another has involved forming theater groups committed to producing their work, and thus involving them directly in "learning the only way you can in the theater," according to Sondheim, "by doing it. It can't be taught academically." Philadelphia's American Music Theater Festival (now the Prince Music Theater); Washington's "In the Works" at the Kennedy Center; Waterford, Connecticut's O'Neill Music Theater Conference; Arlington, Virginia's Signature Theater—these are among the many venues in the United States today that provide regular outlets for mounting new musical stageworks by little-known writers. Yet New York still remains the center of aspiration and opportunity, with or without the prospect of Broadway in sight. Here, the activities of a number of small, not-for-profit, Off Broadway and Off-Off Broadway companies have played crucial roles in the development of new work—the Manhattan Theater Club (formed in 1970), Vineyard Theater (1981), and the now defunct Musical Theater Works (1983–2004). New York Theater Workshop (1979), another of these companies, produced what has become by far the most successful of all new musicals of the younger generation to date, *Rent* (1996).

Rent began as something of an antimusical. That it turned into a Broadway musical sensation is one of several ironies connected with the work and its success. A product chiefly of the talent and drive of songwriter-librettist Jonathan Larson (1960–1996), *Rent* went through seven years of workshopping and revising before reaching its final form. Yet Larson never quite finished it. He died of an aortic aneurysm on the day public previews were to begin on the New York Theater Workshop's stage in the East Village. Larson was thirty-five. He had regarded *Rent* as the hoped-for breakthrough of his career; his death galvanized the company to take it up as a mission on his behalf. "From the time of Jonathan's death to the opening," said director Michael Greif, "I was operating with a more focused sense of urgency than perhaps I have in other situations, because I really wanted to succeed for him." The *New York Times*, too, took up the cause. In an article in its Sunday edition, it drew poignant parallels between Larson and the show he wrote—especially one of the show's leading characters, Roger, also a songwriter, who sings of writing "one song before I go . . . one song to leave behind." And it hailed *Rent* as a potential breakthrough for the musical theater itself. It quoted Stephen Sondheim, who said that Larson, whom he had mentored, had tried "to blend contemporary pop music with theater music, which doesn't work very well; he was on his way to finding a real synthesis." Word spread; interest mounted. The show became such an unexpected Off-Off Broadway hit that its producers decided to move it to Broadway. An ensuing blitz of interviews, media hype, ads, even *Rent*-inspired costumes in a Bloomingdale's boutique—all contributed to a whirlwind atmosphere in which it became ever harder to distinguish between Larson and *Rent*; aspiration and achievement. At the height of this hoopla, Larson won the Pulitzer Prize in drama for *Rent*—posthumously—before the show ever opened on Broadway. More than a show, *Rent* had become a cultural event no one could afford to miss.

In such a climate it was easy to overlook the show's flaws, especially in the unfolding of its narrative. But at the time Broadway offered nothing quite like *Rent* in raw talent, musical energy, and amplitude of spirit. Larson thought of it as "a *Hair* for the '90s." And like *Hair* a generation earlier, *Rent* brought a downtown sensibility uptown as it presented a group portrait of a community of young people who reject the norms of contemporary society, and who express themselves in doing so in a rock-based musical idiom. *Rent*'s story, however, involves a free updating of *La Bohème* in which the bohemians of nineteenth-century Paris in Puccini's opera (and the novel on which it is based) become the alternative artists of Manhattan's East Village as the twentieth century ends. Privation, disease, and death pervade both works, but *Rent* remains celebratory where *La Bohème* approaches the tragic. Moreover, *Rent* depicts characters who are, among other things, homeless, transvestite, gay, lesbian, HIV-positive and drug-addicted. For example, Puccini's Rodolfo, originally a poet, has become Roger (Adam Pascal), a punk rocker and recovering heroin addict with HIV; his lover, Mimi (Daphne Rubin-Vega), originally a seamstress, keeps her name but is now an S & M dancer and a junkie with HIV; Marcello, Mark (Anthony Rapp), is an aspiring filmmaker; Musetta, Maureen (Idina Menzel), is a bisexual performance artist; Colline and Schaunard, Collins (Jesse L. Martin) and Angel (Wilson Jermaine Heredia), are gay lovers, respectively black and Hispanic. *Rent* simply takes divergence from mainstream culture as a given. Indeed, it "exalts 'Otherness,'" Larson said, "glorifying artists and counterculture as necessary to a healthy civilization."

Rent's score consolidates the celebration of this counterculture. Performed by the cast of fifteen and a five-piece band, it contains some thirty-five songs. Many of them are fun, funny, or informed by a savvy humor that mixes the worlds of *La Bohème* and contemporary New York. "Light My Candle," a duet for Roger and Mimi, for example, evokes Puccini's touching scene of Rodolfo's and Mimi's first meeting even as it undercuts it with an edgy eroticism and wit. And where in *La Bohème* Musetta made a shameless public display of herself to the strains of Puccini's waltz for her, Maureen performs "Over the Moon" as a send-up of the avant-garde performance artists typical of the cultural scene of the East Village of the 1980s. On the other hand, many songs are also sobering. No song better captures the show's dark theme and hopeful spirit than "Seasons of Love," a list song in a gospel style. With its keen awareness of the need for cherishing the moment as time passes, it amounts to the virtual anthem of the show:

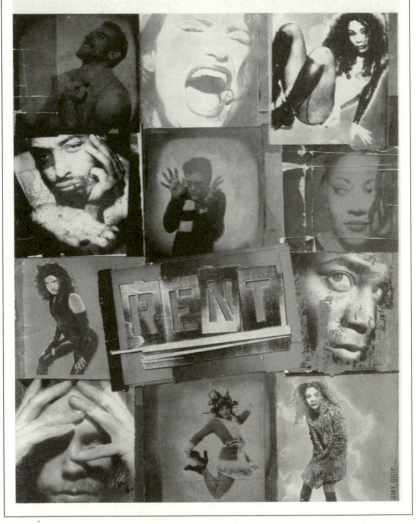

Playbill cover for *Rent* showing members of the cast, l. to r., top row: Adam Pascal (Roger Davis), Idina Menzel (Maureen Johnson), Daphne Rubin-Vega (Mimi Marquez); next row down: Jesse L. Martin (Tom Collins), Anthony Rapp (Mark Cohen), Fredi Walker (Joanne Jefferson); next row down: Menzel, Taye Diggs (Benjamin Coffin III); bottom row: Pascal, Wilson Jermaine Heredia (Angel Schunard), and Rubin-Vega.

Five hundred twenty-five thousand
Six hundred minutes
How do you measure—measure a year?
In daylights—in sunsets
In midnights—in cups of coffee
In inches—in miles
In laughter—in strife

In—five hundred twenty-five thousand
Six hundred minutes
How do you measure
A year in the life?

How about love?

"Seasons of Love" (*Rent*)

What accounts for *Rent*'s inordinate success has to do in large part with its contemporary story, its sense of social inclusion, its optimism in "celebrating life in the face of death and AIDS," and its ingratiating soft-rock score. Such qualities have worked to narrow the generation gap and put at least one major Broadway musical of serious intent back into the cultural mainstream. Thus *Rent*, originally an un-Broadway musical, has ironically come to symbolize the musical revival of Broadway itself. "Jonathan, in his heart of hearts, felt that there was something about this alternative theater scene and something about commercial musical Broadway that could come together," said the show's choreographer, Marlies Yearby. "He really felt that this piece was it, that it could bridge those worlds."

The success of *Rent* remains an anomaly, however. Comparable works by Larson's most gifted contemporaries are still little known by theatergoers at large. To help improve this situation, several of the more prominent nonprofit companies have committed themselves not only to producing distinguished new shows by such writers, but also to using the very prominence of their productions as leverage to transfer them to Broadway when possible. Three of these companies stand out from the rest: the Public Theater/New York Shakespeare Festival (now the Joseph Papp Public Theater), Playwrights Horizons, and Lincoln Center Theater. The Public Theater, founded as the Shakespeare Workshop by Papp in 1954, served as the original home of *Hair* and *A Chorus Line*, and it has continued both to develop unusual musical stageworks of merit and to move the more successful of these to Broadway (*Bring in 'Da Noise/Bring in 'Da Funk; The Wild Party; Caroline, or Change*). Playwrights Horizons, which began operating in 1971, has been "dedicated solely to the creation and production of new American plays and musicals." It developed Sondheim's *Sunday in the Park with George* and *Assassins*, and it has also nurtured high-quality new musicals by less established writers (*Falsettos, Floyd Collins, Grey Gardens*). Lincoln Center Theater is unusual in that, while located outside the Times Square district, it qualifies technically as a Broadway house in one of its theaters, which seats over five hundred. Since its founding in 1985, it has staged memorable revivals of classic shows (*Anything Goes, Carousel*) and premiered notable new ones as well (*Marie Christine, Parade, The Light in the Piazza*).

Critics sometimes speak of the "Sons of Sondheim" in referring to a handful of show writers whose works such companies have produced. This is a mixed blessing perhaps as far as Broadway is concerned, but a clear homage to the man who forged the creative path such writers have been traveling as they dramatize complex and mature subject matter with sophisticated musical means. (Others sometimes refer to them as "Friends of Audra," in recognition of Broadway diva Audra McDonald [b. 1970], their contemporary, who anthologized most of them on her 1998 debut recording "Way Back to Paradise," and who continues to champion their work in live performance and on later albums.) While such writers are far too maverick a group to form any kind of a school, the ones that critics most often single out do constitute something like a musical theater "Mighty Handful": Ricky Ian Gordon (b. 1956), Jeanine Tesori (b. 1961), Michael John LaChiusa (b. 1962), Adam Guettel (b. 1964), and Jason Robert Brown (b. 1970). But it remains to be seen whether "the hope of the American musical theatre," as David Patrick Stearns suggests, really rests with these five—all or even any of them.

Their talents vary. Tesori writes music only; LaChiusa tends to do all the writing himself: book, lyrics, and music. Their accomplishments vary as well. Gordon, the most classically trained of the group, is better represented in the nation's opera houses than in the New York theater; only two of his shows thus far have enjoyed Off Broadway musical productions: *Dream True* and *My Life with Albertine* (2003). Tesori, perhaps the most wide-ranging musician of the five, followed her Off Broadway debut, *Violet*, with three different kinds of Broadway productions: a musical comedy, *Thoroughly Modern Millie* (2002), a musical drama for which Tony Kushner (b. 1956) wrote the book and lyrics, *Caroline, or Change*, and an animated movical, *Shrek The Musical.* LaChiusa, provocative, prolific, and largely self-taught, has seen half a dozen of his pieces produced Off Broadway, beginning with *First Lady Suite* (1993) and *Hello Again*; and he has had Broadway productions of two impressive works written more in the spirit of music theater, with its operatic bent, than musical theater:

Audra McDonald (Lizzie Curry) in the Roundabout Theater Company's 2007 revival of *110 in the Shade*.

Marie Christine (1999), and *The Wild Party* (2000), for which George C. Wolfe coauthored the book. Guettel and Brown, finally, the youngest of the quintet, are also the only ones so far to have won Tony Awards, both on the occasion of their Broadway debuts: Guettel with *The Light in the Piazza* (2005), for which Craig Lucas (b. 1951) wrote the book; Brown with *Parade* (1998), with its book by Alfred Uhry (b. 1936).

Seven productions thus reflect the total Broadway work of the five writers, all of whom are now at least in their forties. Of these shows, moreover, only three ran longer than four months (*Millie, Light in the Piazza*, and *Shrek*). This low and commercially low-yielding output from so highly regarded a pool of artists in midcareer says as much about their own inclinations, however, as it does about the difficulties of getting produced on Broadway at all. If, for all the excellences of their work, the ambition of such writers often exceeds their grasp, the point is not simply that they are ambitious. It is rather that their ambition moves them in directions and in ways not likely to subject them to the discipline that communicating with a broad public imposes, and yields results not easily accommodated by the musical theater mainstream. And so these children of Sondheim, if you will, have not left much of a mark on Broadway, nor do they seem poised to do so. This is cause not for celebration, but for concern.

Consider the case of Adam Guettel (rhymes with "shtetl" he says). Particularly now that his work has finally made its initial appearance on Broadway, his unusual gifts and background together give pause for reflection on the current state of the musical as it relates both to its future and its past. Hailed by the *New York Times* as "one of the bright young hopes of Broadway," Guettel may not have yet fully lived up to the promise of his 1996 New York debut, Off Broadway, with *Floyd Collins*. But what extraordinary promise—especially when the true-life story of Floyd Collins (a man who spends two weeks trapped in a cave and dies) hardly seemed like material for any kind of musical: Is there enough air down there for him to sing, and any room at all to dance? Composer-lyricist Guettel and librettist-lyricist Tina Landau (b. 1963) transformed this unlikely material into a moving piece of musical theater that not only sings but soars at times with radiant imagination—from "The Call," a duet Floyd sings with the echoes of his own voice as he sounds out a cave at the start of the show, to "How Glory Goes" at the end, when Floyd wonders what he can expect to find in heaven as he prepares himself for death.

Set in rural Kentucky in 1925, *Floyd Collins* focuses on two concerns—the quiet world of Floyd Collins (Christopher Innvar): his family, his faith, his dreams; and the busy world around Floyd Collins: the failed attempt to rescue him, which mushrooms into a nationwide media frenzy. The music underscores this duality. With the help of a banjo, guitar, harmonica, and fiddle, it blends the sounds of bluegrass picking and country singing with the aural vistas of the likes of Aaron Copland. The effect is fresh, vernacular, American. "How Glory Goes" shows one aspect of this style, as fragments of melody contract and expand on a bed of luminously dissonant chords (Ex. 16-2).

This is not what one expects to find on Broadway nowadays, however—neither in its subject nor its treatment. Maybe one will find it there at some future date, as playwright John Guare playfully projects:

I don't know what the future's going to be, but I'd place a bet that years from now, the writers of those musicals of the future will look back [at

Ex. 16-2. Adam Guettel, music and lyrics: "How Glory Goes," *Floyd Collins*

the 1996 theater season] and say it wasn't Rent, *it wasn't* Bring in 'Da Noise *that changed it for them back in the '90s, it was that show on 42nd Street called* Floyd Collins.

But Guettel's work can be seen as an emblem of something more than future promise. It bears a strong connection to the past as well. Indeed, as the grandson of Richard Rodgers, Adam Guettel represents a certain continuity in musical theater, perhaps even a sense of Broadway renewal. (At the time he was born, in fact, Rodgers was working on *Do I Hear a Waltz?*, the only show he ever wrote with Sondheim, who has become something of a mentor to Guettel.) Guettel himself, however, is more circumspect about his historical position: "I can't say that I studied my grandfather's work in an academic way, or in any systematic way, or even in a chaotic way. . . . The more I try to do this work, the more respect I have for him, though." That respect extends both to the artistic accomplishment of his grandfather's finest shows and to their sense of cultural rightness, their ability to connect directly with an audience: "The basic dramatic techniques and the surefire instincts that he had about where a number should go, how a scene builds toward a number. . . . The time and place of his shows and how they synchronized with where America was at that time."

Rodgers's time coincided with the Golden Age of Broadway musicals; not ours. Yet if any principles from that time carry over to the present, Guettel and his contemporaries may face their greatest challenge writing for the medium today in balancing these twin prerogatives.

It is this equilibrium of artistic and cultural forces that made the American musical at its best a popular art, not only in Rodgers's hands but in those of many others whose work this account has touched on. It was popular both demographically and stylistically—because of the large number of people whose lives it touched, if only by way of a song, and because of the broad appeal of its crowd-pleasing vulgarities (think of the "Honey Bun" burlesque, for instance, in *South Pacific*). And it was art in the sense of both craftsmanship and aesthetic ambition— because of the skill with which it matched form to content in its greatest moments, and because of its intellectual and expressive striving for a certain gravitas (think of the "Twin Soliloquies" scene in the same show). Above all, it was popular and art at once.

Today, that kind of balancing act seems both more difficult to achieve and also somehow less worth achieving. This may reflect an erosion of faith in the American ideal of a melting pot, a common culture based on European models, which most influential musicals of the Golden Age embraced. As a nation, our cultural frame of reference has widened considerably over the past half century. And as it has, we have become accustomed to the splintering of our entertainments into niches aimed at different segments of the American population. Such fragmentation is nothing new, of course, even in the history of Broadway shows. For example, 1938 saw the opening on Broadway of *The Cradle Will Rock*, Marc Blitzstein's antimusical before the fact—a vehemently ideological piece, more notorious than popular. The same year also saw the Broadway opening of *Hellzapoppin*, the Olsen and Johnson romp with no greater aim than to be, as Brooks Atkinson put it, "loud, low, and funny!"—an unprecedentedly popular musical, but hardly art. Rough equivalents exist on today's musical stage for the kinds of shows each of these represents. But we now tend to view them antithetically: the one, too arty ever to be popular; the other, too popular ever to be art. The question is whether we have similar equivalents today for 1938 musicals that fell in between these two extremes, such as *Knickerbocker Holiday*, *Leave It to Me*, and *The Boys from Syracuse*.

On the popular side today, Broadway continues to succumb to the pull of mass culture. As ever, it focuses on where the money is—in form: musicals with traditionally structured books and soft-rock scores; in content: on feel-good material already proved successful, above all in mass-media entertainment forms such as the movies. The movical trend, in fact, shows no sign of abating as the biggest hit-makers continue to mine the vein for new hits. Within months of the Broadway closing of *The Producers*, for example, Mel Brooks was ready with his next movical, *Young Frankenstein* (2007); and within months of *Beauty and the Beast*'s closing, Disney opened *The Little Mermaid* (2007). Of late, even television has entered the musical lists. "High School Musical," a made-for-TV film on the Disney Channel, became such a preteen sensation in 2006 that it spawned sequels and, among other spinoffs, a live concert tour and even a staged version, which opened in Chicago. (Might not a Broadway booking already be more than a twinkle in some Disney executive's eye?) NBC even ran a reality TV series in 2007, "*Grease*: You're the One That I Want," to audition contestants for the star spots in an upcoming Broadway revival of *Grease*, and cast them on the basis of viewers' votes. (NBC apparently had no fear that turning the process of casting a Broadway show into an entertainment might ultimately prove more entertaining than the show itself.)

Unquestionably, today's electronic media play far more definitive roles in shaping popular culture than do live entertainments. So it is not surprising that major producers of commercial theater in New York ally their interests with those of the culturally dominant media: They spend the bulk of their time, energy, and money trying to stage the products of the motion picture, recording, and television industries. With few exceptions, however, the shows that result from these efforts never quite manage to shed their aura of reconstituted forms of entertainment. Moreover, when considered together with revivals of former Broadway hits, such shows serve to diminish whatever stature Broadway currently enjoys as the creative epicenter of original musical theater in the United States. Indeed, the abundance of such offerings gives the impression that Broadway has become—even more than it was in the days of *Uncle Tom's Cabin* and *The Black Crook*—a gathering place of derivative culture. In this sense, despite Broadway's being alive with all manner of theatrical activity, one hears talk aplenty nowadays of the musical itself as dead. Such talk is exaggerated, to be sure. But the feeling it expresses isn't.

"People who complain about the demise of the American musical have simply been looking in the wrong places," writes Ben Brantley—and by wrong, of course, he means Broadway. Where, then, might the right places be? Surely, the not-for-profit companies of Off Broadway, Off-Off Broadway, and regional theater—almost anywhere, that is, but Broadway. Such companies have come to represent the art side of musical theater today, not because the musicals they produce are necessarily works of art, but because such companies are less bound by commercial constraints in their choice of what to produce altogether. While operating under their own financial constraints, they remain more open to the "cerebral," "earnest," and "emotional" shows that for Michael John LaChiusa constitute "the real thing" in musicals as opposed to what he calls Broadway's faux musicals, which offer "no challenge, no confrontation, no art." In pursuit of the real thing, moreover, LaChiusa himself has chosen to create works that blur traditional distinctions between musicals and operas. (In 2006, Houston Grand Opera premiered *Send (who are you? i love you)*, a-one-act, one-woman opera he wrote for Audra McDonald.) He is not alone in this pursuit. In 2006, Lincoln Center Theater joined the Metropolitan Opera in a project to commission new "opera/theater works" from several promising writers, including Tesori, Guettel, and LaChiusa. The Metropolitan's general manager, Peter Gelb, explained the rationale for those a move: "As Lincoln Center Theater continues its support of serious musical theater at a time when Broadway has turned increasingly to pop music, it is logical that The Met and LCT should join forces, since we believe that the thin border between opera and serious musical theater can easily be crossed."

However exciting the results of such collaborations may or may not prove, it is unlikely that they will prove to be musicals. Nor are they even likely to resemble the Broadway operas of the past since such shows, by opting for commercial productions from the start, tended to anchor their musical discourse in American popular song no matter how sophisticated the composers who wrote them (Kurt Weill, Leonard Bernstein). For some of Sondheim's children to shift the institutional focus of their talents now puts them at the risk of distancing themselves both from the marketplace that has characteristically shaped popular musical theater in America and from its audience. Jason Robert Brown, whose first book show Lincoln Center Theater produced, now looks back at the whole experience with dissatisfaction in part because "We were very much writing *Parade*," as he puts it, "in an ivory-tower place" that failed to take its audience into account. As he has since come to understand:

> The work we do ultimately must relate always to what the audience's experience of that event is. We do not just happen to be putting things up on a stage. The commercial musical theater must ask of itself that the audience respond to and respect the work that we're doing in a way that more experimental theater does not have to do. The musical theater, in my view, cannot be separated from its commercial aspect. . . . A commercially successful show is, by some definitions, a better work [than a show that is fine artistically but commercially fails]. . . . While I'm disappointed that my work is not financially successful and has not been commercially well received, that's still the standard to which I'm holding myself.

As long as ivory-tower shows offer the only real alternatives to the prevailing musical fare of the Times Square arena, it is clear why faux musicals will endure.

Is there a future, then, for Broadway musicals as a genuinely popular art, caught as they are today between the conflicting lures of Las Vegas and La Scala? It may be that American culture itself has become too fragmented and conflicted to support the kind of entertainment that can still hold in balance the diverging interests of commerce and art. In that case, the story of that entertainment whose history this book has charted has come to an end. That, however, is probably not the case. Musical theater may have come relatively late to North America as a distinct form of cultural practice. But there is no sign of its leaving early. By now it has worked its way too deeply into our national psyche (and our national pockets) to pack it up anytime soon.

Over half a century ago, Leonard Bernstein described the American musical as "an art that arises out of American roots, out of our speech, our tempo, our moral attitudes, our way of moving." Musicals, he felt, reflect not just our external characteristics as Americans but also our internal makeup: our national character. Indeed, beyond the sheer joy of doing them, and doing them well, lie deeper questions of why continue doing them at all. What is the value of musicals and their meaning? Do musicals even matter in American life today? If so, do they matter in the same way they did, say, in 1954, when some seventy million people, then the biggest entertainment audience in history, watched *The Rodgers and Hammerstein Cavalcade* broadcast nationwide on all four television networks simultaneously? Or in the way they must still have mattered when, as late as 1970, President Richard M. Nixon had *1776* performed at the White House and cared enough about the show's meaning to try to have its content altered? And have our moral attitudes not changed since Bernstein spoke of them, especially among Americans who have come of age after the upheavals of the Vietnam era shook our faith in many of the basic tenets of national belief? Since the 1970s, in fact, musicals of consequence have tended to deal awkwardly with the meaning of what was once called the American Dream, whether understood as abiding by certain abstract principles of freedom and equality or in terms of seizing opportunities for amassing material goods. Some shows have questioned it, even debunked it, without offering anything comparable in its place. Other shows have offered hollow reassurances that little of importance about it has changed. The former fail to satisfy; the latter fail to convince. Perhaps it is too much to ask of a popular art that it succeed at both.

But so sharply dialectical a reading of the current state of things in musical theater may misrepresent the genius of Broadway to reinvent itself to meet the concerns of each generation as it, so to speak, "just got here." Indeed, despite a tendency toward self-promotion that makes even the less extravagant claims of Broadway suspect, popular musical theater has never comprised only one kind of entertainment, nor has it ever stood still over time. It has changed as a medium, bent to the imaginative wills of those intent on catching us and showing us to ourselves as we change as a nation. It may flounder from time to time as it grapples with the difficulties of coming to terms with an American Dream itself subject to change over time. But in doing so, it will undoubtedly discover new ways of doing what it has always done in transforming our experience as Americans into the stuff of an art that entertains: sensationalize, sentimentalize, trivialize, vulgarize—and, every now and again, also penetrate and exalt. "You can always count on Americans to do the right thing," Winston Churchill once remarked, "after they've tried everything else."

NOTES

1: Transition Stages

21 ceremonies on the continent: Specific discussions of the Navajo chantways, the Pueblo *matachines*, and the Mayan dance-dramas, for example, can be found in Huntsman, 363–65; Kurath, 265–68; and Sell, 3–28, respectively. On the difficulties in historical studies of Native American music, which circulated orally rather than in written form, see R. Crawford, *America's Musical Life*, 3–14.

21 in New France as well: Castañeda, 10–13; Olavarría y Ferrari, Vol. 1, 1–15; B. Kennedy, 5; P. A. Davis in Wilmeth and Bigsby, Vol. 1, 216–18.

21 considerably less: Key studies of the musical stage in colonial America include Sonneck, "Early American Operas," 428–95; Sonneck, *Early Opera in America*; Silverman; Virga; Ogasapian, 131–33, 159–64.

21 William and Mary College: Fischer.

22 (*Harlequin Collector*): Dunlap, 8–9.

22 both ballad operas: Rubsamen, facsimiles of *Flora, or Hob in the Well* in vol. 16; and *The Disappointment* in vol. 28; Cibber, 14; Barton.

22 such theatrical genres: S. L. Porter, ix.

24 "still been in England": Jeremy, 101.

24 center of theatrical entertainment: R. Crawford, notes to *Music of the Federal Era*.

25 James Hewitt: On German musicians in eighteenth-century America, see Sonneck, "German," 64–66. On Pelissier, see Kroeger. On Carr and Hewitt, see Lowens, 89–114, 194–202; Siek, 158–84.

25 single song survive: The libretto to *The Archers* in Mates, ed. *Dunlap*; the music in Marrocco and Gleason, 211–12; see also Mates, *American Musical Stage*.

25 more or less intact: Yellin, Notes to *The Ethiop*.

25 "to it in the first place": Mast, 2.

26 even the tragedies of Shakespeare: S. L. Porter, ix.

26 "take it into account": Root, "Introduction," vol. 2, vii.

26 genres and traditions of its own: Bernheim, 31–33; Wickham, 209–10; McConachie, "American Theatre in Context," 147–48.

27 "general prosperity": Buckley, *Opera House*, 57.

27 a *metropolis*: Spann, 216–21; Bender, 108–9.

28 the United States: Lindstrom, 4, 6, 14: Root, *Popular Stage Music*, 4.

28 up to its time: Buckley, "Paratheatricals," 460. Benjamin Baker (1818–1890) found his first success as a playwright with *A Glance at New York* (1848), a tour of the less savory parts of the city with songs interspersed that set new lyrics to familiar tunes. The play

had a democratizing effect on audiences, and it was published by Samuel French (Acting Edition, 1857?). It also introduced the character of Mose, a feisty butcher and volunteer fireman, who became New York's emblematic "Bowery b'hoy." Played by Frank S. Chanfrau (1824–1884), Mose proved so popular that Baker rewrote the play with his b'hoy as the central character, retitling it *New York As It Is*, and found even greater success than with the original.

28   of the nation's theatrical life: M. C. Henderson, *City*, 50–88; G. Wilson, 66; Qinnn, 202.

29   "smelling, of course, most horribly": Toynbee, 423.

29   "original music for *Macbeth*": Moody, *Riot*, 110; the *New York Herald Tribune*'s account is cited in Downer, *Macready*, 297–99.

30   "Another volley, and another!": Toynbee, 425–26; Moody, *Riot*, 115–16.

30   people lay dead or dying: Full account in Moody, *Riot*, 101–75; see also Cliff.

31   Astor Place was clearly not that: Bank, 111.

31   in the city's history: Buckley, *Opera House*, 11, 77.

31   riot *about* the theater: Ibid., 64.

31   Robert Montgomery Bird: Ranney, 15; Moody, *Riot*, 85–97, 117–25; Buckley, *Opera House*, 41; see also McConachie, "Theatre of the Mob," 17–46.

31   "dear to every true American heart": Moody, *Riot*, 179.

32   "and a *low* class." L. W. Levine, 66. As George Templeton Strong, a noted diarist of the period, summed it up: "What appeared on the surface to be the violent culmination of a quarrel between rival actors in fact revealed a complex web of social, political, and ethnic conflicts, causes, inequities, rivalries, intolerances, and animosities—some directly attributable to the socially elitist structuring of the opera establishment at Astor Place" (V. B. Lawrence, 580).

32   gallery of the house: Bank, 51.

32   "all ranks of the people together": Grimsted, *Melodrama*, 52–56.

32   "and promote digestion": Robert Ewing in ibid., 99.

33   Macready's *Macbeth*: Toynbee, 423; Downer, *Macready*, 318–38; Moore, 22–40. Between the Restoration and the mid-nineteenth century, so much music accrued to productions of this Shakespeare play that contemporary accounts of it abound as "being in the nature of an Opera," on the one hand (E. W. White, *History*, 86), and of its effect in "turning the theatre into a concert hall," on the other (M. Rosenberg, 9). On the history of the music used in *Macbeth*, see R. E. Moore, 22–40.

33   "exclusive place of amusement": Maretzek, *Revelations*, 214; McConachie, "New York Operagoing," 181–91.

33   "barbarism to culture": In Moses, *Forrest*, 246; James's view of culture seems close to Matthew Arnold's classic formulation in chapter 1 of *Culture and Anarchy*: "A study of perfection . . . which consists . . . in an inward condition of the mind and spirit, not in an outward set of circumstances. . . . It seeks . . . to make the best that has been thought and known in the world current everywhere." This is at variance with more recent views whose early articulation can be found in the work of Arnold's contemporary Edward B. Tylor: "Culture or Civilization, taken in the widest ethnographic sense, is that complex whole which includes knowledge, belief, art, morals, law, custom, and any other capabilities and habits acquired by man as a member of society" (vol. 1, 1).

33   suspect Metropolitan Opera: Browne, 326–32; R. C. Allen, 73–76.

33   held together in American life: Buckley, *Opera House*, 76; L. W. Levine, 68; Grimsted, *Melodrama*, 74–75.

33   "theater and separate audience": Grimsted, *Melodrama*, 75.

34   the company would disband: Bernheim, 10, 26, 32; M. C. Henderson, *City*, 135–37.

35   the theaters that featured them: Bernheim, 31; Poggi, 26–27.

35   "speculating on a dangerous issue": Twain, 176.

35   "Direct from Broadway": M. C. Henderson, *City*, 134.

36   "a system necessarily cruel and unjust": Stowe, 9.

36 "five bad plays to one good one": Gossett, 261.

36 grim and necessary work of survival. Dulles, 4–5; R. C. Allen, 45.

37 play of any kind until 1862: Barish, 158; R. C. Allen, 46–51; Gossett, 261.

39 Stowe herself: Birdoff, 27, 48–49, 75, 87; Underwood in Gossett, 266.

39 killing him off at the end: Uncle Tom's virtue was ultimately rewarded in Conway's play, which not only kept the hero alive at the end but also gave him his freedom and reunited him with his family.

39 institution of slavery itself: Grimsted, "Uncle Tom from Page to Stage," 240–41.

40 and The Octoroon: Wickham, 184–90.

40 and incomplete: Modern editions of the Aiken play can be found in Moody, Dramas; Riis, vol. 5 The latter edition includes musical cues that the former does not. See also A. D. Shapiro, "Action Music," 49–72; McLucas, vol. 4.

40 music often describe this function: The modern use of the terms "diegetic" and "non-diegetic" comes from film studies; see Gorbman, 20–26.

41 instrumental forces on hand: Mayer and Scott, 1–2.

42 "to patch together the story of it": Riis, "Music and Musicians," 277–78, 280, 282.

43 verbal, even literary and intellectual: Cohen, 11–13.

43 the case with The Black Crook: Quinn and G. A. Richardson omit The Black Crook from consideration in their comprehensive histories of American drama. On the other hand, comparable studies of American theater may well include it, as do Hornblow, vol. 2, 100–101, and Taubman, American Theater, 105–6.

43 most popular musical stageworks of the age: This German Romantic opera with spoken dialogue was first performed in New York in 1825, adapted and translated into English, and often performed therafter in significantly different versions. See Upton, 217–24.

43 combine with something else: Whitton, 10.

43 "without being particularly original": Cohen-Stratyner, 210.

45 reviewer called it "rubbish": Freedley, 69.

45 "to the rescue, he is defeated": Dickens in Johnson and Johnson, p. 352.

45 stage tableaux and ballets: Some of the Baker dance pieces have survived in published keyboard arrangements. These are discussed in Root, Stage Music, 90–94. Other conductor-composers such as Edward Mollenhauer, Giuseppe Operti, and Harvery Dodworth provided the music for later Black Crook productions in New York. Most of this music is now lost. The text of the play, however, remained in manuscript for more than a century before it was published in Matlaw, 323–74.

46 popular songs of the period: Appelbaum, 2–6.

46 "FIFTY THOUSAND DOLLARS": New York Times (hereinafter NYT), Sept. 12, 1866, p. 7. Such a staggering sum of money at the time (even if the figures were exaggerated) made a long run necessary for The Black Crook to turn a profit, and the success of the venture made its precedent persuasive.

47 all radiant and covered with "girls": Gintautiene, 86.

47 "wonders of the Arabian Nights realized": Twain, 85–86

47 "the effect is almost painful": Gintautiene, 89; Freedley, 70.

47 from prurience to indignation: Browne, 180–81.

47 "describing the ancient heathen orgies": Rev. Charles B. Smythe in Root, Stage Music, 81.

48 "public decency and morality": Whitton, 23. According to Whitton, the negative publicity from the editorials that appeared in the Herald were meant to have a positive effect on Black Crook's box office.

48 Twain said, were "everything": Twain, 85.

48 rectitude where they were not: R. C. Allen, 105.

49 that dwarfed virtually all competition: Root, Stage Music, 94; R. C. Allen, 114. P. T. Barnum indirectly disputed Black Crook's moneymaking supremacy in 1867, which may or may not have been another exercise in his art of "humbug." See Barnum, 694–95.

49   1876, 1882, 1883, 1886, 1889, 1892: Mates, "*The Black Crook* Myth," 39. With the 1870 revival, a variety show was inserted in the Act 3 Ballroom Scene at Wolfenstein's Palace, and it became a staple in later productions regardless of its irrelevance to the plot (Gintautiene, 169). In the 1892 revival the variety sequence included a pantomime depicting various New York City street toughs found in the shows of Edward Harrigan, then at the peak of his popularity—all within *The Black Crook*'s rural, German, seventeenth-century setting (*NYT*, Sept. 2, 1892).

49   in the late nineteenth century: M. C. Henderson, *City*, 136; R. C. Allen, 306; Root, *Stage Music*, 79, 94.

50   than any other single work: McSpadden, claiming to be "the first survey of these fields," does not mention *The Black Crook* at all though it has an extended section on what it calls "American Opera" (257–350), which begins with *The Little Tycoon* and ends with *No, No, Nanette* and *The Connecticut Yankee*. Among the most reputable studies that more or less begin with *The Black Crook* are C. Smith; Bordman, *American Musical Theatre: A Chronicle*; and Henderson and Bowers. A major objection to the historiographical practice of starting with the show is lodged by Mates, "*The Black Crook* Myth," 31–43. For a more amusing summary of alternative historiographical beginnings, see Borroff, 101–11.

50   nineteenth century in America: Odell, vol. 5, 481–84; vol. 6, 237–38, 309–13; vol. 8, 152–56.

2: Variety Stages

55   the new social construct, leisure?: Buckley, *Opera House*, 19.

55   "with our leisure when we get it": Dulles, 209.

56   "theatrical entertainment," vaudeville: E. F. Albee in Stein, 214.

56   according to journalist Bert Lowry: Stein, 8.

56   entertainment with refreshment: Garrett, 9.

57   no demands of literacy on its audience: Engle, xxi–xxii.

57   distinctly American form of show business: Toll, *On with the Show*, 81. Other important books on the American minstrel show include Wittke; Nathan; Toll, *Blacking Up*; Lott; Cockrell; Bean et al.; Mahar; Lhamon, *Raising Cain* and *Jump Jim Crow*.

57   "Ethiopian delineators": Rice also established significant models for the minstrel show afterpiece with his brand of "Ethiopian operas." See Lhamon, *Jump Jim Ctrow*, 147–383.

57   (castanetlike clappers): Cockrell, 151–52. Representative songs from the minstrel stage's first decade, 1842–1853, are performed in *The Early Minstrel Show*.

58   washed himself ashore: Toll, *Blacking Up*, 54.

58   "clamurous rooster": Ibid., 55.

59   "She descends. They embrace": Engle, 63.

59   the cakewalk, the soft shoe, tap: The first great vernacular dancer to exert a lasting influence on the American musical stage was William Henry Lane, aka "Master Juba" (1825–1852), a free-born black who appeared as a headliner over the all-white Ethiopian Minstrels with whom he performed. Charles Dickens seems to have had Lane in mind in the memorable description he left of the movements of the dancer he saw in a Negro dance hall in New York: "Single shuffle, double shuffle, cut and cross-cut, snapping his fingers, rolling his eyes, turning in his knees, presenting the backs of his legs in front, spinning about on his toes and heels like nothing but the man's fingers on the tambourine; dancing with two left legs, two right legs, two wooden legs, two wire legs, two spring legs—all sorts of legs and no legs—what is this to him?" Dickens in Bean et al., 229.

59   "addition to histrionic art": Howells, 315.

59   native tradition on the American stage: Lott, 64; Dennison, 88.

59   "their white fellow citizens": Douglass in Bean et al., 3.

60   earlier on the stage by whites: Trotter, 271; Lott, 234.

60   other variety-based entertainments of the era: Toll, *On with the Show*, 105–9.

61   "respectable vile house" in New York: Zellers, "Cradle of Variety," 580. See also McNamara, *The New York Concert Saloon*, 109–16.

62   "and even without suspicion": Rodger, 388–89.

62   by the end of the nineteenth century: Major books on vaudeville include D. Gilbert; Laurie, Jr.; McLean, Jr.; Dimeglio; Snyder; and Kibler.

62   Frank Kerns, and Charley White: Rodger, 389–91, 397.

62   ties to working-class culture: Zellers, *Tony Pastor*, 41–45; R. C. Allen, 179–80; Slide, 1, 390–92; see also Kattwinkel.

63   "did not hesitate to appear there": Russell in Stein, 11.

64   Rialto district in Venice: Frick, 50–57.

64   any phase of theatrical art: Slide, 5–7, 275–85; R. C. Allen, 189, 180; Bernheim, 40–41.

64   ostensibly been coined: R. C. Allen, 179; Slide, xiv.

66   legitimate theater audience was working class: Michael M. Davis, Jr., *The Exploitation of Pleasure: A Study of Commercial Recreations in New York City* (New York: Russell Sage Foundation, 1911) in Snyder, 199.

67   "(animals, exotic costumes, trapeze artists)": George Gottlieb in Page, 7–12.

67   "from a bad play, there is no escape": Wilson in Slide, v

67   "vaudeville was nothing and everything": R. C. Allen, 185–86.

68   New Yorkers of the Gilded Age: Major studies concerning Harrigan and Hart include Kahn, Jr.; Burns; Moody, *Ned Harrigan*; Koger; and Franceschina, *David Braham*.

69   (Thirty-fourth Street) and beyond: Root, *Stage Music*, 8–10, 174.

69   Hoyt's remains unclear: Moody, *Harrigan*, 249; Moody, *Dramas*, 632–34. *A Trip to Chinatown* appears regularly in histories of Broadway musicals on the strength of the popularity of three of the songs that were performed in it: "The Bowery" and "Reuben and Cynthia," both by Hoyt and composer Percy Gaunt, and the famously interpolated "After the Ball," by songwriter Charles K. Harris. *A Trip to Chinatown* is published in Hunt, *America's Lost Plays*, vol. 9, 105–48. See also Hunt, *Life and Works*.

69   "which is now animating fiction": Howells, 315–16. Howells wrote the libretto to a failed comic operetta, *A Sea Change or Love's Stowaway* (1885), with music by George Henschel. Hoyt, too, scripted a comic operetta libretto with almost equal lack of success, *The Maid and the Moonshiner* (1886), with music by Edward Solomon, and starring Lillian Russell and Tony Hart.

70   previously deemed unfit for art: Dahlhaus, *Nineteenth-Century Music*, 264.

70   Harrigan at one time or another: Dormon, 35; Moody, *Harrigan*, 166.

70   verisimilitude in costume and stage design: Finson, vol. 1, xxiii–xxvi.

70   tolerance in later ones: Koger, 145, 152; W. H. A. Williams, 170–71.

70   by bringing them together: There were narrative plays, too, that fed the public appetite for ethnic types depicted separately on the stage. Certain stars pursued successful careers by specializing in one to the exclusion of all others. Frank Chanfrau made a career portraying the same Irish immigrant Mose in play after play, beginning with *A Glance at New York* (1848). Joseph K. Emmet did much the same later, portraying a German immigrant from one play to the next, starting with *Fritz, Our Cousin German* (1870).

71   (*McSorley's Inflation*, 1882): Kahn, 64.

71   "colored people are bad colored people": Howells, 316.

71   were of Irish descent: Harrigan was born in New York. His parents had come to Canada in the eighteenth century. Hart was born in Massachusetts of Irish immigrant stock.

71   social spectrum that Harrigan and Hart depicted: Dormon, 37. Nearly half of New York City's nearly one million population in 1870 were non-native born and of these almost half were Irish.

71   generally lasted a month: Finson, xv.

72   stage Irishman of the period: Dormon, 25–27.

74   "General melee and curtain": Harrigan in Moody, *Dramas*, 565; the full play, 549–65.

74   "They are nightmares to me": Kahn, 263–65.

74   "champion oarsman and club swinger": Moody, *Harrigan*, 91–92.

74   three acts with about eight songs: On the difficulties of determining the actual use of music in the production, see Preston, xxi–xxiii.

74   for Braham to set to music. Moody, *Harrigan*, 154–55; Five Harrigan and Braham songs are performed in *Don't Give the Name a Bad Place*.

76   To wear the trousers, oh! . . .: *Cordelia's Aspirations*, New York Public Library (herein-after NYPL), Harrigan Papers, Box 2, 7B: 63–66. None of Harrigan's plays was pub-lished in his lifetime. The lyrics are from the sheet music published by William A. Pond in 1880 when the song first appeared in *The Mulligan Guards' Surprise*, three years before its reuse in *Cordelia's Aspirations*.

76   Broadway musical *Harrigan 'n' Hart*: Stewart, 8. The musical, based on the partners' lives and songs, failed on Broadway in 1985.

76   "appurtenances of the musical stage": Quinn, vol. 1, 102; C. Smith, 35; Moses, *American Dramatist*, 277–91.

76   "upon which to hang the specialties": Koger, 8.

76   America in the Gilded Age: Preston, xvii.

77   "stage is the burlesque of events": Hutton, 147–48.

78   the music as a point of reference: *Po-ca-hon-tas or The Gentle Savage* in Moody, *Dramas*, 397–421,

78   original musical numbers: The text and music for *Evangeline* are in R. Jackson.

78   travesty, pantomime, and extravaganza: R. C. Allen, 101–3.

78   "An Ethiopian Burlesque": *Desdemonum* in Engle, 52–67.

78   *Humpty Dumpty* (1868): See Senelick.

78   which might also apply to *The Black Crook*: Clinton-Baddeley, 109.

78   Thomas Edison in their efforts: B. Baker, 93–94, 227–28.

79   transgressive speech and behavior: R. C. Allen, 121–56; Gänzl, *Lydia Thompson*.

79   New York's Mayor Fiorello LaGuardia: H. L. Mencken coined the term "ecdysiast" to mean a stripper in 1940. Besides R. C. Allen, the major books on burlesque and bur-lesque shows include Sobel, *Burleycue* and *A Pictorial History*; Zeidman; Corio with Joe DiMona; Minsky and Machlin; and Shtier.

79   a cheaper version of vaudeville: R. C. Allen, 221.

79   after a popular soap product: Isman, 247.

80   of something more current: Fields and Fields, 140, 144, 172.

82   as being racially demeaning: Dennison, "Coon Song," in *New Grove Dictionary of Ameri-can Music* (hereinafter *NGDAM*), vol. 1, 493–94; Hill and Hatch, 141.

82   *Quo Vadis* . . . set in ancient Rome: Fields and Fields, 160–62.

82   "others are going to do or say": May Robson in Isman, 261.

83   "a part of the play": Mitchell in Fields and Fields, 163.

83   gave the genre its name: Important books on the history of the revue include Baral; Boardman, *Revue*; Lee Davis, *Scandals and Follies*.

83   "political, historical and theatrical": Bordman, *Chronicle*, 128; Bordman, *Revue*, 14–21.

83   several generations of comic performers. At the turn of the century, major comic teams were already modeling their acts directly on Weber and Fields, the Rogers Brothers among them, and possibly Williams and Walker as well, See "Dahomey on Broadway," *NYT*, Feb. 19, 1903.

84   meant to contrast with their own: Fields and Fields, 12–14, 132–33.

84   Hebrew comedy even in its dialect: The "Dutch" dialect of Weber and Fields can be heard in *Music from the New York Stage*, vol. 1, discs 1–2 (see Historical Discography).

85   and an absence, as it were: In surveying the history of American entertainment on the musical stage, even sympathetic writers since the 1960s have seen fit to keep a separate

chapter for the contributions of African Americans. See Toll, *On with the Show,* 111–39; Gottfried, *Broadway Musicals,* 329–39.

85 greater variety of purposes than before: In 1967, three years into the original Broadway run of *Hello, Dolly!,* producer David Merrick turned a "white" show into a "black" one simply by switching casts accordingly. Critic Martin Gottfried wrote indignantly in 1979 (*Broadway Musicals,* 329): "The practice of selling color still persists. Productions are still identified as 'black musicals' and we cannot pretend that a show cast solely with black performers isn't a 'black musical.' Nor can we pretend that race isn't part of the show." But all-black musicals have since appeared on Broadway in which race was in fact an intrinsic "part of the show," and in a more artistic and penetrating sense than Gottfriend seems to have had in mind—*Jelly's Last Jam; Bring in 'Da Noise, Bring in 'Da Funk.*

85 "by, about, or involving African Americans": Woll, xiii–xiv; see also Peterson, Jr.

86 the first modern black musical: J. W. Johnson, 95; Southern, *African American Theater,* xv–xvi. *The Creole Show's* more ambiguous relationship to minstrelsy is summarized in Hill and Hatch, 91–92.

86 "Moses of the colored theatrical profession": Riis, *Just Before Jazz,* 40.

86 "were going a long, long way": Southern, *Readings,* 233.

86 neither in house nor in season: Eubie Blake presents another perspective on the matter: "The purse makes Broadway. Williams and Walker, Cole and Johnson, and Ernest Hogan, they were the big-time shows. They played Broadway . . . but it *wasn't* Broadway because it was dollar top. It didn't class as Broadway until it gets to two dollars and fifty cents. They played the same theatres, but it wasn't Broadway." In E. G. Seller, 44.

86 premiere on that account: Gayle, Jr., 87.

87 into the shows of others: Before the ideas of unified "scores" and compositional ownership of shows became widespread on Broadway in the 1930s, individual songs by writers white and black were commonly interpolated into productions with which such writers were otherwise unaffiliated. Generally carried out at the insistence of singing stars, the practice continued as long as songs were generic enough to suit the purpose, books flexible enough to accommodate them, and stars powerful enough to override the objections of writers whose contracts might have given them grounds to consider a show "theirs." Notable Cole-Johnson interpolations include Anna Held, Ziegfeld's wife, singing "The Maiden with the Dreamy Eyes" in *The Little Duchess* (1901) and Marie Cahill singing "Under the Bamboo Tree" in *Sally in Our Alley* (1902). Both songs—albeit with Thomas Seabrooke singing the first in another 1901 production—can be heard in *Music from the New York Stage,* vol. 1, disc 2 (see Historical Discography). See Riis, *Just Before Jazz,* 191–93.

87 Roof Garden the year before: S. B. Johnson, 54.

88 in a different persona: Hill and Hatch, 162.

88 "saddest man I ever knew": W. C. Fields in Toll, *On with the Show,* 131.

88 "inconvenient—in America." B. Williams, 34. Major books on Williams include Rowland; Charters; E. L. Smith; and Chude-Sokei.

89 at the time in published form: Unusual for a work of its type at the turn of the century, a piano-vocal score for *In Dahomey* was published in London (Keith, Prowse & Co., [1903?] 1902). A moderm critical edition is also available: T. L. Riis, *Music of the USA,* vol. 5. See also T. L. Riis, *Just Before Jazz,* 91–105; Riis, *More Than Just Minstrel Shows,* 48–55; D. Krasner, *Resistance,* 41–74. On the distinction between a score with *a prescriptive* purpose (that is, one giving directions for future performances) and a score whose purpose is purely *descriptive* (one leaving a record of a past performance), see T. Kelly, 30–31.

89 performance over scripted matter: T. L. Riis, *In Dahomey,* xv, xxix; Graziano in Loney, *Musical Theatre,* 218–19.

89 "Williams in particular": Bordman, *American Musical Theatre,* 2d ed., 191.

90 to the broader audience to be found there: J. W. Johnson, 151, 173; Woll, 6.

90   "On Emancipation Day": See M. G. Carter, 209–11.

91   "the toes must turn well out": Beerbohm, 13; D. Krasner, *Resistance*, 75–98.

92   without being *merely* racial. T. L. Riis, *Minstrel Shows*, 55.

92   "no spoon in sight": B. Williams, 33.

92   "Nobody, no time": The music to "Nobody" is by Bert Williams, the text by Alex Rogers. The text cited here is taken from Williams's 1906 recording of the song, to be found in *Music from the New York Stage*, vol. 1, disc 3 (see Historical Discography), and differs somewhat from that of the published sheet music reproduced in Charters, 135–37. See also T. Brooks, 105–47.

93   "resign his post as their entertainer": Douglas, 329–30.

93   "justified the name of comedy": T. L. Riis, *In Dahomey*, xvi.

3: A Transatlantic Muse

97   "unassuming little opera": G. Hughes, 2. Major comprehensive studies of operetta in English include Mackinlay; Lubbock; Bordman, *American Operetta*; Traubner.

97   "irrational" and "exotic": S. Johnson, vol. 2, 160: "the Italian opera, an exotick and irrational entertainment, which has been always combated and always has prevailed."

97   applied to this genre quite well: Emerson, 99.

98   has endured to the present: Dizikes, 166–67, 216–17; Bereson, 131–47.

98   order of *popular* musical theater: Bordman, *Operetta*, 10.

98   the musical play: Bordman, *Operetta*, 150–54; and Traubner, *Operetta*, 402.

98   music they composed: Galand, 15.

99   was a comic one: Unlike "the more obvious operetta," wrote Hugo von Hofmannsthal while working on *Der Rosenkavalier*, "*Meistersinger* or [*The Marriage of*] *Figaro* . . . contain little to make one laugh and much to smile at." In Hammelmann and Osers, 10.

99   customarily housed opera: Lamb, "Operetta," *New Grove Dictionary of Music and Musicians* (hereinafter *NGDMM*) 18:497; Crittenden, 10.

99   in the twentieth: Traubner, 111, 147, 243, 276.

100 "climb any higher": Faris, 56–57.

101 of consenting adults: Rick Altman, 134; Galand, 15; Crittenden, 10.

101 the different strains: Traubner, x–xi; Lamb, "Operetta," *NGDMM* 18:493.

101 late nineteenth century: Lamb, ibid.

102 parody, and skepticism: Samson, "Music and Society," 41–42. T. W. Adorno's famous remark on the split between modernism and mass culture—"torn halves of an integral freedom to which, however, they do not add up"—is discussed in Denning, "The End of Mass Culture."

102 mocking pretension: The meaning of Offenbach's oft-cited phrase "primitif et vrai" becomes clearer when one considers it in light of comparable references to the old opéra-comique throughout the essay in which it appears, "Concours Pour une Opérette," 230–31: "la simplicité d'autrefois" (the simplicity of the past), "le genre gracieux et léger des premiers jours" (the graceful and light genre of the early days), "l'opéra-comique dans sa naïveté première" (the opéra-comique in its first innocence), etc., my translation. Dahlhaus, *Nineteenth-Century Music*, 226–27, substitutes "*gai*" for "*vrai*," a misquotation as common as the misunderstanding it engenders.

102 "means of communication": my translation; Kraus, 134–37, See also Janik and Toulmin, 84–85; Iggers, 85–88.

103 "modern Major-General": W. S. Gilbert, 132–34.

105 any particular performance: In practice, American companies frequently altered the operettas they performed with interpolations and deletions of all kinds to suit their strengths, cover their weaknesses, or simply play to local tastes. Into one New York performance of Johann Strauss's operetta *Prince Methusalem*, comic baritone De Wolf Hopper inserted a recitation of the baseball poem that would notoriously hound him

for the rest of his career, "Casey at the Bat." See also R. Aronson, 93–94; Traubner, 139; Dizikes, 209; and Bordman, *American Operetta*, 37.

106 *The Queen's Lace Handkerchief* in 1880: Unlike *Grand Duchess* or *Pinafore*, *Handkerchief* does not represent a major work in the output of its composer or national school. On such grounds, a better choice would be Johann Strauss's own *Die Fledermaus*, now widely considered the finest example of classic Viennese operetta and a work still in the standard repertoire. If, generically, the choice of *Handkerchief* thus seems misgauged here, historically, it is nonetheless on the mark. *Handkerchief*, though now largely forgotten, scored the biggest success of any Strauss operetta in nineteenth-century America, while *Fledermaus* made virtually no impression at the time.

106 theaters of New York: Morgan, 64–97; Root, *American Stage Music*, 115–16; Traubner, 30.

106 success in the United States: Root, *American Stage Music*, 118.

106 "worn to shreds": Odell, vol. 8, 296.

107 entertainments might reach. Root, *American Stage Music*, 132.

107 "and then leaving": Offenbach, *Orpheus*, 70.

108 "today you ask them!": Ibid., 72.

108 "an Englishman himself": Dizikes, 207.

109 "as much as that": W. S. Gilbert, 117.

109 "but not imbecile": G. Smith, 65; Prestige in Helyar, 123.

109 "to raise a laugh": Sablosky, 165.

110 "we proved our case": Traubner, 154–55.

110 unimproved by others: G. Smith, 63. See also R. Allen.

110 1988–2003: The company made some concessions to American tastes, however. For the 1879 tour impresario Richard D'Oyly Carte assembled an especially high-spirited cast. Americans, he said, "like 'emotional' singing and acting. The placid English style won't do." G. Smith, 64. Even G & S themselves apparently introduced certain "Americanisms" into *The Pirates of Penzance*. See Dolan.

110 "been really sung": Barnabee, 308.

110 stage in America: Boardman, *American Operetta*, 21.

111 "writers or opera": Barbabee, 306, 424; E. N. Waters, 91.

111 hit New York: R. Aronson, 66.

112 "father of comic opera": Bordman, *Oxford Companion*, 446–47; *NYT*, Jan. 17, 1892, Nov. 14, 1894.

112 arts in Washington, D.C.: R. Aronson, 263–68.

112 "Queen of Comic Opera": Dizikes, 211; B. F. Gordon; Hopper; Morell; F. Wilson; A. Fields; Strang, *Prima Donnas* and *Celebrated Comedians*.

112 "Austria, Germany and France": Hopper, 55.

112 in the United States: R. Aronson, 235, 221.

115 razed in 1930: R. Aronson, 61, 103–11; Bordman, *American Operetta*, 28–29; M. C. Henderson, *City*, 168, 219; Hirsch, *Boys*, 40–41.

115 at the Casino: S. B. Johnson, 13; Briggs, 15–16; Dizikes, 208–11, 217–18; Ahlquist in Saffle, 41–45.

116 from the *Pinafore* craze: Kaufman, v. 12, xviii.

117 "to the backbone": *London Daily Telegraph* (April 13, 1898). This, by contrast, from a London reviewer in the *Illustrated Sporting and Dramatic News* (April 23, 1898): "I did not see a great deal in the production identifying it with any special national type. For weaknesses of plot the story is not distinguishable from one of our own musical comedies, and if the setting is American—well, I do not remember any air in the piece so out of common as to prove to the doubter that the music of light opera is *not* of one exceedingly common race." See also Gänzl, *The Musical*, 120–22.

117 Romberg, and Berlin: Bordman, *Oxford Companion*, 629; H. B. Smith, *First Nights*, 3–4; *Stage Lyrics*.

118 "some of these conspiracies": Smith in Franceschina, *H. B. Smith*, 138.

118 had been forgotten: O. L. Krasner, *New Grove Dictionary of Opera* (hereinafter *NGDO*), vol. 1, 1108–9. A modern reprint of the vocal score to *Robin Hood* is in Schleifer, vol. 5. The libretto and vocal score of *The Highwayman* are in Krasner, *Later Operetta, Part II.* See also Krasner, *Reginald de Koven.*

118 Gilbert and Sullivan: H. B. Smith, *First Nights,* 109.

119 (*The Highwayman*): O. L. Krasner, *Later Operetta, Part II,* 92, 308–9.

119 lyrical than dramatic: For this his music was also taken to task by Gilbert, who turned down a proposal from de Koven to collaborate with him, saying that the composer's output "does not display certain qualities that I hold ... to be essential to the music that is to illustrate the libretto I am writing." In Stedman, 441.

119 "light opera in America": Farwell, 124.

119 "not American music": Bordman, *American Operetta,* 49.

120 country for four years: Bierley, *Descriptive Catalogue,* 9–29; *The Works,* 13–35; *An American Phenomenon;* Bordman, *American Operetta,* 59–64.

120 a colony of Spain: The libretto and vocal score of *El Capitan* are in Bierley, *Later Operetta, Part I.* See also Jorgensen.

120 Spanish-American War: The show was still on tour in 1898 when, as Commodore Dewey's flagship sailed out to attack the Spanish fleet in Manila Bay, the band on board played the "El Capitan March" Sousa had arranged from two of its vocal numbers ("You See in Me, My Friends/Behold El Capitan" and "Against the Spanish Army/ Unsheath the Sword"). For Sousa this was standard practice. Aside from a few revivals of note—*El Capitan* (Goodspeed Opera House, 1973) and *The Glass Blowers* (New York City Opera, 2002)—little of Sousa's theater music survives today except those instrumental arrangements made by cobbling together melodies originally sung on the stage into marches for his band. See Hess, 7, 17–19.

122 top musical form: Norton in Newsom, 43–52. Marches provided the most memorable music in *El Capitan.* Even those who thought the score lackluster agreed—"humdrum," one critic called it, "with an accent on the drum."

122 "first-class librettos": Sousa, 345.

122 "time for this work": Ibid.

122 (*The Fall of a Nation,* 1916): E. N. Waters; Mordden, *Broadway Babies,* 7–21; Debus.

123 that validated it: Samson, "The Great Composer," 259.

124 crisscrossed the land: E. N. Waters, 136–38; P. C. Lewis, 9; Poggi, 29–33.

124 around Times Square: McDermott, 456; Bernheim, 46–63; M. C. Henderson, *City,* 189; Poggi, 11–28.

126 *The Wizard of Oz* (1903): See A. Fields, *Fred Stone.*

126 even by comedians: Historical performances of both songs can be heard in *Music of Victor Herbert* (see Historical Discography). The tempo of the 1923 recording by Amelita Galli-Curci of "Kiss Me" (side G) is ♩ = ca. 104; the tempo of the 1906 recording of "Streets" (side D) is ♩ = ca. 192. Herbert's 1912 conducting of "Kiss Me Again" played by an orchestra without singer (side C) gives a sense of the kind of rubato he expected of the *valse lente,* especially pronounced here with no third beat in the accompaniment.

126 was mostly spent: W. J. Henderson in Bordman, *American Operetta,* 64.

127 "free American Style": E. N. Waters, 406.

128 "by musical comedy": Hopper, 55.

4: The Native Wit

133 "upon the comedy": Hopper, 56.

133 lowbrow vulgarities of the other: Newbury, 381–82.

134 like a revue: Gänzl, *The Musical,* 104.

134 "be called one": M. Knapp, "Watch Your Step," 248; Bergreen, 109. Use of the term musical comedy has changed since the turn of the twentieth century, when the genre

first took hold in the United States. In its heyday between the two world wars, musical comedy often lent its name to almost any kind of popular musical stagework. The term was thus ambiguously applied not just to a species of theater but also to the genus that subsumed it: both to a type of production on the spectrum of musical stage entertainment and to the spectrum itself. The subject of Smith's *Musical Comedy in America* includes the full spectrum except for opera; that of Bordman's *American Musical Comedy* excludes everything but the specific genre. More recently the term has been commonly applied in the narrower sense, while use of musical comedy in the broader sense has given way to the less restrictive term musical theater. See Kislan, *The Musical*, 164; Lamb, "Musical," *NGDAM*, vol. 3, 291, and *NGDO*, vol. 3, 525–26.

134   "on 'musical comedy'": Ade, "Musical Comedy," 193.

134   Lionel Monckton: Lamb, *150 Years*, 116–21. Edwardes operated two flagship theaters in London; the Gaiety mainly presented musical comedies and Daly's, mainly musical plays. However legitimate the generic distinction, the nomenclature acknowledging it was often inconsistently applied. The "Bill of the Play" at Daly's Theater in London for July 1, 1896, refers to *The Geisha* as a "Japanese Musical Play," while that at Daly's Theater in New York for September 18, 1896, refers to the same work as a "Japanese Musical Comedy." See also Mander and Mitchenson, 9–22; Lamb, "Music of the Popular Theatre," 97–104; Gänzl, *The Musical*, 102–19.

135   than anyone else: Banfield, "Bit by Bit," 221–22.

136   by the Shubert brothers: *Florodora* is discussed in Lamb, *Leslie Stuart*, 82–111. Touted retroactively as "The World's First Ever Original Cast Album," original London *Florodora* recordings were compiled and reissued in England on Opal/Pearl CD 9835 in 1989. "Tell Me, Pretty Maiden" as originally recorded in New York can be heard in *Music from the New York Stage*, vol. 1, disc 2 (see Historical Discography).

136   "of theatrical productions": McNamara, *Shuberts*, xxvi; P. A. Davis, "Syndicate/Shubert War," 147–57. The Shuberts abandoned producing after World War II and they sold many of their theaters after an antitrust suit in 1955 in which the U.S. Supreme Court ruled that theatrical amusements qualified as "articles of trade and commerce." The Shubert Organization, formed in 1973, still owns about half of all Broadway theaters today. See Poggi, 17–18; Liebling; Stagg; F. Hirsch, *Boys*; Chach et al.

137   comedy in the twentieth: Cohan, *Twenty Years*; Morehouse; McCabe; Vallillo, 233–44.

137   "I wanted to ring": Cohan, *Twenty Years*, 192, 198; McCabe, 60, 65.

138   "*Other* countries": Hischak, *Boy Loses Girl*, 1–10; McCabe, 60; Vallillo, 236.

138   "and back again": McSpadden, 260.

139   "to suit themselves": Cohan, "Why My Plays Succeed," 9, 58.

139   accepted the union: On the strike and its background, see Harding, 132–37; on its effect on Cohan, see McCabe, 147–61.

140   "even subtle performance": Rodgers, *Musical Stages*, 184.

140   one of his own: Cohan used a pinched tenor voice, delivering songs in a half-spoken *parlando* style rather than through outright singing. Some of his performances can be heard on *Music from the New York Stage*, vols. 1 and 2 (see Historical Discography).

140   "piano in F sharp": Cohan, *Twenty Years*, 103.

140   "vitality of his songs": Rodgers, *Musical Stages*, 154.

140   without offending anyone: R. Crawford, *America's Musical Life*, 530.

140   "*and* the brave": Though it would not formally become the national anthem until 1931, "The Star-Spangled Banner" had already received official recognition from several national organizations, including the U.S. Navy in 1889.

140   "and call poetry": Metcalfe in McCabe, 77.

141   columnist, and playwright: If historians of American drama consider Cohan's work at all, they tend to compare it with Ade's: Quinn, vol. 2, 113–18; Moses, *American Dramatist*, 288–90; G. B. Wilson, 325. Ade's published writings were free to develop a distinctive American vernacular—his *Fables in Slang* (1899) served as a model for writers of the 1920s. Yet his writings for the stage seem constrained by an expected high-toned

comic opera style of the period. Ade wrote five librettos in his prime playwriting years, the most successful being *The Sho-Gun* (music: Gustav Luders, 1904). More notable perhaps was *The Fair Co-ed* (1909), since it was a musical adaptation of his most popular play, *The College Widow* (1904), which, in turn, became the basis for the Princess Theater hit *Leave It to Jane* (1917). For his views on musical theater, see Ade, "Light Opera," 145, and "George Ade Talks," 287–88.

141 (*The Sultan of Sulu*): *The Best of George Ade*, 125; complete libretto, 122–76.

141 a policy, at least implicity: With the box-office in mind, Ade equivocated on the subject of satire on the musical stage. "A good many people praised the purpose of 'The Sultan of Sulu' because it is satirical—in a way a comment on current events. But I don't believe that sort of a thing in comic opera is a go with the public any more. It is all very well to attempt the Gilbertian trick; the critics will stand by you. But the rest won't." Ade, "Slang and the Stage," 9.

141 "at the same time": Mc Cabe, 50–51.

141 "to sentimental clichés": Furia, *Poets*, 31.

142 the "New Rialto": R. Aronson, 220–21.

142 Forty-second Street and Seventh Avenue: M. C. Henderson, *City*, 134–36; Frick, 3–5.

144 Forty-seventh Street and beyond: W. R. Taylor, xiii–xvi; M. Knapp, "Introductory Essay," 120.

144 "grandfathers had migrated": Hammerstein, *New York Times Magazine* (hereinafter *NYTM*), May 5, 1957.

144 involvement in Vietnam: McGilligan, 11–64.

145 "the nearest buck": Melnick, 39; Caesar in Furia, *Poets*, 19.

145 (the 1890s to the 1950s): Ewen, *All the Years*, 153; Hamm, *Yesterdays*, 286; R. Crawford, *America's Musical Life*, 471–91; Goldberg, *Tin Pan Alley*; Ewen, *Life and Death.*

145 a style (or styles): Melnick, 31.

145 "oral-tradition music": Hamm, *Yesterdays*, 379.

146 "strictly verboten": Forte, 28–29.

146 ("All Alone," 1924): Few musicians explain the basis for their choice of letters in analyzing popular songs. When the song clearly fits the form, there is no need to. It is when a song deviates from the standard schemes that one realizes the insufficiency of self-evident claims for the process. If, for example, the letters for the chorus structure of Irving Berlin's "All Alone" are to indicate the melodic design, then the sectional recurrences of the song's title in a rising 3-note step-wise motif might be represented as AAAB. If, on the other hand, the letters are to indicate the harmonic areas of the sections, this would be better represented as ABCA—a discrepancy that puts to question the usefulness of the letter scheme here at all. Wilder, 98, even goes so far as to indicate the form of Berlin's "The Girl on the Magazine Cover" (1915) as ABCD.

146 "standards": Hamm, "Popular Music," *NGDAM*, vol. 3, 595, 597; "Early Tin Pan Alley," xliv–xlvi.

150 to the title: A musical analysis of "Blue Skies" is in Forte, 87–91.

152 "for the public": C. K. Harris, 36.

152 "You Made Me Love You": Fremont; and Appelbaum reprint of the original sheet music.

153 possible to his public: For a compilation of the shows and song interpolations, see H. G. Goldman. 334–50. On Jolson and the Shuberts, see McNamara, *Shuberts*, 84–91, 115–17; Chach et al., 267–79; F. Hirsch, *Boys*, 85–88. Less reliable are Freedland, *Jolson*; Oberfirst.

153 "many opera glasses": Nathan in Bloom, 185.

153 "at the back of it": Benchley in Bloom, 188.

153 "health and gaiety": Seldes, *Arts*, 175, 176.

154 "on the biggest scale": Banfield, "Entertainers," 70.

154 with scripted material: Jolson can be heard performing throughout *Music from the New York Stage*, vols. 2, 3, and 4, with his June 4, 1913, recording of "You Made Me Love You" (Columbia A-1374) in vol. 3, disc 1 (see Historical Discography). On dealing with

the "rearticulation" of notated popular music in performance, see Tagg, 37–68; Middleton, 104–6.

154 them in blackface: Rogin, 435–56; Alexander, 133–79.

154 "entertainment" in America: Douglas, 348, 352, 363, 364; Banfield, "Entertainers," 70.

154 "it makes 'em laugh": Seldes, *Arts*, 177.

154 "the legitimate theater": Berlin in Bergreen, 101.

155 Lower East Side: Biographcal studies other than Bergreen's include Woolcott; Freedland, *Irving Berlin*; Whitcomb; Barrett; Furia, *Irving Berlin*; Jablonski, *Irving Berlin*; Leopold.

156 to opera burlesques: On Berlin's pre-1914 songs, see Hamm, *Songs from the Melting Pot*. The songs are published in Hamm, *Irving Berlin: Early Songs*, 3 vols.; the lyrics in Kimball and Emmet.

157 the fun out of it: On the Castles, see Mr. and Mrs. V. Castle; I. Castle; Golden.

157 domain of popular song: Dillingham hired Berlin again the following year for *Stop! Look! Listen!* (1915), this time without the Castles. *Watch Your Step*'s musical numbers were published in their staged sequence as a score by Berlin in 1914. *Stop! Look! Listen!* was similarly prepared for publication by Waterson, Berlin and Snyder but never printed. The manuscript is in the Burnside Collection (JPB 83–48: 1097), Music Division, NYPL, Lincoln Center.

157 "against a rhythmic melody": Berlin in Bergreen, 107; Kresa in Kimball and Emmet, 434.

157 differences it contained: Bergreen, 106–7.

158 the same stars in vaudeville: M. Knapp, "Watch Your Step," 247.

158 "AMERICAN MUSIC": Kern in Woolcott, 216.

158 more often understood: Bergreen, 54, 68, 121.

159 "for the commercial": Douglas, 355.

159 "made financially successful": Marbury, 253–54.

159 number of musicians: "No more than eleven musicians" in the pit is often claimed. But according to conductor and music archivist John McGlinn, based on instrumental parts discovered in the early 1980s, there were sixteen musicians in the pit for *Very Good Eddie*—flute, two bassoons, two trumpets, two pianos (grand and upright), percussion, four violins, two violas, cello, and bass—seventeen for *Oh Boy!*, and twenty for *Oh, Lady! Lady!!*

160 show rehearsal pianist: Major studies of Kern include Freedland, *Jerome Kern*; Bordman, *Jerome Kern*; Lamb, *Jerome Kern*; Banfield, *Jerome Kern*.

160 long remain indebted: Bordman, *Kern*, 300; and *American Musical Comedy*, 56; Lamb, *150 Years*, 151–54.

160 with an Englishman: The anecdote appears in Wodehouse and Bolton, 139–40, but not in Marcosson and Frohman.

160 only modestly well: Bordman, *American Musical Theatre*, 305.

160 "peppered with attractive music": Wodehouse, "Summer Stuff," 47; see also his *Vanity Fair* articles.

160 salt to it himself: Major studies of Wodehouse include French; Jasen; Hall; B. Green, *P. G. Wodehouse*; Connolly; McCrum. See also Day. A perhaps too delightful account of the triumvirate's first meeting is in Wodehouse and Bolton, 7–12. Its accuracy is questioned in Bordman, *Kern*, 120–21. G. Bolton, "Improvement," 7, mentioned Wodehouse collaborating on *Nobody Home*; and Bolton had no qualms later telling Livesey, 95, that "when [Wodehouse] and I wrote that joint autobiography, we never allowed literal truth to get in the way of the story."

160 Princess Theater auspices: See Olin; Lee Davis, *Bolton and Wodehouse and Kern*; Hischak, *Boy Loses Girl*, 11–22. That the entire series consisted of six shows is confirmed by the producers later advertising *Sitting Pretty* in 1924 as "The Seventh of Their Series of the Princess Musical Comedies." See Bordman, *Kern*, 246.

160 Bolton, Wodehouse, and Kern: *Have a Heart* (1917) and *Leave It to Jane* were both writ-

ten by the triumvirate but did not open at the Princess Theater, so they are not considered among the six in Olin, 1. Of the Princess Theater productions, Louis Hirsch replaced Kern on *Oh, My Dear!* (1919) and none of the three contributed to *Go To It* (1916), so these two are not considered among the six in Bordman, *Kern,* 170.

162   "New York institution": Wodehouse and Bolton, 6.

162   "lyricists still are shooting": Seldes, "Looking Back," 10.

162   play *Over Night:* G. Bolton, "Working with Wodehouse," 111.

162   "in our musical comedies": G. Bolton, "Improvement," 7.

162   the most likely suspect: *Oh Lady! Lady!!* was so well regarded by its authors as having the best story of the bunch that in 1927 Wodehouse turned it into a novel, *The Small Bachelor.*

163   "as you will, without music": G. Bolton, "Improvement," 7.

163   "recognition—and royalties": In Bordman, *Kern,* 149.

163   "intensity of effect": Seldes, *Arts,* 156.

163   "my own mantle": Herbert in Freedland, *Kern,* 34.

163   "English composers": Kern in Reid, 5. See Lamb, *Kern,* 56–65; Suskin, *Show Tunes,* 3–26.

164   "the song did not fit": Wodehouse in Wilk, *Playing Our Song,* 18.

164   "democratization of the genre": B. Green, "Wodehouse the Writer," 22.

165   "it doesn't *scan*": Wodehouse in Furia, *Poets,* 39–40.

165   fun at the contrivance: Lee Davis, *Bolton and Wodehouse and Kern,* 87.

165   "casually into the songs": Parker in B. Green, *Wodehouse,* 110.

165   "every one of which counts": Wilder, 42.

166   old Princess style: Often overlooked among the key contributors to the Princess style and later bearers of its influence is Edward Royce (1870–1964). The director-choreographer, born and trained in England, worked in New York regularly after 1916. His most distinguished work after the Princess shows was for *Irene, Sally, Kid Boots,* and *No, No, Nanette.*

5: The Cult of Romance

171   "heavy light opera": Traubner, 282.

171   "and romantic passions": Friml in Dizikes, 448.

172   "and heroines in tears": Gilbert W. Gabriel in Bordman, *American Operetta,* 120.

172   "the traveling salesman": Kraus, 136–37 (my translation).

173   of a Silver Age: Traubner, 243–44. Not until the 1920s did unabashed romanticism overwhelm the gaiety in Lehár's operettas to make their connection to the products of the Golden Age sufficiently remote to justify the concept of a new age altogether. See Gänzl, *The Musical,* 144.

173   various species of shows: Traubner, 377.

174   with the rubric "operetta": Galand, 15.

175   "That's not music!": Wilhelm Karczag in Schneidereit, 173; Traubner, 247.

175   "you love me so!": This, the first English translation used in America, was prepared by librettist Edward Morton and lyricist Adrian Ross for the London premiere earlier in 1907. The original German text reads:

> *Lippen schweigen, 's flüstern Geigen, hab' mich lieb!*
> *All die Schritte sagen bitte, hab' mich lieb!*
> *Jeder Druck der Hände deutlich mir's beschrieb.*
> *Er sagt klar, 's ist wahr, 's ist wahr, ich hab' dich lieb!*

175   "by way of their toes": O. L. Krasner, "Merry Widow," 9.

175   "or on a dance floor": Dizikes, 371.

175   Among the most memorable: In the cultural history of Broadway, *Die Fledermaus (The Bat)* belongs with these works though it was the artistic creation of an earlier generation. The American discovery of the piece dates from its 1912 Broadway incarnation as

The Merry Countess, which, as the mistranslated title suggests, was itself a product of the Viennese operetta craze that swept America in the wake of *The Merry Widow*.

177 "all the songs by heart": Rodgers, *Musical Stages*, 8.

177 "concealed sexual interest": O. L. Krasner, "Merry Widow," 10.

177 revision a year later: Mordden, *Broadway Babies*, 10.

177 Metropolitan Opera Company wouldn't: See Sheean; Cone.

179 sense of a score: That the act 1 dream melody fragments do not appear in the published score is explained in Roffman, 16.

180 "music, is his invention": Mordden, *Broadway Babies*, 21.

180 inherit it—Jerome Kern: Cf. S. Green, *World of Musical Comedy*, 31, and Bordman, *American Operetta*, 99–100.

180 "the actual firing-line": George Creel in Tischler, 70.

180 "liberty cabbage": D. M. Kennedy, 41.

180 and Roderick Freeman: Lamb, *150 Years*, 165; Bordman, "Friml," *NGDO*, 308.

181 United States in 1909: On Romberg, see E. Arnold; Everett; L. A. McLean, 117–41.

182 "the operettas were formed": John Shubert in F. Hirsch, *Boys*, 117.

182 Shubert Organization: Ibid., 144.

182 by German-speaking audiences: The success of *Blossom Time* gave rise to a series of pastiche Broadway operettas in which new stories and songs were fashioned around the existing music of "classical" or "semi-classical" composers: Offenbach, *The Love Song* (1925); Tchaikovsky, *Natja* (1925); Chopin, *White Lilacs* (1928). All failed except for the 1934 Johann Strauss pastiche *The Great Waltz*. Later the practice was consistently revived by the team of Robert Wright and George Forrest with varying degrees of success: Grieg, *Song of Norway* (1944); Herbert, *Gypsy Lady* (1946); Borodin, *Kismet* (1953); Rachmaninoff, *Anya* (1965).

183 remake of it for Broadway: *Blossom Time* and *Das Dreimäderlhaus (The House of the Three Girls)* are compared in Gänzl, *The Musical*, 197–98; Mordden, *Make Believe*, 39–41.

183 *Merry Widow* vein: The song seems to have been Romberg and Donnelly's inspiration. The only citation of the "Unfinished Symphony" theme in *Dreimäderlhaus* appeared not as a song but in the orchestral underscore at the end of act 2 (Ludwig Döblinger: Leipzig, Vienna, 1916), 73.

183 closer to kitsch: Taruskin, 36.

183 "and Al Jolson": P. Wood, 99.

184 "100% Americanism": Despite growing aversion to the cultural products of the Central Powers after 1914, Broadway producers continued to import German operettas fitted to American books, but with much of their original scores intact. At first these met with success: *The Blue Paradise*, 1915 (Edmund Eysler's *Ein Tag im Paradies*, 1913); *Alone at Last*, 1915 (Lehár's *Endlich Allein*, 1914); *Miss Springtime*, 1916 (Kálmán's *Zsuzsi Kisasszony*, 1915). Later, as hostilities drew America into the fray, such ventures failed: *Her Soldier Boy*, 1916 (Kálmán's *Gold gab ich für Eisen*, 1914); *My Lady's Glove*, 1917 (Strauss's *Die schöne Unbekannte*, 1915); *The Riviera Girl*, 1917 (Kálmán's *Die Csardasfürstin*, 1915).

184 with more poignant ones: Romberg nevertheless did appropriate some of the original Walter Kollo score, doing so apparently on purely musical grounds. For instance, the music to Ottillie's song, "Die Männer sind alle Verbrecher!" (*Wie einst im Mai*: act 2, no. 9) appears in the chorus of apprentices "Come boys it's noon we can stop now" (*Maytime*, act 1, no. 2), though neither the corresponding texts nor book situations have anything to do with one another.

184 "'gripping' and 'poignant'": Heilman, "Speculations," 212. Theatrical discussions of American melodrama are in Rahill; Grimsted, *Melodrama*. For a musical discussion, see A. D. Shapiro, "Melodrama," *NGDAM*, vol. 3, 202–4.

185 "a child in every adult": Bentley, *Life of the Drama*, 216–18.

185 total lack of humor: The scenes are taken from the *Wie einst im Mai* "Regiebuch," 17–18 (my translation) and the *Maytime* "Prompt Book and Stage Guide," 1–30 to 1–32. Both are now housed in The Shubert Archive.

188 "writers and composers": Hamm, "Musical Theater," *NGDAM*, vol. 3, 304.

188 *The Three Musketeers* in 1930: Gänzl, *The Musical*, 196, gives the figures for the initial runs of nine Broadway operettas of the 1920s in New York, London, and Paris.

189 spoken melodramas: Rahill, 83.

189 "were done long ago": Friml in S. Green, *World*, 47.

190 finale of act 1: Readers familiar with *Rose-Marie* through film versions may be surprised to learn how far these deviated from the Broadway original. In the early decades of talking films Hollywood approached the purchase of a hit Broadway property less intent on adapting it to the new medium than on transforming it for what a studio considered maximum screen effect. Thus the very films that now epitomize Broadway operetta for many often differ substantially from the real thing—including those in the Jeanette MacDonald–Nelson Eddy series, five of which derive from the Silver Age representatives of the genre: *Naughty Marietta* (1935), *Rose-Marie* (1936), *Maytime* (1937) *Sweethearts* (1938), and *New Moon* (1940). See Knowles.

190 succeed without it: Mordden, *Make Believe*, 168.

190 as totem poles: Operettas commonly were split down the middle between comedy and romance: in *Rio Rita*, between its scripted parts (book: Guy Bolton and Fred Thompson; music: Harry Tierney; lyrics: Joe McCarthy) and the screwball antics of comedians Bert Wheeler and Robert Woolsey; in *Rosalie* (book: William Anthony McGuire and Bolton), between half a score written by Romberg and P. G. Wodehouse and the other half by George and Ira Gershwin. See Mordden, *Make Believe*, 168, 176–78.

191 showing of silent films: With the advent of sound films by the early 1930s, operettas could finally be heard as well as seen on the screen. Many motion pictures of the type were produced in Hollywood, the most famous being the eight operetta films Jeanette Macdonald and Nelson Eddy made together for MGM. Though such films gave only a flavor of the originals whose titles they bore, they did much to popularize the genre at home and abroad and to link the work of Herbert, Romberg, and Friml in the public mind. See Traubner, 379.

191 another character in the show: The dialogue appears in the *Rose-Marie* "Prompt-Book," 1–42 to 1–43; the music appears in the piano-vocal "Conductor's Score," 104. Both are from the Tams-Witmark Music Library.

192 "as separate episodes": S. Green, *Rodgers and Hammerstein Fact Book*, 293.

192 remain a major issue: Of the forty-three Broadway shows for which Harbach created librettos and/or lyrics, six were for Karl Hoschna, eleven for Friml, and five for Kern.

192 "Father of Times Square": See Carroll.

193 "operatic musical comedy": Hammerstein, "Voices," 14, 70.

193 "human to be entertaining?": Ibid., 70.

194 "for the music throughout": Kern in Gordon and Funke, 147.

194 something else entirely: Important studies of *Show Boat* include Kreuger; Fordin, 70–90; Ziegfeld and Ziegfeld, 132–48; Bordman, *Kern*, 275–92; Swain, 15–49; Berlant, 399–442; Block, *Enchanted Evenings*, 19–40; Mordden, *Make Believe*, 205–32.

195 "crammed with plot": [G. S. Kaufman?], *NYT* (n.d.), 26.

195 "musical-comedy bookmakers": Alison Smith in S. Green, *Rodgers and Hammerstein Fact Book*, 353.

195 "of literary works": Watts, Jr., *New York Herald Tribune* (n.d.).

195 "distort its values": [G. S. Kaufman?], *NYT* (n.d.), 26.

197 "is unbearably sweet": Engel, *American Musical Theater*, 13.

198 own standard—black: On the history of American miscegenation law, see Pascoe, 44–69.

198 critics of the piece: On issues pertaining to racism in *Show Boat*, see http://en.wikipedia .org/wiki/Show_Boat#Racism_and_Controversy; and in the show's film versions, see Stanfield, 147–56; S. Smith, 9–24.

198 musically interesting songs: The less than favorable critique of key *Show Boat* songs in

Wilder, 55–60, is based on purely musical criteria, and thus, as James Maher points out in the book's introduction (xxx) is "*not* concerned with how well [such songs] worked, or failed to work, in the dramatic situation for which they were written."

199   strands of the plot: Even the show's pivotal performers worked in an operetta vein, both vocally (Howard Marsh [?–1969], the tenor who created the role of Ravenal, also created the romantic leading roles in *Blossom Time* and *The Student Prince*) and dramatically (Helen Morgan [1900–1941] played Julie with a melodramatic pathos most apparent in her act 2 pantomime). In the words of *Show Boat*'s director, "Without any spoken word, [she] conveyed joy, the hopelessness of her own condition, and the fact that she was sacrificing her job." Colvan, 82–83.

199   when she first heard it: Fordin, 83.

199   rising transformation of the former: See Swain, 42–47.

199   without being grandiose: "Ol' Man River" is often associated with the black bass-baritone Paul Robeson (1898–1976), who played the role of Joe in the 1928 London production of *Show Boat*, the 1932 Broadway revival, and the 1936 film. Bringing "a rich sonority and even a sort of racial significance to the singing" (Henry Hazlitt, *The Nation*, June 8, 1932), Robeson later turned the song into his own cultural property and significantly altered Hammerstein's text to replace what he felt were racially denigrating lyrics with more activist ones. See "Lyric Changes," http://www.scc.rutgers.edu/njh/PaulRobeson/lyrics.htm; "On Revising 'Old Man River,'" http://www.theatermirror.com/glhriver.htm; R. Knapp, *Formation*, 190.

200   Herbert, Friml, and Romberg: Hamm, "Musical Theater," 305.

200   Broadway in December 1927: Ziegfeld in Kreuger, *Show Boat*, 20.

200   (1994, Broadway): On the differences between the various versions, see Kreuger, *Show Boat*, 76ff; Block, *Enchanted Evenings*, 23–27; McGlinn, 26–38.

201   "after *Show Boat*": Kreuger, "Some Words," 18.

201   "musical coaxed into one form": Mordden, "'Show Boat' Crosses Over," 80–81.

201   "theater into a credible drama": Swain, 15.

201   "suitably mature fashion": Kreuger, "Some Words," 18.

201   "comedy as an art form": Robert Coleman in S. Green, *Rodgers and Hammerstein Fact Book*, 353.

201   *Show Boat* might have failed: Ziegfeld thought an early version of the book "too serious" and insisted Hammerstein revise it because, as he put it in a telegram to Kern, "in present shape has not got a chance except with critics but the public no, and I have stopped producing for critics and empty houses." In Bordman, *Kern*, 282.

6: A Shadow of Vulgarity

205   "and what was fun?": Fitzgerald, 13–14. See also Erenberg, 233–63.

205   "movies," and "jazz": Loeb in Douglas, 346–67. Hemingway used Loeb as a model for his literary dabbler Robert Cohn in *The Sun Also Rises*.

205   culture during the 1920s: Kammen, 83.

205   experience of African Americans: Woolcott in Douglas, 377.

206   utter the word "jazz": Hill and Hatch, 215.

206   "excited the baser instincts": Sousa in Ogren, 156; Pattison, 5–6.

206   "then dancing, then music": Fitzgerald, 16.

206   "intellectual bad manners": Seldes in Kammen, 84–85.

206   with "the great arts": Kammen, 80.

207   "at most of our museums": Seldes, *Arts*, 3.

207   "and the polished fake": Ibid., 294–95; Seldes in Kammen, 80, 91–92.

207   "or workplace identities": Hammack, 36.

207   end of the decade: T. G. Moore, 9; M. C. Henderson, *City*, xi; Mordden, *Make Believe*, 233–34.

207   about fifty were musical: Poggi, 47–49; Bordman, *American Musical Theatre*, 425; A. Shaw, 231–84.

208   different guises throughout: F. Hirsch, *Boys*, 303.

209   for spectacle and dance: Mordden, *Make Believe*, 76; F. Hirsch, *Boys*, 140.

209   "That's for the book": Rodgers, *Musical Stages*, 172–73.

210   kept them moving forward: Some shows generally regarded as musical comedies had sufficiently compromised plots to admit of a genre identity problem: *I'd Rather Be Right* was published as "A Musical Revue" while *Face the Music* hedged its bets by calling itself "A Musical Comedy Revue."

210   "reprise is just a repetition": Dietz, 137.

211   *The Ziegfeld Follies* (1946): Major studies of Ziegfeld include Cantor and Freedman; Farnsworth; Baral, "Ziegfeld"; Higham; R. Carter; Ziegfeld and Ziegfeld.

211   in their own fashion: Baral, *Revue*, 44–115, 136–39; Bordman, *Revue*, 29–51; Mordden, *Make Believe*, 83–98.

211   "don't have much to change": Will Rogers in Mizejewski, *Ziegfeld Girl*, 6.

211   Theater on Forty-second Street: M. C. Henderson, *The New Amsterdam*, 60–87.

212   "New Stagecraft" of European modernism: Urban; A. Aronson, *Architect of Dreams*, 33–36, 72–77; Carter and Cole, 70–97, 233–45.

212   chorus girls into "showgirls": Duff Gordon, 243–50, 289–90; Etherington-Smith, 178, 260; Matheson, 15–19.

212   staircases and ramps: Duff Gordon, 245; Gilmartin, 275; Lasser, 445; Mizejewski, *Ziegfeld Girl*, 1.

212   above all, inaccessible: Mizejewski, *Ziegfeld Girl*, 11.

212   "A Pretty Girl Is Like a Melody": The song can be heard in *Ziegfeld Follies of 1919*. Other relevant archival LPs include *Stars of the Ziegfeld Follies* and *Follies, Scandals, & Other Diversions* (see Historical Discography for all three recordings).

212   in a different light: R. C. Allen, 282, 245–46; Lasser, 442, 445; Erenberg, 206–19.

212   "fantasy of American womanhood": Mizejewski, *Ziegfeld Girl*, 3.

212   "disrobing his goddess": E. Wilson, 51.

212   to rival the *Follies*: Chach et al., 285–95.

213   "the evening dress—wasn't": Alan Dale in F. Hirsch, *Boys*, 91.

214   "fundamental of all commodities": Murray, viii.

214   "Cards as Women Do": The two sketches are in Oliver, *Revue Sketches*, 1–7, 15–23.

215   *As Thousands Cheer* (1933): Smithsonian issued archival recordings of *The Band Wagon* and *At Home Abroad* (see Historical Discography).

215   "'I Love Louisa'": Gordon and Funke, 136.

217   Program with Running Times: Programs and timings come from Gordon's *Band Wagon* typescript (Walter Hampden-Edwin Booth Theater Collection and Library); Dietz's typescript (Museum of the City of New York Theater Collection); and the synopsis in Billman, 67–68.

218   a unified tone and point of view: M. Goldstein, *Kaufman*, 188–90.

218   "check your brains with your hat": Atkinson in Gordon and Funke, 139.

219   "proceed with the examination": "Warburton" and "Claghornes" are in Oliver, *Revue Sketches*, 113–21, 123–31.

220   *As Thousands Cheer*: The program comes from Sam Harris's typescript of *As Thousands Cheer* (Princeton University Library); the synopsis is in S. Green, *Ring Bells!*, 83–39.

222   "the right running order": Coward in Lee Davis, *Scandals*, 16–17.

222   "not interfere with the continuity": Hammerstein, *Kern Songbook*, 51.

224   "not be too dignified": Schwab, 37.

224   "which to spread the laughs": H. Fields, 41.

224   "out of the way of other things": Kerr, "Musicals That Were Playful," 25.

225   (as Aristotle put it) catharsis: Cohen, 33–34.

225   Marx Brothers movie, for example: Heilman, "Introduction," xxxii.

225   "responsibilities of adulthood": Bentley, *Life of the Drama*, 298.

225   "generic quality of wine": Potts, 151–52.

225   "'Moore-type yuks'": Merman and Martin, 103.

226   "Mine are very good": In S. Green, *Great Clowns*, 182.

227   "value at the end": Wodehouse and Bolton, 221.

227   as lasting sixty-two seconds: Lahr, *Notes*, 120.

227   "Scotch, by absorption": In S. Green, *Great Clowns*, 110.

228   "(BLACKOUT)": In Lahr, *Notes*, 119.

228   "the audience won't accept it": Ibid., 120.

229   phrasing called swing: Tucker, *NGDMM*, vol. 12, 903–4.

229   "*Rhapsody in Blue*": Ibid., 910.

229   "mass-marketed popular music": D. Schiff, *Gershwin*, 83.

229   as he put it, "but American": G. Gershwin, "National Anthem," 30; Hamm, "Blues for the Ages," 348–49.

229   its more "classical" bent: Bordman, *American Musical Theatre*, 388.

229   "staccato, not legato": G. Gershwin, "National Anthem," 30.

229   jazzy duple-meter tune: Tempting though it is to assume Youmans wrote the music for "My Boy and I," his hand in the composition is not entirely clear. The copyright registration for "No, No, Nanette" (July 31, 1924; E-594501) lists Youmans as the song's composer, while that for its obvious source, "My Boy and I" (Jan. 7, 1924; E-578611), lists the song's composer as Herbert Stothart.

229   with the modern urban life: Ogren, 144–45.

230   Bobby Connolly: Cohen-Stratyner, 321, 536.

230   "does he attempt to express it": H. A. Gilbert, 27; Ries, "Sammy Lee," 82.

230   dance director of the day: Over a forty-year career, Wayburn filled the stages of vaudeville and Broadway with dancers and dance routines. Both as a showman (he invented the "Ziegfeld Walk" for parading showgirls to navigate the *Follies'* staircases with grace) and as a teacher (he ran successful dance studios in Chicago and New York), Wayburn exerted a formative influence on the careers of countless chorines as well as stars such as Marilyn Miller, Ann Pennington, and Adele and Fred Astaire. See Stratyner. For other views on the number and classification of theater dance types of the period, see Ries, "Sammy Lee," 5–9; Kislan, *Hoofing*, 24–40.

230   on Wayburn's part: Wayburn, 57–60.

231   "the other features, at times": Ibid., 83–85.

231   "I Want to Be Happy": Ries, "Sammy Lee," 33–41, 86. Lee's written notes for *Nanette*'s dances have survived in the files at MGM in Culver City, California, affording a glimpse at what musical comedy choreography of the period might actually have looked like on the stage.

231   "with the story at hand": Ibid., 84–85.

232   on a truly international scale: Schmidt-Joos, 156; Gänzl, *The Musical*, 185–86.

232   as a "dummy" lyric: Bordman, *Days to be Happy*, 78.

233   "Feeling you're all mine": "Thé Pour Deux," lyrics de Colline de Merry (Paris, Éditions Salabert, 1926), my translation.

233   "You wind up going all the way": "Wenn ein Mädel 'Ja' gesagt," deutscher Gesangstext von Artur Rebner (Berlin, Rondo Verlag, 1925), my translation.

234   "after the great war": In Bulloch, vol. 40 (1925), 47.

234   her husband had named: Bordman, *Days to Be Happy*, 3–6.

234   "More Than You Know": Wilder, 311–12, on the distinction between theater and pop songs: "I can't claim [Youmans] as one of the great writers of theater songs, for with few exceptions, his songs were [only] better-than-average pop songs. . . . [Yet] *Hallelujah!*, *Rise 'N' Shine*, *Great Day*, and *I Know That You Know* are distinctly theatrical in flavor and not just because they are in *alla breve* rhythm or syncopate the fourth beat, though those factors help. It's because the canvas is larger, the line broader, the intensity greater."

235   felt they had escaped: D. Krasner, *Beautiful Pageant*, 266–67.

235   name of entertainment: Woll, 111; Graziano, 108; D. Krasner, *Beautiful Pageant*, 247.

235   "sculpture, music, and dancing": L. Hughes, 370.

235   a "Musical Melange": Douglas, 378.

235   ragtime-inspired numbers: The work of both teams can be heard in *Shuffle Along* (see Historical Discography).

236   "know further downtown": Alan Dale in Woll, 71.

237   "never be no black mayor": *Shuffle Along* Electronic Edition, http://www.alexander street4.com/cgi-bin/asp/philomain/getojbect_?c.30:2:1./project.

237   "absence of street lights": Southern, *Music of Black Americans*, 427–28, which conflicts with Woll, 78, in its view of *Shuffle Along*'s cultural significance. Douglas, 378,384, proposes a synthesis: "*Shuffle Along* was hailed by blacks and whites as a critical step away from minstrelsy and its coon songs toward a modern black musical art, yet in some ways its importance stems precisely from its *return* to minstrelsy. The so-called years of exile [from Broadway] for Negro performers had resulted, not in a diminution of modern Negro musical art, but in a proud intensification and creative complication of it. . . . Anything, but anything, from the latest and hottest Negro dances to the oldest of white blackface routines, was grist for the *Shuffle Along* mill. . . . The point [here] was not the choice but the freedom of choice."

237   "jazz rhythms visible": Stearns and Stearns, xiv.

237   "these girls DANCED!!!": Blake in Huggins, 337.

237   teach his own chorines the movements: Kimball and Bolcom, 148.

238   *Scandals of 1926*: Stearns and Stearns, 110–111; Erenberg, 250.

238   to visit Harlem vicariously: Woll, 94–95; Erenberg, 254–59.

238   Lena Horne (b. 1917) in 1939: See respectively Egan; E. Waters; Bourne; Horne.

238   black musicals of the 1920s: Singer, *Black and Blue*, 209–12, claims that the hit song of *Blackbirds of 1928*, "I Can't Give You Anything But Love," was written not by McHugh and Fields but by "Fats" Waller and Andy Razaf.

239   before moving downtown: Woll, 131–32.

239   definition, Louis Armstrong: Both Waller and Armstrong can be heard in *Souvenirs of Hot Chocolates* (see Historical Discography).

7: Broadway Songbook

243   more than one writer: Even when identifiable, the separate contributions of the members of librettist teams rarely divide neatly along the lines of book and lyrics, though Giuseppe Giacosa was the versifier of Luigi Illica's prose for Puccini, and generally, Ludovic Halévy supplied the verse and Henri Meilhac the spoken dialogue for Offenbach. P. J. Smith, 292; Trowell, *NGDO*, vol. 2, 1191ff.

244   "plot and are part of it": Herbert in Sanjek, *American Popular Music*, vol. 3, 98.

244   "keeps the numbers apart": Wodehouse, "Agonies," 39.

245   "What's a finale?": Thomson, *Reader*, 552. That nearly all his shows before 1930 have an act 1 finale makes it unlikely that Rodgers was unfamiliar at least with the term—only perhaps with its more traditional use as a through-composed concerted number.

245   Berlin was musically illiterate: On Berlin's reliance on musical "secretaries" (Helmy Kresa, et al.), see Bergreen, 278–79.

245   in time for opening night: On Porter's reliance on Dr. Albert Sirmay and others, see C. Schwartz, *Porter*, 170–71.

245   Bennett (1894–1981): See Ferencz.

246   "all sound like a 'work'": L. Bernstein, *Joy of Music*, 173.

246   a complete theater production: See J. A. Conrad; Collinson; R. R. Bennett. The 1993 *Collective Bargaining Agreement*, 45, defines orchestration as "the art of scoring the vari-

ous voices of an already written composition in complete form." It describes arranging in terms of "reharmonization, paraphrasing, development, etc." and establishes that arranging, "including, as it does, the creative work of harmonic, melodic, rhythmic, and contrapuntal nature, belongs to the province of creative work."

246 a show without the other: Boosey and Hawkes published full scores to Leonard Bernstein's *Candide* (Scottish Opera edition) and *West Side Story* in 1994, a first for Broadway shows. The Kurt Weill Edition began its planned publication of critical edition full scores to all of Weill's Broadway works with *The Firebrand of Florence* in 2002.

247 what exactly this might mean: Considered purely as words, lyrics arguably are more nearly part of a show's book though they are frequently regarded as part of its score (see Hart and Kimball, xxv). This may relate to the fact that the composer who receives credit for "the music" of a Broadway show is the only musician of the many who shape its score whose work *necessarily* involves the lyrics. (The contributions of the other musicians are primarily musical in nature, by contrast, and compositionally uncredited.)

247 sheer variety of numbers: L. Hart; Nolan, *Hart*, 225.

247 also discernibly alike: Rodgers, "How to Write Music," 743; and *Musical Stages*, 293.

247 survive the show itself: In the last chapter of *American Musical Landscape*, Crawford traces the diffusion of the Gershwins' song "I Got Rhythm" from its origin in *Girl Crazy* through various levels of American musical culture.

247 scattered and frequently lost: Krasker and Kimball list the whereabouts of such extant materials, when known, for all the book shows of Berlin, the Gershwins, Porter, and Rodgers and Hart. Recent discoveries of presumed lost show materials from Warner Brothers Music in 1982 and Tams-Witmark Music Library in 1987 have helped enormously with this kind of work.

248 and motion pictures: Sanjek, *Print to Plastic*, 13; Crawford, *Musical Life*, 672–75.

248 as they never had before: Forte, 3–4; Bordman, *Musical Theatre*, 388; Maher in Wilder, xxx–xxxvi; Hamm, *Yesterdays*, 326–90; Pessen, 180–97.

250 immigrants in America: D. Schiff, *Gershwin*, 94–95.

250 "He was a composer": Berlin in Bolcom, "A Serious Composer."

250 recognize him as one of their own: D. Schiff, *Gershwin*, 82–83; Forte, 149.

250 any American composer before: Ewen. Other general studies of one or both of the Gershwin brothers include Goldberg, *George Gershwin*; Armitage; Jablonski and Stewart; Schwartz, *Gershwin*; Kimball and Simon; Jablonski, *Gershwin*, and *Gershwin Remembered*; D. Rosenberg; Peyser, *Memory of All That*; S. E. Gilbert; Furia, *Ira Gershwin*; Schneider; Pollack.

250 "made of better material": In Goldberg, *Gershwin*, 81.

251 "Try Ira": In Furia, *Ira Gershwin*, 45–46.

251 "everything at once": In ibid., 4.

251 *The American Language*: W. R. Taylor, 214.

251 its first public exposure: Foremost among such columns was Franklin P. Adam's "Conning Tower," in which future comedy writers such as George S. Kaufman, Morrie Ryskind, Yip Harburg, and Howard Dietz also made early appearances in print. Dietz, 19–21: "The reign of F.P.A. was an era of golden laughter. While the contribution of F.P.A.'s light verse and paraphrasing was not profound, it was literature that simulated a forum of readers who were proud of their standards. The contributors lived by a code of scansion and were united in a war against assonance. . . . We turned to F.P.A. first thing in the morning to see if we had made it, or if not who had."

251 *Park Avenue*, 1946: See Kimball, *Lyrics of Ira Gershwin*; Jablonski in Schneider, 255–77.

252 "evaluation, for taste": Harburg in Peyser, *Memory*, 28.

252 "just a songwriter": Ira Gershwin in Furia, *Ira Gershwin*, 193.

252 "in concept and design": Astaire, 128.

253 "is highly improbable": I. Gershwin, ix, 42.

253   "an ear for the current phrase": Ibid., 120

254   "full of outdoor pep": In Kimball and Simon, xvi.

254   "Park Avenue hot": In Meredith, 438. Led by the already well-known cornetist "Red"
       Nichols, the *Girl Crazy* pit band included such soon-to-be swing-band luminaries as
       Benny Goodman, Jack Teagarden, Glenn Miller, and Gene Krupa.

254   eighth-notes in every bar: For attempts to account for this song's rhythmic fascination,
       see Copland, 38; Wilder, 131; Mast, 72–73.

255   "new [Broadway] genre": Jablonski, "The Gershwins Go to War," 25. Smithsonian-
       issued archival compilations of *Lady, Be Good!*, *Oh, Kay!*, and *Funny Face* (see Historical
       Discography).

257   to work on the stage: Hischak, *Boy Loses Girl*, 45–54.

258   to that of *The Mikado*: L. Bernstein, *Joy of Music*, 171.

258   "satirical operetta": Ruhl.

258   "satire on American politics": In Kaufman and Ryskind, 115.

258   "old-line musical comedy": Atkinson, "Pulitzer Laurels," 7:1.

259   "a kiss that conquers": Schlesinger, "How History Upstaged," 2:6.

259   a real political agenda: M. Goldstein, *Kaufman*, 201.

259   "*Young President Ought to Know*": A play on the title of William J. Fielding's 1924 best-
       seller, *What Every Young Man Should Know*, a book of sex instruction for boys.

260   "enjoys the despair, masochistically": Grigson, v.

260   "world's potential goodness": Mason. 80.

260   "no interest in politics at all": Fitzgerald, 14.

260   but not strictly satire: Comparisons of the two versions are in Mason, 88–89; Krasker,
       17–20.

261   in the *New York Times*: Anderson, "On Government," 9:1; and *Off Broadway*, 81–86.

261   much tamer than intended: E. Rice, 380; Logan, 109–112; Sanders, 272–78; F. Hirsch,
       Weill, 167–69.

261   that runs out of steam: The nature of *Cradle*'s success remains controversial. On the one
       hand, Mellers, 420: "Blitzstein [achieved], within his self-imposed limitations, a range
       and depth of experience comparable with that of much more complex 'art' music." On
       the other, Bentley, "Comedy," 56: "Blitzstein's attitude, though it can be called extreme
       by those who think in political terms, was conventional and conformist in cultural, and
       so ultimately in human, terms. He did not rebel except politically, i. e., on the surface. On
       the contrary, he accepted most of what a real rebel would be rebelling against: the way of
       feeling and thinking and behaving, of the established regime."

261   as much as private ones: Revues traditionally used their separate sketches to poke
       fun at timely items in the public arena; and they continued to do so during the Great
       Depression, only sometimes giving overt expression to a consistent political point of
       view—*Parade*, 1935, on the left; *One for the Money*, 1939, on the right.

261   "satire on Practically Everything": I. Gershwin, 162

262   toward political relevance: See Vacha, 573–90.

262   insecurity about the medium: Anderson on *Knickerbocker Holiday*: "I seem to be getting
       along very well with the operetta but it's a new form for me and I can't be sure." Avery,
       73; Logan, 109

262   less than legitimate enterprise: Kaufman, for one, harbored a lifelong ambivalence over
       the musical medium which expressed itself with humor in the following 1948 letter
       to the producer of *Gentlemen Prefer Blondes*: "I've quit completely as a musical book
       writer. Don't know enough about it and can't stand the corny songs that get stuck in.
       I'm aware that the corny songs are necessary, but I'm a crotchety old bastard." Herman
       Levin Papers, 79 AN/21-1, Wisconsin State Historical Archives. See also M. Gold-
       stein, *Kaufman*, 130, 294, 398.

263   *Porgy and Bess*: Mast, 77.

264   "adjectives—or aspired to be": Hamm, *Yesterdays*, 377–78.

264   "Porter's so . . . thirties!": Mercer in Furia, *Poets*, 153.

264   Protestant, and privileged: Biographical studies of Porter include Eells; Kimball, *Cole*; Siebert; Schwartz, *Cole Porter*; Grafton; Citron, *Noël and Cole*; Morella and Mazzei; McBrien.

264   "Gilbert and Sullivan crazy": Millstein, "Words Anent Music," 16.

265   words and music: Brendan Gill in Kimball, *Cole*, xv, xii–xiii.

265   "to be pursued by it": Ibid., xiii.

265   comprised a "lost generation": Kimball, *Complete Lyrics of Cole Porter*, xvii; Douglas, 41, 88.

265   apprenticed to a trade: Stein in Thomson, *Reader*, 546.

266   (1893–1966)—their first: See Crouse.

266   shows at the time: "Billy Gaxton . . . had to keep out of sight of his boss, who was on the ship; and he had to keep out of sight of the girl's mother, who also knew him. So it was a succession of disguises for Bill. We would ask Bill, 'what are you good at?' He said, 'well, I do Chinese very well. I do an imitation of a woman.' And things like that. And then we would begin to fit scenes around it." Lindsay, 21.

266   major new production: Block, *Enchanted Evenings*, 42–53, 325–27, compares the original production with the 1962 Off Broadway revival (on which Bolton himself worked) and the 1987 Lincoln Center revival. See also Holden, "Glimpse of the Olden Days," 5H, 32H.

267   rests chiefly on its score: Nonetheless, revivalists have had few qualms about cutting the original's lesser-known numbers and replacing them with even more hit songs taken from other Porter shows. Contrary to the claims of apologists for the practice such as Mast, 194, Florence Leeds of the Cole Porter Musical and Literary Property Trusts in New York confirmed to me during the 1980s that Porter's will did not sanction the switching of his songs from one show to another.

267   "I'd do a crossword puzzle": In Millstein, "Words Anent Music," 16, 55.

268   Reno's one-sided obsession: See Mast, 188–89.

268   came to crafting librettos: Taubman, "Porter Is 'The Top.'" "When his book writer has provided him with a comprehensive outline of the show, Porter prepares a chart that shows at a glance the nature and spotting of the required numbers. He rarely interferes with the book. Without false pride he confesses, 'I have no book sense.'" Cf. Swain, 129–30, who faults *Anything Goes* for not being an integrated musical play, and Block, *Enchanted Evenings*, 48–49, who refreshingly questions assumptions underlying modern critical approaches to the show and the applicability of the musical play model altogether.

268   represents the case: Already as a show writing undergraduate, Porter wrote to a college collaborator: "I have had to insert arrows indicating the approach of certain songs, at which points the conversation must 'lead up' . . . Finish the second act. I can do nothing until you do. You see my only means of making the songs relevant is by writing verses which give the idea of belonging to the person that sings them." Siebert, vol. 2, 827.

269   "is much too sad to be told": *Anything Goes*, 1935 London version, typescript in Billy Rose Theater Collection, New York Public Library for the Performing Arts.

269   often playfully ironic: Hoping to bring cheer into a gloomy situation in *Oh, Kay!*, for example, a comedian addresses the chorus, "It's the philosophy of sunshine, girls. I learned it at the knee of my old mammy. Do you want to hear a Mammy song?" When the girls reply with a resounding "No!" he responds, "Very well, then, I'll sing you the song she used to sing to me," and he goes into the Gershwins' "Clap Yo' Hands." L. Bernstein, *Joy of Music*, 169–70.

270   in the second act: Merman and Eells, 127; Fields and Fields, 519, cite an instance in *Let's Face It* in which an old Lew Fields routine directly influenced one of Herbert's books for Porter.

270   "Bluebird," *Anything Goes*: Mast, 194.

270   Ethel Merman (1908–1984): On Merman, see Merman and Eells; Merman and Martin; Thomas; Bryan; Kellow; C. Flinn.

271   "or a beautiful one": Osborne, 61.

271   "And she is so damned apt": C. Porter, "Notes." See Mordden, *Babies*, 114–19. Marilyn
       Miller, who recorded infrequently and not in her prime, can be heard online at http://
       www.archive.org/details/MarilynMiller-01-05. Merman can be heard singing her earli-
       est Porter shows in *Anything Goes* and *Red, Hot and Blue!* (see Historical Discography).

273   no mistaking what he meant: Such frankness incurred resistance. What might get by
       in the theater would not pass muster in other media with a broader audience base, and
       censorship in various forms haunted Porter throughout his career. Theater songs, from
       the sobriety of "Love for Sale" to the frivolousness of "But in the Morning, No," with its
       double entendres, were banned from the radio. When his songs were retained, their lyr-
       ics were often altered on recordings or in translation from stage to screen—even as late
       as the filming of Porter's last Broadway show, *Silk Stockings*, in 1956. See correspondence
       in "Silk Stockings" folder, Porter Collection, Music Division, Library of Congress.

273   "sound downright provincial": Moss Hart, *Porter Song Book*, 2.

273   "brittle, bright poesy": Eells, 159. Lahr, *Notes*, 203, dubbed Porter "the Alexander Pope of
       American musical comedy, [who] created lyrics whose complexity captured the veneer
       and the exuberance of a world as confident in its coherence as the heroic couplet."

273   aspect of the human condition: Leithauser, Book Review, 27; Lounsberry, xiii; Latou-
       che and Moross, xi–xiii. Earlier on, anthologies of light verse in English such as those
       edited by Auden (1938) and Amis (1978) did not include Broadway song lyrics, though
       an exception is that edited by Kronenberger (1935), which saw fit to cite an example
       each of George Ade and Ira Gershwin. Broadway lyrics are well represented, however,
       in more recent anthologies, such as those edited by Harmon (1979), Baker (1986), and
       Gross (1994); and in these Porter's work appears more often than that of any other
       Broadway lyricist.

274   differences are no less revealing: "O Tell Me the Truth About Love" was one of sev-
       eral Auden poems that Benjamin Britten set to music between 1937 and 1938. If "the
       model, for the text and the music, was clearly Cole Porter," as D. Mitchell claims,
       that model would probably not have been "At Long Last Love," which was published
       shortly after the Auden-Britten collaboration. D. Mitchell, 109–11, 128–29; Kimball,
       Complete Lyrics of Cole Porter, 229–30.

274   dualistic mode of perception: J. Smith, 48, 50.

275   "musical comedy not beckoned": Updike in Kimball, *Complete Lyrics of Cole Porter*, xiii.

275   commercial culture they scorned: In *The Snows of Kilimanjaro* Hemingway disparaged
       the moral ambivalence of Porter's song "It's Bad for Me." Adorno impugned Kurt
       Weill's music for Broadway by claiming that it was "hard to distinguish from Cole
       Porter" (in Kowalke, "Kurt Weill, Modernism," 36, 64). Even the more conservative
       Maxwell Anderson once rejected a proposed collaboration: "I'm afraid it's more Cole
       Porter's dish than mine. It's perfect material for a Broadway musical . . . but it couldn't
       possibly carry any meaning, and I find myself unable to take an interest in a play that
       doesn't say something" (in Avery, 241).

276   "knew that we had to try": Rodgers, *Musical Stages*, 27–28. Other important books on
       Rodgers and/or Hart include Ewen, *Richard Rodgers* and *With a Song in His Heart*;
       Marx and Clayton; D. Hart, *Thou Swell*; Hart and Kimball; Rodgers, *Letters to Dorothy*;
       Nolan, *Lorenz Hart*; Hyland; Secrest, *Somewhere for Me*; Block, *Richard Rodgers Reader*
       and *Richard Rodgers*.

276   "I wanted to be led": Rodgers, *Musical Stages*, 20.

276   films in Hollywood (1931–1935): In Marx and Clayton, 195.

276   produced all three musicals: On the influence of the burlesque tradition of Herbert's
       father on these musical comedies, see Fields and Fields, 442–43, 456–57, 465.

277   burlesqued the subject: Cox, 92; Kaplan, 293–94.

277   "rough Broadway wit": Mantle in S. Green, *Fact Book*, 72.

277   "with the Round Table, Lancelot": *A Connecticut Yankee*, 1927 typescript, Billy Rose
       Theater Collection, New York Public Library for the Performing Arts

277   "more important than the sense": In Darrell, 12.

278   in order to make it make sense: Rodgers, *Musical Stages*, 80. See also Wilder, 169; Forte, 179–82.

278   "at the fun it's having": Kerr, "Musicals That Were Playful," 28.

278   Gershwins would do the same: Furia, *Poets*, 110–14.

279   one year later (*Girl Crazy*): Kimball, "Broadway and the Depression," 48–49; McNamara in W. R. Taylor, 179–82; Poggi, 65–96.

280   "anything Broadway had ever known": de Mille, *America Dances*, 187.

280   credit be replaced by "Choreography": Balanchine's own account of *Slaughter* appears in Balanchine and Mason, 538–40.

280   But Balanchine choreographed: As the "Czarina of Broadway," Albertina Rasch had earlier claimed the "choreographer" distinction for herself. See Ries, "Albertina Rasch," 95ff.

280   "not merely physical ones": Balanchine, "Notes," 202.

281   down-to-earth American styles: To achieve this mix, the Russian-born Balanchine was assisted by Herbie Harper, a protégé of the most successful black American dance director of the period, Buddy Bradley. See Stearns and Stearns, 167; Moulton, 202; Rodgers, *Letters*, 216.

281   advance the plot from within: For different views of *Slaughter*, see Lerman, 81; Copeland, 34; Block, *Enchanted Evenings*, 89–90.

282   "ignominious and to be scorned": de Mille, *America Dances*, 188.

282   "comedy with the meaning left out": Potts, 151.

282   "took a long step toward maturity": Watts and Gibbs in S. Green, *Fact Book*, 219–20.

282   which the letters had spawned: O'Hara in Rodgers, *Musical Stages*, 198.

283   "the luck you're going to need": *Pal Joey*, 1940 typescript, The Rodgers and Hammerstein Theater Library.

283   "happy ending—no ending at all": Mast, 181.

283   also an eminently musical one: "Comedy," *Webster's New International Dictionary*, 2nd ed. (Springfield, MA, 1939), 535.

284   "but they're going to like *you*": Kelly in Hirschhorn, 98; Yudkoff, 75–83; Hyland, 126–32.

284   "he expressed himself to that extent": Rodgers, *Rodgers and Hart Song Book*, 2.

286   "unsentimental and self-mocking": Rodgers, *Musical Stages*, 201.

286   romance without the illusions: Furia, *Poets*, 123–34.

286   "sweet water from a foul well?": In Block, *Reader*, 69–70.

286   "with a knowing point of view": Ibid., 158–59.

286   original substantially intact: On the differences between the two versions, see T. Taylor, 163; Block, *Enchanted Evenings*, 105–7.

287   *I Married an Angel*, *By Jupiter*: See Ewen, *All the Years*, 366. Only in "What Is a Man?," a song during which Vera is actually shown to change her mind, did *Pal Joey* move with the kind of musical dramaturgy the term musical play now implies, where the story is told *through* the songs. There is some doubt, however, whether this number was performed in the original production. See Hart and Kimball, 272.

287   for future developments: On *Pal Joey* as the first in a new breed of Broadway musical, see Engel, *American Musical Theater*, 35; Dizikes, 503.

287   had so richly taken part: Furia, *Poets*, 17–18, 124–25, 175–76.

287   musicals had come to an end: Joshua Logan in Marx and Clayton, 256.

8: The Script Angle

291   had to be able to sing well: Mander and Mitchenson, 21; Gänzl, *The Musical*, 112–23.

292   "to trite or light subjects": Hammerstein, *Lyrics*, 20–21. Hammerstein's earliest published writings use the term musical play more or less synonymously with operetta: "Voices," 14, 70.

292 "routinely melodramatic plot": Traubner, 402; Bordman, *American Operetta*, 151, 154.

292 making such offerings "illegitimate": Bowman and Ball, 178; R. K. White, 101.

292 "farce, musical comedy, and revue": See Jerrold and Macready in L. Levine, 75–76. The distinction also applies to ways of acting: representational versus presentational. In a conventional musical, according to Bert Lahr, "You go down front; you talk to an audience. Where in a dramatic play you cannot do that. You've got to look at one another and play perfectly legitimate." In Lahr, *Notes*, 316.

292 "other than popular": Wentworth and Flexner, 316.

293 "I write plays—*only* plays": M. Hart, *Act One*, 227. S. Bach, 367–68, who concedes that Hart "enriched," "fictionalized," and "improved" portions of *Act One* for artistic effect, concludes: "It didn't matter whether or not it was literally true; it rang with what George Abbott had called that 'Truth-ier Truth.'"

294 *Lady in the Dark* was Hart's brainchild: S. Bach, 216–30; F. Hirsch, *Weill*, 181–203. See also mcclung in Kowalke and Edler, 235–64; mcclung, *American Dreams*; mcclung, Lee, and Kowalke; mcclung, *Lady in the Dark*.

294 "no interest for either of us": M. Hart, *Lady in the Dark*, vocal score, 5. The libretto is in S. Richards, *Great Musicals*, vol. 2, 55–123.

294 "describe the [heroine's] dreams": In F. Hirsch, *Weill*, 182.

295 "a new musical form": M. Hart, *Lady*, vocal score, 5.

295 "the stage no longer produces": F. Hirsch, *Weill*, 184.

296 "one sequence to the next": Horner, 266; F. Hirsch, *Weill*, 196–97.

297 worked with completed librettos: mcclung in Kowalke and Edler, 247.

297 large-scale operetta finales: F. Hirsch, *Weill*, 186; Drew, 315.

298 and take control again: mcclung in Kowalke and Edler, 259–63, traces the different forms Liza's melody takes in the course of her various dreams.

298 with musical side dishes: K. Allen viewed the show favorably purely as a play: "Even without the music and its artistic dances . . . "Lady in the Dark" would be a successful straight play." Brown did not: "Though billed as a musical play . . . it does not belong in the realm of those activities behind the footlights where words supply their own music, where ideas bear close inspection, or where even an unguessable story is told so absorbingly that it holds attention on its own merits."

298 "becomes very good theater": Kronenberger, "Review."

298 "dramatically and psychologically": Hart, *Lady*, vocal score, 5.

299 such works as *Cabaret* (1966) and *Chicago* (1975): Bob Fosse, for example, wrote me of how much *Lady*'s "Circus Dream" had influenced him in the creation of *Chicago*.

299 and saved the guild: Other Theater Guild-related straight plays were also later turned into guild musicals—*Lilliom* (1921) became *Carousel* (1945); *The Pursuit of Happiness* (1933) became *Arms and the Girl* (1950); *The Great Adventure* (1947) became *Darling of the Day* (1968). The Theater Guild also produced several original book musicals, including *Allegro* (1947), *Bells Are Ringing* (1956), *The Unsinkable Molly Brown* (1960), and musical revues, including *The Garrick Gaieties* (1925, 1926, 1930), *Parade* (1925), and *Sing Out, Sweet Land* (1944).

300 example of the genre: E. Norton, "Broadway After World War II," 44, gives pride of place to *Knickerbocker Holiday*.

300 immediate and far-flung: Libretto in Rodgers and Hammerstein, 1–84. Major studies of the work include S. Green, "*Oklahoma!*," 88–94; Swain, 73–97; Mordden, *Rodgers and Hammerstein*, 16–49; Wilk, *O.K.!*; T. Carter.

301 "the script angle of the production": Bone.

301 "No Gags. No gals. No chance": Helburn, 285. On the attribution of this famous quip to Rose Bigman, an assistant to columnist Walter Winchell, see Sagolla, 274, n. 6.

302 "Just 'Aaaaaah!'": Jeffrey Lunden in Secrest, *Somewhere*, 255.

302 be the rousing final number: W. Goldman, 377.

302 "and you mustn't mislead them": Hammerstein in Ormsbee.

303 "talent and personality": de Mille, *Dance to the Piper*, 323.

304 than it was joyous: In a 1985 interview with the author, de Mille said that the point of Hammerstein's original ballet scenario was no more than "spectacle and girls and tights," and that she changed its tenor. "There's no sex in your play," she told me she told Hammerstein. "I want to see the postcards [the girlie pictures hanging in Jud's room]—not as Jud knew them, but as Laurey *thought* he knew them. Now this is a good girl's idea of bad girls. And they're stereotyped, of course . . . full of horror and threat . . . A very sinister ballet, actually." Hammerstein's scenario draft is in a November 16, 1942, typescript in the Rodgers and Hammerstein Library. The final scenario used is in Rodgers and Hammerstein, 49–51. See T. Carter, 121–36.

304 "a musical comedy and failed": Hammerstein in Fordin, 199–200.

305 even called it a "folk operetta": Kronenberger and Nichols in Bordman, *American Operetta*, 149.

305 "song is the servant of the play": Hammerstein, *Lyrics*, 19.

305 "not just *with* its songs": Sondheim, "Musical Theater," 232.

305 musical layouts of the two works: The layout of the songs for *Green Grow the Lilacs* is a composite based on three sources: the typescript in the Berg Collection, NYPL; the "reading version" published by Samuel French; and the Playbill of the 1931 Theater Guild production.

307 "any well-made musical play": Hammerstein, "In Re '*Oklahoma!*'"

307 unaware of any singing at all: "Oh What a Beautiful Mornin'" replaced "Git Along, Little Dogies"; "The Farmer and the Cowman" replaced "Skip to My Lou." Rodgers, *Musical Stages*, 220, made a point of avoiding "authentic" music in the show, a practice he later exalted into an aesthetic principle. With reference to *The King and I*, see Rodgers, "The Background Is Siam."

307 "not to jump but to ooze": In T. Carter, 26.

308 de Mille (1905–1993): Rouben Mamoulian came to Broadway via Hollywood, where he worked notably with Rodgers and Hart on *Love Me Tonight* (1932) and with Hammerstein and Kern on *High, Wide and Handsome* (1936). On Broadway he directed six musical plays, from *Porgy and Bess* to *Lost in the Stars*. Agnes de Mille came to Broadway via ballet (*Rodeo*, 1942) and choreographed fourteen book shows, from *Oklahoma!* to *Come Summer* (1969), with perhaps her finest work in *Brigadoon* and *Paint Your Wagon*.

308 "—the play would stop": Mamoulian in Hutchens.

308 "to describe itself as art": Mamoulian in Palmer, 128.

309 "afraid that Jud will murder Curly": de Mille, "Musical Comedy Tonight."

309 "rest of the play. This was new": de Mille in Newquist, 94–95.

309 "was called musical play." Lerner, *The Musical Theatre*, 160.

310 "production in a specific place": Rodgers, *Musical Stages*, 227.

310 sets of Lemuel Ayers: Gibbs, 34.

311 a better postwar world: Donovan, "Beautiful Mornin'," 483–84; Hasbany, 642–65.

311 feel good about doing so: Most, "'We Know We Belong,'" 81.

311 "tells its friends to buy tickets": In Donovan, "Beautiful Mornin'," 482; Ranney and Fried in S. Green, *Fact Book*, 520–21.

311 *the Moon, Annie Get Your Gun*: Donovan, "*Annie Get Your Gun*," 532–33.

311 sounded like in the theater: Sanjek, vol.3, 239, 352–54. Jack Kapp (1901–1949), president of Decca Records, masterminded his company's recording in 1943 of most of *Oklahoma!*'s songs performed by the Broadway cast, chorus, and orchestra. These were released in a boxed-set album containing six 10-inch double-sided 78-rpm discs (DA 359). When the album sold over a million copies, Decca returned to the studio to record the omitted songs—"It's a Scandal," "Lonely Room," and "The Farmer and the Cowman"—and released them in a separate album as *Oklahoma! Volume Two* (DA-383).

312 American culture, the Broadway musical: Wildbihler and Volklein, xxii.

312 the other way around: Most, *Making Americans*, 122.

313 Annie Oakley (1860–1926): The show is discussed in Fordin, 242–47; Bergreen, 446–60; Jablonski, *Berlin*, 235–46.

313   Wild West Exhibition: Brasmer, 207–14; Toll, *On with the Show*, 163–68; D. Russell.

316   "ANNIE: Why didn't I think of that!": Act 2, scene 3. A composite of *Annie Get Your Gun as a Straight Play Without Music Based on the Original Musical Play* (Chicago: The Dramatic Publishing Company, 1952?), 83, and the *Annie Get Your Gun* typescript (1946?) in the Billy Rose Theater Collection, New York Public Library for the Performing Arts.

316   defense industries in a positive light: Hein, 1–3. See also Hartmann; Honey; Rosen.

316   *Bloomer Girl* was overtly political: Meyerson and Harburg, 187–212.

317   "women's emotions in war": de Mille, *Promenade*, 194.

317   meaning now largely forgotten: Hein, 6–7.

317   "Merman to play her!": Fields in Wilk, *Our Song*, 289.

317   books as well as lyrics: Of an earlier generation, the few consistently successful female lyricists and librettists on Broadway included Rida Johnson Young (1888–1926): *Naughty Marietta* and *Maytime*; Anne Caldwell (1867–1936): *Chin-Chin* (1914) and *The Night Boat* (1920); and Dorothy Donnelly (1880–1928): *Blossom Time* and *The Student Prince*. Those of Dorothy Fields's generation included Betty Comden (1915–2007): *On the Town* and *Bells Are Ringing*; and Carolyn Leigh (1926–1983): *Wildcat* (1960) and *Little Me* (1962). Successful female composers of Broadway musicals have been even fewer and their successes less sustained. They include Kay Swift (1897–1993): *Fine and Dandy* (1930); Mary Rodgers (b. 1931): *Once Upon a Mattress*; and Carol Hall (b. 1936) *The Best Little Whorehouse in Texas*. See also L. A. McLean; Ohl; Forte, 310–30.

317   "one of the boys": Jonathan Schwartz in Winer, 174. Desowitz, 27, maintains Fields actually conceived the show "as a metaphor for her own success as a lyricist in a male-dominated profession."

318   write the music as planned: Bergreen, 446–47.

318   "And with a moon up above": In Fordin, 245.

319   as that of the book writers: Fordin, 244; Bergreen, 450.

319   "Merman acting like Annie Oakley": Garland, "'Annie Get Your Gun.'"

319   "what she really wanted, Frank": Logan, 182.

319   "healthier-minded than when they arrived": Ibid., 113.

320   "Any literate play," Anderson replied: Ibid., 113.

320   "judging it as literate": Bentley, *Playwright as Thinker*, 4–5.

320   "stuff that keeps the numbers apart": Wodehouse, "Agonies," 39.

320   (but often in preproduction versions): Among the other published librettos were *Let'Em Eat Cake* (Alfred A. Knopf, 1933), *I'd Rather Be Right* (Random House, 1937), *The Cradle Will Rock* (Random House, 1938), *Knickerbocker Holiday* (Anderson House, 1938), *Johnny Johnson* (Crown, 1939), *Pal Joey* (Duel, Sloane and Pearce, 1941) and *Lady in the Dark* (Random House, 1941).

320   accorded the status of literature: *Guys and Dolls* was printed in Bentley, *From the American Drama*, vol. 4; *Lost in the Stars* was printed in Hewes. *The Fantasticks* and *Fiddler on the Roof* were printed in Gassner and Barnes, in which Barnes, ix–x, justified their inclusion: They "do have a literary quality apart from the music [although] . . . these are not plays but the febrile, heaving skeletons of the musical theatre. They were fleshed out by music, but they have their own fever, their own strength, and, I think, their own validity." Gassner, on the other hand, justified omitting *Oklahoma!* from *Best Plays of the Modern American Theatre* (1947), xxx: "It would pain me . . . to see *Oklahoma!* shorn of its proper glories, its Richard Rodgers music, and Agnes de Mille choreography. Although good drama can always be good theatre, it does not follow that good theatre always makes good drama."

321   as a text into print: The libretto was published by Alfred A. Knopf in 1953. The show is discussed in McBrien, 300–320; Swain, 129–52; Block, *Enchanted Evenings*, 179–96.

321   "original off which it feeds": Lawson-Peebles, 96; Swain, 136–38.

321   "literate without being highbrow": Robert Garland in Suskin, *Opening Night*, 369.

322   chunks of it verbatim: The Shakespeare sources for *Kate*'s "Shrew" scenes are as follows:

Kiss Me, Kate	*The Taming of the Shrew*
Act 1, scene 5	Act 1, scenes 1 & 2; Act 2, scene 1
Act 1, scene 9	Act 3, scene 2
Act 2, scene 3	Act 4, scenes 1 & 3
Act 2, scene 8	Act 5, scene 2

322   love affairs of his bachelor days: On the original song "Where Is the Life That Late I Led?," see J. H. Long, 4; Seng, 1–2. The line also appears in *Henry IV*, Part 2, V, iii.

324   moved in half steps: "Easy to Love" ultimately appeared in the 1936 film "Born to Dance," sung by James Stewart. See Kimball, *Complete Lyrics of Cole Porter*, 172, 299–301. An unusual instance of Porter revising a song in response to a singer's limitations rather than writing a new one altogether is "Blow, Gabriel, Blow!," which he wrote and rewrote for Merman in *Anything Goes*. The "First Version" is in the Cole Porter Manuscript Collection, Beinecke Library, Yale University.

324   "such a beautiful set": Porter in Millstein, "Words Anent Music," 16.

324   "Shakespeare takes twenty": Spewack, xvi–xvii.

325   at the end of the show: The connections between *Kiss Me, Kate* and *Lady in the Dark* are tenuous but apparently traceable to a common source in an unfinished musical on which the Spewacks collaborated with Weill and Harburg in 1937. See Drew, 286–88.

326   *The Taming of the Shrew* itself: See Block, 193–96; Lawson-Peebles, 95. Studies of musicals of the period from a feminist perspective include R. M. Goldstein, 1–8; Mendenhall, 57–69; S. E. Wolf, "Queer Pleasures," 51–63; and *A Problem*. By contrast, see also Hanson, 13–33.

326   moreover, was seldom choice: McBrien, 223.

326   single show he ever wrote: Spewack, xiii.

326   "harder for everybody else": In Millstein, "Words Anent Music," 55.

327   "she'll thank you for it": Spewack, viii.

327   tongue in cheek, to be sure: The words are actually those of Bella, who seems to have been more central than her husband to the creation of *Kate*. See McBrien, 303–18, 350–51.

327   specifics of a given production: In 1976 *Leave It to Me* was published in S. Richards, *Great Musicals*, more perhaps as a historical curiosity. Apart from *Kiss Me, Kate*, only the London version of *Anything Goes* (Samuel French, 1936) was published during Porter's lifetime.

327   that superseded their events: "An event generates its own specific script, which can be quite different from the actual text of the work. A script is a 'marked-up' text, with deletions, additions, and performance directions pertinent to the production at hand, with a given set of performers and for a specific venue. There is a tension, then, between the generality of text and the individuality of scripts assembled and edited for particular occasions . . . [though] in practice, the boundaries between text and script are fluid." Hinton and Harsh, foreword, 8.

9: Musical Theater: The New Art

331   now often mass, culture: R. Williams, 76–82.

332   "from the masses themselves": Adorno, 43. The concept was originally developed in the chapter "The Culture Industry: Enlightenment as Mass Deception" in Adorno and Horkheimer.

332   "sentimentalities of *South Pacific*": Macdonald, 4, 38–39; Bentley, *Playwright*, 6–7; Jensen, 20–30.

332   never directly part of it: Surely because of *Oklahoma!*'s high profile and prestige, Bentley, *Playwright*, 281–84, used it as a whipping boy for the whole "theatricalist" ethos of

Broadway musicals, which found greater meaning in the integration of a show's artistic elements than in the primacy of its text. See T. Carter, 206–11.

332   "redefine itself as art": Most, *Making Americans*, 155.

333   "a vital, vibrant American art": Gottfried, *Broadway Musicals*, 189; Ewen, *Story*, 233,
      243.

333   "a new dramatic art form": E. Norton, "Some Lovely Music."

333   "in the English-speaking world": Bentley, *Playwright*, 281.

333   "would be more appropriate": Isaacs and Gilder, 452, 493. The term "musical theater"
      was already in circulation but not necessarily limited in this way. On the relationship
      between this *Theatre Arts* issue and the first full-length history of Broadway musicals,
      see Beiswanger, 21, 25–26, 29; C. M. Smith; Stempel, "The First History." See also Kat-
      ter; Canning.

333   choice for the medium itself: Trends in book titles are good indicators of change.
      Examples of the old nomenclature include McSpadden; C. M. Smith; S. Green, *World*.
      Early significant shifts to the new terminology can be seen in Ewen, *Complete Book* and
      Story and *Composers*; Engel, *American Musical Theater*.

333   "(*West Side Story*)": In Engel, *American Musical Theater*, xii.

333   *Fiddler on the Roof* (1964): See Bordman, *American Musical Theatre*, 530; Lerner, *Musical
      Theatre*, 153, 211; Suskin, *Opening Night*, 3–14; Schubert, vol. 6, 701–5.

334   "the emotionality of melodrama": Beidler, 214–15.

334   became the stars themselves: Nichols, 47.

335   *The Sound of Music* (1965): General studies of the Rodgers and Hammerstein collabo-
      ration include D. Taylor; S. Green, *Story* and *Fact Book*; Kislan, "Nine Musical Plays";
      Nolan, *Sound of Their Music*; Mordden, *Rodgers and Hammerstein*.

335   the biggest box office draws: Rodgers and Hammerstein, *Six Plays*; Mast, 201–18.

335   leaves even *Oklahoma!* behind: On Hammerstein's career as a librettist, see Hischak,
      Boy Loses Girl, 27–44; J. B. Jones, 140–60.

335   "*Carousel* is about life and death": In Mordden, *Rodgers and Hammerstein*, 78.

337   "the way the costumes look": Rodgers, *Musical Stages*, 277.

337   unlike that of any other: Swain, 110, claims: "'The Carousel Waltz' has an extraor-
      dinary relationship with the songs in the musical play. Like a classical overture, it
      sets the musical terms of the entire composition and is the main source of musical
      material." Yet there is no indication of the polytonal sounds to which Swain refers
      in Rodgers's holograph of the waltz in the Library of Congress. The idea may have
      been Robert Russell Bennett's, whose orchestration of the waltz, now lost, is used in
      the original cast album recorded in May 1945 (New York: Decca DA) and was later
      replaced by an orchestration of Don Walker's. Stempel, "Composers of Less Than
      Compositions," 3–4.

338   "to the salvation of souls": Bentley, *What Is Theatre?*, 192.

338   "from which *Carousel* was fashioned": Langner, *Magic Curtain*, 391. Molnár previously
      refused both Puccini and Weill the rights to musicalize his play. D'Andre, 6–20. The
      early R & H ballets were the work of de Mille and a dance-music arranger: Buddy
      Lewis for *Oklahoma!*, Trude Rittman for *Carousel* and *Allegro*; and, for *The King and
      I*, Rittman and choreographer Jerome Robbins. *South Pacific* had no choreography as
      such.

338   "would only return in spirit": Mast, 210. See D'Andre, 185–88.

338   "were like musical plays": Dorothy Rodgers in Holden, "Remembering."

338   one continuous dramatic fabric: The *Carousel* numbers directly derived from *Lilliom*
      are usually solos or duets. "June Is Bustin' Out All Over," "Blow High, Blow Low," "A
      Real Nice Clambake," and other chorus and dance ensembles in the show have less to
      do with *Lilliom* than with musical comedy or operetta conventions. See Swain, 99–127;
      Block, *Enchanted Evenings*, 159–78.

339   "unexacting taste and refinement": Gassner, *Dramatic Soundings*, 571.

340   "to do this play" in the first place: James Michener in Fordin, 271.

340 based on *Uncle Tom's Cabin*: For a history of stage transformations of *Uncle Tom's Cabin*, see M. Wood. On historical misrepresentations in the musical, see "*The King and I*: Fact or Fiction?" http://www.thaistudents.com/kingandi.

340 what takes place inside it: On larger cultural interpretations of *South Pacific* and *The King and I*, see McConachie, "'Oriental' Musicals," 385–98; Beidler, 207–22; Klein, 143–222; Most, *Making Americans*, 153–96.

340 "philosophy inspired by Moscow": In Fordin, 270.

340 "World War II sentiments": Gassner, *Dramatic Soundings*, 571.

341 "reappearance of certain characters": Michener, "Happy Talk."

342 "a man worthy to be loved": Michener, *Tales*, 104–6.

343 "the show became great," said Logan: Logan, 230.

343 "toward opera but *in our own way*": L. Bernstein, *Joy of Music*, 178.

343 "as if it were a form of literature": In Engel, *American Musical Theater*, xii.

344 *Man of La Mancha*: Auden's lyrics were ultimately replaced by those of Joe Darion who, while no Auden, was more adept at the task to hand: writing lyrics easily sung, readily understood, and made to work in a show context. See "Song of the Quest" in chapter 12, p. 504.

344 "which came to Daly's last night": E.K.

345 "enough on which to experiment": Lerner, "Advice," ix. Engel, *American Musical Theater*, 38–39, 56, elevates this stance into a principle: "The paucity of thoroughly original librettos is due to a general lack of understanding of the requirements of the musical theater as opposed to those of non-musical plays. The dramatic form of the musical is necessarily a different one, and one of its aspects—the skeletal quality which allows music and lyrics to assume functional roles—is not generally known by many of even our best writers . . . Whatever might account for it, the fact is that 'original' books for musical shows have not been as workable as adaptations of existing material."

346 Shaw's *Caesar and Cleopatra*: Why these shows failed is discussed in Mandelbaum, *Not Since "Carrie."* On "flops," see also Rosenberg and Harburg, 107, 171, 303–33.

347 "among Nazi Germany's victims": R. Knapp, "History," 135–36. The immediately perceived issues, however, were rather Catholic principles and Austrian nationalism. See Trapp, 127–42.

347 "in the forties and fifties": Atkinson and Tynan in S. Green, *Fact Book*, 634–35.

347 "conventional musical comedy": Hammerstein, "Turns." By contrast, R & H admit their preference in *Pipe Dream* for characters whose "problems are simple. . . . We find pleasure that their worries, this time, are not concerned with the future of a kingdom [*King and I*] or with miscegenation [*South Pacific*]. Just like other beasts, we need desperately to have change in our lives." In Mandelbaum, *Not Since "Carrie,"* 99.

348 "to pay for being Rodgers and Hammerstein": Steinbeck in Fordin, 327–28.

348 concluding it couldn't be done: Lerner, *Street*, 38; Langner, *G.B.S.*, 244–45.

348 "to the origins they provided": Lerner, *Musical Theatre*, 186.

348 two teams largely overlapped: General studies of Lerner and/or the Lerner and Loewe collabortation include Lerner, *Musical Theatre*; B. Green, *Hymn to Him*; Lees; D. Shapiro; Citron, *The Wordsmiths*; Jablonski, *Alan Jay Lerner*.

349 (*Paint Your Wagon*), and beyond: While Loewe still wrote the dance and vocal arrangements for *Brigadoon*, he entrusted more of these responsibilities to Trude Rittman over time so that by *Camelot* it was she who did them all. See Pomahac.

349 "part of his plays in rhyme": B. Green, *Hymn to Him*, 7–8.

350 "Nevertheless, that is what I am": Lerner, *Street*, 23.

350 "orchestrated Scottish idyll": In Suskin, *Opening Night*, 103.

350 "plays, novels or short stories": Lerner, *Musical Theatre*, 162. See also Hischak, *Boy Loses Girl*, 199–230.

350 literary source for *Brigadoon*: Theater critic George Jean Nathan openly accused Lerner of lifting *Brigadoon*'s plot from "Germelshausen," a nineteenth-century German tale by Friedrich Gerstäcker. Lerner vehemently denied this. (At stake was the

author's honor, as there was no financial interest involved; Gerstacker's work was in the public domain.) For Lerner's views on book adaptations, see his *Musical Theatre*, 162; "Reader Questions Origin"; "Advice," vii–ix. See also Lees, 49–50; B. Green, *Hymn to Him*, 29–30.

350   was based so much as *adopt* it: Mordden, *Roses*, 154. Key studies of the show include Swain, 179–200; Garebian, *Making of My Fair Lady*; Block, *Enchanted Evenings*, 225–44; S. Bach, 334–65. Lerner's account is in *Street*, 30–135.

351   "write a non-love song?": Lerner, *Street*, 36–37.

351   "dramatized in music and lyrics": Lerner, *Street*, 43; *Musical Theatre*, 186.

352   only implied in the original: On Shaw's afterthoughts on his play and his subsequent reworking of it for the film, see Silver, 107–30; Goodman, 303, 313–15. Lerner's first libretto drafts reveal how far off the mark he was until he realized the film version gave him virtually all the structure he needed (S. Bach, 340). Even Loewe was influenced by the film through Arthur Honegger's score: The xylophone's "How kind of you to let me come" in the film's whole-tone setting crops up again in "The Rain in Spain," albeit in a more diatonic form.

352   "nor a great lyric," Lerner admitted: Lerner, "Creation." The lyrics are semantically close to empty—hardly lyrics at all. But because the rhymed exercise for the long vowel "a" in English happened to have the word "Spain" in it, Loewe set it as a tango: a kind of musical pun. Ironically, the musical allusion to Spain (or at least Latin culture), now so inextricably part of the song, often gets lost in translation. The exercise Eliza sings to the same music in the Japanese version of the show is meant to rid her of her inner-city Tokyo accent (*shitamachi*) and it means, when rendered into English, "The Sun Rises in the East/The Sun Sets in the West" (*He wa hegashi ni noboru/He wa nishini shizumu*).

352   "the spirit of the Irish Pope": Lerner, *Street*, 45.

353   "any other musical to date": Ibid., 67.

353   some of its writing: S. Bach, 342–43.

353   "either the musical or dramatic stage": Atkinson, "Everybody's Lady."

353   W. S. Gilbert to Noël Coward: Gama's song in *Princess Ida* may not have been a conscious model for Higgins's "I'm an Ordinary Man," but Noël Coward's "Mad Dogs and Englishmen" certainly was a model for "Why Can't the English?" An early version of the song, which shows the Coward touch, can be found on the overside sheets to Loewe's piano-vocal holographs for "Show Me" and "I Could Have Danced All Night" in the Loewe Collection, Music Division, Library of Congress.

354   "speaks and acts his songs admirably": Bentley, *What Is Theatre?*, 283. Harrison's spoken delivery of Higgins's lines also determined the entrance and pacing of the music he sang, not the other way around. "I could not use [conductor Franz Allers] in the way a singer does. I never waited for the beat, he had to catch mine. I never looked at him, he had to follow me. This was quite revolutionary. I would start a number straight out of dialogue and go into the song, without changing tempo, and this was something he'd never had to cope with, and created a problem for him in bringing the orchestra in at the exact moment. But he always managed to do it, and although my rhythm patterns were never quite the same from night to night we always caught up with each other fore or aft" (Harrison, 163).

354   as *My Fair Lady*'s logo: Al Hirschfeld (1903–2003) became Broadway's preeminent caricaturist and cartoonist over a phenomenally long carrer in which his work appeared most influentially in the *New York Times*. See Hirschfeld, *World*; *Hirschfeld*; *Hirschfeld: Art*; *Hirschfeld On Line*.

354   "mineral oil of the musical's dénouement": Gassner, *Crossroads*, 206.

354   "over the obstacles of social class": Mast, 309.

355   "to misfit all stories": B. Shaw, 782.

355   "I am not certain he is right": Lerner, "Note," 7.

355   formed the basis of the show: T. H. White, "What It's Like," 117.

356   subject better suited to comedy: Lerner, *Street*, 190; see also 188–254.

356   "if he were Ibsen": T. H. White, "What It's Like," 117.

356   "not wholly an Ibsen tragedy": Ibid., 116–17. On the problems of *Camelot*, see Schroth, 36; Swain, 200–204. Lerner himself revised the work several times: three months into the Broadway run, for the West End, for Hollywood, and for a 1981 Broadway revival.

356   "that was known / As Camelot": Jacqueline Kennedy in T. H. White, "For President Kennedy," 159.

356   "a noble message and a bittersweet ending": Beidler, 219. As Camelot became synonymous with Kennedy's presidency, Lerner's lines informed the historical writing about it, from the titles of books (Manchester) to their rhetoric (Schlesinger, Jr., 1031): "Above all he gave the world for an imperishable moment the vision of a leader who greatly understood the terror and the hope, the diversity and the possibility, of life on this planet and who made people look beyond nation and race to the future of humanity."

357   "Broadway had hitherto envisioned": Walsh and Platt, 116.

357   but again without great success: More than three decades after its Broadway premiere, *Rex* has been meeting with audience approval in a newly revised version, most recently produced in 2010 by Toronto's Civic Light Opera Company.

358   *Catch a Star!*, 1955: See LoMonaco. Tamiment was a training ground for many talents, including Bea Arthur, Carol Burnett, Danny Kaye, Jerome Robbins, Neil Simon, and Woody Allen. Harold Rome, who gained early experience at Green Mansions, wrote the songs to *Wish You Were Here* (1952), whose setting was a Green Mansions–style adult summer camp. On the Harnick and Bock collaboration, see Kasha and Hirschhorn, 152–69.

358   their response was: "The book": Harnick, 38.

358   "the feeling of time and place": Such songs stood in opposition to what Harnick called "the institution of the divertissement—that is, songs (or dances) which are actually extraneous to the book, no matter how entertaining. There's nothing wrong with divertissements, whether inserted as moments of sheer frolic, or as editorial comment, but they have little to do with the kind of collaboration between librettist, lyricist, and composer that I am writing about." Harnick, 38–39.

361   a respected literary vehicle: Ozick, 99. On *Fiddler*'s relation to Aleichem, see Slobin, "Some Intersections," 41–42; Wolitz, 514–36; Whitfield, "Fiddling," 105–25.

362   John Kander and Fred Ebb: On Stein's career, see Hischak, *Boy Loses Girl*, 190–96. On *Fiddler*, see Altman and Kaufman; Guernsey, *Broadway Song and Story*, 115–34; Swain, 247–74.

362   "IN TERMS OF HIS DAUGHTERS AND THEIR SUITORS": Robbins in Altman and Kaufman, 43. For the full text, see Harnick Papers, Manuscript Archives, Wisconsin State Historical Society, Madison.

363   journey from exclusion to acceptance: Altman and Kaufman, 90; Most, *Making Americans*, 3.

363   "He said, 'It's so Japanese!'": Stein in Guernsey, *Song & Story*, 132.

364   "the very thing he repudiated": Ozick, 103.

364   but a place of exile: Wolitz, 516, 519, 527.

364   American popular culture: On the idea of "disproportionate" cultural representation, see Most, *Making Americans*, 7. On American Jews and Broadway musicals, see W. Goldman, 146–53; Steyn, 74–87; Whitfield, *In Search*, 59–87; Mast, 34–37, 296.

364   as Jews—though most perhaps did: Oscar Hammerstein II was raised by his mother as an Episcopalian, although his father was Jewish. See Fordin, 16; Most, *Making Americans*, 225.

364   as Jews—even though some were not: Gentile theater producer and Boston Red Sox owner Harry Frazee sold Babe Ruth to the New York Yankees allegedly to finance *No, No, Nanette*. Vilified in newspaper reports that portrayed him as a Jew, he did not dis-

pute the claim because he felt "it helped him in New York for some to believe he was Jewish." Stout and Johnson, 148; Levesque. (Ruth was actually sold to the Yankees in 1919; *Nanette* was not produced until 1924. In 1919, however, Frazee did produce the play *My Lady Friends*, on which *Nanette* was later based. See Bordman, *Days to be Happy*, 75–76.)

364   *Oklahoma!'s* "Persian" peddlar: D'Andre, 181; J. B. Jones, 146–47; Kadison and Bul-off. The R & H shows also reveal a general, perhaps not unrelated secularizing trend. *Carousel's* inspirational but worldly "You'll Never Walk Alone" replaces a reading of St. Matthew's Beatitudes in *Lilliom*. And the nuns' "Morning Hymn," sung in Latin in *The Sound of Music*, is a textually appropriate "Jesu Rex admirabilis" (attributed to St. Bernard of Clairvaux), but with "Jesu" omitted. (Accounts vary over the compo-sition of the music to this and other liturgical-style numbers in the show: Rodgers, *Musical Stages*, 301; Clarke, 9. Trude Rittmann, the show's rehearsal pianist, wrote the author in 1996: "Mother Morgan's recollections [in Clarke] sound much 'truer' to me than do Dick's. He did *not* write the liturgical pieces but, as usual, things were often mixed with lots of input by T[rude] R[ittmann] and Russell Bennett.")

365   annihilated by the Second World War: Harnick in Guernsey, *Song & Story*, 121, relates that Robbins wanted to "put the shtetl life onstage to give another twenty-five years of life to that shtetl culture which had been devastated during World War II. That was his vision." Harnick goes on in a 2006 letter to the author: "In my opinion, [Robbins] was obsessed with that mission from the time he became our director until the curtain went up on opening night." The show's nostalgia, however, confounded Russian com-poser Dmitri Shostakovich, who saw the film of *Fiddler* while on a trip to the United States: "What astounded me about it: the primary emotion is homesickness. . . . Even though the motherland is a so-and-so, a bad, unloving country, more a stepmother than a mother." Shostakovich, 158. While the authenticity of *Testimony's* authorship has been the subject of much debate, the perception remains valid whether or not it was Shostakovich's own.

365   those values were meaningful: On "Jewish" musicals of the period, see J. B. Jones, 205–24.

365   that began with *Oklahoma!*: Lerner, *Musical Theatre*, 211, 153. See also Bowers, which ends with *Fiddler*.

10: Opera, in Our Own Way

369   male lead, bass Ezio Pinza: The differences between operatic or "legit" vocal produc-tion and singing of the Broadway kind—bel canto vs. can belto—are discussed in Osborne; Banfield, "Entertainers," 63–67, 74–81. On Pinza's leaving the Metropolitan Opera to star in *South Pacific*, see Taubman, "Metropolitan's Basso"; Pinza, 3–4; Pinza and Magidoff.

369   "that precisely this was happening": Graf, 133, 150.

370   "I tried to emotionalize everything": Loesser in Millstein, "Loesser," 22. Even parts of the work now spoken were originally meant to be sung. See Frank Loesser Manu-scripts, Music Division, New York Public Library for the Performing Arts. Important studies of *Fella* can be found in Block, "Loesser's Sketchbooks," 60–78; and *Enchanted Evenings*, 211–23; Swain, 153–78.

370   get it all onto an original cast recording: *The Most Happy Fella*, 3 LPs. New York: Columbia 03L-240, 1956.

370   "a musical play of operatic proportions": Weill, Notes to *Street Scene*; and "Musical The-atre," 1.

371   "those with operatic pretensions": In Gruen, *Menotti*, 98–99.

371   "concerted move to chuck them": In H. Burton, 271.

371   "for any goddamned Bernstein opera!": In Zadan, 14. Laurents, 329, denies ever saying

anything of the sort, claiming Bernstein was not above "proxy attribution . . . to justify what he considered his capitulation, because *West Side* wasn't an opera."

371   the more they avoided "the O word": M. Walsh, *Who's Afraid of Opera?*, 154.
371   "rather term it a dramatic musical": Weill, "Broadway Opera," 42. When published, *Street Scene* was called "An American Opera."
372   "a musical—with a lot of music": F. Loesser, 17.
372   "more unconventional music than *South Pacific*": L. Bernstein, "Prelude."
372   his musicals of the later 1940s: Stempel, "*Street Scene*," 321–34; Kowalke, "Weill and the Quest," 283–301.
372   no more suitable generic designation: On different uses of the term, see Graf, 133–50; Engel, *American Musical Theater*, 132–54; Stempel, "Musical Play," 147–55.
373   grand in the operatic sense: Grand opera generally denotes any serious, large-scale, all-sung stagework produced by an opera company. In the historically specific sense however, the term refers to a particular subgenre of opera that flourished from the 1830s to the 1860s at the Paris Opera and which is associated above all with the collaborations of composer Giacomo Meyerbeer and librettist Eugène Scribe—*Robert le diable*; *Les Huguenots*; *Le Prophète*.
373   "but *in our own way*": L. Bernstein, *Joy of Music*, 178.
374   through which opera had become popular: DiMaggio, 22, 30; McConachie, "New York Operagoing," 187; L. W. Levine, 85–104.
375   "a continuum of aesthetic practice": DiMaggio, 43.
375   "social salvation" that Henry James called it: James in J. Horowitz, 37.
375   educating and improving audiences: DiMaggio, 21–22, 31; Dizikes, 435–37.
375   "not granted to the amusement trades": Thomson, *Reader*, 352.
376   "Opera was a way people lost money": Hammerstein, *Carmen Jones*, xiii.
376   ran on Broadway for over two years: Ardoin, 83.
376   and nearly lost their shirts: The Company also produced such unusual musicals as *Knickerbocker Holiday* and *Juno*. See Wharton, 151–56, 185–86, 190–93.
376   "something richer, truer, deeper": C. Crawford, 173. Crawford, 93–97, 114–44, 163–82, also produced *Johnny Johnson*, *One Touch of Venus*, *Brigadoon*, and *Paint Your Wagon*, and would have produced *West Side Story* but for a falling out with its authors before rehearsals.
377   "inadequate to handle the dramatic line": Thomson, "*Regina*."
377   presented in opera houses ever since: On Blitzstein's revisions of *Regina*, see E. A. Gordon, 364–65, 434–35.
377   "has the controlling interest": Banfield, "Bit by Bit," 220.
377   "In *The Medium* the drama is the music": Atkinson in Suskin, *Opening Night*, 429–30.
378   "than in most opera": Banfield, *Sondheim*, 6–7. See also Osolsobe; Bolcom, "Parallel Universes," 34–36, 57.
378   gave access to a wider audience: Weill, "Future of Opera," 187; Menotti in Gruen, *Menotti*, 124.
378   than opera alone appeared to offer: G. Gershwin, "Rhapsody"; Loesser in Millstein, "Great Loesser," 22; Bentley, *What Is Theatre?*, 192.
379   an offer more to the composer's liking: Stravinsky and Craft, 404. Craft relates that while Stravinsky imagined a Broadway production for *Rake* along the lines of *The Consul*, potential backers were reluctant to invest without first hearing the score, which Stravinsky refused to permit for nonmusicians. "Eventually, Billy Rose's opinion was sought (if not his money); but, like the others, he wanted to hear the piece and therefore had to be smuggled, like Odysseus among Polyphemus's sheep, into a group of Stravinsky's musician friends for whom the composer had agreed to play the opera. After a very few minutes, Mr. Rose's countenance clearly implied that Tom Rakewell could expect a crueler fate in the commercial theater than in Bedlam."
379   "a musical play, based on an opera": Hammerstein, *Carmen Jones*, xv.
379   "battle for artistic honors": Hammerstein, "Voices," 70.

379   "the *genre* of *opéra-comique*" with his: Bizet in McClary, 16, 44–45. Like Hammerstein, Bizet was aware of his own limitations. He wrote to his friend Ernest Guiraud: "Your place is at the Opéra; I'm afraid of making a poor showing there, of not having the necessary fullness. I shall shine at the Opéra-Comique; I shall enlarge and transform the genre." With *Carmen*, he did.

379   edifying characters, and happy endings: McClary, 45.

380   "to the pleasures of 'high art'": McClary, 121. See also Dahlhaus, *Realism*, 88–92.

380   more focused on the audience: Hammerstein, *Carmen Jones*, xiv–xv.

380   "improve the audience or even instil a vision": Banfield, "Bit by Bit," 221.

381   an African American, was similarly marginalized: Having chosen a black milieu for Carmen Jones and her intimates because of its parallels with that of the gypsies in Spain, Hammerstein may have made all of the characters in the show black to avoid the racial disparity between Bizet's lovers, which would have been intolerable for American audiences at the time. On the musical's racial dimensions, see McClary, 132; Woll, 184–89.

381   "singable, understandable, and dramatic": Hammerstein, *Carmen Jones*, xvii. On the impediments to textual intelligibility in opera generally, see P. Robinson, 328–29, 333–41.

381   to replace it in *Carmen Jones*: The *Carmen* vocal score Hammerstein used is in the Library of Congress, Music Division; Robert Russell Bennett's full score and parts are in the Rodgers and Hammerstein Music Library. Here is the original French text:
      Rien n'y fait, menace ou prière,
      L'un parle bien, l'autre se tait;
      Et c'est l'autre que je préfère.
      Il n'a rien dit, mais il me plaît.

382   *Antony and Cleopatra*, 1966: M. Rich et al., vol. 3, 419–20; Dizikes, 435–37, 451–52.

382   a grant from the Ford Foundation: M. Rich et al., vol. 3, 420; Dizikes, 460–70.

383   Curtis Institute of Music: Studies of Menotti include Gruen, *Menotti*; Ardoin; Casmus; Wlaschin.

383   "I proved with *The Medium* and *The Consul*": In Ardoin, 99–100.

384   he saw as "the opera problem": Boulez in Buzga.

384   as through-composed music dramas: Swain, 357, dismisses "the whole terminological business" because, by whatever name, "the matter at hand is music drama." Stravinsky is less ecumenical: "I believe 'music drama' and 'opera' to be two very, very different things. My life work is a devotion to the latter." In E. W. White, 452.

384   Elton John and Tim Rice's *Aida*, 2000: Whether *Carmen Jones* was itself a parody is discussed in Rosenfield; Nichols, "Carmen Jones."

385   Weill, Blitzstein, Loesser, and Bernstein: Major studies of *Porgy and Bess* include Durham; Alpert; Kimball, *Complete Lyrics of Ira Gershwin*, 235–41; Swain, 51–72; Block, *Enchanted Evenings*, 60–84.

385   "neither of the theatre nor entertaining": G. Gershwin, "Rhapsody."

385   "Gershwin wrestling with his medium": Thomson, "George Gershwin," 18.

386   ragtime, spirituals, blues, and jazz: R. Crawford, "Porgy and Bess," vol. 3, 1062.

387   to the brink of despair: Ibid., 1063.

389   "that amazingly impede the action": Atkinson, "'Porgy and Bess.'"

389   "sheer Broadway entertainment": Downes, "'Porgy and Bess.'"

389   "sure-fire rubbish": L. Gilman.

389   "falling between two stools": Thomson, "Gershwin," 17.

389   where its folk element was concerned: R. Crawford, "Ain't Necessarily Soul," 26–30.

389   "folk-opera about Negroes": Cruse, 103.

389   culture the show purported to represent: H. Johnson, 26.

390   followed by a national tour: Thomson in Dizikes, 461.

390   fifty years after its premiere: Hamm, "Theatre Guild Production," 495–532.

391   Gershwin's own wishes in this regard: Drew, 354.

391 "without benefit of subsidy my life work": In Kowalke, "Weill, Modernism," 58.

392 "tragedy of racism (*Lost in the Stars*)": Feingold, "Weill Party," 5. Major discussions in English of Weill's American career are in Sanders, 209–403; Kowalke, *A New Orpheus*, 269–341; Drew, 274–435; Spoto, 121–343; R. Taylor, 216–334; Kilroy; Schebera, 236–337; Kowalke and Symonette, 191–493; F. Hirsch, *Kurt Weill*, 124–366.

393 "then the sudden, swift catastrophe": Andrew Porter in Lee et al., 48.

393 no tragedy in the strict sense: Heilman, *Tragedy and Melodrama*. Bentley, *Playwright as Thinker*, 86–89, argues that opera is generically incapable of tragedy.

394 "creates a unity of drama and music" Weill in Lee et al., 28.

394 theme song, "Lonely House": Weill in Hinton, "*Street Scene*," vol. 4, 580.

394 at the climax of their duet: Weill in F. Hirsch, *Weill*, 271: The duet "reaches the climax . . . when Sam asks her to kiss him, and here the lilac-bush theme should sing out in the orchestra."

396 "elite adulation in a single stroke": Douglas, 70.

396 "without the quality of self-involvement": Wilder, 133.

396 "the concept of a composer as such": Adorno in Kowalke, *A New Orpheus*, 218–19; Hinton, "Kurt Weill," vol. 4, 1124–29.

396 "regardless of the style I am writing in": Weill, letter to Sablosky, July 24, 1948 (Kurt Weill Foundation).

397 "a post-modernist before his time": Hinton, "Kurt Weill," 1127; Kowalke, "Weill, Modernism," 56–69.

397 TV show that focused on the arts: See Buck; Rose.

397 "musical theater has ever known": L. Bernstein, *Joy of Music*, 164, 174.

398 "creative talent at this precise time": Ibid., 179.

398 "musical or plot materials": C. M. Smith, 204.

398 "like Mozart; but not probable": Kerman, 269.

399 *1600 Pennsylvania Avenue* (1976): Major studies of Benstein include Peyser, *Bernstein*; Gradenwitz; Ledbetter; Fluegel; S. Chapin; H. Burton; Secrest, *Leonard Bernstein*; W. W. Burton; Oja, *Leonard Bernstein*.

400 after Koussevitzky's death in 1951: Peyser, *Bernstein*, 147–48; H. Burton, 136–37.

400 "notwithstanding, a serious musical work": In H. Burton, 470.

400 "opera, which is not operetta, either": D. Schiff, "Re-hearing," 68.

400 Sondheim, writing his first Broadway lyrics: Major discussions of *West Side Story* include Guernsey, *Song & Story*, 40–54; Garebian, *West Side Story*; Swain, 205–46; Block, *Enchanted Evenings*, 245–73; Banfield, *Sondheim*, 31–38.

401 their wedding, in a dress shop: For a synopsis of the Shakespeare/Laurents parallels, see Engel, *Words*, 234–42; for an interpretation of the divergences, see G. Jackson, 97–101.

401 "of one of the play's protagonists": Houghton, *Romeo and Juliet*, 11.

401 "merely an exhibition of bad taste." J. Martin "'West Side Story,'" 2:15.

401 Hispanics and Latino culture altogether: See Rusk, L 83; Sandoval-Sánchez, 66–82; Wells.

402 "That was the true *gesture* of the show": In Guernsey, *Song & Story*, 54.

402 "the characters are so inarticulate": Atkinson, "Jungles," 14; Taubman, "Foot," 2:9.

402 "the whole piece, inverted, done backwards," etc.: Bernstein in H. Burton, 274.

403 words where now it has none: Bernstein in Guernsey, *Song & Story*, 44. For the original words, see *West Side Story* typescript #549, Billy Rose Theater Collection, New York Public Library for the Performing Arts.

404 "into circling pools of hostility": Kerr, "'West Side Story.'"

404 "never falling into the 'operatic' trap": Bernstein, *Findings*, 144.

405 into "I Have a Love": See Stempel in Ledbetter, 49–51.

405 "I don't *want* pear-shaped tones": Lawrence in W. W. Burton, 178. In what seems like an act of self-indulgence, Bernstein later conducted and recorded a singularly unidiomatic version of the show with opera singers (2CDs, New York: Deutsche Grammo-

phon 415 253–2, 1985), which demands comparison with the original cast recording (LP, New York: Columbia OL 5230, 1957) for its implications to be understood.

405 "clean decision not to set it at all": In H. Burton, 275; Guernsey, *Song & Story*, 44.

405 "in this genre that is not opera": Banfield, *Sondheim*, 290.

405 "a new age in the theater": Ewen, *Story*, 242.

406 "This, to my regret, has not really happened": In Gruen, "In Love," 18.

406 "quite contrary or at least wholly new": G. Martin, "On the Verge," 79. See also Verdino-Sullwold, 31–43.

407 "*The Music Man* as Best Musical": Lerner, *Musical Theatre*, 192.

11: The Great American Showshop

411 "whoever heard of such a thing?": In Oliver, *By George*, 191. The *NYT* had earlier published a less inspired debate on the matter between Fred Lounsberry, "Down with Sense" (June 22, 1952), and Richard Rodgers, "In Defense of Sense," (June 29, 1952).

412 the artifice of the musical stage: See Mordden, *Babies*, 147; Banfield, *Sondheim*, 92.

412 for distinguishing between the two: Lamb, "Musical Comedy," vol. 12, 815; "Musical," vol. 3, 289; Kowalke, "Das Goldene Zeitalter," 137–78. "Musical" was adopted by the *NYT* in its annual listing of theater productions beginning in 1944. See Beckerman and Siegman, xxii.

413 "a hit even before the curtain went up": Styne in Kislan, *The Musical*, 222.

414 musical plays in the postwar period: For structural comparison of musical comedies and musical plays, see Engel, *American Musical Theater*, 71–121; and *Words*, 224–27; Frankel, 95–117; Kislan, *The Musical*, 190, 221–34; Kowalke, "Das Goldene Zeitalter," 158–61.

415 Germany is said to have begun: Jansen, 29–30; Schubert, vol. 6, 704–5.

415 "theatergoers around the world flowed": Gänzl, *The Musical*, 283. Gänzl, 337, lists seventy-three Broadway musicals that played London between 1945 and 1970.

415 "the great American showshop": Garland, "*Carmen Jones*."

416 107 million people watched: Mordden, *Roses*, 204–5; *Rodgers and Hammerstein*, 179–80. Baxter, 157–58, cites over sixty new musicals and operas presented on television between 1955 and 1959, far more than in any comparable period before or since.

416 Broadway show into a hit almost overnight: Lerner, *Street*, 244–46.

417 "*Foxy* was damaged": Blyden in Lahr, *Notes*, 315.

418 "They took over the show": C. Feuer, 180–81.

419 behind American musical comedy: Studies of Abbott include his memoir, *Mister Abbott*; F. Hirsch, *Harold Prince*, 22–39; Hischak, *Boy Loses Girl*, 72–83.

420 *Three Men on a Horse*, 1935: These plays became the basis for three non-Abbott musicals during Abbott's lifetime: *Chicago* (1975), *On the Twentieth Century* (1978), and *Banjo Eyes* (1941).

420 "wear and tear on the nervous system": Abbott in Berger.

421 "common sense into the musical": In F. Hirsch, *Prince*, 23.

421 "what is put in and what is taken out": Abbott, *Mister Abbott*, 263–64.

422 missing from Bissell's book: See Atkinson, "Pajama Game."

423 "an hour or two and see what happens": Bissell, 46–48. *Say Darling* became the basis for a 1958 musical for which Bissell and his wife, Marian, coadapted the book with Abe Burrows.

424 caught in the zipper of his pants: Walter Kerr in Suskin, *Opening Night*, 535.

424 just what it needed to know: Mordden, *Roses*, 101.

424 backers from investing in it: Prince, *Contradictions*, 8–10.

424 "with no propaganda either way": Abbott, "Musicals Take Over," 96.

425 "capital and labor? The audience's!": In F. Hirsch, *Prince*, 29.

426   as Broadway would allow: Studies of Harburg include Meyerson and Harburg; Hischak, *Boy Loses Girl*, 101–7. Harburg also published two volumes of non-song light
verse: see Harburg, *At This Point* and *Rhymes*.

426   "Listen to our songs": Harburg in Brahms and Sherrin, 126–27.

426   Hammerstein's musical plays: Mordden, *Babies*, 147; Meyerson and Harburg, 184.

427   a showcase for Lena Horne: Meyerson and Harburg, 227.

427   and *Saratoga*, 1959: Studies of Arlen include Jablonski, *Happy*; and *Rhythm*; Bach and
Mercer; Furia, *Skylark*.

427   "form of the American musical": Meyerson and Harburg, 221.

427   told in two interlocking fables: Kronenberger in Suskin, *Opening Night*, 213.

429   "skin making such a difference": Harburg in A. Wolf.

429   "back for another glimpse of it." Kronenberger in Suskin, *Opening Night*, 213.

430   the names of former associates: Navasky, 74.

430   "optimism, essential superiority": L. Bernstein, "Colloquy." The discussion of *Candide*
here stems from the show's political and satirical ties to *Finian* and *Flahooley*. Yet it
constitutes a digression, since *Candide* does not fully fit the terms of this chapter: It
resembles an operetta more than a musical comedy; it does not come out of any of the
four networks of collaborators; and it is not a representative product of the "great
American showshop."

430   to be read into the record: Rollyson, 572–73.

431   "at the naming of names": *Candide* typescript, 1–2–13, Billy Rose Theater Collection,
NYPL for the Performing Arts.

431   "So there's nothing we can buy!": Random House (1957) published the Broadway version of *Candide*; Avon (1970) published the original version.

432   "it's real garment-trade stuff": Miller in W. W. Burton, 109, 113.

432   concert version (1989, rev. 1993): On the differences between the versions, see J. A.
Conrad, vol. 1, 713–14; N. Bernstein, 4.

432   Bernstein said, to European music: In H. Burton, 260.

433   "You're a whore": Ibid., 263.

433   "the exposure of false ones": Guthrie, 241. See also Engel, *Words*, 250–54.

433   "Your paycheck": In Mordden, *Roses*, 39.

433   of the postwar generation: Studies of Loesser include A. Loesser; Mann; Burrows,
Honest Abe; S. Loesser; C. Feuer. See also Kimball and Nelson; Garebian, *Making of
Guys and Dolls*.

434   culture that they disdained: A. Loesser, 217–39; S. Loesser, 6–17; Konas, 264–75.

434   "best of all American musical comedies": Bentley, *From the American Drama*, ix.

434   to create a new one: Mann, 68; Hischak, *Boy Loses Girl*, 153–56.

434   "more Runyonesque than Runyonese": Eyre, 36.

435   "songs that were already written": Burrows, *Honest Abe*, 149; Burrows, "Making of *Guys
and Dolls*," 40–47, 50–52.

439   "to have certain other rules," he said: In Millstein, "Greater Loesser," 22.

440   "the thing a bond salesman does": Loesser in Drutman, 5:2.

441   a Broadway *Beggar's Opera*: Burrows in Mann, 69.

441   her trade she caught a cold: See Runyon, 300.

441   "for more than just one joke": Loesser in Drutman.

442   its characters remained one-dimensional: Burrows, "How to Succeed," 59. See also S.
Miller, *From "Assassins,"* 95–108.

443   a direct influence on their work: S. Loesser, 222–29.

443   with the book and score for the first: See Willson's three memoirs, *And There, Eggs I
Have Laid*, and *Territory*, which recounts the making of *The Music Man*. See also Skipper; Hischak, *Boy Loses Girl*, 156–58.

443   ("Minuet in G"): Brantley, "Rogue"; S. Miller, *Deconstructing Harold Hill*, 73–94.

444   "a ballad waltz for her": Willson, *Territory*, 37–38.

445   "the musical as a con game": Brantley, "Rogue."

446   "our unofficial city anthem": http://www.leonardbernstein.com/events/news/news_
       page.asp?id=69.

446   their own satiric material: See Comden; Comden and Green; Kasha and Hirschhorn,
       62–73; Hischak, *Boy Loses Girl*, 109–17.

446   "the Marx Brothers rolled into one": Stone in Haun, "Comden & . . ."

447   "and promoting a production": F. Rich, "David Merrick." See also Kissel.

447   "sophisticated taste of Yogi Berra": Schapp, 43–44.

447   55–60 percent for all his shows: Rosenberg and Harburg, 7, 58.

447   was the most distinguished: On *Gypsy*, see T. Taylor, 192–219; Guernsey, *Song & Story*,
       55–74; Zadan, 36–62; Garebian, *Making of Gypsy*; S. Miller, *Assassins*, 84–94; Kasha and
       Hirschhorn, 286–301.

449   "filled out by the songs they sing": Laurents in Zadan, 61–62.

449   the life of a famous stripper: Laurents in T. Taylor, 197–98.

449   "you'll destroy yourself": Laurents in Millstein, "Culled."

450   "language of pure musical comedy": Lerner, *Musical Theatre*, 195.

451   "sublime ambition in such vernacular terms": Banfield, "Ironbridge," 88.

453   "and true to the situation": Sondheim in Guernsey, *Song & Story*, 69.

453   "choose one of those two things": Hammerstein in ibid., 69–70.

454   "But it's not very cheerful": Sondheim in Zadan, 52.

12: Away from Broadway

461   called the Off Broadway musical: D. M. Flinn, *Musical!*, 332–37; Mordden, *Open Win-
       dow*, 175–91.

461   whose heart was Times Square: On earlier New York theater districts, see M. C. Hen-
       derson, *City*; Frick.

461   a hit or a flop: Lacking the state subsidies common in European theaters, a Broadway
       show was usually financed as a speculative business venture by an ad hoc group of pri-
       vate investors who collectively risked large sums of money to meet the show's start-up
       and running expenses in the hope of ultimately reaping profits from a long run in New
       York and its economic consequences. See T. G. Moore; Langley; Rosenberg and Har-
       burg, 3–68; Fink, 285–93.

461   at the top in the American theater: See R. Gilman, 77.

462   "decommercialization of the American theatre": Houghton, *Entrances*, 6, 279.

462   loosely applied since the 1930s: Burns Mantle used the term "Off Broadway" in the
       1934–35 theater season. See M. C. Henderson, *Theater in America*, 282; Price, 21.

462   "damaging the theater as an institution": Styne. On *Once Upon a Mattress*, see Kasha and
       Hirschhorn, 240–49.

463   find their way onto the Broadway stage: Schneider in Greenberger, 77–76.

463   "personally, are more satisfying": Ibid., 64, 75.

464   they could not get anywhere else: T. G. Moore, 20.

464   political New Theater of the 1930s: Gassner, *Crossroads*, 116–23. Poggi, 102, traces the
       start of America's noncommercial theater to the production of James Herne's *Marga-
       ret Fleming* in Boston in 1891. Greenberger, 3, locates Off Broadway's beginnings in
       the dramas of social reform produced by the Progressive Stage Society in New York in
       1905. Berkowitz, 23–24, relates Off Broadway also to the Yiddish Theater and to the
       African American theater district that flourished in New York in the 1920s.

465   all over the United States: Moody, "Little Theatre," 590; Wertheim, 3, 149–51.

466   as Anton Chekhov and Bernard Shaw: Wertheim, 153–57.

466   relocated permanently to Broadway: Ziegfeld and Ziegfeld, 86; Baral, *Revue*, 122. As an
       Off Broadway and thus non-Equity venture, *Greenwich Village Follies* did a brisk busi-
       ness on Broadway during the Actors' Equity strike of 1919, when most other Broad-

way productions had to close. See also Bordman, *Musical Revue*, 58–59; Mordden, *Make Believe*, 94–97.

466   referred to as "simplicity itself": J. M. Anderson, 62; See also Baral, *Revue*, 118; Cocuzza, 147–55; J. E. Hirsch, 157–77.

468   (*Porgy and Bess, Oklahoma!, Carousel*): On Theater Guild's troubled role in the genesis of *My Fair Lady*, see D'Andre, 242–57; Somerset-Ward, 138–39. On Theater Guild generally, see Langner; Helburn; Nadel; Waldau.

468   on the map of popular culture: Rodgers, *Stages*, 60–67; Hart and Kimball, 46–54, 69–76.

468   "Ziegfeld produced up on Broadway": J. M. Anderson, 62.

469   "check your brains with your hat": In M. Gordon, 139.

469   also been the show's coproducer: Waters and Samuels, 222; Furia, *Berlin*, 157–58; Plotkins, 177.

470   "episodic structure, type characters": I. A. Levine, 139.

470   *Pink Slips on Parade*: M. Goldstein, *Political Stage*, 173–74, 187–88, 214. Related left-wing musical productions of the period include a comic opera, *Maid in Japan*; a cantata, *Life in a Day of a Secretary*; and numerous nightclub acts of Cabaret TAC (Theatre Arts Committee).

470   "sex and love and the moon above": In E. A. Gordon, 103.

470   what was left of its furniture: The two sketches are in Oliver, *Revue Sketches*, 205–18.

471   "such as the Grand Street Follies": In Harry Goldman, 27.

471   refused to pay double union dues: Ibid., 40.

471   from a working-class point of view: Dubinsky.

471   "war, fascism, and censorship": In Gassner, *Soundings*, 429–30.

471   "Easter Parade" ("Sunday in the Park"): Rush, 57.

471   "who have no time for them": M. Goldstein, *Stage*, 208.

472   on behalf of middle-class values: I. A. Levine, 145.

472   "the very sources from which it evolved": In Harry Goldman, 22.

472   "deprives it of social significance": Adorno, 460.

472   "ashamed to be in its audience": In Harry Goldman, 32.

473   "but for terse dramatic punches": Moross, 13, 33.

474   musical production invariably demands: Sanders, 232; Gassner, *Soundings*, 470. *Johnny Johnson*'s stage history is told in Clurman, 187–91; C. Crawford, 93–97; Strasberg, 152.

474   to the artifice of the stage: Baxandall, 70.

474   "*Das ist Scheisse*": In M. Goldstein, *Stage*, 221; Willett, 81–84.

474   the "democratization of culture": Hopkins in Zuck, 159.

475   *Sing for Your Supper* (1939): See Mathews, vii; Rabson (1983), 14–17; Rabson (1984), 1–2; Loney, *Musical Theatre*, 187–99, 381–88.

475   "were its new manifestation": Clurman, 200.

475   Weill had used in *Johnny Johnson*: J. B. Robinson, 133–52; Schwind, 161.

475   "new and better than either": Flanagan, 201.

476   "dignity to the powers that be": Brecht in Houseman, 245–46. Whether or not *Cradle* can be seen as prefiguring the concept musical of the 1970s, Brecht saw early on that it was one of a new genre of "plays in the form of revues," as he put it. "The linear story has been thrown on the scrap heap, the story itself as well as its line, for the new plays have no story, hardly even a connecting thread." In Willett, 153.

476   ("Nickel Under the Foot," "Joe Worker"): See Block, *Enchanted Evenings*, 121–28; Zuck, 211–27; Oja, "Marc Blitzstein," 445–75.

478   "mythology of the labor movement": Thomson, *Reader*, 301. On the aesthetic-political problematic in Blitzstein's work, see Shout, "Marc Blitzstein," 414–19.

478   proceed with the work as planned: Flanagan, 202–3; Blitzstein. See also Flanagan in E. A. Gordon, 161–62.

478   "gained in this kind of presentation": Engel, *Bright Day*, 84–85. See Lehrman. Helpful

if less authoritative are S. Miller, *Rebels*, 1–17; T. Robbins, which relates more directly to his 1999 film of the same title (minus "The"), mixing fact and fancy in reconstructing the context of Blitzstein's *Cradle*.

479   "ROOSEVELT TO INTERVENE": *NYT*, June 17, 1937.

480   productions of the piece have done the same: Block, *Enchanted Evenings*, 117–18.

480   toward Broadway also more ambivalent: Poggi, 168–71.

481   "34th Streets, in the City of New York": In Cordell and Matson, xiii. A secondary area running from Fifth Avenue to the Hudson River and from Fifty-sixth to Seventy-second streets was also excluded: Farber, 3; Sergel, 149; M. C. Henderson, *Theater in America*, 198.

481   "comes alive in that environment": Atkinson, "At the Theatre."

482   "production styles were seminal": Berkowitz, 37.

483   "either their dignity or their way": Atkinson, "Made with Music," 2:1.

484   all kinds of plays Off Broadway than on: Kowalke "*Threepenny Opera* in America," 117; Poggi, 189–90; F. Hirsch, *Weill*, 323–33.

484   "expression of all that is American": Brecht, *Collected Plays*, vol. 7, 420, 423. On Brecht's American period, see Lyon; Cook.

484   "and that of the criminal world": Brecht, "Use of Music," 85.

485   "would otherwise shamefully conceal": Canetti in Hinton, *Threepenny Opera*, 192; see also Kowalke, "Accounting," 18–38.

485   It was emblematic of the whole: Brecht, "Use of Music," 85; Weill in Hinton, *Threepenny Opera*, 188. The original abortion reference, excised from the 1954 production, was reinstated in the 1976 Lincoln Center production, which hewed more closely to Brecht's text. On the audience's misunderstanding of the work's songs as "hit tunes, hostile as these songs are both to themselves and to this audience," see Adorno, 409.

485   "to challenge us to change them": Barish, 455–56.

485   "elements of entertainment offered": Brecht, "Use of Music," 85.

486   "[were made to] conflict openly": Brecht, "Experimental Theatre," 132.

486   on the English-speaking stage: Kowalke, *Threepenny Opera* in America," 81; Drew, 200–201. Though softened in its bite and generally less faithful to Brecht's text than several later renderings, Blitzstein's version has not been superseded as far as English-language performances are concerned in its sheer musicality and uncanny ability to capture the popular imagination. On the relative merits of the Blitzstein translation, see Papp; Feingold, "Two by Four," 139–41.

487   to suit Broadway tastes: Lenya in S. Green, Notes to *The Threepenny Opera*.

487   "Songs were sung straight out": Little, 80.

488   "as an alternative version of it": Berkowitz, 1st ed., 39.

488   "within the means of everyone": Hambleton and Houghton, 29.

488   "in the thrust of its programming": Little, 153.

489   "too special for Broadway": Houghton, 229.

489   "Nobody'll come to see it": In Peck, 2:3.

489   musical comedies without great success: Latouche's brief career as lyricist and librettist was extraordinarily eclectic, ranging from musical comedy and revue to opera and operetta: "Ballad for Americans," *Sing for Your Supper*, 1939 (Earl Robinson, music); *Cabin in the Sky*, 1940; *Banjo Eyes*, 1941; *The Lady Comes Across*, 1942 (Vernon Duke); *Rhapsody*, 1944 (Fritz Kreisler); *Polonaise*, 1945 (Chopin); *Beggar's Holiday*, 1946 (Duke Ellington); *Ballet Ballads*, 1948; *The Golden Apple*, 1954 (Jerome Moross); *The Vamp* (James Mundy); *The Ballad of Baby Doe*, 1956 (Douglas Moore); *Candide*, 1956 (Leonard Bernstein). In 2489 the York Theater Company mounted a retrospective revue of his work, *Taking a Chance on Love, the Lyrics and Life of John Latouche*.

489   "Paris a traveling salesman": Latouche and Moross, xiv–xv.

490   "ragtime, blues, vaudeville turns, etc.": Ibid., xv.

491   rather than a limitation placed on it: Berkowitz, 48.

491   *The Boys from Syracuse*, 1938/rev. 1963: Not all such "revivals" were undertaken in the

same spirit. *Anything Goes* dropped much of the show's original score for more commercially viable hit songs cribbed from other Porter shows ("Friendship," "It's Delovely," etc.); *Leave It to Jane* harbored an antiquarian respect for the show's original songs. The books to both shows, however, were rewritten.

492   "1950s rock 'n' roll movies": Bentley, *What Is Theatre?*, 318: "The joke against the generation immediately preceding one's own is vulgar, provincial, second-rate. First-rate jokes are against one's own generation." On *The Boy Friend*, originally a one-act London offering, see Gänzl, *British Musical Theatre*, vol. 2, 641–51.

492   *Alive and Well and Living in Paris*, 1968: Blau; S. Miller, *Rebels*, 91–124.

492   "to do it as tiny as we could": Schmidt in Guernsey, *Song & Story*, 77. See also Schmidt; Farber and Viagas; T. Jones, 101–6, 165–68; Hischak, *Boy Loses Girl*, 206–8.

493   "of the space carried it even further": Schmidt in Guernsey, *Song & Story*, 79.

494   "growing up that would touch people": T. Jones, 102–3.

495   "back to a more romantic time"; Ibid., 148.

495   "designer could possibly devise": In S. Green, *World*, 340.

495   "a set of timeless values": Gornick, 2:5.

496   People's Republic of China: Farber and Viagas, 205–6, 210–11.

496   "that still hadn't seen *Oklahoma!*": Hischak, *Boy Loses Girl*, 206.

496   mini-musicals of all kinds: See "Short Plays, Small Musicals" in Guernsey, *Song & Story*, 413–20; Frankel, 60–62; T. Jones, 82–84.

496   (*Colette*, 1970; *Philemon*, 1975): See T. Jones, 121–40.

496   part of its raison d'être: Poggi, 191–94.

497   "Off Broadway's aesthetic freedom": Brustein, *Seasons of Discontent*, 43.

498   "deals for backers, producers and agents": Brustein, "Siren Song."

499   (Actors' Workshop, 1952): Wilmeth, 821–22.

499   Schwartz's *The Baker's Wife*, 1976: Before New York producers and managers consolidated their virtual monopoly over professional theater in America not long after the turn of the twentieth century, several regional centers were important sources of original musicals: Boston (*Robin Hood*, 1890; *The Serenade*, 1897), Chicago (*The Sultan of Sulu*, 1902; *The Time, the Place and the Girl*, 1907).

500   "and the intimacy inspiring": Wasserman, *Impossible Musical*, 108.

500   "new works to add to the repertoire": Goodspeed Opera House program and promotional blurb. In 1984, Goodspeed opened the Norma Terris Theater in Chester, Connecticut, for the purpose of developing new musicals.

501   "ANTA was the only such theater available": W. Bolton.

501   "praise for the production's 'stereophonic effects'": Wasserman, *Impossible*, 122.

501   "It is all new ground": Gottfried, "Man of La Mancha."

503   "the most meaningful function of his imagination." Wasserman, "Preface," 11. See also S. Miller, *Assassins*, 139–49.

503   "dancers wearing horse head masks": S. Green, *World*, 345.

504   "they're having a religious experience": Albert Marre in Wasserman, "Preface," 11.

505   motto song for Don Quixote: Although Auden wrote about sixteen "lyrics" for *Man of La Mancha*, none of his work was ultimately used. "He had no impact on the show," wrote Wasserman to the author in 1985, "other than as a warning of what not to do. . . . We parted ways on two issues: first, he wrote poems rather than lyrics, and second, he and I differed sharply on the play's story and theme. In brief, he wished to be true to the novel. I wished to be true only to my intention, however willful it might be." "Song of the Quest" is in "Unused lyrics by W. H. Auden relating to the musical *Man of La Mancha*," Dale Wasserman Papers, Archives Division, State Historical Society of Wisconsin, Madison. See also Wasserman, *Impossible*, 82–95.

505   stigmatized them as "The Establishment": Berkowitz, 125–26; Poggi, 198. A still later generation of alternative theater activists has sought to replace the Off-Off Broadway designation altogether with Indie (for independent) Theater.

506   "off-off is basically improvisational": W. Goldman, 132.

506 theaters of not more than ninety-nine seats: Solomon, 732; Berkowitz, 126.

506 starring a then-unknown Bernadette Peters: See Stone.

506 *The Faggot* (1973): Feingold, "Al Carmines." As composer, lyricist, librettist, director, and/or performer, the prodigious Al Carmines created some sixty Off-Off Broadway musical theater pieces. *In Circles* is based on Gertrude Stein, whose plays formed the backbone of his Judson musicals. *Promenade*'s libretto, by María Irene Fornés, is published in S. Richards, *Rock Musicals*, 507–60.

506 the piece into a full-fledged musical: On *Godspell*, see Swain, 275–92; S. Miller, *Assassins*, 74–83.

507 characterized the work of these groups: Berkowitz, 146–47.

507 in lower Manhattan's East Village: Papp in Epstein, 202.

507 "bringing in rewrites every day": Freedman in ibid., 211. On *Hair*, see Davis and Gallagher; Horn; S. Miller, *Sun Shine*; Jonathan Johnson; Wollman, *Theater Will Rock*.

509 mean it as a compliment: Berkowitz, 145–46; Bigsby, 73; Horn, 46.

509 "opposed the war because they were hippies": Horn, 45. On the two versions, see Horn, 21–46, 51–92; W. Goldman, 381–87.

509 referred to the dances as "non-dances": Hentoff; Gold, 28–30; Schoettler, 189–93.

509 "the music said it all": Davis and Gallagher, 37–38.

509 theatricality on its own terms: See Engel, *Words*, 292–310; Mordden, *Foot*, 310–14; Hamm, "Musical Theater," *NGDAM*, vol. 3, 307–8.

510 "describe a social epoch in full explosion": O'Horgan in Davis and Gallagher, 12.

511 from one performance to the next: *Hair* constituted more of an event than most shows of its vintage. Convention fixes the status of a show as of its opening-night performance. Davis and Gallagher, 92–101, give an account of *Hair*'s Broadway premiere. Yet, given the very processive nature of a performance-driven musical that was subject to perpetual change after its premiere, to what extent that performance can be considered definitive is debatable.

511 "the same confidence and equanimity as before": Brustein, *Third Theatre*, 63.

511 "supporting artistic talent in others": Berkowitz, 46.

512 *The Umbrellas of Cherbourg* (1979): Berkowitz, 1st ed., 177–83.

512 that turned into runaway hits: There were also original productions of non-Broadway shows that took their cues from *Threepenny Opera* and *Fantasticks* and enjoyed memorably long runs Off Broadway: *Your Own Thing* (1968), 933 performances; *I'm Getting My Act Together and Taking It On the Road* (1978), 1,165; *Little Shop of Horrors* (1982), 2,209.

512 of the Broadway theater district: Berkowitz, 157.

512 "could be excused for hardly noticing": Ibid., 151.

513 "a significant part of the center": Ibid., 63.

13: The Metaphor Angle

517 and "left-wing musicals": Gottfried, "Something's Coming, Something Good," in *Theater Divided*, 171–211.

517 "as opposed to a literary idea": Ibid., 190.

517 "coming to replace the idea of a 'book'": Gottfried in Suskin, *More Nights*, 994.

517 "began with *West Side Story*": Gottfried, "Flipping."

517 "the vogue theatrical word of the '40s": Sondheim in J. Gordon, *Art*, 7.

518 "how to describe a plotless piece": Sondheim in *Broadway: A History*, tape 5, segment 18.

518 a production might lack focus: Cartmell, 94–105.

518 the playwrights themselves or the performers: Cole and Chinoy, 13–70. International terminology can be cause for confusion here. The person called "director" in America is known in England as the "producer," and as the *régisseur* in Germany and Russia, but

not in France, where *régisseur* refers to the stage manager and the director is called the *metteur en scène.*

518 "all the disciplines and elements of production": Banfield, *Sondheim*, 147.

519 literal generative sense: Such notions of auteurship reflect perceptions that may change over time, however—especially as new productions by new directors in a sense replace the original, but do not replace the words and music of the original, which remain largely intact. If at one time, then, one spoke of *Company* and *Follies* as Prince shows, today one speaks of them more often as Sondheim's. The point is that at no time in all likelihood did anyone speak of *Oklahoma!* or *Carousel* as Mamoulian's.

519 "like cubist painting or sculpture": Banfield, *Sondheim*, 147.

520 "the tale that is told": Kislan, *Musical*, 179.

520 "a vaudeville with a plot": Lerner in *NYT*, Oct. 3, 1948.

520 "too young at the time to realize that": Prince in F. Hirsch, *Weill*, 297.

520 "to recreate *Allegro* all the time": Sondheim in Secrest, *Sondheim*, p. 56.

521 Aristotle, for one, deemed a lesser art: According to Aristotle: "The Spectacle has, indeed, an emotional attraction of its own, but of all the parts [of drama] it is the least artistic, and connected least with the art of poetry." In A. Aronson, *Set Design*, ix. *Follies* differs from the shows mentioned, as it "was conceived by James Goldman and me, its plotlessness and revue-style included, long before Harold Prince read it." Sondheim, 2007 communication to the author.

521 "a coherently packaged topic": Banfield, *Sondheim*, 148.

521 "reconstitute it in a modernist form": Walsh and Platt, 135.

522 "to fit the new cultural times": Mast, 320–21. *Follies*, however, is the exception that proves Mast's rule: The show alternates songs of "metaphoric comments" with songs that are indeed "psychological expressions of specific characters."

522 concept musical than Harold Prince (b. 1928): Major studies of the director include Prince, *Contradictions*; Ilson; F. Hirsch, *Harold Prince*.

522 "George Abbott and Jerome Robbins": In F. Hirsch, *Prince*, 2.

523 the modern concept musical: On *Cabaret*, see Masteroff, Kander, and Ebb; Garebian, *Making of Cabaret*; Guernsey, *Song & Story*, 135–50; F. Hirsch, *Prince*, 59–68; Mizejewski, *Divine Decadence*, 159–99.

523 effectively ended with the show: See Hischak, *Boy Loses Girl*, 212–15.

523 the team of Kander and Ebb: See Kander, Ebb, and Lawrence; Kasha and Hirschhorn, 96–111, 190–205.

523 "who wears his wit and insecurities on his sleeve": Kander et al., 4.

523 "quintessentially Broadway show business": Prince in ibid., xviii.

524 change the show by the time it opened: Gottfried, *Divided*, 202.

524 often described as camp: On camp, see Christopher Isherwood; Sontag; Booth, which posits the following, 18: "To be camp is to present oneself as being committed to the marginal with a commitment greater than the marginal merits."

524 "new kind of musical, but Hal knew": In F. Hirsch, *Prince*, 60.

524 metaphoric approach to convey a theme: The shift is assiduously traced in Rinaldi.

524 "*Cabaret* evolved from Hal Prince's concept": In Kander et al., 60: "For months Hal and Joe Masteroff and [Fred Ebb] and I would sit in a room and play a game that I call 'What if?' The director, writers, and composer sit in a room together and imagine the characters and elements of the story. That's an area where Hal's strength as a leader of collaboration shone through. We were inventing incidents that were going to be part of the story. What if such and such happens? What if somebody throws a brick through the window? Hal was a master of that process. He was able to free us in a way that we all jumped in without any inhibitions whatsoever. If it was a bad idea, it was a bad idea. . . . As the captain of the collaboration, Hal was able to be selective and to bring us together in agreement about what should be done."

524 "a metaphor for Germany": Prince, *Contradictions*, 126.

526 "you could fall into a trap of prejudice": In Guernsey, *Song & Story*, 142. The song's final line proved so disturbing to audiences that a less offensive line replaced it on Broadway: "She isn't a *meeskite* at all." Later productions of the show have gone back to the original.

527 "tone and point than emotion and character": Willard, 5.

527 "You've given everything away": In F. Hirsch, *Prince*, 64.

527 "our country in the 1960s": Prince, *Contradictions*, 67, 125. Prince had in mind the kind of racism in America that sparked the Civil Rights movement. But his choice of metaphor also capitalized on a cultural climate in which the postwar silence over what was increasingly being called "the Holocaust" was broken, and a broad American public became more personally aware of the horrific dimensions of Nazism through film (*The Diary of Anne Frank*, 1959; *Judgment at Nuremberg*, 1961) and print (William Shirer's *The Rise and Fall of the Third Reich*, 1960; Hannah Arendt's *Eichmann in Jerusalem*, 1963). See Mizejewski, *Divine*, 186–87.

528 "been doing instead of being there": Shout, *Kiss*, 128ff.

528 metaphor for the meaning of a play: Larsen, 114, 174–76.

529 "Boris was an author": In Rich and Aronson, 188. On the major musical stage designers of the period, see Mielziner; Bay; Burdick et al.; A. Aronson, *American Set Design*; Goodwin; Larsen; Mikotowicz; M. C. Henderson, *Mielziner*; A. B. Harris.

529 "Limbo Area, and the audience understood": Prince, *Contradictions*, 126.

529 "and becomes a celebration": Masteroff in F. Hirsch, *Prince*, 68.

529 on a visit to Moscow in 1966: Winkler, 50–55; Ilson, 137–44.

530 shaped by Prince in Broadway terms: Prince came to see several of his directorial decisions in the original production as "compromises" and changed them accordingly in the 1987 Broadway revival, in which Cliff was a homosexual and the final line of "If You Could See Her" was restored.

530 "the emotional patterns of the plot": Kerr, *Thirty Plays*, 201–2.

530 succeeded two years before, *Zorba* failed: On *Zorba*, see Kander et al., 85–94; F. Hirsch, *Prince*, 69–70; Mordden, *Open Window*, 210–13.

531 the values of a musical playwright: See Sondheim, "Theater Lyrics," 61–97; "Musical Theater," 228–50. Major studies of Sondheim include Zadan; Huber; J. Gordon, *Art Isn't Easy*; and *Sondheim, A Casebook*; Gottfried, *Sondheim*; Banfield, *Sondheim's Broadway Musicals*; Secrest, *Sondheim*; Goodhart; Citron, *Sondheim*; T. Chapin; M. E. Horowitz.

531 "from where he was emotionally at the beginning": Sondheim in Kanfer et al., 72–73.

531 "a lot of good work to be done": Sondheim in Zadan, 363.

531 "the makers of the self-reflexive musical": F. Hirsch, *Prince*, 71.

532 "problem was to find the form for it": Sondheim in Zadan, 124, 117.

532 "central character to examine these marriages": Prince in ibid., 117.

532 another human being ("Being Alive"): "Being Alive" was one of the four songs written for the final spot, the others in no way inferior to it and each mapping a different path through the marriage Robert now envisioned. While "Marry Me a Little," "Multitudes of Amys," and "Happily Ever After" were not used in the original production, in the absence of an emotional trajectory inevitably leading to "Being Alive," Banfield, *Sondheim*, 162–64, suggests including these songs in future productions if we are to take the show's concept seriously: "Do we really believe that Robert's only 'adult' option is to couple, sooner or later, for good and/or ill, or remain a cipher? There are many worlds impinging on the characters in *Company* that the exclusive dramatic concentration on one issue is in danger of distorting through omission. . . . [If] we step back from the concept musical for a moment and decline the scriptural authority of *Company*'s original production, its decisions and solutions and collaborations, we may be able to grasp more facets of the conceptual truth by allowing the alternative endings equal validity, to suggest that all four songs ought to be in the score. Perhaps

this is a corner that the concept musical was not ready to turn in 1970 but can countenance now; or maybe *Company* should be allowed to mature from a museum artifact (the original production) into a public domain text, complete with its variants and critical apparatus, evidence that is just as liable to undermine the notion of an authoritative text as to establish one." See Guernsey, *Playwrights*, 92–97; J. Gordon, *Casebook*, 50–51; Lawson-Peebles, 137–60.

533 "that's what *Company* is about": In F. Hirsch, *Prince*, 86; Sondheim, "Musical Theater," 234–35.

533 "*Company*," he said, "is about the set": Sondheim, "Musical Theater," 238.

534 "as comment and counterpoint" In Zadan, 117.

534 "integrity of the whole, complement it": T. P. Adler, 516.

535 "psychological stresses, inadvertent revelations": Prince, *Contradictions*, 149.

536 "kosher about what this guy is saying": Sondheim, "Theater Lyrics," 71.

537 "That's the entire plot": Sondheim in *Broadway: A History*, tape 5, segment 18.

538 "is the content, what it's all about": Prince, *Contradictions*, 162.

538 ("The Story of Lucy and Jessie"): Sondheim claims Porter as his model here (Zadan, 147). Perhaps he was thinking of "I Get a Kick Out of You," in which the singer wants what she can't have and disdains what she can. But *Lady in the Dark*'s "The Saga of Jenny" (Ira Gershwin–Weill) seems a more direct model and "Ah, Paris!" as *Follies'* more obvious Porter-style number.

539 and a rising one in the other: Compare the weak-beat motifs on scale steps 5-6-5-^{b}7 in Gershwin, and 3-4-3-5 in Sondheim; and the chromatic inner voices between chords descending G-G^{b}-F-E in Gershwin and ascending B^{b}-B-C-D^{b} in Sondheim. See Block, *Enchanted Evenings*, 281–82.

541 "its distinctive sweet and sour pungency": F. Hirsch, *Prince*, 85.

541 "there's music going on in the pit": Sondheim in Zadan, 248.

542 "an entertainment, but with a subversive edge": Holden, "Smile."

542 "go home and not be able to sleep": In Zadan, 119.

543 "requiring a total brain adjustment": In Mandelbaum, *A Chorus Line*, 58.

543 "fresh stock of their imaginative energies": Kerr in Suskin, *More Nights*, 603–4.

543 "instead of the regional theatre": In F. Hirsch, *Prince*, 131.

544 for anyone to bear, even hyperbolically: Lahr, *Light Fantastic*, 289.

544 "classic or in the historical or popular repertoire": Zinoman. See definition of revivals in chapter 16, p. 645.

545 *Night Music, Sweeney Todd*: On Sondheim's librettists, see Hischak, *Boy Loses Girl*, 161–82.

545 "the experience you have in a school play": In Zadan, 301.

545 "not stuff that was reliant on a text": Lapine in Zadan, 296.

545 verbal discourse and its meanings: See http://www.visualtheater:co.il/visual.html.

546 "I knew there was a real play there": In Zadan, 296–97.

547 are all by now traditional in the extreme: See Bonahue in J. Gordon, *Casebook*, 171–83.

547 "My beliefs are conservative, but my work is not": In J. Gordon. *Art Isn't Easy*, 300.

547 the nature of the creative process itself: See Adler in Goodhart, 51.

547 "where reality and representation meet": Walsh and Platt, 132.

547 imbue it with an astonishing consistency: See Banfield, *Sondheim*, 364–68.

548 "as if I had taken his Christmas away": In M. E. Horowitz, 99.

549 "someone or something is to blame": Weidman in Bishop, *Assassins*, x–xi.

549 any traditional emotional "payoff": See Miller in J. Gordon, *Casebook*, 188.

550 "horrifying acts that these people did": Sondheim in *Assassins*.

551 "a show which makes such a demand": Sondheim and Weidman, www.playbill.com (January 11, 2002).

554 "may lose its ability to entertain": Walsh and Platt, 146.

14: A Dancing Place

559   "dance sensibility into realms beyond dancing": Review of *Dreamgirls* in R. E. Long,
      258. See also Challender, Schlundt; Grody and Lister; Mordden, *Babies*, 165–81; Steyn,
      178–95.

560   during the First World War: Schoettler, 54.

560   the show's dance directors: R. E. Long, 14.

560   "social-dance routines for Miller": Ries, "Sammy Lee," 10.

561   "'high' art and spiritual ennoblement": R. E. Long, 14.

561   movement patterns of choreography: Blocking, choreography, and musical staging are
      generally defined in Kislan, *Hoofing*, 95. See also Champion in Giordano, 75.

561   the rehearsal process of a show: Not only direction and choreography, but virtually
      all aspects of production were compartmentalized. See Craig in J. Gordon, *Casebook*,
      93–96.

562   "don't have to depend on words all the time": Verdon in Coleman, 27.

562   "and they call themselves that": Abbott, *Mister Abbott*, 249–50.

562   "to my head, to the words": Prince in Thelen, 13–14.

562   "the stage in a musical number": Kislan, Hoofing, 95. As it became common to spread
      more and more music throughout a Broadway show, musical staging came to imply
      the staging of virtually anything that moved. While shows thus often seemed choreo-
      graphed from start to finish, the more the choreographer-directors concerned them-
      selves with overall staging, the less time they had for specifically choreographic tasks.
      These they often entrusted to others: Peter Gennaro did some of the choreography for
      Robbins in *West Side Story*; Bob Avian for Bennett in *A Chorus Line*; Thommie Walsh
      for Tune in *Nine*.

562   musical dream scenes in yet a third: Hart at the Music Box Theater; Rasch at the Alvin
      Theater; Short at the Lyceum Theater. Hassard Short (1877–1956) staged musical
      sequences for other book shows (*Face the Music; Jubilee; Carmen Jones*), directed shows
      like *The Great Waltz* ("Production Conceived and Directed by"), and took on all the
      staging for *The Hot Mikado*, 1939 ("Entire Production, Book, and Ensembles Staged
      by"). On how the stage itself figured in the production of *Lady in the Dark*, see Horner,
      265–75.

563   "that it seems perfectly natural": In Hutchens.

564   many still thought of as a man's job: Mordden, *Rodgers and Hammerstein*, 95. On the
      stage, dancing women had commanded the focus of male attention in musicals at least
      since *The Black Crook*. Behind the scenes, women had not usually held commanding
      positions except as choreographers—notably, through de Mille's generation, Alber-
      tina Rasch (1896–1967): *Rio Rita, The Band Wagon*; Anna Sokolow (1915–2000): *Street
      Scene, Regina*; Helen Tamiris (1905–1966): *Annie Get Your Gun, Fanny*; Hanya Holm
      (1893–1992): *Kiss Me, Kate; My Fair Lady*.

564   by the time of *Allegro* in 1947: On de Mille, see Gherman; Easton. In addition to her
      work as a choreographer, de Mille authored numerous books of memoirs and reflec-
      tions on American dance, which are both incisive and invaluable contributions to the
      historiography of the Broadway musical. Among these are *Dance to the Piper; And
      Promenade Home; Speak to Me, Dance with Me; America Dances*.

565   scenic designer Jo Mielziner (1901–1975): A leader of the new stagecraft movement
      in America, Mielziner helped transform the craft of the "stage decorator" into the art
      of the "scene designer." Notably in *I Married an Angel, Allegro*, and *South Pacific*, he
      designed sets that eliminated the need for long pauses during changes of scenery—
      as he said, "To overcome the episodic and rigid format of writing stories in acts and
      scenes as opposed to employing the technique of connected thoughts and freedom of
      movement enjoyed by such mediums as the motion pictures." In Larsen, 140–41. See
      Mielziner, 21–22, 136–37; M. C. Henderson, *Mielziner*.

565   and a singing chorus of thirty-eight: Mordden, *Rodgers and Hammerstein*, 97.

565   her credit as the show's director: R. E. Long, 47.

565   "material with little of either to boast of": J. Martin, "Allegro."

565   "so other choreographers rode over her": Mitchell in R. E. Long, 59.

567   forms of dance and theatrical expression: On Robbins, see C. Conrad; G. Lawrence; Jowitt. Robbins worked with brilliance in both the cultivated and commercial worlds of his métier. In this respect he was much like Leonard Bernstein, to whose music he created dances for the concert stage (*Fancy Free*, 1944; *Facsimile*, 1946; *Dybbuk*, 1974) as well as for Broadway (*On the Town, Wonderful Town, West Side Story*).

567   "the way I make ballets": In R. E. Long, 130.

568   "Then the whole show began to switch": In Thelen, 207.

568   from his *Fancy Free* ballet scenario: Osato, 243.

569   "you feel that way about the dance": Biancolli in Giordano, 22–23.

569   "'No we have to cut this'": Robbins in Guernsey, *Song & Story*, 8. Robbins internalized the lesson. Some twenty years later, it was Robbins-the-director of *Fiddler on the Roof* who cut the ten-minute "Chava Ballet" by Robbins-the-choreographer when it didn't "work" in the show.

569   subsequent work both in ballet and on Broadway: R. E. Long, 82. Carol Lawrence, *West Side Story*'s Maria and both a ballet dancer and a singer, described the differences in working with Robbins-the-director and Robbins-the-choreographer (W. W. Burton, 171–72): "Jerry came from a ballet background in which the choreographer is the master and the *corps-de-ballet* the absolute slaves. Dancers get used to that treatment only because it works. When you intimidate and humiliate a dancer and say: 'You *can't* jump higher, you *can't* jump further . . .' his or her attitude is: 'Goddamn you, I'll show you.' And you do it, because the adrenalin flies through your system, and you literally do it to show them up. And so it's rebellion that the choreographer is calling on to serve his ends. Now, that works in a dancer, but it does not work in an actor. You cannot force, for example, an actor to be more poignant. But you see Jerry . . . had come from where he was—as a choreographer—with the only tools that he knew how to use."

570   "of an effort that I began in *Allegro*": de Mille, *America Dances*, 192.

570   "interrupting the continuous flow of dance": In R. E. Long, 110.

572   "'Tradition' because he insisted on it": Harnick in Altman and Kaufman, 30–32.

572   "his idea of what the book was changed": Bock in Guernsey *Song & Story*, 123.

572   "choreographers"—and the most powerful: Mordden, *Babies*, 181.

572   "the musical's commander-in-chief": R. E. Long, 142.

572   "require the approval of the writers": R. Rodgers, "Stardust," 95.

573   "Robert Fosse and Gower Champion": de Mille, *America Dances*, 193.

573   of strip-joints and burlesque: R. E. Long, 219.

573   "lasting stamp on the national style": de Mille, *America Dances*, 187. See also Loney, *Unsung*; Andreu, 4–25; Kislan, *Hoofing*, 161–62; www.theatredance.com/choreographers/cole.html; www/danceart.com/gotjazz/cole.htm.

574   dance team with his wife Marge: On Champion, see Payne-Carter; Gilvey, *Gower Champion*; and *Before the Parade Passes By*.

574   books by Michael Stewart (1929–1987): On Stewart, see Hischak, *Boy Loses Girl*, 183–90. The songwriters were: *Birdie*, Lee Adams, lyrics, Charles Strouse, music; *Carnival*, Bob Merrill; *Dolly!* Herman; *I Do! I Do!*, Tom Jones, lyrics and book, Harvey Schmidt, music; *42nd Street*, Al Dubin, lyrics, Harry Warren, music.

574   took it down at the end: In conventional wing and drop sets, flat pieces of scenery are painted to create a specific illusion onstage and must be replaced with each new change of scene: horizontally from the sides (wings) and vertically from the fly space above (drops). Unit sets, by contrast, remain onstage throughout a performance since they are more abstractly suggestive and so more broadly suited for reuse in different scenes. The unit set is particularly favored in concept musicals for the palpable way it serves as a metaphor and constant reminder of the show's theme. See Waterhouse, 17.

574   "it was the wrap around the orchestra": Champion in W. Goldman, 293.

575   League of New York Theaters in 1962: Schoettler, 179–82. Champion and Merrick
      worked together on seven musicals. See Kissel, 9–23, 209–11, 287–92.

575   comedic highs to song and dance: For example, Act 4's mistaken identities and cross-
      gender dressing were cut, while Dolly's Act 4 soliloquy on rejoining the human race
      became the musical's Act 1 finale, "Before the Parade Passes By." See Bogard in Bogard
      and Oliver, 368–70; Kasha and Hirschhorn, 177–78.

575   showtune evocations of a bygone age: On Herman, see Herman and Stasio; Herman
      and Bloom; Citron, *Jerry Herman.* At a crisis point during the tryouts in Detroit, Mer-
      rick called in additional songwriters to help with the *Dolly* score. Bob Merrill osten-
      sibly collaborated with Herman on "Elegance" and "Motherhood March." Charles
      Strouse and Lee Adams wrote a song called "Before the Parade Passes By," which was
      not used in the show; Herman claims not to have heard it when he later wrote his own
      song of the same title, which was. The conflicting views on who wrote what appear,
      on one hand, in Suskin, *Show Tunes,* 445, 471, 497; and, on the other hand, in Herman,
      Showtune, 80–84, and Citron, *Herman,* 94–100. Neither party seems to have considered
      the internal evidence of the earlier song (unpublished) on deposit in the Library of
      Congress, with which the familiar later song (published) shares certain gestural affini-
      ties. This suggests that if Herman did not actually hear the earlier song, he may in fact
      have seen it. The Strouse-Adams "Parade" was copyrighted on January 15, 1964 (EU
      807268); the Herman "Parade" was copyrighted on March 5, 1964 (EU 185768).

575   "theater humming a showtune": Herman, *Showtune,* 226–27.

575   reputedly receiving $275,000: Suskin, *Show Tunes,* 445, 497; Kissel, 292–94.

576   "That's how Gower got his level": Channing in McGovern and Winer, 127; Jerry Her-
      man 1990 interview with the author.

577   "begin the evening's title song": Kerr, "Hello, Dolly!"

578   "has been absolutely no preparation": Canby, "Excitement," 62.

578   "happening off-set behind a curtain": Stone in Rosenberg and Harburg, 134–36. On
      Stone (1930–2003), see Hischak, *Boy Loses Girl,* 196–202; Bell, 133–55.

579   until his own death in 2000: Corry; Rich, "David Merrick."

579   "blend with the dance movements": Fosse in Gottfried, *All His Jazz,* 251. See also
      Grubb; Beddow.

579   "satire of our sexual nature": Doctorow.

579   against the conventions of musical comedy: Brantley, "Album of Fosse."

580   proved inadequate to the book: R. E. Long, 149.

580   "value to me for the rest of my career": Fosse in Jowitt, 243.

580   "the medium and the main event": McGovern and Winer, 137

581   "You got rid of the author": In Grubb, 206.

581   "I wanted to keep it pure": In Gardner, 59. On the differences between the two *Cabarets,*
      see Mast, 321–24; Mizejewski, *Divine Decadence,* 159–235.

581   "perverted into a Broadway whore": Ostrow, 116.

581   original concept, and the show failed: Gottfried, *Jazz,* 262.

582   fellow murderess Velma Kelly (Chita Rivera): In vaudeville, historically, truth was often
      stranger than fiction. Nan Patterson, for example, a onetime *Florodora* girl, was actu-
      ally billed at Hammerstein's Victoria Theater as "The Singing Murderess." Ewen, *All
      the Years,* 180. More particularly, "*Chicago* was an entertainment but it also said some-
      thing about celebrity, about our celebrating killers. At the time Squeaky Fromme of the
      Manson family was on the cover of *Time,* and that sort of infamy was initially what the
      show was about." Ebb in Kander et al., 128.

583   "His tragedy was wanting to believe it": Ostrow, 123.

584   "only long cues to the next number": Fosse in Grubb, 206.

584   "if only a book to fight with": Kerr, "Dancin'."

585   a "living archive" of American theater dance: Theodore, 275–77.

585   shows for which they were created: *Bye Bye Birdie* was the first musical to be fully laba-

notated. Artistic bias against commercial dance precluded the preservation of even single Broadway numbers in labanotation until the 1940s. Union demands and technological constraints, on the other hand, prevented the preservation of Broadway shows as originally performed on videotape until Betty Corwin formed the Theater on Film and Tape Archive at the Library for the Performing Arts at Lincoln Center in 1970. *Company* was the earliest complete staged Broadway production in its collection (recorded in Washington in 1972 at the end of its national tour). Hollywood has also preserved the work of some of the great Broadway director-choreographers: Cole's can be seen in *Gentlemen Prefer Blondes* (20th Century Fox, 1953) though de Mille choreographed the Broadway original; de Mille's in *Oklahoma!* (Magna Corporation: Todd-AO, 1955; RKO Pictures: CinemaScope, 1956) and *Carousel* (20th Century Fox, 1956); Kidd's in *Guys and Dolls* (Goldwyn 1955) and *L'il Abner* (Paramount, 1959); Robbins's in *The King and I* (20th Century Fox, 1956) and *West Side Story* (United Artists, 1961); Fosse's in *The Pajama Game* (Warner Brothers, 1957), *Damn Yankees* (Warner Brothers, 1968), *Sweet Charity* (Universal, 1969), and his cinematic rethinking of the Prince-Field *Cabaret* (ABC, 1972). Performing as Hollywood dancers themselves, Gower can be seen with Marge Champion in *Show Boat* (MGM, 1951), Kidd in *It's Always Fair Weather* (MGM, 1955), Fosse in *Kiss Me, Kate* (MGM, 1953) and together with Verdon in *Damn Yankees*.

585   Broadway was once indeed a dancing place: On Broadway dance reconstructions, see Loney, "On Broadway"; Rothstein; Canby, "Fosse."

586   died of AIDS in his early forties: On Bennett and his *magnum opus*, see Mandelbaum, *A Chorus Line*; D. M. Flinn, *What They Did for Love*; K. Kelly; Viagas, Lee, and Walsh; Stevens and George. See also Grody and Lister, 95–115; Hamlisch and Gardner, 135–60.

587   "Fosse did for musical comedy": Gene Foote in McGovern and Winer, 138.

587   "forget he's watching an actor": John Cunningham in ibid., 131–32.

588   "it was what musical theater should be": Laurents in Zadan, 137, 236.

588   which he maintained dance was *by nature*: Bennett in Kislan, *Hoofing*, 116.

589   "workshop allows you to be wrong, then fix it": Bennett in Mandelbaum, *Chorus Line*, 92, 114.

592   and composer Marvin Hamlisch (b. 1944): "You could not talk to writers about dramatizing a rehearsal scene, or dramatizing what a dancer goes through, working very hard to look like every other dancer in the room," Bennett said. "I had to 'dummy' chunks of the show on people before the writers could write it" (Mandelbaum, *Chorus Line*, 114). Even nonchoreographic director Prince similarly "dummied" the Act 1 finale of *A Little Night Music* onstage before Sondheim came up with the song "A Weekend in the Country" for it (Prince, *Contradictions*, 179).

592   presentational rather than representational: D. M. Flinn, 266; Challender in R. E. Long, 247.

593   beneath the pizzazz of "One": Note the unprepared crash gear-box harmonic changes: "else will do"—G minor; "you know who"—F-sharp minor; "One"—E-flat major.

594   "always harder than to say something": Kleban in Mandelbaum, *Chorus Line*, 163.

594   "It's got to be about something": Bennett in Philp, 65.

594   "the job they love and we expect": Schoettler, 248.

595   state subsidies that theaters received in Europe: D. M. Flinn, 270; Mandelbaum, *Chorus Line*, 316.

595   "a musical about Broadway gypsy-dancers": Ostrow, 162–63.

596   (*The Producers*, 2001): On Daniele and Stroman, see R. E. Long, 274–87; Bell, 114–31, 174–91; Eichenbaum, 12–15, 20–23.

597   earlier version with a conceptual one: Tune, 96–106. See also Grody and Lister, 142–54.

597   spaces of the Grand Hotel itself: See Gottfried, *More Musicals*, 108–24.

597   "becomes inseparable from composition": Mordden, "Inside."

598   "half-thought for the half-educated": Feingold, "Tunesmithing," 114.
598   "fact that it lacked a plot": Tune, 97.
598   "The director/choreographer is dead": Tune in R. E. Long, 273.
598   throroughly kinetic form of entertainment: Canby, "New Fosse Vehicle."
599   associate director, Gillian Lynne: Lynne (b. 1927), a former soloist with the Sadler's
      Wells Ballet, helped to develop jazz dance in Britain. In the 1960s she choreographed
      three fairly undistinguished Merrick shows on Broadway, in the last of which, *How
      Now, Dow Jones* (1967), she was replaced by then unknown (and uncredited) Michael
      Bennett.

15: Distancing Effects

603   "'Cause I just got here": Bennett, Kirkwood, Dante, Hamlisch, and Kleban, 130–31.
603   "the worst block in town": Reichl, 43–76.
603   *Let My People Come* (1976): Both shows originated Off Broadway—*Calcutta!* in 1969,
      People in 1974—and later transferred to Broadway, where the former succeeded and
      the latter failed. In revival, moreover, *Calcutta!* enjoyed an astonishing Broadway run
      of nearly 6,000 performances (1976–1989), its success resting perhaps on its espousal
      of traditional and rather unenlightened views of sexuality at the height of the women's
      and the gay liberation movements. More "enlightened" shows of the type—*The Dirtiest
      Show in Town* (1970), *Stag Movie* (1971), *The Faggot* (1973)—originated Off Broadway
      and prudently remained there. See Ward.
603   undercurrent of racial and ethnic tension: Reichl, 3, 44.
604   during their Broadway runs: Rosenberg and Harburg, 7.
604   "for less than $5 million": Ibid., 18.
604   90 percent of Broadway's legitimate houses: Ibid., 23–35.
605   "What they lack is artistic *passion!*": Schwartz in Kasha and Hirschhorn, 268.
605   whose age fell under that benchmark: That *Hair*'s creators (except possibly Ragni)
      were over thirty was conveniently downplayed in the press, if not deliberately obscured:
      McDermott (b. 1928), Rado (b. 1932), Ragni (b. 1935? or 1942 ?–d. 1991).
605   described one of Sondheim's shows: Whitfield, *In Search*, 84.
605   "stopped writing for the market": Kander in Eyre and Wright, 176
606   "entertainment flourished in this country": Rich in Prince, *Contradictions*, 169–70.
607   "*A Chorus Line* is, in effect, the last Broadway musical": Feingold, 1976, repr. in *Village
      Voice*, May 21, 1985, 91.
608   "Europeans should stay out of here": Ulvaeus in Palm, 474.
609   *Half a Sixpence*, 1965: Snelson, "'We said,'" 107. For a list of shows that constituted the
      "American invasion" of the West End between 1945 and 1970, see Gänzl, *The Musical*,
      337.
609   "whether consciously or not": Bricusse in Steyn, 166–67.
609   the exception that proved the rule: On Lloyd Webber, see McKnight; Gänzl, *Lloyd Web-
      ber*; Mühe; Richmond; M. Walsh, *Lloyd Webber*; Coveney; Citron, *Sondheim and Lloyd
      Webber*; Snelson, *Lloyd Webber*. On Lloyd Webber shows, see Nassour and Broderick;
      Perry, *Phantom*; and *Sunset*; Gänzl, *Aspects of Love*; Hanan. On Rice, see T. Rice; Lassell.
609   "instead of aping Broadway badly": In Richmond, 14.
609   "more like *Hair* than *Oklahoma!*": In M. Walsh, *Lloyd Webber*, 63.
609   "bring Broadway up to date": Richmond, 58.
610   "helped us to be original": Rice in Kasha and Hirschhorn, 232.
610   to the masses in their thrall: Swain, 294.
611   rather than a divine one: F. Hirsch, *Prince*, 159.
611   "and a very proper one at that": In M. Walsh, *Lloyd Webber*, 62.
612   commercial music industry in the 1960s: Rockwell, vol. 3, 1365.

612   status as an outsider genre: Warfield, 239.

612   vapid, irrelevant, and downright phony: Whitfield, *In Search*, 109–13. If it had once been common to speak of "the music theater as a primary source of 'quality' popular music" (Wilder, xxx–xxxvi) and of the Broadway show tune as the most distinguished form of expression in American popular song (Shapiro and Pollock, 61), with the rise of rock in the 1960s a rift between popular music and Broadway music soon grew so wide that it was no longer possible to measure both by the same standard. See Wollman in Washburne and Derno, 311–30.

612   Motown (*Dreamgirls*): Warfield, 232. S. Richards, *Great Rock Musicals* contains the librettos to *Hair*, *Tommy*, *Your Own Thing*, *Superstar*, *Grease*, and *The Wiz*, among others.

613   "can't express mood or establish tone": Mordden, *Better Foot*, 310.

613   "orgiastic, rather than dramatic": G. Martin, *Twentieth-Century Opera*, 71, 78.

615   but as LP concept albums: *Jesus Christ Superstar*, 2 LPs. London: Decca DXSA 7206, 1970; *Evita*, 2 LPs. London: MCA MCX 503, 1976.

615   "sung . . . *incessantly*": Laurents in Steyn, 278.

615   the Metropolitan Opera House: See Christgau, 42.

615   "Roll Over, Chuck Berry!": See Rockwell, vol. 3, 1365. "We were worried about the airy-fairy connotations of calling [*Tommy*] an opera. After all, The Who were a rough, streetwise bunch of London kids. . . . [But] rock touring was really shitty. We thought, Why should rock audiences have to listen to music in fuckin' aircraft hangars? What attracted us to the rock-opera idea was that opera houses were run by committee, and not by greedy carnival people, who were always looking to rip us off at the gate. We hit up the opera managers with 'This is opera and opera's for the people.' We thought we'd be able to browbeat them into giving us their opera houses, and we did." Chris Stamp in Lahr, *Light Fantastic*, 296.

615   *Tommy*, after all, *without* The Who?: See Wollman, *Theater Will Rock*, 24–41, 158–70. In *Tommy*-like fashion, though preceding it to Broadway, the Beatles' finest concept album was mounted in New York in 1974 as *Sgt. Pepper's Lonely Hearts Club Band on the Road* (without dialogue and with seventeen added Lennon-McCartney songs) by Tom O'Horgan, who sought to capitalize on his earlier successes in the vein with *Hair* and *Superstar*. Similarly, ABBA's 1984 recording of *Chess* was successfully staged by Trevor Nunn in London in 1986, and in New York two years later, albeit unsuccessfully.

616   "a continuous musical event like opera": Lloyd Webber in F. Hirsch, *Prince*, 157.

616   "a rock concert of a favorite album": Gottfried, *More Nights*, 56.

616   stageworthy and turn it into a scene: Rosenberg and Harburg, 46.

616   Evita herself had once manipulated hers: F. Hirsch, *Prince*, 159–65. Also see Swain, 293–307; Walsh and Platt, 166–71.

618   buzzword by the end of the 1980s: Sternfeld, 1–3.

620   "rather than just another musical": Mackintosh in Morley and Leon, 62.

620   *Cats* from the cats' perspective: Napier in Goodwin, 149.

620   ran one publicity line: Lamb, *150 Years*, 334; Gänzl, *The Musical*, 380. Mackintosh was deeply influenced by the work of Sean Kenny, the original stage designer for *Oliver!* and the designer of *Cats'* New London Theater, an arena-style house with a revolving stage. "You are totally pulled into another world. That's what I've come to demand of all my shows. It all stems from *Oliver!* The sets have to dance with the action." Mackintosh in Morley and Leon, 48.

620   "hit me with the experience": Nunn in Richmond, 92.

621   the Broadway musical as a "live" experience: Walsh and Platt, 158. See also J. K. Moore, 169–88; Grant, 188–203.

621   "no cultural barriers to be stormed": Morley in Flinn, *Musical!*, 485.

622   "a piece of hokum": In Snelson, *Lloyd Webber*, 81. See also Hogle, 173–204.

622   something closer to the "real thing": Gänzl, *The Musical*, 341–42, 374, 395.

622   or, more archly, poperettas: D. Richards.

622 pop recording industry in France: On Boublil and Schönberg, see Vermette; Behr; Behr and Steyn.

623 force into a multinational coalition: Several nations that later ventured into the fray on their own, however, fared poorly. Russia's *Junon and Avos* (1990), Poland's *Metro* (1992), and Holland's *Cyrano, The Musical* (1993) all had disastrous receptions in New York.

623 retranslated into French—and failed: Sternfeld, 175, 180–81, 218; Behr, 71–78. For a comparison of the musical numbers on the original French recording and in the English stage production, see Swain, 392–93.

624 took on lives of their own: Swain, 402–3, discusses such musical references and their sometimes questionable dramatic appropriateness.

625 Puccini's *Madam Butterfly* itself suggests: Sternfeld, 202.

625 "from time to time and used": Napier in Goodwin, 151.

626 "as if they'd been written in tears": Eyre and Wright, 344.

626 *Dracula, The Musical,* 2004: Sternfeld, 313–19, 328–29.

626 "sound are constitutive of its nature": Walsh and Platt, 163.

626 positioning them for Broadway: Kislan, *The Musical,* 269–70.

627 "it might not have got off the ground": Nunn in Eliot, 11.

627 He made his shows, in a phrase, critic proof: Sternfeld, 3–5.

627 "breath for breath" fidelity to the original: Morley and Leon, 71–73. In the 1960s, when such British musicals as *Irma La Douce, Stop the World,* and *Oliver!* came to Broadway, they played as David Merrick productions.

628 more than twenty years on Broadway alone: Rosenberg and Harburg, 64, 331–33.

629 "its final journey around the world": Mackintosh in *Broadway: The American Musical,* vol. 3.

629 "essential element of the musical's identity": Snelson, *Lloyd Webber,* 188.

630 "deepest pockets and, in truth, the most skill": F. Rich, "Detour."

630 Magic Kingdom on the Great White Way: Henry, 72.

630 "'These shows made how much?'": Mackintosh in Maslon, 438.

631 objects into peoplelike characters: Lahr, *Light Fantastic,* 286–88. On Disney on Broadway, see Frantz; Taymor and Greene; Marcus; Blumenthal, 210–17. For more thoughtful discussions, see Nelson, 71–85; Wickstrom, 285–98.

631 "to mind is the modern Broadway musical": Henry, 72.

632 "Broadway and avant-garde theater": Taymor in R. Cohen, 317–18.

633 "heart of a Hollywood production": Lahr in Maslon, 423.

633 to its former glory and to active use: M. C. Henderson, *New Amsterdam,* 7: Hugh Hardy, Disney's architect, described the theater's reconstruction as "an 'interpretive' restoration that still enables this glorious old playhouse to be a viable performance venue."

633 rubric: historic preservation: Nelson, 83.

633 "by the forces of good over evil": Reichl, 157.

634 "tourist version of its former self": Nelson, 83. See also S. Adler, 201–10.

634 "producers profit from all sales": Wollman, "Economic," 449–50.

634 shows that exemplified it movicals: See Shenton. On American movie musicals, see Rick Altman; J. Feuer; Hischak, *Film It with Music;* Muir. On the relationship between musicals for the stage and for the screen, see Druxman; Mast; G. Wood, 212–30; Hischak, *Screen Door.*

635 the films from which they derived: See Hischak, *Screen Door,* 179–96, 263–72.

636 screen musical for the stage: Ibid., viii.

637 with a new beginning and ending: Brooks and Meehan, 14. See also Denman.

638 "he wants to be on top again": Stroman in *The Producers.* In comparable fashion, Rob Marshal's film version of *Chicago* (2002) uses close-ups to indicate that the musical numbers take place in Roxie Hart's mind, whereas in Fosse's original staging, the numbers played directly to the audience as a vaudeville.

639 "kitsch (like *Mamma Mia!*)": Brantley, "His Songs."

640 (John Lennon, mostly without the Beatles): See Scott.

640   rise of rock had severed it: Wollman, "Economic," 446.

640   "the work you get, once you get it": In ibid., 455.

641   "the distancing tool of technology": Charles Isherwood, "'Movin' Out.'"

16: Another Broadway . . . Another Show . . .

646   "preceding the Eligibility Date": American Theatre Wing, 5.

647   the radically reconceived *Cabaret*, 1998: The situation resembles that in most opera houses today, though opera texts are less subject to change than Broadway ones in revival. "Three separable views have become current . . . as to what, from the staging point of view, an operatic text up for revival is: first, that it is the record of an event that deserves repeating; second, that it is a set of instructions asking to be put into effect in the best possible way; and third, that it is a pure, sheer, non-prescriptive stimulus to the free play of theatrical imagination." Savage, 401–4.

647   in that illusory safe bet: Far from safe bets, most revivals flop. Those that succeed tend to make less money than successful new shows. According to producer Barry Weissler: "Revivals are a little easier to market because you know what you have. But original shows generally have a longer and more fruitful life because all the subsidiary and ancillary rights are open." In Pacheco.

647   but who simply created its lead roles: See Kowalke, "Goldene Zeitalter," 142.

648   starring the record's Joey, Harold Lang: Engel, *Bright Day*, 170–71. See also Penndorf. Vivienne Segal, the original Vera Simpson in 1940, re-created the role on the *Pal Joey* LP (New York: Columbia 4364, 1950) and in the 1952 revival.

649   *Guys and Dolls*; and *My Fair Lady*: Lieberson, 20–21, 29. At the time of his writing, Lieberson headed a committee to oversee the preservation past Broadway show materials by the Yale University Library. See Barlow, 25–32.

649   more than one or two (1951–52 saw five): Kowalke, "Goldene Zeitalter," 138–39.

649   for limited engagements each spring: The company presented some twenty-five such shows during the fifteen seasons it lasted, among them *Show Boat*; *Kiss Me, Kate*; *Guys and Dolls*; *Carousel*; and *The Music Man*. See Dalrymple, 273–79; Severo.

649   "the concert hall and the opera house": Rodgers, "Enshrined," 20.

650   had nothing at all to do with the original: Choreographer Berkeley, then seventy-six, and tap-dancer Keeler, then sixty-two, had become celebrities through their work in movie musicals of the 1930s.

650   were content simply to be musicals: J. Burton, 277.

650   "must be our valentine to the audience": Shevelove in Dunn, 211. For a comparison of the 1925 and 1971 productions, sere Mordden, *Make Believe*, 78–81.

651   restoration of his orchestrations: On the differences between the 1936 and 1983 productions of *On Your Toes*, see Block, *Enchanted Evenings*, 91–103.

651   "the American musical theater heritage": Mauceri, Notes to *On Your Toes*.

652   "a star vehicle for the director": Steyn, 250.

652   "too serious *for a musical*": Prince, "Show Boat," 35; Prince in Haun, "Can't Help," 14. On Prince's and earlier *Show Boat* productions, see Block, *Enchanted Evenings*, 23–27, 319–24.

653   more than half a century earlier: Prior to 1994, special awards were occasionally given for an "innovative production of a revival" (*Porgy and Bess*, 1977) or a "reproduction" of a play or musical (*The Pirates of Penzance*, 1981; *On Your Toes*, 1983). See Stevenson.

653   as *Cabaret* did when it was new: Roundabout's *Cabaret* ran for 2,377 performances; the original for 1,165. Adapted by British director Sam Mendes from his own Donmar Warehouse production, it went far beyond the customary revisions of a Broadway show. It infused the old material with a new set of meanings, inverting the premises of the original relationship between the staging and the story, and so complicating the very notion of spectatorship. "It turns out to be the club that puts on the story

rather than a story that contains within it a club." Mendes in Masteroff et al., 99. It also radically shifted the conceptual focus of the original, including the meaning of the show's focal character, the emcee. "In the original, the emcee was a figure for the encroachment of Naziism. . . . Here he represents the world the Nazis will destroy." Clum, 279.

653   "light of day [again] as full productions": Judith Daykin in Morris, 35.

654   "high-stepping pizzazz": P. Marks.

654   articles in fan magazines (*Show Music*): *Show Music*, a quarterly magazine devoted to musical theater and issued under the auspices of the Goodspeed Opera House since 1985, stopped publication in 2002.

655   "our flowering with the American musical theater": Hart in Mandell.

655   the view expressed is widely held: There is no critical consensus on how long the Golden Age of the Broadway musical lasted or on precise criteria for determining of what it consisted. For Bordman (*A Chronicle*) it is based on songs; for Engel (*A Consideration*) it is based on librettos. Most commentators agree that it started in the early 1940s, emblematically with either *Pal Joey* (Engel, *A Consideration*, vii; L. Bernstein, *Joy*, 174) or *Oklahoma!* (Suskin, *Opening Nights*, 5), and ended in the late 1950s or early 1960s, with *West Side Story* (Atkinson in Engel, *A Consideration*, xii; Kingman, 253) or *Fiddler on the Roof* (Bordman, *A Chronicle*, 530; Suskin, *Opening Nights*, 11). See Block, "Broadway Canon."

655   "until *Show Boat* broke the mold": Atkinson in Engel, *American Musical Theater*, xii.

655   "progress . . . toward general artistic excellence": C. M. Smith, ix–x, 203.

655   *The Rise and Fall of the Broadway Musical*: Grant.

656   "past will wind up stifling its future": Tommasini, "Old Musicals," 2:1, 24–25.

656   "they are choking out new shows": Sondheim in ibid., 1.

657   "upends a traditional native form": Rich, "Sondheim," C19.

657   "pretty much made their peace with that": Childs in Singer, *Ever After*, 272–73.

658   "this status if it *isn't* popular": Hausam, xviii–xix.

658   "this is no way to be popular": Ibid., xix, xx.

658   "gender, sexual orientation, and disability": Minow.

659   accolades and respectable Broadway runs: On *Falsettos* and *Jelly*, see Thelen, 58–73, 208–25; Bell, 16–31, 46–73.

659   "Particularly in all-black shows": Wolfe in Thelen, 214, 217–18; Bell, 55.

660   self-styled inventor of jazz: Gioia, 39: "Although Morton did not invent jazz, he was perhaps the first to think about it in abstract terms, and articulate—both in his remarks and in his music—a coherent theoretical approach to its creation."

660   as his wife once delicately put it: In Lomax, 208–10.

661   "make up 'da Funk that's underneath": Wolfe in Hill and Hatch, 439.

661   a strikingly new kind of equilibrium: Regarding identity politics, the interests of racial and ethnic groups other than African Americans have been less well represented on the Broadway musical stage. On Asian American concerns about *Miss Saigon*, see Brustein "Use and Abuse," 31–34; Yoshikawa, 275–94; Hisama. About the 2002 revival of *Flower Drum Song*, see Wang, ix–xiv; D. H. Lewis; Tchen. On Latino American concerns about the 1979 play with music *Zoot Suit*, see Sandoval-Sánchez, 110–13. About *The Capeman* (1998) see Simon; Sebesta, 183–98. A harbinger of change in this regard perhaps can be seen in the 2008 Tony Award for best musical going to *In the Heights*, a Broadway musical not only about but also by Latino Americans (book: Quiara Alegría Hudes; songs: Lin-Manuel Miranda).

662   Ethel Merman, Carol Channing: Broadway divas of a younger generation might include Bette Middler (b. 1945), Betty Buckley (b. 1947), Bernadette Peters (b. 1948), and Patti LuPone (b. 1949). On diva musicals, see Clum, 167–96. On transvestism in musicals, see Toll, *On with the Show*, 239–63; Roger Baker. On gender and sexuality in musicals, see Van Leer; D. A. Miller; S. E. Wolff, "Queer Pleasures"; and *A Problem Like Maria*; Steyn, 146–212; Kirle, 161–200.

662 "to become the text in some shows": Clum, 9.

662 sexless, ashamed, or the butt of humor: N. Hart, 5.

662 "And that's what makes it count!": Fierstein in *Broadway: The American Musical*, vol. 3.

662 "merely a 'gay version' of it": D. A. Miller, 130. N. Hart, 19: "Just what did *La Cage aux Folles* ultimately end up being about? Laurents wanted it to be about illusion and disorientation; Herman wanted it to be about 'standing up for yourself and fighting bigotry'; Fierstein wanted it to be about the universality of love and marriage; and Hearn and Barry wanted it to be about *anything* but the intimation that they themselves might be homosexual."

663 "his own son's bigotry toward homosexuals": In Herman and Stasio, 226, 223–46; Citron, *Herman*, 225–53.

663 "was a guy in a frock": Steyn, 201.

663 confounded conventional musical expectations: Clum, 269–73; S. Miller, *Deconstructing*, 52–72. See also Kasha and Hirschhorn, 112–17.

663 regardless of one's age or sexuality: Finn in E. Schiff, 263; Rich, "'Falsettos.'"

663 that would come with maturity: S. Miller, *Deconstructing*, 56–57.

665 "gay men in the 1980s and beyond": Bishop, Notes to *Falsettoland*. The theater community formally responded to the crisis with the founding in 1988 of Broadway Cares/ Equity Fights AIDS, an enterprise aimed at raising funds and awareness to combat the disease.

665 but not in the least operatic: Though generally less compelling than *Falsettos*, Finn's other major theater work of recent decades includes a revision of *In Trousers* (1985), *Romance in Hard Times* (1989), *A New Brain* (1998) and *The 25th Annual Putnam County Spelling Bee* (2005).

666 for a musical of any kind: On *Hedwig*, see Clum, 193–97; Wollman, *Theater Will Rock*, 180–90.

666 a "well-known rock icon": Mitchell and Trask, 19.

666 as allowing them to coexist: Wollman in Washburne and Derno, 322; Wollman, *Theater Will Rock*, 181.

666 contrary to the practices of musical theater: See Wollman, *Theater Will Rock*, 186–90.

668 "mysteries both poignant and comic": Clum, 195–96.

669 Baum's classic *The Wonderful Wizard of Oz*: See Cote. The musical *Wicked* actually draws directly on Gregory Maguire's 1995 novel *Wicked: The Life and Times of the Wicked Witch of the West*. Alice Walker's novel *The Color Purple* and Frank Wedekind's drama *Frühlings Erwachen* (*Spring Awakening*) provide the bases for the musicals of the same name.

670 who created it in New York in 1961: See Engel, *Bright Day*, 278–85; Evans.

671 "It can't be taught academically": Sondheim in Tommasini, "Composer's Death."

672 before reaching its final form: On Larson and *Rent*, see McDonnell and Silberger (with libretto); Schulman; S. Miller, *Rebels*, 183–98; Wollman, *Theater Will Rock*, 170–76.

672 "I really wanted to succeed for him": In McDonnell and Silberger, 55; Rapp, 124–36.

672 "his way to finding a real synthesis": Sondheim in Tommasini, "Composer's Death." See also Tommasini in McDonnell and Silberger, 50.

673 "a *Hair* for the '90s": Larson in McDonnell and Silberger, 8.

673 "necessary to a healthy civilization": Ibid., 6.

675 "life in the face of death and AIDS": Ibid., 37.

675 "that it could bridge those worlds." Yearby in ibid., 48.

676 these five—all or even any of them: D. P. Stearns.

677 George C. Wolfe coauthored the book: On music theater see Labroca, 8–9; Bawtree, 2–15; Salzman and Desi, 253–59.

678 "the bright young hopes of Broadway": Brantley, "Autumnal American."

678 as he prepares himself for death: On *Floyd Collins*, see S. Miller, *Rebels*, 148–82. Hausam contains the librettos to *Floyd Collins*, *Rent*, *Parade*, and LaChiusa's *The Wild Party*.

680 "on 42nd Street called *Floyd Collins*": Guare.

680 "where America was at that time": Guettel in Singer, *Ever After*, 121. See also J. Green.

681 popular musical, but hardly art: Atkinson in Stumpf. *Cradle* is remembered today despite its short Broadway run, while *Hellzapoppin*, the long-running record-holder before *Okalahoma!*, is largely forgotten. An "Audience Guide" published in conjunction with the American Century Theater's 2007 reconstruction of *Hellzapoppin* provides invaluable insights into the show, most of the success of which relied on nonscripted elements. See Marshall.

682 of the musical itself as dead: Teachout, 47: "The Broadway musical is dead. Such, at any rate, is the conventional wisdom."

682 by wrong, of course, he means Broadway: Brantley in McDonnell and Silberger, 57.

682 "no challenge, no confrontation, no art": LaChiusa, 30–35.

683 "serious musical theater can easily be crossed": Gelb.

683 "the standard to which I'm holding myself": Brown in Bryer and Davison, 29–30.

684 "our moral attitudes, our way of moving": L. Bernstein, *Joy of Music*, 178.

684 four television networks simultaneously?: Grant, 1.

684 try to have its content altered?: While the Nixon administration failed to have a number like "Cool, Cool Considerate Men" cut from the 1970 White House performance of *1776*, it may well have been instrumental in having it cut from the 1972 film version of the show. See Calta; Ostrow, 100; Spencer.

WORKS CITED

Abbreviations

JAMS: *Journal of the American Musicological Society*
NGDAM: *New Grove Dictionary of American Music*
NGDMM: *New Grove Dictionary of Music and Musicians*, 1st edition
NGDMM2: *New Grove Dictionary of Music and Musicians*, 2nd edition
NGDO: *New Grove Dictionary of Opera*
NYT: *New York Times*

Abbott, George. *"Mister Abbott."* New York: Random House, 1963.
———. "The Musicals Take Over." *Theatre Arts*, July 1954.
Ade, George. "George Ade Talks of His Stage Ideals." *Theatre Magazine*, 1904.
———. "Light Opera Yesterday and Today." *Theatre Magazine*, 1903.
———. "Musical Comedy." In Lazarus, *The Best of George Ade.*
———. "Slang and the Stage." *New York Daily Tribune*, July 31, 1902.
Adler, Steven. *On Broadway: Art and Commerce on the Great White Way.* Carbondale: Southern Illinois University Press, 2004.
Adler, Thomas P. "The Musical Dramas of Stephen Sondheim: Some Critical Approaches." *Journal of Popular Culture* 12:3 (Winter 1978).
Adorno, Theodor W. *Essays on Music.* Edited by Richard Leppert. Translated by Susan H. Gillespie. Berkeley: University of California Press, 2002.
Adorno, Theodor W., and Max Horkheimer. *Dialectic of Enlightenment* (Philosophische Fragmente). New York: Social Studies Association, Inc., 1944.
Albee, Edward F. "Twenty Years of Vaudeville." In Stein, *American Vaudeville.*
Allen, Kelcey. Review of *Lady in the Dark. Women's Wear Daily,* January 24, 1941.
Allen, Reginald, *Gilbert and Sullivan in America: The Story of the First D'Oyly Carte Company American Tour.* New York: Gallery Association of New York State, 1979.
Allen, Robert C. *Horrible Prettiness: Burlesque and American Culture.* Chapel Hill: University of North Carolina Press, 1991.
Alexander, Michael. *Jazz Age Jews.* Princeton. NJ: Princeton University Press, 2001.
Alpert, Hollis, *The Life and Times of "Porgy and Bess": The Story of an American Classic.* New York: Alfred A. Knopf, 1990.
Altman, Richard, with Mervyn Kaufman. *The Making of a Musical: Fiddler on the Roof.* New York: Crown, 1971.
Altman, Rick. *The American Film Musical.* Bloomington: Indiana University Press, 1987.

American Theatre Wing. *Rules and Regulations of the American Theatre Wing's Tony Awards, 2005–2006.*

Amis, Kingsley, ed. *The New Oxford Book of Light* Verse. New York: Oxford University Press, 1978.

Anderson, John Murray. *Out Without My Rubbers.* New York: Library Publishers, 1954.

Anderson, Maxwell. *Off Broadway: Essays about the Theater.* New York: William Sloan, 1947.

———. "On Government: Being a Brief Preface to the Politics of 'Knickerbocker Holiday.'" *NYT*, November 13, 1938.

Andreu, Helene. *Jazz Dance.* Englewood Cliffs, NJ: Prentice Hall, 1983.

Appelbaum, Stanley, ed. *Show Songs from "The Black Crook" to "The Red Mill."* New York: Peter Smith Publishers, Inc., 1974.

Ardoin, John. *The Stages of Menotti.* New York: Doubleday, 1985.

Armitage, Merle. *George Gershwin, Man and Legend.* New York: Duell, Sloan and Pearce, 1958.

Arnold, Elliott. *Deep in My Heart.* New York: Duell, Sloan and Pearce, 1940.

Arnold, Matthew. *Culture and Anarchy.* London, 1869.

Aronson, Arnold. *American Set Design.* New York: Theatre Communications Group, 1985.

———. *Architect of Dreams: The Theatrical Vision of Joseph Urban.* New York: Columbia University Press, 2000.

Assassins, VHS. New York: Music Theatre International, Video Conversation Piece, 1996?

Astaire, Fred. *Steps in Time.* New York: Harper & Brothers, 1959.

Atkinson, Brooks. "At the Theatre." *NYT*, April 25, 1952.

———. "Everybody's Lady." *NYT*, June 3, 1956.

———. "The Jungles of the City." *NYT*, September 27, 1957.

———. "Made With Music." *NYT*, March 21, 1954.

———. "The Pajama Game." *NYT*, May 30, 1954.

———. "'Porgy and Bess,' Native Opera, Opens at the Alvin." *NYT*, October 11, 1935.

———. "Pulitzer Laurels." *NYT*, May 8, 1932.

Auden, W. H., ed. *The Oxford Book of Light Verse.* London: Oxford University Press, 1938.

———. "Unused lyrics by W. H. Auden relating to the musical *Man of La Mancha.*" Dale Wasserman Papers, Archives Division, State Historical Society of Wisconsin, Madison.

Avery, Laurence G., ed. *Dramatist in America: Letters of Maxwell Anderson, 1912–1958.* Chapel Hill: University of North Carolina Press, 1977.

Bach, Bob, and Ginger Mercer, eds. *Our Huckleberry Friend: The Life, Times, and Lyrics of Johnny Mercer.* Secaucus, NJ: Lyle Stuart, 1982.

Bach, Steven. *Dazzler: The Life and Times of Moss Hart.* New York: Alfred A. Knopf, 2001.

Baker, Barbara, ed. *Bolossy Kiralfy, Creator of Great Musical Spectacles: An Autobiography.* Ann Arbor, MI: UMI Research Press, 1988.

Baker, Roger. *Drag: A History of Female Impersonation in the Performing Arts.* New York: New York University Press, 1994.

Baker, Russell, ed. *The Norton Book of Light Verse.* New York: W. W. Norton, 1986.

Balanchine, George. "Notes on Choreography." In Chujoy and Manchester, *The Dance Encyclopedia.*

Balanchine, George, and Francis Mason. *Balanchine's Complete Stories of the Great Ballets.* New York: Doubleday, 1977.

Banfield, Stephen. "Bit by Bit: Five Ways of Looking at Musicals." *Musical Times* 135:1814 (Apr. 1994).

———. "The Ironbridge Letters." *American Music*, Spring 1992.

———. *Jerome Kern.* New Haven, CT: Yale University Press, 2006.

———. *Sondheim's Broadway Musicals.* Ann Arbor: University of Michigan Press, 1993.

———. "Stage and Screen Entertainers in the Twentieth Century." In Potter, *The Cambridge Companion to Singing.*

Banham, Martin, ed. *The Cambridge Guide to World Theatre.* Cambridge: Cambridge University Press, 1988.

Bank, Rosemarie K. *Theatre Culture in America, 1825–1860.* Cambridge: Cambridge University Press, 1997.

Baral, Robert. *Revue: A Nostalgic Reprise of the Great Broadway Period.* New York: Fleet Publishing Company, 1962.

———. "Ziegfeld and His Follies." *Variety,* January 9, 1957.

Barish, Jonas A. *The Antitheatrical Prejudice.* Berkeley and Los Angeles: University of California Press, 1981.

Barlow, Robert. "A University Approach to the American Musical Theater." *Notes,* December 1955.

Barnabee, Henry Clay. *My Wanderings: Reminiscences of Henry Clay Barnabee.* Boston: Chapple Publishing Company, 1913.

Barnum, Phineas Taylor. *Struggles and Triumphs; or, Forty Years' Recollections of P. T. Barnum.* Buffalo, NY: The Courier Company, 1882.

Barrett, Mary Ellin. *Irving Berlin: A Daughter's Memoir.* New York: Alfred A. Knopf, 1994.

Barton, Andrew. *The Disappointment: or the Force of Credulity. A Critical Edition of the First American Drama.* Edited by David Mays. Gainesville: University Presses of Florida, 1976.

———. *The Disappointment: or, the Force of Credulity. Musical Accompaniments and an Original Overture by Samuel Adler.* Edited by Jerald C. Graue and Judith Layng. Madison, WI: A-R Editions, 1976.

Bawtree. Michael. *The New Singing Theatre: A Charter for the Music Theatre Movement.* New York: Oxford University Press, 1991.

Baxandall, Lee. "Brecht in America." *The Drama Review,* Fall 1967.

Baxter, Joan. *Television Musicals.* Jefferson, NC: McFarland & Company, 1997.

Bay, Howard. *Stage Design.* New York: Drama Book Specialists, 1974.

Bean, Annemarie, James V. Hatch, and Brooks Mcnamara, eds., *Inside the Minstrel Mask: Readings in Nineteenth-Century Blackface Minstrelsy.* Hanover, NH: Wesleyan University Press, 1996.

Beckerman, Bernard, and Howard Siegman. "The Passing—and Everlasting—Show." In *On Stage: Selected Reviews from the New York Times, 1920–1970.* New York: Arno Press, 1973.

Beddow, Margery. *Bob Fosse's Broadway.* Portsmouth, NH: Heinemann, 1996.

Beerbohm, Constance. "The Cakewalk and How to Dance It." *The Tatler,* July 1, 1903.

Behr, Edward. *The Complete Book of Les Misérables.* New York: Arcade, 1989.

Behr, Edward, and Mark Steyn. *The Story of Miss Saigon.* New York: Arcade, 1991.

Beidler, Philip D. *"South Pacific* and American Remembering; or 'Josh, We're Going to Buy This Son of a Bitch!'" *Journal of American Studies,* August 1993.

Beiswanger, George. "Theatre Today: Symptoms and Surmises," *Journal of Aesthetics and Art Criticism* 3, nos. 9–10 (1944): 19–29.

Bell, Marty. *Broadway Stories: A Backstage Journey through Musical Theatre.* New York: Limelight Editions, 1993.

Bender, Thomas. *New York Intellect.* New York: Alfred A. Knopf, 1987.

Bennett, Michael, James Kirkwood, Nicholas Dante, Marvin Hamlish, and Edward Kleban. *A Chorus Line: The Book of The Musical.* New York: Applause Theatre Book Publishers, 1995.

Bennett, Robert Russell. *Instrumentally Speaking.* New York: Belwin-Mills, 1975.

Bentley, Eric. "Comedy and the Comic Spirit in America." In Downer, *American Theater Today.*

———. *From the American Drama.* New York: Doubleday, 1956.

———. *The Life of the Drama.* New York: Atheneum, 1983.

———. *The Playwright as Thinker.* New York: Reynal & Hitchcock, 1946; repr. San Diego: Harcourt Brace Jovanovich, 1987.

———. *What Is Theatre?* New York: Limelight, 1968.

Bereson, Ruth. *The Operatic State: Cultural Policy and the Opera House.* London: Routledge, 2002.

Berger, Marilyn. "George Abbott, Broadway Giant with Hit after Hit, Is Dead at 107." *NYT,* February 2, 1995.

Bergreen, Laurence. *As Thousands Cheer: The Life of Irving Berlin.* New York: Viking, 1990.

Berkowitz, Gerald M. *New Broadways: Theatre Across America Approaching a New Millennium.* Totowa, NJ: Rowman & Allenheld, 1997.

Berlant, Lauren. "Pax Americana: The Case of *Show Boat.*" In Lynch and Warner, *Cultural Institutions of the Novel.*

Bernheim, Alfred L. *The Business of the Theatre: An Economic History of the American Theatre, 1750–1932.* New York: Benjamin Blom, 1932.

Bernstein, Leonard. "Colloquy in Boston." *NYT,* November 18, 1956.

———. *Findings.* New York: Simon & Schuster, 1982.

———. *The Infinite Variety of Music.* New York: Simon & Schuster, 1966.

———. *The Joy of Music.* New York: Simon & Schuster, 1959; repr. 1993.

———. "Prelude to a Blitzstein Musical Adaptation." *NYT,* October 30, 1949.

———. *The Unanswered Question.* Cambridge, MA: Harvard University Press, 1976.

Bernstein, Nina. "Candide's Travels." *prelude, fugue & riffs,* Spring/Summer 1997.

Bierley, Paul E *John Philip Sousa: An American Phenomenon.* Englewood Cliffs, NJ: Prentice-Hall, 1973.

———. *John Philip Sousa: A Descriptive Catalogue of His Works.* Urbana: University of Illinois, Press, 1973.

———, ed. *Later Operetta: Nineteenth-Century American Musical Theater,* vol. 14. New York: Garland, 1994.

———. *The Works of John Philip Sousa.* Columbus, OH: Integrity Press, 1984.

Bigsby, C.W.E. *A Critical Introduction to Twentieth-Century American Drama,* vol. 3: *Beyond Broadway.* Cambridge: Cambridge University Press, 1985.

Billman Larry. *Fred Astaire: A Bio-Bibliography.* Westport, CT: Greenwood, 1997.

Birdoff, Harry. *The World's Greatest Hit: Uncle Tom's Cabin.* New York: S. F. Vanni, 1947.

Bishop, André. Preface to *Assassins.* New York: Theatre Communications Group, 1991.

———. Notes to *Falsettoland,* CD. New York: DRG CDSBL-12601, 1990.

Bissell, Richard. *Say Darling.* Boston: Little, Brown, 1957.

Blau, Eric, *Jacques Brel Is Alive and Well and Living in Paris.* New York: E.P. Dutton, 1971.

Blitzstein, Marc. *Marc Blitzstein Discusses His Theater Compositions,* LP. New York: Westminster/Spoken Arts 717, 1956.

Block, Geoffrey Holden. "The Broadway Canon from *Show Boat* to *West Side Story* and the European Operatic Ideal." *The Journal of Musicology,* Fall 1993.

———. *Enchanted Evenings: The Broadway Musical from "Show Boat" to Sondheim.* Oxford and New York: Oxford University Press, 1997.

———. "Frank Loesser's Sketchbooks for *The Most Happy Fella.*" *The Musical Quarterly* 73 (1989).

———. *Richard Rodgers.* New Haven, CT: Yale University Press, 2003.

———, ed. *The Richard Rodgers Reader.* New York, 2002.

Bloom, Ken. *Broadway: An Encyclopedic Guide to the History, People and Places of Times Square.* New York: Facts on File, 1991.

Blumenthal, Eileen. *Julie Taymor: Playing with Fire.* New York: Harry Abrams, 1999.

Bogard, Travis, and William Oliver, eds. *Modern Drama: Essays in Criticism.* New York: Oxford University Press, 1965.

Bolcom, William. "Parallel Universes." *Opera News,* July 1993.

———. "A Serious Composer with Broadway Style." *NYT,* August 30, 1998.

Bolton, Guy. "The Improvement in Musical Comedy Standards." *Dramatic Mirror,* February 23, 1918.

———. "Working with Wodehouse." In Cazalet-Keir, *Homage to P.G. Wodehouse.*

Bolton, Whitney. "Man of La Mancha, a Treasure." *The Morning Telegraph,* November 24, 1965.

Bone, [Harold]. "Away We Go!" *Variety,* March 11, 1943.

Booth, Mark. *Camp.* London: Quartet, 1983.

Bordman, Gerald Martin. *American Musical Comedy: From "Adonis" to "Dreamgirls."* New York: Oxford University Press, 1982.

————. *American Musical Revue: From "The Passing Show" to "Sugar Babies."* New York: Oxford University Press, 1985.

————. *American Musical Theatre: A Chronicle.* New York: Oxford University Press, 1978; 2nd ed., 1992.

————. *American Operetta: From "H.M.S. Pinafore" to "Sweeney Todd."* Garden City, NY: Doubleday, 1981.

————. *Days to Be Happy, Years to Be Sad: The Life and Music of Vincent Youmans.* New York: Oxford University Press, 1982.

————. "Friml." *NGDO.*

————. *Jerome Kern: His Life and Music.* New York: Oxford University Press, 1980.

————. *The Oxford Companion to American Theatre.* New York: Oxford University Press, 1984; 2nd ed., 1992.

Borroff, Edith. "Origin of Species: Conflicting Views of American Musical Theater History." *American Music* (1984): 101–11.

Bourne, Stephen. *Ethel Waters: Stormy Weather.* Lanham, MD: Scarecrow Press, 2007.

Bowers, Dwight Blocker. Notes to *American Musical Theater: Shows, Songs, and Stars,* 4CDs. Washington, DC, and New York: Smithsonian/CBS, 1989.

Bowman, Walter Parker, and Robert Hamilton Ball. *Theatre Language: A Dictionary of Terms in English of the Drama and Stage from Medieval to Modern Times.* New York: Theatre Arts Books, 1961.

Brahms, Caryl, and Ned Sherrin, eds. *Song by Song: The Lives and Work of 14 Great Lyric Writers.* Bolton, UK: Ross Anderson, 1984.

Brantley, Ben. "An Album of Fosse." *NYT,* January 15, 1999.

————. "His Songs Abound, but Where's Johnny." *NYT,* March 13, 2006.

————. "Rogue Sells Horns; Hope Is Free." *NYT,* April 28, 2000.

————. "A Wise Autumnal American in Florence." *NYT,* April 19, 2005.

Brasmer, William. "The Wild West Exhibition: A Fraudulent Realty." In Matlaw, *American Popular Entertainment.*

Brecht, Bertolt. *Collected Plays,* vol. 7. Edited by Ralph Manheim and John Willett. London, 1976.

————. "On Experimental Theatre." In Willett, *Brecht on Theatre.*

————. "On the Use of Music in an Epic Theater." In Willett, *Brecht on Theatre.*

Briggs, John. *Requiem for a Yellow Brick Brewery: A History of the Metropolitan Opera.* Boston: Little, Brown, 1969.

Broadway: A History of the Musical, 5 Videotapes. Irvine, CA: Chesney Communications VC 1392–1396, 1989.

Broadway: The American Musical, 3 DVDs. Directed by Michael Kantor. Hollywood, CA: Paramount, 2004.

Brooks, Mel, and Tom Meehan. *The Producers [How We Did It].* New York: Miramax, 2001.

Brooks, Tim. *Lost Sounds: Blacks and the Birth of the Recording Industry, 1890–1919.* Urbana: University of Illinois Press, 2004.

Brown, John Mason. Review of *Lady in the Dark. New York Post,* January 24, 1941.

Browne, Junius Henri. *The Great Metropolis: A Mirror of New York.* Hartford, CT: American Publishing Company, 1969.

Brustein, Robert. *Seasons of Discontent.* New York: Simon & Schuster: 1967.

————. "The Siren Song of Broadway Is a Warning." *NYT,* May 22, 1988.

————. *The Third Theatre.* New York: Alfred A. Knopf, 1969.

————. "The Use and Abuse of Multiculturalism." *The New Republic,* September 16 and 23, 1991.

Bryan, George B. *Ethel Merman: A Bio-Bibliography.* Westport, CT: Greenwood, 1992.

Bryer, Jackson R., and Richard A. Davison, eds. *The Art of the American Musical: Conversations with the Creators.* New Brunswick, NJ: Rutgers University Press, 2005.

Buck, Kirstin. *Cultivating the Wasteland.* New York: American Council for the Arts, 1983.

Buckley, Peter George. "To the Opera House: Culture and Society in New York City, 1820–1860." PhD diss., SUNY, Stony Brook, 1984.

————. "Paratheatricals and Popular Stage Entertainiment." In Wilmeth and Bigsby, *The Cambridge History of American Theatre*, vol. 1.

Bulloch, John Malcolm. "A Collection of Theatre Programmes and Newspaper Cuttings Relating Thereto." The British Library, London.

Burdick, Elizabeth B., Peggy C. Hansen, and Brenda Zanger, eds. *Contemporary Stage Design—U.S.A.* Middletown, CT: Wesleyan University Press, 1974.

Burns, Warren Thomas. "The Plays of Edward Green Harrigan: The Theatre of Intercultural Communication." PhD diss., Pennsylvania State University, 1969.

Burrows, Abe. *Honest Abe.* Boston: Atlantic-Little, Brown, 1980.

————. "How to Succeed in (Show) Business . . ." *Show Business Illustrated*, January 23, 1962.

————. "The Making of *Guys and Dolls.*" *Atlantic Monthly*, January 1980.

Burton, Humphrey. *Leonard Bernstein.* New York: Doubleday, 1994.

Burton, Jack. *Blue Book of Broadway Musicals.* New York: Century House, 1952.

Burton, William Westerbrook, ed. *Conversations about Bernstein.* New York: Oxford University Press, 1995.

Buzga, Jaroslav. "Sprengt die Opernhäuser in die Luft." *Der Spiegel*, September 25, 1967.

Calta, Louis. "White House Books Uncut '1776.'" *NYT*, January 23, 1970.

Canby, Vincent. "Excitement Fills Premiere of 'Dolly.'" *NYT*, December 18, 1969.

————. "In a New Fosse Vehicle, a Headlong Joy Ride." *NYT*, January 24, 1999.

Canning, Charlotte. "Directing History: Women, Performance and Scholarship." *Theatre Research International* 30:1 (2005): 49–59.

Cantor, Eddie, and David Freedman. *Ziegfeld, the Great Glorifier.* New York: Alfred H. King, 1934.

Carroll, John F. "Oscar Hammerstein I, 1895–1915: His Creation and Development of New York's Times Square Theatre District," PhD diss., CUNY, 1998.

Carter, Marva Griffin. "Removing the 'Minstrel Mask' in the Musicals of Will Marion Cook." *The Musical Quarterly* 84:2 (Summer 2000) 206–20.

Carter, Randolph. *The World of Flo Ziegfeld.* New York: Praeger, 1974.

Carter, Randolph, and Robert Reed Cole. *Joseph Urban: Architecture, Theatre, Opera, Film.* New York: Abbeville Press, 1992.

Carter, Tim. *Oklahoma!: The Making of an American Musical.* New Haven, CT: Yale University Press, 2007.

Cartmell, Don J. "Stephen Sondheim and the Concept Musical." PhD diss., University of California, Santa Barbara, 1983.

Casmus, Mary Irene. "Gian Carlo Menotti: His Dramatic Techniques: A Study Based on the Works Written 1937–1954." PhD diss., Columbia University, 1962.

Castañeda, Carlos E. "The First American Play." *Preliminary Studies of the Texas Catholic Historical Society* 3:1 (1936).

Castle, Irene. *Castles in the Air.* As told to Bob and Wanda Duncan. New York: Da Capo, 1958.

————. [Mrs. Vernon]. *My Husband.* New York: Da Capo, 1919.

Castle, Mr. and Mrs. Vernon. *Modern Dancing.* New York: World Syndicate Company, 1914.

Cazalet-Keir, Thelma, ed. *Homage to P. G. Wodehouse.* London: Barrie & Jenkins, 1973.

Chach, Maryann, Reagan Fletcher, Mark E. Swartz, and Sylvia Wang. *The Shuberts Present: 100 Years of American Theater.* New York: Harry Abrams, 2001.

Challender, James W. "The Function of the Choreographer in the Development of the Concept Musical: An Examination of the Work of Jerome Robbins, Bob Fosse, and Michael Bennett on Broadway between 1944 and 1981." PhD diss., Florida State University, 1986.

Chapin, Schuyler. *Leonard Bernstein: Notes from a Friend.* New York: Walker & Company, 1992.

Chapin, Ted. *Everything Was Possible: The Birth of the Musical "Follies."* New York: Alfred A. Knopf, 2003.

Charters, Ann. *Nobody: The Story of Bert Williams.* New York: Macmillan, 1970; repr. 1983.

Christgau, Robert. "Whooopee!" *The Village Voice*, June 12, 1969.

Chude-Sokei, Louis. *The Last "Darky": Bert Williams, Black-on-Black Minstrelsy, and the African Diaspora.* Durham, NC: Duke University Press, 2005.

Chujoy, Anatole, and P. W. Manchester, eds. *The Dance Encyclopedia.* New York: Touchstone, 1967.

Cibber, Colley. *The Plays of Colley Cibber.* Edited by Timothy J. Viator and William J. Burling. Madison and Teaneck, NJ: Fairleigh Dickinson University Press, 2001.

Citron, Stephen. *Jerry Herman: Poet of the Showtune.* New Haven, CT: Yale University Press, 2004.

———. *Noël and Cole: The Sophisticates.* New York: Oxford University Press, 1993.

———. *Sondheim and Lloyd Webber: The New Musical.* Oxford and New York: Oxford University Press, 2001.

———. *The Wordsmiths: Oscar Hammerstein 2nd and Alan Jay Lerner.* New York: Oxford University Press, 1995.

Clarke, Clorinda. "The Sound of Music." *Manhattanville Alumnae Revue,* Spring 1960.

Cliff, Nigel. *The Shakespeare Riots: Revenge, Drama, and Death in Nineteenth-Century America.* New York: Random House, 2007.

Clinton-Baddeley, Victor. *The Burlesque Tradition in English Theatre after 1660.* New York: Benjamin Blom, 1971.

Clum, John M. *Something for the Boys: Musical Theater and Gay Culture.* New York: St. Martin's Press, 1999.

Clurman, Harold. *The Fervent Years: The Group Theatre and the Thirties.* New York: Alfred A. Knopf, 1945; repr. 1975.

Cockrell, Dale. *Demons of Disorder: Early Blackface Minstrels and Their World.* Cambridge: Cambridge University Press, 1997.

Cocuzza, Ginnie. "The Greenwich Village Follies of 1919." In Loney, *Musical Theatre in America.*

Cohan, George M. *Twenty Years on Broadway and the Years It Took to Get There.* New York: Harper & Brothers, 1924.

———. "Why My Plays Succeed." *Theatre Magazine,* May 1924.

Cohen, Robert. *Theatre,* 5th ed. Mountain View, CA: Mayfield Publishing, 2000.

Cohen-Stratyner, Barbara Naomi. *Biographical Dictionary of Dance.* New York: Schirmer, 1982.

Cole, Toby, and Helen Krich Chinoy, eds. *Directing the Play.* Indianapolis: Bobbs-Merrill, 1953.

Coleman, Emily. "The Dance Man Leaps to the Top." *NYT,* April 19, 1959.

Collective Bargaining Agreement between the League of American Theatres & Producers, Inc., and Associated Musicians of Greater New York, Local 802, AFM, AFL-CIO. 1993.

Collinson, Francis M. *Orchestration for the Theatre.* London: John Lane, 1941.

Colvan, E. B.["Zeke"]. *Face the Footlights!: A New and* Practical *Approach to Acting.* New York: Whittlesey House, 1940.

Comden, Betty. *Off Stage: My Non–Show Business Life.* New York: Simon & Schuster, 1995.

Comden, Betty, and Adolph Green. *The New York Musicals of Comden and Green: On The Town, Wonderful Town, Bells Are Ringing.* New York: Applause Theatre & Cinema Book Publishers, 1997.

Cone, John Frederic. *Oscar Hammerstein's Manhattan Opera Company.* Norman: University of Oklahoma Press, 1966.

Connolly, Joseph, *P.G. Wodehouse.* London: Haus, 2004.

Conrad, Christine. *Jerome Robbins: That Broadway Man, That Ballet Man.* London: Booth-Clibborn, 2000.

Conrad, Jon Alan. "Broadway Orchestration." Unpublished monograph.

———. "Candide." *NGDO,* vol. 1.

Cook, Bruce. *Brecht in Exile.* New York: Holt, Rinehart and Winston, 1982.

Copeland, Roger. "Broadway Dance." *Dance Magazine,* November 1974.

Copland, Aaron. *What to Listen for in Music.* New York: Mentor Books, 1957.

Cordell, Richard, and Lowell Matson, eds. *The Off-Broadway Theatre.* New York: Random House, 1959.

Corio, Ann, with Joe DiMona. *This Was Burlesque.* New York: Madison Square Press, 1968.

Corry, John. "Gower Champion Dies Hours before Show Opens." *NYT,* August 26, 1980.

Cote, David. *Wicked: The Grimmerie, A Behind-the Scenes Look at the Hit Broadway Musical.* New York: Hyperion, 2005.

Coveney, Michael. *Cats on a Chandelier: The Andrew Lloyd Webber Story.* London: Hutchinson, 1999.

Cox, James M. "A Connecticut Yankee in King Arthur's Court: The Machinery of Self-Preservation." *Yale Review,* Autumn 1960.

Crawford, Cheryl. *One Naked Individual: My Fifty Years in the Theatre.* Indianapolis: Bobbs-Merrill, 1977.

Crawford, Richard. *The American Musical Landscape.* Berkeley: University of California Press, 1993.

———. *America's Musical Life: A History.* New York: W. W. Norton, 2001.

———. "It Ain't Necessarily Soul: Gershwin's *Porgy and Bess* as a Symbol." *Yearbook for Inter-American Musical Research* 8 (1972): 26–30.

Crawford, Richard. Notes to *Music of the Federal Era,* LP. New York: New World 299, 1978.

———. "Porgy and Bess," *NGDO,* vol. 3.

Crawford, Richard, Allen Lott, and Carol J. Oja, eds. *A Celebration of American Music: Words and Music in Honor of H. Wiley Hitchcock.* Ann Arbor: University of Michigan Press, 1990.

Crittenden, Camille. *Johann Strauss and Vienna: Operetta and the Politics of Popular Culture.* Cambridge: Cambridge University Press, 2000.

Crouse, Russel. "Explaining That Anything Goes." *NYT,* November 25, 1934.

Cruse, Harold. *The Crisis of the Negro Intellectual.* New York: Morrow 1967.

Dahlhaus, Carl. *Nineteenth-Century Music.* Translated by J. Bradford Robinson. Berkeley: University of California Press, 1989.

———. *Realism in Nineteenth-Century Music.* Translated by Mary Whittall. Cambridge: Cambridge University Press, 1985.

Dalrymple, Jean. *From the Last Row.* Clifton, NJ: James T. White & Company, 1975.

D'Andre, David Mark. "The Theatre Guild, Carousel, and the Cultural Field of American Musical Theatre." PhD diss., Yale University, 2000.

Darrell, Margery, ed. *The Rodgers and Hart Song Book.* New York: Simon & Schuster, 1951.

Da Silva, Howard. Notes to *The Cradle Will Rock,* 2 LPs. New York: MGM SE 4289-2, 1965.

Davis, Lee. *Bolton and Wodehouse and Kern: The Men Who Made Musical Comedy.* New York: James H. Heineman, 1993.

———. *Scandals and Follies: The Rise and Fall of the Great Broadway Revue.* New York: Limelight, 2000.

Davis, Lorrie, with Rachel Gallagher. *Letting Down My Hair.* New York: Arthur Fields, 1973.

Davis, Peter A. "Plays and Playwrights to 1800." In Wilmeth and Bigsby, *The Cambridge History of American Theatre.*

———. "The Syndicate/Shubert War." In W. R. Taylor, *Inventing Times Square.*

Day, Barry, ed. *The Complete Lyrics of P. G. Wodehouse.* Lanham, MD: Scarecrow Press, 2004.

Debus, Allen G. "The Early Victor Herbert: From the Gay Nineties to the First World War." Notes to *Music of Victor Herbert,* 3 LPs. Washington, DC, and New York: Smithsonian/RCA R-017, 1979.

de Mille, Agnes. *America Dances.* New York: Macmillan, 1980.

———. *And Promenade Home.* Boston: Little, Brown, 1958.

———. *The Book of Dance.* New York: Golden Press, 1963.

———. *Dance to the Piper: Memoirs of the Ballet.* Boston: Little, Brown, 1952.

———. *Martha: The Life of Martha Graham.* New York: Random House, 1991.

———. "Musical Comedy Tonight." 1979 TV script. In Agnes de Mille Papers, Dance Collection, New York Public Library for the Performing Arts, Lincoln Center.

———. *Portrait Gallery.* Boston: Houghton Mifflin, 1990.

———. *Reprieve: A Memoir.* New York: Doubleday, 1981.

———. *Speak to Me, Dance with Me.* Boston: Little, Brown, 1973.

————. *To a Young Dancer: A Handbook*. Boston: Little, Brown, 1962.

————. *Where the Wings Grow: A Memoir of Childhood*. New York: Doubleday, 1978.

Denman, Jeffrey. *A Year with "The Producers."* New York: Theatre Arts, 2002.

Denning, Michael. "The End of Mass Culture." In Naremore and Brantlinger, *Modernity and Mass Culture.*

Dennison, Sam. *Scandalize My Name: Black Imagery in American Popular Music.* New York: Garland, 1982.

Desowitz, Bill. "Another Revival of 'Annie Get Your Gun.'" *NYT*, January 7, 2001.

Dietz, Howard. *Dancing in the Dark*. New York: Quadrangle, 1974.

DiMaggio, Paul. "Cultural Boundaries and Structural Change: The Extension of the High Culture Model to Theater, Opera, and the Dance, 1900–1940." In Lamont and Fournier, *Cultivating Differences.*

Dimeglio, John E. *Vaudeville U.S.A.* Bowling Green, OH: Bowling Green University Popular Press, 1973.

Dizikes, John. *Opera in America: A Cultural History*. New Haven, CT: Yale University Press, 1993.

Doctorow, E. L. "Tap-Dancer among the Literati." *NYT*, October 4, 1987.

Dolan, Marc J. "Transoceanic Irony, or the Poetic Justice of *The Pirates of Penzance*." http://hcs.harvard.edu/hrgsp/productions/pir81/pir81arg.htm.

Donovan, Timothy P. "*'Annie Get Your Gun'*: A Last Celebration of Nationalism." *Journal of Popular Culture* 12:3 (Winter 1978).

————. "Oh, What a Beautiful Mornin': The Musical *Oklahoma!* And the Popular Mind in 1943." *Journal of Popular Culture* 8:3 (Winter 1974).

Don't Give the Name a Bad Place: Types & Stereotypes in American Musical Theater, 1870–1900, LP. New York: New World 265, 1978. Notes by Richard M. Sudhalter.

Dormon, James H. "Ethnic Cultures of the Mind: The Harrigan-Hart Mosaic." *American Studies* 33:2 (Fall 1992).

Douglas, Ann. *Terrible Honesty: Mongrel Manhattan in the 1920s*. New York: Farrar, Straus and Giroux, 1995.

Downer, Alan Seymour. *The Eminent Tragedian William Charles Macready*. Cambridge, MA: Harvard University Press, 1966.

————, ed. *American Theater Today*. New York: Basic Books, 1967.

Downes, Olin. "'Porgy and Bess,' Native Opera, Opens at the Alvin." *NYT*, October 11, 1935.

Drew, David. *Kurt Weill: A Handbook*. London: Faber, 1987.

Drutman, Irving. "Song-Writing Sensation: Frank Loesser." *New York Herald Tribune*, December 17, 1950.

Druxman, Michael B. *The Musical, from Broadway to Hollywood*. South Brunswick, NJ: A. S. Barnes, 1980.

Dubinsky, David. Notes to *Pins and Needles*, LP: Twenty-fifth Anniversary Edition. New York: CBS AOS 2210, 1962.

Duff Gordon, Lady ["Lucile"]. *Discretions and Indiscretions*. London: Jarrolds, 1932.

Dulles, Foster Rhea. *America Learns to Play: A History of Popular Recreation, 1607–1940*. New York: Peter Smith, 1952.

Dunlap, William. *A History of the American Theatre from Its Origins to 1832*. New York: [Burt Franklin], 1832; repr. Urbana and Chicago: University of Illinois Press, 2005.

Dunn, Don. *The Making of NO, NO, NANETTE*. Secaucus, NJ: Citadel Press, 1972.

Durham, Frank. *DuBose Heyward, The Man Who Wrote Porgy*. Columbia: University of South Carolina Press, 1954.

The Early Minstrel Show, LP. New York: New World 338, 1985. Notes by Robert B. Winans.

Easton, Carol. *No Intermissions: The Life of Agnes de Mille*. Boston: Little, Brown, 1996.

Eells, George. *The Life That Late He Led: A Biography of Cole Porter*. New York: Putnam, 1967.

Egan, Bill. *Florence Mills: Harlem Jazz Queen*. Studies in Jazz, No. 48. Lanham, MD: Scarecrow Press, 2004.

Eichenbaum, Rose. *Masters of Movement: Portraits of America's Great Choreographers.* Washington, DC: Smithsonian Books, 2004.

E.K. Review of *A Connecticut Yankee. Daily Telegraph* (London), October 11, 1929.

Eliot, T. S. *Cats: The Book of the Musical.* San Diego: Harcourt Brace, 1983.

Emerson, Ralph Waldo. *Selected Essays, Lectures, and Poems.* Edited by Robert D. Richardson, Jr. New York: Random House, 1990.

Engel, Lehman. *The American Musical Theater: A Consideration.* New York: Macmillan, 1967; rev. 1975.

———. *This Bright Day.* New York: Macmillan, 1974.

———. *Words with Music: The Broadway Musical Libretto.* New York: Associated Music Publishing, 1981.

Engle, Gary D., ed. *This Grotesque Essence: Plays from the American Minstrel Stage.* Baton Rouge: Louisiana State University Press, 1978.

Epstein, Helen. *Joe Papp: An American Life.* Boston: Little, Brown, 1994.

Erenberg, Lewis A. *Steppin' Out: New York Nightlife and the Transformation of American Culture, 1890–1930.* Westport, CT: Greenwood, 1981.

Etherington-Smith, Meredith, and Jeremy Pilcher. *The "It" Girls: Lucy, Lady Duff Gordon, the Couturiere "Lucile," and Elinor Glyn, Romantic Novelist.* San Diego: Harcourt Brace, 1986.

Evans, Frank. "The Rebirth of the Great American Song, Part Two: The BMI-Lehman Engel Musical Theatre Workshop." http://www.aislesay.com/BMI.html.

Everett, William. Sigmund Romberg's Operettas 'Blossom Time,' 'The Student Prince,' 'My Maryland,' and 'My Princess.'" PhD diss., University of Kansas, 1991.

Everett, William A., and Paul R. Laird, eds. *Cambridge Companion to the Musical.* Cambridge: Cambridge University Press, 2002.

Ewen, David. *All the Years of American Popular Music.* New York: Prentice Hall, 1977.

———. *Complete Book of the American Musical Theater.* New York: Holt, 1958; rev. 1976 as *New Complete Book of the American Musical Theater.*

———. *Composers for the American Musical Theatre.* New York: Dodd, Mead and Company, 1968.

———. *A Journey to Greatness: The Life and Music of George Gershwin.* New York: Henry Holt, 1956.

———. *The Life and Death of Tin Pan Alley: The Golden Age of American Popular Music.* New York: Funk and Wagnalls, 1964.

———. *Richard Rodgers.* New York: Holt, 1957.

———. *The Story of the American Musical Theater,* rev. ed. Philadelphia: Chilton, 1968.

———. *With a Song in His Heart: The Story of Richard Rodgers.* New York: Holt Rinehart and Winston, 1963.

Eyre, Richard. "Directing Guys and Dolls." In *The Guys and Dolls Book,* edited by Matt Wolf. London: Royal National Theatre/Nick Hern Press, 1982.

Eyre, Richard, and Nicholas Wright. *Changing Stages: A View of British and American Theatre in the Twentieth Century.* New York: Random House, 2001.

Farber, Donald C. *From Option to Opening: A Guide for the Off-Broadway Producer.* New York: DBS, 1968.

Farber, Donald C., and Robert Viagas. *The Amazing Story of the Fantasticks, America's Longest-Running Play.* New York: Carol Publishing Group, 1991.

Faris, Alexander. *Jacques Offenbach.* New York: Scribner, 1980.

Farnsworth, Marjorie. *The Ziegfeld Follies: A History in Text and Pictures.* New York: Bonanza, 1956.

Farwell, Anna [Mrs. Reginald de Koven]. *A Musician and His Wife.* New York: Harpers, 1926.

Feingold, Michael. "Al Carmines." *The Village Voice.* September 6, 2005.

———. "Tunesmithing." *The Village Voice.* November 21, 1989.

———. "The Two by Four Is a Whorehouse Again." *The Village Voice,* May 10, 1976.

———. "The Weill Party." *Kurt Weill Newsletter,* Spring 2001.

Ferencz, George J., ed. *"The Broadway Sound": The Autobiography and Selected Essays of Robert Russell Bennett.* Rochester, NY: University of Rochester Press, 1999.

Feuer, Cy. *I Got the Show Right Here.* New York: Simon & Schuster, 2003.

Feuer, Jane. *The Hollywood Musical,* 2nd ed. Bloomington: Indiana University Press, 1987.

Fields, Armond. *Fred Stone: Circus Performer and Musical Comedy Star.* Jefferson, NC: McFarland, 2002.

———. *Lillian Russell: A Biography of "America's Beauty."* Jefferson, NC: McFarland, 1999.

———. *Tony Pastor: Father of Vaudeville.* Jefferson, NC: McFarland, 2007.

Fields, Armond, and L. Marc Fields. *From the Bowery to Broadway: Lew Fields and the Roots of American Popular Theater.* New York: Oxford University Press, 1993.

Fields, Herbert. "The Laugh Is on the Author." *Theatre Magazine,* March 1930.

Fink, Michael. *Inside the Music Industry,* 2nd ed. New York: Schirmer, 1966.

Finn, William, and James Lapine. *Falsettos.* New York: Samuel French, 1995.

Finson, Jon W., ed. *Edward Harrigan and David Braham, Collected Songs: Music of the United States of America,* vol. 7. Madison, WI: A-R Editions for the American Musicological Society, 1997.

Fischer, Lisa E. "Douglas-Hallam Theater: Excavation of an 18th-Century Playhouse." Colonial Williamsburg Research Division Web site.

Fitzgerald, F. Scott. "Echoes of the Jazz Age." In *The Crack-Up,* edited by Edmund Wilson. New York: New Directions, 1945.

Flanagan, Hallie. *Arena: The History of the Federal Theatre.* New York: Duell, Sloan and Pearce, 1940.

Flinn, Caryl. *Brass Diva: The Life and Legends of Ethel Merman.* Berkeley: University of California Press, 2007.

Flinn, Denny Martin. *Musical! A Grand Tour: The Rise, Glory, and Fall of an American Institution.* New York: Schirmer, 1997.

———. *What They Did for Love: The Untold Story Behind the Making of A CHORUS LINE.* New York: Bantam, 1989.

Floyd, Samuel S., Jr. *Black Music in the Harlem Renaissance.* Westport, CT: Greenwood, 1990.

Fluegel, Jane, ed. *Bernstein Remembered.* New York: Carroll & Graf, 1991.

Fordin, Hugh. *Getting to Know Him: A Biography of Oscar Hammerstein II.* New York: Random House, 1977.

Forte, Allen. *The American Popular Ballad of the Golden Era, 1924–1950.* Princeton, NJ: Princeton University Press, 1995.

Franceschina, John Charles. *David Braham, the American Offenbach.* New York: Routledge, 2003.

———. *Harry B. Smith, Dean of American Librettists.* New York: Routledge, 2003.

Frankel, Aaron. *Writing the Broadway Musical,* rev. ed. New York: Da Capo, 1999.

Frantz, Donald. *Disney's Beauty and the Beast: A Celebration of the Broadway Musical.* New York: Hyperion, 1995.

Freedland, Michael. *Irving Berlin.* New York: Stein & Day, 1974.

———. *Jerome Kern: A Biography.* London: Robson, 1978.

———. *Jolson.* New York: Stein & Day, 1972.

Freedley, George. "The Black Crook and the White Fawn." *Chronicles of the American Dance: From the Shakers to Martha Graham.* Edited by Paul Magriel. New York: Da Capo Press, 1978.

Fremont, Robert A., ed. *Favorite Songs of the Nineties.* New York: Dover, 1973.

French, Robert B. D. *P. G. Wodehouse.* Edinburgh: Oliver & Boyd, 1966.

Frick, John W. *New York's First Theatrical Center: The Rialto at Union Square.* Ann Arbor: UMI Research Press, 1985.

Furia, Philip. *Ira Gershwin, the Art of the Lyricist.* New York: Oxford University Press, 1996.

———. *Irving Berlin: A Life in Song.* New York: Schirmer, 1998.

———. *The Poets of Tin Pan Alley: A History of America's Great Lyricists.* New York: Oxford University Press, 1990.

————. *Skylark: The Life and Times of Johnny Mercer.* New York: St. Martin's Press, 2003.

Galand, Joel. Introduction to *The Firebrand of Florence.* Kurt Weill Edition I:18. New York: European-American Music, 2002.

Gänzl, Kurt. *The British Musical Theatre.* London: Macmillan, 1986.

————. *The Complete Aspects of Love.* New York: Viking, 1990.

————. *The Encyclopedia of the Musical Theatre,* 2nd ed., 3 vols. New York: Schirmer, 2001.

————. *Gänzl's Book of the Broadway Musical. 75 Favorite Shows, from H.M.S. Pinafore to Sunset Blvd.* New York: Schirmer, 1995.

————. *The Musical: A Concise History.* Boston: Northeastern University Press, 1997.

————. *Lydia Thompson: Queen of Burlesque.* New York: Routledge, 2002.

————. *The Music of Andrew Lloyd Webber.* London, 1989.

Gardner, Paul. "Bob Fosse Off His Toes." *New York,* December 16, 1974.

Garebian, Keith. *The Making of Cabaret.* Oakville, ONT: Mosaic, 2002.

————. *The Making of Guys and Dolls.* Oakville, ONT: Mosaic, 2002.

————. *The Making of Gypsy.* Toronto: ECW Press, 1993.

————. *The Making of My Fair Lady.* Toronto: ECW Press, 1993.

————. *The Making of West Side Story.* Toronto: ECW Press, 1995.

Garland, Robert. "'Annie Get Your Gun' at Imperial Theatre." *New York Journal-American,* May 17, 1946.

————. Review of *Carmen Jones. New York Journal-American,* December 3, 1943.

Garrett, John M. *Sixty Years of British Music Hall.* London: Chappell & Co., 1976.

Gassner, John, ed. *Best Plays of the Modern American Theatre.* New York: Crown, 1947.

————. *Dramatic Soundings.* New York: Crown, 1968.

————. *Theatre at the Crossroads.* New York: Holt, Rinehart, and Winston, 1960.

Gassner, John, and Clive Barnes, eds. *Best American Plays.* New York: Crown, 1971.

Gayle, Addison, Jr. *Oak and Ivy: A Biography of Paul Laurence Dunbar.* Garden City, NY: Doubleday, 1971.

Gelb, Peter. "The Metropolitan Opera and Lincoln Center Theater Announce Met/LCT Opera/Theater Commissions." http://www.metoperafamily.org/metopera/news/detail.aspx?id=166.

Geraths, Armin, and Christian Martin Schmidt, eds., with Rüdiger Bering. *Musical: Das unterhaltende Genre, Handbuch der Musik im 20. Jahrhundert,* Bd. 6. Laaber, Germany: Laaber Verlag, 2002.

Gershwin, George. "Our New National Anthem." *Theatre Magazine,* May 1925.

————. "Rhapsody in Catfish Row." *NYT,* October 20, 1935.

Gershwin, Ira. *Lyrics on Several Occasions.* New York: Alfred A. Knopf, 1959.

Gherman, Beverly. *Agnes de Mille: Dancing Off the Earth.* New York: Atheneum, 1990.

Gibbs, Wolcott. "The Theatre [?]." *The New Yorker,* April 10, 1943.

Gilbert, Douglas. *American Vaudeville: Its Life and Times.* New York: Whittlesey House, 1940.

Gilbert, H. A. "Sammy Lee Commands——ON WITH THE DANCE!" *Jewish Tribune,* April 19, 1929.

Gilbert, Steven E. *The Music of George Gershwin.* New Haven, CT: Yale University Press, 1995.

Gilbert, William Schwenck. *The Complete Plays of Gilbert and Sullivan.* New York: W. W. Norton, 1976.

Gilman, Lawrence. "George Gershwin's New Opera, 'Porgy and Bess,' Produced by the Theater Guild." *New York Herald Tribune,* October 11, 1935.

Gilman, Richard. "Celebrating 30 Years of Off-Broadway." *The Village Voice,* May 2, 1985.

Gilmartin, Gregory. "Joseph Urban." In William Taylor, *Inventing Times Square.*

Gilvey, John Anthony. *Before the Parade Passes By: Gower Champion and the Glorious American Musical.* New York: St. Martin's Press, 2005.

————. "Gower Champion as Director: An Analysis of His Craft in Four Broadway Musicals, 1961–1968." PhD diss., New York University, 1996.

Gintautiene, Kristina. "*The Black Crook*: Ballet in the Gilded Age, 1866–1876." PhD diss., New York University, 1984.

Gioia, Ted. *The History of Jazz*. New York: Oxford University Press, 1997.

Giordano, Gus, ed. *Anthology of American Jazz Dance*. Evanston, IL: Orion, 1978.

Gold, Ronald. "It's 'Non-Choreography' but 'All Dance': An Interview with Julie Arenal, Choreographer of 'Hair.'" *Dance Magazine*, July 1968.

Goldberg, Isaac. *George Gershwin. A Study in American Music*. New York: Simon & Schuster, 1931.

———. *Tin Pan Alley: A Chronicle of the American Popular Music Racket*. New York: John Day, 1930.

Golden, Eve. *Vernon and Irene Castle's Ragtime Revolution*. Lexington, KY: University Press of Kentucky, 2007.

Goldman, Harry. "When Social Significance Came to Broadway: 'Pins and Needles' in Production." *Theatre Quarterly*, Winter 1977–78.

Goldman, Herbert G. *Jolson: The Legend Comes to Life*. New York: Oxford University Press, 1988.

Goldman, William. *The Season: A Candid Look at Broadway*. New York: Limelight, 1969.

Goldstein, Malcolm. *George S. Kaufman: His Life, His Theater*. New York: Oxford University Press, 1979.

———. *The Political Stage*. New York: Oxford University Press, 1974.

Goldstein, Richard M. "'I Enjoy Being a Girl': Women in the Plays of Rodgers and Hammerstein." *Popular Music and Society*, Spring 1989.

Goodhart, Sandor, ed. *Reading Stephen Sondheim: A Collection of Critical Essays*. New York: Garland, 2000.

Goodman, Randolph G. *From Script to Stage: Eight Modern Plays*. San Francsisco: Rinehart Press, 1971.

Goodwin, John, ed. *British Theatre Design: The Modern Age*. New York: McGraw-Hill, 1989.

Gorbman, Claudia. *Unheard Melodies: Narrative Film Music*. Bloomington: Indiana University Press, 1987.

Gordon, Barclay F. "Lillian Russell and the Casino." www.operetta.org.

Gordon, Eric A. *Mark the Music: The Life and Work of Marc Blitzstein*. New York: St. Martin's Press, 1989.

Gordon, Joanne. *Art Isn't Easy: The Achievement of Stephen Sondheim*. Carbondale: Southern Illinois University Press, 1990.

———, ed. *Stephen Sondheim: A Casebook*. New York: Garland, 1997.

Gordon, Max, with Lewis Funke. *Max Gordon Presents*. New York: Bernard Geis Associates, 1963.

Gornick, Vivian. "'The Fantasticks': At 29, a Pacifier More than a Play." *NYT*, May 14, 1989.

Gossett, Thomas F. *Uncle Tom's Cabin and American Culture*. Dallas: Southern Methodist University Press, 1985.

Gottfried, Martin. *All His Jazz: The Life and Death of Bob Fosse*. New York: Bantam, 1990.

———. *Broadway Musicals*. New York: Harry Abrams, 1979.

———. "Flipping over 'Follies.'" *NYT*, April 25, 1971.

———. "Man of La Mancha." *Women's Wear Daily*, November 23, 1965.

———. *More Broadway Musicals Since 1980*. New York: Harry Abrams,1991.

———. *Sondheim*. New York: Harry Abrams, 1993.

———. *A Theater Divided: The Postwar American Stage*. Boston: Little, Brown, 1967.

Gottlieb, George A. "Psychology of the American Vaudeville Show." In Page, *Writing for Vaudeville*.

Gradenwitz, Peter. *Leonard Bernstein: The Infinite Variety of a Musician*. London: Berg Publishers, 1987.

Graf, Herbert. *Opera for the People*. Minneapolis: University of Minnesota Press, 1951.

Grafton, David. *Red, Hot & Rich!: An Oral History of Cole Porter.* New York: Stein & Day, 1987.

Grant, Mark N. *The Rise and Fall of the Broadway Musical.* Boston: Northeastern University Press, 2004.

Graziano, John. "Black Musical Theater." In Floyd, Jr. *Black Music in the Harlem Renaissance.*

Green, Benny. *P. G. Wodehouse: A Literary Biography.* London: Pavillion, 1981.

———. "Wodehouse the Writer of Lyrics." In Heineman and Bensen, eds., *P. G. Wodehouse: A Centenary Celebration.*

———, ed. *A Hymn to Him: The Lyrics of Alan Jay Lerner.* New York: Limelight, 1987.

Green, Jesse. "A Complicated Gift." *NYT*, July 6, 2003.

Green, Stanley. *Encyclopedia of the Musical Theatre.* New York: Dodd, Mead and Company, 1976.

———. *The Great Clowns of Broadway.* New York: Oxford University Press, 1984.

———. "Oklahoma! Its Origin and Influence." *American Music*, Winter 1984.

———. *Ring Bells! Sing Songs!—Broadway Musicals of the 1930s.* New Rochelle, NY: Arlington House, 1971.

———. Notes to *The Threepenny Opera*, LP. New York: MGM SE-3121, 1954.

———. *The World of Musical Comedy*, 4th ed. San Diego: A. S. Barnes, 1980.

———, ed. *Rodgers and Hammerstein Fact Book: A Record of Their Works Together and with Other Collaborators.* New York: Lyn Farnol Group, 1980.

———. *The Rodgers and Hammerstein Story.* New York: John Day, 1963; repr. New York: Da Capo, 1980.

Greenberger, Howard. *The Off-Broadway Experience.* Englewood Cliffs, NJ: Prentice Hall, 1971.

Grigson, Geoffrey. *The Oxford Book of Satirical Verse.* Oxford: Oxford University Press, 1980.

Grimsted, David. *Melodrama Unveiled: American Theatre and Culture, 1800–1850.* Chicago: University of Chicago Press, 1968.

———. "*Uncle Tom* from Page to Stage: Limitations of Nineteenth-Century Drama." *The Quarterly Journal of Speech*, October 1970.

Grody, Svetlana McLee, and Dorothy Lister. *Conversations with Choreographers.* Portsmouth, NH: Heinemann, 1996.

Groos, Arthur, and Roger Parker, eds. *Reading Opera.* Princeton, NJ: Princeton University Press, 1988.

Grosch, Nils, Joachim Lucchesi, and Jürgen Schebera, eds. *Kurt-Weill Studien*, vol. 1. Stuttgart, Germany: [Olms Verlag], 1996.

Gross, John. *The Oxford Book of Comic Verse.* Oxford: Oxford University Press, 1994.

Grubb, Kevin Boyd. *Razzle Dazzle: The Life and Works of Bob Fosse.* New York: St. Martin's Press, 1989.

Gruen, John. "In Love with the Stage." *Opera News*, September 1972.

———. *Menotti: A Biography.* New York: Macmillan, 1978.

Guare, John. Notes to *Floyd Collins*, CD. New York: Nonesuch/Time Warner 79434-2, 1997.

Guernsey, Otis L. Jr., ed. *Broadway Song & Story.* New York: Dodd, Mead and Company, 1985.

———, ed. *Playwrights, Lyricists, Composers on Theater.* New York: Dodd, Mead and Company, 1974.

Guthrie, Tyrone. *A Life in the Theatre.* New York: McGraw-Hill, 1959.

Hall, Robert A., Jr. *The Comic Side of P. G. Wodehouse.* Hamden, CT: Archon Books, 1974.

Hambleton, T. Edward, and Norris Houghton. "Phoenix on the Wing." *Theatre Arts*, November 1954.

Hamlisch, Marvin, with Gerald Gardner. *The Way I Was.* New York, Scribner, 1992.

Hamm, Charles. "A Blues for the Ages." In Crawford et al., *A Celebration of American Music.*

———. "Irving Berlin and Early Tin Pan Alley." In Hamm, ed., *Irving Berlin, Early Songs.*

———. "Musical Theater." *NGDAM* (1986), vol. 3, 300–309.

———. "Popular Music." *NGDAM* (1986), vol. 3, 589–610.

———. "The Theatre Guild Production of *Porgy and Bess.*" *JAMS* 40:3 (Fall 1987).

————. *Yesterdays: Popular Song in America*. New York: W. W. Norton, 1979.

————, ed. *Irving Berlin, Early Songs, 1907–1914: Music of the United States of America*, vol.2. Madison, WI: A-R Editions, 1994.

————. *Irving Berlin, Songs from the Melting Pot: The Formative Years, 1907–1914*. New York: Oxford University Press, 1997.

Hammack, David. Introductory Essay. In Taylor, *Inventing Times Square*.

Hammelmann, Hanns, and Ewald Osers, trans. *A Working Friendship: The Correspondence Between Richard Strauss and Hugo von Hofmansthal*. New York: Vienna House, 1961.

Hammerstein, Oscar II. "In Re 'Oklahoma!'" *NYT*. May 23, 1943.

————. Introduction to *Carmen Jones*. New York: Alfred A. Knopf, 1945.

————. Introduction to *The Jerome Kern Songbook*. New York: Simon & Schuster and T. B. Harms, 1955.

————. *Lyrics*. New York: Simon & Schuster, 1949; repr. Milwaukee: Hal Leonard, 1985.

————. "Tribute to Yankee Doodle Dandy." *NYT Magazine*. May 5, 1957.

————. "Turns On a Carousel." *NYT*, April 15, 1945.

————. "Voices Versus Feet." *Theatre Magazine*, May 1925.

Hanan, Stephen Mo. *A Cat's Diary: How the Broadway Production of Cats Was Born*. Hanover, NH: Smith and Kraus, 2001.

Hanson, Laura. "Broadway Babies": Images of Women in the Musicals of Stephen Sondheim." In Gordon, *Stephen Sondheim*.

Harburg, E. Y. ["Yip"]. *At This Point in Rhyme*. New York: Crown, 1976.

————. *Rhymes for the Irreverent*. New York: Grossman, 1965.

Harding, Alfred. "A Brief History of the Actors' Equity Association." In Bernheim, *Business*.

Harmon, William, ed. *The Oxford Book of American Light Verse*. New York: Oxford University Press, 1979.

Harnick, Sheldon. "What Comes First in a Musical? The Libretto." In Guernsey, *Playwrights, Lyricists, Composers*.

Harris, Andrew B. *The Performing Set: The Broadway Designs of William and Jean Eckart*. Denton, TX: University of North Texas Press, 2006.

Harris, Charles K. *After the Ball: Forty Years of Melody*. New York: Frank-Maurice, 1926.

Harrison, Rex. *Rex*. London: Macmillan, 1974.

Hart, Dorothy. *Thou Swell, Thou Witty: The Life and Lyrics of Lorenz Hart*. New York: Harper & Row, 1976.

Hart, Dorothy, and Robert Kimball, eds. *The Complete Lyrics of Lorenz Hart*. New York: Alfred A. Knopf, 1986.

Hart, Lorenz, "Running Up a Score." *NYT*, October 29, 1939.

Hart, Moss, *Act One: An Autobiography*. New York: Random House, 1959.

————. Foreword to *The Cole Porter Song Book*. New York: Simon & Schuster, 1959.

————. Foreword to *Lady in the Dark, A Musical Play*, vocal score. Chappell Music Co.: New York, 1941.

Hart, Norman. "The Selling of *La Cage aux Folles*: How Audiences Were Helped to Read Broadway's First Gay Musical." *Theatre History Studies*, June 2003.

Hartmann, Susan M. *The Home Front and Beyond*. Boston: Twayne, 1982.

Hasbany, Richard. "Bromidic Parables: The American Musical Theatre during the Second World War." *Journal of Popular Culture* 6:4 (Spring 1973).

Haun Harry. "Can't Help Lovin' That SHOW BOAT." *Playbill* 94:10 (1994). Gershwin Theatre.

————. "Comden & ..." *Playbill Magazine*, December 3, 2003.

Hausam, Wiley, ed. *The New American Musical: An Anthology from the End of the Century*. New York: Theatre Communications Group, 2003.

Heilman, Robert B. *Tragedy and Melodrama*. Seattle: University of Washington Press, 1968.

————. "Tragedy and Melodrama: Speculations on Generic Form." In *Tragedy: Vision and Form*, edited by Robert W. Carrigan. New York: Harper, 1981.

————. "Introduction" in *William Shakespeare: The Taming of the Shrew*, Robert B. Heilman, ed. New York: Signet, 1986.

Hein, James G. "The Men Are Back, Annie, Forget Your Gun." Unpublished ms.

Heineman, James H., and Donald R. Bensen, eds. *P. G. Wodehouse: A Centenary Celebration.* New York: Pierpont Morgan Library/Oxford University Press, 1981.

Helburn, Theresa. *A Wayward Quest.* Boston: Little, Brown, 1960.

Helyar, James, ed. *Gilbert and Sullivan: Papers Presented at the International Conference Held at the University of Kansas in May 1970.* Lawrence: University of Kansas Libraries, 1971.

Henderson, Amy, and Dwight Blocker Bowers. *Red, Hot & Blue: A Smithsonian Salute to the American Musical.* Washington, DC: Smithsonian Institution Press, 1996.

Henderson, Mary C. *The City and the Theatre.* Clifton, NJ: James T. White and Co., 1973; rev. ed. New York: Back Stage Books, 2004.

———. *Mielziner: Master of Modern Stage Design.* New York: Back Stage Books 2001.

———. *The New Amsterdam: The Biography of a Broadway Theatre.* New York: Hyperion, 1997.

———. *Theater in America.* New York: HNA Books, 1986.

Henry, William A., III. "Disenchanting Kingdom." *Time,* May 2, 1994.

Hentoff, Nat. Notes to *Hair,* LP. New York: RCA LSO-1150, 1968.

Herman, Jerry, and Ken Bloom. *Jerry Herman: The Lyrics.* New York: Routledge, 2003.

Herman, Jerry, with Marilyn Stasio. *Showtune: A Memoir.* New York: Dutton, 1996.

Hess, Carol A. "John Philip Sousa's *El Capitan*: Political Appropriation and the Spanish-American War." *American Music,* Spring 1998.

Hewes, Henry, ed. *Famous American Plays of the 1940s.* New York: Dell, 1960.

Higham, Charles. *Ziegfeld.* Chicago: Henry Regnery, 1972.

Hill, Errol G., and James V. Hatch. *A History of African American Theatre.* Cambridge: Cambridge University Press, 2003.

Hinton, Stephen. "Kurt Weill," "Street Scene." *NGDO,* vol. 4.

———, ed. *The Threepenny Opera,* Cambridge Opera Handbooks. Cambridge: Cambridge University Press, 1990.

Hinton, Stephen, and Edward Harsh, eds. *Die Dreigroschenoper.* Kurt Weill Edition I:5. New York: European-American Music, 2000.

Hirsch, Foster. *The Boys from Syracuse: The Shuberts' Theatrical Empire.* Carbondale: Southern Illinois University Press, 1998.

———. *Harold Prince and the American Musical Theatre.* Cambridge: Cambridge University Press, 1989.

———. *Kurt Weill on Stage; From Berlin to Broadway.* New York: Alfred A. Knopf, 2002.

Hirsch, John E. "The American Revue Costume." In Loney, *Musical Theatre in America.*

Hirschfeld, Al. *Hirschfeld: Art and Recollections from Eight Decades.* New York: Scribner, 1991.

———. *Hirschfeld by Hirschfeld.* New York: Dodd, Mead, 1979.

———. *Hirschfeld on Line.* New York: Applause, 1999.

———. *The World of Al Hirschfeld.* New York: Harry Abrams, 1968.

Hirschhorn, Clive. *Gene Kelly: A Biography.* Chicago: Regnery, 1974.

Hisama, Ellie M. "'The American Dream': *Miss Saigon* and the Politics of Memory." Paper delivered at American Musicological Society meeting, November 5, 1999.

Hischak, Thomas S. *Boy Loses Girl: Broadway's Librettists.* Lanham, MD: Scarecrow Press, 2002.

———. *Film It with Music: An Encyclopedic Guide to the American Movie Musical.* Westport, CT: Greenwood, 2001.

———. *The Oxford Companion to the American Musical: Theatre, Film, and Television.* New York: Oxford University Press, 2008.

———. *Through the Screen Door: What Happened to the Broadway Musical When It Went to Hollywood.* Lanham, MD: Scarecrow Press, 2004.

Hogle, Jerrold E. *The Undergrounds of "The Phantom of the Opera": Sublimation and the Gothic in Leroux's Novel and its Progeny.* New York: Palgrave, 2002.

Holden, Stephen. "A Glimpse of the Olden Days, via Cole Porter." *NYT,* October 18, 1987.

———. "Remembering the Maestro of Broadway." *NYT,* April 11, 1990.

————. "To Its Creators, 'Smile' Was Always a Beauty." *NYT*, November 23, 1986.

Honey, Maureen. *Creating Rosie the Riveter*. Amherst: University of Massachusetts Press, 1984.

Hoover, Cynthia Adams. "Music in Eighteenth-Century American Theater." *American Music* 2:4 (Winter 1984): 6–18.

Hopper, De Wolf, with Wesley Winans Stout. *Once a Clown, Always a Clown*. Garden City, NY: Little, Brown, 1925.

Horn, Barbara Lee. *The Age of Hair: Evolution and Impact of Broadway's First Rock Musical*. Westport, CT: Greenwood, 1991.

Hornblow, Arthur. A *History of the Theatre in America: From Its Beginnings to the Present Time*. Phildelphia: J. B. Lippincott Company, 1919.

Horne, Lena, and Richard Schickel. *Lena*. Garden City, NY: Doubleday, 1965.

Horner, Harry. "Designer in Action." *Theatre Arts*, April 1941.

Horowitz, Joseph. *Understanding Toscanini*. New York: Alfred A. Knopf, 1987.

Horowitz, Mark Eden. *Sondheim on Music: Minor Details and Major Decisions*. Lanham, MD: Scarecrow Press, 2003.

Houghton, Norris. *Entrances and Exits*. New York: Limelight, 1991.

————. Introduction to *Romeo and Juliet/West Side Story*. Edited by John Bettenbender. New York: Laurel Leaf, 1965.

Houseman, John. *Run-Through: A Memoir*. New York: Simon & Schuster 1972.

Howells, William Dean. "Editor's Study." *Harpers New Monthly Magazine*, July 1886.

Huber, Eugene R. "Stephen Sondheim and Harold Prince: Collaborative Contributions to the Development of the Modern Concept Musical, 1970–81." PhD diss., New York University, 1990.

Huggins, Nathan Irvin, ed. *Voices from the Harlem Renaissance*. New York: Oxford University Press, 1976.

Hughes, Gervase. *Composers of Operetta*. London: Macmillan, 1962.

Hughes, Langston. "The Big Sea." In Huggins, *Voices from the Harlem Renaissance*.

Hunt, Douglas L., ed. *Five Plays by Charles H. Hoyt: America's Lost Plays*. Princeton, NJ: Princeton University Press, 1941.

————. *The Life and Works of Charles H. Hoyt*. Nashville, TN: Vanderbilt University Press, 1945.

Huntsman, Jeffrey H. "Native American Theatre." In Seller, *Ethnic Theatre in the United States*.

Hutchens, John K. "About a Man on a Tightrope." *NYT*, May 6, 1945.

Hutton, Laurence. *Curiosities of the American Stage*. New York: Harper & Brothers, 1892.

Hyland, William G. *Richard Rodgers*. New Haven, CT: Yale University Press, 1998.

Iggers, Wilma Abeles. *Karl Kraus, A Viennese Critic of the Twentieth Century*. The Hague: Martinus Nijhoff, 1967.

The Illustrated Sporting and Dramatic News (London).

Ilson, Carol. *Harold Prince: From "Pajama Game" to "Phantom of the Opera."* Ann Arbor: UMI Research Press, 1989.

Isaacs, Edith J. R., and Rosamond Gilder. "American Musical Comedy: Credit It to Broadway." *Theatre Arts*, August 1945.

Isherwood, Charles. "'Movin' Out' Moves Out, And Just When It Was Really Getting Going." *NYT*, November 20, 2005.

Isherwood, Christopher. *The World in the Evening*. New York: Methuen, 1954.

Isman, Felix. *Weber and Fields: Their Tribulations, Triumphs and Their Associates*. New York: Boni & Liveright, 1924.

Jablonski, Edward. *Alan Jay Lerner: A Biography*. New York: Henry Holt, 1996.

————. *Irving Berlin: American Troubadour*. New York: Henry Holt, 1999.

————. *Gershwin*. Garden City, NY: Doubleday, 1987.

————. *Gershwin Remembered*. Portland, OR: Amadeus Press, 1992.

————. "The Gershwins Go to War." Notes to *Strike Up the Band*, 2 CDs. New York: Elektra Nonesuch/Roxbury 79273-2, 1991.

————. *Harold Arlen: Happy with the Blues.* Garden City, NY: Doubleday, 1961.

————. *Harold Arlen: Rhythm, Rainbows, and Blues.* Boston: Northeastern University Press, 1996.

Jablonski, Edward, and Lawrence D. Stewart. *The Gershwin Years.* New York: Doubleday, 1958; repr. New York: Da Capo, 1996.

Jackson, Gertrude. "West Side Story: Thema, Grundhaltung und Aussage." *Maske und Korthurn,* 1970.

Jackson, Richard, ed. *Early Burlesque in America: Nineteenth-Century American Musical Theater,* vol. 13. New York: Garland, 1994.

Janik, Allan, and Stephen Toulmin. *Wittgenstein's Vienna.* New York: Simon & Schuster, 1973.

Jansen, Wolfgang. *My Fair Lady: Die deutsche Erstaufführung 1961 im Berliner "Theater des Westens."* Berlin: Weidler Buchverlag, 1992.

Jasen, David A. *P. G. Wodehouse: A Portrait of a Master.* New York: Mason & Lipscomb, 1974.

Jenson, Joli. *Redeeming Modernity: Contradictions in Media Criticism.* Newbury Park, CA: Sage, 1990.

Jeremy, David John, ed. *Henry Wansey and His American Journal, 1794.* Philadelphia: Gregg Press, 1970.

Johnson, Edgar, and Eleanor Johnson, eds. *The Dickens Theatrical Reader.* Boston: Little, Brown, 1964.

Johnson, Hall. "*Porgy and Bess*—A Folk Opera." *Theatre Arts Monthly,* January 1936.

Johnson, James Weldon. *Black Manhattan.* New York: Alfred A. Knopf, 1930; repr. New York: Arno, 1968.

Johnson, Jonathan. *Good HAIR Days: A Personal Journey with the American Tribal Love-Rock Musical HAIR.* New York: iUniverse, 2004.

Johnson, Samuel. *Lives of the English Poets.* Edited by George Birbeck Hill. Oxford, 1905; repr. New York, 1967.

Johnson, Stephen Burge. *The Roof Gardens of Broadway Theatres, 1883–1942.* Ann Arbor: University of Michigan Press, 1985.

Jones, John Bush. *Our Musicals, Ourselves: A Social History of the American Musical Theatre.* Hanover, NH: Brandeis University Press, 2003.

Jones, Tom. *Making Musicals: An Informal Introduction to the World of Musical Theatre.* New York: Limelight Editions, 1998.

Jorgensen, Michael R. "John Philip Sousa's Operetta 'El Capitan': A Historical, Analytical and Performance Guide." PhD diss., Ball State University, 1994.

Jowitt, Deborah. *Jerome Robbins: His Life, His Theater, His Dance.* New York: Simon & Schuster, 2004.

Kadison, Luba, and Josef Buloff. *On Stage, Off Stage.* Cambridge, MA: Harvard University Press, 1992.

Kahn, E. J., Jr. *The Merry Partners: The Age and Stage of Harrigan and Hart.* New York: Random House, 1955.

Kammen, Michael. *The Lively Arts: Gilbert Seldes and the Transformation of Cultural Criticism in the United States.* New York: Oxford University Press, 1996.

Kander, John, and Fred Ebb, as told to Greg Lawrence. *Colored Lights: Forty Years of Words and Music, Show Biz, Collaboration, and All That Jazz.* New York: Faber, 2003.

Kanfer, Stefan, et al. "The Once and Future *Follies.*" *Time,* May 3, 1971.

Kaplan, Justin. *Mr. Clemens and Mark Twain.* New York: Simon & Schuster, 1966.

Kasha, Al, and Joel Hirschhorn. *Notes on Broadway.* Chicago: Contemporary Books, 1985.

Katter, Nafe Edmund. "'Theatre Arts' under the Editorship of Edith J. R. Isaacs." PhD diss., University of Michigan, 1963.

Kattwinkel, Susan. *Tony Pastor Presents: Afterpieces from the Vaudeville Stage.* Westport, CT: Greenwood, 1998.

Kaufman, Charlotte R., ed. *Early Operetta in America: Nineteenth-Century American Musical Theater,* vol. 12. New York: Routledge, 1994.

[Kaufman, George S.?] "'Show Boat' Proves Fine Musical Show." *NYT,* December 28, 1927.

Kaufman, George S., and Morrie Ryskind. *Of Thee I Sing.* New York: Samuel French 1935.

Kellow, Brian. *Ethel Merman: A Life.* New York: Viking, 2007.

Kelly, Kevin. *One Singular Sensation: The Michael Bennett Story.* New York: Doubleday, 1990.

Kelly, Thomas. *First Nights.* New Haven, CT: Yale University Press, 2000.

Kennedy, Brian. *The Baron Bold and the Beauteous Maid: A Compact History of Canadian Theatre.* Toronto: Playwrights Canada Press, 2004.

Kennedy, David M. "Victory Proved Easier Than Peace." In *Our Century in Pictures,* edited by Richard B. Stolley. Boston: Little, Brown, 2000.

Kerman, Joseph. *Opera as Drama.* New York, 1956; rev. ed. Berkeley: University of California Press, 1988.

Kerr, Walter. "'Dancin' Needs More Than Dancing." *NYT,* April 9, 1978.

———. "Hello, Dolly!—A Musical about Matchmakers." *New York Herald Tribune,* January 17, 1964.

———. "Musicals That Were Playful, Irresponsible, and Blissfully Irrelevant." *NYT Magazine,* April 11, 1971.

———. *Thirty Plays Hath November: Pain and Pleasure in the Contemporary Theatre.* New York: Simon & Schuster, 1969.

———. "West Side Story." *New York Herald Tribune,* April 28, 1960.

Kibler, M. Alison. *Rank Ladies: Gender and Cultural Hierarchy in American Vaudeville.* Chapel Hill: University of North Carolina Press, 1999.

Kilroy, David M. "Kurt Weill on Broadway: The Postwar Years (1945–1950)." PhD diss., Harvard University, 1992.

Kimball, Robert. "Broadway and the Depression." Notes to *Girl Crazy,* CD. New York: Elektra Nonesuch 79250-2, 1990.

———, ed. *Cole.* New York: Holt, Rinehart and Winston, 1971.

———. *The Complete Lyrics of Cole Porter.* New York: Alfred A. Knopf, 1983.

———. *The Complete Lyrics of Ira Gershwin.* New York: Alfred A. Knopf, 1993.

Kimball, Robert, and William Bolcom. *Reminiscing with Sissle and Blake.* New York: Viking, 1973.

Kimball, Robert, and Linda Emmet, eds. *The Complete Lyrics of Irving Berlin.* New York: Alfred A. Knopf, 2001.

Kimball, Robert, and Steve Nelson, eds. *The Complete Lyrics of Frank Loesser.* New York: Alfred A. Knopf, 2003.

Kimball, Robert, and Alfred Simon. *The Gershwins.* New York: Atheneum, 1973.

Kingman, Daniel. *American Music: A Panorama,* rev. ed. New York: Schirmer, 2002.

Kirle, Bruce. *Unfinished Show Business: Broadway Musicals as Works-in-Process.* Carbondale: Southern Illinois University Press, 2005.

Kislan, Richard. *Hoofing on Broadway: A History of Show Dancing.* New York: Prentice Hall, 1987.

———. "Nine Musical Plays of Rodgers and Hammerstein: A Critical Study in Content and Form." PhD diss., New York University, 1970.

———. *The Musical: A Look at the American Musical Theater,* rev. ed. New York: Prentice Hall, 1995.

Kissel, Howard. *David Merrick: The Abominable Showman.* New York: Applause, 1993.

Klein, Christina. *Cold War Orientalism: Asia in the Middlebrow Imagination, 1945–1961.* Berkeley: University of California Press, 2003.

Knapp, Margaret. Introductory Essay. In Taylor, *Inventing Times Square.*

———. "Watch Your Step: Irving Berlin's 1914 Musical." In Loney, *Musical Theatre in America.*

Knapp, Raymond. *The American Musical and the Formation of National Identity.* Princeton, NJ: Princeton University Press, 2005.

———. *The American Musical and the Performance of a Personal Identity.* Princeton, NJ: Princeton University Press, 2006.

———. "History, 'The Sound of Music,' and Us." *American Music* 22:1 (Spring 2004).

Knowles, Eleanor. *The Films of Jeanette MacDonald and Nelson Eddy.* Cranbury, NJ: A. S. Barnes, 1976.

Koger, Alice Kane. "A Critical Analysis of Edward Harrigan's Comedy." PhD diss., University of Michigan, 1984.

Konas, Gary. "Frank Loesser's Hidden Class." *Biography* 16:3 (Summer 1993): 264–75.

Kowalke, Kim H. "Accounting for Success: Misunderstanding *Die Dreigroschenoper.*" *Opera Quarterly* 6 (Spring 1989): 18–38.

———. "Das Goldene Zeitalter des Musicals." In Geraths, *Musical.*

———. "Kurt Weill and the Quest for American Opera." In *Amerikanismus, Americanism, Weill: die Suche nach kultureller Identität in der Moderne,* edited by Hermann Danuser and Hermann Gottschewski. Schliengen, Germany: Edition Argus, 2003.

———. "Kurt Weill, Modernism, and Culture: Öffentlichkeit als Stil." *Modernism/Modernity* 2 (1995): 27–69.

———. "The Threepenny Opera in America." In Hinton, *The Threepenny Opera.*

———. ed. *A New Orpheus: Essays on Kurt Weill.* New Haven, CT: Yale University Press, 1986.

Kowalke, Kim H., and Horst Edler, eds. *A Stranger Here Myself: Kurt Weill Studien.* Hildesheim, Germany, and New York: Olms Verlag, 1993.

Kowalke, Kim H., and Lys Symonette, editors and translators. *Speak Low (If You Speak Love): The Letters of Kurt Weill and Lotte Lenya.* Berkeley: University of California Press, 1996.

Krasker, Tommy. "What Price Cheese?" Notes to *Strike Up the Band,* 2 CDs. New York: Elektra Nonesuch/Roxbury: 79273-2, 1991.

Krasker, Tommy, and Robert Kimball. *Catalog of the American Musical.* Washington, DC: National Institute for Opera and Musical Theater, 1988.

Krasner, David. *A Beautiful Pageant: African-American Theatre, Drama, and Performance in the Harlem Renaissance, 1910–1927.* New York: Palgrave Macmillan, 2002.

———. *Resistance, Parody, and Double Consciousness in African-American Theatre, 1895–1910.* New York: St. Martin's Press, 1997.

Krasner, Orly Leah, ed. *Later Operetta, Part II: Nineteenth-Century American Musical Theater,* vol. 15. New York: Garland, 1994.

———. "DeKoven, Reginald." *NGDO,* vol. 1. London, 1992.

———. "Reginald DeKoven and American Comic Opera at the Turn of the Century." PhD diss. CUNY, 1994.

———. "Wien, Women and Song: *The Merry Widow* in New York." *The Sonneck Society Bulletin,* Spring 1996.

Kraus, Karl. *Sprüche und Widersprüche,* 3rd ed. Munich: A. Langen, 1914.

Krauss, Anne McClenny. "Alexander Reinagle, His Family Background and Early Professional Career." *American Music* (1986): 425–56.

Kreuger, Miles. *Show Boat: The Story of a Classic American Musical.* New York: Oxford University Press, 1977.

———. "Some Words about 'Show Boat.'" Notes to *Show Boat,* 3 LPs. Hayes Middlesex, England: EMI Angel 49108, 1988.

Kroeger, Karl, ed. *Pelissier's Columbian Melodies: Music for the New York and Philadelphia Theaters.* Madison, WI: A-R Editions, 1984.

Kroeger, Karl, and Victor Fell Yellin, eds. *Early Melodrama in America: Nineteenth-Century American Musical Theater,* vol. 2. New York: Garland, 1994.

Kronenberger, Louis, ed. *An Anthology of Light Verse.* New York: Modern Library, 1935.

———. Review of *Lady in the Dark. PM,* January 24, 1941.

Kurath, Gertrude Prokosch, and Antonio Garcia. *Music and Dance of the Tewa Pueblos.* Santa Fe: Museum of New Mexico Press, 1970.

Labroca, Mario. "Music Theatre—Yesterday and Today." *International Congress: Contemporary Music Theatre,* Hamburg, Germany, 1964. Paris: International Music Council, 1964.

LaChiusa, Michael John. "The Great Gray Way." *Opera News* 70:2 (August 2005).

Lahr, John, *Light Fantastic: Adventures in Theatre.* New York: Dial Press, 1996.

———. *Notes on a Cowardly Lion: The Biography of Bert Lahr.* New York: Ballantine, 1969.

Lamb, Andrew. *Jerome Kern in Edwardian London.* Brooklyn: Institute for Studies in American Music, 1985.

———. *Leslie Stuart: The Man Who Composed Florodora.* New York: Routledge, 2002.

———. "Music of the Popular Theatre." In *Music in Britain: The Romantic Age, 1800–1914.* Edited by Nicholas Temperley. London: Athlone Press, 1981.

———. "Musical." *NGDAM.* London, 1986.

———. "Musical Comedy." *NGDMM.* London, 1982.

———. *150 Years of Popular Musical Theatre.* New Haven, CT, and London: Yale University Press, 2000.

———. "Operetta." *NGDMM.* London, 1982.

Lamont, Michele, and Marcel Fournier, eds. *Cultivating Differences: Symbolic Boundaries and the Making of Inequality.* Chicago: University of Chicago Press, 1992.

Langley, Stephen. *Theatre Management in America.* New York: Drama Book Specialists, 1974.

Langner, Lawrence. *G.B.S. and the Lunatic.* New York: Atheneum, 1963.

———. *The Magic Curtain.* New York: Dutton, 1951.

Larsen, Orville K. *Scene Design in the American Theatre from 1915 to 1960.* Fayetteville: University of Arkansas Press, 1989.

Lassell, Michael. *Elton John and Tim Rice's Aida: The Making of a Broadway Show.* New York: Disney, 2000.

Lasser, Michael. "The Glorifier: Florenz Ziegfeld and the Creation of the American Showgirl." *The American Scholar,* Summer 1994.

Latouche, John, and Jerome Moross. *The Golden Apple.* New York: Random House, 1954.

Laurents, Arthur. *Original Story By.* New York: Alfred A. Knopf, 2000.

Laurie, Joe, Jr. *Vaudeville: From the Honky-Tonks to the Palace.* New York: Henry Holt and Co., 1953.

Lawrence, Greg. *Dance with Demons: The Life of Jerome Robbins.* New York: Putnam, 2001.

Lawrence, Vera Brodsky, ed. *Strong on Music: The New York Music Scene in the Days of George Templeton Strong.* Vol. 1, *Resonances.* New York: Oxford University Press, 1988; repr. Chicago: University of Chicago Press, 1995.

Lawson-Peebles, Robert, ed. *Approaches to the American Musical.* Exeter, UK: University of Exeter Press, 1996.

Lazarus, A. L., ed. *The Best of George Ade.* Bloomington: Indiana University Press, 1985.

Ledbetter, Steven, ed. *Sennetts and Tuckets: A Bernstein Celebration.* Boston: Boston Symphony Orchestra/David R. Godine, 1988.

Lee, Joanna, Edward Harsh, and Kim Kowalke, eds. *Street Scene. A Sourcebook.* New York: Kurt Weill Foundation, 1996.

Lees, Gene. *Inventing Champagne: The Worlds of Lerner and Loewe.* New York: St. Martin's Press, 1990.

Lehrman, Leonard. *Marc Blitzstein: A Bio-Bibliography.* Westport, CT: Greenwood, 2005.

Leichtman, Ellen C., ed. *To the Four Corners: A Festschrift in Honor of Rose Brandel.* Warren, MI: Harmonie Park Press, 1994.

Leithauser, Brad. "Light Verse: Dead But Remarkably Robust." *NYT,* June 7, 1987.

Leopold, David. *Irving Berlin's Show Business, Broadway, Hollywood, America.* New York: Harry Abrams, 2005.

Lerman, Leo. "Theatre Dance in My Time." *Dance News Annual.* New York, 1953.

Lerner, Alan Jay, "Advice to Young Writers." In *Paint Your Wagon.* New York: Coward-McCann, 1952.

———. "Creation of a Lady." New York: Tams-Witmark, 1963.

———. *The Musical Theatre: A Celebration.* London: Collins, 1986.

———. Note to *My Fair Lady.* New York: Signet, 1956.

———. "Reader Questions Origin of 'Brigadoon' and Gets Author Lerner's Reply." *NYT,* March 30, 1947.

———. *The Street Where I Live.* New York: W. W. Norton, 1978.

Levesque, John. "For Harry Frazee III, 'The Curse' Has a Different Meaning." *Seattle Post-Intelligencer*, September 26, 2003.

Levine, Ira A. *Left-Wing Dramatic Theory in the American Theatre*. Ann Arbor: UMI Research Press, 1985.

Levine, Lawrence W. *Highbrow/Lowbrow: The Emergence of Cultural Hierarchy in America*. Cambridge, MA: Harvard University Press, 1988.

Lewis David H. *Flower Drum Songs: The Story of Two Musicals*. Jefferson, NC: McFarland, 2006.

Lewis, Philip C. *Trouping: How the Show Came to Town*. New York: Harper & Row, 1973.

Lhamon, W. T., Jr. *Jump Jim Crow: Lost Plays, Lyrics, and Street Prose of the First Atlantic Popular Culture*. Cambridge, MA: Harvard University Press, 2003.

———. *Raising Cain: Blackface Performance from Jim Crow to Hip Hop*. Cambridge, MA: Harvard University Press, 1998.

Lieberson, Goddard. "The Ten Musicals Most Worth Preserving." *NYT Magazine*, August 5, 1956.

Liebling, A. J. "The Boys from Syracuse." *The New Yorker*, November 18 and 25, December 2, 1939.

Lindsay, Howard. "Howard Lindsay . . . Recalls the Original Production with Miles Kreuger." Notes to *Anything Goes*, CD. Hayes Middlesex, England: EMI Angel 7 49848-2, 1989.

Lindstrom, Diane. "Economic Structure, Demographic Change, and Income Inequality in Antebellum New York." In *Power, Culture and Place: Essays on New York City*, edited by John Hull Mollenkopf. New York: Russell Sage, 1988.

Little, Stuart W. *Off-Broadway: The Prophetic Theatre*. New York: Coward, McCann & Geoghegan, 1972.

Livesey, Herbert B. "The Last Playwright." *New York Magazine*, February 20, 1978.

Loesser, Arthur. "My Brother Frank." *Notes* 7:2 (March 1950).

Loesser, Frank. "Some Notes on a Musical." *Playbill*. Broadway Theatre, 1956.

Loesser, Susan. *A Most Remarkable Fella: Frank Loesser and the Guys and Dolls in His Life*. New York: D. I. Fine, 1993.

Logan, Joshua. *Josh: My Up and Down, In and Out Life*. New York: Delacorte, 1976.

Lomax, Alan. *Mister Jelly Roll*. Berkeley: University of California Press, 1973.

LoMonaco, Martha Schmoyer. *Every Week a Broadway Revue: The Tamiment Playhouse, 1921–1960*. Westport, CT: Greenwood, 1992.

Loney, Glenn. "On Broadway: American Dance Machine." *Ballet News*, January/February 1980.

———. *Unsung Genius: The Passion of Jack Cole*. New York: Franklin Watts, 1984.

———, ed. *Musical Theatre in America: Papers and Proceedings of the Conference on the Musical Theatre in America*. Westport, CT: Greenwood, 1984.

Long, John H. *Shakespeare's Use of Music: The Final Comedies*. Gainesville: University of Florida Press, 1961.

Long, Robert Emmet. *Broadway, The Golden Years: Jerome Robbins and the Great Choreographer-Directors, 1940 to the Present*. New York: Continuum, 2001.

Lott, Eric. *Love and Theft: Blackface Minstrelsy and the American Working Class*. New York: Oxford University Press, 1993.

Lounsberry, Fred. Introduction to *103 Lyrics of Cole Porter*. New York: Random House, 1954.

Lowens, Irving. *Music and Musicians in Early America*. New York: W. W. Norton, 1964.

Lowry, Bert. "In the Days of Variety." *Sunset Magazine*, September 1927. In Stein, *American Vaudeville*.

Lubbock, Mark. *The Complete Book of Light Opera*. New York: Appleton-Century-Crofts, 1962.

Lynch, Deidre, and William B. Warner, eds. *Cultural Institutions of the Novel*. Durham, NC: Duke University Press, 1996.

Lyon, James K. *Bertolt Brecht in America*. Princeton, NJ: Princeton University Press, 1980.

Macdonald, Dwight. "Masscult & Midcult." In Macdonald, *Against the American Grain*. New York: Vintage, 1962.

Mackinlay, Sterling. *Origin and Development of Light Opera*. London: Hutchinson, 1927.

Mahar, William J. *Behind the Burnt Cork Mask: Early Blackface Minstrelsy and Antebellum American Popular Culture*. Urbana and Chicago: University of Illinois Press, 1999.

Manchester, William. *One Brief Shining Moment*. Boston: Little, Brown, 1983.

Mandell, Jonathan. "The Un-Spectacle." *Newsday*, November 19, 1996.

Mandelbaum, Ken. *"A Chorus Line" and the Musicals of Michael Bennett*. New York: St. Martin's Press, 1989.

——. *Not Since "Carrie": Forty Years of Broadway Musical Flops*. New York: St. Martin's Press, 1991.

Mander, Raymond, and Joe Mitchenson. *Musical Comedy: A Story in Pictures*. London: Peter Davies, 1969.

Mann, Martin Arthur. "The Musicals of Frank Loesser." PhD diss., CUNY, 1974.

Marbury, Elisabeth. *My Crystal Ball*. New York: Boni and Liveright, 1923.

Marcosson, Isaac Frederick, and Daniel Frohman. *Charles Frohman: Manager and Man*. New York: Harper & Brothers, 1916.

Marcus, Joan. *Disney Presents The Lion King*. New York: Disney Press, 1998.

Maretzek, Max. *Crotchets and Quavers, or, Revelations of an Opera Manager in America*. New York: Samuel French, 1855; repr. as *Revelations of an Opera Manager in 19th-Century America*. New York: Dover, 1968.

Marks, Edward B. *They All Sang*. New York: Viking Press, 1934.

Marks, Peter. "Thanks for the Lift: Broadway as It Used to Sound." *NYT*, February 8, 1998.

Marrocco, W. Thomas, and Harold Gleason, eds. *Music in America*. New York: W. W. Norton, 1964.

Marshall, Jack. "The Secrets of Hellzapoppin." http://www.americancentury.org/ag_hellza poppin.pdf.

Martin, George. "On the Verge of Opera, Stephen Sondheim." *Opera Quarterly* 6:3 (Spring 1989): 76–85.

——. *Twentieth-Century Opera: A Guide*. New York: Limelight, 1999.

Martin, John. "The Dance 'Allegro.'" *NYT*, January 18, 1948.

——. "'West Side Story' as an Experiment in Method." *NYT*, October 27, 1957.

Marx, Samuel, and Jan Clayton. *Rodgers & Hart: Bewitched, Bothered, and Bedeviled*. New York: Putnam, 1976.

Maslon, Laurence. *Broadway: The American Musical*. Based on the documentary film by Michael Kantor. New York: Bulfinch, 2004.

Mason, Jeffrey D. *Wisecracks: The Farces of George S. Kaufman*. Ann Arbor: UMI Research Press, 1988.

Mast, Gerald. *Can't Help Singin': The American Musical on Stage and Screen*. Woodstock, NY: Overlook, 1987.

Masteroff, Joe, John Kander, and Fred Ebb. *Cabaret: The Illustrated Book and Lyrics*. New York: Newmarket Press, 1999.

Mates, Julian. *The American Musical Stage Before 1800*. New Brunswick, NJ: Rutgers University Press, 1962.

——. "The Black Crook Myth." *Theatre Survey* 7 (1966): 31–43.

——. ed. *Musical Works of William Dunlap*. Delmar, NY: Scholars' Facsimiles and Reprints, 1980.

Matheson, Rebecca Jumper, and Molly Frances Sorkin. *Designing the It Girl: Lucile and Her Style*. Exhibition Catalogue. New York, 2005.

Mathews, Jane De Hart. *The Federal Theatre, 1935–1939*. Princeton, NJ: Princeton University Press, 1967.

Matlaw, Myron, ed. *American Popular Entertainment*. Westport, CT: Greenwood, 1979.

——, ed. *The Black Crook and Other Nineteenth-Century American Plays*. New York: Dutton, 1967.

Mauceri, John. Notes to *On Your Toes*, LP. New York: Polydor 813 667-1, 1983.

Mayer, David, and Matthew Scott. *Four Bars of 'Agit': Incidental Music for Victorian and Edwardian Melodrama.* London: Samuel French, 1983.

McBrien, William. *Cole Porter: A Biography.* New York: Alfred A. Knopf, 1998.

McCabe, John. *George M. Cohan: The Man Who Owned Broadway.* New York: Doubleday, 1973.

McClary, Susan. *Georges Bizet: Carmen.* Cambridge: Cambridge University Press, 1992.

mcclung, bruce d. "American Dreams: Analyzing Moss Hart, Ira Gershwin and Kurt Weill's Lady in the Dark." PhD diss., University of Rochester, 1994.

————. *Lady in the Dark: Biography of a Musical.* Oxford and New York: Oxford University Press, 2007.

mcclung, bruce d., Joanna Lee, and Kim Kowalke, eds. *Lady in the Dark: A Sourcebook.* New York, 1996.

McConachie, Bruce. "American Theatre in Context." In Wilmeth, *Cambridge History of American Theatre.*

————. "New York Operagoing, 1825–50: Creating an Elite Social Ritual." *American Music* 6 (1988): 181–92.

————. "The 'Oriental' Musicals of Rodgers and Hammstein and the U.S. War in Southeast Asia." *Theatre Journal* 46 (October 1994): 375–88.

————. "'The Theatre of the Mob': Apocalyptic Melodrama and Preindustrial Riots in Antebellum New York." In *Theatre for Working-Class Audiences in the United States, 1830–1980,* edited by Bruce A. McConachie and Daniel Friedman. Westport, CT: Greenwood, 1985.

McCrum, Robert. *Wodehouse: A Life.* New York: W. W. Norton, 2004.

McDermott, Douglas. "Syndicate, Theatrical." In Wilmeth and Miller, *Cambridge Guide to American Theatre.*

McDonnell, Evelyn, with Katherine Silberger. *Rent by Jonathan Larson.* New York: Rob Weisbach Books, 1997.

McGilligan, Patrick. Introduction to *Yankee Doodle Dandy.* Madison: University of Wisconsin Press, 1981.

McGlinn, John. "Notes on 'Show Boat.'" Notes to *Show Boat,* 3 LPs. Hayes Middlesex, England: EMI/Angel 49108, 1988.

McGovern, Dennis, and Deborah Grace Winer. *Sing Out, Louise!* New York: Macmillan, 1993.

McKnight, Gerald. *Andrew Lloyd Webber.* New York: St. Martin's Press, 1984.

McLean, Albert G., Jr. *American Vaudeville as Ritual.* Lexington: University of Kentucky Press, 1965.

McLean, Lorraine Arnal. *Dorothy Donnelly: A Life in the Theatre.* Jefferson, NC: McFarland, 1999.

McLucas, Anne Dhu, ed. *Later Melodrama in America: Nineteenth-Century American Musical Theater,* vol. 4. New York: Garland, 1994.

McNamara, Brooks. *The New York Concert Saloon: The Devil's Own Nights.* Cambridge: Cambridge University Press, 2002.

————. *The Shuberts of Broadway: A History Drawn from the Collections of the Shubert Archive.* New York: Oxford University Press, 1990.

McNamara, Brooks, and Peter A. Davis. "The Syndicate/Shubert War." In Taylor, *Inventing Times Square.*

McSpadden, Joseph Walker. *Light Opera and Musical Comedy.* New York: Thomas Y. Crowell, 1936.

Mellers, Wilfrid. *Music in a New Found Land: Themes and Developments in the History of American Music.* London: [Sheed & Ward], 1964.

Melnick, Jeffrey. "Tin Pan Alley and the Black-Jewish Nation." In *American Popular Music,* edited by Rachel Rubin and Jeffrey Melnick. Amherst: University of Massachusetts Press, 2001.

Mendenhall, Christian. "American Musical Comedy as a Liminal Ritual of Woman as Homemaker." *Journal of American Culture* 13:3 (Winter 1990): 57–69.

Meredith, Scott. *George S. Kaufman and His Friends.* New York: Doubleday, 1974.

Merman, Ethel, with George Eells. *Merman: An Autobiography.* New York: Simon & Schuster, 1978.

Merman, Ethel, and Pete Martin. *Who Could Ask for Anything More.* Garden City, NY: Doubleday, 1955.

Meyerson, Harold, and Ernie Harburg. *Who Put the Rainbow in "The Wizard of Oz"?: Yip Harburg, Lyricist.* Ann Arbor: University of Michigan Press, 1993.

Michener, James A. "Happy Talk: Tribute to the Writers of 'South Pacific.'" *NYT,* July 3, 1949.

———. *Tales of the South Pacific.* New York: Macmillan, 1947.

Middleton, Richard. *Studying Popular Music.* Philadelphia: Open University Press, 1990.

Mielziner, Jo. *Designing for the Theatre: A Memoir and a Portfolio.* New York: Bramhall House, 1965.

Mikotowicz, Tom. *Oliver Smith: A Bio-Bibliography.* Westport, CT: Greenwood, 1993.

Miller, D. A. *Place for Us: Essay on the Broadway Musical.* Cambridge, MA: Harvard University Press, 1998.

Miller, Flournoy, and Aubrey Lyles. *Shuffle Along.* Electronic Edition by Alexander Street Press, L.L.C. 2005. http://alexanderstreet4.com/cgi-bin/asp/philomain/getobject?c.30:2:1./project.

Miller, Scott. *Deconstructing Harold Hill: An Insider's Guide to Musical Theatre.* Portsmouth, NH: Heinemann, 2000.

———. *From "Assassins" to "West Side Story": The Director's Guide to Musical Theatre.* Portsmouth, NH: Heinemann, 1996.

———. *Let the Sun Shine In: The Genius of HAIR.* Portsmouth, NH: Heinemann, 2003.

———. *Rebels with Applause: Broadway's Groundbreaking Musicals.* Portsmouth, NH: Heinemann, 2001.

———. *Strike Up the Band: A New History of Musical Theatre.* Portsmouth, NH: Heinemann, 2007.

Millstein, Gilbert. "Culled from a Stripper's Past." *NYT,* May 17, 1959.

———. "The Great Loesser." *NYT Magazine,* May 20, 1956.

———. "Words Anent Music by Cole Porter." *NYT Magazine,* February 20, 1955.

Minow, Martha. *Not Only for Myself: Identity, Politics, and the Law* (1997). New York: New Press, 1999. http://books/first/m/minow-myself.html.

Minsky, Morton, and Milt Machlin. *Minsky's Burlesque.* New York: Arbor House, 1986.

Mitchell, Donald. *Britten and Auden in the Thirties: The Year 1936.* Woodbridge, UK: Boydell Press, 1981.

Mitchell, John Cameron, and Stephen Trask. *Hedwig and the Angry Inch.* Woodstock, NY: Overlook Press, 2000.

Mizejewski, Linda. *Divine Decadence: Fascism, Female Spectacle and the Making of Sally Bowles* Princeton, NJ: Princeton University Press, 1992.

———. *Ziegfeld Girl: Image and Icon in Culture and Cinema.* Durham, NC: Duke University Press, 1999.

Moody, Richard. *The Astor Place Riot.* Bloomington: Indiana University Press, 1958.

———, ed. *Dramas from the American Theatre, 1762–1909.* Cleveland: World Publishing Co., 1966.

———. "Little Theatre Movement." In Banham, *Cambridge Guide to World Theatre.*

———. *Ned Harrigan: From Corlear's Hook to Herald Square.* Chicago: Nelson Hall, 1980.

Moore, J. Kenneth. "The Mixing and Miking of Broadway: Changing Values of a Sound/Music Aesthetic." In Leichtman, *To the Four Corners.*

Moore, Robert E. "The Music to Macbeth." *Musical Quarterly* 47 (January 1961): 22–40.

Moore, Thomas Gale. *The Economics of the American Theater.* Durham, NC: Duke University Press, 1968.

Mordden, Ethan. *Better Foot Forward.* New York: Grossman Publishers, 1976.

———. *Broadway Babies.* New York: Oxford University Press, 1983.

————. *Coming Up Roses: The Broadway Musical in the 1950s.* New York: Oxford University Press, 1998.

————. "Inside a State-of-the-Art Kaleidoscope." *NYT*, February 25, 1990.

————. *Make Believe: The Broadway Musical in the 1920s.* New York: Oxford University Press, 1997.

————. *Open a New Window: The Broadway Musical in the 1960s.* New York: St. Martin's Press, 2001.

————. *Rodgers and Hammerstein.* New York: Harry Abrams, 1992.

————. "'Show Boat' Crosses Over." *The New Yorker*, July 3, 1989.

Morehouse, Ward. *George M. Cohan, Prince of the American Theater.* Philadelphia: J. B. Lippincott, 1943.

Morell, Parker. *Lillian Russell: The Era of Plush.* New York: Random House, 1940.

Morella, Joseph, and George Mazzei. *Genius and Lust: The Creativity and Sexuality of Cole Porter and Noël Coward.* New York: Carroll & Graf, 1995.

Morgan, James Oliver. "French Comic Opera in New York, 1855–1890." PhD diss., University of Illinois, 1959.

Morley, Sheridan, and Ruth Leon. *Hey, Mr. Producer! The Musical World of Cameron Mackintosh.* New York: D. McKay Co., 1998.

Moross, Jerome. "New Musical Revues for Old." *New Theatre*, October 1935.

Morris, Rebecca. "The Bare Essentials." *Show Music*, Fall 1994.

Moses, Montrose J. *The American Dramatist.* Boston: Little, Brown, 1925.

————. *The Fabulous Forrest: The Record of an American Actor.* Boston: Little, Brown, 1929.

Most, Andrea. *Making Americans: Jews and the Broadway Musical.* Cambridge, MA: Harvard University Press, 2004.

————. "'We Know We Belong to the Land': The Theatricality of Assimilation in Rodgers and Hammerstein's *Oklahoma!*" *Publications of the Modern Language Association*, January 1998.

Moulton, Robert Darrell. "Choreography in Musical Comedy and Revue on the New York Stage from 1925 through 1950." PhD diss., University of Minnesota, 1957.

Mühe, Hansgeorg. *Die Musik von Andrew Lloyd Webber.* Hamburg: Verlag Dr. Kovač, 1993.

Muir, John Kenneth. *Singing a New Tune: The Rebirth of the Modern Film Musical, from "Evita" to "De-Lovely" and Beyond.* New York: Applause, 2005.

Murray, Ken. *The Body Merchant: The Story of Earl Carroll.* Pasadena: Ward Ritchie Press, 1976.

Nadel, Norman. *A Pictorial History of the Theatre Guild.* New York: Crown, 1969.

Naremore, James, and Patrick Brantlinger, eds. *Modernity and Mass Culture.* Bloomington: Indiana University Press, 1991.

Nassour, Ellis, and Richard Broderick. *Rock Opera: the Creation of Jesus Christ Superstar . . .* New York: Hawthorn Books, 1973.

Nathan, Hans. *Dan Emmett and the Rise of Early Negro Minstrelsy.* Norman: University of Oklahoma Press, 1962.

Navasky, Victor. *Naming Names.* New York: Viking Press, 1980.

Nelson, Steve. "Broadway and the Beast: Disney Comes to Times Square." *The Drama Review* 39:2 (Summer 1995): 71–84.

Newbury, Michael. "Polite Gaiety: Cultural Hierarchy and Musical Comedy, 1893–1904." *Journal of the Gilded Age and Progressive Era* 4:4 (2005): 381–408.

Newquist, Roy. *Showcase.* New York: William Morrow, 1966.

Newsom, Jon, ed. *Perspectives on John Philip Sousa.* Washington, DC: Library of Congress/Government Printing Office, 1983.

Nichols, Lewis. "Carmen Jones." *NYT*, December 3, 1943.

————. "R & H Co." *The Saturday Review of Recordings*, October 25, 1947.

Nolan, Frederick. *Lorenz Hart: A Poet on Broadway.* New York: Oxford University Press, 1994.

————. *The Sound of Their Music: The Story of Rodgers and Hammerstein.* London: Dent, 1978.

Norton, Elliot. "Broadway After World War II." In Downer, *American Theater Today.*

————. "Some Lovely Music and Some Errors in *Carousel*." *Boston Post*, April 1, 1945.

Norton, Richard C. *A Chronology of American Musical Theater*, 3 vols. New York: Oxford University Press, 2002.

Nunn, Trevor. "The Great British Musical." In Goodwin, *British Theatre Design*.

Oberfirst, Robert. *Al Jolson: You Ain't Heard Nothin' Yet*. San Diego: A. S. Barnes, 1980.

Odell, George Clinton Densmore. *Annals of the New York Stage*, 15 vols. New York: Columbia University Press, 1927–1949.

Offenbach, Jacques. "Concours Pour une Opérette en un Acte." *Revue et Gazette Musicale de Paris*, July 20, 1856.

————. *Orpheus in America: Offenbach's Diary of His Journey to the New World*. Translated by Lander MacClintock. Bloomington: Indiana University Press, 1957.

Ogasapian, John. *Music of the Colonial and Revolutionary Eras*. Westport, CT: Greenwood, 2004.

Ogren, Kathy J. *The Jazz Revolution: Twenties America and the Meaning of Jazz*. New York: Oxford University Press, 1989.

Ohl, Vicki. *Fine and Dandy: The Life and Work of Kay Swift*. New Haven, CT: Yale University Press, 2004.

Oja, Carol. *Leonard Bernstein*. New Haven, CT: Yale University Press, 2007.

————. "Marc Blitzstein's *The Cradle Will Rock* and Mass-Song Style of the 1930s." *Musical Quarterly* 73:4 (1989).

Olavarría y Ferrari, Enrique de. *Reseña Histórica del Teatro en México, 1538–1911*, vol. 1. Mexico City: Porrua, 1961.

Olin, Reuel Keith. "A History and Interpretation of the Princess Theatre Musical Plays: 1915–1919." PhD diss., New York University, 1979.

Oliver, Donald, ed. *By George: A Kaufman Collection*. New York: St. Martin's Press, 1979.

————, ed. *The Greatest Revue Sketches*. New York: Avon Books, 1982.

Ormsbee, Helen. "'Oklahoma!' Enters Choice Company of Shows That Top Thousand Performances." *New York Herald Tribune*, July 8, 1945.

Osato, Sono. *Distant Dances*. New York: Alfred A. Knopf, 1980.

Osborne, Conrad L. "The Broadway Voice: Just Singin' in the Pain." *High Fidelity Magazine*, January/February 1979.

Osolsobě, Ivo. *The Theatre Which Speaks, Sings, and Dances: Semiotics of the Musical Theatre*. Prague: Supraphon, 1974.

Ostrow, Stuart. *A Producer's Broadway Journey*. Westport, CT: Praeger, 1999.

Ozick, Cynthia. "Sholem Aleichem's Revolution." *The New Yorker*, March 28, 1988.

Pacheco, Patrick. "Going Back to the Book." *Newsday*, August 27, 2000.

Page, Brett. *Writing for Vaudeville*. Springfield, MA, 1915.

Palm, Carl Magnus. *Bright Lights Dark Shadows: The Real Story of ABBA*. London: Omnibus, 2002.

Palmer, Tony. *All You Need Is Love*. Middlesex, UK: George Weidenfeld and Nicolson, 1976.

Papp, Joseph. "Bring Back Threepenny Opera!" Notes to *Three Penny Opera*, LP. New York: Columbia PS 34326, 1976.

Pascoe, Peggy. "Miscegenation Law, Court Cases, and Ideologies of 'Race' in Twentieth-Century America." *The Journal of American History* 83:1 (June 1996): 44–69.

Pattison, Robert. *The Triumph of Vulgarity*. New York: Oxford University Press, 1987.

Pauly, Thomas H. Introduction to Maureen Watkins, *Chicago*, edited by Thomas H. Pauly. Carbondale: Southern Illinois University Press, 1997.

Payne-Carter, David. *Gower Champion: Dance and American Musical Theatre*. Westport, CT: Greenwood, 1999.

Peck, Seymour. "'Apple' Among Bagels." *NYT*, March 7, 1954.

Penndorf, Ron. "Musical Theater on Record." http://www.ronpenndorf.com/journalof recordedmusic2,html.

Perry, George C. *The Complete Phantom of the Opera*. New York: Henry Holt, 1987.

————. *Sunset Boulevard: From Movie to Musical*. New York: Henry Holt, 1993.

Pessen, Edward. "The Great Songwriters of Tin Pan Alley's Golden Age: A Social, Occupa-
    tional and Aesthetic Inquiry." *American Music* 3 (Summer 1985): 180–97.
Peterson, Bernard L., Jr. *A Century of Musicals in Black and White: An Encyclopedia of Musical
    Stage Works By, About, or Involving African Americans.* Westport, CT: Greenwood, 1993.
Peyser, Joan. *Bernstein: A Biography.* New York: Beech Tree, 1987.
———. *The Memory of All That: The Life of George Gershwin.* New York: Simon & Schuster,
    1993.
Philp, Richard. "Michael Bennett and the Making of 'A Chorus Line.'" *Dance Magazine*, June
    1975.
Pinza, Ezio. "Why I Went to South Pacific." *Etude*, September 1949.
Pinza, Ezio, with Robert Magidoff. *Ezio Pinza, An Autobiography.* New York: Rinehart, 1958.
Plotkins, Mary Jane. "Irving Berlin, George Gershwin, Cole Porter and the Spectacular
    Revue: The Theatrical Context of Revue Songs from 1910 to 1937." PhD diss., Tufts Uni-
    versity, 1982.
Poggi, Jack. *Theater in America: The Impact of Economic Forces, 1870–1967.* Ithaca: Cornell Uni-
    versity Press, 1968.
Pollack, Howard. *George Gershwin: His Life and Work.* Berkeley: University of California Press,
    2006.
Pomahac, Bruce. "Frederick Loewe Message Board." http://www.frederickloewe.org/bbs/
    messages/169.html.
Porter, Andrew. "Town and Country." In Lee, *Street Scene.*
Porter, Cole. *Anything Goes.* First version in the Cole Porter Manuscript Collection. Beinecke
    Library, Yale University.
———. "Notes on the Morning After an Opening Night." *NYT*, November 8, 1936.
Porter, Susan L. *With an Air Debonair: Musical Theatre in America, 1785–1815.* Washington,
    DC: Smithsonian Institution Press, 1991.
Potter, John, ed. *The Cambridge Companion to Singing.* Cambridge: Cambridge University
    Press, 2000.
Potts, L. J. *Comedy.* New York: Chandler, 1966.
Preston, Katherine K., ed. *Irish American Theater: Nineteenth-Century American Musical Theater,*
    vol. 10. New York: Garland, 1994.
Price, Julia. *The Off-Broadway Theatre.* New York: Scarecrow Press, 1962.
Prince, Harold. *Contradictions: Notes on Twenty-six Years in the Theatre.* New York: Dodd, Mead
    and Company, 1974.
———. "*Show Boat*: Director's Notes." *Playbill* 94:10, Gershwin Theatre, 1994.
The Producers, DVD. Directed by Susan Stroman. Universal City, CA: Universal Studios, 2006.
    Feature Commentary.
Quinn, Arthur Hobson. *A History of the American Drama from the Beginning to the Civil War.*
    New York: Appleton-Century-Crofts, 1923.
Rabson, Carol. "*Disappointment* Revisited." *American Music,* Spring 1983 and Spring 1984.
Rahill, Frank. *The World of Melodrama.* University Park: Pennsylvania State University Press,
    1967.
Ranney, H. M. *Account of the Terrific and Fatal Riot at the New-York Astor Place Opera House.*
    New York: H. M. Ranney, 1849.
Rapp, Anthony. *Without You: A Memoir of Love, Loss, and the Musical RENT.* New York: Simon
    & Schuster, 2006.
Reichl, Alexander J. *Reconstructing Times Square.* Lawrence: University Press of Kansas, 1999.
Reid, Louis R. "Composing While You Wait." *Dramatic Mirror,* June 2, 1917.
Rice, Elmer. *Minority Report: An Autobiography.* New York: Simon & Schuster, 1963.
Rice, Tim. *Oh, What a Circus: The Autobiography, 1944–1978.* London: Hodder and Stoughton,
    1999.
Rich, Frank. "David Merrick, 88, Showman Who Ruled Broadway, Dies." *NYT*, April 27, 2000.
———. "Detour for American Theater, Direction Uncertain." *NYT*, October 18, 1998.
———. "'Falsettos': Broadway Boundary Falls Amid Reunions." *NYT*, April 30, 1992.

———. "Sondheim and Those Who Would Kill." *NYT*, January 28, 1991.

Rich, Frank, with Lisa Aronson. *The Theatre Art of Boris Aronson.* New York: Alfred A. Knopf, 1987.

Rich, Maria F., and Victor Fell Yellin/H. Wiley Hitchcock. "Opera." *NGDAM*, vol. 3 (London, 1986).

Richards, David. "The 'Saigon' Picture Is Worth 1,000 Words." *NYT*, April 21, 1991.

Richards, Stanley, ed. *Great Musicals of the American Theatre*, 2 vols. Radnor, PA: Chilton, 1973–1976.

———, ed. *Great Rock Musicals.* New York: Stein & Day, 1979.

Richardson, Gary A. *American Drama from the Colonial Period through World War I: A Critical History.* New York: Twayne, 1993.

Richmond, Keith. *The Musicals of Andrew Lloyd Webber.* London: Virgin, 1995.

Ries, Frank W. D. "Sammy Lee: The Broadway Career." *Dance Chronicle* 9:1 (1986): 1–95.

———. "Albertina Rasch: The Broadway Career." *Dance Chronicle* 6:2 (1983): 95–137.

Riis, Thomas L. *Just Before Jazz: Black Musical Theater in New York, 1890–1915.* Washington, DC: Smithsonian Institution Press, 1989.

———. *More Than Just Minstrel Shows: The Rise of Black Musical Theatre at the Turn of the Century.* Brooklyn: Brooklyn College Institute for Studies in American Music, 1992.

———. "The Music and Musicians in Nineteenth-Century Productions of *Uncle Tom's Cabin.*" *American Music* 4:3 (1986): 268–86.

———, ed. *The Music and Scripts of In Dahomey: Music of the United States of America*, vol. 5. Madison, WI: A-R Editions for the American Musicological Society, 1996.

———, ed. *Uncle Tom's Cabin: Nineteenth-Century American Musical Theater*, vol. 5. New York: Garland, 1994.

Rinaldi, Nicholas G. "Music as Mediator: A Description of the Process of Concept Development in the Musical 'Cabaret.'" PhD diss., Ohio State University, 1982.

Robbins, Jerome. "Book Changes by April [1964]." In Altman and Kaufman, *Making of a Musical.*

Robbins, Tim. *Cradle Will Rock: The Movie and the Moment.* New York: Newmarket Press, 2000.

Robinson, J. Bradford. "Kurt Weills Aneignung des amerikanischen Theaterliedes: Zur Entstehungsgeschichte von *Johnny's Song.*" In Grosch, *Kurt-Weill Studien.*

Robinson, Paul. "A Deconstructive Postscript: Reading Libretti and Misreading Opera." In Groos and Parker, *Reading Opera.*

Rockwell, John. "Rock Opera." *NGDO*, vol. 3.

Rodger, Gillian. "Legislating Amusements: Class Politics and Theater Law in New York City." *American Music* 20:4 (2002): 381–98.

Rodgers, Richard. "The Background Is Siam, The Music Is Pure Broadway." *New York Herald Tribune*, March 25, 1951.

———. "How to Write Music in No Easy Lessons." *Theatre Arts Monthly*, October 1938.

———. *Letters to Dorothy.* Edited by William Appleton. New York: Random House/New York Public Library, 1988.

———. *Musical Stages.* New York: Random House, 1975.

———. "Now the Musical Theater Is Enshrined." *NYT Magazine*, June 21, 1964.

———. "Stardust & Sweat: How a Broadway Musical Is Put Together." *Writer's Yearbook*, 1965.

Rodgers, Richard, and Oscar Hammerstein, II. *Six Plays by Rodgers and Hammerstein.* New York: Random House, 1955; repr. Modern Library, 1959.

Roffman, Frederick S., and Bruce and Rosemary Steeg. "*Naughty Marietta*—A Guide to the Opening Night Version." Notes to *Naughty Marietta*, 2 LPs. Washington, DC: Smithsonian American Musical Theater Series R-026, 1981.

Rogin, Michael. "Blackface, White Noise: The Jewish Jazz Singer Finds His Voice." *Critical Inquiry* (1992): 435–56.

Rollyson, Carl. *Lillian Hellman.* New York: St. Martin's Press, 1988.

Root, Deane L. *American Popular Stage Music, 1860–1880.* Ann Arbor: UMI Research Press, 1981.

————. "Introduction to the Series." In *Nineteenth-Century American Musical Theater*, vol. 2.

Rose, Brian. *Televising the Performing Arts*. Westport, CT: Greenwood, 1992.

Rosen, Marjorie. *Popcorn Venus: Women, Movies & the American Dream*. New York: Coward, McCann & Geoghegan, 1974.

Rosenberg, Bernard, and Ernest Harburg. *The Broadway Musical: Collaboration in Commerce and Art*. New York: New York University Press, 1993.

Rosenberg, Deena. *Fascinating Rhythm, The Collaboration of George and Ira Gershwin*. New York: Dutton, 1991.

Rosenberg, Marvin. *The Masks of Macbeth*. Berkeley: University of California Press, 1978.

Rosenfield, John. "'Carmen Jones' and the Minor Art of Parody . . ." *Dallas News*, January 7, 1947.

Rothstein, Mervyn. "Old Casts Hark Back to Recreate 'Ballet' For Jerome Robbins." *NYT*, September 19, 1988.

Rowland, Mabel, ed. *Bert Williams, Son of Laughter: A Symposium of Tribute to the Man and to His Work by His Friends and Associates*. New York: The English Crafters, 1923; repr. Negro Universities Press, 1969.

Rubsamen, Walter H., ed. *The Ballad Opera*, vol. 16: *Country Operas II*, and vol. 28: *American Ballad Operas*. New York: Garland, 1974.

Ruhl, Arthur. Review of *Of Thee I Sing*. *New York Herald Tribune*, December 28, 1931.

Runyon, Damon. "Neat Strip." In *Take It Easy*. New York: Triangle, 1941.

Rush, David Alan. "A History and Evaluation of the ILGWU Labor Stage and its Productions of Pins and Needles, 1937–1940." MA thesis, University of Iowa, 1965.

Rusk, Dr. Howard A. "The Facts Don't Rhyme: An Analysis of Irony in Lyrics Linking Puerto Rico's Breezes to Tropic Diseases." *NYT*, September 29, 1957.

Russell, Don. *The Wild West, or A History of the Wild West Shows*. Fort Worth, TX: Amon Carter Museum of Western Art, 1970.

Russell, Lillian. "Lillian Russell's Reminiscences." *Cosmopolitan Magazine*, February 1922. In Stein, *American Vaudeville*.

Sablosky, Irving. *What They Heard: Music in America, 1852–1881*. Baton Rouge: Louisiana State University Press, 1986.

Saffle, Michael, ed. *Music and Culture in America, 1861–1918*. New York: Garland, 1998.

Sagolla, Lisa Jo. *The Girl Who Fell Down: A Biography of Joan McCracken*. Boston: Northeastern University Press, 2003.

Salzman, Eric, and Thomas Desi. *The New Music Theater: Seeing the Voice, Hearing the Body*. Oxford and New York: Oxford University Press, 2008.

Samson, Jim. "Music and Society." In *The Late Romantic Era: From the Mid-19th Century to World War I*, edited by Jim Samson. Englewood Cliffs, NJ: Prentice Hall, 1991.

————. "The Great Composer." In *The Cambridge History of Nineteenth-Century Music*, edited by Jim Samson. Cambridge: Cambridge University Press, 2001.

Sanders, Ronald. *The Days Grow Short: the Life and Music of Kurt Weill*. New York: Holt, Rinehart, and Winston, 1980.

Sandoval-Sánchez, Albert. *José, Can You See? Latinos On and Off Broadway*. Madison: University of Wisconsin Press, 1999.

Sanjek, Russell. *American Popular Music and Its Business: The First Four Hundred Years*, 3 vols. New York: Oxford University Press, 1988.

————. *From Print to Plastic: Publishing and Promoting America's Popular Music (1900–1980)*. Brooklyn: Institute for Studies in American Music, 1983.

Savage, Roger. "The Staging of Opera." In *The Oxford Illustrated History of Opera*, edited by Roger Parker. Oxford: Oxford University Press, 1984.

Schaap, Dick. "Imp in a Monster Mask." *Life*, December 13, 1968.

Schebera, Jürgen. *Kurt Weill, An Illustrated Life*. Translated by Caroline Murphy. New Haven, CT: Yale University Press, 1995.

Schiff, David. *Gershwin: Rhapsody in Blue*. Cambridge: Cambridge University Press, 1997.

———. "Re-hearing Bernstein." *Atlantic Monthly*, June 1993.

Schiff, Ellen, ed. *Fruitful & Multiplying: 9 Contemporary Plays from the American Jewish Repertoire*. New York: Mentor, 1996.

Schleifer, Martha Furman, ed. *American Opera and Music for the Stage: Eighteenth and Nineteenth Centuries*. Boston: G. K. Hall, 1990.

Schlesinger, Arthur M., Jr. "How History Upstaged the Gershwins." *NYT*, April 5, 1987.

———. *A Thousand Days: John F. Kennedy in the White House*. Boston: Houghton Mifflin, 1965.

Schlundt, Christena L. *Dance in the Musical Theatre: Jerome Robbins and His Peers, 1934–1965. A Guide*. New York: Garland, 1989.

Schmidt, Harvey. *The Fantasticks: With Special 30th Anniversary Foreword and Illustrations by the Authors*. New York: Applause, 1990.

Schmidt-Joos, Siegfried. *Das Musical*. Munich: Deutscher Taschenbuch Verlag, 1965.

Schneider, Wayne, ed. *The Gershwin Style*. New York: Oxford University Press, 1999.

Schneidereit, Otto. *Operette A–Z: Ein Streifzug durch die Welt der Operette und des Musicals*. Berlin [DDR]: Henschel, 1981.

Schoettler, Eugenia Volz. "From a Chorus Line to 'A Chorus Line': The Emergence of Dance in the American Musical Theatre." PhD diss., Kent State University, 1979.

Schroth, Evelyn. "Camelot: Contemporary Interpretation of Arthur in 'Sens' and 'Matière.'" *Journal of Popular Culture* 17:2 (Fall 1983): 31–43.

Schubert, Gisela. "Musical." In *Die Musik in Geschichte und Gegenwart*, 2nd ed. Kassel: Bärenreiter, 1997.

Schulman, Sarah. *Stagestruck: Theater, AIDS, and the Marketing of Gay America*. Durham, NC: Duke University Press, 1998.

Schwab, Laurence. "How to Write a Successful Musical Comedy." *Theatre Magazine*, February 1929.

Schwartz, Charles. *Cole Porter: A Biography*. New York: Dial Press, 1977.

———. *Gershwin: His Life and Music*. Indianapolis: Bobbs-Merrill Company, 1973.

Schwind, Elisabeth. "'Weill Hasn't Changed, I Have': Zur Ästhetik des Komponisten Marc Blitzstein." In Grosch, *Kurt-Weill Studien*.

Scott, Alec. "Movin' Out and the Rise of the Jukebox Musical." November 21, 2005. http://www.cbc.ca/arts/theatre/movinout.html.

Sebesta, Judith A. "Just Another Puerto Rican with a Knife? Racism and Reception on the 'Great White Way.'" *Studies in Musical Theatre* 1:2 (August 2007):183–97.

Secrest, Meryle. *Leonard Bernstein: A Life*. New York: Alfred A. Knopf, 1994.

———. *Somewhere for Me: A Biography of Richard Rodgers*. New York: Alfred A. Knopf, 2001.

———. *Stephen Sondheim: A Life*. New York: Alfred A. Knopf, 1998.

Seldes, Gilbert. "Looking Back at the Princess Shows." *Theatre Magazine*, July 1924.

———. *The 7 Lively Arts*. New York: Harper & Brothers, 1924; new ed. New York: Sagamore, 1957.

Sell, Barry D. "Nahuatl Plays in Context." In *Nahuatl Theater*, edited by Barry D. Sell and Louise M. Burkhart. Norman: University of Oklahoma Press, 2004.

Seller, Maxine Schwartz, ed. *Ethnic Theatre in the United States*. Westport, CT: Greenwood, 1983.

Senelick, Laurence. *The Age and Stage of George L. Fox., 1825–1877*. Hanover, NH: University Press of New England, 1988.

Seng, Peter J. *The Vocal Songs in the Plays of Shakespeare, A Critical History*. Cambridge, MA: Harvard University Press, 1967.

Sergel, Sherman Louis, ed. *The Language of Show Biz: A Dictionary*. Chicago: Dramatic Publishing, 1973.

Severo, Richard. "Persuasive Dreamer Who Brought Theater to City Center Dies at 96." *NYT*, November 17, 1998.

Shapiro, Anne Dhu. "Action Music in American Pantomime and Melodrama, 1730–1913." *American Music* 2:4 (1984): 49–72.

———. "Melodrama." *NGDAM*, vol. 3 (London, 1986).

Shapiro, Doris. *We Danced All Night: My Life Behind the Scenes with Alan Jay Lerner.* New York: Barricade Books, 1990.

Shapiro, Nat, and Bruce Pollock, eds. *Popular Music, 1920–1979*, vol. 1. Detroit: Gale, 1985.

Shaw, Arnold. *The Jazz Age: Popular Music in the 1920s.* New York: Oxford University Press, 1987.

Shaw, Bernard. *Pygmalion: The Bodley Head Collected Plays*, vol. 4, edited by Dan H. Laurence. London: Bodley Head, 1972.

Sheean, Vincent. *Oscar Hammerstein I: The Life and Exploits of an Impresario.* New York: Simon & Schuster, 1956.

Shenton, Mark. "'Movicals' Reign on Broadway and in the West End." September 13, 2005. http://www.thestage.co.uk/shenton/2005/09/movicals_reign_on_broadway_and-in_t .php-20k.

Shostakovich, Dmitri. *Testimony: Memoirs of Dmitri Shostakovich as related and edited by Solomon Volkov.* Translated by Antonia W. Bouis. New York: Harper & Row, 1979.

Shout, John D. "The Kiss That Conquers: Interpreting the American Musical." Unpublished ms.

———. "The Musical Theater of Marc Blitzstein." *American Music* 3:4 (Winter 1985): 413–28.

Shtier, Rachel. *Striptease: The Untold Story of the Girlie Show.* New York: Oxford University Press, 2004.

Siebert, Lynn Laitman. "Cole Porter: An Analysis of Five Musical Comedies and a Thematic Catalogue of the Complete Works." PhD diss., CUNY, 1975.

Siek, Stephen. "Benjamin Carr's Theatrical Career." *American Music* 11:2 (1993): 158–84.

Silver, Arnold. "The Playwright's Revenge." In *Modern Critical Interpretations: Pygmalion*, edited by Harold Bloom. New York: Chelsea, 1988.

Silverman, Kenneth. *A Cultural History of the American Revolution.* New York: Crowell, 1976.

Simon, Paul. Interviewed by Don Imus. http://www.rhhardin.home.mindspring.com/ trascript.simon.text

Singer, Barry, *Ever After: The Last Years of Musical Theater and Beyond.* New York: Applause, 2004.

———. *Black and Blue: The Life and Lyrics of Andy Razaf.* New York: Schirmer, 1992.

Skipper, John C. *Meredith Willson: The Unsinkable Music Man.* El Dorado Hills, CA: Savas Woodbury Publishers, 2000.

Slide, Anthony. *The Encyclopedia of Vaudeville.* Westport, CT: Greenwood, 1994.

Slobin, Mark. "Some Intersections of Jews, Music, and Theater." In *From Hester Street to Hollywood*, edited by Sarah Blacher Cohen. Bloomington: Indiana University Press, 1983.

———, ed. *Yiddish Theater in America: Nineteenth-Century American Musical Theater*, vol. 11. New York: Garland, 1994.

Smith, Susan. *The Musical: Race, Gender and Performance.* London: Wallflower Press, 2005.

Smith, Cecil Michener. *Musical Comedy in America.* New York: Theatre Arts Book, 1950; 2nd ed. with Glenn Litton, 1981.

Smith, Eric Ledell. *Bert Williams: A Biography of the Pioneer Black Comedian.* Jefferson, NC: McFarland, 1992.

Smith, Geoffrey. *The Savoy Operas.* New York: Universe Books, 1985.

Smith, Harry B. *First Nights and First Editions.* Boston: Little, Brown, 1931.

———. *Stage Lyrics.* New York, R. H. Russell, 1900.

Smith, June. "Cole Porter in the American Musical Theatre." In *Themes in Drama*, edited by James Redmond. Cambridge: Cambridge University Press, 1981.

Smith, Patrick J. *The Tenth Muse.* New York: Alfred A. Knopf, 1970.

Snelson, John. *Andrew Lloyd Webber.* New Haven, CT: Yale University Press, 2004.

———. "'We Said We Wouldn't Look Back': British Musical Theatre, 1935–60." In Everett and Laird, *Cambridge Companion to the Musical.*

Snyder, Robert W. *The Voice of the City: Vaudeville and Popular Culture in New York.* New York: Oxford University Press, 1989.

Sobel, Bernard. *Burleycue: An Underground History of Burlesque Days.* New York: Farrar and Rinehart, 1931.

———. *A Pictorial History of Burlesque.* New York: Bonanza Books, 1956.

Solomon, Alisa. "Off-Off Broadway." In Banham, *Cambridge Guide to World Theatre.*

Somerset-Ward, Richard. *An American Theatre: The Story of Westport Country Playhouse.* New Haven, CT: Yale University Press, 2005.

Sondheim, Stephen. "The Musical Theater." In Guernsey, *Broadway Song & Story.*

———. "Theater Lyrics." In Guernsey, *Playwrights, Lyricists, Composers on Theater.*

Sonneck, Oscar G. "Early American Operas." *Sammelbände der internationalen Musikgesellschaft* (1904–1905): 428–95.

———. *Early Opera in America.* New York: G. Schirmer, 1915; repr. Benjamin Blom, 1963.

———. "German Influence on the Musical Life of America." In *Oscar Sonneck and American Music,* edited by William Lichtenwanger. Urbana and Chicago: University of Illinois Press, 1983.

Sontag, Susan. "Notes on 'Camp.'" *Partisan Review* 31:4 (Fall 1964).

Sousa, John Philip. *Marching Along: Recollections of Men, Women and Music.* Boston: Hale, Cushman & Flint, 1928.

Southern, Eileen, ed. *African American Theater: Nineteenth-Century American Musical Theater,* vol. 9. New York: Garland, 1994.

———. *The Music of Black Americans,* 2nd ed. New York: W. W. Norton, 1983.

———. *Readings in Black American Music,* 2nd ed. New York: W. W. Norton, 1983.

Spann, Edward K. *The New Metropolis: New York City, 1840–1857.* New York: Columbia University Press, 1981.

Spencer, David. "1776." http://www.aislesay.com/NY-1776.html.

Spewack, Samuel, and Bella Spewack. "How to Write a Musical Comedy." In *Kiss Me, Kate.* New York: Alfred A. Knopf, 1953.

Spoto, Donald. *Lenya: A Life.* Boston: Little, Brown, 1989.

Stagg, Jerry. *The Brothers Shubert.* New York: Random House, 1968.

Stanfield, Peter. "From the Vulgar to the Refined: American Vernacular and Blackface Minstrelsy in *Show Boat.*" In *Musicals: Hollywood and Beyond,* edited by Bill Marshall and Robynn Stilwell. Exeter, UK: Intellect, 2000.

Stearns, David Patrick. "The Smart Set." http://www.tcg.org/publicatons/at/2000/smart.cfm

Stearns, Marshall, and Jean Stearns. *Jazz Dance: The Story of American Vernacular Dance.* New York: Macmillan, 1968.

Stedman, Jane. "Then Hey! For the Merry Greenwood: Smith and de Koven and Robin Hood." *Journal of Popular Culture* 12:3 (Winter 1978): 432–45.

Stein, Charles W., ed. *American Vaudeville as Seen by Its Contemporaries.* New York: Da Capo, 1984.

Stempel, Larry. "Composers of Less Than Compositions/Songwriters of More Than Songs: Problems of Authorship in the Music of the Musical." Unpublished paper, AMS, 1996.

———. "The First History of the American Musical." Unpublished paper. Musical Theater Conference, CUNY, 2008.

———. "The Musical Play Expands," *American Music* 10:2 (Summer 1992): 136–69.

———. "Street Scene and the Enigma of Broadway Opera." In Kowalke, *A New Orpheus: Essays on Kurt Weill.*

Sternfeld, Jessica. *The Megamusical.* Bloomington: Indiana University Press, 2006.

Stevens, Gary, and Alan George. *The Longest Line: Broadway's Most Singular Sensation, A Chorus Line.* New York: Applause, 1995.

Stevenson, Isabelle, ed. *The Tony Award.* Portsmouth, NH: Heinemann, 1994.

Stewart, Michael. Author's Note to *Harrigan 'n' Hart.* New York: Samuel French, 1986.

Steyn, Mark. *Broadway Babies Say Goodnight: Musicals Then and Now.* London: Faber, 1997.

Stone, Wendell C. *Caffe Cino: The Birthplace of Off-Off Broadway*. Carbondale: Southern Illinois University Press, 2005.

Stout, Glenn, and Richard A. Johnson. *Red Sox Century*. Boston: Houghton Mifflin, 2000.

Stowe, Harriet Beecher. Preface to *Uncle Tom's Cabin*. New York: Bantam, 1982.

Strang, Lewis C. *Celebrated Comedians of Light Opera and Musical Comedy in America*. Boston: L. C. Page, 1901.

———. *Prima Donnas and Soubrettes of Light Opera and Musical Comedy in America*. Boston: L. C. Page, 1900.

Strasberg, Lee. *A Dream of Passion*. Boston: Little, Brown, 1987.

Stratyner, Barbara. *Ned Wayburn and the Dance Routine: From Vaudeville to the Ziegfeld Follies*. Studies in Dance History No. 13. Hanover, NH: Society of Dance History Scholars, 1996.

Stravinsky, Vera, and Robert Craft. *Stravinsky in Pictures and Documents*. New York: Simon & Schuster, 1978.

Stumpf, Charles. "Olsen and Johnson, The Zaniest of the Zanies." http://www.classicimages .com/1998/october98/olsenandjohnson.html.

Styne, Jule. "Off-Broadway, We Love You Ardently, But . . ." *New York Herald Tribune*, August 2, 1959.

Suskin Steven. *More Opening Nights on Broadway*. New York: Schirmer, 1997.

———. "On the Record": *Gypsy, Brownstone and Marc Blitzstein*." *Playbill*, September 7, 2003.

———. *Opening Night on Broadway*. New York: Schirmer, 1990.

———. *Show Tunes, 1905–1985*. New York: Dodd, Mead and Company, 1986.

Swain, Joseph P. *The Broadway Musical*, 2nd ed. New York and Oxford: Oxford University Press, 2002.

Tagg, Philip. "Analysing Popular Music: Theory, Method and Practice." *Popular Music* 2 (1982): 37–67.

Taruskin, Richard. "The Golden Age of Kitsch." *The New Republic*, March 21, 1994.

Taubman, Howard. "A Foot in Each Camp: Bernstein's Score of 'West Side Story' Falters between Musical and Opera." *NYT*, October 13, 1957.

———. "Cole Porter Is 'The Top' Again." *NYT*, January 16, 1949.

———. *The Making of the American Theatre*. New York: Putnam, 1967.

———. "Metropolitan's Basso at Home on Broadway." *NYT*, May 1, 1949.

Taylor, Deems. *Some Enchanted Evenings: The Story of Rodgers and Hammerstein*. New York: Harper, 1953; repr. Westport, CT: Greenwood, 1972.

Taylor, Ronald. *Kurt Weill: Composer in a Divided World*. Boston: Northeastern University Press, 1992.

Taylor Theodore. *Jule, the Story of Composer Jule Styne*. New York: Random House, 1979.

Taylor, William R., ed. *Inventing Times Square: Commerce and Culture at the Crossroads of the World*. New York: Russell Sage Foundation, 1991.

Taymor, Julie, with Alexis Greene. *The Lion King: Pride Rock on Broadway*. New York: Hyperion, 1997.

Tchen, John Kuo Wei. "*Flower from Drum Song*—The Reviews Are In, Critics Are Clueless about New Emergent American Sensibility." *Maynard Institute for Journalism Education*, November 2002.

Teachout, Terry. "Is Musical Comedy Dead?" *Commentary*, June 2004.

Thelen, Lawrence. *The Show Makers: Great Directors of the American Musical Theatre*. New York: Routledge, 2000.

Theodore, Lee. "Preserving American Theatre Dance: The Work of the American Dance Machine." In Loney, *Musical Theatre: Papers and Proceedings*.

Thomas, Bob. *I Got Rhythm: The Ethel Merman Story*. New York: Putnam, 1985.

Thomson, Virgil. "George Gershwin." *Modern Music*, November/December 1935.

———. Review of *Regina*. *New York Herald Tribune*, November 1, 1949.

———. *A Virgil Thomson Reader*. New York: Houghton Mifflin, 1981.

Tischler, Barbara L. *An American Music: The Search for an American Musical Identity*. New York: Oxford University Press, 1986.

Toll, Robert C. *Blacking Up: The Minstrel Show in Nineteenth-Century America*. New York: Oxford University Press, 1974.

———. *On with the Show*. New York: Oxford University Press, 1976.

Tommasini, Anthony. "A Composer's Death Echoes in His Musical." *NYT*, February 11, 1996.

———. "A Crowd of Old Musicals Squeezes the New." *NYT*, August 16, 1998.

Toynbee William, ed. *The Diaries of William Charles Macready*. London: Chapman & Hall, 1912; repr. New York: Benjamin Blom, 1969.

Trapp, Maria Augusta. *The Story of the Trapp Family Singers*. Philadelphia: Lippincott, 1949.

Traubner, Richard. *Operetta; A Theatrical History*. New York: Doubleday & Co., 1983.

Trotter, James Monroe. *Music and Some Highly Musical People*. Boston: Lee and Shepard, 1880; repr. Chicago: Johnson Reprint, 1969.

Trowell, Brian. "Libretto." *NGDO* (London, 1992).

Tucker, Mark. "Jazz." *NGDMM2* (London, 2001).

Tune, Tommy. *Footnotes, A Memoir*. New York: Simon & Schuster, 1997.

Twain, Mark. *Mark Twain's Travels with Mr. Brown*. Edited by Franklin Walker and G. Ezra Dane. New York: Alfred A. Knopf, 1940.

Tylor, Edward B. *Primitive Culture*. London: Murray, 1871.

Upton, William Treat. "Max and Agathe vs. Rodolph and Agnes, et al." *Notes* (March 1947): 217–24.

Urban, Joseph. *Theatres*. New York: Theatre Arts Press, 1929.

Vacha, J. E. "Posterity Was Just Round the Corner: The Influence of the Depression on the Development of the American Musical Theater in the Thirties." *South Atlantic Quarterly*, Autumn 1968.

Vallillo, Stephen M. "George M. Cohan's *Little Johnny Jones*." In Loney, *Musical Theatre in America*.

Van Leer, David. *The Queening of America: Gay Culture in Straight Society*. New York: Routledge, 1995.

Verdino-Süllwold, Carla Maria. "Opera, Operetta, or Musical? Vanishing Distinctions in Twentieth-Century Music Drama." *Opera Journal* 23 (December 1990) 31–43.

Vermette, Margaret. *The Musical World of Boublil and Schönberg: The Creators of Les Misérables, Miss Saigon, Martin Guerre, and The Pirate Queen*. New York: Applause, 2007.

Viagas, Robert, Baayork Lee, and Thommie Walsh. *On The Line: The Creation of A CHORUS LINE*. New York: William Morrow, 1990.

Virga, Patricia H. *The American Opera to 1790*. Ann Arbor: UMI Research Press, 1982.

Waldau, Roy S. *Vintage Years of the Theatre Guild, 1929–1939*. Cleveland: Press of Case Western Reserve University, 1972.

Walsh, David, and Len Platt. *Musical Theatre and American Culture*. Westport, CT: Praeger, 2003.

Walsh, Michael. *Andrew Lloyd Webber: His Life and Works, A Critical Biography*. New York: Harry Abrams, 1997.

———. *Who's Afraid of Opera?* New York: Simon & Schuster, 1994.

Wang, David Henry. *Flower Drum Song*. New York: Penguin, 2002.

Ward, Jonathan. "Come in My Mouth: The Story of the Adult Musicals of the '70s." http://www.furious.com/Perfect/adultmusicals.html.

Warfield, Scott. "From *Hair* to *Rent*: Is 'Rock' a Four-Letter Word on Broadway?" In Everett and Laird, *Cambridge Companion to the Musical*.

Washburne, Christopher J., and Maiken Derno, eds. *Bad Music: The Music We Love to Hate*. New York: Routledge, 2004.

Wasserman, Dale. *The Impossible Musical: The Man of La Mancha Story*. New York: Applause, 2003.

———. Preface to *Man of La Mancha, A Musical Play*. New York: Dell, 1968.

Waterhouse, Robert. "Direction and Design: The Partners Hal Prince and Boris Aronson." *Plays and Players*, March 1972.

Waters, Edward N. *Victor Herbert: A Life in Music.* New York: Macmillan, 1955.

Waters, Ethel, and Charles Samuels. *His Eye Is on the Sparrow.* Garden City, NY: Doubleday, 1951.

Watts, Richard, Jr. "'Show Boat' Here with Cargo of Song and Color." *New York Herald Tribune,* December 29, 1927.

Wayburn, Ned. *The Art of Stage Dancing. The Story of a Beautiful and Profitable Profession: A Manual of Stage-Craft.* New York: The Ned Wayburn Studios of Stage Dancing, 1925.

Weill, Kurt. "Broadway and the Musical Theatre." *The Composer's News-Record* 2 (May 1947).

———. "Broadway Opera: Our Composers' Hope for the Future." *Musical Digest* 28 (December 1946).

———. "The Future of Opera in America." *Modern Music,* May/June 1937.

———. Letter to Caspar Neher, February 16, 1947. In Lee, Harsh, and Kowalke, *Street Scene.*

———. Notes to *Street Scene,* LP. New York: Columbia OL 4139, 1947.

Wells, Elizabeth A. *"West Side Story* and the Hispanic." *ECHO,* Spring 2000.

Wentworth, Howard, and Stuart Berg Flexner. *Dictionary of American Slang,* 2nd ed. New York: Thomas Y. Cromwell, 1975.

Wertheim, Arthur Frank. *The New York Little Renaissance: Iconoclasm, Modernism, and Nationalism in American Culture, 1908–1917.* New York: New York University Press, 1976.

Wharton, John F. *Life among the Playwrights: Being Mostly the Story of the Playwrights Producing Company, Inc.* New York: Quadrangle, 1974.

Whitcomb, Ian. *Irving Berlin and Ragtime America.* London: Century Hutchinson, 1987.

White, Eric Walter. *A History of English Opera.* London: Faber, 1983.

———. *Stravinsky: The Composer and His Works,* 2nd ed. Berkeley: University of California Press, 1979.

White, R. Kerry. *An Annotated Dictionary of Technical, Historical and Stylistic Terms Relating to Theatre and Drama.* Lewiston, NY: Mellen, 1995.

White, Terence Hanbury. "For President Kennedy, An Epilogue." *Life,* December 6, 1963.

———. "What It's Like to be Translated into 'Camelot.'" *Vogue,* February 15, 1961.

Whitfield, Stephen J. "Fiddling with Sholem Aleichem: A History of *Fiddler on the Roof.*" In *Key Texts in American Jewish Culture,* edited by Jack Kugelmass. New Brunswick, NJ: Rutgers University Press, 2003.

———. *In Search of American Jewish Culture.* Hanover, NH: Brandeis University Press, 1999.

Whitton, Joseph. *"The Naked Truth!" An Inside History of the Black Crook.* Philadelphia: H. W. Shaw, 1897.

Wickham, Glynne. *A History of the Theatre.* Cambridge: Cambridge University Press, 1985.

Wickstrom, Maurya. "Commodities, Mimesis, and *The Lion King*: Retail Theatre for the 1990s." *Theatre Journal* 51:3(1999): 285–98.

Wildbihler, Hubert, and Sonja Völklein. *The Musical: An International Annotated Bibliography.* Munich: K. G. Saur, 1986.

Wilder, Alec. *American Popular Song: The Great Innovators, 1900–1950.* New York: Oxford University Press, 1972.

Wilk, Max. *O.K.! The Story of Oklahoma!* New York: Grove, 1993.

———. *They're Playing Our Song.* New York: Atheneum, 1973.

Willard, Charles. "'Life's Progress': *Love Life* Revisited." *Kurt Weill Newsletter,* Fall 1984.

Willett, John, ed. and tr. *Brecht on Theatre: The Development of an Aesthetic.* London: Methuen, 1964.

Williams, Bert. "The Comic Side of Trouble." *American Magazine,* January 1918.

Williams, Raymond. "Culture." In *Keywords: A Vocabulary of Culture and Society.* New York: Oxford University Press, 1976.

Williams, William H. *'Twas Only an Irishman's Dream: The Image of Ireland and the Irish in American Popular Song Lyrics, 1800–1920.* Urbana and Chicago: University of Illinois Press, 1996.

Willson, Meredith. *And There I Stood with My Piccolo.* Garden City, NY: Doubleday, 1948.

———. *But He Doesn't Know the Territory.* New York: G. P. Putnam's Sons, 1959.

————. *Eggs I Have Laid.* New York: Holt, 1955.

Wilmeth, Don B. "Resident Non-profit Professional Theatre in the USA." In Banham, *Cambridge Guide to World Theatre.*

Wilmeth, Don B., and Christopher Bigsby, eds. *The Cambridge History of American Theatre*, 3 vols. Cambridge: Cambridge University Press, 1998.

Wilmeth, Don B., and Tice L. Miller, eds. *Cambridge Guide to American Theatre.* Cambridge: Cambridge University Press, 1993.

Wilson, Edmund. *The American Earthquake: A Documentary of the Twenties and Thirties.* New York: Doubleday, 1958.

Wilson, Francis. *Francis Wilson's Life of Himself.* Boston: Houghton Mifflin, 1924.

Wilson, Garff B. *Three Hundred Years of American Drama and Theatre.* Englewood Cliffs, NJ: Prentice Hall, 1973.

Wilson, Woodrow. *The New York Dramatic Mirror*, January 20, 1915. In Slide, *Encyclopedia of Vaudeville.*

Winer, Deborah Grace. *On the Sunny Side of the Street: The Life and Lyrics of Dorothy Fields.* New York: Schirmer, 1997.

Winkler, Elizabeth Hale. *The Function of Song in Contemporary British Drama.* Newark: University of Delaware Press, 1990.

Wittke, Carl. *Tambo and Bones: A History of the American Minstrel Stage.* Durham, NC: Duke University Press, 1930.

Wlaschin, Ken. *Gian Carlo Menotti on Screen: Opera, Dance, and Choral Works on Film, Television and Video.* Jefferson, NC: McFarland, 1999.

Wodehouse, P. G. "The Agonies of Writing a Musical Comedy." *Vanity Fair*, March 1917.

————. "On the Writing of Lyrics." *Vanity Fair*, June 1917.

————. "Summer Stuff." *Vanity Fair*, September 1915.

————. "Take Your Choice of Musical Comedies." *Vanity Fair*, April 1915.

————. "Writing the Show at the Century." *Vanity Fair*, December 1917.

Wodehouse, P. G., and Guy Bolton. *Bring on the Girls!* New York: Simon & Schuster, 1953.

Wolf, Arlene. "How They Made That 'Rainbow.'" *NYT*, March 9, 1947.

Wolf, Stacy Ellen. *A Problem Like Maria: Gender and Sexuality in the American Musical.* Ann Arbor: University of Michigan Press, 2002.

————. "The Queer Pleasures of Mary Martin and Broadway: *The Sound of Music* as a Lesbian Musical." *Modern Drama* 39 (1996).

Wolfe, George C., and Susan Birkenhead. *Jelly's Last Jam.* New York: Theatre Communications Group, 1993.

Wolitz, Seth L. "The Americanization of Tevye or Boarding the Jewish *Mayflower.*" *American Quarterly* 40 (December 1988).

Woll, Allen. *Black Musical Theatre: From Coontown to Dreamgirls.* Baton Rouge: Louisiana State University Press, 1989.

Wollman, Elizabeth L. "The Economic Development of the 'New' Times Square and Its Impact on the Broadway Musical." *American Music* 20:4 (Winter 2002).

————. *The Theater Will Rock: A History of the Rock Musical from "Hair" to "Hedwig."* Ann Arbor: University of Michigan Press, 2006.

Wood, Graham. "Distant Cousin of Fraternal Twin? Approaches to the Film Musical." In Everett and Laird, *Cambridge Companion to the Musical.*

Wood, Marcus. "A Cabinet of Curiosities." http://www.common-place.org/vol-04/no-13/wood.

Wood, Peggy. *How Young You Look: Memoirs of a Middle-sized Actress.* New York: Farrar & Rinehart, 1941.

Woolcott, Alexander. *The Story of Irving Berlin.* New York: G. P. Putnam's Sons, 1925.

Yellin, Victor Fell. "Rayner Taylor's Music for *The AEthiop.*" *American Music* 4:3 (1986): 249–67, and 5:1 (1987): 20–47.

————. Notes to *The Ethiop* [sic] and *The Indian Princess*, LP. New York, New World 232, 1978.

Yoshikawa, Yoko. "The Heat Is on *Miss Saigon* Coalition: Organizing Across Race and Sexuality." In *The State of Asian America: Activism and Resistance in the 1990s*, edited by Karin Aguilar San-Juan. Boston: South End Press, 1994.

Yudkoff, Alvin. *Gene Kelly: A Life of Dance and Dreams.* New York: Watson-Guptill, 1999.

Zadan, Craig. *Sondheim & Co.*, 2nd ed. New York: Harper & Row, 1986.

Zeidman, Irving. *The American Burlesque Show.* New York: Hawthorne, 1967.

Zellers, Parker. "The Cradle of Variety: The Concert Saloon." *Educational Theatre Journal* 20:4 (December 1968): 578–85.

———. *Tony Pastor: Dean of the Vaudeville Stage.* Ypsilanti: Eastern Michigan University Press, 1971.

Ziegfeld, Richard, and Paulette Ziegfeld. *The Ziegfeld Touch: The Life and Times of Florenz Ziegfeld, Jr.* New York: Harry Abrams, 1993.

Zinoman, Jason. "On Stage and Off: Can 1991 Be New for a Musical?" *NYT*, April 23, 2004.

Zuck, Barbara A. *A History of Musical Americanism.* Ann Arbor: UMI Research Press, 1980.

SELECTED HISTORICAL DISCOGRAPHY

In the early decades of the twentieth century, English record companies made the first regular recordings of excerpts of musicals from America with their London casts. But it was Decca Records that launched original cast recordings of Broadway musicals as a mass-market phenomenon *in* America when it issued most of the songs from *This Is the Army* (1942) and then *Oklahoma!* (1943), sung by those who first performed them on the stage, in disc sets of 78-rpms packaged together as albums—scrapbooks of the shows in three-minute snapshots of sound. Thus preserved as units, these shows are not hard to find today as they were later reissued in long-playing (LP) and compact disc (CD) formats as the technology changed. Subsequent Broadway shows similarly recorded by other companies as well either followed this pattern or, in the case of post-1950 shows, were originally issued in the newer formats.

Original cast recordings involving Broadway musical productions before 1942, however, are more difficult to find. If extant and still in listenable condition, they exist in older formats that usually preserved only a few numbers from a production and that were generally issued as self-contained items in isolation from one another. (Brunswick's 1932 recordings of *Blackbirds* and *Show Boat* in revival as well as Musicraft's of *The Cradle Will Rock* in 1938, all in sets of 78s, provide the earliest notable exceptions.) Thus LP and CD reissues of archival reconstructions and compilations of such materials, preserving in conceptual units as they do the earliest "living" traces of the performance legacy of America's musical theater, are invaluable for the pleasures and insights they afford, and eminently worth seeking out. Some of the more accessible of these include:

American Musical Theater: Shows, Songs, and Stars, 4 CDs. Washington, DC, and New York: Smithsonian/CBS, 1989. Notes by Dwight Blocker Bowers.

Blake, Eubie, and Noble Sissle. *Shuffle Along.* New York: New World 260 [Recorded Anthology of American Music], 1976. Notes by Robert Kimball.

Blitzstein, Marc. *The Cradle Will Rock.* New York: Musicraft, 1938. Reissued, *Marc Blitzstein: Musical Theatre Premieres* [*The Cradle Will Rock*; *No for an Answer*; etc.], 2CDs. Wadhurst, England: Pearl/Koch, 1998.

Follies, Scandals & Other Diversions: From Ziegfeld to the Shuberts. New York: New World 215 [Recorded Anthology of American Music], 1977. Notes by George Oppenheimer.

Gershwin, George, and Ira Gershwin. *Fascinating Rhythm: The Broadway Gershwin, 1919–1933.* New York: BMG Classics, 1998. Notes by Dwight Blocker Bowers.

———. *Funny Face.* Washington, DC, and New York: Smithsonian/RCA R-019 [American Musical Theater Series], 1980. Notes by Deena Rosenberg.

———. *Lady, Be Good.* Washington, DC, and New York: Smithsonian/CBS R-008 [American Musical Theater Series], 1977. Notes by Edward Jablonski.

———. *Oh, Kay!* Washington, DC, and New York: Smithsonian R-011 [American Musical Theater Series], 1978. Notes by Wayne Shirley.

———. *Porgy and Bess.* New York: Decca, 1940, 1942. Reissued, Universal City, CA: MCA, 1992. Notes by Louis Untermeyer and Max O. Preeo.

Herbert, Victor. *Music of Victor Herbert.* Washington, DC, and New York: Smithsonian/RCA R-017, 3 LPs [American Musical Theater Series], 1979. Notes by Allen G. Debus.

Kahn, Gus, Walter Donaldson, and others. *Whoopee.* Washington, DC, and New York: Smithsonian/RCA R-014 [American Musical Theater Series], 1978. Notes by Stanley Green.

Kern, Jerome. *Show Boat.* New York: Brunswick, 1932–1933. Reissued, New York: Columbia AC-55, 1974. Notes by Alfred Simon.

McHugh, Jimmy, and Dorothy Fields. *[Lew Leslie's] Blackbirds of 1928.* New York: Brunswick, 1932. Reissued, New York: Columbia OL-6770, 1968. Notes by Miles Kreuger.

Music from the New York Stage 1890–1920, 12 CDs. Wadhurst, England: Pearl GEMM 9050-61, 1993. Notes by Dwight Blocker Bowers.

Originals: Musical Comedy, 1909–1935. New York: RCA LPV-560 [Vintage Series], 1968. Notes by Dan H. Laurence.

Porter, Cole. *Anything Goes.* Washington, DC, and New York: Smithsonian/RCA R-007 [American Musical Theater Series], 1977. Notes by Richard C. Norton.

———. *Let's Face It*; *Red, Hot and Blue*; and *Leave It to Me.* Washington, DC, and New York: Smithsonian/CBS R-016 [American Musical Theater Series], 1979. Notes by Richard C. Norton.

———. *From This Moment On: Songs of Cole Porter,* 4 CDs. Washington, DC, and New York: Smithsonian/Sony, 1992. Notes by Dwight Blocker Bowers.

Schwartz, Arthur, and Howard Dietz. *At Home Abroad.* Washington, DC, and New York: Smithsonian/RCA R-024 [American Musical Theater Series], 1981. Notes by Stanley Green.

———. *The Band Wagon.* [New York: RCA, experimental 33⅓-rpm disc not issued, 1931.] Washington, DC, and New York: Smithsonian/RCA R-021 [American Musical Theater Series], 1979. Notes by Richard C. Norton.

Souvenirs of Hot Chocolates. Washington, DC, and New York: Smithsonian/CBS R-012 [American Musical Theater Series], 1978. Notes by Dan Morgenstern.

Stars of the Ziegfeld Follies. Pelican LP-102, 1972.

Star-Spangled Rhythm: Voices of Broadway and Hollywood, 4 CDs. Washington, DC, and New York: Smithsonian/BMG, 1996. Notes by Dwight Blocker Bowers.

They Stopped the Show. New York: Audio Fidelity Audio Rarities LPA-2290, 1969. Narration by Chamberlain Brown.

Toward an American Opera, 1911–1954. New York: New World 241 [Recorded Anthology of American Music], 1978. Notes by Patrick J. Smith.

The Ultimate Broadway Composers, 12 CDs. Wadhurst, England: Pearl, 2000–2004. Notes by Dwight Blocker Bowers.

Ziegfeld Follies of 1919. Washington, DC, and New York: Smithsonian/CBS R-009 [American Musical Theater Series], 1977. Notes by Stanley Green.

Music and Lyrics

W. H. Auden, 274: "Twelve Songs: XII," from *Collected Poems* by W. H. Auden. Copyright © 1976 by Edward Mendelson, William Meredith, and Monroe K. Spears, Executors of the Estate of W. H. Auden. Used by permission of Random House, Inc., and Faber and Faber Ltd.; **504**: From "Song of the Quest." Copyright © 1981 by The Estate of W. H. Auden. Reprinted by permission of Curtis Brown, Ltd.

Irving Berlin, 149: "Blue Skies" by Irving Berlin. Copyright © 1926, 1927 by Irving Berlin. Copyright © Renewed. International Copyright Secured. All Rights Reserved. Reprinted by Permission; **318**: "They Say It's Wonderful" from *Annie Get Your Gun*. Words and Music by Irving Berlin (Williamson Music).

Marc Blitzstein, 477: "The Cradle Will Rock" from *The Cradle Will Rock*. Words and Music by Marc Blitzstein (Warner Chappell Music).

Alain Boublil, Herbert Kretzmer, and Claude-Michel Schönberg, 624: "Bring Him Home" from *Les Misérables*. Words by Alain Boublil and Herbert Kretzmer, Music by Claude-Michel Schönberg (Alain Boublil Music Ltd).

Betty Comden, Adolph Green, and Leonard Bernstein, 445: "New York, New York" (from *On the Town*). Lyrics by Betty Comden and Adolph Green. Music by Leonard Bernstein. Copyright © 1945 (Renewed) WB Music Corp. All Rights Reserved. Used by permission from Alfred Publishing Co., Inc.

Joe Darion, 504: "The Impossible Dream." ("The Quest") Lyrics by Joe Darion. Reprinted by permission of the Estate of Joe Darion.

Howard Dietz and Arthur Schwartz, 219: "New Sun in the Sky" from *The Band Wagon*. Words by Howard Dietz, Music by Arthur Schwartz (Warner Chappell Music).

William Cary Duncan, Oscar Hammerstein II, Herbert Stothart, and Vincent Youmans, 230: "My Boy and I" from *Mary Jane McKane*. Words by William Cary Duncan and Oscar Hammerstein II, Music by Herbert Stothart and Vincent Youmans (Warner Chappell Music).

Photo Credits

Frontispiece

ii (*clockwise from top left*): The New York Public Library/Astor, Lenox and Tilden Foundations; Bettmann/Corbis; The Shubert Archive, a project of the Shubert Foundation; The New York Public Library/Astor, Lenox and Tilden Foundations; Photofest; Photofest; Photofest.

Introduction

2: Philadelphia Museum of Art/Corbis; 3: Philadelphia Museum of Art/Corbis.

Part One: Out of the Nineteenth Century

17: Bettmann/Corbis.

1: Transition Stages

18: The New York Public Library/Astor, Lenox and Tilden Foundations; 23: Bettmann/Corbis; 30: Bettmann/Corbis; 48: The New York Public Library/Astor, Lenox and Tilden Foundations.

2: Variety Stages

52: Harvard Theater Collection; 61: The New York Public Library/Astor, Lenox and Tilden Foundations; 63: The New York Public Library/Astor, Lenox and Tilden Foundations; 65: Corbis; 73: The New York Public Library/Astor, Lenox and Tilden Foundations; 81: The New York Public Library/Astor, Lenox and Tilden Foundations; 90: Museum of the City of New York.

3: A Transatlantic Muse

94: From the Collection of Harold Kanthor, the University of Rochester Library; 113: Museum of the City of New York, Byron Collection; 114: Bettmann/Corbis; 116: Bettmann/Corbis; 121: The New York Public Library/Astor, Lenox and Tilden Foundations; 125: Museum of the City of New York, Byron Collection.

Part Two: Into the Twentieth Century

129: The New York Public Library/Astor, Lenox and Tilden Foundations.

4: The Native Wit

130: Collection of The New-York Historical Society; 135: Museum of the City of New York/Byron Collection/Hulton Archive/Getty Images; 143: Bettmann/Corbis; 151: The Shubert Archive, a project of the Shubert Foundation; 156: The New York Public Library/Astor, Lenox and Tilden Foundations.

5: The Cult of Romance

168: Courtesy of The Rodgers & Hammerstein Organization; 176: The New York Public Library/Astor, Lenox and Tilden Foundations; 178: All photos Bettmann/Corbis; 187: The Shubert Archive, a project of the Shubert Foundation; 190: Museum of the City of New York; 196: The New York Public Library/Astor, Lenox and Tilden Foundations.

6: A Shadow of Vulgarity

202: The Shubert Archive, a project of the Shubert Foundation; 213: The New York Public Library/Astor, Lenox and Tilden Foundations; 216: The New York Public Library/Astor, Lenox and Tilden Foundations; 221: The New York Public Library/Astor, Lenox and Tilden Foundations; 232: The New York Public Library/Astor, Lenox and Tilden Foundations; 236: The New York Public Library/Astor, Lenox and Tilden Foundations.

7: Broadway Songbook

240: Hulton Archive/Getty Images; **252:** Al Hirschfeld. Reproduced by arrangement with Hirschfeld's exclusive Representative, the Margo Feiden Galleries LTD., New York, www.alhirschfeld.com; **256:** Photofest; **272:** Michael Ochs Archives/Corbis; **281:** Photofest.

8: The Script Angle

288: Courtesy of The Rodgers & Hammerstein Organization; **297:** Photofest; **304:** Bettmann/Corbis; **314–15:** Eileen Darby/Time & Life Pictures/Getty Images; **323:** Photofest.

9: Musical Theater: The New Art

328: Al Hirschfeld. Reproduced by arrangement with Hirschfeld's exclusive Representative, the Margo Feiden Galleries LTD., New York, www.alhirschfeld.com; **339:** Courtesy of The Rodgers & Hammerstein Organization; **344:** Courtesy of The Rodgers & Hammerstein Organization; **352:** Leonard Mccombe/Time Life Pictures/Getty Images; **361:** Photofest.

10: Opera, in Our Own Way

366: Photofest; **382:** Courtesy of The Rodgers & Hammerstein Organization; **386:** Everett Collection; **392:** Culver Pictures, Inc.; **399:** RSA Venture, renewed 1990. Licensed by Broad Reach Enterprises, Inc.; **404:** The New York Public Library/Astor, Lenox and Tilden Foundations.

11: The Great American Showshop

408: Ray Fisher/Time Life Pictures/Getty Images; **412:** Al Hirschfeld. Reproduced by arrangement with Hirschfeld's exclusive Representative, the Margo Feiden Galleries LTD., New York, www.alhirschfeld.com; **418:** Eileen Darby Images; **423:** Will Rapport Archive, The Harvard Theatre Collection, Houghton Library; **428:** Yip Harburg Foundation; **440:** Museum of the City of New York; **448:** Courtesy of Queens Library, Long Island division; **452:** The New York Public Library/Astor, Lenox and Tilden Foundations.

Part Three: Toward the New Millennium

457: Photofest.

12: Away from Broadway

458: Photofest; **467:** The New York Public Library/Astor, Lenox and Tilden Foundations; **479:** The New York Public Library/Astor, Lenox and Tilden Foundations; **487:** Courtesy of the Weill-Lenya Research Center, Kurt Weill Foundation for Music, New York; **493:** The New York Public Library/Astor, Lenox and Tilden Foundations; **502:** The New York Public Library/Astor, Lenox and Tilden Foundations; **508:** Photofest.

13: The Metaphor Angle

514: Photofest; **525:** Photofest; **539:** Martha Swope; **550:** Martha Swope; **552:** Copyright © Fraver 2002.

14: A Dancing Place

556: The New York Public Library/Astor, Lenox and Tilden Foundations; **566:** Gjon Mili/Time Life Pictures/Getty Images; **571:** Photofest; **577:** The New York Public Library/Astor, Lenox and Tilden Foundations; **582:** Martha Swope; **589:** Martha Swope; **590–91:** Photofest.

15: Distancing Effects

600: Photofest; **617:** Martha Swope; **625:** Photofest; **628:** All photos Photofest; **632:** Joan Marcus.

16: Another Broadway . . . Another Show . . .

    642: Philip Greenberg; **660:** Photofest; **664:** Martha Swope; **667:** Photofest; **674:** Photofest; **677:** Joan Marcus.

First Color Insert

    C-1 top: The Pierpont Morgan Library/Art Resource; **C-1 bottom:** Museum of the City of New York; **C-2:** The New York Public Library/Astor, Lenox and Tilden Foundations; **C-3 top left:** The New York Public Library/Astor, Lenox and Tilden Foundations; **C-3 top right:** The New York Public Library/Astor, Lenox and Tilden Foundations; **C-4 top left:** Courtesy Special Collections Gladys Marcus Library, Fashion Institute of Technology - SUNY; **C-4 right:** The New York Public Library/Astor, Lenox and Tilden Foundations; **C-4 bottom left:** Courtesy of Sevenarts Ltd.; **C-5 top:** The New York Public Library/Astor, Lenox and Tilden Foundations; **C-5 bottom:** The New York Public Library/Astor, Lenox and Tilden Foundations; **C-6 top:** Museum of the City of New York; **C-6 bottom:** Image by Fernand Bourges, The New York World, Color Gravure section, January 22, 1928. Courtesy of the Rare Book, Manuscript, and Special Collections Library, Duke University, Durham, North Carolina; **C-7 top left:** Ray Lee Jackson/Time Magazine/Time & Life Pictures/Getty Images; **C-7 top right:** Time Life Pictures/Time Magazine, Copyright Time Inc./Time Life Pictures/Getty Images; **C-7 bottom right:** Paul Dorsey/Time Inc./Time Life Pictures/Getty Images; **C-7 bottom left:** Time Life Pictures/Time Magazine, Copyright Time Inc./Time Life Pictures/Getty Images. **C-8:** Courtesy of The Rodgers & Hammerstein Organization.

Second Color Insert

    C-1: Virginia Museum of Fine Arts, Richmond. The Council Graphic Arts Fund; **C-2:** Hank Walker/Time Life Pictures/Getty Images; **C-3:** Mark Kauffman/Time Life Pictures/Getty Images; **C-4:** Photofest; **C-5 top:** The New York Public Library/Astor, Lenox and Tilden Foundations; **C-5 bottom:** Martha Swope; **C-6:** Martha Swope; **C-7:** Photofest; **C-8:** Photofest.

INDEX

Page numbers in *italics* refer to illustrations.
Page numbers beginning with 687 refer to notes.